RENAISSANCE PASTORAL
and its English Developments

RENAISSANCE PASTORAL

and its English Developments

SUKANTA CHAUDHURI

CLARENDON PRESS · OXFORD
1989

Oxford University Press, Walton Street, Oxford OX2 6DP
Oxford New York Toronto
Delhi Bombay Calcutta Madras Karachi
Petaling Jaya Singapore Hong Kong Tokyo
Nairobi Dar es Salaam Cape Town
Melbourne Auckland
and associated companies in
Berlin Ibadan

Oxford is a trade mark of Oxford University Press

Published in the United States
by Oxford University Press, New York

British Library Cataloguing in Publication Data
Chaudhuri, Sukanta
Renaissance pastoral.
1. *English pastoral literature, 1400–1702.*
Critical studies
I. Title
820′.91
ISBN 0–19–811736–1

Library of Congress Cataloging in Publication Data
Chaudhuri, Sukanta, 1950–
Renaissance pastoral and its English developments / Sukanta Chaudhuri
p. cm.
Bibliography: p. Includes index.
1. *English poetry—Early modern, 1500–1700—History and criticism.* 2. *Pastoral poetry, English—History and criticism.* 3. *English poetry—European influences.* 4. *Pastoral poetry—History and criticism. I. Title.*
PR539 P3C4 1989 821′.3′09321734—dc 19 88–37923
ISBN 0–19–811736–1

Typeset by Joshua Associates Ltd., Oxford
Printed in Great Britain
by Biddles Ltd.
Guildford and King's Lynn

To my wife

Preface

This book aims at a critical history of English Renaissance pastoral. It also surveys the context of continental pastoral, much though English practice diverged from it. In addition to a general account, I have offered analytic studies of most important pastoral writers and works in the age.

The standard English guide to Renaissance pastoral is still W. W. Greg's *Pastoral Poetry and Pastoral Drama*, first published in 1906. I hope this book will supplement Greg's classic work, using the extensive scholarship of the intervening eighty-two years. The results of this labour have appeared piecemeal in accounts of single authors or general studies of the mode; but a full historical and analytic study of Renaissance pastoral has never been undertaken. Perhaps no single book can serve, but I hope mine will partly meet the need.

Half the book (not the first half as printed) was written during three years' concentrated research in Oxford; the other half while coping with a full-time job and innumerable commitments in Calcutta. I would like to think that the difference is not readily discernible.

Through Mr John Buxton and Dr Helen Cooper, I have profited from the finest scholarship of two generations in the field. Friends who have advised me over particular works, authors and areas are too numerous to mention. Mr Ashok Ghosh and Ms Paola di Robilant gave invaluable help with the Latin and Italian translations respectively. Needless to say, the errors in this and all other respects are my own.

I must particularly thank the staff of the Bodleian Library and the Taylor Institute in Oxford and the Presidency College Library in Calcutta. The Inlaks Foundation, the Indian Council for Cultural Relations, the British Council, and the Deutsch Shakespeare-Gesellschaft (West) have all, directly or indirectly, given me financial help for the project. I am grateful to them all.

Contents

Conventions Used

The spelling of 'eclogue' has been standardized, except in direct quotation, and the English word applied to poems in all languages.

In rendering humanists' names, I have preferred vernacular forms to Latin where the difference lies solely in the ending. For the rest, I have used my judgement, always choosing a familiar Latin form to an unfamiliar vernacular one. I have used 'Mantuan' rather than 'Spagnoli', 'Stephanus' rather than 'Estienne', and, as a *via media*, 'de Ponte' rather than the confusing 'Pontanus' or the unfamiliar 'Van der Brugge'.

The style 'Virgil I' etc. has been used to refer to one of a numbered series of eclogues by the same poet.

Quotations from Latin, French, and Italian texts are accompanied by translations (my own, unless otherwise indicated). Greek and Spanish texts have been read and quoted in translation only; so has d'Urfé's *L'Astrée*, except for its prefatory material.

In the notes, the first reference to any work has been fully documented. Later references within the same chapter are usually by author's name only. The first reference in every subsequent chapter includes a short title or other suitable indication. Short titles have always been used to distinguish two or more works by the same author.

1

Introduction: The Nature of Pastoral

THIS book provides a critical history of English Renaissance pastoral and its European antecedents. My view of the pastoral mode will, I hope, emerge fully from the treatment of specific works. But it seems necessary to define my primary assumptions at the outset.

It is superfluous to point out at this date that pastoral is not folk literature; nor does it aim at presenting country life as it is. It selects details from that life, adds to them, and reorders them to create a world of the imagination, invested with urban longing for an ideally simple life in nature. In other words, it is subtle and sophisticated, exploring the gap between the complex existence of poet and reader and the designedly naïve dream of rural simplicity. All pastoral implies this duality, this awareness of two opposed worlds: country and city, simple and complex, imaginary and real.

Yet the contrast is ultimately spurious, because this country world is a creation of the urban imagination and must necessarily embody its values, with whatsoever degree of obliqueness or inversion. The opposed principles ultimately merge; the adversaries are fighting on the same side. In the crudest form of such a merger, the shepherds talk and act like courtly lovers and poets. In subtler forms, they modify sophisticated sentiments only to heighten and purify them (in aesthetic, not moral terms), producing something perceptibly different from the common urban or courtly experience but fulfilling the latter's demands in a more intense or at least more piquant form.

Sometimes the shepherds can stand for courtly characters in a more direct way, through simple point-to-point allegory. The activities of the conventional shepherd (which I shall soon list in more detail) reflect all the chief human concerns and activities. They have a clear affinity to the pursuits of more advanced societies. This power to embody representative human states, not merely to provide a comparison or veiled reference, gives pastoral an extraordinary scope for symbol and allegory. The danger is that such reference easily approaches the stage where the correspondence ceases to matter. We talk of a ruler as a shepherd not because we are struck by the resemblance between their pursuits, but only as a fashionably or diplomatically oblique style of reference. The symbol becomes first metaphor and then a mere cipher. Much so-called pastoral belongs to this class. It presents shepherd-rulers fighting battles and shepherd-poets singing for kings at court. Such direct allegory oversteps all admissible limits of imaginative convention and turns the shepherds flagrantly into opposites of themselves.

The distance between 'court' and 'country' constantly fluctuates in pastoral: their relationship assumes all possible proportions from direct to inverse.[1] Hence each can be assessed in terms of the other to any desired degree of interpenetration. Further, the rustic ideal generated by the convention can be assessed in terms of a more genuine rusticity brought into the picture as a secondary development. So too the courtier's behaviour in the country can be assessed against the general values of court life. So subtle and variable are these contrasts that the assessment often remains ambiguous, balancing opposite virtues or probing layer after layer of cross-ironies until all sense of judgement is lost. Or else, cutting the Gordian knot—as when the leading shepherds prove to be of noble birth—the opposites might merge in a satisfactory narrative end whose thematic implications remain uncertain or obfuscatory.

From medieval *pastourelle* to *As You Like It*, attempts at genuine encounters between the two worlds make for a challenging complexity, lapsing into confusion in inexpert hands. It is important to realize that the same complexity underlies what appears to be a contrary and more fundamental feature of pastoral: a cultivated *naïveté*, a direct, lucid primarity and simplicity of apprehension. The shepherd of pastoral functions as basic or representative man, though frequently at the price of an excessive simplism. He enacts certain well-defined roles, the two foremost being those of poet and lover. He is also the type of the ruler, reigning over his sheep. In Christian pastoral he becomes a priest, a shepherd of souls. Already in Virgil, he is a conscious country-dweller, in contrast to the townsman. From the Renaissance, he is moreover the type of man in conscious contact with nature. While watching his flocks by night, he studies the stars, tells tales, contemplates philosophy. As a 'wise shepherd', he acquires another dimension to his nature.

Hence, as I remarked earlier, the shepherd's life comes to epitomize

[1] Cf. Andrew V. Ettin's account of 'contrasting' and 'binding' opposites in pastoral: *Literature and the Pastoral* (New Haven, 1984), 29–30.

the chief human concerns and activities. It becomes a calling of dignity and value. But it reflects these concerns in an unusually simple setting, free of the counter-currents of hostile and distracting circumstances that bedevil more complex societies. It can therefore reveal very clearly the original impulses behind human action.

The simplicity and psychological purity of the impulse is not merely a matter of tone or atmosphere; it is a primary theme of pastoral in its own right. At times it comes practically to imply a moral purification, a wholeness and innocence in the exercise of faculties that we realize only corruptly and imperfectly in our own lives.

> When we have run our Passions heat,
> Love hither makes his best retreat.[2]

At such moments the pastoral world comes closest to its Christian and pagan prototypes, Eden and the Golden Age, assuming a kind of moral primitivism.

There is another matter as well. 'I play to please my selfe,' says Spenser's Colin Clout.[3] A remark by Renato Poggioli brings out the implications of this declaration: 'If the artist or the poet dons so often a pastoral disguise, it is only because he wishes to emphasise his personality in private rather than in public terms.'[4] So too with the shepherd's other roles. Because he has no 'image' to project, no circumstances to control, he can be more purely absorbed in the activity itself, with its own fulfilment.

Such non-utilitarian activities are essentially hedonistic. Rosenmeyer writes illuminatingly about the Epicurean nature of pastoral.[5] The action becomes its own justification, reduced by the simplifying process I have described to sense, order, and harmony. Of course, the justification is aesthetic, not necessarily material or moral. Shepherds often face the frustration of an unkind love, an interrupted song, an oppressive master, a dead friend. But they succeed in reducing such experience to a defined and hence acceptable form. Even death merely lends a sober colour to the

[2] Marvell, 'The Garden', ll. 25–6. All Marvell refs. to the *Poems*, ed. Hugh Macdonald (The Muses' Library; 2nd edn. London, 1956; repr. 1972).

[3] *The Shepheardes Calender*, 'Iune', l. 72. All Spenser refs. to the 1-vol. *Poetical Works*, ed. J. C. Smith and E. de Selincourt (Oxford, 1912; repr. 1970).

[4] Renato Poggioli, *The Oaten Flute. Essays on Pastoral Poetry and the Pastoral Ideal* (Cambridge, Mass., 1975), 23. Poggioli makes the remark in a somewhat different context, of an inward-turned 'pastoral of the self'.

[5] Thomas G. Rosenmeyer, *The Green Cabinet. Theocritus and the European Pastoral Lyric* (Berkeley, 1969; repr. 1973), *passim*, especially ch. iv.

perspective without distorting it or blotting it out. We see this in Sannazaro, and in Virgil himself in his tenth eclogue:

> 'tamen cantabitis, Arcades' inquit,
> 'montibus haec vestris, soli cantare periti
> Arcades. o mihi tum quam molliter ossa quiescant,
> vestra meos olim si fistula dicat amores . . .' (ll. 31–4)

[(He said) 'Yet ye, O Arcadians, will sing this tale to your mountains; Arcadians only know how to sing. O how softly then would my bones repose, if in other days your pipes should tell my love!'][6]

Once again, the primitivism of pastoral proves to be sophisticated, even factitious. Its simplicity is a concomitant of its stylized, representative quality, sometimes charged with clear symbolism. E. W. Tayler finds in pastoral a vindication of the principle of 'nature'.[7] But there is nothing naturalistic about nature in pastoral. It is balanced by an equal insistence on aesthetic ordering.[8] The elements of an experience are sifted, shaped, and distanced to form a 'realm in itself, an absolute realm, detached from all that is not art and literature', as Bruno Snell says of Virgil's Arcadia.[9]

This clarifying, ordering vision, worked by a controlling simplicity of syntax, diction, and total poetic form, is the most characteristic achievement of pastoral, but also its characteristic danger. The artifice is often too patently artificial or trivial: pleasant and untaxing, deliberately confined to superficialities instead of penetrating to the primary impulse. Escapism and nostalgia are traits commonly associated with pastoral.[10] Some have even viewed them as the mother elements to which the mode is always reaching out, or reaching back.

Further, such stylized simplicity inevitably leads to the creation of stereotypes. Much Renaissance pastoral resembles the drawings made with a child's pack of stencils, a set repertory of undemanding motifs in a limited number of combinations. Very little pastoral poetry realizes the

[6] All Virgil refs. and trs. to and from the Loeb Classics edn. by H. R. Fairclough (rev. edn. Cambridge, Mass., 1978). The Eclogues are in vol. i.

[7] E. W. Tayler, *Nature and Art in Renaissance Literature* (New York, 1964), *passim*, esp. pp. 4–9, 56–71.

[8] This is true even of the Theocritean 'pleasance' described by Rosenmeyer (ch. ix, esp. pp. 196–8), which conveys the beauty of the setting necessarily free of aesthetic—let alone allegorical—design.

[9] *The Discovery of the Mind*, tr. Thomas G. Rosenmeyer (1953; repr. New York 1960), 290.

[10] The most obvious instance, as the title makes clear, is Laurence Lerner's *The Uses of Nostalgia. Studies in Pastoral Poetry* (London, 1972); but perhaps significantly, the actual chapter on this theme (ch. ii) takes nearly all its examples from works not formally pastoral.

potential of the form. One may almost say that the 'otherness' of the pastoral setting frustrates its own purpose: it trivializes its deepest assumptions, makes un-serious what is most serious about the mode.

Yet the root pastoral impulse lies in this otherness and imaginative integrity. I have taken it as my guiding principle in this study, adopting Laurence Lerner's distinction between 'pastoral as convention' and 'pastoral as theme'.[11] The basic pastoral mode, inspiring and justifying the rest, assumes an imaginary shepherd world depicted for its own sake, symbolically reflecting and concentrating important aspects of the human condition but not passing into specific allegory. This is conveniently, if sometimes inadequately, referred to by W. L. Grant's term 'art-pastoral'.[12] It degenerates all too often into prettification and imitative triviality; but where vividly recreated, it marks the central working of the pastoral imagination. The symbolic potential of this pastoral is exploited by applying it to particular situations. Such application becomes increasingly nominal and jejune, the arid region of the allusive eclogue. But the degree of allusion can vary, as can the degree of pastoralism. 'Art-pastoral' and 'allegorical' pastoral are best viewed as the opposite ends of a graded series of possibilities rather than as black-and-white alternatives.[13]

My study suggests that the chief tendency of Renaissance pastoral is towards the allusive pole. Virgil's Eclogues were read almost exclusively in such terms in the Renaissance, and eclogues on the Virgilian model, in Latin, French, and Italian, are largely allusive and didactic, even where they contain a vivid pastoral setting. Such art-pastoral as was composed constitutes a subsidiary trend in the eclogue, a more important one in Italian romance and drama. Moreover, the eclogue disintegrates into an assortment of lyric models treating of increasingly disparate themes.

All these tendencies are reflected in English poetry before *The Shepheardes Calender*. But the *Calender* virtually inaugurates English Renaissance pastoral, and its original synthesis of conventions sets English pastoral on a completely different course from the continental. Even its allusions reach out towards the universal, and they are overshadowed by the shepherd's more general roles: as poet, lover, and

[11] Ibid. 27.

[12] W. Leonard Grant, *Neo-Latin Literature and the Pastoral* (Chapel Hill, 1965), *passim*. The nearest Grant comes to a formal definition is on p. 117.

[13] Even this may be putting it too crudely, as Rosenmeyer holds, deriding 'an orderly grid of limiting terms' (p. 277). Rosenmeyer's whole section on the subject (pp. 267–82) is subtle and illuminating.

dweller in nature. Neither Spenser nor his successors write art-pastoral exclusively; but the primacy of the vein is established to an unusual degree.

From Spenser to Drayton, the main body of English Renaissance pastoral provides a rich, solid, and distinctive body of work, though curiously precarious in its imaginative identity. Meanwhile, the Renaissance had evolved the genres of pastoral drama and pastoral romance: the former entirely new, the latter nearly so, barring the late classical *Daphnis and Chloe* and some partial medieval precedents. Within this more expansive compass, there grows a cyclic pattern of action whereby court and country take on a new productive interrelation. This fertile innovation produces the complex and suggestive versions of pastoral in Book VI of *The Faerie Queene*, *As You Like It*, and *The Winter's Tale*.

As the mainstream of pastoral poetry grows diffuse in Jacobean and Caroline times, the influence of these wider developments ensures new and stimulating compounds: *Britannia's Pastorals*, *The Muses Elizium*, the pastorals of Milton and Marvell. They are sometimes conventional in form, sometimes innovative; but their inner concerns reflect the full range of pastoral possibilities.

Such a substantial line of development can never be said to end; but Milton and Marvell provide a good stopping-point. The formal pastoral of later generations is a conventional shadow of its old self; while the vital inner concerns of the mode are conveyed through new types of nature-poetry and country literature which, though associated with formal pastoral and in many ways genuinely akin to it, are essentially different and in some respects opposed. The end of the Renaissance also marks the end of a long course of development in pastoral. It is this course that I intend to trace in this book.

PART I

Pastoral in the Continental Renaissance

2
Virgil Allegorized

FOR THE Renaissance, the great model for pastoral poetry was Virgil's Eclogues or Bucolics. The precedence of Theocritus was always granted, and sometimes his superior excellence as well. But Latin prevailed far more than Greek; the Bucolics were universally read in the schoolroom; and the reflected glory of the *Aeneid* shone upon Virgil's other works as well. Renaissance commentaries on the Eclogues thus took on a great importance,[1] and inevitably affected the new pastorals being composed in that age.

Commentaries on the Bucolics, and on the pastoral generally, bring out a curious dichotomy in Renaissance views. Both elements go back to late classical commentators. On the one hand, pastoral poetry is related to primitivist ideals. The fragment of fourth-century commentary ascribed to Aelius Donatus[2] holds it

probabilissimum, bucolicum carmen originem ducere a priscis temporibus, quibus vita pastoralis exercita est et ideo velut aurei saeculi speciem in huiusmodi personarum simplicitate cognosci, et merito Vergilium processurum ad alia carmina non aliunde coepisse nisi ab ea vita, quae prima in terris fuit.[3]

[most probable, that bucolic poetry derives its origin from ancient times, when the pastoral life was practised; and therefore, in such simplicity in the characters is recognized, as it were, the image of the Golden Age; and Virgil, progressing to other poetry, rightly did not begin elsewhere but from that life which was the first on earth.]

[1] See Richard Jenkyns, 'Classical Sources for English Pastoral Literature, 1575–1635' (B.Litt. diss., Oxford, 1975). See also Fred J. Nichols, 'The Development of Neo-Latin Theory of the Pastoral in the Sixteenth Century', *Humanistica Lovaniensia*, 18 (1969), 95–114; J. M. Evans, 'Lycidas, Daphnis and Gallus', *English Renaissance Studies Presented to Dame Helen Gardner* (Oxford, 1980); B. R. Smith, 'On Reading *The Shepheardes Calender*', *Spenser Studies*, 1 (1980), 69–93.

[2] I shall refer to it as 'Donatus'. The authorship is immaterial to my purpose.

[3] ll. 240–6 in J. Brummer (ed.), *Vitae Vergilianae* (Leipzig, 1912). The Renaissance texts of late classical commentators do not always correspond to the modern. I have checked Brummer's text against that in Virgil's *Opera* (Venice, 1544).

Puttenham is unusual in recognizing pastoral as a late and sophisticated genre.[4] J. C. Scaliger represents the more general view: 'Vetustissimum igitur Poematis genus ex antiquissimo viuendi more ductum esse par est.'[5] [Therefore it is right that the oldest genre of poetry should be drawn from the oldest manner of life.] Nomadic hunters marked the earliest phase of civilization; herdsmen, next to appear, instituted poetry.

The next stage in the argument also goes back to the fourth century, to Donatus and Servius: 'primo enim pastoralis fuit in montibus vita, post agriculturae amor, inde bellorum cura successit.'[6] [For pastoral life in the mountains came first; then followed love of tillage, and later the conduct of war.] This 'naturalis ordo' was followed by Virgil in his three principal works: the Eclogues, the Georgics, and the *Aeneid*.

A parallel assumption relied upon the composition of society at a single point of time. The idea grew in the feudal Middle Ages. John of Garland writes:

> Tria genera personarum hic debent considerari secundum tria genera hominum, que sunt curiales, ciuiles, rurales . . . Secundum ista tria genera hominum inuenit Uirgilius stilum triplicem . . .
>
> [Three kinds of characters ought to be considered here, according to the three types of men, which are courtiers, city dwellers and peasants . . . According to these three types of men, Virgil invented a triple style.][7]

In the Renaissance, Jodocus Badius Ascensius (whose commentary was first published in 1500) fits these occupations into the life-span of individual Romans:

> Nam prima est rusticis pecoris cura: deinde agrorum quorum cultu indurati tandem ad arma gerenda idonei censentur.[8]
>
> [For first, to rustics, comes the care of flocks; then of fields, hardened by the cultivation of which, they are at length judged fit to wield arms.]

Minturno proposes a slightly different pattern. A well-governed *civitas* has three spheres of activity: *urbanum*, *bellicum*, *rusticum*. The *Aeneid*

[4] *The Arte of English Poesie*, I. xviii G. Gregory Smith (ed.), *Elizabethan Critical Essays* (Oxford, 1904; repr. 1964), ii. 40, ll. 9–23. I am assuming for the sake of convenience that the *Arte* is entirely Puttenham's work.

[5] *Poetices libri septem* (Lyons, 1561), I. iv, p. 6, col. 2.

[6] Servius, ed. G. Thilo (Leipzig, 1887), III. i, p. 3, l. 30–p. 4, l. 1. (Henceforth 'Thilo', cited by volume, part, page, and line no.) I have checked Thilo's text against the Renaissance version in Virgil's *Opera* (Lyons, 1528) and found substantial, if not exact, correspondence in the passages cited here.

[7] Text and translation as in *Parisiana Poetria*, ed. T. Lawler (New Haven, 1974), 10.

[8] Virgil's *Opera* (Lyons, 1528) fo. †7v. All citations from Badius from this edn.

deals with the first two, while the Eclogues and Georgics concern the third, which is the oldest of all.[9]

This leads to another distinction, the *stilus triplex* of John of Garland's account. Donatus, followed by Servius, established the idea that Virgil's three works illustrate the three principal oratorical modes: the simple, middle, and grand. These were related to the three classes of men. In Servius's words (Thilo, III. i. 2. 2–5; cf. Donatus, ll. 253–9),

nam in Aeneide grandiloquum [stilum] habet, in georgicis medium, in bucolicis humilem pro qualitate negotiorum et personarum: nam personae hic rusticae sunt, simplicitate gaudentes, a quibus nihil altum debet requiri.

[For in the *Aeneid* he has a grand style, in the Georgics an intermediate, and in the Bucolics a humble, after the quality of the actions and characters: for the people here are rustics, delighting in simplicity, from whom nothing profound should be required.]

Medieval and Renaissance commentators consistently repeat this.

Here then is a strong assumption of pastoral simplicity in the Eclogues. But at the same time, there are important considerations prompting the very opposite view. After all, the Eclogues are written by the poet of the *Aeneid*: there is an implicit *gravitas* in all his works. Minturno practically finds in the Eclogues the grandeur of heroic poetry:

Quam puro simplicique & uerborum & sententiarum genere haec eadem exprimenda sint, Theocritus ostendit . . . Itaque Virgilius quominus eam tenuitatem assequeretur, & diuinam poetae maiestatem, & grauitatem Romanam in causa fuisse putandum est. (*De poeta*, p. 166)

[Theocritus shows in what plain and simple manner, of both words and observations, these same matters can be expressed . . . Hence the fact that Virgil attains less to this sparseness, is to be thought owing to both the divine majesty of the poet and to Roman *gravitas*.]

'Divinum' is Minturno's customary epithet for heroic poetry.[10]

Also, as we shall see in a moment, the Eclogues were scoured for references to Virgil's life and times, which could scarcely be identified with a simple pastoral culture. As the Deventer school commentary, published at the end of the fifteenth century, puts it,

[9] *De poeta . . . libri sex* (Venice, 1559), 99.

[10] There is another special, and irrelevant, sense in which Minturno considers pastoral to be a species of 'epic': for by that term, he signifies all poems 'quibus neque cantu, neque saltatione opus sit' [in which there is no use of either song or dance]: *De poeta*, p. 417. There seems little point in seeing this as a general association of pastoral and heroic poetry, though the attempt has been made by Rosenmeyer (*The Green Cabinet*, pp. 4–5) and F. J. Nichols, pp. 107–10.

Intentio autem virgilij scribentis bucolica fuit sub iocundis verbis & in persona rusticorum pastorum laudare augustum caesarem . . . laudare etiam protectores suos pollionem et mecenatem. In quo relucet magnum ingenium virgilij scilicet comprehendere magnam rem in parua videlicet imperatores senatores & alios praesides in persona pastorum.[11]

[However, Virgil's intention in writing the Bucolics was to praise Augustus Caesar using light words and in the guise of simple shepherds . . . and also to praise his protectors, Pollio and Maecenas. Whereby Virgil's great genius shines forth, even to comprise great things in small, namely emperors, senators, and other rulers in the guise of shepherds.]

At about the same time, Cristoforo Landino wrote his more advanced commentary on the same assumption of an 'opus duplici argumento ornatum'[12] [work adorned with a double subject].

Theocritus's Alexandria and Syracuse were scarcely primitive rural communities either, but this was remembered less often because of the standard contrast between Theocritus's simple pastorals and Virgil's more complex and allusive ones. Servius, as usual, provides the *locus classicus*: Virgil

aliquibus locis per allegoriam agat gratias Augusto vel aliis nobilibus . . . in qua re tantum dissentit a Theocrito: ille enim ubique simplex est. (Thilo, III. i. 2. 17–20)

[at some points, he might render thanks through allegory to Augustus or to other noblemen . . . in which respect he differs from Theocritus, for the latter is always simple (i.e. literal, non-allegorical)]

Virgil's ingenuity was particularly admired where he reworked Theocritus so as to incorporate an allusion. Jodocus Badius writes:

Si ad Theocritum respexerimus dixerimus omnia simpliciter dicta. . . . uerum multa est Maronis ars qui Theocritum imitando institutum suum persequi nouit. (fo. 24ᵛ, col. 1)

[If we were to look back to Theocritus, we would say that everything was simply said . . . great, indeed, is Virgil's art, who, while imitating Theocritus, knew how to pursue his own design.]

Though Theocritus's non-pastoral Idylls are full of allusions, only once perhaps does his pastoral turn allegorical: in Idyll VII, the shepherds may stand for his poetic circle, with himself as Simichidas. Rare too are the intrusions of the poet's own personality (as at the opening of Idyll XI). Virgil goes much further in this direction. The Bucolics undoubtedly

[11] *Bucolica. P. Virgilii Maronis cum commento familiarissimo* (Deventer, 1492), sig. A2ʳ.
[12] Virgil's *Opera* (Nuremberg, 1492), sig. Π2ᵛ.

contain a fair amount of allusion, though its extent is a fertile source of controversy.[13] Tityrus in Eclogue I has been customarily taken to be Virgil himself. His farm, it is said, was nearly seized by a veteran of Philippi, but saved by the intervention of Octavian, whom he thanks in this poem. Modern scholars dispute this, but are inclined to grant that the dispossessed Menalcas of Eclogue IX may be the poet. It is highly probable that Daphnis in Eclogue V is Julius Caesar, deified after his death.

Other eclogues refer explicitly to the poet's friends and patrons. Eclogue X treats of Cornelius Gallus's misfortune in love, against a background of cryptic references to his poetic career. There is also a puzzling compliment to him in Eclogue VI. 64ff.; compliments to Asinius Pollio in III. 84ff., IV. 11 ff., and VIII. 6–13, and to Publius Alfenus Varus[14] in VI. 6ff. Above all, of course, there is the mystifying prophecy of the miraculous child in Eclogue IV, who shall be born during Pollio's consulship. Eclogue VI has a didactic aspect—Silenus singing of the creation and of various myths—as well as an allusive: the compliment to Gallus appears to be a literal interlude in a continuous sequence of allusions to neoteric poetry.

But this catalogue of external matter misrepresents the quality of Virgil's pastoral. Some of the allusions are brief and incidental: an opening aside, a passing exchange in a singing-match. Others are organically woven into the pastoral: the literally rural affairs of Eclogues I and IX, the consistent pastoral metaphor of Eclogue V—if indeed there is any allusion here at all. We cannot tell. The imaginary pastoral world remains the dominant reality; the Roman world is admitted only where it conforms. As R. D. Williams puts it, 'It is an involvement of mood and emotion, not of external resemblances . . . We are not dealing in the *Eclogues* with substitution, but we are sometimes dealing with an enlargement of the pastoral world through its partial alignment with the real world.'[15] 'Virgil's influence,' writes Frank Kermode, 'is therefore not without its dangers: it is easier to reproduce the letter than the spirit.'[16] Virgil's Renaissance imitators habitually succumb to this danger, inspired by an exaggeratedly allegorical reading of the Eclogues.

[13] In this paragraph and the next, I have taken my information about commonly accepted allegory in the Eclogues from H. J. Rose, *The Eclogues of Virgil* (Berkeley, 1942), and R. Coleman (ed.), *Vergil: Eclogues* (Cambridge, 1977). Rose and Coleman do not themselves always agree with the interpretations.

[14] The identification is uncertain.

[15] *Virgil* (1967), 9–10.

[16] F. Kermode (ed.), *English Pastoral Poetry from the Beginnings to Marvell* (London, 1952), 27.

Servius, influential throughout the Renaissance, is sometimes credited with discrimination in this matter. As we saw in an earlier quotation, he posits allegory only at certain points. Elsewhere he says, 'refutandae enim sunt allegoriae in bucolico carmine, nisi cum . . . ex aliqua agrorum perditorum necessitate descendunt' (Thilo, III. i. 33. 13–15).[17] [For allegories are to be opposed in the Bucolics, unless they derive from some exigency connected with the lost lands.] He says this while denying that 'fures' [thieves or knaves] in Eclogue III. 16 alludes to Virgil's alleged pursuit of Quintilius Varus's wife. Similarly, he does not grant that the ten apples sent by Menalcas to Amyntas (III. 71) stand for the ten eclogues.

But, on the whole, Servius is sympathetic to allegory. He dismisses the preposterous, but admits everything short of it. He endorses the belief that Eclogue III. 95, 'ipse ariem etiam nunc vellera siccat' [the ram himself is even now drying his fleece], refers to Virgil's plunging into the Mincio to escape his evictor, the (probably mythical) centurion Arrius. About Eclogue II, Servius repeats several theories: Alexis is Augustus Caesar, or a slave-boy given to Virgil by Pollio, or one owned by Caesar himself (Thilo, III. i. 18. 3–8). He mentions, without explicitly supporting, the view that the singers in Eclogue VII are Virgil and a rival contending before Augustus (Daphnis) (Thilo, III. i. 85. 14–17). In Eclogue V he admits that 'puer' [boy] in line 54 cannot refer to Caesar; but that, in line 30, 'thiasos inducere Bacchi' [to lead on the dances of Bacchus], must refer to him, 'quem constat primum sacra Liberi patris transtulisse Romam' [of whom it is well known that he first carried the worship of Bacchus to Rome]: Thilo, III. i. 58. 1. Badius plaintively comments, 'si vt Seruius docet haec sequentia manifeste de caesare dicta sunt: non video cur reliqua de eo dicta negem' (fo. 24^{v}, col. 1). [If, as Servius teaches, these things that follow are manifestly said of Caesar, I do not see why we should deny that the rest is said about him as well.]

By and large, Renaissance commentators are avid for allegory. Much of it comes from Roman history, real or imaginary. In Eclogue I, not only is Tityrus Virgil, but (after Probus[18] of the first century AD) Meliboeus is Gallus. In Eclogue II Alexis is Augustus, or else the same Gallus, a

[17] Cf. Donatus (ed. Brummer, ll. 295–6): 'in bucolicis Vergilii neque nusquam neque ubique aliquid figurate dici, hoc est per allegoriam.' [In the Bucolics of Virgil, neither nowhere nor everywhere can something be said to be spoken figuratively, that is in allegory.]

[18] Thilo, III. ii. 329. 3–4. Here too I have ignored the controversy over the authorship of the commentary attributed to Probus.

courtier spurning Virgil (Corydon), a mere poet.[19] The slave-boy theory also finds many adherents. Eclogues III and VII are said to reflect Virgil's poetic rivalries, with courtly patrons as the singers' sweethearts.[20] The contests may also be seen as reflecting the rivalries of other poets or citizens.[21] In Eclogue V, Daphnis is usually Julius Caesar, but sometimes Quintilius Varus or the poet's apocryphal brother Flaccus Maro.[22] Eclogue IV forecasts Augustus Caesar's 'golden' reign.[23] In Eclogue X, Gallus's suffering in love stands for his political downfall, with Augustus cast as Lycoris![24] Abraham Fleming even sees in the Pharmaceutria's (or Sorceress's) efforts (Eclogue VIII) 'the poets seeking of *Agustus* his fauour for the recouerie and hauing againe of his lands and cattell'.[25]

On the whole, Eclogue VI remains unscarred. Even the indefatigable Juan-Luis Vives, of whom more anon, confesses (fo. 28ʳ) 'Nulla est hic opus allegoria, ipsa per se sunt satis magna, & cantari digna.' [There is no need of allegory here; they are great enough in themselves, and fit to be sung.] But Servius provides an allusive touch: the two lads Chromis and Mnasyllos are Virgil and Alfenus Varus, and Silenus is Siron, who taught them Epicurean philosophy. Aegle stands for Epicurean hedonism, seen as a feminine trait (Thilo, III. i. 66. 22–7).

Most ingenious of all are Stefan Reich (Riccius) and Vives. Riccius provides two paraphrases for each poem, a literal and an *ecphrasis allegorica*. Even the former has moral and allegorical elements. The allusions can be matched piecemeal from other commentators; Riccius's speciality is to assume a double strand of meaning right through. Landino had earlier postulated a 'dupl[ex] argument[um]' without working out the details. Melanchthon goes further, postulating that all pastoral, even the earliest, carries an allegorical intent: 'Semper enim fuerunt cantilenae, & rusticis figuris alias res ac personas cantilenis significare mos fuit' (sig. B1ʳ). [For there have always been songs, and it was the practice to intend other matters and persons in the songs under rustic forms.]

19 See the *Paraphrastica interpretatio* of the Eclogues by Stephanus Riccius (Stefan Reich) appended to Melanchthon's *Argumenta seu dispositiones rhetoricae in eclogas Virgilii* (Gorlitz, 1568), sig. I1ʳ. (Henceforth 'Melanchthon' or 'Riccius' as appropriate.)

20 See Juan-Luis Vives, *Vergilii Bucolica . . . in eadem allegoriae* (Milan, 1539), fos. 12ᵛ, 15ᵛ, 29ᵛ. (Henceforth 'Vives': refs. to the 2nd sequence of foliation, containing the commentary.)

21 See Melanchthon, sig. C8ʳ.

22 See Riccius, sig. Q5ʳ; *The Bucolikes of Publius Virgilius Maro*, tr. A. Fleming (London, 1575), 13–14.

23 See Riccius, sig. P7ᵛ.

24 See Vives, fo. 34ᵛ.

25 *The Bucoliks of Publius Virgilius Maro . . . Together with his Georgiks*, tr. A. Fleming (London, 1589), sig. D3ᵛ.

But the first prize for allegorizing must go to Vives. He finds it inconceivable that Virgil would have wasted three years over pastoral toys, or that Augustus and other noble Romans would have read him if he had. He is impatient even with Servius's occasional rejection of allegory, in places where to Vives it is 'manifestissima' (fo. 2^{v}).

Less acute wits may be astonished at Vives' ingenuity. Meliboeus of Eclogue VII, looking for his he-goat, becomes Virgil coming to Rome to recover his land. True, the poem is clearly located on the banks of the Mincio—that is, in Virgil's native land rather than Rome—but that is to conceal the allegory, 'ad tegendam allegoriam' (fo. 30^{r}).[26] With such an appetite for *lucus a non lucendo*, there are plainly no limits to what Vives can discover.

In one direction, he is absorbed in the Christian allegory. Eclogue IV was commonly read as a prophecy of Christ—usually unwitting on Virgil's part. Vives draws this to unprecedented allegorical lengths, involving the whole history of the Church. As a crowning touch, he claims it is not allegory at all but a literal reading: 'Taceant impij. nam vel simplici verborum sensu, absque vllis omnino allegorijs, de nullo prorsus alio potest intelligi quod hic dicitur, quam de CHRISTO' (fo. 18^{r}). [Let the impious be silent. For in the simple literal sense, removed from all allegory whatsoever, what is said here can truly be understood of none other than Christ.] Here Vives is at least extending a long tradition. His interpretation of Eclogue V is, as far as I know, unique: he relates it to the death of Christ as prophesied in Sibylline verses. (Eclogue IV is commonly traced to such verses.) Virgil, however, was borrowing from those verses to mourn the death of Caesar (fo. 21^{v}) 'ex ignorantia veri sensus' [from ignorance of the true meaning]. This must rank as a staggering instance of double allegory, Christ as well as Caesar.

In the process, of course, Vives totally ignores the pastoral framework and details, barring the occasional bucolic touch dictated, it seems, by the decorum of the *mos pastoricius*. This is a virulent form of a common malady. All too often in the age, appreciation of pastoral poetry seems to entail a contempt for the pastoral world, an impatience with its terms in the urge to penetrate to the 'real' and more exalted meaning beneath it. The Renaissance cult of the pastoral often conceals a basically anti-pastoral stand.

Yet at the same time, the range of possible themes for the pastoral metaphor is greatly expanded. The eclogue is given a new validity in

[26] Fleming explains this to his satisfaction: as Daphnis belonged to Sicily, his appearing by the Mincio is a clear sign of allegory. (*Bucoliks* [and] *Georgiks* (1589), sig. D2^{r-v})

terms that hold meaning for the age. This is the first of many ways in which, as we shall see, the pastoral is simultaneously enriched and impoverished.

There is yet another sort of 'figure' that the allegorists constantly discover in the Eclogues, generally despite the poet. Eclogue II. 8 ff. is a favourite passage: 'nunc etiam pecudes umbras et frigora captant . . .' [Now even the cattle court the cool shade . . .]. Vives interprets this as follows, and Riccius repeats his very words: 'In tanta pace Italiae, in tanta quiete omnium, & securitate Octauiani virtute parta . . .' (Vives, fo. 9^r; Riccius, sig. 11^v). [In such peace in Italy, in such repose of all things, and safety engendered by the virtue of Octavian . . .] Obviously this is not the same as holding Tityrus to be Virgil. That was an act of identification, A taken to be B. Thenceforth the poem could be read more or less literally, applying to B what is said about A. Here, on the contrary, the noontide setting is read as metaphor; the literal meaning disappears. We may call this a figural or symbolic mode of expression. Melanchthon calls it the true allegorical, as opposed to the tropological, where the literal meaning runs parallel to the figurative.[27]

This sort of allegory was encouraged by Servius. The beech-tree in Eclogue I. 1 is, he says, an 'arbor glandifera, quae fuit victus causa' [a nut-bearing tree that was a source of food], thus standing for Tityrus–Virgil's land and possessions (Thilo, III. i. 4. 24–5. 1). In Eclogue IX. 15, the croaking raven in the hollow oak stands for the clamorous soldiers destroying the land (Thilo, iii. i. 111. 19–21).

The Renaissance was not slow to follow such a lead. The technique can lend gravity to the trivial exchanges of the amoebean eclogue. Menalcas's query (Eclogue III. 1) 'Dic mihi, Damoeta, cuium pecus?' [Tell me, Damoetas, who owns the flock?] is said to be a hit at pastoral poetry: 'Carmen hoc pastoricium, quo tantopere te effers, cuius nam est? An est Poetae alicuius ignobilis, Meuij puta uel Bauij?' [This pastoral song for which you give yourself such airs, whose is it really? Is it some ignoble poet's, Maevius's for instance, or Bavius's?]: Riccius sig. I 8^v. Gallus's intemperate passion stands for Virgil's love of his lost farm.[28] The fauns, beasts, and oaks moved by Silenus's song (Eclogue VI. 27–8) stand respectively for rational, animal, and vegetable existence, indicating that 'musica & sapientes & efferatos atque imanes ac denique stupidos ac pene a sensu destitutos delectat'.[29] [Music delights both the

27 *Institutiones rhetoricae* (Cologne, 1522), ch. xiii (sig. D4^v–E1^r).
28 The Deventer commentary (ed. cit.), sig. H2^r.
29 Landino's commentary (Virgil's *Opera*, Nuremberg, 1492), fo. 14^r.

wise and the savage and monstrous, and even the dull and those almost devoid of understanding.] Badius has a readier explanation for this universal joy: Silenus nursed Bacchus, and Bacchus signifies wine, which is 'nursed' in a pleasant climate and surroundings (fo. 27^{v}, col. 1).

From Vives, I have room for only a few choice examples. In Eclogue III. 36 ff., the beechwood cups stand for 'elegantiam, facetumque dicendi genus' [elegance and fineness of style]: fo. 14^{v}. In Eclogue V the lions are the pagans who mourned Christ's death, like Pilate or the centurion. The shepherds, unsurprisingly, are the apostles (fo. 22^{v}). Nature's lament at Gallus's death (Eclogue X. 13 ff.) is elucidated thus: 'lauri, hoc est poetae ac studiosi, myricae, plebes, saxa, id est infimi in vulgo, & imperitissimi ac rudissimi' (fo. 35^{r}) [laurels, that is poets and scholars; tamarisks, common men; stones, that is the lowest of the rabble, the most ignorant and uncultured]. The shepherds and swineherds (Eclogue X. 19) indicate 'omnium & plebis & procerum admirationem' [the admiration of all, both the vulgar and the eminent].

The pastoral setting dissolves before such 'figural' interpretations. Trees and animals are really persons; shepherd maidens turn to elder statesmen; cattle and lizards, fragrant soups and beechwood cups are reduced to such abstract concepts as peace and poetry. The pastoral world cannot take on a true existence. Its features are evoked, as necessity requires, to suggest aspects of the courtly or 'real' world, but they cannot yield a coherent picture of shepherds' lives.

One final class of 'inner meanings' may be introduced by Vives' reading of Eclogue VIII. Mopsus's marriage to Nysa suggests the rewards reaped by the undeserving. The Pharmaceutria's rites show how a person who cannot succeed by fair means resorts to foul (fos. 31^{v}–32^{r}). This is not so much allegory as moralization, and indeed is compatible with a literal reading of the poem. Erasmus even moralizes 'that horrid one | Beginning with "Formosum pastor Corydon"'.[30] It is said to show the frustration of an ill-matched love.

Corydon rusticus, Alexis vrbanus; Corydon pastor, Alexis aulicus; Corydon indoctus . . . Alexis eruditus; Corydon aetate prouectus, Alexis adolescens; Corydon deformis, hic formosus. Breuiter dissimilia omnia.[31]

[Corydon rustic, Alexis urban; Corydon a shepherd, Alexis a courtier; Corydon untaught . . . Alexis learned; Corydon advanced in age, Alexis adolescent; Corydon ugly, the other handsome. In brief, everything is dissimilar.]

[30] Byron, *Don Juan*, i. 42.

[31] *De ratione studii*, ed. J.-C. Margolin: *Opera omnia*, i. 2 (Amsterdam, 1971), 142.

Time brought its revenge. As we shall see, Erasmus's own love-eclogue was unmercifully moralized. At the other, unacademic extreme, Abraham Fleming misunderstands the nature of the Epicureanism in Eclogue VI to provide an edifying depiction of vice: 'So that in *Silenus* we haue the portraiture of drunkennesse & drowzinesse, and in the others the representation of Venerie and fleshlie pleasures.'[32] Gallus's love, of course, was readily, and habitually, used as an exemplum of lust and inconstancy.[33]

Elsewhere the moral is drawn from a few lines only. Silenus's salacious quip (Eclogue VI. 25–6) 'carmina vobis, | huic aliud mercedis erit' [you shall have your songs, she another kind of reward] is given an amusingly grave interpretation by Vives: 'Vos viri accipietis eruditionem, quam eligetis, hoc erit precium laboris vestri. animo autem foemineo, pecunia erit curae suae precium' (fos. 27ᵛ–28ʳ). [You men shall accept learning, which you choose: that shall be the reward of your labours. But to the feminine soul, riches shall be the reward of its toils.] Eclogue VIII. 43, 'Nunc scio, quid sit Amor' [Now I know what Love is], is itself a moral observation; but Vives double-refines it (fo. 33ʳ) to refer to 'omnem animi cupiditatem, siue auri, siue decoris, gloriae, magistratus, veneris' [all desires of the soul, for wealth, beauty, glory, office, or love].

Ultimately the moral may not even lie within the poem but be marked in a digression. Landino takes the first step in this direction. *Pace* Bruce Smith (p. 75), Landino does not provide a detailed Platonic or other philosophic interpretation of any eclogue. But he does provide long explanatory notes of particular lines and phrases that may approach philosophical definitions, like that of *formosu[s]* (Eclogue II. 1) cited by Smith, or *pec[us]* (Eclogue II. 20), or *bon[us]* (Eclogue V. 1). By Vives' day, this has turned into didactic excursus. Vives comments on the same *formosus*: 'Quid formosius, quam animi lineamenta, vt dicunt Stoici, & amico suus amicus, & doctus docto, candido vtique?' (fo. 8ᵛ) [What is more beautiful than the lineaments of the soul, as the Stoics say, particularly to the pure-minded? So friend to friend, so the wise to the wise.] Corydon's passion acquires a mystic turn (fo. 12ʳ): 'Talis est hominum vita, quoad iungatur & vnum fiat cum Deo.' [Such is the life of men, until it is conjoined and made one with God].

But Riccius goes furthest in this direction. His *paraphrasis* of Eclogue V is followed by a long meditation on *contemptus mundi*. He quotes Genesis, Job, and Corinthians, and ends:

[32] *Bucoliks* [and] *Georgiks* (1589), sig. C4ᵛ.
[33] For examples see J. M. Evans, pp. 237–8.

Quis autem tam ferreus est, tam saxeus, tam omnis humanitatis expers, Si Heroicas Caesaris uirtutes ob oculos ponat ... qui non idem nobiscum in moestissimas uoces erumpat & nostrum luctum suum esse ducat. Ea est humanae uitae conditio, ea sors, ea imbecillitas (sig. L1r).

[But who is so unfeeling, so stony-hearted, so devoid of all humanity that, if he places the heroic virtues of Caesar before his eyes, does not break out with us in saddest tones and hold our sorrow to be his own? This is the state of man's life, his destiny, his helplessness.]

This scarcely suggests the joyful spirit of the apotheosis of Daphnis.

As far as moral meanings went, Theocritus's 'simple' pastorals were as promising as Virgil's 'allegorical' ones.[34] Idyll XXI, on a fisherman's dream of wealth, was a moralist's favourite. The lover in Idyll III is, according to Eobanus Hessus, 'impotentis animi typum mire repraesentans' [the type of the immoderate soul, wonderfully represented].[35] Riccius makes a thorough job of Idyll XIX, on Cupid stung by a bee: it treats 'de amoris uoluptate' [of the pleasure of love]: '... ut nil nisi mel in ea appareat, sed sub hoc melle uenenum, & dolores non paucos nec modicos tandem subesse ... confidebamus' (sig. O 6v) [so that there appears to be nothing in it except honey; but we have been convinced that finally there is poison beneath the honey, and sorrows neither few nor small]. Much later, Isaac Casaubon also finds here the theme 'Dulcia sic tristi semper sunt mixta dolore.' [Pleasures are always mixed thus with sad pain.][36] This is strikingly anticipated in Thomalin's emblem in Spenser's 'March'. Casaubon reads Idyll XXVII, a love-exchange ending in seduction, as weighing the advantages and disadvantages of marriage (p. 221). The shepherd and his girl have been reduced to a pair of discoursing moralists.

Casaubon also holds (p. 179) that Idyll XXIII (where a heartless youth is crushed under a statue of outraged Eros) teaches that 'nemo debet superbire propter formam' [no one should be proud of his looks]. More important, he reads Idyll XX allusively: the shepherd's complaint against a proud city girl is a rebuke to certain deriders of pastoral poetry (p. 153). The idea is older: we find it in the English *Sixe Idillia* of 1588.

Amidst all this theme-hunting, Ramus's commentary on the Bucolics

[34] I shall refer to all poems in the Theocritean canon by the poet's name, although his authorship of some of the pieces is doubted or rejected. The same applies to poems ascribed to Bion and Moschus.

[35] *Theocriti Syracusani Eidyllia*, tr. Eobanus Hessus (Basle, 1531), sig. C1r.

[36] *Theocriti Syracusii Idyllia & Epigrammata ... Iosephi Scaligeri & Isaaci Casauboni Emendationes seorsim dabuntur* ([Heidelberg], 1596), 151.

makes a pleasant change. He admits the 'autobiography' in Eclogues I and IX. Beyond this, his remark on Eclogue II indicates his position. He reports the attempted identification of Alexis, but protests

mihi magis placet communem locum, & communem affectum fictis nominibus a poeta cantari, ut sine tropo res simpliciter intelligatur, praesertim cum Theocriti imitatio constet.[37]

[It seems better to me that a common subject or common emotion should be sung by the poet under imaginary names, so that the matter can be understood simply, without rhetoric, particularly as the imitation of Theocritus is manifest.]

For Ramus, the fact that Virgil is imitating Theocritus argues that he must be writing simply. In Eclogue V again (p. 91), 'res simpliciter intelligi potest, ficti nempe argumenti, cum Theocriti imitatio appareat' [the matter can be simply understood, though indeed of fictitious subject, when the imitation of Theocritus is made clear]. The curt comment (p. 70) on the ram drying his fleece (Eclogue III. 95) is typical: 'Servius hic allegoriam facit de Virgilio pene per Arrium militem interfecto, nisi se in Mincium abjecisset: quod non placet.' [Here Servius devises an allegory of Virgil being nearly killed by the soldier Arrius, had he not cast himself into the Mincio. This does not seem right.]

I am not trying to promote Ramus as the apostle of simplicity. He subjects the Eclogues to an awesome battery of logical analysis, and indeed only exchanges one brand of pedantry for another. But this change is significant, for it implies a shift in the centre of attention. The complexities turn upon a different axis, based upon the form of the poem and not its external referents.

For Ramus, it is unnecessary to postulate a weighty allegory to lend importance or dignity to a poem. All discourse, even a minor poem in the humble style, even the talk of shepherds, has its inner structure and complexity, shares the same dialectic patterns as an exalted oration. The Ramist Abraham Fraunce says explicitly, 'not so muche as the mylke mayde without reasoninge sellethe her milke'.[38]

The Ramist approach affords the possibility of a rehabilitation of the pastoral, an interest in the shepherd's world for its own sake. It is indeed no more than a possibility. If we are to propose Ramus as an influence on pastoral poets—obviously a matter for extreme caution, that I shall not attempt here—we must recognize that his complex interpretations of

[37] *P. Virgilii Maronis Bucolica, P. Rami . . . praelectionibus exposita* (4th edn. Frankfurt, 1582), 45.

[38] *The Shepherdes Logic* (BL MS Addl. 34361), facsimile (Menston, 1969), fo. 4ʳ.

pastoral could also have a directly opposite effect. It could encourage the treatment of serious and complex themes, and relate the eclogue to larger and more elaborate structures of fiction and discourse.

It would be inordinately speculative to try to trace the influence of Ramus's commentary, or his literary ideas generally, even on a poet supposedly influenced by Ramism, like Sidney. There is nothing to suggest that Ramist notions had any direct effect on the nature of any pastoral work. I simply wish to point out the implications of Ramus's commentary itself. Alone in the age, it gives some support for taking Virgil's pastoral fiction as important in its own right: 'significatur hic Virgilius, ut Servio placet; mihi vero Corydon ipse significatur' (p. 45, on Eclogue II). [Virgil is meant here, as it seems to Servius; but, to me, Corydon himself is meant].

3

Allusive and Didactic Pastoral

It is beyond the scope of this book to afford a connected history of continental pastoral. I shall only outline the principal themes and concerns, with their effects on the nature and wider development of pastoral. While taking care not to offend against biography, geography, and chronology, I shall refer to such matters only to explain allusions or provide some basic historical bearings. I shall also consistently group together poems on the same subject written at different times in different countries. This is not meant to argue for direct influence but simply to record a recurrent development of the same resources of the pastoral convention.

Within this range, there are local groupings and tendencies: the unusually prominent court-compliment at Ferrara, to a lesser extent elsewhere in Italy, and again at the French court; the more didactic, social, and academic concerns of German humanists like Eobanus Hessus, Euricius Cordus, and to some extent Joachim Camerarius the Elder; the importance of local scenery and mythology in the Neapolitan humanists and Tuscan vernacular poets. But ultimately, these appear to be local mutations of the same recurrent developments. Borso d'Este of Ferrara, François I of France, and Philip, Margrave of Hesse, are lauded in the same vein[1] of *paulo maiora*, rising above the *humiles myricae*, as in Virgil IV. There are only minor differences between the Mantuanesque rusticity of Paolo Belmisseri,[2] an Italian sometime resident in France, and that of Camerarius the German, de Ponte the Dutchman, or for that matter Barclay the Englishman. The age discovered a variety of themes in the pastoral, but along with it a synoptic view of the genre. An anthology of thirty-eight pastoral poets, probably selected by Erasmus's former

[1] See respectively Boiardo's Latin Eclogue IV (Boiardo, *Tutte le opere*, ed. A. Zottoli (Milan, 1937), ii. 671); Andrelini I (*Eclogues*, ed. with Arnoullet's Eclogues by W. P. Mustard (Baltimore, 1918), 23); Hessus XIII (Oporinus, p. 568: see n. 3). I have used these edns. throughout for the poets in question.

[2] The name occurs in various forms. I have followed Grant, *Neo-Latin Literature and the Pastoral*.

secretary Gilbert Cousin of Noseroy[3] and published by Johannes Oporinus from Basle in 1546, runs from Calpurnius (fl. AD 50–60) to George Sabinus (1508–60), with the most casual regard for chronology. Petrarch comes after Pontano, Boccaccio between Eobanus Hessus (1488–1540) and Pomponio Gaurico (1481–1530). A 1504 anthology from Giunta of Florence runs from Virgil through Petrarch to Mantuan and Gaurico. We may compare E. K.'s easy association of Theocritus, Virgil, Mantuan, Petrarch, Boccaccio, Marot, Sannazaro (in that order) 'and also diuers other excellent both Italian and French Poetes'.[4] William Webbe spans the centuries with the same nonchalance: 'After *Virgyl* in like sort writ *Titus Calphurnius* and *Baptista Mantuan*, wyth many other both in Latine and other languages very learnedlye.'[5]

Renaissance pastoral (with its classical and medieval antecedents) is too far-flung a phenomenon to be reduced to a simple chronological pattern of contact and influence. Even direct imitation need mean little. Mantuan V is imitated in Barclay IV as well as Spenser's 'October': the two poems are poles apart in character. In 'December', Spenser imitates Marot's 'Eglogue au Roy' to totally different ends. Further, lines of influence run from pastoral to non-pastoral works and vice versa. In this and the next two chapters, I shall attempt to find a way through this complex interplay of themes and models.

1. *Allusion and allegory: The Neo-Latin eclogue*

Given the heavily allegorical reading of Virgil's Eclogues, it is hardly surprising that the Renaissance Neo-Latin eclogue should be allusive to an extraordinary degree. To be sure, there are a certain number of art-pastorals. Grant lists seventy or so; I have come across fifty-four among some 250 eclogues I have examined. Even among these, a few are set in specific localities. Some, while free of allusion, have such a strong moral note (Mantuan I, II, III) or earthy rustic flavour (Camerarius II, III, IV, VIII, XIX) that they scarcely qualify as art-pastoral.

Moreover, at least twenty-eight of Grant's seventy instances actually appear to contain specific allusions. I have listed these in Appendix A. To mention only one crucial example here, among this number are two of

[3] See Grant, p. 410. I have cited this anthology as 'Oporinus'. The title-page reads *En habes lector bucolicorum autores XXXVIII . . . Farrago quidem Eclogarum CLVI*.

[4] Epistle to Gabriel Harvey preceding *The Shepheardes Calender*.

[5] *A Discourse of English Poetrie*: Gregory Smith (ed.), *Elizabethan Critical Essays*, i. 262, ll. 22–5.

(Giovan) Battista Guarino's three eclogues, which Grant (p. 118) calls the earliest art-pastorals of the Italian Renaissance.[6]

As I remarked in my Introduction, allusive pastoral and art-pastoral are not mutually exclusive, and a poem dominated by one mode can touch upon the other. A series of mythical stories or bland amoebean exchanges may suddenly spring a reference to a friend or patron.[7] A shepherd's name may identify him with a real person by way of compliment, like 'Chronidon' (the famous teacher, Guarino da Verona) in Tito Vespasiano Strozzi's eclogues, or 'Beraldus' (Filipo Beroaldo) in Cayado IV.[8] At the very least, an art-pastoral may be prefaced by a dedication or compliment in Virgil's manner, but at much greater length. In Antonio Mario's 'Thyrsis', the complimentary opening occupies 26 out of 84 lines; in Scévole de Sainte-Marthe's 'Damoetas', 29 out of 100.[9]

Allusions vary strikingly in mode, degree, and extent. They may pervade the poem, occur at a single point, or even lie beneath the surface. The shepherd world exists simultaneously, contiguously, with the world of real men and affairs. The poets set out with this dual awareness, and present the two worlds in all possible combinations. Occasionally a particular eclogue may be confined to one end of the spectrum; but the poet always knows he has the full range to draw upon.

The allegorical reading of Virgil would be reinforced by two great exemplars from the earliest Renaissance, Petrarch and Boccaccio. Petrarch's Eclogues were printed, on their own or as part of the *Opera*, seventeen times between 1473 and 1581. They were also included in Oporinus's anthology of 1546. Boccaccio's Eclogues seem to have been printed only once before Oporinus, in 1504.

The allegorical nature of Petrarch and Boccaccio's Eclogues has been brought out in earlier studies.[10] I can therefore be brief. Boccaccio admits the possibility of eclogues whose meaning appears on the 'bark' or

[6] For Guarino's eclogues see his *Poema divo Herculi Ferrari Ensium Duci dicatum* (Modena, 1496).

[7] e.g. in Boiardo III, VII; Giambattista Amalteo V (Appendix to Sannazaro's *Opera* (Amsterdam, 1728), 387); Cornelio Amalteo, 'Proteus' (ibid. 460). These edns. used throughout for the Amalteo brothers.

[8] I have used Strozzi's *Borsias (fragmenta); Bucolicon liber*, ed. J. Fogel and L. Juhasz (Leipzig, 1933); Henrique Cayado, *Eclogues*, ed. W. P. Mustard (Baltimore, 1931).

[9] For Mario, see *Carmina illustrium poetarum italorum* (Florence, 1719–26), vi. 244; for Sainte-Marthe, his *Poemata. Recens aucta* (Limoges, 1596).

[10] See W. W. Greg, *Pastoral Poetry and Pastoral Drama* (1906; repr. New York, 1959), 22–6; Helen Cooper, *Pastoral: Medieval into Renaissance* (Ipswich, 1977), 36–46; T. G. Bergin (ed.), *Petrarch's Bucolicum Carmen* (New Haven, 1974), Introduction.

surface; but in fourteen of his sixteen efforts, it lies 'sub cortice',[11] and even one of the others (Eclogue I) alludes to Neapolitan politics. Petrarch is even more insistent on allegory: 'id genus est quod nisi ex ipso qui condidit auditum, intelligi non possit'.[12] [This genre is such that it cannot be understood unless heard from the very man who composed it.] The need for such commentary appears when we consider the astonishing degree of symbolism in Petrarch's Eclogues. A single instance must serve. In Eclogue I. 8–10, Silvius (Petrarch) goes wandering among mountain-peaks, wildernesses, mossy crags, and cataracts. This is explained:

Inaccessum cacumen . . . fame rarioris et ad quam pauci perveniunt, altitudo est. Deserta . . . sunt studia; hec vere deserta hodie . . . Muscosi scopuli sunt potentes ac divites . . . fontes sonantes literati et eloquentes homines dici possunt . . .[13]

[The inaccessible peak . . . is the height of a rarer fame, to which few attain. The deserts . . . are studies; today these are truly deserted . . . The mossy crags are rulers and rich men . . . the sounding springs can be said to be learned and eloquent men]

The Renaissance credits Virgil with such impossibly taxing allegory, but few poets incorporate it in their own work. Indeed it is impossible without an exegesis of some length—a luxury few could have enjoyed. The intricate play of parallels is reduced of necessity to a basically simple metaphor. Beyond the general correspondence, the pastoral proliferates into a maze of detail where the allegory cannot follow it. Here, for instance, is Mantuan (IX. 133–9) on the threats lying in wait for the 'shepherd' in Rome:

quando inter silvas graderis, defende galero
lumina, namque rubi praetendunt spicula longis
dentibus et curvus discerpit pallia mucro.
nec depone pedum multaque armare memento
cote sinum, ne te subito novus opprimat hostis.
et perone pedem tegito; spineta colubris
plena hominum vitae morsu insidiantur amaro . . .[14]

[When you step among the woods, protect your eyes with a bonnet, for bramble-bushes hold out their long-toothed prickles, and the curved spike tears at cloaks.

[11] Letter to Fra Martino da Signa: *Opere Latine minori*, ed. A. F. Massera (Bari, 1928), 216.

[12] Letter to his brother, *Familiarium rerum libri*, x. 4: see V. Rossi (ed.), *Le familiari* (Florence, 1934), ii. 304. Cf. the letter to the Roman Tribune, July 1347 (*Epistolae variae*, 42), quoted in translation in E. H. R. Tatham, *Francesco Petrarca* (London, 1926), ii. 406.

[13] Letter to his brother, *Familiari*, x. 4: ed. Rossi, ii. 306.

[14] All refs. to W. P. Mustard's edn. (Baltimore, 1911).

Nor should you put aside your sheep-hook; and remember to load your scrip with stones, that you may not be suddenly struck down by some new foe. And cover your feet with raw-hide boots: the thorn-bushes, full of snakes, entrap the life of men with cruel bite.]

The details here have no separate metaphoric function; they all make the same general point. So with the plentiful images of sheep-plague, wolves, and other pastoral perils, in contexts both religious and secular. Conversely, peace and plenty may be described in pastoral or rustic terms, as in Cordus I (Oporinus, p. 348):

> Omnia melle fluent, pia largiter omnia tellus
> Proferet, immensa rumpantur ut horrea messe,
> Magna nec accipiant infusum dolia mustum,
> Plenaque stent saturi noctu ad praesepia tauri.

[Everything flows with honey, the loving earth bountifully offers everything, so that barns burst with the immense harvest, nor can great jars hold the outpoured new wine, and full-fed oxen stand at night at well-stocked mangers.]

Occasionally at least, certain stock figures or roles are presented in genuinely pastoral terms. Foremost among these is the king or ruler. Virgil's Daphnis apart, the earliest model is found in Nemesianus I, where Meliboeus (unidentified, but surely a real person) is presented as a kind of master-shepherd. A more memorable instance is Argus in Petrarch II, standing for King Robert of Naples.

Following these, a genuine metaphor of the ruler as shepherd is applied to Louis XII of France in Belmisseri VI; Wilhelm II, Margrave of Hesse, in Hessus VI; either Wilhelm or his son Philip in Cordus IV; John Frederick, Elector of Saxony, in Johann Stigel's 'Iolas'; and Henri II of France in Jacob de Slupere's Eclogue VI.[15] A few lines from Stigel may speak for all (Oporinus, p. 778):

> Ille lupos repulit Getulis montibus ortos,
> Ille iugo docuit Tyrios subiungere tigres.
>
> . . . .
>
> Hei quoties nostris conuentus egit in agris.
> Iam certus uarias ruris componere lites,
> Et pacem aeternam pecorum stabilire magistris.

[He drove away the wolves sprung from the Gaetulian mountains, he taught how to subjugate Tyrian tigers to the yoke . . . How often, ah me, did he call for

[15] For Belmisseri, I have used his *Opera poetica* (n.pl., n.d.); for Hessus, Cordus, and Stigel, the text in Oporinus. For de Slupere see n. 17 below.

gatherings in our fields. He was sure to reconcile the various disputes of the countryside, and settle the rulers of flocks in everlasting peace.]

The first two lines are obviously modelled on Virgil V. 29 and take on a colouring of heroic myth from that poem. The place-names provide romantic touches: Gaetulia (Morocco) and Tyre could scarcely pose threats to Saxony. We may add that their fauna does not include wolves and tigers.

We cannot tell how many of the poets knew of Homer's description of kings as 'shepherds of armies' (*Iliad*, ii. 243). But they would all know the good and bad shepherds of Isaiah, Ezekiel, the Psalms and the Gospels,[16] and the shepherd as priest became another stock allegorical type. The lack of classical models would be compensated by two powerful eclogues from Petrarch (VI and VII) on the Great Schism and the corruption of the Curia. Of Mantuan's familiar pieces, Eclogues VII, VIII, and X deal with the poet's own Carmelite Order, and IX with the degeneration of the Curia. The last two poems are most vividly pastoral, as the passage quoted above on the dangers waiting for a shepherd may illustrate. Let me now quote instead an account of the Reformation by the Dutch Catholic de Slupere:

> Lanigerique greges, armentorumque magistri
> Errarunt passim, summo rectore carentes,
>
> . . . .
>
> Interea varios orbata per arua tumultus
> Exciuere lupi gregibus, miserisque colonis.
>
> . . . .
>
> Rarus erat, cui cura gregis communii, & idem
> Rura perexigua cum maiestate regebat.[17]

[The woolly flocks and herdsmen wandered here and there, lacking their highest ruler . . . Meanwhile, in the orphaned fields, wolves stirred up many agitations among the flocks and the wretched farmers. . . . It was rare to find one who had care of the common herds, and even he ruled over the fields with very little authority.]

Similar passages occur in de Slupere VI and VIII.

The shepherd may also be a type of the poet. Generally it is his singing that makes him so, even in opposition to his other tasks.[18] But occasion-

[16] See Psalms 23: 1, 80: 1, 95: 7; Isaiah 40: 11, 56: 11; Ezekiel 34; Matthew 7: 15; John 10: 1–16; Hebrews 13: 20, 1 Peter 2: 25, 5: 4.

[17] Eclogue VII: *Iacobi Sluperii . . . Poemata* (Antwerp, 1575), 148. All refs. to this edn.

[18] See Calpurnius IV; and in the Renaissance, Mantuan V. 15–19, Belmisseri I (*Opera poetica*, fo. 1^r), Cordus II (Oporinus, p. 350).

ally his more basic duties provide the metaphor. In Publio Fausto Andrelini XII, Corydon's life of rustic labour clearly stands for Andrelini's life as poet, scholar and teacher:

> Mox tanto ruris flagravi ardore colendi,
> Ut nimio immorerer studio; non frigus adurens,
> Torrida non aestas vetuit, non horrida grando
> Plurimus aut imber calido demissus ab Austro.
>
> . . . .
>
> Primus ego agricolas docui quos Franca tenebant
> Arva rudes; (ll. 166–9, 175–6)

[Soon I burnt with such ardour to till the fields that I wasted away with too much study. Neither could freezing cold stop me, nor scorching summer, nor the fearsome hailstorm, nor thick rain brought down from the warm south wind . . . I first taught the rude husbandmen of the fields of France]

This may well have been a model for Marot's 'Eglogue au Roy', for Andrelini taught in France for some thirty years from 1489, and was connected with the court. His eclogues appeared in 1496,[19] two years before Mantuan's.

Again, the shepherd may be a teacher: by his 'song' or lectures, like Pulitius (Poliziano) in Eclogue II of the Italianate Portuguese Enrique Cayado; by his general role as 'wise shepherd', like Chronidon (Guarino da Verona) in Strozzi I and II; or in a general parallel between the pastoral and academic communities. I shall treat later of Giles Fletcher's Cambridge eclogues. Much earlier, Hessus I uses the same metaphor to describe the poet's entry to the University of Erfurt in 1504. During the Counter-Reformation, de Slupere VIII (p. 169) describes the Academy of Douai as teaching

> morbos pepulisse salubribus herbis,
> Astrorumque minas tempestatisque futurae
> Signa, modumque gregis diuersa per arua regendi . . .

[to expel diseases with health-giving herbs, (tell) the warnings of the stars and the signs of coming storms, and the way to look after flocks in different kinds of pastures]

This also reflects the image of the shepherd as priest.

All these are instances of genuine metaphor. The pastoral mode is playing an organic part in the presentation of non-pastoral experience. From this metaphoric core, the 'allegorical' eclogue may take one of two

[19] Except the twelfth and last, quoted above, which first appeared in 1512.

courses. It may combine its allusive purpose with authentic pastoralism in a more consistent way, as I shall describe in section 4 of this chapter. Or, as happens more frequently, it may treat the pastoral element casually, ineptly, or not at all.

'Pastoral allegory' can sometimes be disconcerting. The poet draws upon a stock image whose details conflict with his specific theme. De Slupere describes in Eclogue VIII (p. 166) how the Pope sent emissaries to Protestant Germany:

> Pan toto Tyberinus ab orbe
> Pastores aetate graues, pecorumque Magistros,
> Cum Satyris etiam Faunos, nemorumque potentes
> Syluanos varijs hinc inde coegerat annis . . .

[From all over the world, Tiberine Pan gathered shepherds venerable in years, rulers of flocks, even Fauns along with satyrs, and sylvans of all ages, lords of the woods, and sent them here from thence]

The correspondence of satyrs and fauns to Church dignitaries is formally unimpeachable, but may raise a smile. Even so, such correspondence is rare. In Pigna's 'Salvius', a eulogy of Cardinal Salviati, fauns and satyrs felicitate the Cardinal, and

> Aspice quam pulchre quatiant ludente Napaea,
> Riteque Hamadryades alternis ictibus agros
> Tunc pedis alterni celeris: Dryadesque puellae
> Aspice . . .[20]

[see how prettily the Napaeans, sportively, and the Hamadryads, in practised manner, beat the ground with alternate blows of their swift feet: see too the young Dryads]

These pagan nymphs are patently unsuitable for praising a churchman; attempts at direct decoding would be out of place. It is simply that the poet's pastoral imagination has run away with him.

The pitfalls of allusive pastoral are very clearly revealed here. The imagery and subject-matter are so far apart that they can only be brought together with difficulty. Given the slightest relaxation of control, their terms will clash, or one side of the equation will swallow up the other.

This is best illustrated from the shepherd-ruler metaphor. As we saw, a king or ruler can be metaphorically presented as a shepherd: he rules his subjects as a shepherd rules his sheep. But in many such eclogues, there are also shepherds representing common subjects—who, in terms of the

[20] Pigna (Giovanni Battista Nicolucci), *Carminum libri quatuor* (Venice, 1553), 156–7.

metaphor, should be sheep. We have here a pretty puzzle involving two distinct images, easily confused. Belmisseri VI commemorates 'Livius' (Louis XII of France) as king of the shepherds but also a shepherd himself, 'pulchri pecoris ductor fidissimus'.[21] Similarly in Jean Arnoullet's Eclogue IV, Louis and Charles II, Count of Nevers, are both pastors, but so is their subject the poet.[22] We shall find some choice instances of such confusion in Alexander Barclay's eclogues.

A clash of metaphors threatens whenever shepherd-subjects praise a shepherd-king. Sometimes the king is made a sort of master-shepherd or overlord.[23] More commonly, the metaphor itself is abandoned. The shepherds, that is to say, are shepherds or common people; the king is a king, an object of awe and wonder, reigning from his distant capital.

This is the commonest method of political allusion in the Renaissance eclogue. It preserves the rustic setting while allowing kings and noblemen to be treated in a direct and adequate way. It also turns to good use the contrast between court and country. We see this already in the early Latin eclogues of Matteo Maria Boiardo (composed *c.*1463–5). In his Eclogue IX (*Opere*, ii. 683), Corydon hesitates before lauding Ercole d'Este of Ferrara:

> Quid faciam? Princeps laudari dignus; at ingens
> Gloria praecipuis jamdudum ornata triumphis
> Cum subit, imbelles trepidant nova pondera Musae.

[What could I do? The prince was worthy to be praised; but when his great glory, adorned with pre-eminent victories, rose to my mind, my unwarlike Muses trembled at this weighty new task.]

The shepherd's diffidence emphasizes the magnitude of courtly events.

This type of allusive eclogue—one cannot really call it allegorical—operates in two principal veins, which we may call the 'suffering shepherd' and the 'admiring shepherd'. Poems about the 'suffering shepherd' are set in the country. No doubt inspired by Virgil I and IX, they describe the ravages of war, tyranny, or other 'courtly' events and policies upon the rustic population. Some combine literal description with metaphor and myth, as in Belmisseri III (on a war I cannot identify), or Andrea Navagero's 'Damon', on the French invasion of Italy in 1512. The grass grows unwillingly, and trees give unwilling shade, for they see how

[21] *Opera poetica*, fo. 13^r.

[22] Arnoullet's *Eclogues*, ed. with Andrelini's by W. P. Mustard: see n. 1 above.

[23] So Nemesianus I; and in the Renaissance, Cordus IV (Oporinus, p. 365), Johann Stigel, 'Iolas' (ibid. 776), Barclay I (in the figure of Morton: see p. 122).

> Ipsi etiam hircipedes fauni, satyrique bicornes,
> Ipsae etiam in solos nymphae fugere recessus:
> Et se se ignotis occultavere latebris.[24]

[The very goat-footed fauns and two-horned satyrs, the very nymphs fled to lonely recesses, and hid themselves in obscure retreats.]

Other poets confine themselves to grimly realistic pictures of the war-torn countryside and ravaged, destitute peasants. There is little difference between the French invasion of Italy (1494–5) as described in Cayado I, the German Peasants' Revolt in Camerarius I, and an unidentifiable war in the ninth eclogue of Petrus de Ponte, a Dutchman settled in Paris whose eclogues appeared in 1512. In de Ponte VII, Virbius, just back from war, recounts its miseries. So does Empirus in 'Autarches', a later poem by Claude du Verdier.[25]

The shepherd also suffers in times of peace. Exploitation by townsmen and courtiers, deplored in general terms in Mantuan VI, is vividly detailed by Euricius Cordus. Cordus IX is a moving poem on the aged Lollus's suffering under a rich neighbour and a tyrannous city official. Eclogue VI castigates the neglect and greed of the clergy. The ecclesiastical metaphor of 'pastoral care' is used with bitter irony (Oporinus, p. 380): the priests are

> Pastores nostri; quibus omnes subdimur agni.
> Aequo animo, si nos tondent, mulgentque, feramus.

[Our shepherds: to whom we lambs are all subject. Let us bear it equably if they shear and milk us.]

These eclogues of the threatened, persecuted shepherd present a basic contrast between rural values and courtly forces. To that extent, they retain the original motives of pastoral, but they do not satisfy its deeper requirements. The shepherd becomes a one-dimensional figure, merely suffering or reacting to forces from the alien courtly world. His special pastoral functions no longer matter: he is not a ruler, lover, or poet, but only a representative of the rural poor. In moral and social terms, this may be a more honest and accurate mode; but formally it marks an atrophy of the pastoral.

This is also true of the 'admiring shepherd', however different he may otherwise be. The model here is Virgil I. 19, where Tityrus marvels at the

[24] Navagero, *Lusus*, ed. A. Wilson (Nieuwkoop, 1973), 36, ll. 15–17.

[25] For Camerarius, I have used his *Libellus continens Eclogas et alia quaedam poematia* (Leipzig, 1568); for de Ponte, his *Decem Aegloge hechatostice* (n.p., 1536); for du Verdier, his *Peripetasis epigrammatum . . . Ecloga . . . & alia poemata* (Paris, 1581).

wonders of Rome. The same awestruck rusticity guides the account of Rome in Calpurnius VII and the eulogies of Nero in Calpurnius I and IV as well. In the Renaissance this becomes a common mode of compliment. In Boiardo I, Pan himself is astonished by the feats of the new Hercules (Ercole d'Este). In Anisio II, rustic wonder is roused by the openly supernatural: a fisherman and two shepherds marvel at portents in the sky when Hernando Gonzalo of Cordoba defeats Louis XII's French army near Naples in 1503.[26]

The more sustained realism of northern poets makes the contrast more effective. In George Sabinus's epithalamium for Albert, Marquis of Brandenberg, Faustus reports the wedding to Palemon. There is a disturbing touch where a door-keeper drives out Faustus with a whip; but by and large, he talks with unmixed admiration of the pageants, feasts, and other celebrations.[27] De Slupere (Eclogue VI: p. 138) describes the Dauphin's wedding in a very similar way. Attention is focused throughout on the court. The shepherds are used to reflect this interest. They function as 'mirror characters', to borrow a term from criticism of the novel.

Even this secondary figure may be dispensed with. As a prologue to the imperial theme, the poet may simply follow Virgil IV and claim to sing of *paulo maiora*. Boiardo IV invokes Urania to inspire the praise of Borso d'Este, in a close imitation of Virgil IV. Hessus XVI pleads the license of *paulo maiora* to justify the paradox of a pastoral praising a city, Nuremberg. In Eclogue I (Oporinus, p. 514) Hessus had already praised Erfurt, 'Vrbs . . . Dicta, potens, opulenta, ingens' [a famous, powerful, rich, and vast city], though seen through shepherd eyes.

In fact, such courtly material needs no announcement or apology. As I remarked earlier, the Renaissance pastoral exists in a continuum of courtly allusion, and may pass at any point into a long passage on the subject. Andrelini is particularly prone to such bald stretches.[28] Boiardo I has a mythological setting, but praises Ercole d'Este in the directest possible terms. Girolamo Vida's Eclogue III presents the widowed Vittoria Colonna as a shepherdess, but her late husband Hernando d'Avalos as a soldier (Oporinus, p. 484):

> ut hostibus unus
> Obstiterit saepe, & prostratas ceperit urbes:

26 I have used the text of Anisio's eclogues in Oporinus, pp. 409–32.

27 Sabinus, *Poemata* ([Leipzig], 1563), sig. s3^{r}ff.

28 See Andrelini II, III, VII, VIII, X.

Vtque duces uictos tot magnis ceperit ausis,
Vna eademque die . . .

[that often he singly withstood armies, and seized overthrown cities; that also he captured vanquished rulers with so many great deeds of daring, on one and the same day]

It is neither possible nor necessary to separate the literal court-references from those couched in formal, transparently pastoral terms. The precise degree of metaphor at any given point has ceased to matter, because the metaphor itself is unimportant.

The Renaissance reversal of the pastoral impulse is best seen in its treatment of the highest and most archetypal pastoral image: the Golden Age, imagined as surviving among shepherds. In Virgil's words from Georgics, ii. 538: 'aureus hanc vitam in terris Saturnus agebat' [such was the life golden Saturn lived on earth]. It is an ideal of the past and a rural ideal, found in this form in Cayado IV, Belmisseri IV, Camerarius VI, and Cordus III. At least as commonly, however, it becomes a present or future state, the outcome of ideal courtly rule. The grand prophecy of Virgil IV becomes in Calpurnius I and IV a simple model for the praise of Nero. Renaissance poets readily follow this lead. Boiardo uses it twice of the Estensi of Ferrara, in Eclogues IV and VI. Later, Giambattista Amalteo applies it in his fifth eclogue to Federico Savorgnan, Doge of Venice, and Cornelio Amalteo sees Don John of Austria as establishing such a millenium. Appropriately for Don John, the victor of Lepanto, navigation will not cease (as was traditionally thought) in his Golden Age, but rather flourish in security![29] All these examples are from Italian poets; but Ronsard's French pastorals provide the most notable instance of this use of the Golden Age myth.[30] The deepest expression of the pastoral ideal is made reliant upon the courtly world and the terms of Iron Age civilization.

2. *Allusion and allegory: The French and Italian eclogue*

The courtly and transparent nature of Renaissance pastoral is best seen in French poets from Marot to the Pléiade. These poets have been treated in

[29] 'Proteus' ll. 78–9: Appendix to Sannazaro (1728), p. 462. For the cessation of navigation, see Virgil IV. 38–9.

[30] See the eclogue 'Deux freres pastoureaux . . .' (Ronsard's *Œuvres complètes*, ed. P. Laumonier, 20 vols. (Paris, 1914–75) xii. 146); the Fontainebleau 'Bergerie', ll. 37ff. (xiii. 78). All Ronsard refs. to this edn.

the context of English pastoral;[31] but so misleadingly by Merritt Y. Hughes[32] that more comment seems necessary. Hughes holds that Spenser absorbed classical pastoral through imitations by the Pléiade. Some of his arguments are convincing; others appear very doubtful.[33] But the overall result, in either case, is to link Spenser to the Pléiade and dissociate him from the classical poets. It becomes the more necessary to demonstrate the basically different, and more limited, nature of French pastoral.

Marot, indeed, shows a finer pastoral vein than his successors. Setting aside two ecclesiastical eclogues that are probably not his work, and two unmemorable genethliaca or birthday poems, we are left with the 'Eglogue sur le Trespas de ma Dame Loyse de Savoye' (1531) and the 'Eglogue au Roy' (1539). Both poems centre upon courtly matters and external occasions.

Louise of Savoy was the Queen Mother. In the elegy on her death, the allegory of government and court life is very clear:

> Plorons, Bergers, Nature nous dispense!
> Plorons la Mere au grand Berger d'icy!
> Plorons la Mere à Margot d'excellence!
> Plorons la Mere à nous aultres aussi![34]

[Let us weep, shepherds: Nature permits us. Let us weep for the mother of the great shepherd of this place! Let us weep for the mother of the good Margot! Let us weep for the mother of the rest of us as well!]

The 'grand Berger', of course, is the king, François I; Margot, his sister Marguerite d'Angoulême; 'nous aultres', the common people. We are led back to the court at every step. At one point, Marot exchanges the larger pastoral scene for a more congenial garden setting, and that explicitly 'le Clos de France' (ll. 141–4).

Similarly, pathetic fallacy is carried beyond the point of simple fitness: a comet appears as a portent, and the sun loses its heat (ll. 102, 186). Spenser, while imitating Marot's poem in 'November', restores decorum by pushing such excesses into the realm of pure metaphor:

[31] See Greg, pp. 61–2; Cooper, pp. 111–14, 134–5.

[32] 'Spenser and the Greek Pastoral Triad', *SP* 20 (1923), 184–215; *Virgil and Spenser* (1929, repr. Port Washington, 1969).

[33] e.g. his treatment of Spenser's 'August' (*Virgil and Spenser*, pp. 272ff.) and his assumption that Sidney's Arcadian eclogues were written before the *Calender*.

[34] ll. 57–60. All refs. to Marot's *Œuvres lyriques*, ed. C. A. Mayer (London, 1964).

The sonne of all the world is dimme and darke:
The earth now lacks her wonted light,
And all we dwell in deadly night . . . (ll. 67–9)

Marot does have more harmonious touches of nature, like a beautiful flower-passage that only grows symbolic at the end (ll. 239–40): 'branches d'Olive, | Car elle estoit la Bergere de Paix' [branches of olive, for she was the shepherdess of peace]. It is a moving poem, but essentially a courtly one. Marot is not really concerned with shepherds, and makes this very plain.

At first sight it is less plain in the 'Eglogue au Roy'. The first part of the poem gives a vivid account of life in the country. Some of the details come from Jean Lemaire des Belges,[35] but Marot adds an impressive charge of symbolism: the four seasons represent the course of human life, and rural activities become a metaphor for the poet's task. The king is Pan, in a hyperbolic but entirely consistent development of the pastoral metaphor.

But gradually the poem changes its course. The woodland gods had wept at Robin's songs; moreover,

Si firent bien les plus souverains dieux,
Si feit Margot, bergere qui tant vault. (ll. 142–3)

[So did even the higher gods; so did Margot, shepherdess of such worth.]

He then describes his contest with 'Merlin' to gain the favour of 'des pastoureaulx le prince' (l. 164). We are back in the world of the *eglogue à clé*. 'Margot' is again Marguerite d'Angoulême. 'Merlin', though not identified, is obviously a rival poet. Robin the shepherd accordingly becomes Clément Marot, and Pan is no longer a god. Now the flattery colours our response to the poetry itself:

Or m'ont les dieux celestes et terrestres
Tant faict heureux, mesmement les silvestres,
Qu'en gré tu prins mes petitz sons rustiques,
Et exaulsas mes hymnes & cantiques,
Me permettant les chanter en ton temple,
Là où encor l'ymage je contemple
De ta haulteur . . . (ll. 175–81)

[Now have the gods of sky and land, and even those of the woods, made me happy in that you take into favour my little rustic sounds, and praise my hymns

[35] *Illustration de Gaule et singularitez de Troye*, i. 21. See Marot, ed. Mayer, pp. 344–5.

and canticles, allowing me to sing in your temple, where I still contemplate the image of your greatness]

It emerges at last that Marot is asking the king to support him in the winter of his life. The anticlimax that concerns us is aesthetic, not ethical: not that Marot is begging for support, but that in so doing he should undermine the poetic possibilities of his mode.

Yet when all is said and done, Marot's eclogues show a certain independent pastoral impulse. Lerner is perhaps over-harsh in saying that 'Au Roy' shows 'a very transparent code, that deceives no one'.[36] But the remark would be entirely just if applied to Ronsard or Baïf.

Ronsard's 'Bergerie', though never performed, was written to be staged by princes and young aristocrats at Fontainebleau in 1564. It opens with talk of the shepherds' 'haute famille', and repeats such references all through,[37] backed by talk of arms and conquests. 'Guisin', the young Henri of Guise, sings of his crook as of a sword:

> Houlette qui soulois par les champs Idumées
> Comme de grands troupeaux conduire des armées . . . (ll. 587–8)

[sheep-hook that was accustomed to lead armies like great flocks on the fields of Palestine]

In an earlier eclogue on the marriage of Charles, Duke of Lorraine, Ronsard hopes that the progeny of this 'shepherd' will reconquer Naples and move on to the Holy Land.[38]

Apart from such cases, where the slip of the allegory is patently showing, there is a consistent focus upon the courtly world. The epithalamium opens by alluding to Meudon, the seat of Charles of Guise, Cardinal of Lorraine and patron of Ronsard and Du Bellay ('Perrot' and 'Bellot'). Hence when 'Pan' crops up, we at once link him with the king, and easily decode the statement that while 'Charlot' will protect Perrot and Bellot's flocks, he in turn will receive wealth and honour from Pan (ll. 101 ff.). Patronage is a constant and open concern. The blessings prayed for Charlot extend to his protégés,

> Puisque tu es si bon, & que tu daignes prendre
> Quelque soing des pasteurs & leurs flutes entendre. (ll. 107–8)

[36] *The Uses of Nostalgia*, p. 29.

[37] See ll. 31, 375–6, 967–8, 1095–6 (*Œuvres*, xiii. 73 ff.).

[38] 'Chant pastoral sur les nopces de Monseigneur Charles Duc de Lorraine, & Madame Claude Fille II. du Roy', ll. 368–70 (*Œuvres*, ix. 94).

[because you are so good, and deign to take some thought for shepherds and listen to their flutes]

The poem closes with an open reference to royal blood and martial prowess.

I need scarcely detail the compliment and political allusion throughout the Fontainebleau 'Bergerie', or the 1559 eclogue on the marriage of Marguerite of France to the Duke of Savoy.[39] In another eclogue,[40] the original Daphnis and Thyrsis are later renamed Carlin and Xandrin, to emphasize that they stand for King Charles IX and his brother Alexandre-Edouard, later Henri III. Pan is Henri II, and the French court (inconsistently enough) is 'le ciel': it was commonly compared to Olympus.[41]

Baïf's first eclogue is addressed 'Au Roy', like Marot's, and with the same purpose. But we have nothing of Marot's vivid pastoral opening. Baïf has alluded to his poverty already by the fourth line, and ends with a wish to celebrate the glories of the king. Eclogue XVII entertains similar hopes of Charles, Cardinal of Lorraine (Ronsard's 'Charlot'). Both poems present the poet as a shepherd; but King François had been a 'grand Berger' too, and his successor Henri II is 'un autre Francin'. Henri is Pan as well, who 'à CHARLE a donné des nos chams le souci' [has given charge of our fields to Charles].[42] The pastoral setting is vividly presented, but its metaphoric bearings are shifting and uncertain.

Elsewhere, Baïf's allusions concern literary affairs. These eclogues sometimes read as self-contained pieces of art-pastoral, but they are allusive every time. In Eclogue III, Toinet (Baïf) disgustedly abandons his pipe, inherited from a 'vieil Sicilien' (Theocritus) through 'Titire' (Virgil), 'Egon' (Sannazaro), and 'Ianet' (Jean Martin, Sannazaro's French translator).[43] Baïf is disputing the claim of another poet (probably Ronsard) to be the first pastoralist among the Pléiade. Eclogue XIX reflects another rivalry. The poet (here 'Pineau') defeats Robin, who has stolen his pipe. In the model, Theocritus VI, the honours were divided. In Eclogue VII, the contesting shepherds are Perrot and Belot (Ronsard and Du Bellay), and the judge is Janot (Jean Dorat, their teacher and mentor). In fact, by an amusing oversight pointed out by Alice Hulubei, we have

[39] 'Monologue, ou Chant pastoral, à . . . Madame Marguerite . . . Duchesse de Savoye' (*Œuvres*, ix. 174ff.).

[40] 'Deux freres pastoureaux . . .' (*Œuvres*, xii. 146ff.).

[41] Ibid., l. 263. See Laumonier's note, *Œuvres*, xii. 162.

[42] Baïf, *Euvres en Rime*, ed. C. Marty-Laveaux (Paris, 1883–6), iii. 93.

[43] Ibid. iii. 16–17.

'Toinet' for 'Janot' at one point: Baïf had originally made himself judge over his fellow-poets![44] In the burlesque Eclogue IV, the contestants quarrel and part before the singing-match can take place. References to the Pléiade indicate that this too is an attack upon rival poets in guise of the foolish Marmot and Jaquin.

Like his associates, Baïf seems unable to write an eclogue unless he is stirred by some external event. In other words, he never talks about shepherds unless he is thinking about something else.

Perhaps owing to a remark by Greg (p. 31), there is an impression that Italian vernacular pastoral is less allusive than its Latin and French counterparts. As far as the formal eclogue is concerned, this is far from correct. The body of Italian eclogues, no less than French and Latin, is solidly allusive. Other elements can be discussed only after this basic admission.

Boiardo wrote ten vernacular eclogues as well as ten Latin ones; and seven of the former are fundamentally allusive. The first two deal with the Venetian invasion of Ferrara (1482–4), also touched upon in Eclogue VIII. Political again is Eclogue IV, mourning the Venetian captivity of 'Teseo' (Nicolò da Correggio) but predicting his rescue by a new 'Ercole' (d'Este, of course). This eclogue has a strong mythological cast, and Eclogue I a strong pastoral one. In Eclogue II, however, both these elements are confined to the framework. They practically disappear in Eclogue X, a panegyric for Alfonso, Duke of Calabria, expected deliverer of Ferrara. Boiardo opens with the formula of *paulo maiora*:

> Questa matera che mia mente avisa,
>   Fuor de gli usati paschi è da cantare,
>   Cum meglior voce e versi d'altra guisa.[45]

[The subject which informs my mind is beyond the accustomed pastures of song, requiring a better voice and a different style of verse.]

Machiavelli also exhorts his 'fistula dolce', 'Più alto ingegno convien che si desti'[46] [it behoves that you arouse yourself to a higher skill], in an eclogue praising 'Iacinto' or Lorenzo de' Medici. Pastoral touches are in fair supply all through, but Iacinto is purely a ruler or patron, with the shepherds as his subjects.

Alamanni, on the contrary, is caught in the usual tangle of metaphors

44 Ibid. iii. 41; Hulubei, *L'Églogue en France au* XVIᵉ *siècle: Époque des Valois (1515–1589)* (Paris, 1938), 392–3.

45 Eclogue x. 4–6; all refs. to Boiardo's Italian eclogues to *Tutte le opere*, ed. Zottoli, vol. i.

46 *Parnaso italiano*, xvi (Venice, 1785), 69.

when praising François I of France. He is both 'il re de' buon pastori' [the king of good shepherds] and himself 'quel buon pastor, di cui le gregge | Givan sicure'[47] [that good shepherd, whose flocks went in safety]. In Eclogue XIII, Alamanni describes France as a happy pasture:

> Ivi per prati, per campagne e colli
> Senza il suo fido can, senz' altra guida,
> Posson sicuri andare armenti e gregge . . .[48]

[There in the fields, the plains and hills, the flocks and herds can move safely without their faithful dog or other guide.]

François himself, however, becomes more and more obviously a king, and his mother and sister are praised in literal terms. Literal too is the praise of the *condottiero* Andrea Doria, invoking the formula of *paulo maiora*. Alamanni tells the Muse of 'Siracusa e Manto' to add the Arno to her haunts:

> Non v'incresca il tornar, ch'oggi altro nome
> Ch'Amarillide, Filli, Tirsi e Mopso
> Cantar convien la mia zampogna tosca.[49]

[Let this new start vex you, that today my Tuscan sampogna should have to sing a name other than Amarillis, Phyllis, Thyrsis, or Mopsus.]

The degree of pastoralism fluctuates in ecclesiastical contexts too. One of the earliest published Italian eclogues, Jacopo Fiorino de' Boninsegni's 'Urania', fiercely condemns the Roman Church in a dark parallel to Virgil IV, but weaves in a good bit of pastoral metaphor, finally invoking Christ the Good Shepherd. The luxury of the prelates is contrasted with the Golden-Age fare of 'chiare linfe, erba tenella, a ghiande' [limpid water, tender herbs, and acorns].[50] Serafino I, on the same subject, also talks of once happy pastures now laid waste, and evil shepherds casting magic spells. But it has more to say about the wheel of Fortune and the downfall of pride. Serafino III passes clearly from the first to the second element: 'Li fulmini precipiti giú piombano | Gran marmori, gran arbori, gran culmini'[51] [the crashing thunderbolts fall upon great marble piles,

[47] Eclogue XII: Alamanni's *Versi e prose*, ed. P. Raffaelli (Florence, 1859), i. 292. All refs. to this edn., but eclogues numbered as in Alamanni's *Opere toscane* (Venice, 1542).

[48] ii. 7.

[49] 'Egloga. Ad Andrea Doria. Ne celebra le lodi', i. 299.

[50] First published in 1481 with Bernardo Pulci's translation of Virgil's Eclogues. Quoted here from G. Ferrario (ed.), *Poesie pastorali e rusticali* (Milan, 1808), 9.

[51] Serafino, *Le rime*, ed. M. Menghini (Bologna, 1894), i. 262.

great trees, great summits]. We have moved from the pastoral to the tragic plane.

Admittedly, open allusion and transparent metaphor are not the commonest modes followed by the Italian allusive eclogue. More often they proceed by another means, still fundamentally 'allegorical' but respecting the terms of the pastoral mode. I shall discuss these poems in section 4. First, I wish to complete my account of the atrophy of the pastoral by considering the moral and didactic eclogue.

3. *Moral and didactic eclogues*

George Puttenham, who seems to have had an acute grasp of the pastoral, draws a distinction between eclogues that 'glaunce at greater matters' and those that 'containe and enforme morall discipline'.[52] The didactic eclogue forms a substantial strand of Neo-Latin pastoral, though only Mantuan's work is remembered today. His ten eclogues were published early on, in 1498; eight of them, written in his youth (*c.*1465) were, by his own account, already circulating in manuscript.[53] Once printed, they became common reading in schools, and their influence was no doubt considerable. But to concentrate on Mantuan alone is to miss the range and variety of the didactic eclogue. To bring this out will be my principal concern.

The simplest didactic eclogues describe the shepherd's duties. Sometimes this serves to stress the toils of the 'suffering shepherd'.[54] Elsewhere it seems chiefly meant to teach such tasks, with Calpurnius V as the model. In Cordus IV, two shepherds discuss medicines and spells to cure cattle and ways to manage them; they then compare the shepherd's and farmer's lives in a fairly realistic manner. Hessus IX deals with a variety of shepherd lore, culminating in a curious debate on the relative merits of the sheep and the goat.

Other rural occupations may also be described. In Andrelini V, a farmer and a vine-grower describe their pursuits. Strozzi's first two eclogues describe the range of rural activities, season by season. The account of spring concentrates on the shepherd, summer on the husbandman, autumn on the vine-grower and honey-gatherer. Cayado IV provides the most idyllic account of this nature, and Camerarius VIII a very homely one.

[52] *Arte of English Poesie*, I. xviii: Gregory Smith, ii. 40, ll. 14–23.

[53] See Mantuan's dedicatory epistle: *Eclogues*, ed. Mustard (Baltimore, 1911), p. 62.

[54] e.g. Mantuan III. 17ff., VI. 94ff. Cordus IX; Camerarius XII.

Such eclogues are less pastorals than georgics. Virgil's model may at times be supplemented by Hesiod's *Works and Days*. Hesiod himself, after all, was a shepherd 'under holy Helicon' (*Theogony*, l. 23), and Virgil associates him with pastoral (Eclogue VI. 69–71). Hesiod's 'Georgica' (so designated) were printed for the first time in Latin translation in the same 1480(?) volume as Theocritus's Idylls. They were also printed together in some early Greek editions like the Aldine of 1495.[55] This could be seen as a Virgilian progression, for Virgil imitated Theocritus in the Bucolics and Hesiod in the Georgics.[56] William Webbe mentions Hesiod and Theocritus together, as writing in supposedly 'homely manner' of 'Sheepeheards talke and of husbandly precepts'.[57] The poets themselves sometimes make the same association. Camerarius says of his Eclogue XIV, a poem of much moral instruction and intermittent rustic lore, 'Ad Eclogam XIIII. pertinent praecepta operae et laboris Hesiodea.'[58] [To Eclogue XIV appertain Hesiod's precepts about tasks and labour.] In Andrelini V. 92, the farmer Amyntas and vine-dresser Corydon are said to have described pursuits 'Tityrus Ascraea lusit quae primus avena' [which Tityrus was the first to sing on the Ascraean pipe]. (Hesiod was born at Ascra in Boeotia.) Eclogues, Georgics, and *Works and Days* are run into a single reference.

There are also medieval precedents for eclogues detailing the shepherd's duties: Jehan de Brie's *Le Bon Berger*, or the long excursus on sheepkeeping in 'Bucarius's' *Pastoralet*.[59] *Le Bon Berger* is a businesslike manual, written to satisfy King Charles V's plan to improve sheep-keeping in France. Known only from an abridged version in several sixteenth-century editions, it describes the shepherd's duties in detail, month by month.

These affinities reverse the pastoral spirit by associating the shepherd with labour rather than *otium*.[60] The shepherd of convention had leisure for contemplation and discussion, poetry and love. As Scaliger says, 'Arator in opere: Pastor otiosus.'[61] [The ploughman is at work: the

[55] In 1516, Giunta printed Theocritus and Hesiod within a few days of each other, and the two edns. are commonly found bound together. See A. S. F. Gow (ed.), *Theocritus* (2nd edn. Cambridge, 1952; repr. 1965), i. p. xlvi n. 1.

[56] See Probus (Servius, ed. Thilo, III. ii. 323. 13–14); Servius (ibid. III. i. 128. 1–4).

[57] *A Discourse of English Poetrie*: Gregory Smith, i. 237, ll. 3–8.

[58] *Libellus continens eclogas*, p. 135.

[59] On *Le Pastoralet* see Cooper, p. 83. The work, primarily allegorical, contains a long disquisition on sheepkeeping.

[60] Cf. Rosenmeyer's remarks on 'Hesiodic' and pastoral poetry: *The Green Cabinet*, pp. 20–30.

[61] *Poetices libri septem* (1566), I. iv, p. 6, col. 2.

shepherd has leisure.] The georgic-pastoral, like certain other types we examined before, dismisses this symbolic shepherd for the true rustic living in a real and often hard world. We are not surprised to find that the eclogue for which Camerarius cites Hesiod also has a strong condemnation of *ocia* (*Libellus*, p. 58):

> Ocia regna, domos, vrbes perdentia totas.
> Ocia perpetuo fortunae inimica secundae,
> Ocia virtutis semper contraria laudi.
> Eneruatur ab his animus, fit debile corpus.

[Ease, destructive of entire kingdoms, families, and cities: ease, always the enemy of favourable fortune: ease, ever hostile to the praise won by virtue. The soul is enervated by it, the body enfeebled.]

Such eclogues can have two further motives of directly opposite import. First, they may be so oriented as to emphasize the beauty of the countryside and the delights of rural life. This is seen very simply in Cayado IV, and with more tempering realism in Strozzi I and II. Against these examples from southern poets we have the earthy realism of the German Camerarius's fictional farmer, staunchly upholding his way of life in Eclogue VIII (*Libellus*, p. 38):

> Neque splendidior me
> Sollicitum fortuna tenet, satis estque carere
> Ad mala traducente fame mihi.

[Nor does a grander fate keep me anxious; it is enough for me to be free of the hunger that leads to calamities.]

These poems lead on to the country idyll, which I shall treat in Chapter 5. But they also belong to the eclogue that treats rustic life as a moral ideal.

The ideal may sometimes take a sterner cast than in the examples above. In Cayado III. 1–38, Tirrhus calls Lycidas into the shade; but he prefers the sun, as being fitter for the shepherd's hard life. Ever since Theocritus, shepherds had sat singing in the shade of tree or cave. Such repose now yields to moral rigour. More elaborate praise of rustic toil comes in Andrelini XII. The shepherd Corydon is a figure of the poet, but his labours hold good on the literal as well as the symbolic plane:

> Difficilis rigidos res est tolerare labores,
> Mopse, homini plumis nutrito in mollibus; at qui
> Iam rerum longo durarum incalluit usu
> Huic notum grata est pondus subiisse voluptas. (ll. 206–9)

[Mopsus, to endure hard labour is a difficult task for a man coddled in soft down; but to the man toughened by long experience of hard things, it is an agreeable pleasure to have submitted to a familiar burden.]

More often than not, praise of rural life is balanced by a denigration of the city. The classic instance is Mantuan VI, with Fulica supporting the town and Cornix refuting him. This is clearly imitated in Belmisseri IV, where Philogaeus ('Earth-lover') defends the country against Politicus. Andrelini VII. 31 ff. has an equally clear contrast, published even before Mantuan's poem. Later, Gervais Sepin makes it one of the many concerns of his Eclogue I.

An important variation, deriving from Theocritus XX, sets the rustic lover against the scornful city girl. Scaliger III uses the model in a purely courtly context;[62] but de Slupere II shows a genuine opposition, warning Tityrus against the town-dwelling Thisbe. The implications become clearer in de Slupere III (*Poemata*, p. 84), where Sylvius rejects Tityrus's preference:

> nec turrigeris in moenibus vnquam,
> Ob rabiem belli, turbasque, dolosque latronum
> Me Superi posthac iubeant habitare coactum.
> Iam valeant vrbes, valeat tua, Tityre, vita . . .

[henceforth, may the gods never decree that I be forced to dwell within turreted walls, exposed to the fury of war and brawls and the guiles of thieves. So farewell to cities; farewell, Tityrus, to your way of life . . .]

Another interesting variation contrasts shepherd and soldier, as in de Ponte VII and du Verdier's 'Autarches'.[63] One may add Camerarius XI, though this is basically mythological: Oenone chides Paris for leaving his lowly but happy shepherd life for the vicissitudes of war and government. In fact, every eclogue on the ravages of war carries the same implicit contrast. The moral shepherd passes into the suffering shepherd.

The town–country debate reflects the deeper opposition of rich and poor. This is very clearly seen in Mantuan VI. Even earlier, in Boccaccio XIII, Daphnis the poet defends his mistress Saphos (poetry) against the merchant Stilbon's beloved Crisis (wealth). With this go more specific complaints against the neglect of poetry and learning. The classic attack on niggardly patrons comes in Mantuan V, with slightly earlier printed examples in Andrelini VIII and X and Cayado III, and later ones in Belmisseri I and Cordus II: the theme, not unnaturally, moves poets

[62] For Scaliger's eclogues, I have used his *Poemata in duas partes diuisa* (n.p., 1574).
[63] See above, at n. 25.

equally in France, Italy, and Germany. Some poems contain an appeal to the patron and thus approach the eclogue of court-compliment. Others are anti-courtly, complaining about poverty and social abuse:

> nec pecus in stabulis, nec in agro farra, nec aurum
> in loculis; et vis positis me vivere curis? . . .
> plena domus curas abigit, cellaria plena,
> plena penus plenique cadi plenaeque lagenae . . .[64]

[No cattle in my stalls, corn in my field, or money in my pocket: and do you wish me to live free of cares? . . . A full house drives away cares—full store-rooms, a full larder, full jars, full flagons]

Some so-called pastorals like Gaurico III dismiss the shepherd altogether and treat directly of the neglect of poets. As usual, we have northern examples to match the Italian. De Ponte I begins in pastoral terms, but soon speaks more plainly (*Decem aegloge*, sig. A3ᵛ):

> Magnates etenim fuluo merguntur in auro.
> Illecebrisve animos dedunt: nil carmina curant:
> Doctrinam insano tumefacti pectore spernunt.

[Truly, the great men are submerged in shining gold, or else they give their souls to allurements: none cares for songs. They spurn instruction with raging, swollen breast.]

Hessus XII presents an interesting variation. Polyphemus has a wonderful dream where the Muses offer him a crown, but he is warned by others that it leads to empty fame, pride, and eventual penury.

In the matter of love, the eclogues are divided. Once at least, in Hessus III, love is an urban affliction opposed to happy rusticity. Elsewhere, as we saw, simple rustics are warned against town girls. Yet shepherds habitually fall in love, and often come to grief thereby. Old shepherds moralize on such amorous folly—perhaps with a contrasting example of virtuous love. This is seen *in extenso* over Mantuan's first three eclogues. The first, 'De honesto amore et felici eius exitu' [Of virtuous love and its happy outcome], is exemplified from Faustus's courtship. The second and third treat 'De insani amoris exitu infelici' [Of the unhappy outcome of crazed love] as experienced by Amyntas. But even Eclogue I speaks of love as a painful and deranging experience, punctuating the narrative with Fortunatus's comments (ll. 114–18):

[64] Mantuan V. 73–4, 78–9.

FOR. Quisquis amat servit: sequitur captivus amantem,
fert domita cervice iugum, fert verbera tergo
dulcia, fert stimulos, trahit et bovis instar aratrum.
FAU. Tu quoque, ut hinc video, non es ignarus amorum.
FOR. Id commune malum, semel insanivimus omnes.

[FORTUNATUS. Whoever loves, is a slave: captive, he follows the beloved, bears the yoke on his subdued neck, endures sweet lashes on his back, endures goads, draws the plough like an ox.
FAUSTUS. I see from this that you too are not ignorant of love.
FORTUNATUS. It is a general misfortune, we have all been deranged by it some time.]

Again, Andrelini XII. 112ff. has a long attack on love, and Cayado V. 130ff. a brief one, both printed before Mantuan's Eclogues. Later, in Antonio Maria Visdomini's 'Sylvanus', two shepherds flee from an old beech, a favourite haunt of Cupid, after carving a warning on its bark in place of the usual love-song.[65] Camerarius is more directly didactic, as the northern Neo-Latinists often are. His Eclogue IX retells Theocritus's account of the death of Daphnis, with much sermonizing on the evils of love. The unworldly vitality of the classical shepherd-hero is exchanged for the cautious common sense of orthodox morals.

We also find much open satire of lovers and, most savagely, of women. The great model is Mantuan once again. His Eclogue IV is closely echoed in Belmisseri V and with more originality in de Ponte IV, where Crispus's son Amyntas has run girl-mad. Canus tells Crispus it is the common malady of youth, and the two old men join in cursing women (*Decem aegloge*, sig. c2ᵛ):

Incautos iuuenes et nescia pectora rerum
Forma, blandicijs, lingua, vi, fraudibus, astu
Plena doli mulier centum per crimina verrit.

[Woman, full of wiles, impels heedless youths and inexperienced minds with a hundred misdeeds, through looks, caresses, words, force, frauds, and cunning.]

In de Ponte X, the sardonic Lemnus deplores Cordolus's betrothal and tells him he has more cause to mourn than to rejoice.

Erasmus's sole eclogue is an interesting case. It is a totally undidactic poem on the love of Rosphamus (later changed to Pamphilus) for Gunifolda (or Galatea). But the commentator Alardus brings the poem into moral line. In a 1539 edition, the eclogue disappears amidst some

[65] I have used the text of Visdomini in Oporinus, pp. 215–19.

ninety pages of moralizing, largely on the evils of love and womankind, the excellence of virginity, and the ethics of marriage. The Argument is a misogynic composition echoing Mantuan IV:

> Non sic scorpius improbus timendus,
> Vt lasciua, salax & impudica
> Vitanda est Galataea, blanda Siren . . .[66]

[The evil scorpion is not to be feared so much as the wanton, lustful, and shameless Galatea, fawning siren, is to be shunned . . .]

If moralizing turns on the one hand to satire, it leads on the other to what can only be called philosophic discussion. Mantuan III opens with a debate on Heaven's justice. In line 12 Fortunatus castigates 'quis ventos tempestatesque gubernat' [whoever rules the winds and storms] for a disastrous hailstorm; Faustus says (l. 35) it is a just retribution for their 'Iurgia, furta, irae, Venus et mendacia, rixae' [quarrels, tricks, rages, lust, lies, and brawls]. Such debates occur all through Renaissance pastoral. The earliest and finest are in Petrarch II and IX. A later example, obviously inspired by Mantuan, is in de Ponte VIII. Cayado V. 66ff. laments the triumph of evil over good, but holds out some hope—as later, more forcefully, does Camerarius IV. Andrelini X. 103–20 and Cayado VIII. 83ff. reverse the pattern by warning recipients of good fortune to be prepared for worse.

Other moral matters may be treated as well. Boccaccio XV is an impressive instance. Phylostropus, the 'converting friend' (Petrarch) leads Typhlus, the 'blind man' (Boccaccio) from Crisis and Dyones (wealth and lust) towards the ascent to Paradise. Hessus VIII, mainly on the joys of country life, contains a meditation on death. A much more elaborate one comes in Arnoullet IV. Camerarius XIV is a compendium of good advice given by a father to his son. Particularly important is the praise of modesty (*pudor*); but, as we saw earlier in this section, there is a strong attack on *ocia*. Pastoral repose is routed by an early expression of the Protestant work ethic.

All Camerarius's eclogues are followed by his own moralizing commentary, often sitting uneasily upon the text. Eclogue II, a farmer's rich curse upon a marauding wolf, becomes directed (*Libellus*, p. 126) against 'violentia & crudelitas & scelerata saeuitia in imbecilliores, perniciosa rebus communibus' [violence, cruelty, and wicked savagery in

[66] *D. Erasmi . . . Bucolicon . . . cum scholijs Alardi Aemstelredami* (Cologne, 1539), sig. A3r. For the eclogue, see Erasmus's *Poems*, ed. C. Reedijk (Leiden, 1956), 136.

the rabble, destructive of the common weal]. In Eclogue XIX, Thestylis complains to Phyllis of her drunken husband and is advised patience. The racy, earthy poem takes on a different colouring in the notes (p. 138): 'Sunt autem & iam in hac sententiae consolantes incommoda aduersae fortunae, & celebrantes patientiam' [but we have here sayings offering consolation for the blows of adverse fortune, and lauding patience]. Mantuan had been more skilful in turning earthy rusticity to didactic purpose.

Spenser's 'February' is anticipated in de Ponte VI with its debate between the young Amyntas and the aged Pinus; and as in Spenser, we find a balance struck between the generations. Pinus deplores Amyntas' youthful profligacy. Amyntas protests that old men condemn the pleasures they cannot enjoy, idealize their own youth, and have the senile vice of avarice. We have passed beyond moralizing into acute satire of basic human foibles.

At the other extreme, the didactic eclogue turns mystical. Anisio III, entitled 'Sapientia', pastoralizes the fifth chapter of the Song of Songs. The daughters of Jerusalem become *nymphae*, and shepherd lads are asked to protect them.

Something very like genuine nature-mysticism appears in Gervais Sepin's Eclogue I. The old shepherd Menalcas has a philosophic concept of nature:

> Parentemque canes & oues ouiumque magistri
> Arcano sensu agnoscentes Numen adorant.[67]

[Dogs and sheep, and the masters of the sheep, adore the God who engendered them, knowing him by a mysterious faculty.]

He has had near-mystical experiences of this deity (p. 751):

> Ecce inopina mihi Natura oblata repente
> Egregia specie stupidos perstrinxit ocellos:
> Hei mihi quis decor? & quantum fulgoris in illa?
> In lauro & violis flauos redimita capillos,
> Bina serenatae pandebat sidera frontis
>
> . . . .
>
> Intentos figens oculos diuina colebam
> Ora Deae; at mecum, heu, cupiens retinere parumper,
> Effugit, & tenues euanida cessit in auras.

[67] *Delitiae C. poetarum Gallorum* (Frankfurt, 1609), iii. 750.

[Behold, unheralded Nature, suddenly revealed in marvellous shape, stunned my dazzled eyes. Ah me, what beauty, & how much of brightness there was in her! Her yellow locks wreathed with laurel and violets, she opened twin stars upon her serene countenance . . . Fixing rapt eyes upon her divine face, I worshipped the Goddess: but, alas, she fled me, who desired to retain her for a little while, and vanished upon the light breezes.]

The inaccessibility and interminable length of Sepin's eclogues have obscured their merits. Grant (p. 403) considers them unworthy of comment.

Basically, though, Sepin's first six eclogues are didactic pieces for his pupil Henri du Bellay. (The seventh and last mourns his death.) This brings us to a last group of eclogues, aiming simply at dispensing information. The figure of the discoursing 'wise shepherd' provided a conventional mouthpiece for miscellaneous instruction. The classic precedent was the popular French manual *Le Compost et kalendrier des bergiers*, many times printed in English as well. There is little or nothing pastoral in the work; but the shepherd appears all through as a sage instructor. 'Shepherds say . . .', 'Shepherds know . . .' is the stock opening to every chapter. In the library of Captain Cox of Coventry, 'The shepards Calender' is the first item under 'Poetrie & Astronomie, and other hid Sciencez'.[68] In a pastoral interlude in *The Complaynte of Scotland*, the knotty discourse of the chief shepherd—largely on astronomy—sits incongruously against the background of idyllic pastoral life.

Shepherds were held to be astronomers, from watching their flocks by night. Hence Meliseus (Pontano) can sing of the heavenly bodies in Zanchi I. In de Slupere IV, a nautical eclogue, Damastor the hero seems to stand for a navigator or explorer: he obviously knows about stars and the weather. The poem also covers European geography and, most notably, the history of the world, chiefly from Genesis.

There are other 'histories' in eclogue form, on the pattern of Virgil VI. Boiardo VI recounts the history of Italy from the earliest times, ending with an elaborate eulogy of Borso and Ercole d'Este. Instruction and compliment are also combined in Sannazaro IV, a marine eclogue with Proteus instead of Virgil's Silenus. His discourse stretches from the Titans' attack on heaven to the death of Federigo of Aragon, ex-King of Naples, in 1504. The poem opens on the note of *paulo maiora*: 'Nunc

[68] John Laneham, *A Letter:* . . . [Containing] *the Entertainment vntoo the Queenz Maiesty, at Killingwoorth Castl* (n.p., 1575), 35.

primum notas velis majoribus undas | Currimus' [now first we run over familiar waters with a larger spread of sail].[69]

Sepin's pedagogic eclogues are the most compendious of all. The first, for instance, opens with a discussion of floods; passes on to seasons, animals, flowers, crops, and other rustic matters; and then, more systematically, to the creation and the various orders of plants. He too declares that his shepherds were taught by those who 'non arbusta solum & humiles myricas sed paulo maiora persecuti syluas etiam canere sciant'[70] [know how to sing not only of orchards and lowly tamarisks but, seeking after somewhat greater things, of forests too].

Once again, the contents of the Renaissance eclogue have drawn us beyond the imagined narrow confines of the pastoral. At the same time, this is only made possible by straining, altering, or simply ignoring the basic implications of the mode.

4. *The two worlds of allusive pastoral*

In section 1 I pointed out the allusive nature of Petrarch's Eclogues. I must now redress the balance by describing the vivid pastoralism that accompanies the allusions. Scholars have been so caught in the tangles of Petrarch's allegory that they have neglected the richness of the pastoral itself. The wild scenery of Eclogue I is a good instance; another is the description in Eclogue IV against which the allegory of poetic inspiration is set:

> . . . vidit [me] ab alto
> Dedalus annosas inter considere fagos;
> Accessit, citharamque ferens:—puer, accipe, dixit;
> Hac casus solare tuos, hac falle laborem.
>
> . . . .
>
> . . . rigidas hac sepe per Alpes,
> Perque nemus vacuum, perque atra silentia noctis
> Fisus eo; plaudunt volucres et concava saxa . . .[71]

[Dedalus saw me from above, sitting among the old beeches. He approached, carrying his cithara. 'Take this, lad,' he said. 'Let your misfortune be soothed by it, your hardship beguiled.' . . . With this I often go boldly through the rude Alps, the desolate wood and the black silence of the night; the birds and hollow rocks applaud me . . .]

[69] ll. 1–2. Refs. to Sannazaro's *Piscatory Eclogues* as ed. and tr. (with a translation of the *Arcadia*) by Ralph Nash (Detroit, 1966).

[70] *Delitiae C. poetarum Gallorum*, iii. 829.

[71] Eclogue IV. 19–22, 58–60; all refs. to Bergin's edn. The trans. are my own.

Such vividly realized settings give a special permanence to the pastoral metaphor. In a different way, so do the ravaged landscape and grotesque, infected flocks of Eclogues VI and VII.

Even though allusive, these poems accept the special nature of the pastoral mode and recreate the shepherd world as a valid fictional entity. Boccaccio reveals the same awareness in his metaphors:

> Video sine vitibus ulmos;
> vix hedere vivunt. Solitos flavescere campos
> en vacuis plenos prospecto horrescere avenis;
> piscosique lacus, pontus fluviique quiescunt;
> cortex nullus inest, resonant nec litora tonsis,
> et passim video sparsas, heu! vasta per arva
> infectas tabo pecudes morbisque capellas . . .[72]

[I see elms without vines; the very ivy is scarcely alive. I see fields, accustomed to grow yellow (with crops), bristle full of hollow reeds; fish-filled lakes, sea, and rivers lie stagnant; not a cork floats upon them, nor do the shores echo with the sound of oars; and everywhere, alas, I see scattered upon the stricken fields sheep and goats infected with the plague . . .]

The problem with such luxuriant pastoralism is its uneasy yet necessary alliance with the external subject-matter. Except perhaps in Petrarch, the details are independent of the allegory; yet the allegory governs it all, so that the pastoral has only a qualified validity. At its most successful, however, the two run *pari passu*, almost like independent worlds coincidentally imaging each other. This is most finely seen in Giovanni Pontano.

Pontano's eclogues were all published posthumously: I to IV in the 1505 Aldine edition of his poetry, V and VI with three prose dialogues in Sigismund Mayr's 1507 edition. The first five eclogues are all allusive. (The sixth, 'Quinquennius', has nothing pastoral.) Eclogues IV and V express Meliseus or Pontano's love for his wife Adriana ('Ariadna')—in Eclogue IV, against a background of war. But both poems open with metamorphic tales. Eclogue V concludes with another myth, of Cupid blessing Ariadna after she frees him from captivity. Adriana was dead by this time, and Eclogue II mourns her death. Meliseus's own lament is preceded by that of Patulcis, the nymph of Virgil's burial-mount near Naples.

The personal and topical allusions are deeply imbued with myth.

[72] Eclogue V. 104–10; as in G. Lidonnici's edn. of *Il 'Buccolicum Carmen'* (Florence, 1914).

There is also a substantial presence of conventional shepherd life. This can grow very realistic: in Eclogue II. 24ff., the shepherds praise Ariadna's skill in hoeing and spinning, and in Eclogue IV. 20ff. Pontano himself comes clothed in skins, belching leeks and onions.[73] Yet all this is only a genial metaphor for the poet's life as a country gentleman. The pastoral is intense in effect but circumscribed in application, drawing us back to Pontano's own world.

The same duality is seen on a much larger scale in Pontano's treatment of the Neapolitan countryside. In Eclogue IV. 99–101, Meliseus's sheep graze there:

> balatum referunt colles Gaurique recessus
> Et Cumae vacuae et cryptae graveolentis Averni,
> antraque Musconis et opaca sepulcra Tuennae.

[The hills, the hidden nooks of Mount Gauro and deserted Cumae, the caverns of noisome Avernus, the caves of Musco and the dark tombs of Tuenna, echo the call of the sheep.]

This scene is strikingly depicted and mythologized in Eclogue I, which celebrates, in seven *pompae*, the marriage of Parthenope (Naples) to the river Sebeto, attended by rural gods representing the local regions and features of the landscape. The final marriage song is sung by Antiniana, the nymph of Pontano's own estate of Antignano.

The mythic figures image the features of the landscape. Mount Gauro carries a huge pine with forest animals, his consort Campe (the Campi Flegrei, west of Naples) a green alder laden with fruit. Butine, a quarter of Naples given to the meat trade, is 'dives haedis, sed ditior agnis' [rich in kids, but richer in lambs]; Ulmia, another quarter, 'libis et cognita buccellatis | . . . et intortis tantum laudata torallis' [renowned for its cakes and biscuits, and equally famous for its twisted *taralli* [a kind of bread]]. The nymph of the spring Pistasis gathers dills and endives and weaves baskets.[74] We pass from the grand to the homely and rustic. Country men and women lead the very first pageant. And the whole is cast in a pastoral framework featuring Macron and Lepidina, shepherd and shepherdess: Pontano and Adriana once again.

In this poem, local and personal matters are lost in pure myth and pastoral. The Neapolitan landscape is genuinely transformed into an idealized poetic world like Theocritus's own Cos or Sicily, though with

[73] All refs. to Pontano's *Carmina*, ed. J. Oeschger (Bari, 1948).

[74] See Pompa V. 44ff. (Gauro and Campe), Pompa IV. 3ff. (Butina), 6ff. (Ulmia), 17ff. (Pistasis).

much more mythopoeia. Elsewhere the imaginative exercise is less complete—as also in the eclogues on Pontano's death by Giano Anisio and Basilio Zanchi. Anisio I peoples the funeral with mythic figures out of Pontano's own pastorals, as well as Bacchus, Silenus, and Tethys. Zanchi evokes the local scenery with much pathetic fallacy, placing the 'Lament for Bion' in Pontano's own landscape, as it were. The dirge is sung by Amilcon:

> e scopulo, summique cacumine montis,
> Qua pelagi horrentes late despectat in undas,
> Et Baccho felix, felix uiridantibus umbris,
> Et cantu, & calamis Neptunia Mergilline.[75]

[from the cliffs and the summit of the highest mountain, where he widely overlooks the bristling waves of the ocean, and Mergellina by the sea, blessed with vines, with green shades, and songs and [the music of] pipes [Mergellina was Sannazaro's villa, overlooking the Bay of Naples].]

In Anisio V, Janus tells Mycon his grandfather's stories of Vesuvius and the surrounding region.

Similarly, Alamanni's vernacular eclogues are specifically set in Tuscany. Some are clearly art-pastorals. Eclogue VIII is practically a translation of Theocritus VIII, except for the change of setting—as later, Benedetto Varchi's Eclogue I is of Theocritus III. Alamanni VII rewords Theocritus II, making the erstwhile lovers meet beside the river Mugnon. Eclogue III hopes that Tuscany will become another Arcadia, 'Che più chiare d'Alpheo fian l'onde d'Arno'[76] [that the waters of the Arno may be brighter than those of the Alpheus].

This last poem, however, is not a Theocritean imitation but an allusive eclogue. Alamanni I and II combine both motives, mourning the dead poet Cosimo Rucellai ('Cosmo') in close imitations of Theocritus I and Moschus's 'Lament for Bion'. In Eclogues III and IV, Alamanni provides his own pastoral fiction for the allusive matter. Here too he alludes to Cosimo's death, but more centrally to the Florentine conspiracy of 1522 which sent the poet into exile and his companions Jacopo del Diacceto and Luigi di Tommaso Alamanni ('Menalca' and 'Mosso') to their deaths.[77] All this is turned to pastoral; Florence herself is 'la bella Flora', Melibeo or Alamanni's erstwhile love. The Florentines suffer as shepherds and rustics, not as city-dwellers (i. 68; Eclogue IV):

[75] Zanchi I: *Poematum libri VIII* (Basle, 1555), 164.
[76] Alamanni, ed. Raffaelli, i. 63.
[77] i. 61; see Raffaelli's note.

I campi che solean dal buon cultore
Prender riposo, senza pace o tregua
Portan d'aspra sementa il peso ogn'anno;
Onde gli armenti i quai fur freschi e lieti
Più che altri mai, son or debili e infermi . . .
Or son pei campi da infelice arena
E steril loglio vinti e l'orzo e il grano.

[The fields which used to repose under a good husbandman, now bear each year, without peace or respite, the burden of a bitter crop; so that the flocks, which were once stronger and happier than any others, are now feeble and infirm . . . Now, in the fields, the barley and the wheat have been vanquished by the wretched sand and the sterile darnel.]

In Eclogue XI, the death of a lady in childbirth is similarly transformed by the pastoral context.

Yet obviously such eclogues would not have been written except for their central, non-pastoral concerns. This vigorous but circumscribed pastoralism appears again and again in Italian eclogues. Varchi II concerns the Stufas of Florence, ending with dirges for a dead lady of the family. But the poem opens with a vivid Tuscan scene and is full of pastoral matters. One lament begins

O Driade, ò Naiade, ò Napee,
O Pane, ò Bacco, ò Cerere, ò Pomona,
O Pecorelle, ò Agne, ò Manzi, ò Tori . . .[78]

[O dryads, O naiads, O napaeae, O Pan, O Bacchus, O Ceres, O Pomona, O sheep, O lambs, O steers, O oxen]

Bernardo Tasso has an eclogue mourning his friend Antonio Broccardo, and two on the widowhood of Vittoria Colonna. Again we find vivid settings of nature, with some mythology and pointed 'art-pastoral' effects. These poems merge into Bernardo's other eclogues, which seem to carry no allusion at all; but some of them feature 'Batto'—Bernardo himself—and 'Galatea' may be his early mistress Ginevra Malatesta.[79]

The combination of allusion with independent pastoralism can be very superficial, as where Minturno provides three political poems with elaborate pastoral frameworks.[80] In the second and third, this takes the form of substantial sequences where Menalca tells Licida of his love. These can stand as eclogues on their own, and would perhaps have been

[78] Varchi, *Componimenti pastorali* (Bologna, 1577), sig. K4ᵛ.
[79] See E. Williamson, *Bernardo Tasso* (Rome, 1951), 58–9.
[80] For Minturno's eclogues, I have used his *Rime et prose* (Venice, 1559), 208 ff.

better left that way. At the other extreme, allusion, pastoral, and myth may be very closely combined. Boiardo's sixth Italian eclogue is an impressive fantasy: a hunter, pursuing a white goat sacred to Pan, talks to a shepherd by a pool sacred to Love. As Carrara says, this may be an allegory of love for a girl in a convent, or of poetic inspiration;[81] but it has an imaginative life of its own.

The most complex examples are provided by Girolamo Benivieni, the Florentine Platonist. He is perhaps the only pastoral poet to follow Petrarch's prescription of copious commentary. His eight eclogues operate more or less simultaneously at several levels. One is that of simple topical allusion. In Eclogue I, Phileno directs Moelibeo to the happy pastures of Varo—that is, Iulio Cesare da Varano, the poet's patron. But Moelibeo is also the poet, Phileno his desire for fame, and the flocks his eclogues. There is, moreover, a 'senso mystico': the higher faculties of the soul exhort the lower to enter the pastures of Christ.

Benivieni seems set on the classic course towards the abstract world of pastoral metaphor and 'allegory'. But his pastoral setting is remarkably substantial: it engages us by its literal terms. The city of Camerino becomes a vivid *locus amoenus*:

Nella piu uaga parte & piu amena
Del diletteuol coll'un prato siede
Bel si ch'imaginar non puossi appena.
Iui tra l'herba i fior lieti si uede
Mille pastor, che sicur ocio pasce
Et riposo tranquill' & pura fede.[82]

[In the prettiest and most agreeable part of the pleasant hill, there is a meadow so beautiful that one can scarcely imagine it. There among the grass and flowers a thousand happy shepherds meet, who feed their flocks on secure ease, tranquil repose, and simple faith.]

Sometimes at least, the symbolism seems an afterthought. Eclogue VII appeared first in a 1481 collection.[83] There, Titiro and Pico sang of a bevy of loves, with Mopso as judge. In the *Opere* of 1519, Mopso disappears. The singing shepherds are Pico (now very plainly Pico della Mirandola) and Lauro (Lorenzo de' Medici), and their loves are given

[81] Enrico Carrara, *La poesia pastorale* (Milan, n.d.), 184.

[82] Benivieni, *Opere* (Venice, 1524), fo. 82^r.

[83] Including eclogues by Benivieni, Boninsegni, and Francesco Arsocchi, appended to Pulci's translation of Virgil's Eclogues. (See n. 50 above.) I have consulted a 1494 edn. from Florence.

explicit philosophic meanings. The poem also alludes to the destruction of Otranto by the Turks.

Eclogue IV too has a double allegory. At one level, it describes the state of Florence after the death of Juliano de' Medici; at another, it reflects moral matters:

per Borea uento impetuoso et di natura freddo & secco, si significano le tentationi del Mondo, della carne et di Sathana . . . Per la oscurita della notte, le tenebre della ignorantia & la cecita dello intelletto. Per le Nymphe, per e pastori, & per le gregie lacere & abbattute, ogni buona cogitatione, opera & affetto (*Opere*, fo. 94^{r}).

[By Boreas, a fierce wind, cold and dry in nature, are signified the temptations of the world, the flesh, and the devil. . . . By the darkness of night, the darkness of ignorance and the blindness of the intellect; by the nymphs, the shepherds and the flocks exhausted and overthrown, every good thought, deed, and emotion.]

All this appears through a luxuriant growth of pastoral detail, as the last sentence makes clear. The misery of Florence becomes a matter of dying sheep and ruined cottages. The poet's personal ruin in Eclogue VIII takes on the harrowing image of the sheep-plague. In Eclogue II, the lament for Pico's death is couched as a love-plaint by Tirsi (Benivieni) for Daphni (Pico), modelled on Virgil II! This approaches the inept metaphoric excesses, where nymphs capered in praise of churchmen, cited in section 1. By and large, however, Benivieni keeps his medium under good control.

I shall end this section by describing, chiefly from Latin examples, what I can only call 'allusive art-pastoral'. Such poems give no internal indication of their allegory. It emerges only from the title, a note, the shepherds' names, or perhaps simply the reader's knowledge of the background. Only the title tells us that Buchanan's 'Desiderium Lutetiae' [Longing for Paris] is not an imaginary shepherd's yearning for his love but the poet's longing from Portugal—perhaps from prison—to return to his intellectual home. Earlier, in Italy, Anisio V conceals references to his circle in an account of a pastoral wedding-feast, even as Theocritus is thought to have done in the harvest-feast in Idyll VII, Anisio's model. In section 2 of this chapter, I noted some similar French pieces by Baïf. Also from France, J. C. Scaliger's Latin Eclogues III and V reflect actual love-affairs behind imitations of Theocritus XXVII and XX. The deserted shepherdess of his Eclogue IV was probably the victim of a court scandal.[84]

[84] Grant (p. 345) mistakenly identifies this shepherdess, Andis, with Ippolita Torelli, Castiglione's wife. In fact, Ippolita is Aegla, who merely reports Andis' lament.

By their nature, such hidden allegories will often be overlooked by the modern reader. De Slupere's first five eclogues seem to present imaginary shepherds. But a parallel group of poems (misleadingly entitled 'Lusus Pastorales')[85] feature the same shepherds in the same situations, but this time obviously as the poet's circle of friends. One title practically identifies Amyntas with a friend;[86] a verse-epistle (not part of the 'Lusus') names his love Aegle as Maria Wynther.[87]

The crucial point is that knowledgeable readers were meant to recognize the allusions. They provide the poem with its *raison d'être*. The pastoral details are so many signs alerting the reader to look out for allusions. Whatever intrinsic beauty it may contain, the metaphor is really reduced to a system of ciphers. The pastoral fiction is limited and undermined even as it is created.

The pastoral relies basically on a contrast between the country and the city or court. For all its frequent unreality, it has a potentially subversive function, questioning urban values by the mere fact of contrast or escape. In most allusive eclogues, this threat is brought under control. Here the two worlds coincide: however vivid the pastoral details, the controlling interest remains courtly or external. Such works may show vigorous exercise of the pastoral imagination, but the most distinctive functions of pastoral appear in them imperfectly or not at all.

[85] See Ch. 5, sect. 2, for the usual sense of the term.

[86] 'Ad Amicum singularem Marium Laureum Hyprensem. Vt Aeglae suae moestissimus supremum dicat vale. Carm[en] Troch[aicum] Amyntas', *Poemata*, p. 210.

[87] *Poemata*, p. 267: 'Ad Iacobum Yertzwertum', *Epistolarum ad amicos Liber I*, epistola iii.

4
Art-Pastoral

1. *Boccaccio and Sannazaro*

ALONGSIDE the allusive eclogue exists a certain body of art-pastoral. But in formal eclogues on the Virgilian model, it constitutes a precarious and subsidiary element; and even in other poetic forms, its independence is constantly threatened. Italian drama provides it with its most stable medium. Its three most important progenitors, however, are all technically romances: Boccaccio's *Ameto* (or *Comedia delle ninfe fiorentine*) and *Il ninfale fiesolano*, and Sannazaro's *Arcadia*.

Ameto and the *Ninfale* are only partially or obliquely pastoral. The *Ninfale* deals with the love of the shepherd Africo for Mensola, a nymph in Diana's virgin train. Diana turns her into a river, and Africo kills himself, though they leave a son to establish their line. Thus the pastoral world shades off into the mythological: the goddess walks the earth, and we hear of metamorphoses other than Mensola's. In another direction, Africo's world extends to his parents, Girafone and Alimena, who are true rustics of Boccaccio's own day. The idealized shepherd, Africo, stands between the real rustic world and an imaginary or mythological one. The two are contiguous yet opposed, and Africo and Mensola's love is a tragic meeting of these basically disparate worlds.

More happily, both worlds lead up to the political and courtly matter of the conclusion. The aged Girafone becomes counsellor to Attalante, the founder of Fiesole. His grandson Pruneo, offspring of the luckless couple, grows to be a landed lord and courtier. The poem ends with a history of Florence and Fiesole. It thus spans the entire area over which later pastoral literature was to range: the rustic, the mythic, the courtly, with idealized shepherd life as an uneasy nexus between them all.

Ameto goes far beyond the pastoral into a complex range of concerns, operating simultaneously at various levels through the work. There is the historical and political element, with its climax in the histories of Naples and Florence (chs. xxxv and xxxviii). Seven ladies relate life-stories that can be traced to actual Italian families. Among them is Emilia, and the career of her wounded warrior-protégé is Boccaccio's own, thinly veiled.

At the same time, the ladies stand for the four cardinal and three theological virtues: the work is knit together by the moral allegory, explicitly outlined in ch. xlvii. There is some incidental allegory too, as in the shepherd Teogapen, 'the love of God' (ch. x). Allegory apart, we have open discussion of moral, philosophical, and theological issues.

At yet another level, love is an important concern. The allegory is conveyed in startlingly erotic, generally adulterous narrative. But matters of love are seriously debated, and the love-stories obviously function as allegories of spiritual enlightenment. The *Ninfale* had shown the triumph of love over chastity: *Ameto* probes the deepest premisses underlying the theme.

The symbiosis of erotic and spiritual is matched by that of Christian and pagan. The ladies worship classical goddesses, and the work is full of Ovidian mythopoeia. Lia, one of the ladies, is Narcissus's sister, daughter of the river Cephisus (ch. iv), while Pacifico, beloved of Adiona, was born from a pear tree (ch. xxvi). The Muses appear in Mopsa's story (ch. xviii), and the early history of Florence incorporates a synod of the gods (ch. xxxviii).

Ameto thus reaches out to the political and topical in one direction, the remote and mythical in another, and the moral and theological in a notable third: all this in a continuum of amatory narrative in truly courtly style. The pastoral element lies in presenting all this through the eyes of Ameto the hunter-shepherd, against an idealized nature-setting. Ameto meets Lia while hunting and falls in love with her. His wooing-song echoes Virgil's Eclogue II with the roles reversed:

> E ciascheduna cosa i blandimenti
> ora dell'ombre cerca; ma tu sola,
> Lia, trascorri per l'aure cocenti;[1]

[And everything now seeks the solace of the shade; but you alone, Lia, wander in the burning air.]

Ameto hears Lia sing, and approaches her like a typical Petrarchan lover:

con pronto viso e timido cuore . . . e con quelle poche e non composte parole che egli dir seppe, nel grazioso coro si mescolò delle donne . . . (ch. v, p. 27).

[with eager face and fearful heart . . . and with those few inchoate words which he knew how to speak, he mingled with the gracious chorus of ladies . . .]

[1] Ch. viii, ll. 28–30; all refs. to *Ameto* as in Boccaccio's *Opere minori in volgare*, ed. M. Marti (Milan, 1971): chapter and line for verse, chapter and page for prose.

His lowly shepherd's station gives a special intensity to his Petrarchan adoration. The ladies' stories are prefaced by a purely pastoral singing-contest between Alcesto and Acaten. This reflects poetic and academic rivalries on one plane, and spiritual concepts on another; but in aesthetic quality it is purely pastoral. Boccaccio has discovered the capacity of pastoral for presenting sophisticated emotions, apparently inimical to its nature, with unusual directness and purity.

But in the central courtly narrative, this sophistication is carried so far that the pastoral element takes on a second, opposite function, that of contrast. Right from the beginning, Ameto is presented (ch. v) as a crude rustic unworthy of Lia's love, 'in abito rozzo, ne' boschi nato e nutricato' [rude in attire, born and nurtured in the woods]; then a 'novello signore' taking the first halting steps in love. The governing values are courtly: Ameto is judged by them and found wanting. He judges himself most harshly of all. Over and over, he curses the 'rozza vita' he has led all this time.[2] The climax comes in ch. xlvi, where the hunter-shepherd's life is explicitly compared to the sinful, loveless state of the soul. Then he was a beast; now, through the love of Lia, he feels he has become a man (p. 198). A parallel may be found in the career of Apaten, Acrimonia's lover in ch. xxix.

The basic metaphor of *Ameto* is feudal and aristocratic: spiritual elevation is linked to high birth and courtly love. In such a context, the rustic or shepherd life can only be a metaphor for inferior spiritual states. The pastoral has not come into its own. Rather, it works in conjunction with other elements: courtly love, mythology, or political, moral, theological, and mystical principles. Boccaccio's vastly popular works[3] provided the Renaissance with models of a variously operating pastoral spirit.

Sannazaro's *Arcadia* (1502, 1504)[4] shows how these various interests may be absorbed in an overall pastoralism. In *Arcadia*, the pastoral has come into its own. The work is primarily concerned with the activities of imaginary shepherds in an idealized landscape.

fra queste deserte piagge agli ascoltanti alberi, et a quei pochi pastori, che vi saranno, racontare le rozze Ecloghe da naturale vena uscite . . .

[2] See e.g. ch. xii, p. 49, ch. xvi, ll. 24–5.

[3] By the end of the 16th cent., there had been 17 edns. of *Ameto* and 12 of the *Ninfale*. The *Ninfale* was also translated into French in 1556, and thence into English in 1597.

[4] An early draft appears to have been composed by 1489. The work was printed in a partial and unauthorized version in 1502, and fully in 1504.

[among these deserted places recount to the listening trees, and to those few shepherds that will be there, the rude eclogues issued from a natural vein . . .][5]

The claim to artless simplicity is part of the pastoral artifice, of course. What is important is that Sannazaro forms his entire work round this artifice. In the tenth *prosa* he recounts the history of the genre, developed by 'un pastore Siracusano' and 'Mantuano Titiro'. The concluding address to his sampogna reaffirms this absorption in the pastoral. It is a deliberate, self-conscious attempt to revive the mode.

The work is full of shepherds' activities, relating to an ideal *otium* rather than a herdsman's actual tasks. The opening scene is a *locus amoenus* where shepherds gather to play and sing; their very departure in the evening is festive, with songs and jests. They spend day after day ('più e più giorni', p. 12) in such sport; and even afterwards, their shepherding is continuously mingled with games and singing-contests. There is a cultivated *naïveté* about such descriptions. Removed from actual rusticity in spirit even more than in detail, they are equally free of courtly allusion. The pastoral setting preserves its independence, even at a certain cost of unreality.

The work opens with a catalogue of trees whose 'ordine non artificioso' (p. 5) does not conceal the artificiality of its composition. Sannazaro's setting is remote and exotic, merging into the stuff of myth, an Ovidian landscape:

al capo d'un fiume chiamato Erimanto pervenimmo; il quale da pie' di un monte per una rottura di pietra viva con un rumore grandissimo e spaventevole, e con certi bollori di bianche schiume si caccia fore nel piano . . . La qual cosa di lontano a chi solo vi andasse, porgerebbe di prima intrata paura inestimabile: e certo non senza cagione; con ciò sia cosa che per commune opinione de' circunstanti populi si tiene quasi per certo, che in quel luogo abiteno le Nimfe del paese (*prosa* 5, p. 38)

[we came to the head of a stream called Erymanthus. Through a fissure in the natural rock at the foot of a mountain it hurls itself forth with a mighty and fearful uproar, and with a kind of boiling of white spume, onto the plain . . . From a distance, for anyone travelling there alone, this would at first encounter breed incalculable fear; and indeed not without reason; inasmuch as in the general opinion of the surrounding populace it is held almost for certain truth that the Nymphs of the countryside make their dwelling in that place (Nash, p. 57)]

[5] All refs. to the Italian text as ed. E. Carrara (Turin, 1926); this passage is from p. 4. Trans. as by Nash (see Ch. 3 n. 69); this passage is from p. 29.

Reality blends into fiction and art. The temple of Pales is adorned with paintings scarcely different from the actual settings of the narrative: 'alcune selve e colli bellissimi, e copiosi di alberi fronzuti, e di mille varietà di fiori' (*prosa* 3: p. 20) [some woods and hills, very beautiful and rich in leafy trees and a thousand kinds of flowers (Nash, p. 42)].

Above all, this exotic pastoral landscape is created by the complex 'pastoral religion' that Sannazaro institutes in his work. The passing mentions of Pan and Pales in the classical eclogue are erected into a complete cult that later pastoralists would freely draw upon. *Arcadia* has two sets of funeral rites; a feast of Pales; and, at the centre of the faith, a temple of Pan with the high priest Enareto. Shepherd life is drawn into the exotic remoteness of romanticized pagan ritual. It is given a fully formed metaphysics and thus made absolutely independent, truly a world in itself.

This is not to deny that *Arcadia* contains many allusions to court and academy. But they are so completely absorbed in the pastoral context that they create little or no formal tension. Rather, they lose their centrifugal tendencies and themselves grow idyllic. The most notable 'external' element is of course the presence of the poet himself as Sincero, a Neapolitan aristocrat. But his love soon settles down into the very same Petrarchan languishment that the authentic shepherd-lovers indulge in. The rustic Carino's love-story in the eighth *prosa* provides a close parallel to Sincero's in the seventh. In a complete inversion of the values of *Ameto*, 'courtly' love has passed wholly within the province of the shepherd.

The eclogues in *Arcadia* partake of the nature of the Petrarchan canzone.[6] Their concerns are repeated in the prose interludes, creating there the same static, elaborate introspection and love-lament. The Petrarchan lover's nature-retreat turns into Sannazaro's pastoral setting and links it to the theme of love. Thus the classical shepherd-lover's passion is transformed, for the Renaissance, into Petrarchan love. After this, whenever Renaissance pastoral actually concerns itself with shepherd life, such love—whether fulfilled or frustrated—is its integral element.

There are many courtly references apart from Sincero's story. The tenth *prosa* celebrates the Renaissance in thinly veiled pastoral terms:

[6] On Petrarchan elements in Sannazaro see David Kalstone, *Sidney's Poetry: Contexts and Interpretations* (Cambridge, Mass., 1965), ch. i, and William J. Kennedy, *Jacopo Sannazaro and the Uses of Pastoral* (Hanover, NH, 1983), 36ff. and the more detailed evidence on pp. 117–27.

il nobile secolo, il quale di tanti e tali pastori si vedeva copiosamente dotato; con ciò fusse cosa che in nostra età ne era concesso vedere et udire pastori cantare fra gli armenti, che dopo mille anni sarebbono desiati fra le selve. (p. 99)

[the distinguished generation that saw itself plenteously endowed with so many shepherds of such quality; inasmuch as in our age it had been granted us to see and hear shepherds singing among their flocks who after a thousand years would be in demand in the forests. (Nash, p. 109)]

The theme is continued in Eclogue 10; but the major part of the poem, as of Eclogue 6, consists of cryptic allegory of social and political disorder. The eleventh *prosa* opens with the praise of Naples. Eclogue 12 mourns the death of Adriana, wife of Sannazaro's fellow-academician Pontano, and borrows from Pontano's own eclogue on the subject. But the allusions are completely absorbed in the pastoral metaphor. Here, for example, is a passage from Eclogue 10 (p. 105; Nash, pp. 114–15):

secche son le viole in ogni piaggia:
ogni fiera selvaggia, ogni ucelletto
che vi sgombrava il petto, or vi vien meno;
e il misero Sileno vecchiarello
non trova l'asinello ov'ei cavalca.
Dafni, Mopso e Menalca, oimè, son morti.

[Withered are the violets on every hillside:
every woodland creature, every little bird
that unladed its breast now wastes away.
And poor old Silenus
cannot find the ass whereon he should ride.
Daphnis, Mopsus, and Menalcas, alas are dead.]

In an age when the pastoral was continually rejecting its own premisses for other concerns and other modes of expression, Sannazaro provides a vital model for the otherness of pastoral and its special transformation of experience. His romance is the classic expression of pastoral as a state of mind. There are overtones of melancholy: unfulfilled love that seems to relinquish all hope as it submerges itself in the unvarying rhythm of pastoral life. This elegiac dimension of love passes into the actal contemplation of death and transience, a recurrent theme. There are two elegies among the eclogues (5 and 11), the first preceded by a prose version of Nemesianus I, another epicedium. But the melancholy is nurtured in a setting of nature; it acts as a bond with other shepherd-lovers and, above all, provides the stimulus for poetry. It thus acquires a compensating aesthetic fulfilment, becomes part of a consistently pleasing pastoral artefact.[7]

Few writers of eclogue, drama, or romance follow Sannazaro's model in its entirety. Most of them only draw upon it for a stock bucolic setting against which to develop their non-pastoral concerns. Even so, they thereby retain some vestige of the classic pastoral milieu, providing at least a minimal justification for using the pastoral mode at all. And in Italian pastoral drama we have a substantial, if thematically limited, body of works in this vein.

2. *Italian pastoral drama*

Although many of the plays treated here are obscure, I have not provided a chronological or descriptive survey in view of the full account in Greg's *Pastoral Poetry and Pastoral Drama*. My purpose is rather to define the overall nature and impact of this body of drama, commencing much earlier than its two famous examples, Tasso's *Aminta* (acted 1573, printed early 1581) and Guarini's *Il pastor fido* (completed 1584, printed December 1589 with 1590 on the title-page).[8]

Italian pastoral drama develops the theme of love, the stylized nature-setting, and the mythological affinities of art-pastoral. Sannazaro is obviously a basic influence; but the 'otherness' and independence of this drama is also linked to the partially pastoral mythic tale like Boccaccio's *Il ninfale fiesolano*. In fact, we may see here a confluence of these two models. The first Italian 'pastoral' plays are essentially mythological. In Poliziano's *Orfeo* (1471), the shepherds are subsidiary. In Nicolò da Correggio's *Cefalo* (1487), Cefalo (Cephalus) is himself a hunter and thus by extension a pastoral figure. But, perhaps more significantly, there are true shepherds in the background. Though the plots do not require it, both plays make the shepherd a part of the mythological setting.

Gradually the pastoral element supersedes the mythological; but the latter continues to be important. In Cinthic Giraldi's *Egle* (acted 1545) sylvan and celestial gods contend for the love of the nymphs. Luigi Groto's *Calisto* (first composed 1561, but surviving only in a 1577 revision) brings Jupiter, Mercury, and Apollo to earth in pursuit of mortal women in a pastoral version of Plautus's *Amphitruo*. Groto's *Il*

[7] Mia Gerhardt comments on this pleasurable melancholy as an element of the total idyll: *La Pastorale* (Assen, 1950), 100–3, 106–7.

[8] See the edn. by J. H. Whitfield with Richard Fanshawe's trans. (Edinburgh, 1976), 7. All refs. to this edn., but the trans. are my own.

pentimento amoroso (1575) has Pan as presiding deity. Diana is present in many plays, as leader of the virgin nymphs whom gods, sylvans, and shepherds alike pursue. Satyrs and fauns are everywhere.

Metamorphoses may be woven into the plot. Giraldi's *Egle* (whose plot comes from Sannazaro's metamorphic eclogue *Salices*) ends in a great collective transformation of the threatened nymphs into trees, rocks, and streams. In Agostino Beccari's *Il sacrificio* (1554) an inconvenient elder brother is changed into a wolf (not a boar, as Greg would have it, p. 175).

Italian pastoral drama becomes a major repository of the 'pastoral religion' we found in Sannazaro. Beccari's play centres upon the sacrifice to Pan, the great event of the shepherd's calendar. Tasso's Aminta throws himself off a rock for thwarted love, but first binds Ergasto, who witnesses this, with

> scongiuri orribili, chiamando
> e Pane e Pale e Priapo e Pomona
> ed Ecate notturna . . .[9]

[fearsome invocations, calling on Pan, Pales, Priapus, Pomona, and Hecate of the night]

This 'religion' reaches its climax in Guarini's *Il pastor fido*. The play is full of oracles and supernatural signs, and the whole action is providentially controlled. The strictly pastoral cult is here modified by the influence of Greek romance, but this merely alters, without destroying, the fantasy-religion of these plays.

This 'religion' is an important factor in creating an independent pastoral milieu. Another is the gradual weeding-out of courtly references. This is the more remarkable in that such drama derives in part from dramatized eclogues of courtly compliment, and was almost invariably acted at courts and noblemen's houses. (The court of Ferrara was the great cradle of pastoral drama.) But the compliment becomes an increasingly smaller and more detachable part of the whole. In Luigi Tansillo's *I due pellegrini* (1527), the body of the piece is taken up with a banal but formally independent love-debate. Only at the very end does the poet praise the court of Nola and its rulers. In Poliziano's original *Favola di Orfeo*, Orpheus had appeared singing a Latin poem in praise of Cardinal Francesco Gonzaga of Mantua (ll. 138–89). In the revised *Orphei tragedia* this is replaced by a brief reference to Ercole d'Este

[9] ll. 1684–6; all refs. to the edn. by M. Fubini and B. Maier (Revised edn. Milan, 1976).

(ll. 198–201).[10] Courtly compliment thus becomes no more than a diversion during a suitable lull in the action. Luigi Groto's *Calisto* has a long song by Apollo, ostensibly praising the river Po but actually Ferrara and its rulers (III. i).[11] *Il pentimento amoroso* has an inset passage on the ladies of Adria (III. iii).[12] (This imitates the long poem in Montemayor's *Diana* on the ladies of the Spanish court.)[13] Such passages are easily separated from the body of the drama. There the shepherds lead an ideal, autonomous existence, contrasted with the *evils* of court and city.

In the first of Alessandro Caperano's pastoral *Comoedie* (printed 1508), the hermit-shepherd Orphen has a long account of his idyllic life, drawing on Virgil's Georgic II and Horace's Epode II.[14] Tansillo's Alcinio also echoes Georgic II: he was born

> Ne l'inclita, felice
> (se lodarla a' suoi lice), alma campagna . . .
> non tra superbe mura o vane pompe . . .
> non di porpora, d'ostro o d'or coverto . . .[15]

[In the famous, happy, and holy country (if it be permitted to those who belong there to praise it) . . . not among proud walls and vain shows . . . not covered with purple or gold . . .]

Beccari's Carpalio moves back modestly from the sleeping Stellinia, for

> Ch'anco servar la fe si dee ne' boschi.
> Deh, non si serva pur ne le cittadi.[16]

[Faith ought still to be kept in the woods: alas, it is no longer kept in the cities.]

Groto, in the Prologue to *Il pentimento*, asserts that it is not in the woods but in the cities that tigers and bears abound. Most important is Silvio's soliloquy in Agostino Argenti's *Lo Sfortunato* (1567), I. iv, with its detailed account of the shepherd's day, stressing his peace and content. Again there is obvious Horatian influence:

> S'alcun si truoua in questa nostra etade
> Colma di uitij, e de miserie piena,

[10] Both texts as in Poliziano's *Rime*, ed. N. Sapegno (Rome, 1949). The revision was probably carried out by Antonio Tebaldeo; see Greg, p. 157. The original version was acted at Mantua, the revised at Ferrara.

[11] *La Calisto nova favola pastorale* (Venice, 1583), fos. 32ʳff.

[12] *Il pentimento amoroso* (Venice, 1592), fos. 42ʳ–43ʳ.

[13] See Yong's translation of *Diana*, ed. J. M. Kennedy (Oxford, 1968), 144ff.

[14] Caperano, *Opera noua* (Venice, 1508), sig. K2ʳ.

[15] *I due pellegrini*, ll. 71 ff.; as in Tansillo's *L'Egloga e i poemetti*, ed. F. Flamini (Naples, 1893).

[16] *Il sacrificio*, IV. vi, *Parnaso italiano*, xvii (Venice, 1785), 310.

Che si chiami felice, i son quell' io,
Che scarco, e sciolto da più graui impacci
Meno fra bei piacer, tranquilla uita . . .[17]

[If there is anyone in this our age, full of vices and miseries, who can call himself happy, that am I, who, free and unconstrained by graver troubles, lead a tranquil life amid beautiful pleasures . . .]

Whereas the pastoral romance brings in more and more aristocratic lovers, reserving shepherds for an inferior or even comic role, pastoral drama shows the shepherds themselves as practising a higher vein of love. In the Prologue to Tasso's *Aminta* (l. 83), Cupid refuses to confine his attention to the courtiers: he will work 'ne' pastori non men che ne gli eroi' [among shepherds no less than among heroes]. This is confirmed in a later chorus, addressed to Amor:

tu di legger insegni
a i più rustici ingegni
quelle mirabil cose . . . (ll. 1159–61)

[you teach the most rustic wits to read those miraculous matters . . .]

All the same, the tone implies a certain surprise that shepherds should love. In most earlier plays, this had been taken for granted. Unexpectedly enough, it is in Tasso and Guarini that the autonomy of the pastoral is less than complete.

Courtly compliments and allusions are sprinkled more thickly than usual in *Aminta*. With them goes an admiration for courtly values.[18] In Act I, scene ii, Tirsi (Tasso) recounts how Mopso had given him the conventional warning against town and court. In fact, he found court life full of talent and virtue. Elpin (the poet Pigna) reigns there, and under his inspiration Tirsi scorns rustic song. Even now his pipe is not 'umil come soleva' [humble as it used to be] but 'emula de le trombe' [a rival of the trumpets]: ll. 641–3. In the courtly eclogue, we often find this yearning for a higher heroic song;[19] it is new in pastoral drama. Later Tirsi repeats this ambition in a eulogy of Alfonso II of Ferrara (ll. 1006 ff.).

Similarly in *Il pastor fido* Carino's love of poetry leads him *away* from Arcadia to Elis and Pisa, where he meets the famous Egon (Cardinal Scipione Gonzaga).[20] Carino does indeed condemn the courtier's life; but courtly and heroic values survive in his unfulfilled ambition (p. 334):

17 *Lo Sfortunato* (Venice, 1573), 30.
18 Cf. Gerhardt, pp. 121–2, on the subject.
19 See below, Ch. 7 n. 26.
20 Whitfield's edn. (cit. n. 8), p. 330: v. i.

con sì sublime stil forse cantato
avrei del mio signor l'armi e gli onori . . .

[in such a lofty style would I have sung of my master's arms and honours]

In *Aminta* and *Il pastor fido* the horizon of pastoral drama expands. *Aminta* shows an unusually strong presence of the court. In Guarini, the influence of Greek romance introduces adventures far beyond the fields and woods, guided by divine and providential powers. But the basic independence of dramatic pastoral remains even in these plays. We are still nearly as much as ever in a remote rustic world, governed by its own powers of love and divinity: unreal, ultimately untenable, but heightened, simplified, and perfected in artificial isolation from reality. Such drama preserves an invaluable interest in the actual stuff of pastoral, all too often lost in the allusive eclogue and the courtly romance.

The plays are full of references to sylvan settings and *loci amoeni*. Such references take on meaning from the fact that there seems to have been a distinct style of stage setting for pastoral plays and entertainments. Commentators on Vitruvius—above all, the influential Sebastiano Serlio—expanded the master's brief account of tragic, comic, and 'satyric' scenes (*De architectura*, v. 6) so as to identify the last with the pastoral. *Satyre*, says Serlio, comprise 'tutti coloro che licentiosamente uiuono' [all those that live licentiously], which clearly means 'gente rustica' [rustic people].[21] Danielo Barbari actually associates the three types of drama with three levels or classes of men and matters, 'altae, mediae, infimae' [high, middle, and low], in the standard manner of pastoral theorists.[22]

The *scena* for 'satyric' pastoral drama should be 'ornata di arbori, sassi, colli, montagne, herbe, fiori & fontane, vuole ancora che vi siano alcune capanne alla rustica'[23] [adorned with trees, rocks, hills, mountains, grass, flowers, and fountains; there should also be some cottages in rustic style]. Serlio's commentary was commonly illustrated by a woodcut of this setting, repeated even in other works like Barbari's *La pratica della perspettiva*. The enormous influence of such an illustration may easily be imagined.

The sheer presence of a painted pastoral scene must have served to concentrate the dramatist's mind wonderfully. Several playwrights refer to it in their prologues. The second and third prologues to Beccari's *Il*

[21] *Libro primo*[*–secondo*] *d'architettura* (Venice, 1560), ii, fo. 27r.

[22] *M. Vitruvii Pollionis De architectura . . . cum commentariis Danielis Barbari* (Venice, 1567), 193.

[23] Serlio, fo. 27r.

sacrificio both go into some detail over the geography of Arcadia.[24] We may imagine the speaker pointing out the items on a screen or backdrop. Groto follows suit in the prologue to *Calisto*.

This is backed up by endless references to woods, rivers, hills, trees, and other natural features. In Giraldi's *Egle*, the satyrs' feigned farewell to the forest expresses a surprisingly sensitive identification with nature, like that seen in the shepherd-lovers of pastoral:

> Non udran più in Arcadia i nostri accenti
> Tristi e infelici Menalo e Liceo,
> Nè i chiar' rivi e lucenti
> Pel nostro pianto reo
> Saran turbati più per queste selve,
> Nè le selvagge belve
> Qui piangeranno i nostri aspri tormenti.[25]

[Maenalus and Lycaeus will no longer hear our sad and unhappy accents in Arcadia, nor will the clear and sparkling rivers in these woods be troubled any more by our wretched weeping, or the wild beasts here lament our harsh torments.]

Even Petrarchan commonplaces take on a new visual validity. Casalio's Parthenia declares that

> Herbe, prati, montagne, arbori, e fonti,
> Ripe, cauerne, boschi, il cielo, el mare,
> Li augelli, el pesce, il pian, questi alti monti,
> Scian perch' io piango . . .[26]

[Grass, meadows, mountains, trees, and springs, shores, caves, woods, sky, and sea, birds, fishes, the plain, and these high peaks, know why I weep.]

In Groto's *Calisto* Gemulo has a long soliloquy contrasting his state with that of natural objects.[27] It is a tedious account, but by the end the nature-setting is established beyond doubt.

Shepherds' occupations are prominent too. The references come so thick and naturally that illustration is difficult. They are particularly numerous in Argenti's *Lo Sfortunato*. In Groto's *Il pentimento*, the shepherds' loves stem directly from their pastoral and sylvan activities. Ergasto sees Dieromena in the Temple of Pales during a sacrifice to stop a sheep-plague. Nicogino, while hunting birds, rescues her from a satyr. In

[24] Edn. cit. (n. 16 above), pp. 231, 236.

[25] Act II, final chorus: *Parnaso italiano*, xxiv (Venice, 1786), 228–9.

[26] Giambattista Casalio, *Amaranta* (Venice, 1538), sig. A6^v: Act I.

[27] 1583 edn., fos. 17^v–18^r: II. i.

Groto's *Calisto*, Silvio falls in love with Selvaggia during their youthful activities together. This resembles the account of Aminta and Silvia's youth in Tasso's play (ll. 401 ff.), and appears to have been added by Groto in the course of revision after the appearance of *Aminta*. The ultimate source is probably Sannazaro's account of Carino's love (*prosa* 8), perhaps reinforced by *Daphnis and Chloe*, which appeared in Amyot's French translation in 1559. (The Greek was not published till 1598.)

While the pastoral romance drifts further and further away from the classical eclogue, the drama continues to draw upon it. The shepherds' wooing-speeches contain innumerable echoes of Theocritus's Cyclops and Virgil's Corydon. In *Orphei tragedia*, a chorus of dryads mourns Euridice's death,[28] and in *Cefalo* the Muses mourn Procris,[29] both in close imitations of pastoral epicedia. The magical rites in Groto's *Calisto* follow the Pharmaceutria poems.[30] Obviously, the dramatists have retained the simple eclogue as a thematic and stylistic model, though not a structural one. In fact, they refer to their own work as eclogues surprisingly late in the day: Groto in the prologues to both *Calisto* and *Il pentimento*, and Argenti in the dedicatory epistle to *Lo Sfortunato*.[31]

In Italian pastoral drama, the refined courtly imagination largely eschews allusions to itself in order to create a world of pure artifice. But while this makes for a notable reinforcement of the 'pure' art-pastoral tradition, we must also admit that in a subtler way, it modifies the purity of art-pastoral, realigning it along the patterns of courtly conduct. In fact, this is inseparable from the elevation of shepherd characters that I have described earlier, notably of shepherd-lovers in Petrarchan or more generally courtly terms. They repeat the standard words and postures of aristocratic romantic lovers.

Instead of contrasting shepherd and court life, the highest and most attractive features of the court are transferred to shepherd life, whose controlling values become chivalric and aristocratic. In *Lilia*, the shepherdess exhorts Felino to let her go:

> in questo e gentilezza esser cortese,
> & sforzar' vna Donna è villania . . .[32]

[herein lies the nobility of the courteous, while to molest a lady is villainy]

[28] Ed. Sapegno, ll. 151 ff.

[29] IV. 222–46 as in E. Faccioli (ed.), *Il teatro italiano*, 1/2 (Turin, 1975), 502–3.

[30] *Calisto*, edn. cit. (n. 11 above), fo. 53ᵛ: IV. ii.

[31] Cf. also Abraham Fraunce's description of *Aminta* as 'Pastoral, and in effect nothing els but a continuation of *aeglogues*' (*The Countesse of Pembrokes Yuychurch* (London, 1591), dedicatory epistle, sig. A2ʳ).

[32] *Lilia* (Siena, n.d.), sig. A5ᵛ.

In Beccari, Erasto repeatedly calls the shepherd Orenio 'gentil'. In Argenti, Dafne tells Iacinto that he is 'd'ogni uaghezza adorno | In cui douria regnar gran cortesia' [adorned with every beauty, in whom great courtesy ought to reign]: p. 70, III. ii. In a complete inversion of *Ameto*, aristocratic love and conduct become the shepherd's concern, even to the near-comic excesses of Groto's *Pentimento*. The complex codes of honour, the lover languishing in despair when a simple explanation could set him right with his lady, remind one of nothing so much as the code-bound lover-knights of chivalric romance. And Argenti's Sfortunato, like Tasso's Aminta, exemplifies the last melancholy refinement of the Petrarchan lover indulging his own frustration.

More deeply, if subtly, their love is permeated with the Platonism ascribed by the age to aristocratic love. Platonism plays about this entire body of drama as an undefined, almost unconscious presence, coming clearly to the surface in the symbolism of Tasso's *Aminta*, not to mention the even more detailed philosophic allegory ascribed by Guarini to his *Il pastor fido*. Richard Cody has interpreted *Aminta* cogently along these lines;[33] but for a general account of the phenomenon, Harold Toliver proves a briefer and acuter guide:

> The shepherd lover thus undergoes a series of ordeals to demonstrate his observance of the *vita cavalleresca*, represented in its most ethereal trophy, the cold nymph; for sexual we may often read social abstinence and for marriage, union with the princely model . . . The governing force in the 'subplot' of the fauns and their disorder is the sensuality of Cupid while the main plot falls under the jurisdiction of the oracles and a higher Eros.[34]

Thus, 'the cavalier-shepherd of Italian pastorals represents one extreme in the translation of feudal institutions into pastoral form'.[35]

As with the *vita cavalleresca* itself, there is a clear sexual basis to the frequently sucrose or laboured idealization. The Platonic strain of Italian pastoral has a factitious and almost coy character: it seems superimposed on a latent sensuality or indeed to express the last refinement of the sensuality itself. Gerhardt (p. 70) remarks acutely that 'La pastorale italienne ne montrera jamais de traces d'un platonisme convaincu' [Italian pastoral will never show signs of sincere Platonism], that it presents a 'conception païenne de l'amour' [a pagan concept of

[33] Richard Cody, *The Landscape of the Mind. Pastoralism and Platonic Theory in Tasso's Aminta and Shakespeare's Early Comedies* (Oxford, 1969).

[34] Harold Toliver, *Pastoral Forms and Attitudes* (Berkeley, 1971), 25.

[35] Ibid. 31.

love]. Since the Middle Ages, aristocratic *fin amour* had sought pragmatic disguise as well as conceptual complexity by its spiritualizing elaborations. The 'Platonic' pastoral of the Renaissance marks a subtler, more secular version of the same development. The pastoral setting serves to distance and transform the aesthetized, quasi-conceptual sophistications of love and courtship, while permitting both franker erotic expression and freer play of fancy as desired. Its distinctive features might be heightened—in the interest of a sensibility opposed to its own.

Shepherd life is vindicated to a courtly audience by being seen to conform to courtly ideals, even to represent their perfection. The aesthetic remoteness and stylized licence of shepherd life allow these ideals greater room for free expression. Obviously, we have here an ambiguous balance of courtly and pastoral elements: the former provides the governing values, the latter only a fantasized vehicle for them—yet suggesting, by its exceptional fitness as a vehicle, a qualitatively superior mode of existence that can free courtly values from the imperfections of the courtly plane of experience itself.

This contradiction, or at any rate compromise or modification, actually appears in various degrees in most of the art-pastorals I describe in this chapter. In this sense, the absence of allusion cannot of itself be held to indicate authentic pastoralism. (Elizabethan pastoral is unusual in the extent to which it transforms the courtly predilections of art-pastoral into a truly original mode of experience.) The uncertainty may even be traced to Sannazaro's *Arcadia*, the principal inspiration behind this entire body of work. It is unsurprising to reflect that this course of development begins with the *Ameto*, where a shepherd's life declaredly rises to the aristocratic in terms of Christian mysticism. Unsurprising too is the growth of this tradition, in one direction, towards romances such as Montemayor's *Diana*, where courtly characters and values explicitly take precedence over the pastoral.

In the last analysis, Italian pastoral drama rests on the points of a contradiction. Its world is fragile and artificial; but it asserts the formal primacy of the pastoral convention in an age when both the eclogue and the romance were more and more eschewing it.

3. *Art-pastoral in the eclogue and its offshoots*

The Neo-Latin eclogue is overwhelmingly allusive and didactic, though (as we saw) some allusive eclogues contain vivid pastoralism. Genuine art-pastoral plays only a supplementary role. Not only are didactic and allusive eclogues far more numerous; more radically, the impulse to write art-pastorals seems a secondary development in most Neo-Latinists. They conceive of the eclogue as essentially a means of topical allusion or moralizing, perhaps developing the pastoral setting as an optional embellishment. Beyond this, they may sometimes indulge in a piece of 'pure', non-allusive pastoral, but only as an incidental exercise in a mode whose serious purpose lies elsewhere.

Boiardo's Latin eclogues illustrate the point very clearly. Eclogues IV and VI are deeply allusive imitations of Virgil IV and VI, chiefly lauding the Estensi of Ferrara. Eclogues I, IX, and X also centre upon such praise. Eclogues III and VII are amoebean, largely non-allusive but with a few compliments to Ercole d'Este. (In Eclogue III, the contest is held before him.) Eclogue V, an exchange of songs, alludes to Boiardo (Bargus) and Tito Vespasiano Strozzi (Tityrus)[36] at the opening and Ercole at the close. Going a step further, Eclogue II seems to be pure art-pastoral. Tityrus is about to kill himself at his beloved's death, but is rescued and consoled by friends. It seems very likely, however, that this treats of a bereavement suffered by Strozzi.[37] Even in Eclogue VIII, one of the shepherds is Bargus; but otherwise, this poem seems genuinely free of allusion, consisting of an exchange of love-songs between two shepherds. We are at last almost fully in the realm of art-pastoral—but only at one end of a graduated series of adjustments. Art-pastoral in the Neo-Latin eclogue marks one end of a spectrum, not a self-contained realm of the imagination.

Some undeniable art-pastorals are little more than academic verse-exercises, like Pomponio Gaurico's painfully structured pieces, Eclogue I above all.[38] Belmisseri VIII and Camerarius VII (both amoebean eclogues) are somewhat more original, but still low-key poems, casual by-products of a pastoral vein exercised more vigorously in allusive and didactic pieces.

These derivative poems do lead to one or two notable developments, however. One of the finest Neo-Latin love-eclogues, Navagero's 'Iolas', is markedly imitative of Theocritus III and XI. But if only by the greater intensity of the exercise, it invests the classical figure of the

[36] For the identifications, see A. Campani, 'Le ecloghe latine', in *Studi su M. M. Boiardo* (1894), 209–10, 224.

[37] See Carrara, *La poesia pastorale*, p. 252. Carrara identifies Bargus as Bartolomeo Paganelli, but see n. 36 above.

[38] I have used Gaurico's *Elegiae XXIX. Eclogae IIII* (n.p., 1526).

lover-shepherd with new vigour. The same may be said of Francesco Berni's 'Amyntas', where Lycidas dies of love for Amyntas.[39]

Inevitably, Petrarchan elements blend with the classical pastoral:

> Ah formosa silex! ah durum pectora marmor!
> Ipsa vides nostris flammas errare medullis,
> Nostra vides quantae populentur pectora flammae;
> Nil piget, atque mori cogis me ferrea tandem.
> Ibo et qua gelidi tolluntur saxa Fanani
> Dulcibus immoriar lacrymis, et robore querno
> Incumbens solis prodam mea vulnera silvis.[40]

[Ah, beautiful stone! Ah, heart of hard marble! You see for yourself the flames that course through my innermost being, you see by what flames my heart is laid waste. Nothing makes you repent, and steely hearted, you drive me at length to die. I shall go and, where the rocks of cold Fanano are raised, let me waste away in sweet tears and, leaning against the trunk of an oak, relate my sorrows to the desolate woods.]

As we have seen, such love-sentiments form the staple of sixteenth-century Italian pastoral drama. The northern poets, usually not very fertile in art-pastoral, yield some instances too: Hessus III and X, for instance, or Erasmus's sole eclogue without the moral commentary. Stephanus's two eclogues show yet another influence at work: one is practically a translation, the other a partial imitation, from *Daphnis and Chloe*.[41]

Unlike the shepherd-lover, the shepherd-poet is usually an allusive figure[42] or at least a moral mouthpiece.[43] But needless to say, every amoebean eclogue implicitly presents the shepherd as poet. Apart from this, some poems (including Johannes Secundus's only eclogue) present Orpheus, the poet-shepherd raised to a mythic plane.[44] Nowhere,

[39] See Berni's *Rime, Poesie Latine e lettere*, ed. A. Virgili (Florence, 1885), 215.

[40] Boiardo VIII, ed. Zottoli, ii. 682.

[41] See Stephanus's *Moschi, Bionis, Theocriti . . . idyllia aliquot, ab Henrico Stephano Latina facta. Eiusdem carmina* (Venice, 1555), sig. B4^{v}ff. Interestingly enough, Stephanus renders a part of *Daphnis and Chloe* otherwise unknown to the age, as first noted by Alice Hulubei. See G. Dalmeyda, 'Henri Estienne et Longus', *Revue de philologie*, 8 (1934), 159–81.

[42] e.g. in Boccaccio XII; Pontano *passim*; Andrelini *passim*; Giambattista Amalteo I; Hessus I; de Ponte I, V; Buchanan, 'Desiderium Lutetiae' (*Opera omnia*, ed. T. Ruddiman (Leiden, 1725), ii. 329).

[43] e.g. in Boccaccio XIII, Mantuan V, Belmisseri I.

[44] For Johannes Secundus, see Oporinus, *Bucolicorum autores XXXVIII*, pp. 503ff. Cody ignores such poems while discussing Orpheus's role as shepherd in *The Landscape of the Mind*.

however, is his role as shepherd brought out. The importance of the Orpheus eclogues lies in introducing another element: the mythological.

A mythological 'eclogue' like Vida II does not really deserve the name: we merely have a shepherd recounting old myths. Others concern 'pastoral religion' rather than a living presence of the gods. In Giambattista Amalteo's Eclogue III, Coridon sings of the huntress Nisa: he is afraid she may share the fate of Proserpine or of Orithyia, raped by Aquilo. Du Bellay's 'Iolas' describes a rustic festival, with the shepherd Iolas's prayers to Pales, Ceres, and Bacchus.[45] But in Johannes Secundus's eclogue, Calliope actually appears and inspires Lycidas to sing Orpheus's lament. This leads on to eclogues, if we may so call them, set entirely in a mythic world. Giambattista Amalteo's Eclogue IV tells of Sarnus's metamorphosis into a river. Eclogue V is a compendium of myths like Vida II—but told by the river-god Silis, wedded to Galatea and attended by a hundred naiads.

Such poems contain nothing pastoral. They are no more 'eclogues' than the poem (not so designated) by Giambattista's brother Cornelio Amalteo, where a long metamorphic tale involving Cupid, Venus, and Diana explains the origin of the rivers Mesulus and Liquentia; or Basilio Zanchi's epithalamium for Pan and Aega, where Mercury paints the bridal cave with mythological scenes. We are on, or beyond, the borderland between pastoral and myth, the territory of some romances and nearly all pastoral drama. But a romance or play can include both elements; the briefer eclogue must choose between them. The precarious body of art-pastoral quickly merges into allusive pastoral at one end and non-pastoral mythological poetry at the other. Pastoral and myth can sometimes blend in a manner reminiscent of Boccaccio's *Ninfale*. Lorenzo de' Medici's metamorphic tale of 'Ambra' is embellished with a pastoral touch by making the wood-nymph Ambra's original lover 'Lauro gentil, pastore alpino, | d'un casto amor' [the gentle Lauro, an alpine shepherd, of chaste love].[46] Seldom can the moral quality of pastoral life have been brought out by such a brief reference. Luca Pulci uses pastoral more elaborately in *Driadeo d'amore*: the river-god Tavajano, once a shepherd, recounts a debate he had with the courtly Lauro on the respective merits of the country and the city.[47]

[45] For Vida, see Oporinus, pp. 477ff.; for Du Bellay, his *Poésies françaises et latines*, ed. E. Courbet (Paris, 1918). Other poets as in edns. cited earlier.

[46] Lorenzo de' Medici, *Opere*, ed. L. Cavalli (Naples, 1969; repr. 1970), 508. All refs. to Lorenzo's works to this edn.

[47] See Carrara, p. 168. The episode occurs in Part III of *Driadeo d'amore*.

These last two instances were in Italian. Returning to Latin poems, we find that the idealized life of shepherds is more clearly depicted in the brief epigrams known as *lusus pastorales* than in many eclogues. Many poets have written *lusus pastorales*: Pietro Bembo, Francesco Vinta, Marco Publio Fontana, Louis-François Duchat. Many more have a few pieces that may pass under the name.[48] But an adequate idea of the form may be derived from the two greatest exponents, Andrea Navagero and Marcantonio Flaminio.

Navagero's *lusus pastorales* (published 1530; some of them translated in Du Bellay's *Divers jeux rustiques*) present the whole range of rural activities:

> Dat Cereri has Teleson spicas, haec serta Lyaeo,
> Haec nivei lactis pocula bina, Pali.
> Pro quibus arva Ceres, vites fecundet Iacchus:
> Sufficiat pecori pabula laeta Pales.[49]

[These ears of grain Teleson gives to Ceres, these garlands to Bacchus, these twin vessels of snow-white milk to Pales. In return for which, may Ceres make the fields fruitful and Bacchus the vines; may Pales provide abundant food for the herd.]

An epitaph on a sheep-dog is matched by a winnower's address to the breezes, and a farmer's to Vulcan while burning a copse. 'Pastoral religion' is reflected in two hymns to Pan as well as the hymn above. Love is another prominent theme: there are vows to Venus, evocations of potential lovers' haunts, rustic gifts, and declarations to the beloved herself. These brief lyrics build up a surprisingly full, integrated rural world, while their brevity precludes external allusion.[50] The pastoral mode seems to preserve itself by a sacrifice of its habitual form, the eclogue.

Yet the poems cited above take their place among a variety of other pieces. Three of them, indeed, are full-scale eclogues: 'Acon' (XIX), 'Damon' (XX), and 'Iolas' (XXVII). But in another direction, they grade off into an assortment of poems of varying lengths, forms, and concerns. Admittedly, Navagero's volume is intended as a miscellany; but the grading-off is important. Some brief pieces have a vaguely rustic setting

[48] See below, Ch. 5, sect. 2.
[49] *Lusus*, XI. All refs. to Wilson's edn.: see Ch. 3 n. 24.
[50] Only one *lusus*, XVI, on burning a copse (*silva*), appears to be allegorical, alluding to Navagero's burning his poems on hearing them compared to Statius's *Silvae*. See Wilson, p. 85.

('Invitatio ad amoenum fontem', invitation to a pleasant spring), others a vaguely mythological one ('Vota Veneri', prayers to Venus, or 'Defectio Euphronis a Pallade ad Veneris', Euphro's defection from Pallas to Venus). The forms are equally varied: 'In Auroram' is a Horatian ode, 'Veris descriptio' an elegy, as indeed is the eclogue-like 'Acon'.

This is the first instance of a phenomenon I shall treat in detail in Chapter 5: the disintegration of the pastoral in form, setting, and spirit. But there is also a cohesive tendency in the *lusus*, brought out in the work of Marcantonio Flaminio.[51] Book III of Flaminio's *Carmina* contains 29 early *lusus* with memorable pictures of nature and pastoral life. The first is addressed to 'Pan pater, & Siluane senex, Faunique bicornes'[52] [father Pan, and old Silvanus, and the two-horned fauns], asking them to spare the shepherd's plum-trees. There are descriptions of the seasons, of woods and caves, *loci amoeni* inhabited by sylvan gods. But the major theme is love, and in Book IV (composed in 1539) we find a connected love-story woven entirely out of *lusus*. Iolas loved Hyella, but was married to Nisa. Hyella died of grief, thereby arousing Iolas's passionate remorse. This remorse takes up the body of the collection, and finally Iolas prepares to die.

Flaminio is linking *lusus* into a connected narrative as Sannazaro did eclogues. But in fact, Flaminio is bypassing the eclogue: moving from a briefer form, the *lusus*, towards a more elaborate one, the romantic narrative. Art-pastoral and the eclogue-form have again forgone contact. Either the form or the spirit must give way; very often, it is both.

Vernacular Italian pastoral repeats the same lines of growth. There is indeed one special development, but it proves to be a false trail. This is the 'rustic eclogue' inaugurated by Lorenzo de' Medici in his 'Nencia di Barberino'.[53] Nencia's praises are sung by Vallera, a far earthier figure than the conventional shepherd-lover. Her teeth, he says, are whiter than a horse's; she dances like a young goat and a mill-wheel. His heart is knotted and enlaced by love like trellis-work, and he cannot wield a hoe any longer.

There is no doubt that Lorenzo is sincerely attempting a new

[51] Some of these *lusus* were translated by Scévole de Sainte-Marthe as fairly long, substantial pieces in a French setting. See 'Le Tombeau de Brunette', Sainte-Marthe's *Œuvres* (Poitiers, 1600), fos. 190ff.

[52] Flaminio, *Carminum libri IIII* (Florence, 1552), 230.

[53] The poem exists in two versions. I have used the shorter, commoner, and more certainly authentic. See Lorenzo's *Opere*, ed. Cavalli, pp. 45 ff. For a more extended account of these poems, see Gerhardt, pp. 82–6. Gerhardt considers this 'genre rustique' to be separate from and opposed to the pastoral.

primitivism. His treatment of Vallera's love shows not only humour but sympathy and even a certain idealization. But later poems diverge from this model. Luigi Pulci's 'Beca da Dicomano'[54] shows a vein of grotesquerie alongside its tenderness. Unlike the pretty Nencia, Beca is both ugly and sensual. The dialect, too, becomes increasingly difficult and exaggerated, a curiosity and a distancing agent. Rusticity ends up as an object of caricature, patronization easily passing into contempt. 'In morte della Nencia', sometimes ascribed to Lorenzo but actually by Bernardo Giambullari—a great hater of peasants, says Carrara (p. 228)—credits the dead girl with 'cento amadori' [a hundred lovers]. Her devoted Vallera finally returns to his dances and companions, declaring 'Lascin pur piagner chi piagne' [yet let him who weeps, weep].[55] Gabriello Simeoni's Ameto, the very reverse of his namesake in Boccaccio, woos his Tonia with wild threats directed at himself, the community, and even the beloved.[56]

In such unpromising byways does the 'rustic eclogue' spend its force. It indeed supplies a precedent—nothing suggests it is a conscious model—for the rustic dialect of *The Shepheardes Calender*. But if precedent were needed, Theocritus's Doric would provide a readier one, and Spenser certainly had Greek enough to grasp it. And I shall argue that in this matter, Spenser's chief models were English.

More orthodox Italian art-pastorals show much the same traits as in Neo-Latin, and occur in much the same proportion to allusive and moral pastoral. The imitative classical vein may be illustrated from Boiardo's Italian Eclogues III and VII, both amoebean contests. Some pieces grow out of the didactic eclogue or tend towards it. In Antonio Tebaldeo's Eclogue I, Titiro complains of his many woes, crowned by losing his mistress to a richer rival. The pastoral and amorous concerns end in a sort of *contemptus mundi*. Gualtiero San Vitale has an interesting trio of eclogues where the shepherd Torbido and the satyr Siculo woo Florida in terms of a simple moral contrast, wealth and honour versus frugal content. Eclogue II pits Torbido's love against Florida's chastity, for she is vowed to Pan. The poems are poised between art-pastoral and moral concerns.[57]

[54] Ferrario (ed.), *Poesie pastorali e rusticali*, pp. 291 ff.

[55] Farrario, p. 290.

[56] See Simeoni's *Satire . . . con una elegia . . . & altre rime* (Turin, 1549), sig. K1ᵛ.

[57] For Tebaldeo see *Parnaso italiano*, xvi. 23ff.; for San Vitale I, the Appendix to Sannazaro's *Arcadia*, ed. M. Scherillo (Turin, 1888), and San Vitale II and III, G. Rossi, 'Il codice Estense X. 34', *Giornale storico della letteratura italiana*, 33 (1899), 265–87.

For the rest, we again find a blend of Petrarchism with classic pastoral love: in Alberti's 'Tyrsis' and 'Corymbus'[58] or Lorenzo de' Medici's 'Corinto'. I have earlier mentioned this element in the framework of Minturno's eclogues. Tebaldeo II is more elaborate: lovesick Damon rebuffs the sympathetic Tirsi, bids farewell to his flock, and kills himself. Tirsi returns to mourn and write Damon's epitaph.

We also find mythology entering the eclogue. Lorenzo de' Medici's second, unfinished eclogue is an account of Pan's contest with Apollo. In San Vitale's poems, one of the lovers is a satyr. Sperone Speroni's eclogue 'Già il Sirio in ciel col suo leone ardea . . .' is a compendium of myths recounted by the old shepherd Dafni, surrounded by fauns and nymphs.[59]

Just as Latin art-pastoral merges into the *lusus pastoralis*, Italian art-pastoral finds briefer forms. There are some finely turned lyrics by Franco Sacchetti, like the address to mountain girls quoted by Greg (p. 35) or a more dramatic account of girls frightened by a snake while gathering flowers.[60] More important are the *lusus*-like pastoral sonnets of Benedetto Varchi and Bernardo Tasso. (Some of Bernardo's are translations of Navagero's *lusus*.)

Varchi's first sequence, 'Fillidi',[61] is chiefly concerned with shepherds' lives and loves and 'pastoral religion', though Carrara (p. 419) holds the love of Damon and Filli to reflect the poet's relations with Tullia d'Aragona. By the second sequence, however, the elderly shepherd Damon has clearly become the poet, and his beloved Carino is undoubtedly his young patron Giulio della Stufa of Florence. In the third sequence, Carino abandons Damon, who finds a new friend in Tirinto, or Cesare Ercolani of Bologna. There are constant references to the Ercolani family, especially to Cesare's father Count Agostino ('Dafne'). The love-plot involving 'Tirinto' may be allusive too. Many sonnets depict the landscape around Bologna, the Ercolani villa and estates, and their circle of friends. One actually cites the month and year![62] We have moved simultaneously from eclogue to sonnet; from art-pastoral to allusion; and from pastoral to the country idyll.

[58] See Alberti's *Rime e versioni poetiche*, ed. G. Gorni (Milan, 1975).

[59] Ferrario, pp. 20ff.

[60] 'Frottola: Le ricoglitrici di fiori', *Alcune rime* (Venice, 1829), p. xiii.

[61] Varchi's pastoral sonnets were collected posthumously in the *Componimenti pastorali* (Bologna, 1577). They were written at various stages of his life, and some had been published earlier among other sonnets. See Cesare Salvietti's dedicatory epistle to the *Componimenti*, sig. A2^v.

[62] May 1557: *Componimenti* sig. H3^v.

Bernardo Tasso's sonnets (published 1560, but written over a number of years) show a similar change of intent. Some are quintessentially pastoral, particularly a clutch in Book I of the 1560 *Rime*:

> Surgete a salutare il nouo Maggio:
> Cantiam le lodi sue sotto quel faggio,
> Dou'io uinsi a cantar Titiro ancora;
> E tu di uaghi fior Licida honora
> Le corna a Pan . . .[63]

[Rise and salute the new month of May. Let us sing its praises beneath that beech, where also I defeated Tityrus at singing. And you, Lycidas, pay homage with pretty flowers to the horns of Pan . . .]

Shepherds court in pleasing nature-settings; they offer sacrifices to their gods; they describe the landscape in which they live. One even talks of a fountain dear to the Muses, 'Che l'alme inebria di diuin furore' [that intoxicates souls with divine madness].[64] Batto may be the poet himself, but his conduct is that of an imaginary shepherd-swain.

But these pastoral pieces lie scattered among five books of sonnets and canzoni, among them pieces that bridge the gap between pastoral and Petrarchism: the lady walking in nature, or the sorrowful lover retreating to it. Elsewhere a specifically topographical setting is lightly tinged with pastoralism. Once again, the formal decline from eclogue to sonnet first concentrates but ultimately dissipates the pastoral impulse.

Pastoral sonnets are found in other poets as well. Lodovico Dolce has a fairly clear sequence, featuring Leucippo, Aminta, Damon, Tirsi, Lidia, and Coridon:

> Ne in grembo a lherba, o presso un ruscelletto,
> Cantò Pastor con piu leggiadro stile
> Di Coridon . . .[65]

[nor, in the lap of the grass or near a stream, did any shepherd sing with a sweeter style than Coridon]

Again there is the sense of a coherent, well-knit pastoral community. Some details clearly imitate the classical eclogue:

[63] Bernardo Tasso, *Rime* (Venice, 1560), 33. For other pastoral sonnets see pp. 33–41, 55, 67, 74–5, 88, 90, 111, 213, 230; Book IV (separately paginated), 32; Book V (separately paginated), 73.

[64] Ibid., main sequence, p. 67.

[65] *Rime diverse di molti eccellentiss. auttori . . . Libro primo, con nuova additione ristampato* . . . (Venice, 1546), 330.

Duo cerui nati a un parto, & duo capretti:
  Dal cui puro color la neue è uinta;
  Per te serbarti, & duo colombi sono.
Che non promise per hauergli Aminta?[66]

[Two deer, born together, and two kids, whose pure colour vanquishes the snow—these have been kept for you, and two doves. What did not Aminta promise in order to get them?]

Pieces such as these mark one extreme of a general tendency of the Italian love-sonnet to pass into pastoral. The classic 'loving shepherds' vein recurs at regular intervals in the popular anthologies of Italian poetry, among both sonnets and canzoni. 'La bella Filli, e mille accesi cori | Di uaghe nimphe' [the beautiful Phillis, and a thousand enflamed hearts of pretty nymphs] appear in a sonnet by Alessandro Piccolomini:

Vien Tirsi, uien, che'l dolce fucco interno
  Scuopre ogni cor, Damon sol mesto e solo
  Guarda à bei colli Toschi, ou'egli ha'l core.
Altro amor, altre frondi, altro fauore
  Brama ei . . .[67]

[Come, Thyrsis, come: every heart reveals the sweet fire within. Only Damon, sad and lonely, gazes at the beautiful Tuscan hills, where his heart is. He yearns for another love, other branches [as love-offerings], other favours . . .]

A single canzone may provide a detailed pastoral scene, with a wide repertoire of conventional features. Giulio Camillo has a poem, 'Quando'l di parte & l'ombra il monde copre'[68] [When the Day Departs and Shadow Covers the Earth] that reads like a cento of pastoral commonplaces, with many direct borrowings from Virgil.

Yet again, however, while one end of this spectrum of lyrics is rooted in classic pastoral, the other passes into diverse forms and conventions. A few sonnets are akin to *lusus* of the *vœux* type:

Questo odorato Aneto, & questi fiori
  Di caltha, che ne l'horto di Damone
  Cols' hier' il bianco Adone
  Vener consacra à te la tua Licori.[69]

[This scented dill and these kingcups, which the fair Adonis plucked yesterday from Damon's garden, your Lycoris consecrates to you, O Venus.]

[66] Ibid. 329.

[67] *Rime di diversi nobili huomini et eccellenti poeti . . . Libro secondo* (Venice, 1547), fo. 142^r.

[68] Ibid., fo. 150^r.

[69] *Libro terzo delle rime di diversi . . . autori* (Venice, 1550), fo. 86^v.

Others pass into simple Petrarchan convention, with a pastoral veneer of varying depth. Giorgio Gradenico's lover exhorts 'uoi campi, abeti, faggi e dumi | Grato ricetto a i miei felici amori' [fields, firs, beeches, and brambles, pleasant refuge of my happy loves] to attemper themselves to the beloved's gracious presence.[70] Claudio Tolomei's shepherd envies the 'semplicetto Amor' al nuouo Aprile' [the most simple love in the new month of April] of happy lovers while he pines for 'aspra & amara | Amarilli' [the harsh and bitter Amaryllis].[71] We hear of shepherds lamenting their 'dolci nemiche' [sweet enemies][72] and alluding to the mistress as 'Madonna'.[73] There may even be a higher Platonic Petrarchism, as when Tirsi tells Flori

> La dolcezza che pioue
> Da uoi, non è uirtù d'alma che sente,
> Ma con' tutto il diuino alto splendore
> Per darui spirto, si fe spirto Amore . . .[74]

[The sweetness which flows from you is not a property of the sensible soul, but Love, with all high divine splendour, made himself a spirit in order to give you spirit.]

The pastoralism in these poems may sometimes be vivid ('Qui uenne al suon della Sampogna mia | Flori, ò Seluaggio, e qui s'assise, e giacque' [Flora came here at the sound of my sampogna, O Selvaggio: here she sat, here lay]),[75] but it is clearly an incidental or subsidiary element, one component out of many in a large body of erotic sentiment.

Torquato Tasso, Bernardo's son, dots his *Rime amorose* with pastoral and semi-pastoral pieces. Most notable are the poems in Book II written to Laura Peperara during her stays in the Mantuan countryside, particularly the long canzone 'Vaghe Ninfe del Po' (no. 175).[76] This evokes Virgil's landscape, where 'il buon Titiro già pascea la greggia' [the good Tityrus once grazed his flock]. But Laura excels Virgil's nymphs, making flocks and shepherds forget their pastures and outshining the rest at country dances. In a very *lusus*-like piece (no. 133), the poet offers Laura's girdle to Diana in thanks for having caught a marauding fox.

[70] *Libro terzo delle rime*, fo. 97v.

[71] *Rime di diuersi, et eccellenti autori . . . Di nuouo ricorrette e ristampate*, ed. L. Dolce (Venice, 1556), 154.

[72] *Libro terzo delle rime*, fo. 109r (sonnet by Lelio Capilupi).

[73] Ibid., fo. 86r (sonnet by Antonio Girardi).

[74] Ibid., fo. 133v (canzone by Remigio Fiorentino).

[75] Ibid. (sonnet by Remigio Fiorentino).

[76] All refs. to Tasso's *Rime*, ed. A. Solerti (Bologna, 1898), ii.

Lusus-like again are a later group of ten brief lyrics on Tirsi's love for Licori (nos. 239–48). Stray poems celebrate Eleonora, Neera, Fillide, and Galatea (nos. 346, 347, 363, 384). Tirsi may be Tasso, as in *Aminta*; but the allusions, if any, are concealed beneath the opacity of pastoral convention. Once again, however, strictly pastoral poems are few in number. In some, even the nature-setting grows very faint or turns into a metaphor for the lady's beauty. The poems to Laura are courtly in tone: in no. 174, it is Laura's move from city to villa that makes 'Civili i boschi e le città selvagge' [the woods civilized and the cities barbarous]. The allusions are clear, and the landscape is strictly localized. Pastoral passes by degrees into poems of topography and country holidays.

Such art-pastoral as I have found in French shows the same intermingling with other veins. Ronsard has one pastoral of simple love and festivity: the 'Voiage de Tours' (*Œuvres*, x. 214ff.), consisting of two love-plaints set against a rustic wedding. The lovers are still Thoinet and Perrot (Baïf and Ronsard), their loves the Francine and Marie of their other poetry. As elsewhere, Ronsard unbends self-consciously to Marie, the country girl of Bourgeuil, designedly exchanging (ll. 311–14) his 'vers . . . traduit du Pindare Gregeois' [verses translated from the Greek Pindar] for the humbler 'chalumeau du pasteur de Sicille' [pipe of the Sicilian shepherd [Theocritus]]. Yet for all these giveaways, the poem is a pleasing exercise in simple pastoral. The Petrarchan laments are tuned to rustic lips, and there is a delicate feeling for nature. It is significant that Ronsard left this poem among his 'Amours' even when the courtly eclogues were separated, first under 'Elegies' in 1567 and then in a group by themselves in 1578. In the next chapter I shall treat Ronsard's nature-poetry in greater detail; but it remains a disparate vein, not incorporated into the courtly conceits of Ronsard's main body of pastoral.

The greatest attempt at such incorporation is seen in a poet outside the Pléiade, one of Baïf's early associates at Poitiers: Jean Vauquelin de la Fresnaie.[77] His early *Les Foresteries* (1555) includes simple love-poems and mythological tales. In some non-pastoral lyrics, natural settings are described vividly, with a feeling for landscape.[78] In the pastoral pieces, the shepherds often stand for real persons, but their milieu is transformed

[77] Gerhardt (pp. 232–3) points to the interesting possibility of a freer, 'art-oriented' pastoral in the early work of the 'jeunes Poitevins'—Baïf, Tahureau, Sainte-Marthe, Vauquelin. She sees the influence of Ronsard as diverting and suppressing this strain.

[78] See e.g. the opening of Book I, foresterie 2; the first 'Description de l'Aurore' (i. 7); and, particularly, the account of the oak-tree in 'Le chéne creus de Perrin' (i. 12). All refs. to *Les Foresteries*, ed. M. Bensimon (Geneva, 1956).

into genuine pastoral. And once at least, in Book II, foresterie 5 (formally a Horatian ode), Vauquelin concentrates a wealth of classic pastoral detail in a compendious scene: shepherds lead their flocks, weave rushes, catch birds, sing of Daphnis on the green, or complain of their love to the forests, rocks, and rivers. And there are 'd'enhaut aus bois les rondes places' [clearings at the top of the woods] where Venus and the Graces sing and dance, and Minerva, Apollo, and the Muses dwell (ll. 21 ff.). The final piece mingles prose and verse in a close imitation of Sannazaro's last eclogue in *Arcadia*. Although explicitly set on Vauquelin's estate, it turns the scene into a romantic forest where the hunter-lover Philereme carves his love-plaints on the trees and rocks.

Les Foresteries as a whole stands on the borderline of pastoral, rather than strictly within its province; but its promise of a very different line of pastoral to that practised by the Pléiade is realized in Vauquelin's *Idillies et pastoralles*. I would have had to say more about this work if it had not remained in manuscript till 1605, for its diverse lyric pieces resemble an important body of Elizabethan poems. In Book I, the hero Philanon is clearly the poet himself (Book II concerns 'diuers Pasteurs'); the poems are set in his native countryside and are full of references to his life and friends. In the later poems in particular, he speaks very plainly of his life as a country *seigneur*. But despite all these allusions, the *Idillies* present us with a vividly pastoral, idyllic landscape and an appropriate vein of love.

> Pasteurs, voici la Fonteinete
> Ou tousiours se venoit mirer
> Et ses beautez seule admirer,
> La pastourelle Philinete.
> Voici le mont ou de la bande
> Ie la vi la dance mener,
> Et les Nymphes l'enuironner
> Comme celle qui leur commande.[79]

[Shepherds, here is the little fountain where the shepherdess Philinette always comes to gaze at herself and, alone, admire her beauty. Here is the hill where I saw her lead the band in dance, and the nymphs surround her as the one who commands them.]

His poems, says Vauquelin, do not present 'les façons & les mœurs des Pasteurs villageois' [the fashions and customs of rustic shepherds] but 'la simplicité de l'amour de telles gents . . . sans fard & sans feintise' [the

[79] Vauquelin, *Les Diverses Poésies*, ed. J. Travers (Caen, 1870), ii. 503–4.

simplicity of such people's love . . . without deceit or artifice].[80] The love of Phillis and Philanon shows something of the stylized simplicity, the apparent innocence of response, that we shall find on a large scale in the Elizabethan pastoral lyric. The sophistication is very obvious—more so than in Elizabethan poetry—but there is a genuine development of the resources of pastoral.

The same cannot be said of the only French lyrics of this nature that were available in print to the Elizabethan poets: those of Philippe Desportes. The limited nature of Desportes's influence on Elizabethan poetry has been pointed out by Anne Lake Prescott,[81] and there is little that is pastoral about his *Bergeries et masquarades*. In his *Œuvres* of 1583, he gathered a number of earlier published pieces under this title, apparently following the example of Ronsard's 1578 *Œuvres* and the title of Remy Belleau's *La Bergerie*: neither a promising precedent for significant pastoralism. Some of Desportes's poems are aristocratic country idylls. One or two epigrams may pass muster as *lusus pastorales*, as may a sonnet adapted from Navagero where lovers offer vows to Venus.[82] There are two dialogues embodying love-confessions at many removes from Theocritus X, though they begin 'Berger . . .' (pp. 187, 191). There is also a famous address to the unfaithful 'Rozette' (p. 219): 'Nous verrons volage Bergere . . .' [We shall see, fickle shepherdess . . .]. But Rozette is Madeleine de Laubespine; so probably is Florelle of the next sonnet. There are classic instances of 'shepherd' becoming a synonym for 'lover', using the lightest of pastoral touches to achieve a simplicity that can only appeal to the most courtly and sophisticated tastes.

Desportes bequeathed a certain formal legacy to the Elizabethans. I shall record a number of sophisticated Elizabethan lyrics on the periphery of the pastoral tradition where his influence seems most in evidence. But even Lodge, who pays high tribute to Desportes's popularity among the English,[83] does not (indeed, cannot) imitate him in any of the truly pastoral pieces in *Phillis* or *Rosalynde*.[84] The vivid and sustained pastoral of the main body of Elizabethan lyrics in this mode

[80] 'Au lecteur', ibid. ii. 443.

[81] *French Poets and the English Renaissance* (New Haven, 1978), ch. iv.

[82] See *Diverses amours et autres œuvres meslées*, ed. V. E. Graham (Geneva, 1963), 201, 205, 190, respectively. All refs. to this edn.

[83] In *A Margarite of America*: as ed. G. B. Harrison (with Greene's *Menaphon*: Oxford, 1927), 207.

[84] He does, however, follow Desportes in some other pieces in these works, as in a praise of country life appended to *Scilla's Metamorphosis*; see Prescott, pp. 142–4.

owes nothing to Desportes's example. Rather, using other models, they successfully overcome the centrifugal tendencies of the pastoral lyric as exemplified in Desportes.

For a major model, we must turn back to the Italians. In the Italian madrigal of the late sixteenth century, the pastoral becomes the vehicle *par excellence* for an important development of sensibility.

It was a late development. There are indeed early sixteenth-century madrigals which assume a well-established pastoral setting; but the great inflorescence of the pastoral madrigal dates from *c.*1570. It is typified in the work of Andrea Gabrieli and Luca Marenzio. This is the period when Sannazaro was used as an important source for madrigal lyrics, some forty years after the poet's death in 1530,[85] and provided the chief inspiration for a 'hybrid' style, turning the elaborate classic madrigal towards the lighter and more colloquial *villanesca*.[86] The result was a simplicity of expression, even a thinness of verbal texture, that fostered a new pastoral lyricism. Detail, while perhaps telling, had to be brief and of necessity conventional: such songs could only be late secondary outcrops of an older and more elaborate pastoral tradition. They would epitomize the convention, presenting in most direct form the simplification of experience and *naïveté* of expression that are basic assumptions of the art-pastoral tradition.

Sometimes the simplicity is patently refined and factitious:

> 'Fuggiti dal mio raggio,
> Pastor gentil e saggio;
> Fuggiti da quest' onda,
> Che l'un'abbruccia troppo e l'altro innonda,
> E vattene all'armento,
> Se non vuoi quì restar di vita spento!'
> Così dicea Licori,
> Cogliend' erbette e fiori.[87]

['Flee from my beam, courteous and wise shepherd: flee from this flood, which burns one excessively and drowns another. Go to your flock, if you do not wish to remain here, your life extinguished.' Thus spoke Lycoris, gathering grass and flowers.]

[85] See Alfred Einstein, *The Italian Madrigal*, tr. A. H. Krappe *et al.* (Princeton, 1949), i. 205–6, ii. 653ff.

[86] See Einstein, ii, chs. 7, 8; *The New Grove Dictionary of Music*, xi, 'Madrigal': *passim*, esp. p. 470, col. 1; p. 471, col. 2.

[87] From Luzzasco Luzzaschi's 3rd book of madrigals: quoted in Einstein, ii. 699. I have referred to all madrigals by the composer's name; the authorship of the words is often unknown or uncertain.

Operating at the very opposite pole from allegorical or allusive pastoral, such songs may none the less conceal patterns of courtly experience:

> Piangea Filli, e rivolte ambe le luci
> Al ciel ch'anch'ei piangea—
> 'O Tirsi, o Tirsi,' pur mesta dicea,
> 'O Tirsi, o Tirsi,' mormoravan l'onde,
> 'O Tirsi, o Tirsi,' i venti,
> 'O Tirsi, o Tirsi,' i fior l'herb'e le fronde . . .[88]

[Phyllis was weeping, and turned both her eyes to the sky, which was also weeping. 'O Thyrsis, O Thyrsis,' she kept on saying mournfully. 'O Thyrsis, O Thyrsis,' murmured the waves, 'O Thyrsis, O Thyrsis,' the winds, 'O Thyrsis, O Thyrsis,' the flowers, grass, and branches . . .]

As Einstein says, 'It is a *lettera amorosa* from a lady to her cavalier'.[89] Marenzio has a song that may have accompanied a bouquet or gift from a *cavaliero* to his lady.[90] Songs of pastoral festivity celebrate aristocratic weddings with various degrees of opacity.[91]

But whatever the external occasion (and we cannot always be sure there is one), many of these pieces form self-contained pastoral scenes that do not, in formal terms, involve any external referent:

> Ecco piu che mai bella e vaga l'aura,
> Pastor le vostre Ninfe risuegliate,
> Ch'el giorno gia s'inaura,
> Ecco ch'ella di fron' e d'herbe e fiori
> Vi da varij colori
> Tessete ghirlandette e'l crin ornate
> D'amate Pastorelle . . .[92]

[Behold, the dawn, prettier and sweeter than ever. Shepherds, awaken your nymphs. The day is beginning already: behold her, giving you various colours in branches, grass, and flowers. Weave garlands and adorn the hair of your beloved shepherdesses . . .]

The naïve licence of shepherd lovers finds its natural vehicle in the light simplicity of the words of such songs:

[88] From Luca Marenzio's 3rd book of madrigals for six voices: quoted in Einstein, ii. 651.

[89] Ibid.

[90] Marenzio, *Il primo, secondo, terzo, quarto & quinto libro de madrigali a cinque voci* (Antwerp, 1609), fo. 11^{v}.

[91] See e.g. Marenzio, ibid. fos. 25^{r}, 38^{r}; Einstein, iii, p. xxx.

[92] Marenzio, *Madrigali a cinque voci*, fo. 5^{r}. I have ignored the repetition of words in the text for musical reasons.

Quando la mia chiamava
Tutt' a me si monstrava
Scoprendo il bianco petto
E per non dar sospetto
S'adirava
Poi caminava
Ma ritardava
Li suoi passi pian piano: . . .[93]

[When my very own called to me, she would show me her white bosom unveiled: then, so as not to rouse ideas, would grow angry and walk away, but delay her footsteps, softly, softly . . .]

There are happy lovers, weaving garlands for each other, kissing and dallying in the woods, calling upon the birds to rejoice because

l'aspra durezza
Della mia Clori ha intenerito amore
Onde son quasi di me stesso fuore . . .[94]

[love has softened the harsh hardness of my Chloris, so that I am as though beside myself]

Equally, there are unhappy lovers, frequently dying of love: the most popular example, set by nearly every composer and translated into English, being Guarini's 'Tirsi morir volea' [Thyrsis Wished to Die]—not from *Il pastor fido*—where the implications of amorous 'death' are made quite explicit:

La bella Ninfa sua che già vicini
Sentia i messi d'amore,
Disse con occhi languidi e tremanti:
'Mori cor mio ch'io moro.'
Le rispose il Pastore:
'Et io mia vita moro.'[95]

[His beautiful nymph, who already felt the messengers of love drawing near, said, with downcast and trembling eyes, 'Die, my heart, for I die.' And the shepherd replied, 'And I too die, my life.']

By the end of the century, the pastoral madrigal has moved from Sannazaresque delicacy to the more unsubtle eroticism, and by now

[93] Einstein, iii, p. xviii: from *Tiers livre de chansons* (Paris, 1554), music by Jacques Arcadelt.

[94] Einstein, iii, p. xxvii: from Andrea Gabrieli, *Il secondo libro di madrigali a cinque voci* (1570).

[95] Einstein, ii. 542.

stereotyped detail, of Guarini and subsequent pastoral drama. Composers now turn for words to *Il pastor fido* rather than the *Arcadia*. With this heavier and more blasé pastoralism goes a tendency towards dramatic dialogue, to which the last quotation bears witness.[96]

With such elaboration, the madrigal tends to pass beyond the confines of its own form into other genres. Thematically too, there is a clear centrifugal tendency. Pastoral might merely provide an ornamental veil for stock Petrarchism,[97] the standard songs on springtime and the *carpe diem* theme,[98] or even a cuckoo-song of a quasi-'folk' nature:

> Mentre il cuculo il suo cucu cantava
> Lascia dicea Amarilli
> Lascia Damon tua Filli
> E corri in braccio cor mio.[99]

[While the cuckoo sang its note, 'Leave,' said Amaryllis, 'leave your Phyllis, Damon, and run to my arms, my heart.']

But at the core of this body of madrigals, we find not only the full range of pastoral detail but, as I have said, a distinctively pastoral version of experience. It is significant that such madrigals were sung and translated in England towards the end of the sixteenth century, and new songs composed on their model. A number of such songs find their way into *England's Helicon*, and blend by degrees into the simple pastoral lyric. The Italian madrigal must rank as a powerful influence behind the special nature of the Elizabethan lyric as I shall define it.

[96] For other instances, see Einstein, ii. 753; iii, p. xxiii (a monologue with other action); iii, p. xxix.

[97] See Marenzio, *Madrigali a cinque voci*, fo. 10^{v}; Andrea Gabrieli, *Il secondo libro de madrigali a sei voci* (Venice, 1586), 16.

[98] See Marenzio, *Madrigali a cinque voci*, fo. 32^{v}; Einstein, ii. 537, 538.

[99] Einstein, iii, p. xxvi: from Gioseppe Caimo, *Il secondo libro di canzonette a quattro voci* (1584).

5

Pastoral and the Renaissance Lyric

1. *Nature-poetry and the pastoral tradition*

IN THE last chapter, I began to show how pastoral poetry undergoes a fragmentation into other forms and concerns. The departure from pastoral proper occurs in stages, and a subterraneous relation remains. A poet may easily move from 'core' pastoral to these peripheral modes, choosing at will from the network of formal possibilities. Partly to emphasize this point, and partly to keep my enquiry within manageable limits, I shall chiefly discuss the work of poets who have also written formal eclogues.

The best-known model for these extensions of the pastoral is Horace's second epode, lauding in its second line the blessed life of rustic labour, 'ut prisca gens mortalium' [like the pristine race of mortals].[1] As Maren-Sofie Røstvig demonstrates, the Renaissance habitually ignored the fact that Horace makes this ideal a passing fancy of the usurer Alfius.[2] Hence the epode could be readily assimilated to other key passages of classical poetry. Virgil's Georgic II. 458–542 is almost as important as Horace's epode. Horace's epistle I. x, 'Urbis amatorem Fuscum' [To Fuscus, lover of the city], declares the poet's own rustic preferences. Epistles I. xiv and I. xvi open on the same note, describing Horace's own farm before passing on to other matters. One or two elegies by Propertius no doubt provided inspiration, such as II. xix, and the Golden-Age passage at III. xiii. 25–46. So even more certainly did some of Tibullus's. His very first poem, according to the standard arrangement, declares his ideal of being 'contentus vivere parvo' [to live content with my little] in the countryside. Some details are very pastoral indeed: the poet wishes to

[1] Texts and trans. of Horace as in the Loeb edns. of the *Odes and Epodes*, ed. C. E. Bennett (London, 1914; repr. 1968), and *Satires, Epistles and Ars Poetica*, ed. H. R. Fairclough (London, 1926; repr. 1970).

[2] Røstvig, *The Happy Man* (2nd edn. Oslo, 1962), 29 (on Cowley's trans.) and *passim*. Røstvig treats the influence of Horace's epode exhaustively, but unfortunately begins her study at the year 1600.

stimulo tardos increpuisse boves;
non agnamve sinu pigeat fetumve capellae
desertum oblita matre referre domum.[3]

[chide the laggard oxen with the goad, nor [think it] a trouble to carry homewards in my arms a ewe lamb or youngling goat forgotten by its dam and left alone.]

Here, as in I. v, Delia will be the poet's companion in such a life. In a different vein is elegy II. i on the festival of the Ambarvalia.

The influence of such poems may be seen even in the formal eclogue. Cayado IV compares rustic life to the Golden Age:

Nos hodie pecorum custodes, inscia turba,
Seruamus primae saltem uestigia gentis
A uulgi fluctu procul, ambitione carentes. (ll. 43–5)

[We at any rate, guardians of flocks, unlearned crew, preserve today the ways of the first humans, far from the stir of vulgar crowds, devoid of ambition.]

This is followed by a season-by-season account of country activities, as also in Strozzi I and II—where the old shepherd's wife is named Delia, perhaps after Tibullus. Hessus VIII idealizes the country, in much the same way, within a complimentary epistle to the humanist Conrad Mut.

Little but the metre separates these professed eclogues from an elegy like Sannazaro's 'Ad Joannem Pardum Hispanum' (I. ii), where the poet leads goats through the woods and writes Phyllis's name on the trees. He hunts, he plays his pipe, he worships the rural gods; country sports and the sparring of goats and oxen are his *grata theatra*. Finally comes a wish:

Dii facite, inter oveis, interque armenta canendo
Deficiam, & sylvis me premat atra dies:
Ut me non docta deploret pastor avena:
Utque sub umbrosa contumuler platano.
Ossaque pascentes venerentur nostra capellae:
Nec procul a tumulo candida balet ovis.[4]

[Appoint, O gods, that when my strength fails, I should be singing among the sheep and cattle, and the black day [of death] overtake me in the woods; that the shepherd may mourn for me on the unlearned flute; that I may be buried beneath a shady plane-tree. May the grazing goats pay homage to my bones, and the white sheep bleat not far from my tomb.]

[3] Tibullus, I. i. 30–2. Text and trans. as in the Loeb edn. by J. P. Postgate (with Catullus and the *Pervigilium Veneris*) (London, 1913; repr. 1976).

[4] ll. 41–6. Refs. to Sannazaro's *Opera* (Amsterdam, 1728).

Barring the first twelve lines on Pardus's studies, the poem is like a pastoral composed, as it were, from the outside: the urban poet consciously adopts the pastoral convention in a personal poem, instead of taking it for granted in an eclogue. Cornelio Amalteo has a very similar vernacular poem addressed to the 'fortunato pastor' Iola and envying his lot—but the title suggests Iola is the poet's brother Giambattista in his country retreat![5]

Giambattista's own verse-epistle 'Ad Julium' also merges pastoral elements with the spirit of Horace's Epode II.

> Non alias malim quaerere divitias.
>
> . . . . . .
>
> laetas viridi pascam sub valle capellas,
> Maenalios recolet fistula nostra modos.[6]

[Let me not wish to seek any other riches than . . . that I may feed contented goats in a green valley, and my pipe again practise the Arcadian modes. [Maenalus: a mountain in Arcadia]]

He too wishes he may die in the country, and his epitaph read

> Huic semper nemora, huic placuerunt mollia semper
> Gramina, qui viridi nunc quoque gaudet humo. (ll. 65–6)

[Him the woods, him the soft grass always gave delight, who even now takes his delight in the green soil.]

The love of nature, directly expressed, mingles with the more highly wrought attractions of literary pastoral.

A step further from the pastoral lies Stephanus's 'De laudibus vitae rusticae'[7] [On the Praise of the Rural Life]. It begins 'Beatus ille . . .', echoing Horace's epode. There is much satire of the city and court; an account of rustic labours, season by season; rustic tales and myths, including a long account of Pan and Syrinx; some Golden-Age references; and the standard 'pastoral pantheon' of gods that have loved the country. All this falls well within the purview of the pastoral tradition—and there are touches straight out of classical pastoral, like the Mopsus who carries ten apples to his sweetheart (sig. D4r).

[5] 'Di M. Giovanni Battista Amaltheo'; see W. P. Greswell, *Memoirs of Angelus Politianus* (2nd edn. Manchester, 1805), 518–24.

[6] Appendix to Sannazaro's *Opera* (Amsterdam, 1728), 422, ll. 2, 5–6.

[7] *Moschi, Bionis, Theocriti . . . idyllia* [and Stephanus's] *carmina* (Venice, 1555), sig. D2r ff.

Other poems combine pastoral and country idyll with specific topographical detail. Pontano yields a number of important early examples. These have a strong element of local myth, as in the poet's formal eclogues. Shepherd-characters also recur from the eclogues, including 'Meliseus' himself. If I do not describe these pieces in detail, or those of the younger Neapolitans Girolamo Carbone and Bernardino Rota, it is only because this has already been done by Carol Maddison.[8] Instead let me take a more modest and typical example from Pontano's Florentine contemporary Cristoforo Landino's 'Descriptio montis Asinarii' [Description of Mount Asinarius]. Except for an altar to the Virgin on its summit, the description is in very general terms:

> Hinc densis tegitur silvis, & mollibus umbris,
> Floribus hinc rident prata decora novis.
> Nec non & varii passim per gramina rivi,
> Scabra inter rauco murmure saxa fluunt . . .[9]

[It is covered on this side with dense woods and soft shadows, and on that the beautiful meadows smile with fresh flowers. Several different streams, scattered among the grass, flow with a harsh murmuring among the rough rocks . . .]

The poet reclines here 'vmbroso viridis sub tegmine quercus' [beneath the shady cover of a green oak], which echoes Virgil I. He can hunt, fish, snare wolves, and milk his goats, free from the noise and the thievery of the city and the scorn of proud Xandra.

Bernardo Tasso has an Italian elegy which pictures his friend Cesare di Ruggiero in the Neapolitan landscape, 'in un' eterno Aprile | Con la bella Amarilli' [in an eternal April, with the beautiful Amaryllis].[10] The topography is much more specific here. There is less about rural activities, but very much the same impression of rest and peace in a beautiful landscape. Basilio Zanchi's Latin 'Aestas' [Summer], one of three poems on the seasons, is tied specifically to the countryside around Rome; but the shepherds who dwell there have come out of pastoral convention:

> Pastores captare umbras aut ualle sub alta,
> Aut ubi uicinis fontibus antra sonant:

[8] In *Apollo and the Nine* (London, 1960); see pp. 62–4 (Pontano), 98 (Carbone), 136 (Rota).

[9] This and the following quotation from *Carmina illustrium poetarum italorum* (Florence, 1719–26), vi. 95–6.

[10] Elegy II, *Rime* (1560), 189 (main sequence).

Et modo gramineis sese exercere palaestris,
Et modo uictrici cingere fronde caput.[11]

[Shepherds seek the shade, either in some deep valley or where caves resound to neighbouring springs; and now they exercise themselves with wrestling on the grass, and now encircle the head with the garland of victory.]

Navagero also includes a shepherd singing of Amaryllis as a detail in a poem inviting his friend Giambattista della Torre to the country in the spring.[12] We do not enter into the life of these shepherds: they are purely a feature of the landscape. Ronsard's 'De la venue de l'esté' [On the Coming of Summer] has a long description of the shepherd's day (*Œuvres*, ii. 23 ff.). The shepherd has obviously come out of Theocritus or Virgil, but is no more than an ornament. We do not know him as a person or see the countryside through his eyes. He is just one of the things the poet sees, a cardboard cut-out of his traditional self.

Other poems may be more purely descriptive or topographic; but then so are many eclogues. Very clear examples occur in Dutch and German poets. An elegy by Sabinus describes the rich rural setting of Thuringia with an obvious eye to its material benefits: 'Omnibus vtilium rebus abundat opum' [It abounds in all useful things].[13] The same locality is praised in the same way in two eclogues so named, Cordus X and Hessus I. De Slupere's local references in 'In Hypram . . . encomion iocosum' [A Merry Encomium of the River Yperlée] and 'Hodoeporicum Brabanticum' [Brabantine Itinerary][14] are longer than, but no different from, those in his eclogues. The eclogue and other forms of rural poetry run *pari passu*, each contributing to the other.

More complex cases of cross-fertilization involve themes other than nature and rustic life, but still sometimes playing at the borders of pastoral. The first part of Giambattista Amalteo's elegy 'Ad Ludovicum Dulcium' [To Lodovico Dolce][15] is more truly pastoral than many eclogues. The poet invites Dolce to a *locus amoenus* where they may sing of Thyrsis, or woo Neaera until she grants them her love. From this he proceeds to complain of love's tyranny. This is illustrated by many myths, particularly that of Orpheus. All these are common concerns in eclogues. Bernardo Tasso's fourth Italian elegy[16] asks his friend Ligurino

[11] Zanchi, *Poematum libri VIII*, p. 196.
[12] *Lusus* XXV. 18–20 (ed. Wilson, p. 44).
[13] I. v: Sabinus, *Poemata* (1563), sig. B8^r.
[14] De Slupere, *Poemata* (1575), pp. 205 ff., 242 ff.
[15] Appendix to Sannazaro's *Opera*, p. 417.
[16] *Rime*, p. 192 (main sequence).

to descend from the hills to the plains. The happy life that awaits him in the plains is vividly described, and the way 'Icasto' (Niccolò Grazia, another friend)[17] will guard him so that he is not snatched away like Hylas. The story of Hylas is then told in some detail, no doubt inspired by Theocritus XIII.

Buchanan's elegy 'Majae calendae' opens with Venus and Cupid rejuvenating all nature. Then comes a bucolic sequence: sheep graze, lambs frolic, bulls and he-goats fight while the she-goats climb the rocks. Fishing and vine-culture are then described (all, of course, variations upon the pastoral theme); then

> Tityrus in calathis tibi lilia, Thestyli, cana
> Servat, & in calathis aurea mala suis;[18]

[Tityrus keeps white lilies and golden apples for you in his baskets, Thestylis]

Presently, having worked this vein to his satisfaction, Buchanan passes on to the *carpe diem* theme. The pastoral element takes its place within a range of concerns.

I have already described how the pastoral sonnets of Varchi and Bernardo Tasso, and Torquato Tasso's *Rime amorose*, move in one direction towards topographical accounts, in another towards simple Petrarchan love-sonnets. What we earlier saw happening within the confines of the eclogue occurs much more strongly when pastoral and rustic themes are given the freedom of a wide range of forms. Pastoral conventions are evoked only as necessary and cast into any required combination with other themes. The integrity of the mode disappears; it becomes simply a source of images, devices, and descriptive details. Other ways of looking at the country have become more important; and, beyond these, there are other themes that have nothing to do with the countryside at all.

Far from being a rigid and insular tradition, the pastoral mingles with other genres and concerns until it loses its individuality and at times all recognizable features. Only a subterranean link remains, which may be traced by following the deviation step by step.

The results of such deviation can now be more deeply analysed. One obvious effect is a more direct and 'natural' treatment of the countryside and country people. The zest and colour of Buchanan's 'Majae calendae' and Stephanus's 'Oda de laudibus vitae rusticae' provide good examples

[17] For the identification see Williamson, *Bernardo Tasso*, p. 63.
[18] Buchanan, *Opera omnia* (1725), 304ff.: ll. 69–70.

of this lyric spontaneity and vivid detail. In French, Jacques Peletier du Mans has many instances of this sort. His 'Odes des saisons', for instance, open with mythological and astronomical references but proceed to direct description of rural scenes and pursuits. From Ronsard we can cite the graceful yet spontaneous delight of the 'Ode' beginning 'Bel aubepin verdissant',[19] or of

> Dieu vous gard, troupe diaprée
> Des Papillons, qui par la prée
> Les douces herbes suçotez,
> Et vous nouvel essain d'abeilles,
> Qui les fleurs jaunes & vermeilles
> Indifferemment baisotez.[20]

[God save you, many-coloured band of butterflies who suck the sweet plants in the meadow; and you, fresh swarm of bees, who impartially kiss both the yellow flowers and the red.]

In formal pastoral, this simple delight in nature is subsumed in a more patterned, framed-in response. The sense of perceived beauty is regulated by a more complex interpretation of nature: as a repository of ideal aesthetic forms, even more as a setting for man's basic activities, heightened to a stylized, simplified, almost or quite symbolic level. The loss in descriptive or naturalistic terms is balanced by the richness of the synthesis.

The simple nature-lyric has no such symbolic intent. There the landscape is perceived with no more than its actual physical beauty or peace. To the post-romantic consciousness this may seem a strangely negative way of putting things, but the pastoral is not a post-romantic form. The real countryside, like the real rustic, may become the subject-matter of valuable new modes of literary experience,[21] but these cannot be called pastoral in any authentic sense.

Another important phenomenon involves social issues as reflected in literary form. I have noted the peculiarly external use of the shepherd-figure in certain landscape-poems. The poet describes the shepherd as a feature of the scene, but does not enter into his state of being. Rather, the poet (speaking in his own person) is clearly attracted to the country

[19] *Œuvres*, vii. 242–4.

[20] 'Ode': 'Dieu vous gard, messagers fidelles . . .', ll. 13–18 (*Œuvres*, vii. 294).

[21] Such is the 'rural lyricism' illustrated from Ronsard by H. M. Richmond in '"Rural Lyricism": A Renaissance Mutation of the Pastoral', *Comparative Literature*, 16 (1964), 193–210.

because it is *not* his habitual milieu. Flaminio tempts his friend Franciscus Turrianus with the pleasures of his villa: a sumptuous meal, then in a quiet retreat

> legentur
> Lusus Vergilij, & Syracusani
> Vatis, quo nihil est magis uenustum,
> Nihil dulcius, ut mihi uidetur.[22]

[The sports (*lusus*) of Virgil shall be read, and of the Syracusan poet [Theocritus], than which nothing is more sweet or agreeable, as it seems to me.]

Theocritus's and Virgil's pastorals have shrunk to a pleasurable ingredient in a very different picture of rustic ease! Fracastoro's dialogue on poetry, *Naugerius*, provides an interesting parallel where the poet Navagero, presented as the principal speaker, breaks out into a rapt recitation of half a bucolic from Virgil.[23]

In Flaminio's poem, the poet reassures his friend, 'redibis inde ad urbem' [you will then return to town]. Ronsard promises himself the same solace when winter comes, in his epistle on 'Les Plaisirs rustiques' to Ambroise de la Porte.[24] Most surprisingly, Vauquelin's Philanon calls Phillis 'aux villes mieux garnies' [to the best provided cities] in the winter.[25] This is one of the points where Vauquelin's identity breaks through the substantial pastoral of *Idillies et pastoralles*.

The poet goes to the country as an educated city-dweller on a poetic and meditative holiday: for rest, solace, and inspiration, but without surrendering his normal poetic personality. Such an attitude harks back to Petrarch's *De vita solitaria*, or chapter 14 of Boccaccio's *De genealogia deorum*. Petrarch, tellingly enough, takes the shepherd as a type of the active life, full of care and struggle, removed from the contemplative existence of the poet in a landscape.[26] Even where the landscape is the source of poetic inspiration—as with Ronsard and his native Vendomois countryside—the poetry is oriented to the courtly

[22] *Carminum libri IIII*, p. 186.

[23] Girolamo Fracastoro, *Navgerivs sive de Poetica Dialogvs*, with a trans. by Ruth Kelso (Univ. of Illinois Studies in Language and Literature, ix/3; Urbana, 1924), fo. 154^r (in facsimile from the 1555 edn.); translation on p. 51. The dialogue is set in a *locus amoenus* in pastoral country. During lunch, the high-born speakers discuss pastoral matters with the herdsmen who have brought them milk. (See facsimile fos. 153^v, 154^v; trans., pp. 50–2.) The lunch itself is an aristocratic alfresco repast of a sort common in the age (see pp. 341–2 below).

[24] *Œuvres*, vi. 10ff.

[25] *Diverses poésies*, ii. 530.

[26] See *The Life of Solitude*, tr. J. Zeitlin (Illinois, 1924), I. iii. 4.

world beyond it, and its fulfilment comes from that world rather than from nature herself. Where shepherds appear, they play a subsidiary part; their higher functions have been transferred back to the upper-class poet. In 'De l'election de son sepulcre' [On the Choice of His Tomb], Ronsard imagines that shepherds will visit his tomb 'A ma feste ordonnée' [at my appointed feast], sing his praises, and offer sacrifice.[27] Sannazaro had expressed the same wish in Elegy I. ii, quoted near the beginning of this chapter. We have slid into a feudal relationship between poet and shepherd.

Tellingly enough, Ronsard has several poems where he addresses his servant as 'Corydon'.[28] One of them, 'La Salade', is memorable for its praise of the virtue and simplicity of country life.[29] But the praise is almost entirely on an abstract plane: the poet writes as a philosopher in his country retreat. It is all the more remarkable if, as V. L. Saulnier suggests,[30] this sophisticated meditation were indeed inspired by the pseudo-Virgilian *Moretum*, which affords one of the clearest pictures of rural poverty in classical poetry.

An actual translation of the *Moretum* opens Du Bellay's *Divers jeux rustiques*. Its sombre spirit contrasts with the polished, highly wrought little lyrics that follow. Nearly all the *vœux rustiques* are translated from Navagero's *lusus pastorales*, but Du Bellay enhances their sophistication and artificiality. Indeed, the process is carried so far that the country setting practically ceases to matter. The scenes from nature have been refined into the delicate stuff of a pure lyric impulse, referring to nothing outside the delight of its own form and movement. This is best illustrated from the much-anthologized 'D'un vanneur de blé, aux vents' [[The vows] of a Winnower of Wheat, to the Winds]:

> De vostre doulce halaine
> Eventez ceste plaine,
> Eventez ce séjour:
> Ce pendant que j'ahanne
> A mon blé, que je vanne
> A la chaleur du jour.[31]

[27] *Œuvres*, ii. 99–101.

[28] However, the only identifiable 'Corydon', Amadis Jamyn, progressed from being Ronsard's page to higher offices and a closer companionship with the poet. See Laumonier's notes, *Œuvres*, vi. 102, xv. 76.

[29] *Œuvres*, xv. 76ff. The other 'Corydon' poems are all 'odelettes', vi. 102, 105, 174.

[30] In his edn. of Du Bellay's *Divers jeux rustiques* (expanded edn. 1965), 8.

[31] Ibid. 17, ll. 13–18.

[Fan the air with your sweet breath, fan this place: while I toil at my wheat, which I winnow in the heat of the day.]

In Desportes's mistitled *Bergeries*, the element of aristocratic retreat is still more pronounced. Rustic occupations enter, where they enter at all, as a comfortable, distanced, and idyllic dream. The rare pastoral stance ('Douces brebis, mes fidelles compagnes . . .': Sweet sheep, my faithful companions)[32] is all too obviously a poetic affectation.

In 1561, Ronsard's and Desportes's fellow-countryman Scaliger had censured Mantuan for the crude rusticity of his shepherds:

Non meminerunt Agasones isti, nobiles homines, etiam quum rusticantur, animos a nobilitate remittere, non amittere . . . Denique hoc ita censendum est: Agros sine vrbanis delitiis feros esse aut sordidos.[33]

[Nor do these grooms remember that high-born men, even when they go into the country, relax but do not release their minds from nobility . . . In a word, we are to conclude that the fields, without urban pleasures, are either savage or sordid.]

The country-idyllists put the 'agasones' in their place; but in doing so, they destroy the poetic and symbolic possibilities of rustic life which alone can provide authentic pastoral.

2. *Idylls*, lusus, *and lyrics*

An important factor behind the diffusion of the pastoral was the apparent example of Theocritus's Idylls. It was recognized at least as early as Servius[34] that only a proportion of the Idylls are pastoral. On their full range of themes and characters, I may quote from the dedicatory verses to Eobanus Hessus's Latin translation:

> Heroum celebrat laudes, Heroidas ornat
> Carmine, pastorem quod decuisse queat.
> Pastor, uenator, messor, piscator, & auceps,
> Nauita, miles, eques, pictor & agricola est.[35]

[32] 'Chanson': 'O bien-heureux . . .', l. 85: *Diverses amours*, p. 170.

[33] *Poetices libri septem*, VI. iv: p. 304, col. 2. F. J. Nichols (*Humanistica Lovaniensia*, 18 (1969), 111–13) suggests that this passage was crucially influential in inducing the sophisticated, decorative nature of French Renaissance pastoral.

[34] Servius, ed. Thilo, III. i. 3. 20–1: 'sane sciendum, [Virgilii] VII. eclogas esse meras rusticas, quas Theocritus X. habet.' [It should be understood, however, that seven of Virgil's eclogues are purely rustic, of which sort Theocritus has ten.]

[35] *Theocriti Syracusani eidyllia trigintasex . . . Helio Eobano Hesso interprete* (Basle, 1531), sig. A5r.

[He [Theocritus] sings the praises of heroes and adorns heroines with a song befitting a shepherd. He is shepherd, hunter, reaper, fisherman, fowler, sailor, soldier, knight, painter, and farmer.]

Of course, Hessus includes among his thirty-six translations certain poems now ascribed, often doubtfully, to Bion and Moschus. By Stephanus's time, Bion and Moschus's work had been separated; but in 1579, Stephanus appended their poems to an edition of Theocritus because 'itidem idyllia sunt inscripta' [these too are entitled idylls]. Further, he includes 'aliorum aliquot poetarum opuscula, licet alius, & quidem diuersi inter se essent argumenti . . . quod idyllia vocari & ipsa possent'[36] [some small works by other poets, although different and indeed varying among themselves in subject . . . because these too can be called idylls].

These *opuscula* are a varied lot: Orphic hymns, elegies and fragments by Solon, poems from the Greek Anthology, and a number of similar short pieces by minor Greek poets, all devoid of pastoral content. The link with the Greek Anthology is interesting, and I shall take it up again.[37] At the moment, I simply wish to demonstrate that the 'idyll' is identified with any short lyric poem, no matter what its subject. This is the commonest definition found in Renaissance commentaries and criticism.

According to Gow, the word *eidyllion* occurs in Greek only in Theocritean scholia, where the explanations are unsatisfactory.[38] The Renaissance readily devised its own. Gow also mentions two Latin precedents for a wide and vague interpretation of the term. In the first century AD, Pliny describes a collection of occasional poems as 'sive epigrammata sive idyllia sive eclogas sive, ut multi, poematia seu quod aliud vocare malueris'[39] [epigrams or idylls or eclogues or, as many say, short poems, or whatever else you may have preferred to call them]. The term *idyllia* was also applied to Ausonius's short non-pastoral poems. I have found a reference to Pliny in Riccius and to Ausonius in Stephanus.[40]

Like the early scholiasts, the Renaissance interpreters all agree on one point: the brevity of the idyll. Hessus and Trimaninus describe it as

[36] *Theocriti aliorumque poetarum idyllia* (Paris, 1579), sig. * 2r.

[37] See also M. Y. Hughes, 'Spenser and the Greek Pastoral Triad', *SP* 20, pp. 195 ff.

[38] A. S. F. Gow (ed.), *Theocritus*, i, p. lxxi.

[39] Pliny, *Epistolae*, IV. xiv.

[40] Riccius's commentary on Virgil's Eclogues, sig. N4r; Stephanus (ed.), Theocritus, sig. * iir and (in the 2nd sequence of pp.), p. 56.

'parvum carmen' [short song], Andreas Divus and Ramus as 'parvum poema' [short poem].[41] The title-pages of Renaissance editions of Theocritus often give the same definition.[42] The selected English translations of 1588 are entitled *Sixe Idillia that is, Sixe Small, or Petty Poems, or Aeglogues*.

This definition is owing to the fact that *eidyllion* is formed by adding a diminutive suffix to *eidos*, a form or figure. *Idyll(ion)* thus comes to mean something like a 'little picture', a brief scene or vignette. J. J. Scaliger calls it (with special reference to Theocritus XXX) a 'poetica imaguncula'[43] [a small poetic picture]. His father J. C. Scaliger suggests reasons for the diminutive: 'vel propter breuitatem, vel ob modestiam ac rei humilitatem'[44] [either because of their brevity, or owing to the modesty and lowliness of the subject]. Ramus echoes this: 'Consimili nominis humilitate Theocritus Idyllion dixit.'[45] [Theocritus called it Idyllion from a similar humility of nomenclature.]

Vauquelin de la Fresnaie offers interesting though inconsistent definitions in the Preface to his *Idillies et pastoralles*. At one point he talks of 'les vers, que les vns appellent Bucoliques, les autres Aeglogues et les autres Idillies' [the poems which some call Bucolics, others Eclogues and yet others Idylls']. But soon after, he describes his 'idillies' as 'imagetes & petites tabletes de fantaisies d'Amour' [small images and miniatures of the fantasies of love]. In an 'eglogue', on the contrary, 'le sujet en semble desirer des propos et des discours plus longs (que Virgille appelle *deductum carmen*)'[46] [the subject seems to require a lengthier treatment and discourse (which Virgil calls *deductum carmen*)]. Of course this is a misinterpretation of Virgil VI. 5, where *deductum carmen* means 'thinly spun [slender or humble] song'.

Despite such distinctions, the definition of the 'idyll' is commonly transferred to the 'eclogue'. As Stephanus says, Servius calls Theocritus's poems eclogues, so why not call Virgil's idylls?[47] So also Minturno: 'Eclogas (sic ille [Virgil] appellat quae Theocritus Idyllia)'[48] [eclogues (so Virgil calls what Theocritus calls idylls)]. Riccius too equates the two

[41] Hessus, *Theocriti . . . Eidyllia*, sig. A3^r; Trimaninus, *Theocriti Syracusani opera Latine . . . expressa* (Venice, 1539), fo. 4^r; *Theocriti Syracusani . . . Idyllia trigintasex . . . Andrea Diuo . . . interprete* (Basle, 1554), 9; Ramus (ed.), Virgil's Eclogues (1582), 26.

[42] e.g. the 1541 Basle and 1545 Frankfurt edns. both have 'parva poemata' on the title-page.

[43] *Theocriti Syracusii Idyllia*, ed. J. J. Scaliger and I. Casaubon ([Heidelberg], 1596), 230.

[44] *Poetices libri septem*, I. iv: p. 7, col. 1.

[45] Ramus (cit. n. 41), p. 26.

[46] *Diverses poésies*, ii. 443–4.

[47] *Theocriti aliorumque poetarum idyllia*, sig. * 2^r.

[48] *De poeta*, p. 162.

terms, and defines the *ecloga* as 'parvum carmen' [short song].[49] Remy Belleau distinguishes between the 'breue et courte' *eglogue* 'à la façon de Theocrite' and the 'plus long' *chant pastoral*.[50] *Sixe Idillia* uses 'Aeglogues' as equivalent to 'Idillia' and 'Small, or Petty Poems'.

For after all, the eclogue too has no etymological connection with the pastoral. In the Renaissance, it was often wrongly derived from the Greek *aix*, *aigos*, a goat.[51] It really means a 'choice' or 'selection', and was applied by the ancient grammarians to Virgil's Bucolics in a sense roughly equivalent to 'Selected Poems'. Ausonius's collection of short, varied poems were (and are) commonly called eclogues as well as idylls. Ausonius himself applied the word 'ecloga' to his longer mythological poem *Cupido cruciatur*, and also (in the Preface to *Griphus ternarii numeri*) to that very different poem, Horace's Ode III. xix.[52] Statius refers to two of his miscellaneous *Silvae* as 'eglogae', III. v and IV. viii.[53] The first has some description of the Neapolitan landscape, the second no rustic touch at all. Statius is clearly using the word loosely, and could have applied it to any other poem in the collection.

J. C. Scaliger has a slightly involved explanation for such usage. Having written a number of *idyllia*, the poet would select the best from that 'incondita turba' [disordered crowd]: these would therefore be called *eclogae*. The *ecloga* thus shares the *idyllium*'s range of subject-matter: 'Horum materia multiplex'.[54]

In fact, even with Virgil's eclogues, the variety of subject-matter had been acknowledged ever since Servius wrote 'qui enim bucolica scribit, curare debet ante omnia, ne similes sibi sint eclogae.'[55] [Whoever writes bucolic poems ought to take care before all things that the eclogues are not similar to each other.] This is duly repeated in commentaries and even in an eclogue by Andrelini: 'Diversum delectat opus.'[56] [A varied work gives pleasure.] Oporinus, introducing his 1546 collection, praises the versatility of pastoral, in which 'nescio quo pacto omnium aliorum quoque generum materias complecti ueteres consueuerunt' [by some agreement, the ancients were accustomed to include the matter of all other genres]. The list includes:

[49] Riccius, sig. N3^{v}–4^{r}.

[50] Note on Ronsard's 'Le Voiage de Tours' in Ronsard's *Œuvres* (Paris, 1560), i/2, fo. 54^{v}. This part of the note is omitted in later edns.

[51] See Helen Cooper, 'The Goat and the Eclogue', *PQ* 53 (1974), 363–79.

[52] See the Loeb Classics Ausonius (ed. H. G. E. White; London, 1919), i. 206 and 354 respectively.

[53] See the Loeb Classics Statius (ed. J. H. Mozley; London, 1928), i. 140 and 204 respectively.

[54] *Poetices libri septem* I. iv, p. 7, col. 1.

[55] Thilo, III. i. 12–13.

[56] Andrelini VIII. 5.

siue decantandis deorum laudibus, siue fortium uirorum gestis celebrandis: . . . funeribus deplorandis, uel etiam recitandis amoribus, atque alijs querimonijs, uel moribus hominum capendis, uel exprimendae tam principum quam popularium uitae . . .[57]

[either singing the praises of the gods, or celebrating the deeds of brave men; . . . lamenting deaths, or else recounting love-affairs and other complaints, or criticizing the manners of men, or describing the lives of both rulers and common men]

Scaliger has an even longer list.[58] Of course, he stipulates that all this material should be put in rustic guise. Yet his disquisition presents pastoral as an open-ended genre, leading on to a variety of other themes and forms.

In considering this variety, I shall begin with Theocritus himself. Apart from his Idylls, he is credited with a number of epigrams, including some half a dozen pastoral ones (nos. 1 to 6 in modern editions): prayers and offerings to Apollo, Pan, and Priapus; a warning to a hunter to flee Pan and Priapus; an invitation to song; a lament for a kid killed by a wolf. These were printed in Theocritus's works from 1516. Also commonly ascribed to him, or at least printed among his works, was the pattern-poem 'Syrinx' or 'Fistula', taking the shape of a pan-pipe on the page, dedicated to Pan, and narrating the story of Pan and Syrinx in a riddle.

Today we can also read these poems in the Greek Anthology, but only one—no. 4—was available in the shorter Planudean Anthology which alone was known till Salmasius's discovery of the Palatine manuscript in 1605–6. However, other poems in the Planudean Anthology would provide models for pastoral epigrams, particularly the votive epigram. James Hutton shows how some of Navagero's *lusus pastorales* go back to the Anthology.[59] According to Laumonier, the epigrammatic *vœux* composed by the Pléiade draw directly on the Anthology as well as on Navagero's intermediary models.[60] Though I have not seen it suggested anywhere, we may assume that the publication of Theocritus's epigrams in 1516 would reinforce the movement towards the pastoral epigram. At any rate, the spate of *lusus pastorales* begins after this date, though there are stray poems composed earlier that may pass under that description.[61]

57 Oporinus, *Bucolicorum autores XXXVIII*, sig. α 2^{r-v}.
58 *Poetices libri septem*, III. xcix: p. 150, col. 1.
59 J. Hutton, *The Greek Anthology in Italy to the Year 1800* (Ithaca, 1935), 190–2.
60 P. Laumonier, *Ronsard poète lyrique* (Paris, 1909), 128–9.
61 The earliest example I have found is by Antonio Mario (fl. 1450), 'Ad nymphas Bononienses'; see *Carmina illustrium poetarum Italorum* (1720), vi. 250. Navagero's *lusus pastorales* were published in 1530, but the date of composition is uncertain.

But the pastoral pieces in the Anthology are, of course, swamped by the rest. Theocritus's six pastoral epigrams exist alongside a number of others on completely different themes. These formal affinities explain why the *lusus pastoralis* is drawn towards a varied range of epigrams and lyrics. I have described this process in Navagero's *Lusus*. Even Flaminio's, despite their narrative unity, show a measure of fluctuation in their form. And once the general setting and situation have been established, individual poems may contain nothing pastoral, but resemble ordinary epigrams or love-lyrics.

Many collections of Neo-Latin lyrics and epigrams will yield a few examples that may pass as authentic *lusus pastorales*. Girolamo Amalteo has a number of epigrams on the love of Acon and Galla; a few are pastoral, such as the one where Acon overhears Galla weeping for a goat slain by a wolf.[62] Girolamo's brother Giambattista has epigrams about Hyella. At least one of these is truly pastoral,[63] but it does not stand apart from the rest.

The word *lusus* seems to indicate any epigram or short poem, with the *lusus pastoralis* as a subspecies. Jodocus Badius writes:

> Ludere dicitur qui rem iocularem aut non apprime grauem carminibus prosequitur. vt qui epigrammata aut elegias aut tenuia opuscula condunt: quia id facili vena & non elaborata sed seipsam quasi offerente minerua efficiunt. Vnde ea opuscula etiam lusus dici solent & nonnunque nuge.[64]
>
> [He is said to sport (*ludere*) who pursues in song a light matter, or one not pre-eminently serious, like those who compose epigrams or elegies or delicate little pieces, because they accomplish this in a manner smooth and not elaborate, but as if Minerva is offering herself [i.e. through spontaneous inspiration]: whence these little pieces are usually called sports (*lusus*) and sometimes trifles (*nugae*).]

This, we should note, is to illustrate *ludere* in Virgil's Eclogue I. 10, where the word refers to Tityrus's pastoral song. But by extending the term, Navagero's whole heterogeneous collection is entitled *lusus*, and Scévole de Sainte-Marthe has two books of *Epigrammata & lusus* without a single pastoral example.[65] I have described a similar diffusion of subject-matter in the Italian pastoral sonnet.

Among French poets, according to Laumonier, the votary epigram derived from the Anthology was considered a species of 'odelette'; more

[62] Appendix to Sannazaro's *Opera* (1728), 373.
[63] 'Ad arietem Hyellae', ibid. 444.
[64] Virgil's *Opera* (Lyons, 1528), fo. 3r, col. 2.
[65] Except perhaps one, 'Veneri'; see Sainte-Marthe's *Poemata* (Limoges, 1596), 240.

elaborate poems of the same nature would be 'odes'.[66] This brings us to another obvious lyric model, the Horatian ode. At points, Horace's *Carmina* approach the *lusus* in subject-matter. Ode III. xviii is a hymn to Faunus, and III. xxii the dedication of a pine tree to Diana. In I. xvii the poet, speaking as a goatherd, invites the reader to country repose. Other poems simply describe springtime and nature's beauty, occasionally passing into mythology (for example, I. iv, IV. vii, IV. xii). This rural beauty and mythological lore may be drawn upon in any poem on any subject. But neither is an essential ingredient, and may be forgotten for long stretches.

This is the very compound treated in the varied lyric tradition I have been tracing, with pastoral and rustic themes at one end of the spectrum. It is scarcely surprising that many of the poems discussed in section I of this chapter, with others of the same nature, should feature in Carol Maddison's account of the Renaissance ode, and that she should talk of the 'invasion of other lyrical forms by the pastoral'.[67] But the Horatian ode is scarcely an exclusive model. It takes its place within the web of other lyric forms that impinge upon the pastoral.

These complex interrelations are reflected in Scaliger's account of the 'Lyrica' in his second chapter on the subject (III. cxxiv) in *Poetices libri septem*. Brevity and variety are the two great features of the lyric, and Horace the outstanding exemplar: 'Breuitate delectatus est Horatius.' [Horace takes pleasure in brevity]: p. 169, col. 1. In his earlier chapter (I. xliv) however, he is obviously thinking of grander forms of lyric: 'Proxima Heroicae maiestati Lyrica nobilitas.' [Lyric dignity comes closest to the majesty of the epic.] Alongside Horace he now names Pindar, whose odes he calls *melos* and *eidos*, 'vnde diminutiuum Idyllion'.[68] But he also mentions two other great exponents of the 'Melos, siue Ode', Anacreon and Catullus. The latter is commended for his 'Dithyrambica, et . . . Choriambica in Cybelen, Bacchum, Silenum, Pana, Faunum, Priapum' (p. 47, col. 2). This makes Catullus's work sound very like *lusus pastorales*, but it is difficult to see what poems Scaliger has in mind.

Anacreon is more important. Two poems in the Theocritean canon are Anacreontic in nature: Idyll XIX, on Cupid and the Bee, and 'The Death of Adonis'. Henricus Stephanus, who discovered the lost Anacreontea

[66] Laumonier, *Ronsard poète lyrique*, pp. 128–9.

[67] *Apollo and the Nine*, p. 63.

[68] p. 47, col. 1. I may hazard a guess here. If Pindar's 'greater' ode was the *eidos*, would not Horace's 'lesser' ode be the *eidyllion*?

and published them in 1554, repeatedly notes the resemblance, and points out an Anacreontic parallel to Idyll XIX. In a volume containing Pindar, Anacreon, and other Greek poets, he includes 'The Death of Adonis' among 'Anacreontia carmina diversorum' [Anacreontic poems by others].[69] (We should remember that modern scholars do not consider the Anacreontea discovered by Stephanus to be Anacreon's own work.)

In fact, for Stephanus at least, there was a deeper association of pastoral and Anacreontic. 'Gratiae omnes efflorescunt' [all graces bloom] in the brief, light Anacreontic lyrics. They are like tiny ivory carvings 'quae humilia sunt, ac veluti serpunt humi, occultum quendam ornatum habent, cuius sensu non omnes sed sagassimi quique solum afficiuntur'[70] [which are humble and, as it were, crawl on the ground, [but] have some hidden ornament by whose touch not all but only the wisest are moved]. This is the humble style classically exemplified in pastoral poetry. At the same time, Stephanus's description suggests a sophisticated grace and elegance. We may recall that his fellow-countryman Vauquelin describes 'Idillies' (expanding the etymological meaning) as signifying 'diuerses petites images & graueures en la semblance de celles qu'on graue aux lapis, aux gemmes & calcedoines pour seruir quelques fois de cachet'[71] [various small images and carvings like those sometimes engraved on stones, gems and chalcedony to serve as seals]. The *Idillies et pastoralles* include a number of poems based wholly or substantially on poems from the Anacreontea and the Greek Anthology.[72]

Much earlier, in 1555, Henricus Stephanus, failing to print for Giovanni della Casa a volume of Anacreontic poetry, instead dedicated to him some translations from Moschus, Bion, and Theocritus (in that order) with some of his own poems 'non diuersi ab illis argumenti' [of subjects not dissimilar to these].[73] Of the eleven Greek poems, only two are pastoral (Theocritus III and XX). The criterion seems to be brevity and *elegantia*: that is probably why Moschus and Bion precede Theocritus. Robert Stephanus, reprinting the book in 1556, praises his brother Henri's translations because 'quicquid tenerum erat in illis &

[69] *Pindari . . . caeterorum octo lyricorum carmina* (3rd edn. Paris, 1586), 266, 270ff.
[70] Ibid. 73.
[71] *Diverses poésies*, ii. 444.
[72] Vauquelin's editor Julien Travers finds 5 clear imitations of the Anacreontea and 13 of poems from the Anthology. Some of these are variations or partial adaptations rather than exact renderings.
[73] *Moschi, Bionis, Theocriti . . . idyllia*, title-page.

molle, expresserit' [he has brought out whatever was delicate and tender in them].[74] This recalls Henri's praise of Anacreon.

But Henri's own poems suggest other affinities: two eclogues, so designated; an 'Oda, de laudibus vitae rusticae' and two *idyllia* addressed to country youths and maidens. Finally comes an 'Anus querela de forma amissa' [An Old Woman's Complaint for her Lost Beauty], obviously without pastoral or rustic element, and Propertius's equally non-pastoral elegy (II. xii in modern numbering) 'Quicumque ille fuit, puerum qui pinxit Amorem' [Whoever he was who first painted Love in the likeness of a boy]. The distinction between *ecloga*, *oda*, and *idyllium* is interesting, but also the fact that Henri groups them together round the Greek idyll as 'carmina non diuersi ab illis argumenti'.

In *Poetices libri septem* (III. c; p. 150, col. 1) Scaliger defines another brief lyric, the *sylva*:

> Poematia ergo quaedam, vt docet Quintilianus, subito excussa calore syluas nominarunt veteres, vel a multiplici materia, vel a frequentia rerum inculcatarum, vel ab ipsis rudimentis: rudia nanque Poemata, & sane effusa, postea castigabant.

> [Therefore, as Quintilian teaches, certain short poems, struck out from sudden heat, the ancients called sylvae, either from the varied material, or from the multitude of matters packed into them, or from their being early attempts: for later they criticized rough and indeed disordered poems [like these].]

This derives from Quintilian X. iii. 17, where *silvae* are a vice of composition rather than a poetic genre, but even more directly from Statius's Preface to Book I of his *Silvae*: 'hos libellos, qui mihi subito calore et quadam festinandi voluptate fluxerunt' [[these little books] which were produced [by me] in the heat of the moment and a kind of joyful glow of improvisation].[75]

It is all very reminiscent of Scaliger's definition of the *idyllium*. That too had stressed the variety of material. As for sudden inspiration, the *idyllia* 'meditati non essent satis' [were not sufficiently thought-out], but 'subito calore excidissent' [escaped out of sudden heat].[76] That is why they had to be selected as *eclogae*. We may recall Badius's definition of the *lusus*, as also the fact that Navagero's *lusus* were compared (albeit to

[74] The same. Paris edn of 1556, sig. A1v.

[75] Text and trans. as in the Loeb Classics Statius, i. 2–3. Such associations may be due to the habitual derivation of *sylva* from Greek *hylē*, unformed, elemental matter. See, for instance, Servius on *Aeneid*, i. 316; also Ben Jonson, *Underwood*, 'To the Reader'.

[76] Scaliger, *Poetices libri septem*, I. iv; p. 7, col. 1.

his chagrin) to Statius's *Silvae*.[77] Vauquelin uses *Les Foresteries*, a clear translation of *Silvae*, as the title for a wide-ranging collection of poems. The Latin *sylva* has become part of the conglomerate of lyric forms surrounding the pastoral. Sainte-Marthe's *Sylvarum libri tres* includes a single eclogue 'Damoetas' (*Poemata*, p. 81): apparently part of a conscious plan, for it begins

> Hactenus aut superum laudes, aut proelia regum
> Diximus Aeolio cantu: nunc rustica nobis
> Musa placet . . .

[so far we have sung the praises of the gods or the wars of kings in Aeolian song: now the rustic muses please us]

Some of Alamanni's Italian *Selve* are quasi-pastoral treatments of Tuscan and Ligurian landscapes, described with an exile's nostalgia; others are on totally different subjects.

I shall close with a less elegant northern instance of the varied mutations of pastoral and 'idyll'. De Slupere calls a group of poems 'Diversorum carminum Syluula, seu Lusus Pastorales' (*Poemata*, pp. 201 ff.), although they are nothing akin to Navagero or Flaminio's *lusus*, and scarcely more to Statius's *Silvae* or Vauquelin's *Foresteries*. Like nearly all de Slupere's work, these poems are very long. I have already described their allusive content, but they have more prominent themes of a general nature. Some can be called rural idylls for want of a better word, though they are clumsily full of local references. They provide an itinerary instead of creating an atmosphere: one piece is actually called a 'Hodoeporicum' or itinerary (*Poemata*, p. 242).

Most remarkable, however, is that nearly all these pieces contain subdivisions, poems within poems, in a variety of metres and stanza-forms. This is matched by changes of speaker and subject. 'De aurorae vernalis suavitate' [On the sweetness of the spring dawn] opens true to its title, with the poet speaking (*Poemata*, pp. 217 ff.). This section could stand as a poem by itself. Presently he hears Tityrus lamenting his love for Thisbe. He then sings 'De venationis iucunditate' [On the pleasure of hunting], with references to his hunting-companions and the songs *they* sing.

Similarly, the unbucolic 'Convivium bucolicum' (*Poemata*, pp. 227–42) opens with a description of winter, and passes on to a winter feast with Tityrus as host. The *pièce de résistance* is Menalcas's rendering of

[77] See earlier in this section for Badius, and Ch. 4 n. 50 for Navagero.

Iolas's love-complaint, which includes a long and self-contained description of springtime. Even the 'Hodoeporicum Brabanticum' closes with a love-song of Sylvius to Callirhoe.

These lumbering, compendious pieces are distinctively Sluperian, but the impulse behind them is a common one: to bring order to the multifarious forms and subjects gathered round the central pastoral tradition. It is important to realize the double movement of Renaissance pastoral: on one side the formal eclogue, on the other a fragmented body of lyrics. Understandably, historians of Renaissance pastoral concentrate on the former. Regarding the latter, I myself have merely noted some basic affinities and possible lines of investigation. But it is a vital element all the same: suggesting a constant alternative to the eclogue, bringing fresh influences to bear upon the pastoral, offering immense problems of synthesis but also the opportunity for a great enrichment of pastoral literature if such synthesis can be achieved. It is part of the wide-ranging tradition that Sidney and Spenser inherit and from which they choose appropriate elements for their own versions of pastoral.

PART II

English Pastoral Poetry

6
English Pastoral before Spenser

1. *The Latin eclogues of Giles Fletcher*

THERE is nothing in the eclogues of Giles Fletcher the Elder that we have not met in continental pastoral. Most of them seem to have been written at Cambridge while Spenser was an undergraduate there (1569–73); they refer to contemporary events, often also at Cambridge.[1] It seems reasonable to assume that they were circulated in manuscript. Early versions of five poems are found in a manuscript at Hatfield House. This was certainly made in Fletcher's lifetime, and I have chosen its readings (in Lloyd Berry's published transcript)[2] in preference to those in books printed long after Fletcher's death and sometimes without his name.[3]

The longest of Fletcher's eclogues, and the first in the Hatfield manuscript, is 'De literis antiquae Britanniae' (probably modelled on Virgil VI). Here Father Cam sings the history of Britain, especially its learned tradition, emphasizing the antiquity of Cambridge and concluding with a survey of the colleges. Two other poems treat more locally and sordidly of Cambridge: 'Queraela Collegij Regalis' is centrally, and 'Aecloga de contemptu ministrorum' partially, concerned with the dispute between Philip Baker, Provost of King's, and his colleagues. Another Hatfield poem celebrates Ann Cecil's marriage to the Earl of

[1] If 'Lycidas' in 'De literis antiquae Britanniae' is Fletcher, as seems likely, the poem was composed in 1570, for Lycidas says (l. 15) that he has been at Cambridge for five years. (Fletcher came to Cambridge in 1565). Berry (see n. 2 below) does not note this.

[2] L. E. Berry, 'Five Latin Poems by Giles Fletcher, the Elder', *Anglia*, 79 (1961), 338–77.

[3] Fletcher's eclogues have been printed as follows: (*i*) 'De literis antiquae Britanniae' (in the Hatfield MS): Cambridge, 1633. (*ii*) 'Aecloga de contemptu ministrorum' of the Hatfield MS as 'Contra praedicatorum contemptum' in William Dillingham (ed.), *Poemata varii argumenti* (London, 1678), 185 ff. (*iii*) 'Queraela Collegij Regalis' (in the Hatfield MS): ibid. 192 ff. (*iv*) 'De Morte Boneri': ibid. 201 ff. (*v*) 'Queraela de obitu Clerj Haddonj' of the Hatfield MS as 'Adonis eiusdem Fletcheri' among the poems appended to *Poematum Gualteri Haddoni . . . libri duo* (London, 1576). The collection also includes other elegies by Fletcher for Haddon; of these, 'Ad salicem Haddoni' has some pastoral touches. (*vi*) 'Aecloga Daphnis inscripta . . . in obitum . . . Nicolai Carri': appended to Nicholas Carr's translation of Demosthenes (see n. 5 below).

Oxford, and the last mourns the death of Clare Haddon (d. 1570) of Cambridge. Another Cambridge elegy (not in the manuscript) mourns Nicholas Carr, Regius Professor of Greek (d. 1568); and there is a very different satiric elegy for the hated Edward Bonner, Bishop of London during the Marian persecutions.

All the eclogues are fundamentally allusive, and not without lapses from the pastoral metaphor. At one point in the 'Aecloga de contemptu ministrorum', the shepherd is clearly revealed as a scholar-cleric, midnight oil mingling with icicles in the beard:

> quoties offensa videndo
> Lumina conterimus digitis, quotiesque seueris
> Naribus, infestae bibitur fuligo lucernae.
> O quoties aestas, quoties nos frigore Caurus
> Vexat, & hybernae glacialia sydera brumae,
> Longaque concretis dependet stiria barbis. (ll. 45–50)

[How often do we rub our smarting eyes with the fingers in order to see, how often is the soot of the flickering lamp inhaled through coarse nostrils. How often does summer, how often does the north-west wind with its cold oppress us, and the icy stars of midwinter; and the long icicle hangs from congealed beards.]

Sometimes again, the pastoral framework seems purely extraneous. In 'De literis antiquae Britanniae', a particularly amusing feature is that the nymphs accompanying Father Cam are the works of old historians, almost it seems the historians themselves, feminized (ll. 43ff.). This is among the most hilarious excesses of misguided pastoral mythopoeia.

But for the rest, here and elsewhere, Fletcher offers a truly imaginative transformation of the Cambridge scene. Sometimes it is simple nature-myth. Father Cam appears with 'madidum caput' [a wet head],

> Caeruleus tergo dependet carbasus, aures
> Canna tegit, patulis fluit humida naribus vnda. (ll. 40–2)

[A blue garment hangs from his back, reeds cover his ears, and a moist stream flows from his broad nostrils.]

The end of 'De literis' has an elaborately mythologized account of the Cambridge landscape. But, more notably, Fletcher turns the actual landscape into a pastoral setting symbolizing academic life. We see this in the 'Aecloga de contemptu ministrorum', in 'Daphnis', and most vividly in 'Queraela Collegij Regalis', where Melibaeus and Aegon sit exchanging songs 'Molliter in viridj graminis herba' [comfortably upon the green grass]: l. 4. If Hobbinoll's 'Paradise' in Spenser's 'Iune' is really

Cambridge, Fletcher's eclogues provide an obvious precedent for the setting though not the circumstances.

Fletcher translates contemporary matters into patterns of pastoral experience. Walter Haddon mourns the death of his son Clare as the hunter Lycidas mourning for Adonis:

> quis retia mecum,
> Quis iuga, quis tenso cinget nemora auia lino,
> Longa vel e teretj stringet venabula quercu?[4]

[Who now, with me, encircles the hills and pathless woods with net and taut line, or cuts long hunting-spears from the smooth oak?]

In 'Queraela Collegij Regalis', King's College complaining of neglect by the Provost Philip Baker becomes Telethusa lamenting the ways of her husband Daphnis. She even practises magic rites in Pharmaceutria style, but here to dissolve the tie. (Baker was removed on the fellows' petition.)

Such 'translation' does not really explore the possibilities of the pastoral metaphor. Walter Haddon is not ruler-shepherd but hunter, Philip Baker not teacher-shepherd but lover-shepherd. Pastoral is being used as cipher, not as meaningful metaphor. In 'Daphnis', however, Nicholas Carr, Regius Professor of Greek, is presented as a singer and 'wise shepherd':

> Daphnis & Argolicas vobiscum inflare cicutas
> Nouerat, & Latia deducere carmen auena.[5]

[Daphnis knew both how to play the Grecian flutes with you [the Muses] and to draw song from the Latin pipe.]

He is also an expert in the shepherd's specialties, medicine and astronomy.

The shepherd-cleric figure is presented very clearly. In 'De morte Boneri', kings and queens are depicted as such, but the common people are sheep, the clergy shepherds, and Bonner a wolf, 'ferox . . . praedator ovilis' [a fierce preyer upon sheep], who attacks both sheep and shepherds. In 'De contemptu ministrorum', Myrtilus and Celadon lament the opprobrium brought on priests by degenerate pastors like Corydon (Philip Baker once again). Such men are unfit to be shepherds, having been born as smiths, ploughmen, and carters.

[4] 'Queraela de obitu Clerj Haddonj . . . Aecloga Adonis', ll. 29–31.

[5] *Demosthenis . . . orationes . . . e Graeco in Latinum conuersae, a Nicolao Carro* (London, 1571), fo. 79ᵛ.

> Illj nec curare gregem, nec pascere doctj,
> Nec cantare modos, aut respondere peritj,
> Sed pauidum tondere pecus, vacuumque coactj
> Velleris, ad gelidae ventos exponere brumae. (ll. 109–12)

[They are not learned in caring for the flock or feeding it, nor skilled in singing measures or responding [to them], but in shearing the terrified herd and exposing them, stripped of their thick fleece, to the winds of icy midwinter.]

Fletcher's Protestantism is markedly more strident than Spenser's,[6] but his pastoral of the Church is rather like that in *The Shepheardes Calender*. As in Spenser, the shepherds seem to stand for specific clergymen: Myrtilus and Celadon of 'De contemptu ministrorum' recur in 'De morte Boneri' as two of Bonner's victims. But there is very little of Spenser's emphasis on the *principles* of 'pastoral care', and the allegory is more fine-spun than ever in Spenser. Amarillis, it is said, cannot abide even the sweetest shepherd's song, but it is enough if Phyllis is pleased. Who or what Amarillis is I cannot say (the Catholic Church, perhaps?) but a note in the Hatfield manuscript explains that Phyllis is 'Ecclesia' (the Church of England?).[7]

Fletcher's poems are among the more vividly pastoral of allusive eclogues, and his ecclesiastical allegory anticipates Spenser's to an appreciable degree. But there is nothing that Spenser could not have found in continental poets as well. Much more important, the general bent of Spenser's work is (I shall argue) in a completely different direction, moving away from all such didactic and allusive models.

Allusive Latin eclogues continued to be written throughout the Elizabethan age, on births, marriages, and deaths, as well as public and ceremonial occasions. They were also written in English, or even translated from the Latin as with Thomas Watson's 'Meliboeus' on the death of Walsingham. I shall treat these poems in Chapter 9; but the mainstream of vernacular pastoral in England takes a completely different course.

2. *Barclay's Eclogues: Satire and the suffering rustic*

Roughly between 1500 and 1513,[8] Alexander Barclay wrote five Eclogues which must be accounted the most important English ones

[6] Though it is worth noting that Nicholas Carr was a Catholic.

[7] 'De contemptu ministrorum', ll. 174–88. The printed text in Dillingham has no indication of allegory at all.

[8] As estimated by Beatrice White in her edn. of the Eclogues (EETS os 175; Oxford, 1928).

before Spenser's. They are the reverse of Arcadian. Rather, they emphasize the poverty and hardship of the shepherd's life, and are full of satirical and didactic passages. In fact, the first three eclogues are based upon *De curialium miseriis*, a prose satire of court life by Aeneas Silvius Piccolomini, later Pope Pius II. The two other pieces are modelled on Mantuan V and VI.

The Argument to Eclogue I describes the old shepherd Cornix's poverty in spite of a life of toil. The eclogue itself opens with an account of the shepherds' miseries after a storm. Here Barclay borrows from Mantuan III to commence on a note of suffering and questioning that Aeneas Silvius does not provide:

> If God (as men say) doth heauen and earth sustayne,
> Then why doth not he regarde our dayly payne?[9]

As a rule, however, the anger and resentment seek a different object. Cornix has already noted the contrast between their state and that of the rich. At first his speech echoes Mantuan; but Barclay introduces more and more touches of his own, building up to a completely original climax:

> They do nought els but reuell, slepe and drinke,
> But on his foldes the poore shepheard muste thinke.
> They rest, we labour, they gayly decked be
> While we go ragged in nede and pouertie
>
> . . . .
>
> But what bringeth them to this prosperitie,
> Strength, courage, frendes, crafte and audacitie. (ll. 343–6, 351–2)

There are many such passages in Barclay, mostly original to the poet. In Eclogue IV, the poor shepherd Minalcas complains:

> Pouertie to me should be no discomforte
> If other shepheardes were all of the same sorte.
> But Codrus I clawe oft where it doth not itche,
> To see ten beggers and halfe a dosen riche . . .[10]

In Eclogue V the protest and satire reach a climax:

> In lust, in pleasour, and good in aboundaunce
> Passe they their liues, we haue not suffisaunce. (ll. 143–4)

[9] Eclogue I. 213–14; all refs. to White's edn. (cit. n. 8).

[10] Eclogue IV. 97–100. Cf. Eclogue II. 789ff. (based on Aeneas Silvius); Eclogue IV. 305ff. (4 ll. in Mantuan expanded to 30); Eclogue V. 663–4 (original to Barclay).

As in the source-poem, Mantuan VI, the town–country debate is turned into a more basic contrast between rich and poor—and further, between duty and pleasure, moral sense and irresponsibility. Barclay adapts his original towards this end. The interlocutors in Mantuan VI, Fulica and Cornix, had differed in nothing except their views on town and country. But Barclay reallocates their speeches up to line 236 so that Amintas becomes a vain upstart, flaunting his smattering of city ways, while Faustus is the traditional, dour, moralizing shepherd.

Barclay introduces much new matter on the shepherd's toil and poverty. The following six lines from Eclogue IV expand as many words in Mantuan:

> Bye strawe and litter, and hay for winter colde,
> Oft grease the scabbes aswell of yonge as olde.
> For dreade of thieues oft watche vp all the night,
> Beside this labour with all his minde and might,
> For his poore housholde for to prouide vitayle,
> If by aduenture his wooll or lambes fayle. (ll. 173–8)

The idyllic world of classical pastoral is far away. This is shown in Eclogue II by an interesting reference to Virgil III. 70 (again this is Barclay's own addition to Aeneas Silvius):

> Thy princes apples be swete and orient,
> Suche as Minalcas vnto Amintas sent,
>
> In sauour of whom thou onely haste delite,
> But if thou shouldst dye no morsell shalt thou bite. (ll. 879–80, 883–4)

Virgil's shepherd-world (though that was not all Arcadia) becomes a remote Never Never Land associated with the city and the court!

Along with this goes much satire. Of course, Barclay's sources are basically satirical, but he adds to the plenty. Eclogue II contains a long piece of satire against women (ll. 399ff.), and another on eating and drinking at court (ll. 538ff.). The latter sticks to Aeneas Silvius, but the former far exceeds the original. The account of cheating traders in Eclogue V. 686ff. is largely Barclay's own invention. In the same poem (ll. 803–30) he inserts a passage from Mantuan (II. 67–78) on the abuse of the Sabbath in the country. But he prefaces this with an original passage (ll. 779–802) on similar irreverence among city-dwellers. He cannot let the criticism of rural life stand by itself.

In a word, Barclay's Eclogues mark an extreme development of the 'suffering shepherd' vein. They show a pronounced satirical and moral bent, vivid accounts of a shepherd's hardships, and a keen awareness of injustice and exploitation, the contrast between rich and poor. We may relate this to Barclay's concern with the concept of the three estates, as pointed out by Ruth Mohl.[11]

All this strongly suggests an independent influence in addition to Mantuanesque pastoral. The obvious model would be *Piers Plowman*, commonly thought to be the first English satire.[12] It circulated widely in manuscript in the Renaissance,[13] ran into four printed editions in mid-century, and was mentioned by many authors.[14]

Even more influential, perhaps, was an extensive body of 'Plowman literature', inspired by the more satirical and demotic aspects of Langland's work. *Pierce the Ploughman's Crede* was twice printed in addition to manuscript copies. *The Plowman's Tale* was ascribed to Chaucer, included in his manuscripts, and (from 1542) printed in his works. *The Praier and Complaynte of the Ploweman vnto Christe* was printed in 1531 and 1532 and—crowning proof of popularity—included from 1610 in Foxe's Book of Martyrs. Yet another tract was printed *c*.1550 and reprinted some forty years later during the Martin Marprelate controversy.[15]

In his primary identity, Piers was the figure of the common man, and frequently of the oppressed peasant. As is well known, 'Piers Plowman' was a code-name in a letter written by John Ball during the Peasants' Revolt. Langland's own work provides a strong basis for such use,[16] and later Plowman-literature is dominated by protest and criticism. *The Plowman's Tale* makes a sustained attack upon the wealth and power of

[11] *The Three Estates in Medieval and Renaissance Literature* (New York, 1933), 143–9.

[12] See Puttenham, *The Arte of English Poesie* (Gregory Smith (ed.), *Elizabethan Critical Essays*, ii. 62. l. 25, p. 64, l. 34–p. 65, l. 6); Francis Meres, *Palladis Tamia* (ibid. ii. 320, l. 19); Henry Peacham, *The Compleat Gentleman*, ch. 10 (J. E. Spingarn (ed.), *Critical Essays of the Seventeenth Century* (Oxford, 1908), i. 132–3); Milton, *Apology for Smectymnuus* (Milton's *Works*, Columbia edn., iii/1 (New York, 1931), 329, ll. 9–10).

[13] At least 5 new MSS were made: Bodl. MS Digby 145 (see A-Text, ed. G. Kane (London, 1960), 9–10); BL Royal Lib. MS 18 B. xvii (see C-Text, ed. W. W. Skeat (EETS os 54, 1873), p. xlviii); Caius College, Cambridge MS 201, made from the printed 1561 text (see B-Text, ed. W. W. Skeat (EETS os 38; 1869), p. xxx); Cambridge Univ. Lib. MS Gg. 4. 31 (see B-Text, ed. G. Kane and E. T. Donaldson (London, 1975), 8); Sion Coll. MS Arc. L. 40. 2/E(S) (ibid. 15).

[14] For a list see W. W. Skeat (ed.), *Piers Plowman*, iv/2 (EETS os 81, 1885), 863–70. However, many of Skeat's instances actually concern the 'Plowman literature' I shall describe in the next few pages.

[15] STC 19903a, 19903a.5. The 1550 title-page reads 'I playne Piers which can not flatter . . .'.

[16] See e.g. B-Text Passus X. 67–8, Passus XIV. 174–8. (All refs. to the B-Text, ed. Kane and Donaldson.)

the clergy. In *Pierce the Ploughman's Crede*, the humble ploughman knows the Creed while friars sunk in sloth and luxury do not. *The Praier and Complaynte of the Ploweman* is most vehement of all:

> For the pore man mote gone to hys laboure in colde & in hete, in wete & drye, & spende his flesch & hys bloude in the rych mennes workes apon gods grounde to fynde the rych man in ese, & in lykynge, & in good fare of mete & of drinke & of clothinge. Here ys a gret ȝifte of the pore man. For he ȝeueth his own body. But what ȝeueth the rych man hym aȝeynwarde? Sertes febele mete, & febele drinke, & feble clothinge.[17]

The opposition of clergy and laity has become a simple contrast of rich and poor, proud and meek.

Even in a work of humanist affinities like the early Tudor play of *Gentleness and Nobility*, the ploughman tells the knight and the merchant that private possession stems from tyranny and extortion (ll. 608–16).[18] The sober political tract *Pyers Plowmans Exhortation, vnto . . . Parlyamenthouse* (*c.*1550) exposes contrasts of wealth and poverty, ending with a stern warning of 'the plage and vengeaunce of God, ready to be powred doune uppon the whole realme, for this cruell oppression of the pore' (sig. B4^{r}). Earlier, at a more popular level, *God Spede the Plough* had listed the ploughman's burden of taxes and other exactions.

This is precisely the complaint made in the Wakefield Second Shepherds' Play:

> we ar so hamyd,
> ffor-taxed and ramyd,
> We ar mayde hand tamyd,
>   with thyse gentlery men.[19]

The hard labour of the Wakefield shepherds is very like the ploughman's, as described in *God Spede the Plough* and the *Crede*. In the Wakefield First Shepherds' Play too, the First Shepherd's reflections on earthly transience soon focus upon his own poverty and loss. The Second Shepherd complains how the townsmen exploit them:

> If he hask me oght | that he wold to his pay,
> ffull dere bese it boght | if I say nay;   (ll. 73–4)

[17] 1531 edn., sig. E5^{v}.

[18] Refs. to the Malone Society repr., 1950.

[19] ll. 15–18; refs. to *The Towneley Plays*, ed. G. England (EETS ES 71, Oxford, 1897; repr. 1952).

Shepherd and ploughman become kindred figures in this demotic literature, part of a whole gallery of rustic types. Langland himself associates 'Plowmen and pastours and pouere commune laborers, | Souteres and shepherdes' (Passus X. 466–7). In John Ball's 'Piers Plowman' letter, Ball himself is 'Iohan schep' (shepherd),[20] perhaps because he is a priest. Skelton's Colin Clout, a spokesman for the common rustic, bears a name that may already have been applied to shepherds.[21] In the Catholic *Banckett of Iohan the Reve* (BL MS Harley 207), the members of the proletarian symposium are exactly (and perhaps consciously) the same as in the lines quoted from Langland: 'peirs ploughman, Laurens laborer. Thomlyn Tailyer. And hobb of the hill. with other' (fo. 1^r). Hob is a shepherd, the best read among the rustics, and to him falls the honour of the conclusive defence of the doctrine of transubstantiation. In *I playne Piers* ... the Ploughman preaches his subversive message to all fellow-labourers, including 'hoggeherdes sheperhedes and all youre sorte dyspysed'.[22]

From the other direction, in Mantuan VI, God in his curse upon the younger sons of Eve equates the shepherd with all poor labourers in both town and country:

> vester erit stimulus, vester ligo, pastina vestra;
> vester erit vomer, iuga vestra, agrestia vestra
> omnia; ...
>
> . . . .
>
> sed tamen ex vobis quosdam donabimus urbe
> qui sint fartores, lanii, lixae artocopique
> et genus hoc alii soliti sordescere ... (ll. 95–101)

[Yours shall be the goad, yours the mattock, yours the dibbles; yours the plough-share, yours the yokes, yours all things rustic ... Some of you, however, we shall give to the city. They shall be poulterers, butchers, sutlers, bakers, and the tribe of all others accustomed to demean themselves with work ...]

The old *Kalender of Shepardes* has some lines to the ploughman beginning 'Peers go thou to plowe.'[23] In line with such precedents, Barclay in his fourth eclogue equates shepherd and ploughman as similar rustic types:

[20] R. H. Robbins (ed.), *Historical Poems of the XIVth and XVth Centuries* (New York, 1959), 55.

[21] See Cooper, *Pastoral*, p. 153.

[22] 1550 edn., sig. A8^r.

[23] *The Kalender of Shepardes*, printed by Thomas Este for John Wally (1570?), sig. A5^r.

> What should a Ploughman go farther than his plough,
> What should a shepherde in wisedome wade so farre . . . (ll. 792–3)

And again, in Eclogue V:

> It were a maruell if Cornix matter tolde
> To laude of shepheardes, or plowmen to vpholde . . . (ll. 399–400)

These brief touches underscore my earlier point about the 'suffering shepherd': he is not a distinct type or symbol, but a figure of the rustic poor generally. His higher symbolic functions are forgotten. In Barclay's Eclogues, this is particularly in evidence owing to conflation with the 'Piers Plowman' tradition.

Plowman-literature preserves one function of the pastoral metaphor: the ecclesiastical. The clergy are habitually presented as neglectful hireling shepherds or wolves in sheep's clothing.

> Lorde of all schepherdes blessed mote thou be. For thou louedest more the scheep then her wole. For thou fedest thy sheep both in body & in soule. [But the prelates] distroyen thy schepe, . . . that for drede they ben disparpled a brode in mownteynes, & there the wilde beestes of the felde distroyeth hem, & deuoureth hem for defaute of a good schepherde.[24]

For all its forensic detail, this is a single-noted metaphor, an overworked pastoral image rather than genuine pastoralism. Moral approbation, philosophic appeal, such suggestive detail as there might be—all these have passed to the ploughman-figure. Moreover, the ploughman is basically 'real', an actual rustic; the shepherd is a metaphoric or allegorical one, with the ploughman and his fellows as his 'sheep'.

Such division is unfortunate; but union, as we have earlier seen, is nearly impossible. The literal and metaphorical shepherds come to clash. In Barclay I. 485, Christ is 'the shephearde of Nazareth'; in Aeneas Silvius's non-pastoral context, he had been merely 'Salvator noster Iesu' [Jesus our saviour].[25] Morton, Archbishop of Canterbury, becomes 'the riche shepheard which woned in Mortlake' (Eclogue I. 499). But this is spoken by an actual shepherd who would be one of the shepherd-priest's 'flock'. Morton visits Coridon's family cottage as 'the patron of thinges pastorall' (Eclogue I. 511), an aristocrat or overlord rather than a true herdsman. With Alcock, Bishop of Ely, Barclay can avoid this metaphoric maze by exploiting a common pun on Alcock's name: 'He all was

[24] *The Praier and Complaynte of the Ploweman vnto Christe* (n.p., 1531?), sig. E8^{r-v}.
[25] *De curialium miseriis*, ed. W. P. Mustard (Baltimore, 1928), 26.

a cocke, he wakened vs from slepe' (Eclogue I. 521). But incongruously, the cock is also 'a father of thinges pastorall' (l. 531); and in Eclogue III. 470–1 Barclay sadly mixes the two metaphors: 'the gentle Cocke whiche sange so mirily, | He and his flocke were like an vnion'. Exactly the same clash between ruler-shepherd and commoner-shepherd occurs in Eclogue IV in a secular context. In the city,

> The riche and sturdie doth threaten and manace
> The poore and simple and suche as came but late
>
> . . . .
>
> And suche be assigned sometime the flocke to kepe
> Which scant haue so muche of reason as the shepe,
> And euery shepheard at other hath enuy,
> Scant be a couple which loueth perfitely . . . (ll. 124–5, 129–32)

In fact, in line 131, 'euery shepheard' seems to be neither ruler nor subject but mankind generally. The significance of sheep and shepherd differs from line to line. One sees the need to define the pastoral mode clearly once again.

When Spenser set about doing so in *The Shepheardes Calender*, he would have found in Barclay—and in Plowman literature generally—a model for his moral, didactic, and satiric vein.[26] But this is a subsidiary element in Spenser's design. In a general way, he emphatically moves *away* from Barclay's model.

J. R. Schultz failed to find any correspondence, beyond the most accidental, between Barclay's Eclogues and *The Shepheardes Calender*.[27] Yet, as Mustard, Schultz, and White have all noted,[28] it is unlikely that Spenser would not have known of Barclay's work—which was not only appended to John Cawood's edition of *The Ship of Fools* in 1570 but published separately several times before.[29] The probability is increased by the fact that, as Mustard points out, E. K.'s Epistle to Harvey clearly echoes Barclay's 'Prologe'.

In any case, there is one fundamental matter in which Spenser draws upon the poetic tradition of which Barclay's Eclogues form a part. This

[26] The matter has been treated, and through exclusive attention over-emphasized, in Alexander Lyle, '*The Shepheardes Calender* and Its English Antecedents' (B.Litt. Oxford, 1969). See also the brief account in David R. Shore, *Spenser and the Poetics of Pastoral* (Kingston, Ont., 1985), 29–30.

[27] 'Alexander Barclay and the Later Eclogue Writers', *MLN* 35 (1920), 52–4.

[28] W. P. Mustard, 'Notes on the Eclogues of Alexander Barclay', *MLN* 24 (1909), 10; Schultz, *MLN* 35; White (ed.), Barclay's *Eclogues*, p. lxi.

[29] Eclogues I–III (*c.*1530, *c.*1548, *c.*1560), IV (*c.*1521), V (*c.*1518): dates as in STC.

consists in an important element of the language of the *Calender*, E. K.'s 'rusticall rudenesse of shepheards, eyther for that theyr rough sounde would make his rymes more ragged and rustical, or els because such olde and obsolete wordes are most vsed of country folke'.[30] Philologists, most notably B. R. McElderry,[31] have tried to minimize the importance of this element. Others have tried to show that the archaic and dialectal diction is most pronounced in the moral and satiric eclogues, where satiric roughness merges with that demanded by 'pastoral decorum'.[32] But the other eclogues make the same demand, and it seems idle to deny that the language has an archaic and dialectal element all through.[33] Alexander Lyle admits (p. 164) that 'Januarye' has the same substantial presence of archaic and rustic words as 'Februarie', though with a very different effect. I shall cite two other local instances, both at the openings of poems and thus conditioning our response to what follows. The first eighteen lines of 'March' yield *alegge*, *sicker*, *thilke*, *studde*, *bragly*, *vpryst*. 'Aprill' begins

> Tell me good Hobbinoll, what *garres* thee *greete*?
> What? hath some Wolfe thy tender Lambes *ytorne*?[34]

The words italicized (by me) were all archaic at that date, on the testimony of the *OED*.[35] The stress-based rhythm that Lyle and Ingham consider characteristic of the moral eclogues, as of earlier rustic and satiric literature, is found equally in the framework of 'August'—a fact they do not recognize.

I shall make no attempt at a philological or metrical study of the *Calender*. I have cited sample passages only to confirm the presence of this element in Spenser's language all through the work. He is re-creating with his own resources an equivalent for the diction, idiom, and register of utterance that he and his age found in Chaucer and late Middle English literature, especially Plowman literature—whose affinities with

[30] Epistle to Gabriel Harvey preceding *The Shepheardes Calender*.

[31] 'Archaism and Innovation in Spenser's Poetic Diction', *PMLA* 47 (1932), 144–70.

[32] See Lyle (cit. n. 26), ch. vi; P. Ingham, 'Spenser's Use of Dialect', *ELN* 8 (1971), 166–7.

[33] It seems both futile and unnecessary to attempt to separate the archaic from the strictly dialectal, as both are being used to give the language a simultaneously primitive and rustic flavour. Because of the belief in the 'purity' of early Chaucerian English, archaisms would in any case be placed in the same register as unsophisticated and dialectal forms.

[34] All Spenser refs. to Smith and Selincourt's 1-vol. edn. (see Ch. 1 n. 3).

[35] For *ytorne* see McElderry, pp. 156–7. My sample suggests that McElderry is grossly over-cautious in estimating the number of archaisms in the *Calender*. Except for *alegge*, he does not note any of the words listed above.

Barclay's Eclogues I have tried to show. Spenser's debt to Chaucer is well authenticated. He has also been shown to echo *The Plowman's Tale* in 'Maye'.[36] In his concluding verses to the *Calender*, 'the Pilgrim that the Ploughman playde a whyle' may refer to the *Tale* or to *Piers Plowman*. In either case, Spenser is professing formal allegiance to a conservative poetic ideal to which Barclay's Eclogues form an adjunct—with the vital difference that Spenser applies the mode to subject-matter that Barclay and the Plowman-poets know nothing of: love, poetry, simple sport, and the appreciation of nature.

These themes are in line with continental art-pastoral; but the distinctive, purportedly rustic element in Spenser's language invests them with a special simplicity and spontaneity, checks their sophistication with a constant hint at rustic directness and sincerity. This leads us beyond the *Calender* to the considerable body of pastoral lyrics written after it and, I shall argue, in line with it. Such lyrics (epitomized by the collection in *England's Helicon*) have practically nothing in common with Barclay's Eclogues; but from Barclay, via Spenser, they preserve a special strain of the 'honest shepherd' in their treatment of idealized pastoral life.

3. *The Tudor lyric*

Given the nature of Spenser's themes as I have just described them, he may be seen to owe a more apparent debt to early Tudor lyric poetry generally. Most of these poems are devoid of pastoral elements. But drawing upon a number of other conventions, they provide a variety of natural settings and, against them, the figures of lovers and sometimes poets and philosophers. Spenser's success in the *Calender* owes much to his looking beyond his pastoral predecessors to this larger complex of settings and traditions, and incorporating their content into his pastoral work.

One of the commonest types of lyric features the lover in a landscape. Medieval May-morning and spring-song traditions blend with a Petrarchan sense of love and nature in several of Surrey's poems: 'The soote season . . .' (actually adapted from Petrarch), 'How eche thing saue the louer in spring reuiueth to pleasure', or the 'Complaint of a louer, that defied loue . . .'.[37] Thomas Howell has a poem on 'The restlesse

[36] See Variorum notes on ll. 1–8, 39: *The Works of Edmund Spenser: A Variorum Edition*, ed. E. Greenlaw *et al*. (Baltimore, 1932–57), *Minor Poems*, i. 297–8.

[37] Tottel's Miscellany, ed. H. E. Rollins (Cambridge, Mass., 1928–9), nos. 2, 11, and 5

paynes of the Louer forsaken', while all around him reigns happy springtime.[38] Turberville has a more memorable one, 'The Louer hoping in May to haue had redresse of his woes . . . bewailes his cruell hap'. Here the contrast is less with nature than with other, happy lovers who go

> Into the fieldes where *Dian* dwels
> With Nimphes enuirond round aboute . . .[39]

The mythic touch, though slight, should not be missed. Elsewhere, the poet concentrates on nature itself. Poem 278 in the second edition of Tottel's Miscellany (31 July 1557) brings the image of 'Mother Earth' to life. In *A Gorgeous Gallery of Gallant Inventions* (1578) 'A propper Dittie. To the tune of lusty Gallant' describes vividly the flowers and birds whose delights the tormented lover has forsworn.[40]

Sometimes nature mourns with the lover, as in this complaint by Wyatt:

> Oft ye riuers, to hear my wofull sounde,
> Haue stopt your cours, and plainely to expresse,
> Many a teare by moisture of the grounde
> The earth hath wept to hear my heauinesse:
> . . . .
> The hugy okes haue rored in the winde,
> Ech thing me thought complayning in their kinde.[41]

This is virtually the same as the pathetic fallacy in the complaints of shepherd-lovers in pastoral poems. At the same time, it relates—as such pastorals themselves do—to the Petrarchan lover's desire for melancholy retreats. Later poets repeat this vein:

> A wailing wight I walke alone, in desart dennes there to complaine,
> Among the sauage sort to mone, I flee my frends where they remaine: . . .[42]

This desire to make nature match the lover's mood leads to an interesting use of winter scenery. The following poem in the Arundel

respectively. All refs. to Tottel to this edn. I have used Tottel's text of Wyatt's and Surrey's poems in preference to that of modern critical edns. as being the one most familiar to Elizabethans.

[38] *Newe Sonets, and pretie Pamphlets* (London, n.d.), 4.

[39] *Epitaphes, Epigrams, Songs and Sonets* (London, 1570), fo. 109ᵛ.

[40] *A Gorgeous Gallery*, ed. H. E. Rollins (Cambridge, Mass., 1926), 26.

[41] Tottel, no. 59: p. 42, ll. 22–8.

[42] *The Paradise of Dainty Devices*, ed. H. E. Rollins (Cambridge, Mass., 1927), no. 27: p. 29, ll. 26–7.

Harington manuscript is a sequel to Surrey's 'Complaint of a louer, that defied loue'.

> ffirst gan hym hye the horye frost | to feoble flowres fearce
> whose chilling colde bothe roote and Rynde | of hearb and trie do pearce
> eache fowle wext faynt and every beast | muste browce wheare he may best
> of busshe or bryere to lyck the leaves | and thinck hym at a feast
> The lyttle Emyte slowthfull was | within the mowle hill hydd
> to shrowde it from the wynters blast | as nature doth her bydde[43]

In Surrey's 'Complaint of a diyng louer' (Tottel, no. 18) the account of winter is feeble. But the poem is important for actually introducing a shepherd, though only as a confidant to the dying courtier-lover.

We have come to the edge of the pastoral. The stage is set for Spenser's Colin to appear, lamenting his love in a winter landscape. In a more general way, Spenser exploits the pastoral possibilities of the basic situation of these lyrics: a lover (usually recognizably Petrarchan) places his love-sentiments within a strong awareness of nature.

The setting of nature appears elsewhere too—memorably, for instance, in Francis Kinwelmarsh's poem, 'A vertuous Gentle woman in the praise of hir Loue'. Spenser may well have recalled the 'Gentle woman's' catalogue of flowers when writing 'Aprill'. But even more important is the sense of outdoor delight, and the way it is blended with the woman's joy in her lover:

> I walke the pleasant fieldes, adornd with liuely greene,
> And view the fragrant flowres, most louely to be seene:
> The purple Columbine, the Cousloppe and the Lillie,
> The Violet sweete, the Daizie and Daffadillie.
>
> The Woodbines on the hedge, the red Rose and the white,
> And eache fine flowres else, that rendreth sweete delite:
> Among the which I choose, all those of seemeliest grace,
> In thought, resembling them to my deare louers face.[44]

In another direction, the natural setting is related to human life in contexts other than love. The commonest of these, of course, is the peace and innocence of the countryside, perhaps contrasted with the ills of the court. This comes close to, and passes into, the simple 'rural idyll' of the townsman's retreat. We have seen many examples in continental poetry.

[43] *The Arundel Harington MS. of Tudor Poetry*, ed. R. Hughey (Columbus, 1960), no. 272: i. 318, ll. 11–16.

[44] *The Paradise of Dainty Devices*, no. 41: p. 42, ll. 2–9.

In England, about this time, the best examples are from Thomas Churchyard (some of them not published till later).[45] This vein may also pass into the common didactic praise of humble content and the mind's kingdom. Of many possible instances,[46] I shall quote one from Tottel's Miscellany as throwing an interesting sidelight upon the pastoral:

> I hard a herdman once compare:
> That quiet nightes he had mo slept:
> And had mo mery daies to spare:
> Then he, which ought the beastes, he kept.[47]

The standard assumption of pastoral—that the shepherds are owners of their flocks, not hirelings—is reversed here, suggesting rather the Mantuanesque eclogue of the poor but morally superior shepherd.

Yet another sort of moral is drawn very commonly from natural phenomena. The cycle of the seasons becomes an image of frustrated love.

> Alas pore hart thus hast thou spent,
> Thy flowryng time, thy pleasant yeres.
> With sighing voyce wepe and lament:
> For of thy hope no frute apperes,
> Thy true meanyng is paide with scorne,
> That euer soweth and repeth no corne.[48]

Another poem in Tottel (no. 197), adapted from Horace's Ode IV. vii, makes the cycle of the seasons signify mutability. Poem 40 in *The Paradise of Dainty Devices* makes it signify 'All thinges ar Vaine'. Most important is a passage by Thomas Howell, too long to quote, where it becomes a symbol for the course of human life, age by age.[49]

This body of poetic imagery provides an important context for Spenser's use of the seasonal cycle in *The Shepheardes Calender*. More generally in these poems, human actions and emotions are related to, or

[45] See *Churchyard's Chance* (London, 1580), fos. 16^r ('A letter in Maie'), 21^v ('Of the quietnesse that plaine Countrey bryngeth'), 25^v ('A letter to maister Cressie').

[46] e.g. Arundel Harington MS, no. 293; *Paradise of Dainty Devices*, no. 100 (from the 2nd edn., 1578).

[47] Tottel, no. 170: p. 124, ll. 8–11. Also in the Arundel Harington MS (no. 17) and with a somewhat different text in *The Arbor of Amorous Devices* (no. 7 as ed. H. E. Rollins, Cambridge, Mass., 1936).

[48] Tottel, no. 303 (from 2nd edn.): p. 251, ll. 17–22.

[49] 'Being sore sicke, aunswereth his felowe enquiring whether he were willing to die', *The Arbor of Amitie* (London, 1568), fos. 3^v–4^r.

placed against, nature; but there is also a sense of the independent power and interest of nature. These are the two fundamental, balancing awareness of *The Shepheardes Calender*. They are not foreshadowed either in Fletcher's Latin or in Barclay's English. But the elements of such an awareness lie scattered, and unrealized in pastoral terms, in this other lyric poetry. Spenser's achievement was to recognize this potential and give it expression in *The Shepheardes Calender*.

He was not entirely without precedent. Leaving aside Scottish examples like Henryson's 'Robene and Makyne', which he almost certainly could not have known,[50] and a pastoral interlude in the prose *Complaynte of Scotland* (1549), which he might have done, English poetry would have yielded him at least one important example, 'Harpelus complaynt' from Tottel's Miscellany (no. 181).

Pleasant but unremarkable when read in the *England's Helicon* of 1600, 'Harpelus' is a surprising piece to find in 1557. The situation is that of Arcadian love-pastoral. The scorned shepherd Harpelus combines Petrarchan and pastoral elements in his love-lament: the willow wreath, the address to his beasts, his envy of their happy love. Phillida weaves garlands 'Of Couslippes and of Colombine' for Corin, her favoured lover. But as this last detail indicates, the poem has the homely simplicity of texture and diction that later distinguishes the Elizabethan pastoral lyric, assisted here by the ballad-like form (although, rhyming *abab*, it is not strictly the ballad stanza).

Another title in Tottel, 'The complaint of Thestilis amid the desert wodde' (no. 201), suggests that the synthesis of pastoral and Petrarchism was well recognized. The fact that the poem has nothing pastoral indicates the force of the convention. (The *Helicon*, in reprinting this piece with a new ascription to Surrey, adds a few pastoral touches.) But when all is said and done, so little of this material survives that it scarcely detracts from Spenser's achievement. The most substantial body of such pastoral before Spenser, in Barnabe Googe's *Eglogs, Epytaphes, and Sonettes* (1563), is not a promising precedent.

However unattractive Googe's eclogues may be, his pastoral context is certainly wider than Barclay's. His herdsmen interrupt their conversation to direct their work, and know the signs of the weather, even as Barclay's might have done.[51] But also, like classical or Arcadian shepherds, they sing as they shelter from the sun's rays, respond to spring, and reward

[50] The work has come down to us only in a single MS.

[51] See Eclogue I (pp. 31, 32), Eclogue VIII (p. 68). All refs. to Googe's *Eglogs, Epytaphes, and Sonettes*, ed. E. Arber (London, 1871).

each other's songs with gifts.[52] Moreover, they are not devoid of romantic love. In Eclogue II, Dametas kills himself for love after the usual lament and farewell to his flocks. In Eclogue VI (p. 52), Faustus pines like any other sentimental shepherd-lover:

> Syth from my Garlande now is falne,
> this famouse Flowre swete:
> Ley Wyllows wynde aboute my hed,
> (a Wrethe for Wretches mete) . . .

Clearly, Googe shows a faint recognition of the scope of 'art-pastoral' conventions. As clearly, he does not pass beyond convention. A short passage on bird-snaring in Eclogue VI may be traced to Sannazaro's eighth *prosa* as rendered in Spanish in Garcilaso's second eclogue. The most marked incidence of pastoral love, in Eclogue VII, is taken directly out of Montemayor's dialogue between Sirenus, Silvanus, and Selvagia. Beyond this stands Eclogue V, the courtly tale of Faustus, Valeria, and Claudia (again from Montemayor's tale of Felix and Felismena) incongruously told by the shepherd Egon.[53]

More important still, the brief expressions of romantic love are firmly controlled by the moral context. In Eclogue I (p. 33) we find:

> Thus: when the beames, infected hath,
> the wofull Louers blud:
> Then Sences al, do strayght decaye,
> opprest with Furyes flud.
> Then Lybertie withdrawes her self,
> and Bondage beares the swaye,
> Affection blynd then leades the hart,
> and Wyt, is wownde awaye.

In Eclogue IV, Dametas' ghost comes from hell to recount his punishment and deplore his 'wycked Wyll' (p. 45). In Eclogue VI the romantic Faustus is roundly advised by Felix to forsake the town and turn to country labours as a cure for his folly. In Eclogue VIII, Cornix urges all shepherds to leave 'Dame *Venus*' and '*Cupidoes* Camp' (p. 63) and turn to the true God. The romantic impulse is more than countered by the moral.

In many cases, moreover, the pastoral provides merely a detachable frame for the didactic content. This is as true of the satire of love in

[52] See Eclogue I (p. 31), Eclogue VIII (p. 62), Eclogue III (p. 38), Eclogue I (p. 35).

[53] For the identification of sources, see Greg, p. 81; T. P. Harrison, jun., 'Googe's *Eglogs* and Montemayor's *Diana*', *Studies in English* (Univ. of Texas), 5 (1925), 68–78.

Eclogue I as the praise of God in Eclogue VIII. The only point where didacticism touches the pastoral context is in the praise of the shepherd's humble content, as in Eclogue VIII (p. 62):

> We fere not we, the tomblyng world
> we breake no sleaps by nyght.

This is expanded in Eclogue III to an opposition of town and country. The critic-shepherd Coridon's standpoint is anything but egalitarian. He laments the passing of true gentlemen, 'Of whom we Shephardes had reliefe' (p. 40). They have been replaced by upstarts like another Coridon, once a carter.[54] Here the pastoral metaphor comes close to literal satire. There is a clear reference (p. 41) to the enclosure system, doubling, it seems, as an allegory of the Marian persecutions:[55] a unique instance of topical 'allegory' in Googe's pastorals.

> And with the shepe, ye Shephardes good,
> (O hate full Hounds of Hell,)
> They did torment, and dryue them out,
> in Places farre to dwell.
> There dyed *Daphnes* for his Shepe,
> the chiefest of them all.
> And fayre *Alexis* flamde in Fyre,
> who neuer perysshe shall.

Googe's *Eglogs* have a perceptible presence of elements unknown to Barclay, some of the elements that Spenser was to use. More than this we cannot say. There is a much stronger presence of common didacticism. But it seems to be going too far to say, as P. E. Parnell does, that the *Eglogs* are consistently moral, even a designed 'refutation of the pastoral tradition'.[56] Googe lacks the imagination to synthesize the various disparate elements in his work into any consistent conception of the pastoral.

[54] P. E. Parnell identifies Coridon with Stephen Gardiner, Chancellor under Queen Mary; see 'Barnabe Googe: A Puritan in Arcadia', *JEGP* 60 (1961), 276.

[55] Suggested briefly by Arber (p. 18) and developed by F. B. Fieler (ed.), Googe's *Eglogs, Epytaphes, and Sonettes* (facsimile edn. Gainesville, 1968), p. xiii.

[56] Parnell, p. 281. Cf. Cooper, p. 125: 'Googe is in a sense attacking Renaissance pastoral as a whole.'

7
The Shepheardes Calender

1. *Allegory and other matters*

IT SHOULD be unnecessary by now to offer defences for treating *The Shepheardes Calender* at considerably greater length than any other work of English Renaissance pastoral. Even the substantial poetic merits of the *Calender* may not justify such length, but its unique historical importance demands it. As the first major Elizabethan pastoral, it sets the tone for nearly all that follows. It casts the elements of the pastoral tradition into boldly original combinations that influence the wider growth of the genre. Much of what I describe in my later chapters would probably have remained unconceived had Spenser not written the *Calender* as and when he did.

The Shepheardes Calender has a substantial allusive and didactic content. As this readily lends itself to commentary, it has occupied a disproportionate share of recent critical attention. It seems to me, however, to be subsidiary to a very different poetic purpose. The really important thing about the *Calender* is not the allusion and moralizing it contains, but the extent to which it forgoes allusion and moralizing for other functions and concerns. The former is Spenser's legacy from the standard eclogue tradition; the latter his original departure, deepening and reworking the 'art-pastoral' vein with crucial results for later Elizabethan pastoral.

My reasons for holding this view will, I hope, be clear by the end of this chapter. But it will be most convenient to begin with the allusive element and examine its extent and nature.

The most elaborate attempt at allegorizing the *Calender* is probably Paul McLane's reading in terms of Elizabeth's proposed marriage to Alençon.[1] This poses a difficult problem with dates, postulating an impossible degree of revision up to a few weeks before publication.[2] The

[1] P. E. McLane, *Spenser's Shepheardes Calender: A Study in Elizabethan Allegory* (Notre Dame, 1961).

[2] Ruth Luborsky ('*The Shepheardes Calender*: The Book and Its Illustrations' (Ph.D.

premisses of McLane's Procrustean argument have already been refuted in detail.[3] In any case, nothing in the text suggests such pervasive allegory. One could propose it only by a fixed belief that pastoral *must* be allegorical, with a consequent effort to hitch it to the nearest topical event.

Allegory seems more likely in the Fables of the Oak and the Brier ('Februarie') and the Kid and the Fox ('Maye'). Various identifications have been proposed. But the nature of both fables bears out E. K.'s comment on 'Februarie': 'This Aeglogue is rather morall and generall, then bent to any secrete or particular purpose.' The Oak and the Brier may stand for Leicester and Oxford, or more possibly for Archbishop Grindal and Bishop Aylmer,[4] but the story bears a common moral. Again, the Kid may be young King James of Scotland and the Fox his French cousin the Duc d'Aubigny.[5] But it is hard to make the dates fit, and we may feel the less need to do so in view of Anthea Hume's convincing reading in terms of general Protestant propaganda, with the Fox as a covert Catholic and the Kid, in E. K.'s words, as representing 'the simple sorte of the faythfull and true Christians'.[6]

Much more significant is the running vein of allusions to the clergy. It seems more or less certain that behind Algrin stands Grindal; behind Morrell, Aylmer; Diggon Davie, Richard Davies, Bishop of St Davids; Thomalin, Thomas Cooper, Bishop of Lincoln; Piers, John Piers, Bishop of Salisbury; Roffy, John Young, Bishop of Rochester and Spenser's employer. The nature of the 'allegory' must be appreciated, however. The relevant poems are among E. K.'s 'moral' eclogues, illustrating such general matters as 'coloured deceipt' and 'dissolute shepheards and pastours' ('The generall argument'). The specific allusions are anchored in principles of Church government and clerical conduct. Morrell in 'Iulye' may be Aylmer, but only as one ready instance of a 'proude and ambitious Pastour'. The reference to Grindal's sequestration ('Iulye', ll. 215–30) is a postscript to Thomalin's general account of Christian principles.

Temple Univ., 1977), 106–18) has shown that the work took a considerable time to produce, with only a limited amount of late revision, not corresponding to McLane's key passages.

[3] See Henry R. Woudhuysen, 'Leicester's Literary Patronage' (D.Phil. Oxford, 1980), 193–202.

[4] See P. W. Long, 'Spenser and the Bishop of Rochester', *PMLA* 31 (1916), 732–3.

[5] See McLane, ch. vi.

[6] 'Glosse' to 'Maye'. See Anthea Hume, *Edmund Spenser, Protestant Poet* (Cambridge, 1984), 21–8; also H. Stein, 'Spenser and William Turner', *MLN* 51 (1936), 345–51.

The episode of Roffy and the wolf in sheep's clothing ('September', ll. 180–225) raises a more fundamental point. It is no doubt based on an untraceable experience of Bishop Young; but Spenser uses the story to develop genuinely the metaphor of 'pastoral care':

> No sooner was out, but swifter then thought,
> Fast by the hyde the Wolfe lowder caught:
> And had not Roffy renne to the steuen,
> Lowder had be slaine thilke same euen. (ll. 222–5)

This extends the standard image of the wolf in the fold, used *ad infinitum* in religious pastoral. Instead of simply reflecting the stock implications about the clergy, it vitalizes the truth about *shepherd* life implicit in the image, the same reliance upon 'heede and watchfulnesse' as required in the Churchman. Spenser here goes beyond the stock Church-pastoral satire of Mantuan IX, on which the earlier part of 'September' is based.

Similarly in 'Maye', the image of the hireling shepherd is freshly validated by Piers (ll. 37–54, 103–31). In 'Iulye', the standard moral ideal of 'pastoral humility' is adapted to ecclesiastical use, reversing the praise of hills over valleys that Mantuan had made in the special context of Mount Carmel in his Eclogue VIII. In a more general way, the Fables (if indeed they are ecclesiastical at all) conform to the concept of homely shepherd lore, as seen in 'Februarie':

> . . . a tale of truth,
> Which I cond of *Tityrus* in my youth,
> Keeping his sheepe on the hils of Kent . . . (ll. 91–3)

In other words, the allegory is placed on a bedrock of independently valid pastoralism. It marks the coincidence of two worlds, not a nominal reference to the shepherd world colouring a central concern with the real one.[7]

This is also evidenced in the non-ecclesiastical allusions. In 'Aprill', Spenser makes Eliza 'Queene of shepheardes all' in a manner that suggests the May Queen as much as the sovereign of England. There are indeed tell-tale signs: the scarlet robes; the ermine, symbol of both royalty and virginity; the 'Redde rose medled with the White yfere'

[7] This has recently been recognized in two balanced and sensitive treatments of Spenser's politics. Hume (ch. ii) posulates an equal and organic infusion of aesthetic and ecclesiastic, shepherd-poet and shepherd-priest, in the *Calender*. David Norbrook (*Poetry and Politics in the English Renaissance* (London, 1984), 76ff.) admits the importance of courtly aesthetic factors in shaping the external concerns, but unlike Hume, he argues categorically for the latter's primacy (p. 81).

(l. 68), perpetuating the 'Tudor myth' of the union of York and Lancaster; and

> Oliues bene for peace,
> When wars doe surcease:
> Such for a Princesse bene principall. (ll. 124–6)

It is clearly royal compliment; but equally clearly an adaptation of the simple pastoral exercises that, it is implied, shepherds undertake in their own world.

So too in 'November', the metaphor at the core of the pastoral epicedium is validated throughout Colin's dirge for Dido; and where allusion is clearest, it is most pastoralized:

> O thou greate shepheard *Lobbin*, how great is thy griefe,
> Where bene the nosegayes that she dight for thee:
> The colourd chaplets wrought with a chiefe,
> The knotted rushrings, and gilte Rosemaree? (ll. 113–16)

The specific reference is difficult to trace, of course. Of possible originals for Dido, the least unlikely is perhaps Sidney's sister Ambrosia.[8]

The final and most basic vein of allusion is the personal. Colin is Spenser, Hobbinoll is Gabriel Harvey. (Nothing supports McLane's notion that Cuddie is Dyer.) It does not at once follow that the *Calender* is full of autobiography, for the love-lorn persona of the poet is a pastoral convention going back at least to Sannazaro's Sincero. Rosalind may well stand for a real mistress, as E. K. asserts in gossip-column vein: 'Rosalinde is also a feigned name, which being wel ordered, wil bewray the very name of hys loue and mistresse' (Gloss to 'Januarye', l. 60). My point is that it does not matter, as everything has been translated into the terms of a greater pastoral fiction. Indeed, Spenser is notably short on individual detail. Hobbinoll may be Harvey, and his pleasant dale Cambridge.[9] But the opening of 'Iune' repeats a standard pastoral opposition that began with Virgil's Tityrus and Meliboeus. Petrarch's Eclogue I turns this inside out, the central character being the restless wandering Silvius, the poet's own persona:

[8] McLane (p. 48) protests that Ambrosia died too young to fit Spenser's account, at about 14½. (For her dates, 1560–75, correctly established, see J. J. Higginson, *Spenser's Shepherd's Calender in Relation to Contemporary Affairs* (New York, 1912), 235–7.) But, parallels with Elizabeth Drury apart, this is to underestimate the maturity of Elizabethan girls. Ambrosia's sister Mary was married at 15½. More cogent is McLane's objection that Spenser came to know Sidney (and, we may add, formed his Leicester connection) four years after Ambrosia's death in 1575.

[9] Suggested by W. L. Renwick: see Variorum Spenser, *Minor Poems*, i. 311.

Monice, tranquillo solus tibi conditus antro,
Et gregis et ruris potuisti spernere curas;
Ast ego dumosos colles silvasque pererro.
Infelix! (ll. 1–4)

[You, Monicus, hiding by yourself in a quiet cave, have been able to dismiss the cares of both flock and field; but I, unhappy, roam the scrubby hills and woods.]

This is closely echoed in the general situation of 'Iune', though the parallel seems to have escaped notice.[10] Colin and Hobbinoll are concealing their identities, deliberately changing themselves into literary shepherds, merging their individual experience in that of conventional, representative characters. Even at his most allusive, Spenser shows the dual awareness of real and pastoral worlds that, in Chapter 3, section 4, we found in the most complex allusive mode of Neo-Latin and Italian pastoral. Incidental allusions are concealed and quite irrelevant to the poetic effect: would we have known of Colin's movement from north to south, had it not been for E. K.'s gloss to 'Iune', line 18? The pastoral world becomes the primary reality: sometimes used to highlight a contemporary matter by telling association, never the other way about.[11] We have moved from the view of pastoral enshrined in the Virgilian commentaries to one detectable in the Bucolics themselves.

2. *The structure of the* Calender

This sense of a consistent, independent pastoral world is largely created by the linked eclogue-sequence. Theocritus and Virgil could not have written their pastorals as a consciously planned series. But thanks to the latter's authority, there grew up the concept of a loosely knit sequence of eclogues, ideally ten in number. The key passage in Servius (based on Donatus) is worth quoting:

nec numerus hic dubius est nec ordo librorum, quippe cum unus sit liber: de eclogis multi dubitant, quae licet decem sint, incertum tamen est, quo ordine scriptae sint.[12]

[10] Cooper (*Pastoral*, p. 153) points out that there is no proof that Spenser knew Petrarch's Eclogues; but the above parallel may be thought suggestive.

[11] Cf. Nancy Jo Hoffman, *Spenser's Pastorals* (Baltimore, 1977), 11: 'Spenser . . . frees pastoral from the *à clé* tradition, and from attachment to real geographic place. He is the first to sense that pastoral can become an integral, inclusive landscape.' Beyond this very broad similarity of outlook, there is practically nothing in common between Hoffman's analysis and mine, and I differ radically from her on the subject of Spenser's landscape: see sect. 5 below.

[12] Servius, ed. Thilo, III. i. 3. 14–16. Cf. Donatus, ed. Brummer, ll. 302, 316–25.

[Neither the number nor the order of the books is in doubt when there is indeed but a single book; [but] many have doubts about the Eclogues, of which, though there are indeed ten, it is none the less uncertain in what order they were written.]

This establishes the number ten; but also an uncertain order and looseness or even absence of total form. Servius inaugurates a running debate as to whether Virgil's Eclogues constitute a unity or ten separate works. Some people, says Minturno, read the Bucolics as a single work.

Sed qui fieri unum id omne possit, mihi non sane liquet, cum minus ita inter se apta & colligata sint, quae hoc poemate continentur, ut ea, quae una quidem actio comprehendit.[13]

[But it is not clear to me how it can all be made one, when what is contained in these poems is less mutually suited and connected than those which a single action does indeed comprehend.]

Neo-Latin poets often printed a numbered series of eclogues, but the degree of unity is usually most questionable. (One or two seem planned as a conscious series, most notably Boiardo's ten Latin eclogues of 100 lines each.) The sequences of *lusus pastorales* sometimes have a more apparent unity, as do pastoral sonnets when arranged and published as Varchi's were posthumously.[14] (Vauquelin's *Idillies et pastoralles* had not been published, or even perhaps composed in full, when the *Calender* appeared.) Above all, of course, Sannazaro fashions a series of eclogues into the evident unity of the *Arcadia*—ultimately in twelve divisions (though originally, it seems, only ten).

Whether influenced by Sannazaro or not, Spenser hit upon the brilliant idea of a series of twelve eclogues corresponding to the twelve months. This enables him—and the artist of the woodcuts—to touch as they find fit upon the various conventions governing 'the labours of the months' (and seasons) and their metaphorical application to human life. We have learnt much—too much—about the use of such conventions in the *Calender*, and I have relegated a full consideration to Appendix B. Suffice it here that the interpretations are often Procrustean: no set pattern can be satisfactorily applied to all twelve eclogues or even their major part. But all these patterns are suggested at appropriate points, and the total impact is more comprehensive, more enrichening, than a simple formulaic adherence could ever have been.

By his deliberately diffuse and multiple use of convention, Spenser

[13] *De poeta*, p. 165.
[14] See Ch. 4 n. 61.

establishes a loose and varied 'community' of shepherds within the total rhythm of life in a rustic setting. Shepherds recur from one eclogue to another, and Colin provides a constant link.

Within this total structure we have a loose division into separate eclogues rather than a continuous narrative. This permits a wide range of themes and experiences to be included: love, poetry, praise of great men, laments for their deaths, celebration of classical gods—but more importantly, moral and Christian themes, often building up to a sense of waste, frustration, and penitence. The 'cast' of shepherds may be expanded as new themes require, since there is no rigid form or narrative structure to be disturbed. The loosely knit eclogue-sequence provides an ideal formal compromise: it combines the sense of an integral pastoral world with the scope for constant change and addition.

It can therefore provide an excellent solution to the problems of form posed by the disintegration of the pastoral into the welter of the miscellaneous lyric: or rather, in the case of English poetry, lyrics of potential relevance to pastoral but not yet assimilated to the mode. I described a body of such poems in the last chapter. Their range of themes is precisely that of the *Calender* as listed above. Spenser unifies these diverse matters, first by casting them in a pastoral mould, and secondly through the shadowy yet perceptible presence of the 'calendar' structure. This gives the themes a greater seriousness, making them the substance of something more than lyric outpourings or occasional poems. At the same time, the presence of these themes enriches the pastoral, re-endowing the shepherd with dignity, varied experience, and an artist's sensibility. It enables Spenser to explore deeply the possibilities of the pastoral mode.

This is seen in a small way in the relatively neglected 'March' eclogue. It is based on a poem ascribed to Bion from at least as early as 1543, though E. K. attributes it to Theocritus and Remy Belleau, commenting on a translation by Ronsard, to Moschus.[15] Spenser's adaptation of his sources has been studied by several critics,[16] but not one has brought out

[15] E. K., 'Glosse' to 'March'; Belleau, note on Ronsard's 'Ode', 'Un enfant dedans un bocage . . .' (Ronsard's *Œuvres*, ed. Laumonier, 20-vol. edn., vii. 259). Bion's poem was tr. by Baïf as well (ed. Marty-Laveaux, iv. 281). There is also a Latin version in Camerarius XIII. M. Y. Hughes wrongly says that Spenser's is the first extant Renaissance translation (*SP* 20, p. 203). Other critics have confused Ronsard's rendering with another of his poems, 'Elegie ou amour oyseau' (*Œuvres*, xv. 206).

[16] See Leo Spitzer, 'Spenser, *Shepheardes Calender, March* ll. 61–114, and the Variorum Edition', *SP* 47 (1950), 494–505; D. C. Allen, *Image and Meaning* (Baltimore, 1968), ch. i; Hoffman, pp. 79ff.

Spenser's most obvious and basic innovation: he is the first to make a genuine pastoral out of the story, incorporating it into a dialogue between two shepherd boys. Thomalin's fowling adventure occurs on a holiday from his herdsmen's tasks, and the story of Cupid is prefaced by the history of his ewe. A half-courtly, half-mythological *jeu d'esprit* on love is brought within the shepherd's orbit. Spenser thus paves the way for the even more deeply pastoral version of the story in Barnabe Barnes, where Cupid is actually discovered in the sheepfold.[17] It is a small example of the way in which *The Shepheardes Calender* expands the frontiers of pastoral. This expansion relates chiefly to three themes: poetry, love, and the apprehension of nature.

3. *The pastoral aesthetic: The shepherd as poet*

In one important and recurring role, Spenser's shepherds are poets. Five eclogues contain formal songs or tales. The complaints in 'Januarye' and 'December' too are rounded, rhetorically shaped utterances, the latter explicitly dedicated to Pan as a 'rurall song'. 'Iune' and 'October' are concerned with Colin, the shepherd-poet *par excellence*.

The shepherds of classical pastoral had been poets as well. Theocritus's Daphnis, Moschus's Bion, Virgil's Gallus present the shepherd-poet in his loftiest vein; but all the shepherds sing. Theocritus's ten chief pastoral Idylls (I, III to XI) all contain songs or song-contests covering the entire range of pastoral experience: love, nature, the gods, music, poetry itself—and sheepkeeping too.

Virgil keeps the singing shepherds. Except for Eclogue IV, all the eclogues feature poet-shepherds and sylvans and often incorporate their songs. But, given the more allusive nature of the Eclogues, the songs lose their total absorption in pastoral life. The Renaissance reading of Virgil emphasizes the allusive aspect of the eclogues; and following this model, the pastoral artefact loses its integrity in the Renaissance.

As we saw, the Renaissance eclogue is commonly devoted to allusive matters, or else to moral and didactic concerns. Perhaps as a consequence of this, it often grows deficient in its sense of form. The shepherds no longer sing but only talk. Petrarch and Mantuan provide important instances of this. Petrarch has several shepherd-poets, but we never see them practising their art. Mantuan's moral shepherds tend to prolixity: a tendency much emphasized in Barclay. Barclay's shortest eclogue, the

17 *Parthenophil and Parthenophe*, Ode 12, ed. V. A. Doyno (Carbondale, 1971), 108.

third, has 824 lines; the others over a thousand each. The inset songs are no better than versified discourses.

Not that the authentic singing shepherd, in a pastoral setting that naturally seems to inspire song and aesthetic order, is totally missing from Renaissance pastoral. Such a figure may appear in unmistakably allusive contexts: Pontano's Meliseus is the most obvious example. Even the allusive Boiardo sometimes lets his shepherds indulge in pure song.[18] There are many amoebean contests where, even if the shepherds may sometimes stand for real poets, the exchanges seem free of allusive intent.[19] Love-songs sung by imaginary shepherds are still commoner:[20] Johannes Secundus's Lycidas repeats Orpheus's own lament. Even the political-minded Minturno prefaces his Eclogue III with an extraneous love-lament, a double sestina.

But needless to say, the outstanding example is Sannazaro's in *Arcadia*. By the mere fact of putting the narrative in prose, the verse eclogues become conscious poetic artefacts. One or two have external referents. Others are formal compositions for specific occasions within the pastoral fiction: Ergasto's dirge for Androgeo (Eclogue 5) or later for Massilia (Eclogue 11), though this also seems to be an elegy for Sannazaro's mother. Most of the eclogues, however, are composed by the shepherds purely to adorn their sports and loves. More telling still, they may be spontaneously composed. Spontaneous too, of course, are the amoebean contests devised for sport.

In the 'moral' eclogues, Spenser's shepherds may sometimes approach the unregulated flow of earlier didactic pastoral. Even among this group of poems, the longest, 'Maye', is nearly half occupied (144 out of 317 lines) by the Fable of the Fox and the Kid. In 'Februarie', the Fable occupies well over half the length. The 'non-formal' eclogues generally centre upon a formal composition with a structured stanza-form. Even where this is not the case, there is evidence of careful control: in the markedly formalized monologues of 'Januarye' and 'December' and the dialogues of 'Iune' and 'October'. In the last, Mantuan V is recast into a tighter structure. Mantuan's Candidus did most of the talking; in Spenser, Cuddie and Piers speak in balanced alternation.

Spenser's shepherds do not merely talk or experience things, but

[18] See his Latin Eclogues VIII and IX.

[19] e.g. in Belmisseri II; Camerarius VII; Alberti, 'Tyrsis'; Boiardo (Italian) III, VII.

[20] Latin examples are Strozzi III, Giambattista Amalteo III, Cordus III, and Hessus X; Italian ones, Alberti's 'Corymbus', Boiardo V, Serafino II.

present that experience in 'rymes and roundelayes', works of conscious art. As Colin says in 'Iune':

> But pyping lowe in shade of lowly groue,
> I play to please my selfe, all be it ill. (ll. 71–2)

'To please my selfe' are important words. Even Colin's song of Eliza was not composed for a formal audience but 'as by a spring he laye, | And tuned it vnto the Waters fall' ('Aprill', ll. 35–6). Whatever its subject, it is in form and nature a spontaneously inspired pastoral song.

The shepherd world exists in its own right, and the shepherds express a frank pleasure in their inconsequential pastoral actions. This appears most clearly—and perhaps by design—in the subsidiary shepherds. Willy and Thomalin in 'March' are led to love as a natural response to spring:

> Thomalin, why sytten we soe,
> As weren ouerwent with woe,
> Vpon so fayre a morow?
> The ioyous time now nigheth fast . . . (ll. 1–4)

In 'August', Willy and Perigot propose a singing-match with the same spontaneous delight:

> Tell me *Perigot*, what shalbe the game,
> Wherefore with myne thou dare thy musick matche? (ll. 1–2)

These eclogues are generally passed over lightly by critics, as being trivial; but their very triviality is a matter for interest and attention.[21] Spenser is presenting the untroubled, almost unthinking *otium* that, while never the constant state of the pastoral universe, constitutes its basic, ideal element. Somewhere in the pastoral world, at least by implication, there will always be this direct, delighted response to life: song, love, friendship, sport enjoyed in unvexed simplicity.

From this continuum, the activities of the leading shepherds stand out in their rich and perhaps contrary implications. The latter attract the reader's attention, but they acquire full meaning only in context: Colin's sestina must be seen against Willy and Thomalin's roundelay. The contrast gives Colin's complaint a poignancy beyond standard courtly

[21] The only recent critic to take note of this element, and that very briefly with respect to 'August' alone, is Simone d'Orangeon in *L'Églogue anglaise de Spenser à Milton* (Paris, 1974), 156. See also Patrick Cullen, *Spenser, Marvell, and Renaissance Pastoral* (Cambridge, Mass., 1970), 77, 100ff.; but Cullen stresses the comic and ironic aspect of these eclogues in a way that seems to me unwarranted.

Petrarchism. It also affects the nature of the complaint. The naïve artifice imparts something of its own spirit to the sophisticated one, giving the latter a sincerity it would not otherwise attain. Above all, it is valued by the less ambitious shepherd-poet: 'neuer thing on earth so pleaseth me' ('August', l. 147). Colin's sestina fulfils a higher possibility of the same aesthetic as the roundelay of Perigot and Willy: its sophistication, potentially centrifugal, is accommodated within the pastoral.

This may be seen in Spenser's entire presentation of the shepherd-poet in Colin, and partly Cuddie, in 'October'. As Richard Helgerson has persuasively demonstrated, Spenser is introducing in the *Calender* an unusually serious approach to the pursuit of poetry and his own projected career.[22] Further, he seems to be weaving round the figure of the shepherd-poet the most profound critical concepts of the Renaissance. The root concept of 'enthusiasm' is directly cited by E. K. in the Argument to 'October', and implied by Cuddie when he invokes the divine origin of poetry:

> Then make thee winges of thine aspyring wit,
> And, whence thou camst, flye backe to heauen apace. (ll. 83–4)

Filled with the divine afflatus, the poet was thought to induce ravishment or ecstasy[23]—as Cuddie does:

> Soone as thou gynst to sette thy notes in frame,
> O how the rurall routes to thee doe cleaue:
> Seemeth thou dost their soule of sence bereaue . . . (ll. 25–7)

More prosaically, this power was held to effect moral reform, especially in the young:[24]

[22] R. Helgerson, 'The New Poet Presents Himself: Spenser and the Idea of a Literary Career', *PMLA* 93 (1978), 893–911. Cf. D. L. Miller, 'Authorship, Anonymity, and *The Shepheardes Calender*', *MLQ* 40 (1979), 219–36.

[23] See e.g. Minturno, *De poeta*, p. 9: 'mentem auditoris excitet, alliciat, abducat quasi diuino spiritu afflatam . . .' [[poetry] rouses, draws, and ravishes the hearer's mind as though it were inspired by a divine spirit].

[24] Ibid. 48: 'Poetica puerorum os tenerum, mentemque fingi oportere.' [Poetry ought to form the tender bones and minds of children.] Such a view was commonly adopted by merging the Platonic concept of enthusiasm with the Horatian dictum that poetry should both profit and delight (*Ars poetica*, 333). See e.g. A. G. Parrhasio, Commentary on the *Ars poetica* (Naples, 1531), fo. 3^r: the poet can 'suo arbitratu inflammare animos hominum, & extinguere iram, odium . . . aut ab his ijsdem ad lenitatem & misericordiam reuocare' [arouse the souls of men at his will, extinguish anger and hatred, . . . or from these very states recall them to gentleness and mercy].

O what an honor is it, to restraine
The lust of lawlesse youth with good aduice:
Or pricke them forth with pleasaunce of thy vaine,
Whereto thou list their trayned willes entice. (ll. 21–4)

This was a standard defence against Plato's condemnation of poetry in the *Republic*, so contrary to his teaching in *Ion* and *Phaedrus* (to which E. K. alludes to explain Spenser's lines: see the gloss on 'October', ll. 21, 27). It may not be an accident that Spenser makes oblique use of a related argument: that the pagan myths are moral at the core:

Seemeth thou dost their soule of sence bereaue,
All as the shepheard, that did fetch his dame
From *Plutoes* balefull bowre withouten leaue:
His musicks might the hellish hound did tame. (ll. 27–30)

The simile[25] brings out the spiritual force—'ecstatic' in the basic sense—of Cuddie's pastoral song.

For it is unquestionably pastoral, and remains so throughout the eclogue. This brings us to the most remarkable point of Spenser's presentation of the shepherd-poet. At first sight, the course that Piers recommends to Cuddie seems to lead out of the pastoral world: from matter of 'the base and viler clowne' to 'bloody Mars, of wars, of giusts'; to 'fayre *Elisa*' and, above all these, the 'bigger notes' of Leicester's heroism and statecraft (ll. 37–48). This is the progress implicit in the concept of the 'wheel of Virgil', as Cuddie knows:

Indeed the Romish *Tityrus*, I heare,
Through his *Mecoenas* left his Oaten reede . . . (ll. 55–6)

[25] Cf. Boccaccio, *De genealogia deorum*, v. xii: 'Cum naturalis concupiscientia ad Inferos, id est circa terrena, omnino lapsa est, vir prudens eloquentia, id est demonstrationibus veris, eam conatur ad superiora, id est ad virtuosa, reducere. Que tandem aliquando restituitur, et hoc dum appetitus ad laudabiliora dirigitur; . . . Euridicis esse musice designationem, cum Orpheus dicatur quasi orenphone, quod interpretatur vox optima.' (Ed. V. Romano (Bari, 1951), i. 245–6.) [When the natural appetite has sunk entirely to the underworld, that is to the earthly sphere, the prudent man attempts through eloquence, that is through demonstration of the truth, to lead it again to the higher, that is the virtuous sphere. It is at length restored, when the appetite is directed towards the more praiseworthy . . . Euridice is the appellation of music, while Orpheus may be said to be, as it were, *orenphone*, which he [Fulgentius] explains as the finest voice.] In Fulgentius's work, we actually find the form *oreaphone*, which is 'meant for *φωνή*, "voice", and possibly *ὀρείας*, "mountainous", that is highest and purest': L. G. Whitbread (trs. and ed.), *Fulgentius the Mythographer* (Ohio, 1971), 98.

It is invoked in much courtly pastoral.[26] The vital difference in Spenser is that Cuddie rejects such themes: 'all the worthies liggen wrapt in leade' (l. 63). Patronage is not solicited. The scope for courtly compliment is deliberately, indeed pointedly forgone. The potential movement away from the pastoral world is stalled.

Indeed, the movement would have been unnecessary. Above all themes born of 'Princes pallace', there is a final body of poetic themes, the heavenly or spiritual: 'whence thou camst, flye backe to heaven apace' (l. 84). Cuddie cannot achieve this flight, but another shepherd-poet can:

> For *Colin* fittes such famous flight to scanne:
> He, were he not with loue so ill bedight,
> Would mount as high, and sing as soote as Swanne. (ll. 88–90)

This heavenly inspiration seems entirely compatible with Colin's status as shepherd. Cuddie's own aspiration to the tragic buskin and 'queint *Bellona*' seems easily within his reach, if only he were well nourished and roused with drink. Pre-eminent among the Muses struck by wonder at Colin's song ('Iune', ll. 57–64) is Calliope, the epic Muse; and the setting of 'Iune' is recognizably Parnassian, in combination with English folk mythology and the pastoral presence of Pan.[27]

There is no question of removing to the city or court as Piers had earlier recommended. Clearly, Spenser is seeking to reflect the entire range of poetic concerns, as the Renaissance conceived of them, in his shepherd world. He avoids the implicit rejection of the pastoral that is the common concomitant to treating lofty themes in eclogue form, and with which he himself has sometimes been credited.[28] He gives a fresh charge of life to the symbolic equation of pastoral with poetic life and inspiration generally.

[26] e.g. Ronsard, 'Eclogue du Thier' (*Œuvres*, x. 50), last lines; Baïf XIX (ed. Marty-Laveaux, iii. 104); Sannazaro, *Arcadia*, *prosa* 7: 'E sì come insino qui i principii de la tua adolescenzia hai tra semplici e boscarecci canti di pastori infruttuosamente dispesi, così per lo inanzi la felice giovenezza tra sonore trombe di poeti chiarissimi del tuo secolo, non senza speranza di eterna fama trapasserai.' (Ed. Carrara, p. 59.) [And even as up to this point you have fruitlessly spent the beginnings of your adolescence among the simple and rustic songs of shepherds, so hereafter you will pass your fortunate young manhood among the sounding trumpets of the most famous poets of your century, not without hope of eternal fame. (Tr. Nash, pp. 74–5.)]

[27] For Parnassian settings in earlier pastoral, see Petrarch III. 85–125; Arnoullet III. 5–9; Erasmus, 'Carmen bucolicum', *Poems*, ed. Reedijk, p. 138.

[28] See e.g. A. C. Hamilton, 'The Argument of Spenser's *Shepheardes Calender*', *ELH* 23 (1956), 171–82.

4. *The shepherd as lover*

Even more numerous than allegorical readings of the *Calender* are the interpretations that view it in a moral or even theological light. Such interpreters concentrate on Colin's love, taking it unquestioningly in the spirit of Colin's own most pessimistic utterances.[29] Their general intent may be summed up in Isabel MacCaffrey's remark that in the *Calender*, love is a metaphor for sin.[30] M.-S. Røstvig goes further, viewing Colin's career in terms of involved Christian Platonic theology.[31] My own very different reading finds partial support only from D. R. Shore and, still more partially, from B. R. Smith.[32]

We cannot, of course, dismiss the frustration and moral judgement voiced by both Colin and his companions. But this is one side of a conflict that also involves a more positive response to love. Already in 'Januarye', Colin laments,

> And yet alas, but now my spring begonne,
> And yet alas, yt is already donne. (ll. 29–30)

But by a happy irony, we learn that 'Winters wastful spight was almost spent' (l. 2). The controlling image of the seasonal cycle contradicts Colin's gloom.

Colin professes to be destroyed by love; but it seems that this destructive passion is also an enlarging and stimulating one. It sharpens his sensibilities, maturing and fulfulling his spirit even in grief.

> And I, that whilome wont to frame my pype,
> Vnto the shifting of the shepheards foote:
> Sike follies nowe haue gathered as too ripe,
> And cast hem out, as rotten and vnsoote.
> The loser Lasse I cast to please nomore,
> One if I please, enough is me therefore.[33]

[29] e.g. R. A. Durr, 'Spenser's Calendar of Christian Time', *ELH* 24 (1957), 269–95; A. W. Lyle, '*The Shepheardes Calender* and Its English Antecedents', ch. vii; M. D. Bristol, 'Structural Patterns in Two Elizabethan Pastorals', *SEL* 10 (1970), 36–42. See also nn. 30 and 31 below.

[30] 'Allegory and Pastoral in *The Shepheardes Calender*', *ELH* 36 (1969), 88–109.

[31] '*The Shepheardes Calender*—A Structural Analysis', *Renaissance and Modern Studies*, 13 (1969), 49–75.

[32] D. R. Shore, *Spenser and the Poetics of Pastoral*, pp. 80–6; B. R. Smith in *Spenser Studies*, 1.

[33] 'December', ll. 115–20. I am following C. H. Herford's interpretation of 'the loser Lasse' as one of the shepherd girls whom Colin courted before he loved Rosalind (the

At one point at least, in 'October', a fellow-shepherd, Piers, appreciates the possible elevation of Colin's soul through love to a great Platonic height:

> Ah fon, for loue does teach him climbe so hie,
> And lyftes him vp out of the loathsome myre:
> Such immortall mirrhor, as he doth admire,
> Would rayse ones mynd aboue the starry skie. (ll. 91–4)

Clearly, there can be no simple evaluation of love in the *Calender*. Spenser does not merely afford a moral anatomy of love; he explores love as a valid and fascinating, if disturbing, experience.

It may be best to start with the lesser lovers. In the last section, I talked about the background of the common shepherd's poetry against which Colin's inspiration stands out. This is as true in matters of love. There is an element of bitter-sweet, conventionally expressed, in Thomalin's love in 'March' and that of Willye and Perigot in 'August'. But, by and large, this pleasing pain is subsumed in an ideally simple delight, as here in the latter poem:

> PER. But whether in paynefull loue I pyne,
> WIL. hey ho pinching payne,
> PER. Or thriue in welth, she shalbe mine.
> WIL. but if thou can her obteine. (ll. 109–12)

Colin's love is seen against this idyllic background. As with his poetry, it is of a different order, akin to that of the sentimental shepherd-lovers of continental art-pastoral. We cannot assume that Spenser was directly influenced by Sannazaro to any considerable extent, even if the scheme of twelve eclogues might have been inspired by *Arcadia*.[34] What we can surely postulate is a strong influence of Petrarchan love-poetry and nature-settings upon Spenser, largely through the English precedents I have described. Introduced into pastoral, such elements would create a compound similar to that made earlier by Sannazaro. Spenser re-creates out of his own resources the union of pastoral and Petrarchism that, originally effected by Sannazaro more than any other single poet, had

'one'). Cullen (p. 95) proposes a different reading by taking 'one' to refer to Colin himself. Grosart's suggestion that 'the loser Lasse' is Colin's Muse seems fanciful. (For Herford and Grosart, see Variorum Spenser, *Minor Poems*, i. 424–5.)

[34] It seems likely that the woodcuts in the *Calender* are at least partly modelled on those in certain edns. of Sannazaro. (See B. R. Smith, pp. 79–84; Woudhuysen, pp. 204–5. Woudhuysen suggests that Sidney was responsible for basing the woodcuts on those illustrating Sannazaro.) E. K., of course, mentions 'Sanazarus' in his Epistle to Harvey.

grown customary and repetitive. This original re-creation gives an unusual vitality to Spenser's treatment of the customary concerns of art-pastoral.

Ultimately, I believe, Spenser's synthesis exceeds the precedents of Sannazaro and the Italian drama. To judge it adquately, we must look for criteria in Petrarch's own work.

We should not make too much of the stock Petrarchan images and paradoxes—the icy fire, the sweet enemy, the living death.[35] There are deeper, less commonplace conceits as well, like the outcast, wandering lover, as in 'Iune':

> But I vnhappy man, whom cruell fate,
> And angry Gods pursue from coste to coste,
> Can nowhere fynd, to shroude my lucklesse pate. (ll. 14–16)

This reflects not only Petrarch's Eclogue I but a running theme of the *Rime* that love 'Cercar m'à fatto deserti paesi' [has made me search among wildernesses].[36] Beyond such local borrowings, Spenser incorporates a more radical Petrarchism in the *Calender*. Classical shepherds had expressed the bitter-sweet of love, but this had been a simple matter of weighing the lover's joys against the beloved's scorn or faithlessness. Sannazaro, at his finest, deepens this into a more philosophic melancholy touched by the sense of death; but that too is a set mood, and commonly declines in his successors into the sentimental languishing of the scorned 'passionate shepherd'. Sannazaro's Petrarchism stops short at the central and most basic conflict in Petrarch; Spenser comprehends it, at least in part.

Petrarch does evince a simple despair owing to the beloved's inaccessibility. But more than this, he shows a medieval Christian sense of the futility of love, the waste and degeneration of the faculties that it induces. This is opposed to the medieval courtly concept of the ideal, elevating influence of love. In place of the simple 'odi et amo', we have a new moral conflict, seen here in *Rime*, 173:

> Mirando 'l sol de' begli occhi sereno
>
> . . . . . .
>
> dal cor l'anima stanca si scompagna
> per gir nel paradiso suo terreno;

[35] See 'Januarye', l. 54; 'October', ll. 98–9; 'December', ll. 95–6.

[36] *Rime*, 360. l. 46; cf. 23. 141. Text and trans. as in *Petrarch's Lyric Poems*, ed. and trs. R. M. Durling (Cambridge, Mass., 1976). No. 360 was translated by Wyatt (Tottel, no. 64).

poi trovandol di dolce et d'amar pieno,
quant' al mondo si tesse opra d'aragna
vede . . . (ll. 1–7)

[Gazing at the clear sun of her lovely eyes, . . . my weary soul leaves my heart for its earthly paradise; then, finding it so full of sweetness and bitterness, it sees that whatever is woven in the world is cobwebs . . .]

This conflict is brought into the *Calender* by placing Colin's love against an equally strong awareness of his poetic career. In 'December', as in earlier eclogues, Colin sees his unhappy love as thwarting his life's purpose:

Of all the seede, that in my youth was sowne,
Was nought but brakes and brambles to be mowne. (ll. 101–2)

We may compare Petrarch, even down to the pastoral and vegetation images, as in *Rime*, 56:

Qual ombra è sì crudel che 'l seme adugge
ch' al disiato frutto era sì presso?
et dentro dal mio ovil qual fera rugge? (ll. 5–7)

[What shadow is so cruel that it blasts the seed so close to the desired fruit? And within my sheepfold what wild beast roars?]

It would be as simplistic in Spenser's case as in Petrarch's to take this as a plain condemnation of love in moral terms. Piers, as we saw, disagrees in 'October': 'loue does teach him climbe so hie'. In 'Iune' Colin himself can dream of great poetry actually born of his hopeless love, if Tityrus (Chaucer) would inspire him:

Then should my plaints, causd of discurtesee,
As messengers of all my painfull plight,
Flye to my loue, where euer that she bee,
And pierce her heart with poynt of worthy wight: . . . (ll. 97–100)

The June eclogue shows clearly that, though saddened by love and doubtful of his capacities, Colin has by no means stopped singing:

I wote my rymes bene rough, and rudely drest:
The fytter they, my carefull case to frame: . . . (ll. 77–8)

In 'November', he actually sings within the eclogue; and Thenot recalls (ll. 43–4) how earlier, Colin had sung 'rownd and rufull' verses *about* his love.[37] Love, in fact, as that same eclogue notes, is as admissible a subject

[37] This positive attitude in love is emphatically noted by Hume (pp. 52–3).

for poetry as divine or royal matters, depending on whether we take 'Pan' as God or king:

> Whether thee list thy loued lasse aduaunce,
> Or honor *Pan* with hymnes of higher vaine. (ll. 7–8)

The lament in 'December' itself gives proof of Colin's continuous power of song and acuteness of sensibility as testified by the very vehemence of his frustration. What we see in Colin reflects the great Petrarchan conflict: the poet is confounded between the rival fulfilments of poetry and love, while measuring both against a sterner moral ideal.

Certainly we do not find in the *Calender* the highest spiritual developments of Petrarchan love. Piers's contention, that love teaches Colin to 'climbe so hie', cannot be dismissed, but it cannot be taken at face value either: it marks one side of a debate. And Rosalind, of course, has nothing of Laura's 'ragion, vergogna et reverenza' [reason, shame, and reverence]: *Rime*, 140. 7, the virtue that infuses guilt into the very love that it inspires. Colin's love is purely amorous in motive. His pangs and frustrations arise from the less subtle conflict between the claims of love and his duty to his Muse, the emotional fulfilment of love and the waste and degradation it involves.

The moral element is not dismissed; but it is no longer a judgement, an absolute criterion, but only one aspect of a much richer, and in some respects inspiring and fulfilling, concept of love. This is Spenser's decisive advance over earlier English treatments of love, both within and outside the pastoral. The matter is important for the wider history of English Petrarchism and love-poetry generally. For our purposes, it is specially important that this new development should first appear in a pastoral, its exponent a shepherd in love.

Quintessentially Petrarchan too is the lover's craving for solitude, escaping into nature: 'Amor femmi un cittadin de' boschi.' [Love made me a citizen of the woods]: *Rime*, 237. 15. Not only does he escape into nature; he communes with it, finding a receptive spirit in the wilderness, as here in *Rime*, 35:

> Si ch' io mi credo omai che monti et piagge
> et fiumi et selve sappian di che tempre
> sia la mia vita, ch' è celata altrui . . . (ll. 9–11)

[so that I believe by now that mountains and shores and rivers and woods know the temper of my life, which is hidden from other persons]

From this, it is an easy step to pathetic fallacy and an identification of nature's moods with the lover's own. We had found these sentiments in some English lyrics before the *Calender*, also in a number of continental works. The *Calender* takes us more fully through the sequence. In 'August':

> More meete to wayle my woe,
> Bene the wild woddes my sorrowes to resound,
> Then bedde, or bowre, both which I fill with cryes,
> When I them see so waist, and fynd no part
> Of pleasure past. Here will I dwell apart
> In gastfull groue therefore . . . (ll. 165–70)

This is Colin's song, though here sung by Cuddie. In 'Januarye' too, Colin had addressed nature around him as an audience of his grief: 'Thou barrein ground', 'You naked trees'. Pathetic fallacy had duly followed:

> Thou barrein ground, whome winters wrath hath wasted,
> Art made a myrrhour, to behold my plight:
> Whilome thy fresh spring flowrd, and after hasted
> Thy sommer prowde with Daffadillies dight.
> And now is come thy wynters stormy state,
> Thy mantle mard, wherein thou maskedst late. (ll. 19–24)

Classical shepherds had been bound to nature by many ties. In Theocritus I, wild animals mourn for Daphnis, and he bids farewell to them and to his familiar countryside. There is stronger pathetic fallacy in Bion's 'Lament for Adonis', Moschus's 'Lament for Bion', and Virgil's lament for Daphnis in Eclogue V. But nature never holds the centre of attention, never becomes an independent force demanding analysis or a planned response.[38] Its effect upon human life is unobtrusive, almost involuntary. The classical shepherd-lover may be left alone in nature, like Virgil's Corydon; he does not deliberately seek solitude, making the objects of nature his audience, fellow-sufferers, and comforters.

There can be no doubt that the intimate association of nature and love derives from Petrarch. Italian poets and dramatists, following Sannazaro's lead, had already made extensive use of this association in pastoral. It involved a considerable degree of stylization, what I have described as a remote and exotic setting merging into the stuff of myth. Now, the presentation of nature in the *Calender* is generally far from

[38] See Rosenmeyer, *The Green Cabinet*, pp. 183–5, and ch. ix generally.

realistic: I have earlier contrasted pastoral with the country idyll and the nature-lyric in this respect.[39] But compared to Sannazaro, and still more his imitators, Spenser conveys a more inclusive concept of nature. It is not merely a symbolic setting for human states, a 'landscape of the mind', but a considerable entity in its own right, interacting with human concerns. The fact that shepherds live in constant contact with this force gives their lives a philosophic bearing that Spenser exploits to a remarkable extent. This shall be the subject of my next section.

5. *The shepherd in nature*

The natural setting of the *Calender* cannot be simply designated. Sir Kenneth Clark distinguishes four categories of landscape-painting.[40] There are passages in the *Calender* to illustrate them all: the landscape of symbols, the landscape of fact, ideal landscape—even on occasion the landscape of fantasy:

> Where I was wont to seeke the honey Bee,
> Working her formall rowmes in Wexen frame:
> The grieslie Todestoole growne there mought I see
> And loathed Paddocks lording on the same.
> And where the chaunting birds luld me a sleepe,
> The ghastlie Owle her grieuous ynne doth keepe.[41]

Here the nature-setting stands half-way between allegory and pathetic fallacy. It is not demonstrably unreal, yet it matches man's mood with a contrived exactitude. Actual pathetic fallacy can be equally striking, as in 'Januarye':

> I see your teares, that from your boughes doe raine,
> Whose drops in drery ysicles remaine. (ll. 35–6)

Yet this is scarcely a uniform mode. We may contrast the use of a hill-and-plain landscape in 'Iulye', the proud Morrell extolling the hills and the humble Thomalin the plains. This is a purely symbolic landscape, reflecting 'a state of mind in which all material objects were thought of as symbols of spiritual truths or episodes in sacred history'.[42] Both Thomalin and Morrell cite much sacred history while praising the plains

[39] See above, Ch. 5, sect 1.
[40] See *Landscape into Art* (London, 1949; repr. 1952), chs. i–iv.
[41] 'December', ll. 67–72: cf. 'Iune', ll. 19–20, 23–4.
[42] Clark, p. 3.

and the hills. The landscape takes on meaning purely from these analogues and associations.

The 'landscape of fact' is easily illustrated from 'Februarie': Thenot's flock is

> Clothed with cold, and hoary wyth frost.
> Thy flocks father his corage hath lost:
> Thy Ewes, that wont to haue blowen bags,
> Like wailefull widdowes hangen their crags . . . (ll. 79–82)

Spring and summer may provide the same vivid impression of nature and human life in nature. The 'Maye' festivities could have inspired a Brueghel painting as much as the winter-scarred flock:

> Yougthes folke now flocken in euery where,
> To gather may buskets and smelling brere:
> And home they hasten the postes to dight,
> And all the Kirke pillours eare day light . . . (ll. 9–12)

'Ideal landscape' is equally easy to discover. We have already seen the Parnassian landscape of 'Iune'. I may add the spring setting of 'Aprill', with its somewhat unbotanical catalogue of flowers.[43] Spenser is not really depicting springtime: he is using some of its sights, sounds, and colours, in combination with mythological figures, Petrarchan conceits, and royal symbols, even such a fanciful invention as the flower 'chevisaunce'.

Spenser moves easily back and forth between a mythic and a realistic presentation of nature. It has been noted[44] how, in 'March', the first half of a stanza describes an object of nature, while the second half mythologizes it:

> Seest not thilke same Hawthorne studde,
> How bragly it beginnes to budde,
>   And vtter his tender head?
> *Flora* now calleth forth eche flower . . . (ll. 13–16)

In 'Iune', Hobbinoll's praise of Colin's song passes from the easy delight of the 'larke in Sommer dayes' to the pageant of '*Calliope* with Muses moe' (ll. 49–64). There is also a very different style of myth-making, the allegorical portrayal of a season in a somewhat medieval manner as here in 'Februarie':

[43] See Janet Spens, *Spenser's Faerie Queene* (London, 1934), 74–5.
[44] By H. Fujii in *Time, Landscape and the Ideal Life* (Kyoto, 1974), 9–12.

Comes the breme winter with chamfred browes,
Full of wrinckles and frostie furrowes:
Drerily shooting his stormy darte,
Which cruddles the blood, and pricks the harte. (ll. 43–6)

The image of winter has been conflated with the standard allegoric personification of death.

Spenser's various approaches shade into one another so subtly that no precise classification seems possible. He does indeed have an eye for objects of natural beauty: the 'Hawthorne studde' ('March', l. 13), the 'larke in Sommer dayes' ('Iune', l. 51), the 'flowring blossomes, to furnish the prime, | And scarlot berries in Sommer time' ('Februarie', ll. 167–8). He can create a vivid sense of landscape—most obviously in 'Januarye' and 'December', but also in 'Iune' and (here) 'Maye':

thilke same season, when all is ycladd
With pleasaunce: the grownd with grasse, the Woods
With greene leaues, the bushes with bloosming Buds. (ll. 6–8)

Yet, all in all, there are remarkably few passages of such immediate sensory or 'natural' appeal, even if we count Hobbinoll's *locus amoenus* in 'Iune'. These shade off into the basically idealized setting of the Hymn to Eliza, with many emblematic details. The next stage is to introduce mythological figures. The natural landscape is transformed into a shaped, symbolic setting.

The distinctively 'English' elements in the landscape must be viewed in this light. Apart from the trees and plants named, there are the much-cited references to Kent. Popular festivals provide the background to 'Aprill' and 'Maye'; we are also told of Sir John of the Kerke ('Maye', ll. 309–10). Above all there is the constant testimony of the shepherds' names and their rustic diction. The setting is English beyond doubt; but it is not presented simply as such, or for its natural beauty, or the immediate activity it may inspire in man. Spenser was alive to all these aspects, and passages may be quoted to illustrate them all. But basically, he is dignifying the English countryside by linking it to more universal elements, combining realism where appropriate with mythic and symbolic extensions—just as the English rustic, while recognizably such, fulfils the representative functions of the shepherd of classical pastoral. The English landscape partakes now of Parnassus, now of the Garden of Cupid, now of the Golden Age, now of Canaan or Sinai or Olivet, now of 'Paradise . . . whych *Adam* lost'. Spenser could scarcely have invested the landscape with such meaning had he confined himself to the purely local and 'natural'.

Yet I cannot agree with Nancy Hoffman, who finds in the *Calender* nothing more than a landscape of the mind, 'nature in the service of human nature' (p. 79). While Spenser's stylized landscape serves many symbolic purposes, I must demur from such extreme 'internalisation'. Rather, Spenser is remarkable in that within the confines of the formal pastoral (where the setting serves as a stylized backdrop for representative human states) he has also set up nature as an independent entity. Man, seen as shepherd, cannot but admit this entity as an element in his own activities, even beyond its obvious physical effects. He relates to it emotionally, even spiritually. The relation may be one of concurrence or of contrast, or of passive, almost unconscious acceptance. Often, indeed, he may subjugate it to serve as a symbol for mental states and concepts. But Spenser never quite loses his sense of the actual, physical nature that provides the stuff of myth and symbol. The Parnassus-setting in 'Iune' has the 'wastfull hylls' for its backdrop. Elsewhere, nature appears in the full actuality of its being: most extensively in 'Januarye' and 'December', but also in the 'August' sestina and the 'November' dirge, and the settings for such diverse eclogues as 'Februarie', 'March', and 'Maye'.

Sometimes nature and man are presented as coequal in spirit, sometimes as divergent. Very occasionally, nature appears as a superior force controlling man's life. We may detect such an intent at some points of the 'December' lament:

> The carefull cold hath nypt my rugged rynde,
> And in my face deepe furrowes eld hath pight:
> My head besprent with hoary frost I fynd,
> And by myne eie the Crow his clawe dooth wright. (ll. 133–6)

Winter and old age are linked at this point by something more than metaphor: they have become concurrent actions of the same force. But at most points the connection is simply metaphorical: winter provides a parallel to old age and frustration, and hence can be 'made a myrrhour' of the human state.

The *Calender* presents nature as a process or entity concurrent with man's life. It does not impose any attitude or response, but simply exists as a power that man cannot ignore, and with which he can, if he so wishes, link or even merge his being. He may see it as a cyclic force governing his life or at least providing a fundamentally analogous movement, as Colin does not only in 'Januarye' and 'December' but in

'November' too: 'Thilke sollein season sadder plight doth aske' (l. 17). Some lines in 'December' (59–61, 63–4) retrospectively apply the analogy to 'Iune' as well:

> A comett stird vp that vnkindly heate,
> That reigned (as men sayd) in *Venus* seate.
>
> Forth was I ledde . . .
>
> . . . .
>
> whether luck and loues vnbridled lore
> Would leade me forth on Fancies bitte to playe . . .

However, this apparent linking of Colin's life to the seasons may be seen from this quotation to undermine itself. Summer becomes as unfortunate for Colin as winter: he interprets the entire seasonal cycle in his own terms, instead of adapting to its variety. The governing force of the metaphor lies not in nature but in Colin's mind. In 'Januarye', as we earlier saw, Colin's frustration already contradicted the actual movement of the seasons.

Among the other characters, there may be a loose sense of kinship with nature, a light matching of moods as in the cases of Willye or Thomalin in 'March'. Equally, there may be a divergent reaction like that of Piers in 'Maye':

> For Younkers *Palinode* such follies fitte,
> But we tway bene men of elder witt. (ll. 17–18)

The spontaneous, almost animal activity induced by nature contrasts with the moral course of mature humanity. In 'Februarie', Thenot accommodates himself to the climate, but his spirit is that of an independent human stoicism:

> Selfe haue I worne out thrise threttie yeares,
> Some in much ioy, many in many teares:
> Yet neuer complained of cold nor heate,
> Of Sommers flame, nor of Winters threat:
> Ne euer was to Fortune foeman,
> But gently tooke, that vngently came. (ll. 17–22)

Cuddie's response is very different. The same season can activate man's moral being in different directions, but does not control it in one. In 'Iune', similarly, Hobbinoll sits in his paradisal grove, while Colin 'Can nowhere fynd, to shroude my lucklesse pate' (l. 16).

For the history of English pastoral, it is to be welcomed that nature in

The Shepheardes Calender does not limit man's life: it merely enters into a variety of enriching relations with humanity. Spenser leaves open the full range of functions and interpretations. Man may merge with it, submit to it, even see himself as bound to it by necessity; he may bend it to his emotional demands, in symbolism or pathetic fallacy; he may react against it or triumph over it. But it has been established as a significant element of poetic experience, in the first major work of Elizabethan poetry—and that work a pastoral.

This 'open-ended' treatment of nature indicates what I consider most valuable about the *Calender* as a whole. It displays *all* the possibilities of pastoral, presents the imaginary shepherd's life in its full potential, drawing as necessary upon any of its poetic and symbolic functions. The shepherd world preserves its independence, while reaching out at points to topical issues that answer to its symbolism. At the same time, its broad canvas of twelve pieces enables it to draw out its basic concerns of poetry, love, and nature (and even Christian morals) much more than is possible in the normal eclogue. The pastoral thus acquires an unusual depth and resonance, almost a philosophic dimension.

The *Calender* carries within itself the two most important lines of development in subsequent English pastoral, both very different from the continental. It sets the tone for the unusually concentrated expression of basic, non-allusive, independent pastoralism in the Elizabethan lyric; and it lays the foundation for a vein of philosophic pastoral developed in romance and drama. I shall treat these in later chapters. Here let me stress the seminal importance of Spenser's work.

8
The Elizabethan Pastoral Lyric

1. *The evolution of the Elizabethan pastoral lyric*

I NOW come to the attractive but dauntingly large and various body of late Elizabethan pastoral poetry. Though relatively little of it consists of formal eclogues, it constantly echoes the themes and language of *The Shepheardes Calender*. Many poets profess their debt to 'Colin',[1] and, as I shall try to show, their work preserves the most remarkable innovations of the *Calender*.

This spate of pastoral poetry did not reach full strength until a decade after the appearance of the *Calender* in 1579. There was indeed a steady production of pastorals through the 1580s. The *Calender* saw two further editions in 1581 and 1586. The pastoral romance, and to some extent the drama, grew notably during this time. Pastoral poetry too had a respectable following; but, by and large, it seems to have been courtly poetry for manuscript circulation, confined to a select readership and largely lost to posterity.

Sidney's work is in a class by itself. Sir Edward Dyer's extant poems, some with an appreciable pastoral content, seem to belong chiefly to a time (*c.*1579–80) when he frequented Leicester House and associated with Sidney and Spenser.[2] There survives a notable pastoral ballad by Ferdinando Stanley, Earl of Derby.[3] Sir Arthur Gorges wrote three nominal pastorals and a genuine one, 'An Ecloge betwen a Shephearde and a Heardman', later published in *A Poetical Rhapsody* (1602).[4] The line continued in the following decades. Robert Sidney's recently

[1] e.g. Richard Barnfield, *Cynthia*, Sonnet XX; Thomas Lodge, *Phillis*, Induction; William Smith, *Chloris*, first dedicatory poem and Sonnet 50; Drayton, *Endimion and Phoebe*, ll. 993–6.

[2] For the probable dates of Dyer's extant poems, see L. G. Black, 'Studies in Some Related Manuscript Poetic Miscellanies of the 1580's' (D.Phil. Oxford, 1970), i. 145–6.

[3] First published in Grose's *Antiquarian Repertory* (1780), iii. 134, from a MS now lost. See Black, ii. 275 ff.

[4] See Gorges's *Poems*, ed. H. E. Sandison (1953), no. 98, for this eclogue, and nos. 44, 94, and 100, for the other three.

discovered poems include five 'Pastorals' with varying claims to the title. Edward Fairfax wrote twelve eclogues in 1603–4, of which only three survive.[5]

'Professional' poets like Thomas Lodge, Anthony Mundy, and Nicholas Breton also wrote pastorals in the 1580s. But they all had courtly affinities: Mundy followed the Earl of Oxford, Lodge the Earl of Derby, and Puttenham assigns Breton to courtly circles too.[6] Mundy's *Sweete Sobbes and Amorous Complaintes of Shepardes and Nymphes in a Fancye Confusde* was registered in 1583; the work has not survived, though it was printed, on Webbe's evidence.[7] Lodge's *Scilla's Metamorphosis* (1589) has a quasi-pastoral element, and the 'sonnets' that follow include both the pastoral lyric and the rustic ode. Marlowe's 'Come live with me' may have been composed in the 1580s, though not published till 1599. However, none of the pre-1590 parallels cited by R. S. Forsythe are really convincing,[8] and the date of the Thornborough manuscript copy is unreliable.[9]

Breton's poetry also remained in manuscript in the 1580s. Even in the next decade, when he published many volumes of verse, his pastorals and other courtly lyrics appeared only in pirated anthologies, or at least what he claimed to be such.[10] Only in 1604 did he bring out a planned collection of pastorals, *The Passionate Shepherd*. This gradual change strikingly reflects the vogue of published pastoral poetry after 1590. I shall examine some factors behind it, with their effects on the nature of the pastoral that came forth.

Thomas Watson's Latin *Amyntas* appeared in 1585.[11] The English translation by Abraham Fraunce ran to five editions between 1587 and 1596 (including that in *The Countess of Pembrokes Yuychurch*). *Amyntas* is pure art-pastoral: eleven laments (Fraunce added a twelfth) by the shepherd Amyntas for his dead love Phillis. In his dedication, Watson cites an odd trio of precedents: Homer's *Batrachomyomachia*,

[5] See below, Ch. 9, sect 2.

[6] *The Arte of English Poesie*, I. xxxi: Gregory Smith (ed.), *Elizabethan Critical Essays*, ii. 63, l. 35.

[7] *A Discourse of English Poetrie*: Gregory Smith, i. 244, l. 30–p. 245, l. 1.

[8] R. S. Forsythe, '*The Passionate Shepherd*, and English Poetry', *PMLA* 40 (1925), 692–742.

[9] Bishop Thornborough began the MS in 1570, but he lived till 1641.

[10] In the prefatory matter of *The Pilgrimage to Paradise* (1592). See Breton's *Works*, ed. A. B. Grosart (1879; repr. New York, 1966), i (*b*), p. 4.

[11] It seems from recent citations that we still need reminders that Watson's *Amyntas* is an original work, not a trans. of Tasso's play.

Virgil's *Culex*, and Petrarch's *Rime*—but not the allusive eclogues of the two latter poets.

Petrarch's *Rime* are particularly important. As we may expect, *Amyntas* borrows material from the pastoral epicedium; but this is combined with the love-laments of classical pastoral, the grief of Polyphemus or Amyntas at the beloved's scorn now applied to her death. The herd becomes a mirror of the shepherd's grief; all nature mourns with him; he calls himself back to his neglected tasks:

> Infoelix pastor iam nudas gramine ripas
> Deseruit, curuoque pedo munitus, in altos
> Ascendit colles, sed lente et passibus aegris;
> Lanigerosque greges una, tenerasque capellas,
> Et molles hoedos meliora ad pabula duxit:
> Inque via secum sic est affatus euntes.
> Quam vereor, Pecudes, ne, me dum tristis amantem
> Cura tenet, nostros et vos ploretis amores.
>
> [Then that vnhappy shepheard stil plag'd with vnhappily louing,
> Left those barren banks and waters no pity taking,
> And on a crockt sheephooke his lims all weary reposing,
> Climed a loft to the hills, but, alas, very faintily clymed,
> Kiddes, and goats, and sheepe driuing, goodman, to the mountains,
> For sheepe, goats, and kidds with pastures better abounding,
> Then by the way thus he spake, to the sheep, to the goats, to the yong kidds.
> O poore flock, it seems you feele these pangs of a louer,
> And mourne thus to behold your mournful maister Amyntas.][12]

There are also meditations on the power of love.[13] Beyond these classical models, we detect the influence of Petrarch's *In morte* poems, with their image of a lamenting lover in a desolate landscape. In pastoral terms, of course, the affinity is with Sannazaro. We also have glimpses of the happy life of Phillis and Amyntas before her death.[14] This too is emphatically pastoral. They court as they tend their flocks, and their tasks are described in detail, for example, in Eclogue VIII:

> Candida (me miserum) Phyllis caprimulga, capellas
> Qua pascente, domum referebant vbera tenta,

[12] Eclogue II. 8–15; cf. Eclogues I. 58ff., V. 81–91, VIII. 17–18. Text and trans. (by Fraunce) as in *Watson's Amyntas and Fraunce's The Lamentations of Amyntas*, ed. W. F. Staton, jun., and F. M. Dickey (Chicago, 1967).

[13] e.g. Eclogues V. 29–48, VI. 26–63, X. 69–75. See also Eclogue III. 83, echoing Virgil VIII. 50: 'Improbus ille puer'.

[14] e.g. Eclogues VII. 40–55 and VIII. 35–47.

Dulcius effluxit compressis lacque papillis:
Qua praesens aetas miscere coagula nullam
Nouit, et agricolis componere liba priorem,
Aut fragilem viridi fiscellam texere hibisco,
Aut per prata choros pago ductare stupente: . . . (ll. 25–31)

[Phillis who was wont my flocke with care to bee feeding,
Phillis who was wont my mylch shee goats to be milking,
Phillis who was wont, (most handsome wench of a thousand)
Either clouted creame, or cakes, or curds to be making,
Either fine basketts of bulrush for to be framing,
Or by the greene meddows gay dauncing dames to be leading]

There is some sylvan mythology: rather desultory, it is true, but important at the end when Amyntas is metamorphosed into the amaranthus ('Querela ultima', ll. 63 ff.).

Read chiefly in Fraunce's translation (which I have therefore used above), *Amyntas* grew extremely popular and supplemented the classical repertory of the Elizabethans. Meres brackets Watson with Theocritus, Virgil, Mantuan, and Sannazaro, and Fraunce with Sidney and Spenser.[15] Both Watson and Fraunce are frequently praised by other contemporaries too.[16] Spenser (*Faerie Queene*, III. vi. 45) alludes to the metamorphosis of Amyntas (following Watson's own example in *Meliboeus*, an elegy for Walsingham) and William Smith and John Dickenson to his grief.[17]

Hence, most unusually, the predominant Neo-Latin influence on Elizabethan pastoral poets would have been amorous art-pastoral, not courtly or allusive. This would be further reinforced after 1592 by the posthumous publication of Watson's *Amintae gaudia*, describing Amyntas's happy courting of Phillis before her death. In *The Countess of Pembrokes Yuychurch* (1591), Fraunce had already woven Tasso's *Aminta* and Watson's *Amyntas* into a single narrative sequence simply

[15] *Palladis Tamia*: Gregory Smith, ii. 321, ll. 6–11.

[16] See Nashe's Preface to Greene's *Menaphon* (Nashe's *Works*, ed. R. McKerrow, rev. edn., Oxford, 1957; repr. 1966), iii. 320; Lodge, *Phillis*, Induction; Peele, Prologue to *The Honour of the Garter*, ll. 47–8, 57–9 (Peele's *Life and Minor Works*, ed. D. H. Horne (New Haven, 1952), 246); Gabriel Harvey, *Foure Letters* (*Works*, ed. A. B. Grosart (1884), i. 218), and *Pierces Supererogation* (ibid. ii. 83, 290). Barnfield's supposed allusion to Watson as 'Amintas' in *The Affectionate Shepherd* (*Poems*, ed. M. Summers (London, n.d.) 29) is more probably to Ferdinando Stanley (Spenser's Amyntas in *Colin Clouts Come Home Againe*).

[17] Smith, *Chloris*, Sonnets 14 and 24; Dickenson, *Arisbas* (London, 1594), sig. E3^{r}—this last a somewhat garbled ref.

by writing in a connecting passage on Phillis's death. Fraunce gauges rightly that the two works draw upon the same vein of idyllic love.

A weaker but still noteworthy influence is that of Theocritus, with the less allusive, more genuinely rustic context this implies. Italian vernacular pastoral has much more Theocritean content than English.[18] But outside Italian, the only sixteenth-century vernacular renderings of Theocritus are the anonymous *Sixe Idillia* of 1588. Three of the six are non-bucolic, in accord with what we saw earlier of the Renaissance approach to the 'idyll'. What is really noteworthy is that these translations derive their style from *The Shepheardes Calender*: they may almost be said to be Theocritus Spenserized. This is easily seen from the 'Emblems' at the end of each Idyll. Another important sign is the metrical variety in two idylls, the first and the last in the collection, particularly the change of metre for the 'inset' amoebean contest in the first (Idyll VIII).

Above all, Spenserian influence appears in the pronounced rustic and archaic diction. We hear of a 'wennell lambe' (sig. A2^{v}), a 'rundelaie' (sig. A7^{v}), and 'smouch[ing]' (sig. A7^{r}); of ewes with 'strouting bags' (sigs. A2^{v}, A4^{r}, A7^{r}), 'whistles' rather than pipes (sig. A2^{r-v}), and the 'crowtoe' (sig. A4^{r}) for Theocritus's hyacinth. Kathrine Koller has shown how heavily Abraham Fraunce too draws on Spenser for the diction of *The Lamentations of Amyntas*.[19] All this suggests how the *Calender* was already becoming a standard model for pastoral writing—and its predominant influence, as I have tried to show, would lead away from allegory to a more deeply pastoral vein, augmenting the Theocritean elements in this particular case.

[18] I here list several Italian renderings of Theocritus, using **bold** figures for the Idylls. I have not included the many French and Italian versions of **XIX**, sorceress-poems that seem to draw on **II** as well as Virgil VIII, or love-complaints drawing upon **III** and **XI** as well as Virgil II. **I**: Tr. Annibale Caro (*Opere*, ed. S. Jacomuzzi (Turin, 1974), 361 ff.); also, closely imitated in Alamanni I (which adapts the poem to the death of Cosimo Rucellai). **III**: Expanded imitation in Benedetto Varchi I. **V**: Followed by Alamanni V (though this has personal allusions and compliments to King François I of France). **VI**: Alamanni X fits the substance of Bion's 'Lament for Adonis' into the framework of this poem. **VIII**: Closely imitated in Alamanni VIII which places it in a Tuscan setting. **XI**: Imitated in Alamanni VI. In addition there are Ronsard's 'Le Cyclops amoureux' (*Œuvres*, x. 275 ff.) and Baïf VIII ('Le Cyclope'), which are clearly modelled on Theocritus, though influenced by Ovid's Polyphemus in *Metamorphoses*, xiii. 750ff. Finally, Vauquelin de la Fresnaie's French imitation of **XII**, expanded and pastoralized, in *Idillies et pastoralles*, i (no. 76) was published in 1605. None of these are cited by R. R. Bolgar in his list of vernacular translations of Theocritus (*The Classical Heritage* (1954; repr. New York, 1964), 524). On the other hand, I have not been able to trace Marot's French trans. of **XXI** which Bolgar cites.

[19] 'Abraham Fraunce and Edmund Spenser', *ELH* 7 (1940), 108–20, esp. pp. 115–18.

I need not linger over Thomas Bradshaw's *The Shepherds Starre* (1591), a bizarre medley that, only at the very end, fulfils the promise of the heading to provide 'A Paraphrase Vpon the third of the Canticles of Theocritus, Dialogue wise'. More stress must be laid on a major source of the *Helicon* lyrics: the pastoral romances of the 1580s. I shall treat these in detail in Chapter 18. But I must anticipate my account by noting here the store of lyrics woven into these romances, on the model of Montemayor's *Diana*. The first continental pastoral romances with verse interludes incorporate elaborate eclogues and *canzone*, as in Boccaccio's *Ameto* and Sannazaro's *Arcadia*. As the prose narrative gains in importance, the interspersed poems lose their affinity to the eclogue and acquire a more varied character, as in *Diana*. Some of them may still be very long; but at least an equal number are brief lyrics or sonnets. This is the point at which the model of such romances is adopted in English. These early English pastoral romances being relatively short (except Sidney's *Arcadia*, which is *sui generis*), we would expect a preponderance of the briefer verse interlude, and this is what we get. *England's Helicon* (1600), that remarkable anthology of pastoral poetry, draws heavily upon these verses, particularly from Greene's *Menaphon* and Lodge's *Rosalynde*, where the marked degree of genuine pastoralism is reflected in at least a fair proportion of the pieces. Here we already find the salient qualities of the pastoral lyric as I shall describe them in the next section, using these poems among my examples.

What was needed was a new impulse that would widen the compass of the various pastoral influences. Paradoxically, the impetus seems to have been provided by another romance of a rather different, inherently less congenial nature. In 1590 came the first edition of Sidney's *New Arcadia*. It was followed in 1591 by the first, pirated text of *Astrophil and Stella*, and in 1593 by the full text of the 'composite' *Arcadia*. The spate of published pastoral poetry begins about this time. This may be thought a coincidence, and admittedly the arguments for seeing it as cause and effect are purely circumstantial; but they are, I think, of considerable weight, and I have treated them in Appendix C.

Besides *The Shepherds Starre*, 1591 saw *Brittons Bowre of Delights*, the first poetic miscellany to have four undoubted pastorals, plus two others so entitled. It was reprinted in 1597. *The Arbor of Amorous Devices* (1594, reprinted 1597) took over some poems from the 1591 *Bowre*, including 'A Pastoral of Phillis and Coridon'. Contrary to popular impression, the earlier miscellanies had been notably devoid of pastorals. Barring 'Harpelus', the less notable 'Complaint of a diyng louer', and the nominally pastoral 'Complaint of Thestilis' (all from Tottel's Miscellany), none of the pre-1590 miscellanies have any pastoral poems at all, though there are many lover's complaints with Petrarchan nature-settings.

Also from 1591 comes *The Countess of Pembrokes Yuychurch*, where Fraunce adds Tasso's *Aminta* to his earlier rendering of Watson's *Amyntas*. The next year saw his *Aminta's Dale* (Part III of the *Yuychurch*), and Watson's posthumously published *Amintae gaudia*. Five eclogues from the latter were translated in 1594 by 'I. T. Gent.' as 'An Old-Fashioned Love'.

In 1593 came Drayton's *Idea the Shepheards Garland* and two other important works: Barnabe Barnes's *Parthenophil and Parthenophe* and Lodge's *Phillis*. In the last two pastoral enters the sonnet-cycle, apparently without reference to Italian precedent, resulting rather from a general dissemination of pastoral in English poetry. Barnes has few pastoral elements in his chief cycle or the succeeding elegies; but there follows an important group of twenty-seven 'Odes Pastorall', with varying claims to the title but a considerable collective impact. Lodge goes even further, seeing himself as a 'poore and affectionate Sheepheard' in love with 'homlie Phillis'.[20] We also find a quasi-pastoral nature-sequence in *The Teares of Fancie* (nos. 25–31) by a 'T. W.' once thought to be Watson.[21]

In 1594 came Barnfield's *The Affectionate Shepherd*. The next year saw Spenser's *Colin Clout* and the *Astrophel* collection; Francis Sabie's *Pan's Pipe*; and Drayton's *Endimion and Phoebe*, where pastoral is brought into the mythological epyllion. In Barnfield's *Cynthia* (also 1595), the title-piece on the Judgement of Paris again combines myth and pastoral. After this comes a sequence of sonnets, one or two of them fully pastoral, and the ode 'Nights were short, and days were long . . .'.

The Faerie Queene, Book VI, was published in 1596, as was the most highly pastoralized sonnet-sequence of all, William Smith's *Chloris*.[22] We also have John Dickenson's *The Shepheardes Complaint*, where the lyrics are joined by a thin prose narrative. In 1598 comes Yong's

[20] Dedicatory letter: Lodge's *Works*, ed. E. W. Gosse (1883; repr. New York, 1963), ii/5. 4.

[21] For exposure of the Collier forgery, see F. Dickey, 'The Old Man at Work', *Shakespeare Quarterly*, 11 (1960), 41, 46. Of course, this does not prove that the poems are not by Watson.

[22] For an account of the pastoral element in *Chloris*, see L. A. Sasek's edn. of Smith's *Poems* (Baton Rouge, 1970), 7, 19–20.

translation of *Diana* (actually written by 1582)[23] with its important collection of lyrics (chiefly non-pastoral, as we shall see, but assimilated to the pastoral tradition). In 1599, *The Passionate Pilgrim* has two true pastorals (one of them '[Come] Live with me and be my love') and pastoral touches in a few other poems.

But the flood has begun to ebb by now. *England's Helicon* (1600) is no doubt the climax, but also the closing diapason, of one distinctive movement of English pastoral poetry. However, some important pieces form a separate section of the last major miscellany, *A Poetical Rhapsody* (1602). The equally substantial pastoral of the next reign is by and large very different in nature, though the old vein persists in stray works like Breton's *The Passionate Shepherd* (1604).[24] The 'Elizabethan' element in Drayton's Jacobean and Caroline pastorals demands separate treatment.

Alongside the ordinary poetry, a strong pastoral element is to be found in the collections of airs and madrigals. I shall give them only brief mention, as—unlike the poetry described so far—they are directly imitative of continental (specifically, Italian) works. Obortello's detailed comparisons provide interesting evidence.[25] The words of many English madrigals are directly translated from the Italian.[26] The English song-writer may introduce pastoral or country touches where none exist in the Italian;[27] but equally, he may ignore such elements where they do exist.[28] Allowing for this two-way traffic, we find an unusually strong pastoral element in Thomas Watson's *The First Sett, of Italian Madrigalls*

[23] See Yong's *Diana*, ed. Kennedy, p. 5, also p. xxxi, and T. P. Harrison, 'Bartholomew Yong, Translator', *MLR* 21 (1926), 133–4; cf. Ch. 16 n. 9.

[24] Jean Robertson, in her edn. of Breton's *Poems (not hitherto reprinted)* (Liverpool, 1952) suggests (p. cviii) that this work contains poems written as early as 1577 or soon thereafter. This would make them a scarcely credible anticipation of *The Shepheardes Calender*.

[25] A. Obortello, *Madrigali italiani in Inghilterra* (Milan, 1949). See also J. B. Leishman, *The Art of Marvell's Poetry* (2nd edn., London, 1968; repr. 1972), 101–14, for the pastoral element in song-books right through the 17th cent.

[26] e.g. Thomas Watson, *The First Sett, of Italian Madrigalls Englished*, no. 3 (see Obortello, p. 264); Thomas Morley, *The First Booke of Balletts*, nos. 11, 13 (see Obortello, pp. 362, 364). Text in E. H. Fellowes (ed.), *English Madrigal Verse 1588–1632* (3rd edn. rev. F. W. Sternfeld and D. Greer; Oxford, 1967), 273, 150, 151. As earlier with Italian madrigals, I have referred to such pieces by the composer's name, although the authorship of the words is often uncertain.

[27] e.g. Watson, *First Sett*, no. 5 (see Obortello, p. 267), though this replaces an extract from Sannazaro's *Arcadia*: ibid., no. 15 (Obortello, p. 275); Morley, *First Booke of Balletts*, no. 3 (Obortello, p. 354). Texts in Fellowes, pp. 273, 275–6, 148.

[28] e.g. Watson, *First Sett*, nos. 17, 19 (see Obortello, pp. 276, 278); Morley, *First Book of Balletts*, no. 1 (Obortello, p. 352), *First Booke of Canzonets*, no. 10 (Obortello, p. 377). Texts in Fellowes, pp. 276, 277, 147, 145.

Englished (1590), and in the earlier collections of Thomas Morley: *Canzonets . . . to Three Voyces* (1593), *Madrigalls to Fovre Voyces* (1594), and above all *The First Booke of Balletts* (1595). Pastoral and rustic songs form over half the collection in Thomas Weelkes's *Balletts and Madrigals* (1598) and Michael Cavendish uses a good few in *Ayres in Tabletorie* (also 1598).[29] But nearly every composer will yield one or two pieces at least.

The courtly strain of the madrigals is balanced by another class of poems: the extensive range of pastoral broadside ballads, which have been ignored by all historians of the mode. A reasonable number of ballads survive from the sixteenth century, and there is strong reason to take many of those extant in early or even late seventeenth-century versions as originating in Elizabethan times if not earlier. The Shirburn Ballads illustrate this point.[30] Among other examples, *The Countryman's Delight* has been traced from Henry VIII's day to late seventeenth-century broadsides.[31] *King Edward IV and the Tanner of Tamworth* was printed from 1564 to after 1700.[32] As a precaution, however, I shall confine myself to ballads recorded in Jacobean or earlier times.

Many of the refined 'literary' lyrics were issued as broadsides: 'Harpelus', Marlowe's 'Come live with me . . .', Breton's 'On yonder hill . . .', and Barnfield's 'As it fell upon a day . . .'.[33] We may take these as evidence for many others now lost. Some other ballads are equally sophisticated in tone and language: the quasi-pastoral setting of *The Deceased Maiden-Lover* and *The Constancy of True Love*;[34] and the detailed pastoralism, with mythological references, of *The Shepheards Lamentation*, *The Shepherd's Wooing Dulcina*, *The Obsequy of Fair Phillida*, or *An excellent newe dyttye* of Dulcina and Coridon.[35] The even more sophisticated *The Swain's Complaint* has an intermittent pastoral setting.[36]

[29] See Fellowes, pp. 284ff., 419ff.

[30] See A. Clark (ed.), *The Shirburn Ballads* (Oxford, 1907), 6.

[31] See *Roxburghe Ballads* (London, 1871–99), iii. 590ff.

[32] Ibid. i. 529–30.

[33] 'Harpelus' was entered in the SR, 1564–5, as 'A ballett intituled FILIDA was a fayre mayden' (Arber's transcript, i. 271). 'Come live with me', entered in 1603 (ibid. iii. 237), survives in an imprint *c.*1628–9 (*Roxburghe Ballads*, ii. 3; for the date, see revised STC no. 6922.4). 'On yonder hill' survives as a broadside of *c.*1624 (*Roxburghe Ballads*, ii. 528); 'As it fell', expanded as *A Louers newest Curranto*, as a broadside *c.*1620–5 (*Pepys Ballads*, ed. H. E. Rollins (Cambridge, Mass., 1929–32), no. 30: i. 186ff.; revised STC no. 1487. 5).

[34] See *Roxburghe Ballads*, i. 260ff. and i. 175ff. respectively.

[35] See, respectively, *Pepys Ballads*, no. 13; *Roxburghe Ballads*, vi. 164ff., ii. 344ff.; *Shirburn Ballads*, no. 13.

[36] *Roxburghe Ballads*, i. 336ff.: see esp. pp. 337, 340.

In a sense, such pieces are only pseudo-ballads, for they cater to a courtly taste for ballads and folk-poetry. Baskervill outlines the vogue of pastoral love-songs and love-debates at court, and distinguishes 'courtly drolls and pastorals in ballad form' from the genuinely popular ballads by the latter's 'naïveté of tone'.[37] Broadside-printers draw freely on both sources. But the former obviously derives from the latter, and this sometimes precious or romanticized interest serves to gain attention and respectability for the genuine product. A two-way movement grows up between courtly and popular ballads: the popular strain is tinged by the courtly and literary, while infusing the latter with a new authenticity, a formal simplicity that suits the basic assumptions of the pastoral mode.

Some ballads have clear classical elements. A. C. Clark's discovery of Theocritean imitation in *All in a Garden Greene* is highly debatable,[38] but *Phillida Flouts Me* undoubtedly echoes Theocritus XI and Virgil II.

I saw my face, of late,
in a fayre fountaine.
I know ther's non so feat,
in all the mountaine.
Lasses do leave their sleepe
and flocke a-bove me;
And for my love do weepe,
and flocke above me.[39]

We also have the Welsh version, current by 1600, of a ballad whose English version (entitled *The Shepherd's World*) is lost.[40] It is full of simple idyllic appeal, ending in a broader vein of rustic sexuality, but it contains many details from classical eclogues: sheltering from the heat, weaving straw, above all singing in alternate verses. Alongside this we may place *The Mery Life of the Countriman*, with its season-by-season account of rural life and its contrast of rustic content with the prince's 'slippery seate'.[41] This contrast takes on an amorous cast in *The Country Lasse, Coridons Commendation . . . of his Loue the Faire Phillis*, *Jone is as Good as my Lady*, and some of the numerous class of milkmaid-ballads.[42]

[37] C. R. Baskervill, *The Elizabethan Jig* (Chicago, 1929), 156–7.

[38] *Shirburn Ballads*, p. 220.

[39] Ibid. 299: no. 73. Also in *Roxburghe Ballads*, vi. 461.

[40] *Pepys Ballads*, no. 32: i. 195 ff.

[41] *Shirburn Ballads*, pp. 360 ff. Actually taken from a MS (Rawlinson Poet. 185, Bodl.) but copied there from a printed broadside.

[42] See, respectively, *Roxburghe Ballads*, i. 165; *Pepys Ballads*, nos. 12, 24 (i. 78 ff.,

Sometimes in such ballads, we find a not unpolitical populism, as in adaptations of the amoebean debate like *A Pleasant New Dialogue . . . between the Serving-man and the Husband-man*.[43] This is also seen in the numerous class of ballads where the disguised king encounters an honest rustic.[44] Specifically pastoral instances are *The Shepherd and the King* [Alfred] and the manuscript 'King Edward III and the Shepherd'. There is also *The King and the Forester*.[45]

Here formal pastoral is merging with the popular treatment of rustic life, producing a compound that in turn affects literary pastoral: as had happened earlier with the *pastourelle* in medieval France[46] and Plowman poetry in late medieval England.[47] The romance of *King Edward and the Shepherd* is reduced to the folk-ballad level from which it must have sprung. The *pastourelle*, a genre largely absent from the mainstream of Elizabethan poetry, occurs constantly in the ballads. Sometimes the girl outwits the courtier or gets her own back, as in *A Beautiful Shepherdess in Arcadia*.[48] The Arcadian venue of this poem belies its sturdy roots in English balladry. It is in fact a version of the widespread balladic tale of *The Knight and Shepherd's Daughter*, where the shepherdess proves to be of higher rank than her seducer.[49] The mingling of courtly and rustic ingredients is symptomatic of the general vein of late Elizabethan pastoral.

The great 'literary' model for such pastoral, *The Shepheardes Calender*, had used somewhat the same compound of elements to create a pastoral world whose Arcadian spirit is moderated by a perceptible rusticity of language, setting, and descriptive detail. I have already suggested how later Elizabethan poetry preserves this compound in a very large, very distinctive body of pastoral. I shall now try to define its nature.

156ff.); and, for milkmaid-ballads, W. C. Chappell, *Old English Popular Music* (rev. edn. London, 1893), i. 291–2; Baskervill, p. 7; Cooper, p. 58.

[43] *Roxburghe Ballads*, i. 300.

[44] See F. J. Child, *The English and Scottish Popular Ballads* (1956 edn., New York, 5 vols. in 3), v. 67–75.

[45] See *Roxburghe Ballads*, iii. 210ff.; Child, v. 71, 73, 74.

[46] On the folk origins of the *pastourelle* see W. P. Jones, *The Pastourelle* (Cambridge, Mass., 1931), *passim*, esp. pp. 33–47, 187–93.

[47] See Ch. 6, sect. 2 above.

[48] *Roxburghe Ballads*, iii. 451ff.

[49] See Child, ii. 457–77, iv. 492–4, v. 237–9. See also Percy's *Reliques* (Everyman's Lib., London, n.d.), ii. 232ff.

2. *The nature of Elizabethan pastoral poetry*

Very little of this pastoral poetry consists of formal eclogues. The purely public, ceremonial, or declamatory pieces can be laid aside, as being opposed to the rest: in continental pastoral, the two had stood in direct relation, blending into each other. Apart from these, the only substantial example is Drayton's *The Shepheards Garland*, whose special nature I shall discuss in Chapter 10. There are two eclogues in Lodge's *Phillis* and three in Sabie's rather untypical work. We may perhaps include the four so-called 'eclogues' in Lodge's *A Fig for Momus*.[50] Other eclogues were indeed written. I have noted[51] how manuscript eclogues are composed through the 1590s as well as the 1580s, more or less on the continental allusive or 'dual' model. There are even earlier instances, like the lost eclogue addressed by Puttenham to Edward VI, or that lamenting the execution of Seymour.[52] Later eclogues may continue this serious allegory of public and religious affairs, as in Fairfax's three surviving pieces; or they may present a lighter, less exacting, sometimes imperceptible personal allegory, as in Robert Sidney's love-eclogues.[53] The eclogues in *A Poetical Rhapsody* also belong here, though they found their way into print. Some (most obviously Sir Philip Sidney's) were written much earlier.

If these samples are any indication, there is in England in the Renaissance the usual cultivation of the eclogue on lines similar to the continental. I shall treat the matter in some detail in the next chapter. But in England, such poetry chiefly remains in manuscript, among courtly and academic circles. It provides an accepted vein of personal expression or discussion of public events. We may even hold that it reflects a cultivated monopoly of the 'higher' possibilities of the pastoral. But unlike its continental analogues, it does not demand general recognition as the central model of pastoral poetry. It does not so commonly obtain the second and more influential validation of print. It leaves the field free for other models to succeed. The manuscript pastorals of Arthur Gorges or

[50] See below, p. 225.

[51] See the beginning of this chapter.

[52] See at the beginning of Ch. 9.

[53] Of the five 'Pastorals', only one mentions 'Rosis' (*Ro*bertus *Si*dneius) and 'Lysa' (perhaps Elizabeth Carey) (no. 7 among the 'poems in diversified form'; see *The Poems of Robert Sidney*, ed. P. J. Croft (Oxford, 1984), pp. 198–201). Katherine Duncan-Jones holds that the poems describe a single love and constitute a sequence ('"Rosis and Lysa": Selections from the Poems of Sir Robert Sidney', *ELR* 9 (1979), 240–3). But contrast the views of P. J. Croft, pp. 90–5.

Robert Sidney have already moved in the direction of the lighter pastoral lyric; and in the latter, at least, the pastoral content is usually minimal. They read, in fact, like the flatly sophisticated pastoral lyrics of the Jacobean age, of a type I shall describe in Chapter 11.

The chief corpus of published pastoral poetry in England during these years is non-allusive, and equally, not tied to the eclogue form. It is difficult to determine whether its nature is supported by critical theory, as there is so little of this relating to the pastoral. Webbe and Puttenham's works appeared in 1586 and 1589, and are in any case strongly reliant on continental theory, so that they understandably confine themselves to the eclogue. Meres keeps the 'lyrick' and 'Pastoral' separate. He includes Barnfield's work in the latter class, but is perhaps thinking of his longer efforts or simply the title *The Affectionate Shepherd*.[54] It is rather more significant that Sir John Harington should associate 'the pastorall with the Sonnet or Epigramme' as 'many times . . . sauour[ing] of wantonnes and love and toying'.[55] This does not, of course, link the genres mentioned in formal terms.

In any case, the Elizabethan pastoral lyric resembles in many ways the varied body of poetic forms that we found to surround the continental eclogue. But in England, these lyric models acquire a new centrality, become a unified formal tradition. Moreover, the continental pastoral lyrics, being as it were a spillover from the eclogue, pass (as we saw) into non-pastoral and allusive matters. The English pastoral lyric largely frees itself from allusion. It does indeed show a great heterogeneity of theme; but this is countered by an unusually concentrated pastoralism in a substantial core of work. In a less co-ordinated manner, the Elizabethan pastoral lyric effects the same rehabilitation of the pastoral as *The Shepheardes Calender*.

Many of these lyrics may pass muster as 'eclogues' in a loose sense, being fair-sized poems written either in octosyllables or in lyric stanzas. These metres may have first been used experimentally, as possible verse-forms for the English eclogue; even poulter's measure was sometimes so used. The model of *The Shepheardes Calender* would encourage metrical variety and experiment. But once adopted, such forms induce less weighty exercises than the formal eclogue. Even if they are metrically elaborate, it is with the intricacy of a stanza in a dance-song, preserving something of the quality of a lyric outburst. This lighter texture can also

[54] *Palladis Tamia*: Gregory Smith, ii. 319, ll. 10–11, 15–19; p. 321, ll. 6–11.

[55] Preface to his trans. of *Orlando Furioso*; see as ed. R. McNulty (Oxford, 1972), 9, ll. 2–3.

encourage brevity and simplicity of treatment. On the other hand, particularly with easy-flowing octosyllables, the same simplicity can lead to meandering length, without the discreet formal control that guides the apparently unregulated progress of the classical eclogue. Such poems appear less tied to the pastoral milieu, more prone to diverge in other directions—as we have found much pastoral poetry tends to do.

The two long laments in Barnfield's *The Affectionate Shepherd* are good instances. The first is declaredly an expansion of Virgil's Eclogue II.[56] But the expansions all lead us towards mythology and courtly Petrarchism, against a lapidary, pseudo-Ovidian setting. There is a purely digressive story of Death and Cupid, borrowed from Du Bellay perhaps by way of Whitney.[57] The 'Second Lament' opens with a truly pastoral sequence of country activities; but goes on to an eccentrically long eulogy of blackness (expanding Virgil X. 38–9) and ends in an equally long stretch of moralizing with only minor pastoral touches.

Breton's *The Passionate Shepherd* has opening pieces ascribed to five 'pastors' whose pastoralism varies greatly. They are shorter but otherwise very like Barnfield's laments. Then follow two long 'sonets': 'A Farewell to the world' and a 'description and praise' of his beloved, both as patched-up composite pieces as anything in Barnfield. Their first halves have nothing pastoral, the second halves a great deal. The nine briefer 'sonets' that conclude the book are non-pastoral again.

The 'Odes Pastoral' in Barnes's *Parthenophil and Parthenophe* are equally heterogeneous. The variety of terms—'ode', 'canzon', 'sestine'—suggests the varied but connected lyric models gathered round the pastoral in continental poetry. Some of Barnes's pieces are markedly pastoral, involving not only shepherds but satyrs and nymphs. Canzon 2 celebrates Astrophel's birthday, and Ode 11 Parthenophe being crowned Queen of May, both in a striking vein of pastoral festivity: one courtly and formal, the other homely and dialect-strewn. Ode 6 begins with courtly play about the mistress's glove, but goes on to a vivid and delicate pastoralism. Ode 12 gives an authentically pastoral version of Bion's poem on the young fowler: Cupid is now brought into the sheepfold.[58] Other poems have nothing pastoral whatsoever, though there may be some pathetic fallacy. In one or two, a nominal 'shepherd' is scarcely more than a synonym for 'lover'. Some pieces are modelled on Sidney.

[56] See Barnfield's Preface to *Cynthia*, *Poems*, ed. Summers, p. 46.

[57] Ibid. 2–4. See Whitney's emblem, 'De morte & amore: Iocosum': Whitney's *Choice of Emblemes*, facsimile repr. ed. H. Green (London, 1866), 132.

[58] *Parthenophil and Parthenophe*, ed. Doyno, pp. 94, 105, 99, 108 respectively.

The over-sophisticated pastoralism of Ode 8 conceals the design of 'In a grove most rich of shade', the eighth song in *Astrophil and Stella*. Sestina 3 and Odes 18 and 20 are quantitative poems even more clearly based on the Arcadian Eclogues, but only the first is pastoral.[59]

The age saw a great number of 'pastoral' lyrics with only the vaguest touch of the shepherd about them. 'Coridons supplication to Phillis' follows up a memorably pastoral opening with an ordinary love-lyric.[60] Breton's 'Choridon's Dreame' has light pastoral touches, but is basically about an angel singing of Phillis.[61] Going a step further, Breton's 'Pawse awhile . . .' has nothing pastoral barring the names Coridon and Phillis.[62] The same is true of many airs and madrigals.

Lodge's *Phillis* and Smith's *Chloris* are notably pastoralized sequences, but they contain many sonnets with only a stray reference to sheep or, particularly in *Phillis*, not even that. Even *England's Helicon* has many pieces with only the vaguest pastoral element. They include Mundy's celebrated 'Beautie sate bathing by a Spring', and Thomas Watson's '*Amintas* for his *Phillis*'.[63] This last is not a translation out of *Amyntas*, though it echoes a few lines here and there.[64] Its pastoral identity derives entirely from association with the Latin work.

Interesting too is Mundy's '*Montana* the Sheepheard, his loue to *Aminta*' (*Helicon*, no. 76). The poem occurs in *Two Italian Gentlemen; or, Fidele and Fortunio*, a play attributed to Mundy.[65] It is not a pastoral play and has no characters named Montana and Aminta. In it, as in a copy of the song in MS Harley 6910, the text reads 'A mistress' instead of 'Aminta'. The poem is one of several 'converted pastorals' in the *Helicon*.[66] There are such poems elsewhere too. Gorges's 'pastoral' on the laurel is based on a non-pastoral French song; he merely adds a bucolic opening stanza.[67] Dowland takes a poem by Greville on a rural

[59] See, respectively, ibid. 102, 107, 125, 126.

[60] *Brittons Bowre of Delights*, ed. H. E. Rollins (Cambridge, Mass., 1933), no. 47; *England's Helicon*, ed. H. E. Rollins (Cambridge, Mass., 1935), no. 40. (The latter work henceforth cited as *Helicon*: all refs. to this edn., vol. i, unless otherwise mentioned.)

[61] BL MS Addl. 34064, fos. 9^r^–10^r^. See Breton's *Works*, ed. Grosart, i (*t*)/2, no. 10 (pp. 16–17).

[62] The same MS, fo. 24^v^. See *Works*, i (*t*)/2, no. 29 (p. 22), and L. G. Black, ii. 269ff.

[63] *Helicon*, nos. 13 and 92. The latter appeared earlier in *The Phoenix Nest*.

[64] See W. W. Greg, 'English Versions of Watson's Latin Poems', *Modern Language Quarterly* (London), 6 (1903–4), 125–9.

[65] See R. Hosley, 'The Authorship of Fidele and Fortunio', *HLQ* 30 (1967), 315–30.

[66] Others are: 'On a day (alack the day)' from *Love's Labour's Lost* (no. 34); Sonnet 37 from Watson's *Hekatompathia* (no. 58); the Earl of Oxford's 'What cunning can express . . .' (no. 52); Churchyard's 'In peascod time . . .' (no. 134); Lodge's 'The Shepherd's Dump' (no. 72).

[67] See *Poems*, ed. Sandison, p. 200.

love-retreat, and turns the name 'Myra' into 'Joan' to create a more rustic effect.[68] Even Marlowe's 'Come live with me . . .' has nothing clearly pastoral as first published in *The Passionate Pilgrim*. The pastoral touches appear in *England's Helicon*, and one wonders whether they could possibly be editorial. Bowers's account suggests that in any case, they represent a later stratum of the text.[69]

In other words, we are approaching the hybrid lyrics, found earlier in continental poetry, that occupy the borderline of pastoral but pass into a variety of miscellaneous poems. Even where the pastoral element is extensive and organic, it is often subsidiary to some other mode or convention. Lodge and Smith use pastoral to embellish the love-sonnet, but the latter is obviously their central concern. In Barnes's 'Odes Pastoral' the 'Ode' element is everywhere; the 'pastoral', occasional though prominent. In fact Barnes's 'Odes', like the Neo-Latin odes I examined earlier, may be described as a body of varied lyric poetry strongly imbued with pastoralism for a good part of its extent, but not basically reliant upon it.[70]

The lyrics at the heart of the Elizabethan pastoral convention present a very different picture. Formally, they are very much the same as those we have examined. But constituting as they do the pastoral core of this heterogeneous body, they present an attractive and notable development of the mode. At first, indeed, they seem to contribute very little. They ring the changes on a set of established features and conventions, using the same themes and details and reinforcing each other's picture of idealized shepherd life. They deliberately eschew idiosyncrasy, seeking to subscribe to what Hallett Smith calls 'a beauty and simplicity which seems almost impersonal'.[71] The extensive view of pastoral life that the individual piece lacks is provided by the total range. Even a single poem may imply a good deal. 'Good Muse rocke me a sleepe' (*Brittons Bowre*, no. 5, *Helicon*, no. 23) is a typical example. A shepherd bewails the loss of Phillida's love. There is much pathetic fallacy, and 'my little flocke' kills itself for grief. The setting, though lightly sketched, is specific enough. This brief poem assumes a pastoral world that readers will be familiar with, and develops the lyric potential of one small corner of it.

[68] *Caelica*, no. 28, as in Dowland's *Second Booke of Songs or Ayres*, no. 18 (Fellowes, p. 475).

[69] Marlowe's *Complete Works*, ed. Fredson Bowers (Cambridge, 1973), ii. 519–28.

[70] Cf. Maddison, *Apollo and the Nine*, pp. 289–90.

[71] *Elizabethan Poetry* (Cambridge, Mass., 1952), 24.

Often the setting is established by one or two telling details; but there may be many such details scattered through a poem, as in the anonymous 'My Flocks feede not . . .' or '*Phillidaes* Loue-call to her *Coridon*' (*Helicon*, nos. 35, 46). There may even be sustained description:

> The Woods at her faire sight reioyces,
> The little birds with their lowd voyces,
> In consort on the bryers beene,
> To glad our louely Sommer Queene.
>
> The fleecie Flocks doo scud and skip,
> The wood-Nimphs, Fawnes, and Satires trip,
> And daunce the Mirtle trees betweene:
> To glad our louely Sommer Queene.[72]

In one direction, these settings lead on to specific mention of pastoral occupations. We see this in Barnfield's *The Affectionate Shepherd* and in several pieces in Breton's *The Passionate Shepherd*. Elsewhere too, Breton can work such details skilfully into a love-lyric:

> Poore *Coridon* dooth keepe the fields,
>   though *Phillida* be she that owes them:
> And *Phillida* dooth walke the Meades,
>   though *Coridon* be he that mowes them.
> The little Lambs are *Phillis* loue,
>   though *Coridon* is he that feedes them:
> The Gardens faire are *Phillis* ground,
>   though *Coridon* be he that weedes them.[73]

The flocks, or other objects of nature, can image the shepherd's own love:

> I doo loue thee as my Lambs
> Are beloued of their Dams,
>   how blest were I if thou would'st prooue me?[74]

But in another direction, the pastoral element is merged with other lines of nature-poetry, like the 'May morning' convention or poems on the return of spring. Traditions are being run together to provide a notable association of love and nature in a pastoral context:

[72] 'W. H.', '*Wodenfrides* Song in praise of *Amargana*', *Helicon*, no. 43 (p. 65, ll. 19–26).

[73] Breton, 'Faire in a morne . . .', *Helicon*, no. 33 (p. 54, ll. 32–9).

[74] Henry Chettle, '*Damelus* Song to his *Diaphenia*', *Helicon*, no. 68 (p. 96, ll. 6–8). For the identification of 'H. C.' as Chettle, see *Helicon*, ii. 26–7.

Loue is abroade as naked as my nayle,
And little byrdes doe flycker from their nestes
Diana sweete hath sett aside her vaile
And *Phillis* shewes the beawtie of her brestes.[75]

The setting where the mistress walks, invigorating and perfecting it in Petrarchan style,[76] can be made specifically pastoral:

Came *Phillis* sweete owte of the wood
And in her hand a lute
Who when she playde but Robin Hoode
Strooke *Philomela* mute.[77]

So too the Petrarchan lover's retreat into nature can blend with the scorned shepherd's lament:

The banke whereon I leand my restles head,
Placed at the bottome of a mirtle tree:
I oft had watered with the teares I shed,
Sad teares did with the fallen earth agree.
Since when the flocks that grase vpon the plaine,
Doe in their kind lament my woes though dumbe . . .[78]

Love, of course, is practically the native element of these poetic shepherds. From Sidney's 'Go my flocke . . .' (*Astrophil and Stella*, Song 9) and the Earl of Derby's 'There was a shepherd', the poems are full of sorrowing swains. The long complaints in Barnfield's *The Affectionate Shepherd* are echoed in many brief lyrics:

The deepe falls of fayre Riuers,
and the windes turning:
Are the true musique giuers,
vnto my mourning.

Where my flocks daily feeding,
pining for sorrow:
At their maisters hart bleeding,
shot with Loues arrow.[79]

[75] Breton, 'The feildes are grene . . .', BL MS Addl. 34064, fo. 6v: Breton's *Works*, i (*t*)/2, no. 7 (p. 16).

[76] See Petrarch's *Rime*, nos. 160, 162, 165, 192, 243.

[77] Breton, 'Vpon a deintie hill . . .', BL MS Addl. 34064, fo. 15v: *Works*, i (*t*)/2, no. 15 (p. 18).

[78] 'T. W.', *The Teares of Fancie*, Sonnet 27. See Watson's *Works*, ed. E. Arber (London, 1870), 192.

[79] Henry Noel (?), 'Of disdainfull *Daphne*', *Helicon*, no. 136 (p. 184, ll. 4–11).

Breton's 'Choridon, vnhappie swaine . . .' weaves in the shepherd's miseries with the flock's.[80] In Smith's *Chloris*, Corin first contrasts the flock's happy state with his own sorrow (Sonnet 3); but later the flocks are also dejected (Sonnet 15). Pathetic fallacy is carried to its extreme in the anonymous 'My Flocks feede not . . .' (*Helicon*, no. 35: p. 56, pp. 27–30):

> Cleare Wells spring not, sweet birds sing not,
> Greene plants bring not foorth their die:
> Heards stand weeping, Flocks all sleeping,
> Nimphs back peeping fearefully.

In all these cases, unhappy love is experienced in a clearly, even vividly, bucolic setting. An originally Petrarchan impulse has been closely combined with the basic premisses of pastoral.

Equally common is a vein of happy mutual love. Here are Breton's Phillis and Coridon:

> He pitty cryed, and pitty came,
> and pittied so his paine:
> As dying, would not let him die,
> but gaue him life againe.[81]

Mutual love is declared through a series of pastoral details in an anonymous dialogue between another Phillida and Coridon:

> PHIL. I will gather flowers my *Coridon*,
> to set in thy cap:
> COR. I will gather Peares my louely one,
> to put in thy lap.[82]

Social distinctions do not matter in this world, except to draw favourable comparisons with courtiers and city-dwellers. Within the pastoral world, master and servant are equal:

> Poore *Coridon* dooth keepe the fields,
> though *Phillida* be she that owes them:

This egalitarianism shows best in Drayton's 'Dowsabell', which also illustrates the equality of the sexes in these poems. Man and woman woo and enjoy each other on an equal footing, the woman sometimes taking

[80] BL MS Addl. 34064; *Works*, i (*t*)/2, no. 33 (p. 23).
[81] Breton, 'Fair in a morne . . .', *Helicon*, no. 33 (p. 54, ll. 4–7).
[82] 'Phillidaes Loue-call to her *Coridon*', *Helicon*, no. 46 (p. 69, l. 30–p. 70, l. 3).

the lead. Besides Dowsabell, we have Henryson's Makyne, Phillida in 'Harpalus',[83] with respect to her feelings towards Corin, and Lodge's 'Country-Kit' with the 'longing tooth'.[84] There had also been shepherdesses in classical pastoral who showed the same frank enterprise: Theocritus's Clearista (Idyll V. 88) and Virgil's Galatea (Eclogue III. 64) who pelted their lovers with apples, and the bolder girls in Theocritus who invited Polyphemus to their beds (Idyll XI. 77–8). Once again we return to the assumptions and responses basic to pastoral. Obviously, such love disproves Poggioli's contention that 'pastoral is a private, masculine world, where woman is not a person but a sexual archetype',[85] and even his fundamental distinction between decorous 'pastoral of innocence' and hedonistic, free-loving 'pastoral of happiness'.[86] Rather, this love blends innate innocence with unrestrained fulfilment in a valid alternative to Petrarchan and Sannazaresque melancholy.

As the semi-balladic form of 'Robene and Makyne', 'Harpalus', and 'Dowsabell' makes clear, we are close to the conventions of popular poetry. I may repeat Helen Cooper's comments on the earlier *bergerie* literature based on the same recognition of rustic life:

> There, love is joyous and fulfilled; it represents a complete rejection of the courtly conventions of suffering and service, and in its spontaneity it comes close to representing Nature and indicting Art. . . . the reader or listener is invited not to trace the uneven path of true love, or the still more uneven path of false love, but to look in on, and wonder at, the perfection of joy. (p. 105)

This quality is recurrently found in the *Helicon*:

> Iolly Sheepheard, Sheepheard on a hill
> on a hill so merrily,
> on a hill so cherily,
> Feare not Sheepheard there to pipe thy fill,
> Fill euery Dale, fill euery Plaine:
> both sing and say; Loue feeles no paine.[87]

The *Helicon* entitles this a jig, and a light piece from Greene's *Menaphon* (no. 32) another. Lodge's 'In pride of youth . . .' (no. 15) is a 'barginet'.[88] Other titles mention dance-forms such as the brawl, the dump, and the

[83] So spelt in *Helicon*.
[84] '*Coridons* Song' from *Rosalynde*, *Helicon*, no. 81.
[85] *The Oaten Flute*, p. 16.
[86] Ibid. 12, 59, and *passim*.
[87] John Wootton, '*Damaetas* Iigge in praise of his Loue', *Helicon*, no. 28 (p. 48, ll. 7–12).
[88] The word is derived from *bergerette* (*berger*, shepherd).

roundelay.[89] Many very sophisticated pieces are formally carols, though the age was ceasing to appreciate the carol-form.[90] Of the two pieces in the *Helicon* actually called carols (nos. 97, 98) the first is technically not such.

The dance-lyrics—or, as the misnamed 'carols' so clearly indicate, lyrics mentally associated with dance—lead on to a more fundamental connection between such poems and popular song. The formal reliance of all or most Elizabethan lyrics on song, and in fact the partial overlapping of the two, has often been noted.[91] With the pastoral lyric, the subject-matter would tend to reinforce the association, which indeed may be thought a common and natural one. Pattison shows how even Spenser's 'August' roundelay is derived from an authentic popular song.[92] *The Complaynte of Scotland* has a long list of the 'sueit melodius sangis of natural music of the antiquite' sung by the shepherds, and another of their dances.[93]

There was an extensive body of popular song on which the pastoral lyricists could draw. Rustic wooing-dialogues range from the elaborate ballad-like examples cited earlier to lighter song-like pieces like 'Kit and Peg'.[94] R. S. Forsythe lists a number of broadside parallels to Marlowe's 'Come live with me . . .'[95] *Pastourelles* are found throughout the English Renaissance, the best-known being 'Hey troly loly lo! Mayde, whether go you?' from Henry VIII's song-book.[96] 'Where are you going to, my pretty maid?' has been traced, perhaps questionably, to Jacobean times.[97] The *Melvill Book of Roundels* has a cryptic *pastourelle*, 'Malkin was a country maid', and a compressed but simple piece, 'The maid she went a-milking'.[98] One of the few authentic folk-songs surviving from this period is 'Oh! shepherd, oh! shepherd', a love-call to a shepherd-lover.[99] We find mention of other lost songs like 'Shepard hay Shepard

[89] See *Helicon*, nos. 64 (brawl), 72 (dump), 11, 16, 56, 81 (roundelay).

[90] For an account of this form, and of its decline in the 16th cent., see R. L. Greene (ed.), *The Early English Carols* (2nd edn. Oxford, 1977), pp. xxix, xxxii.

[91] See Bruce Pattison, *Music and Poetry of the English Renaissance* (2nd edn. London, 1970), 141–59; John Stevens, *Music and Poetry in the Early Tudor Court* (London, 1961), ch. vii; Catherine Ing, *Elizabethan Lyrics* (London, 1969), 15–24.

[92] Pattison, pp. 173–4.

[93] *The Complaynt of Scotlande*, ed. J. A. H. Murray (EETS ES 17, London, 1872), 64–6.

[94] See Baskervill, pp. 387 ff.

[95] Forsythe, pp. 708 ff.

[96] See Stevens, pp. 424–5.

[97] See I. and P. Opie, *The Oxford Dictionary of Nursery Rhymes* (Oxford, 1951), 282.

[98] Nos. 64–5 and 52 in G. Bantock and H. O. Anderton's edn. of the *Melvill Book* (London, 1916).

[99] See *The Journal of the Folk-Song Society*, 3 (1907), 122–5; Baskervill in *MP* 14 (1916), 247 n. 1.

hee',[100] 'Barley-Break', 'The Shepherd's Daughter', 'The Merry Merry Milkmaids', 'The Milkmaid's Dumps', and 'The Doleful Shepherd'.[101] There are few if any pastoral pieces among love-carols, but of course shepherds figure largely in carols of the Nativity. I do not have space for the variety of festival-songs and country love-lyrics preserved by Thomas Ravenscroft.[102]

Most of these pieces are no doubt not true folk-songs but, like the ballads, 'popular' pieces by Greene's or Stevens's definition: 'neither folk-song nor art-song, but something in-between'.[103] Or else they are even more sophisticated, with classical allusions, like those sung by Walton's milkmaid: 'Come shepherds deck your heads', 'As at noon Dulcina rested', 'Phillida flouts me'.[104] The songs are mentioned along with indisputably popular ballads; but, as with the ballads, such songs were prized by courtly and educated taste, so that it can be hard to distinguish the truly popular from the sophisticated–idyllic.

Sometimes, of course, it is all too easy. 'The Loving Forrester' and 'A Pleasant Countrey Maying-song'[105] treat of country loves with an alien, courtly salaciousness. Even the *pastourelle*—largely a popular genre in sixteenth-century England, whatever its medieval and continental history—can yield such a very sophisticated piece as 'With my flocke as walked I',[106] where the shepherdess is Elizabeth, and the shepherd amazed by her aloof chastity.

Imitations of popular song were composed for the Queen's entertainments and progresses: sung by real or costumed rustics, but aimed at a very different audience. Breton's 'In the merry moneth of May', Watson's 'With fragrant flowers we strew the way', and Ceres' song from the Bisham entertainment of 1592 represent three degrees of sophistication.[107] The songs in *The Triumphes of Oriana* (1601) pass through all grades of sophistication, from idyllic rusticity through sylvan myth to

[100] No. 2413 in H. E. Rollins, *Analytical Index to the Ballad-Entries in the Stationers' Register* (Chapel Hill, 1924). This may be the same as the piece entitled 'Phillis hoe' in BL MS Addl. 27879 fo. 172ʳ.

[101] See Chappell, i. 270, 289, 291–2, and *Roxburghe Ballads*, i. 402.

[102] In *Pammelia* (1609), *Deuteromelia* (1609), and *Melismata* (1611). There are also a number of songs attached to *A Brief Discovrse of the true (but neglected) vse of Charact'ring the Degrees* (1614). See Fellowes, pp. 201–55.

[103] Stevens, p. 41. Cf. Greene, *Carols*, p. cxxxiii.

[104] *The Compleat Angler*, Third Day, ch. iv. For the songs, see respectively *Pepys Ballads*, no. 13 (i. 85); *Roxburghe Ballads*, vi. 164ff.; *Shirburn Ballads*, no. 73.

[105] *Pepys Ballads*, nos. 27 (i. 173) and 47 (ii. 9) respectively.

[106] Chappell, i. 116.

[107] *Helicon*, nos. 12, 26, and 87. The first two were sung at Elvetham in 1591.

extremely exalted non-pastoral settings.[108] More generally, there are songs on rustic themes in plays and masques, as in Nashe's *Summer's Last Will and Testament* or, for that matter, the closing songs in *Love's Labour's Lost* or 'It was a lover and his lass' in *As You Like It*.

The *Helicon* has its crop of such instances. As a rule, of course, they are courtly and 'literary' imitations of popular poetry, though some may grow popular and appear later in broadsides. 'In peascod time . . .' was the name of a popular tune to which such celebrated ballads as *Chevy Chase* and *The Lady's Fall* were sung. Is Churchyard's poem opening with those words (*Helicon*, no. 134) the original song to that tune, or an imitation? Chappell and Rollins assume the first; but the sophisticated allegory of Venus and Cupid may make us pause.[109] 'Iolly Sheepheard, Sheepheard on a hill' (*Helicon*, no. 28) is by a John Wootton believed to be a courtly poet, half-brother to Sir Henry Wootton. But the poem is based on an old song whose many variants are given by Cooper.[110] Breton's 'The feildes are grene . . .' closes with 'Of highest trees the hollye is the Kinge, | and of all flowres faire fall the Quene the Rose.'[111]

Breton's 'Good Muse rocke me asleep . . .' (*Brittons Bowre*, no. 5, *Helicon*, no. 23) resembles in its opening an old song 'O death rock me asleep . . .',[112] though the 'popular' nature of this is perhaps questionable. I have cited several other exceedingly 'literary' poems with carol-like refrains. Elsewhere, a 'refrain' may occur at the *beginning* of each stanza.[113] Or various other repetitive devices may be used, with obvious self-consciousness, to yield a supposedly 'folk' effect.

> *Phaebe* sate,
> Sweete she sate,
> sweet sate *Phaebe* when I saw her . . .[114]

Even these extreme and self-defeating instances show how awareness of popular song makes a difference to the nature of the 'literary' pastoral lyric. It inspires light, song-like verse-forms, of a simplicity demanded both by such forms and by rustic associations, with the occasional phrase

[108] For the three types, see nos. 4, 12, 23; 5, 10, 19; 20, 22 (Fellowes, pp. 158ff.).

[109] See Chappell, i. 89; *Helicon*, ii. 186. For the attribution to Churchyard, see L. G. Black, i. 204.

[110] Cooper, pp. 116–17. I can add a religious imitation, 'A Jollie sheppard that sate on *Sion* hill': see H. E. Rollins (ed.), *Old English Ballads* (Cambridge, 1920), 101ff.

[111] BL MS Addl. 34064 fo. 6v; Breton's *Works*, i (*t*)/2, no. 7 (p. 16).

[112] See Chappell, i. 111.

[113] See *Helicon*, nos. 18, 28, 54, 143.

[114] '*Montanus* praise of his faire *Phaebe*', from Lodge's *Rosalynde*; *Helicon*, no. 29 (p. 49, ll. 16–18). Cf. *Helicon*, nos. 17, 33.

or detail that suggests the actual shepherd or countryman. Usually, indeed, it is 'particularity of . . . the "curds and clouted cream" variety', in Joan Grundy's phrase.[115] The shepherds nearly all have classical names, and there are classical allusions as well. These lyrics reshape rustic life, rustic poetic forms and registers to create a genuinely different ideal of existence, a revision of normal modes of experience. They thereby fulfil the basic function of pastoral. That they should be brief, light, even trivial, is part of their success: they present an uncomplicated, almost childlike world of undistorted sensations and responses.[116]

The title-page of *England's Helicon* carries some Latin verses:

> Casta placent superis,
> pura cum veste venite,
> Et manibus puris
> sumite fontis aquam.

[Chaste things please the gods. Come in pure vestment, and with pure hands take up the water of the spring.]

There seems to be no doubt that Elizabethan poets consciously conceived of pastoral as a means of simplifying and idealizing experience:

> COR[IDON]. Melampus, tell me, when is Loue best fed?
> MEL[AMPUS]. When it hath suck'd the sweet that ease hath bred.[117]

This 'ease' is the *otium* traditionally celebrated in pastoral. More loftily, in Lodge's *Rosalynde*, Phoebe extols true love even as she rejects its sordid 'False semblance':

> Deuoide of all deceite,
> A chast and holy fire: . . .[118]

Ranging beyond love, Edmund Bolton discovers in the shepherd's state not merely a happiness above that of kings, but a happier, purer version of the royal state itself:

> You Sheepheards which on hillocks sit
> like Princes in their throanes:
> And guide your flocks, which else would flit,
> your flocks of little ones:

[115] Joan Grundy, *The Spenserian Poets* (London, 1969), 150. Cf. Cooper, p. 180.
[116] On this quality in pastoral, see Rosenmeyer, *The Green Cabinet*, ch. iii.
[117] '*Coridon* and *Melampus* Song', from Peele's lost *The Hunting of Cupid*; *Helicon*, no. 18 (p. 35, ll. 22–3).
[118] '*Phaebes* Sonnet, a replie to *Montanus* passion', *Helicon*, no. 39 (p. 60, ll. 13–14).

Good Kings haue not disdained it,
  but Sheepheards haue beene named:
A sheepe-hooke is a Scepter fit,
  for people well reclaimed.[119]

'People well reclaimed' suggests the Golden Age: to put it another way, a state of innocence, a sinless world. Breton has a notable poem in MS Addl. 34064, 'In time of yor . . .',[120] celebrating the ideal simplicity of rustic love and rustic values. It is the ideal of a past age, but said to survive among country-dwellers. Generally, however, these lyrics do not express the idea didactically, but embody it in their mode of expression. It does not emerge as a moral concept but rather as a state of mind, an expression of the unreflective happiness obtained by following the ideal.

The shepherds in these poems are invariably happy, except when languishing in love: the one curse of pastoral life, as Barnfield says.[121] But even in love, as we saw, they enjoy more often than not a spontaneous mutual affection. They also know happiness in more general terms: sometimes exuberant joy, sometimes a serene content:

Feede on my Flocks securely,
Your Sheepheard watcheth surely,
Runne about my little Lambs,
Skip and wanton with your Dammes,
  Your loving Heard with care will tend ye:[122]

This may almost be called the general spirit of *all* these poems. As I said earlier in the context of *The Shepheardes Calender*, such happiness is the continuum against which we see specific sorrows. Grief, though inevitable, is not a threat but rather part of the aesthetic design. By the same token, complex emotions are reduced to their simplest primary components and scaled down to a point of easy assimilation. This may occur through absolute simplicity of utterance, passing into *naïveté*:

I wooed hard a day or two,
    Till she bad,
    Be not sad,
Wooe no more, I am thine owne,
  thy dearest little one,
  thy truest pretty one.

[119] 'THEORELLO. A Sheepheards Edillion', *Helicon*, no. 2 (p. 9, ll. 4–11).
[120] Fos. 18^{r-v}; Breton's *Works*, i (*t*)/2, no. 17 (p. 19).
[121] 'The Shepherd's Content', *Poems*, pp. 32–3.
[122] Henry Chettle, 'To his Flocks', *Helicon*, no. 55 (p. 83, ll. 28–32). For the identification of 'H. C.' as Chettle, see n. 74 above.

Thus was faith and firme loue showne,
As behooues
Sheepheards Loues.[123]

The very mention of 'faith and firme loue' seems too serious in such a context. The rhyme-scheme is involved, but this is a dance-lyric; and in any case, such jingling rhymes can suggest naïve abandon, as in 'My Flocks feede not . . .' (*Helicon*, no. 35: p. 56, ll. 17–18):

Hart is bleeding, all helpe needing,
O cruell speeding, fraughted with gall.

This may be reinforced by a series of artless analogies:

MELI[BEUS]. Yet what is Loue, good Sheepheard saine?
FAU[STUS]. It is a Sun-shine mixt with raine,
It is a tooth-ache, or like paine,
It is a game where none dooth gaine,
The Lasse saith no, and would full faine:
And this is Loue, as I heare saine.[124]

One way and another, we find the clear presence of a pastoral sensibility or register of utterance in the Elizabethan lyric, distinguished by deeper traits than the mere mention of fields and flocks. It will be obvious that such pastoralism connects easily with the example of *The Shepheardes Calender*. In the *Calender*, Spenser had gathered into eclogue form, and moreover into a substantial series of poems, the latent tendencies in this direction that had earlier lain, scattered and unrecognized, in lyrics. After the *Calender*, this pastoralism again breaks up into lyric form, losing the special depth and elaboration it had acquired in Spenser's eclogue-sequence but retaining its essential nature. These lyrics preserve the imaginative integrity of the pastoral world. Instead of allusion, they make the more radical comment on reality implied by total absorption in an independent poetic universe.

[123] 'The Sheepheard *Dorons* Iigge', from Greene's *Menaphon*; *Helicon*, no. 32 (p. 53, ll. 2–10).
[124] 'The Sheepheards description of Loue' ('Ignoto'), *Helicon*, no. 54 (p. 83, ll. 8–12).

9
The Pastoral of Allusion

1. *Spenser: The later pastorals*

IT SHOULD be apparent by now that English Renaissance pastoral, seminally influenced by *The Shepheardes Calender*, follows a very different line of development from the continental. Non-allusive pastoral predominates, and the formal eclogue is greatly reduced in importance, leading to a new simplicity of form and tone. Needless to say, there remains a fair proportion of allusive pastorals and of full-scale eclogues, as I have already indicated. The two categories coincide in good measure, but the first is my primary concern in this chapter.

Such allusive pastoral, as in all ages everywhere, effects an uneasy and contrary merger of court and country, shepherds and their masters. At its best, though, it can achieve a genuine union of opposites, an infusion of each scale of values into the other. Pastoral expands its range, but brings its own spirit to bear on the new areas it has annexed.

There are surprisingly early instances of such pastoralizing of experience. We cannot tell the nature of Puttenham's lost eclogue to Edward VI;[1] but there survives a poem said to commemorate the execution of Edward Seymour, Duke of Somerset, in January 1551–2.[2] Its central figure is an oak-tree (Seymour), but the shepherd life beneath it is vividly presented, suggesting the Golden Age at certain points. According to Harrington, the poem's earliest editor, the oak's bounty of acorns and honey indicates the 'great State and Magnificence of [Seymour's] Table and Hospitality'.[3] If so, it is a remarkable anticipation of the Golden-Age motif in the country-house poems of the next century.

As we might expect, Spenser affords the finest syntheses of allusion with authentic pastoral—not equally in every case, needless to say. In

[1] See Cooper, *Pastoral*, p. 124.

[2] See *Arundel Harington MS*, ed. Hughey, i. 385. The lost MS copy of the poem is said to have been dated 1564.

[3] Henry Harrington (ed.), *Nugae Antiquae* (1769), 93–4. Cited in *Arundel Harington MS*, i. 386.

Daphnaida, for instance, the pastoralism is intermittent and conventional. Sir Arthur Gorges mourning his wife Douglas becomes Alcyon, the once 'iollie Shepheard swaine' (l. 54); but there is only one sustained piece of pastoral (ll. 309–57), and even this on conventional lines:

> Let Bagpipe neuer more be heard to shrill,
> That may allure the senses to delight;
> Ne euer Shepheard sound his Oaten quill
> Vnto the many . . . (ll. 323–6)

Pastoral serves simply as a general code or convention: it does not correspond, either allegorically or by a subtler identity of spirit, to any genuinely pastoral trait in the life of Sir Arthur Gorges or his lady.

Astrophel provides a contrast, for in it Sidney's life and ethos take on a truly pastoral tone. If Sir Calidore in *The Faerie Queene* is a portrait of Sidney, Astrophel prefigures Calidore's courtesy with its affinities to pastoral. Astrophel's provenance provides a convenient link:

> A Gentle Shepheard borne in *Arcady*,
> Of gentlest race that euer shepherd bore . . . (ll. 1–2)

'Gentle' shifts meaning from 'soft-natured' to 'noble'; and 'Arcady' relates on the one hand to Sidney's *Arcadia*,[4] on the other to the standard pastoral landscape. Astrophel's role as poet-shepherd is validated at two levels, allegorical and literal, for he was actually a pastoral poet: the pastoral setting becomes Parnassian. Of course, Arcady is clearly the court, and the allegory contains the usual contradictions: this shepherd goes 'Merily masking both in bowre and hall' (l. 28). But these courtly activities express a genuine delicacy and simplicity, a spirit that we primarily associate with pastoral. It extends at points to a deeper 'pastoral innocence':

> His sports were faire, his ioyance innocent,
> Sweet without sowre, and honny without gall . . . (ll. 25–6)

Chivalric pursuits are as fully translated into pastoral as perhaps anywhere:

> In wrestling nimble, and in renning swift,
> In shooting steddie, and in swimming strong:

[4] We may also note that the funeral singing-meet at the end of *Astrophel*, introducing the succeeding pieces in the vol., imitates the 'Eclogues' in Sidney's *Arcadia*, especially the group following Basilius's supposed death.

> Well made to strike, to throw, to leape, to lift,
> And all the sports that shepherds are emong. (ll. 73–6)

The very art of war is allegorized as hunting.[5]

In a word, the allegory is integral and self-contained. The pastoral metaphor generates an independent life that transforms the non-pastoral content, even though we retain our sense of the latter's literal entity. Sidney is not simply a courtier by the end of the poem. He has infused a special grace into court life, the grace which Spenser has extracted and crystallized in its fit medium of the pastoral convention.

This process bears out the common view of a basically pastoral bent to Spenser's sensibility. His varied use of pastoral stems from a core allegiance to an aesthetic and a register of experience that constitute the deepest assumptions of the pastoral mode. The impression is made absolute by *Colin Clouts Come Home Againe*.

Colin Clout presents two pastoral worlds. One is the patently allegorical pastoral of the court. Cynthia is a shepherdess, and the 'learned throng' surrounding her becomes, at certain points, shepherds and shepherdesses too. But there is a second, metaphorically ambiguous shepherd world to which Colin himself belongs. At first glance it seems to consist of actual shepherds, contrasted with courtiers in the classic opposition of pastoral:

> Therefore I silly man, whose former dayes
> Had in rude fields bene altogether spent,
> Durst not aduenture such vnknowen wayes,
> Nor trust the guile of fortunes blandishment . . . (ll. 668–71)

A long passage of court satire follows, to 'warne yong shepheards wandring wit' (l. 684) against the glitter of court life. But elsewhere the contrast favours the court:

> Such loftie flight, base shepheard seemeth not,
> From flocks and fields, to Angels and to skie. (ll. 618–19)

And the courtiers, of course, have also been presented as shepherds. This uncertainty reflects the conflict between real and metaphoric shepherds that we have encountered so often before. This has been noted—by Lerner for instance[6]—and put down to simple inconsistency, brought about by social and careerist pressures on Spenser.

[5] Contrast the lament for Sidney inset in Watson's *Meliboeus* (*Poems*, ed. Arber, pp. 155 ff.) where 'Astrophill' is a warrior pure and simple, though defending shepherds' flocks.

[6] *The Uses of Nostalgia*, pp. 133–5.

But finally, Spenser succeeds in finding a path through the maze. He cannot fully avoid the dangers inseparable from allusive pastoral; but because at a deeper level he has a consistent conception of the pastoral, he can impose a unity of theme despite the vacillations in the metaphor.

Colin's shepherd community in Ireland is allegorical too, standing for a community of poets. Colin, of course, is Spenser. The poets at the English court had been shepherds as well, but there is a difference in the nature of the allegory. In the court-sequence, the allegory lies near the surface, 'shepherd' and 'piping' being used as convenient synonyms for 'poet' and 'poetry'. By contrast Colin himself, his native milieu, and his ideal of poetry are presented in great pastoral detail. All nature mourns Colin's absence:

> The woods were heard to waile full many a sythe,
> And all their birds with silence to complaine:
> The fields with faded flowers did seem to mourne,
> And all their flocks from feeding to refraine: . . . (ll. 23–6)

Spenser presents his entire career in poetic guise:

> Charming his oaten pipe vnto his peres,
> The shepheard swaines that did about him play: . . . (ll. 5–6)

Pastoral allegory is applied to not only the poet's name but the poet's world. There is a telling pun in Colin's 'oaten quill' (l. 194).[7] Thus, although there may be poet-shepherds at court, the poet is basically seen as the true shepherd, humble and unambitious, ill at ease with court life and distrustful of Fortune's gifts. They may at first attract him, but he is really being attracted by his own wondering image of court life, simplifying and idealizing its complexities. He sees the court in terms of his own reconciling pastoral vision, as embodying the ideal of beauty and harmony that he as shepherd has learnt to conceive.

Ultimately, the attractions of 'that liues painted blisse' (l. 685) prove illusory. The very virtues attributed to court life seem more accessible in the country. The praise of Cynthia is first said to be beyond a shepherd's reach; but later it finds vivid expression in pastoral terms:

> The speaking woods and murmuring waters fall,
> Her name Ile teach in knowen termes to frame:
> And eke my lambs when for their dams they call,
> Ile teach to call for *Cynthia* by name. (ll. 636–9)

[7] *OED*, *quill*: 1*c*. 'A musical pipe, made of a hollow stem'; 3*b*. 'The feather of a large bird . . . formed into a pen . . .'.

Contemplation of Cynthia raises Colin to a pitch of divine inspiration, 'like one yrapt in spright' (l. 623). But, at the end, the love of Rosalind is seen to inspire the same elevation:

> So hie her thoughts as she her selfe haue place,
> And loath each lowly thing with loftie eie. (ll. 937–8)

Some time before this, Colin had been rapt into the same 'celestiall rage' (l. 823) of love in the specific context of shepherd life. Courtiers prophane the 'mightie mysteries' of love while shepherds

> Do make religion how we rashly go,
> To serue that God, that is so greatly dred; . . . (ll. 797–8)

More than ever it is apparent that the virtues of the court reflect those of the country and are admissible only in so far as they do so. The pastoral ideal ultimately rejects the court and provides its own fulfilment.

This is realized in a happy, harmonious 'shepherd's nation' in a remote Irish setting. Here the objects of nature retain their pristine mythic entities, as in the story of Mulla and Bregog, and the shepherds (as in the Golden Age) do not know a ship when they see one. Against this background, Spenser invests shepherd life with his poetic, and accompanying ethical, ideal: humble dignity, an aspiration simultaneous with it, and a withdrawn otherness of life.

Thus Spenser manipulates and resolves the basic paradox of courtly pastoral. He uses it to reassert the classic pastoral values as values, not intrinsically linked to any setting. They provide criteria for judging court culture and finding it wanting. And finally, they vindicate an imaginary shepherd life as their ideal repository. Behind the literal pastoral, then, lies a 'pastoral of the mind'.

2. *Allusive pastoral from Peele to Quarles*

A basic commitment to the pastoral distinguishes Spenser's work from the superficially similar compound of, say, Peele's *Eclogue Gratulatory on Essex's Return from Portugal* (1589) or Thomas Watson's *Meliboeus* on the death of Walsingham, published in 1590 in both Latin and English.

Peele's poem is pervaded by pastoral references and a genuine, if somewhat overdone, register of pastoral diction:

> Gray as my cote is, greene all are my cares,
> My grasse to drosse, my corne is turned to tares:

Yet even and morrow will I never lin,
To make my crowd speake as it did begin.[8]

But there is no sense of a genuine pastoral world: it is all patently an allegoric device. Simple shepherds like Piers and Palinode (metaphorically standing for humble poets) are juxtaposed with ruler- and warrior-shepherds like Essex, 'a great Herdgroome, certes, but no swaine' (l. 48). At another level, Essex is a divine shepherd, like Apollo. We may explain these shifts by the shepherd-speakers' need to translate everything, somehow or other, into pastoral terms. But in the absence of a consistent pastoral framework, the translation remains external and mechanical—especially as there are long direct references to martial feats in the latter part (ll. 80–8, 99–116, 126–50).

In Watson's *Meliboeus* too, the pastoral details are extensive but unevenly spread. The speakers, Corydon and Tityrus (Watson, and Walsingham's cousin Thomas), are clearly pastoralized. Corydon in particular is a lowly shepherd, and invokes nature's grief in sustained pathetic fallacy:

O heards and tender flocks, o handsmooth plains,
o Eccho dwelling both in mount and vallie:
o groues and bubling springs, o nimphs, o swains,
o yong and old, o weepe all *Arcadie*.[9]

But Tityrus strikes a higher note: his lament has much celestial imagery but little pastoral. For Watson makes no secret of Walsingham's actual identity: he was distinguished by 'watchfull studie for *Dianaes* health', 'gentle birth which vertues worth did raise', and 'honors titles, [and] abundant wealth' (p. 153). Hence his pastoral functions, detailed later, are patently allegorical. It is Watson's basic purpose to emphasize rather than conceal that Arcadia is England, and the shepherds not really such. The sense of pastoral as code is borne out by the English preface, where Watson laboriously explains 'I figure Englande in *Arcadia*; Her Maiestie in *Diana*; Sir Francis Walsingham in *Meliboeus*, and his Ladie in *Dryas*' (p. 147).

Pastoral is mechanically applied in a few minor pieces in the *Astrophel* volume, chiefly a 'pastorall Aeglogue' between Lycon and Colin by L[udovick] B[ryskett]. More memorable, however, is 'An Elegie, or friends passion, for his *Astrophill*' by Matthew Royden. It has no explicit

[8] ll. 14–17; all refs. to Peele's *Life and Minor Works*, ed. Horne, pp. 224ff.
[9] Watson's *Poems*, ed. E. Arber, p. 165. All refs. to this edn.

pastoralism whatsoever: but its vivid nature-setting and extended pathetic fallacy can only derive from the pastoral convention, and is reminiscent of both Theocritus I and the *Epitaphium Bionis*.

The same may be said of a later lament for Sidney, published in 1602 in *A Poetical Rhapsody*: no. 135, 'Others [more hexameters] vpon the same [the death of Sidney]'.[10] Another elegy on Sidney in this volume (no. 9)[11] is clearly pastoral, a painstaking allegory of the contemporary poetic milieu, in the style and diction of *The Shepheardes Calender* and indeed with a long excursus on Colin's woes.

The most curious eclogue in *A Poetical Rhapsody* is 'Eubulus's Complaint' (no. 8) by Francis Davison, the editor of the volume. It is ostensibly a love-lament by the shepherd Eubulus, a self-contained pastoral fiction. But the beloved is none other than Astraea: the poem is a political allegory, a complaint for Elizabeth's shabby treatment of Davison's father. Allusion and autonomous pastoral have seldom pursued such richly parallel courses. This makes one wonder whether the third eclogue in the *Rhapsody* (no. 10, wrongly headed 'II. Eclogue'), now identified as Sir Arthur Gorges's work, may not conceal a clueless allegory. Here a shepherd declares his love of 'Daphnee' and lives in hope, although another 'Heard-man' warns him he aims too high.

There seems to have been a similar allegory in Sir Walter Ralegh's puzzling poem, *The Ocean's Love to Cynthia*. This is confirmed by Spenser's *Colin Clout*, where Ralegh is 'the shepheard of the Ocean' (l. 66 and later) and Elizabeth, Cynthia. The surviving fragments of Ralegh's poem point to an underlying pastoral motif. They have many prominent images drawn from nature and the seasons.[12] Twice at least, the lover's predicament is presented in clearly, even unusually vivid pastoral terms. In Book XI. 25–32, the lover was once happy with his flock but is now lonely and comfortless. Lines 497–508 are more patently metaphorical: the heart is the sheepfold, false hope the shepherd's staff, poetry his pipe. Allegoric purpose being announced in this way, we are easily led to read the poem in terms of an estrangement between Ralegh and the Queen: perhaps after the seduction of Elizabeth Throgmorton, perhaps on an earlier occasion around 1589.

[10] All refs. to *A Poetical Rhapsody*, ed. H. E. Rollins (Cambridge, Mass., 1931).

[11] The 2nd eclogue in the vol., though wrongly headed 'III. Eglogue'. The 1608 and 1611 edns. actually cite Sidney by name in the text, while the 1602 and 1621 edns. have 'Willy'.

[12] e.g. Book XI. 13, 17–18, 21–4, 71–2, 77–80, 241–8, 275–8; Book XII. 1, 4, 17. Refs. to Ralegh's *Poems*, ed. Agnes Latham (London, 1951; repr. 1962).

In earlier poets too, relations between monarch and courtier could come disguised as standard pastoral situations. Two of Dyer's doubtful pieces, 'Amidst the Fairest mountain tops' and 'Alas, my heart . . .' have been so interpreted.[13] In the Elizabethan lyric, the Queen is thoroughly absorbed into the independent world of pastoral myth.[14] In Canzon 2 in Barnes's *Parthenophil*, 'Eliza' is truly 'Arcadiaes Queene' (l. 43) and finally a '*Delian* Nymphe' (l. 49). The same note is struck more lightly in a number of airs and madrigals.[15] Elsewhere, a largely non-allusive lyric can lead up to Eliza's praise couched in pastoral love-convention, as in Barnfield's 'Nights were short . . .'.[16]

It is indeed hard to tell when an eclogue or lyric may not conceal personal allegory. One of Robert Sidney's manuscript eclogues clearly names the shepherd 'Rosis' after *Ro*bertus *Si*dneius. More conjecturally, Ann Stanford finds the life of Francis Sabie reflected in his *Pan's Pipe* (1595).[17] But the allegory is secondary, almost incidental, overlaid by a lyric impulse in the one case and a fictional one in the other.

More obvious allegories abound, needless to say. From the plentiful crop of laments after Elizabeth's death in 1603, we may select Henry Chettle's *Englandes Mourning Garment*, a prose tract interspersed with verses. As in earlier allusive pastorals, the bucolic metaphors are pervasive but contradictory: shepherds can stand for kings, priests, poets, or common rustics. Pan himself is now Christ and now James I.

It appears that Edward Fairfax wrote twelve eclogues, in 1603.[18] A complete manuscript survived at least into the early eighteenth century. Today only three poems remain, one of them imperfect. Two concern theological and ecclesiastical matters; and though they are accomplished

[13] See, respectively, R. M. Sargent, *At the Court of Queen Elizabeth. The Life and Lyrics of Sir Edward Dyer* (Oxford, 1935), 205; L. G. Black, *Studies in . . . Poetic Miscellanies*, i. 151–2.

[14] I may appear to have dealt very cursorily with the widespread pastoral celebration of Queen Elizabeth by the poets of her reign, extending to a veritable myth and cult of the 'shepherds' Queen'. I need only refer to E. C. Wilson, *England's Eliza* (1939; repr. London, 1966), ch. iv, and Cooper, *Pastoral*, ch. vi. I have nothing to add to these accounts.

[15] e.g. Thomas Watson, *First Sett of Italian Madrigalls*, no. 8; Michael Cavendish, *Ayres in Tabletorie*, no. 24; Thomas Morley, *Canzonets . . . To Three Voyces*, no. 8 (Fellowes, pp. 274, 426, 135); also Nicholas Yonge, *Musica Transalpina*, Book II (London, 1597), 24.

[16] In *Cynthia* (*Poems*, p. 67); also *Helicon*, no. 51.

[17] 'The Life of Francis Sabie', *HLQ* 25 (1961–2), 263–82.

[18] 'These Bucolickes were written in the first yeare of the reign of K. James': Fairfax's son William, as quoted by the poet's great-nephew Brian. See Fairfax's *Godfrey of Bulloigne . . . together with Fairfax's Original Poems*, ed. K. M. Lea and T. M. Gang (Oxford, 1981), 649. See also W. W. Greg, 'Fairfax's Eighth Eclogue', *Collected Papers* (Oxford, 1966), 29ff.

pieces of verse, they hold pastoral motifs in uneasy combination with more complex ones. In 'Eglon and Alexis', Eglon laments how his prize lamb has sickened after being seduced by the Fox; Alexis suggests the blood of a 'holy Lamb', and departs on noting cryptically the swathed 'crow' or knocker—a sign of childbirth—at his own door.

We may read this (as Fairfax's latest editors do)[19] as an allegory of the Fall of Man. But it may also stand for the decline of the Church, probably into Catholicism, and the promise of a Protestant revival. This would agree with the subject of the other eclogue, 'Hermes and Lycaon': the two shepherds hold an amoebean contest about the merits of their respective loves, who clearly represent the two Churches.

As Lea and Gang remark, 'these poems hardly pretend to make sense on the literal level'.[20] Yet the first at least contains a fair degree of pastoral metaphor. What modifies the effect is the predominantly sophisticated diction (with a few rusticities of tone) and the many recondite allusions, chiefly classical. In 'Hermes and Lycaon', the chief source of allusion is the Apocalypse. Its high mysteries conflict with the pastoral, which is in any case much atrophied in this piece.

In the imperfect 'Ida and Opilio', shepherd and shepherdess champion the wealth and achievement of modern and ancient times respectively, culminating in Opilio's praise of the Elizabethan mariners. It is worth noting that Ida does not praise the ancients for restraint or spirituality, but for greater wealth and power.

On available evidence, then, Fairfax had imbibed the mechanics of the eclogue but, like most allusive pastoralists, had perforce to overthrow its spirit and purpose. We also come upon attempts at making pastoral out of all kinds of curious subject-matter. A minor example is George Buc's *Daphnis Polystephanos. An Eclog treating of Crownes, and of Garlandes* (1605), and specially praising the plant 'Genest' or broom. The true object of praise is the House of Plantagenets and its successors, and the pastoral element is insignificant.

A later and more prominent instance occurs in that curious work, Phineas Fletcher's *The Purple Island* (1633). At first sight, the pastoral framework here seems almost grotesquely incongruous: Thirsil, the shepherds' May Lord, sings of man's nature and constitution, sometimes in disconcertingly unromantic detail. As might be expected, the pastoralism is usually nominal, a token stanza at the beginning and end of each

[19] Lea and Gang, p. 660.
[20] Ibid. 650.

canto. But Canto I opens with an elaborate display of stock pastoral motifs, and even the later touches sometimes make vivid use of convention:

> The shepherds in the shade their hunger feasted
> With simple cates, such as the countrey yeelds;
> And while from scorching beams secure they rested,
> The Nymphs disperst along the woody fields,
> Pull'd from their stalks the blushing strawberries,
> Which lurk close shrouded from high-looking eyes;
> Shewing that sweetness oft both low and hidden lies.[21]

Very occasionally, Fletcher can make light but organic use of pastoral. The *paulo maiora* note is struck several times: 'How dare I then forsake my well-set bounds . . .' (Canto VI, stanza 4). The Orpheus legend is retold in Canto V;[22] and in the climactic use of pastoral for Christ, he is given Orphic features in his shepherd state (Canto XII, stanza 7):

> The worlds great Light his lowly state hath blest,
> And left his heav'n to be a shepherd base:
> Thousand sweet songs he to his pipe addrest:
> Swift rivers stood; beasts, trees, stones ranne apace,
> And serpents flew to heare his softest strains:
> He fed his flock, where rolling *Jordan* reignes;
> There took our rags, gave us his robes, and bore our pains.

The final union of Christ with Eclecta (the soul) is celebrated in a brief pastoral epithalamium (Canto XII, stanza 87).

The shepherds' feast takes place beside the 'Chame' (Canto I, stanza 2); but the poet wishes to live in humble content 'under some *Kentish* hill | Neare rowling *Medway*' (Canto I, stanza 28). These are Fletcher's own haunts, of course; and the vein of personal allusion is taken up in other poems, including certain piscatory eclogues. The shepherds' names recur in these pieces: Thirsil, Myrtilus, Thenot, Thomalin—the first two, it seems, personae of Fletcher himself.[23] Clearly, the shepherds in *The Purple Island* are Fletcher and his circle of friends; and the setting is de-allegorized to an urbane nature-retreat in 'To Master W. C.', where they

[21] Canto IV, stanza 1; all refs. to the *Poetical Works* of Giles and Phineas Fletcher, ed. F. S. Boas (Cambridge, 1909), ii.

[22] It is paraphrased there from Boethius, *Consolation of Philosophy*, iii, met. 12. Fletcher uses the passage from Boethius elsewhere too. See Boas's note in Fletcher's *Works*, ii. 364.

[23] This is clearest in the poem 'To my beloved *Thenot* in answer of his verse' (*Works*, ii. 231). See also 'To Master W. C.' (p. 227), 'To *Thomalin*' (p. 235). The longing for a retreat in Kent appears in 'To my ever honoured Cousin W. R. *Esquire*' (p. 228).

By yellow *Chame*, where no hot ray shall burn thee,
Will sit, and sing among the Muses nine;
And safely cover'd from the scalding shine,
We'l read that *Mantuan* shepherds sweet complaining
Whom fair *Alexis* griev'd with his unjust disdaining: . . .[24]

Passages like this point to a clear allusive intent behind *The Purple Island*; and the didactic purpose, needless to say, is pervasive.

We return to the mainstream of allusive pastoral with the poems of Thomas Randolph and William Basse. Randolph's 'An Eglogue to Mr Iohnson' presents Ben Jonson as Tityrus, protégé of Pan (the king), and Randolph as his favourite successor Damon. But Damon is frustrated by the singer's lack of reward, and also by his unhappy exchange of '*Cham's* fair streams' for what appears to be London theatrical life:[25]

Call'd thence to keep the flock of *Corydon*.
Ah woe is me, anothers flock to keep;
The care is mine, the master shears the sheep![26]

The allegorization is skilful, as where Aristotle becomes the 'wise shepherd' of Stagira whose 'deep and learned layes' were sung upon the Cham (ll. 133–6). But the delight in pastoral detail is obviously subservient to the interest of the allusion.

In this it differs from 'An Eglogue occasion'd by two Doctors disputing upon predestination'. Theological arguments are cogently presented through opaque, easy-flowing pastoral metaphor:

Poore lamb alas; and couldst thou, yet unborne,
Sin to deserve the Guilt of such a scorne?
Thou hadst not yet fowl'd a religious spring,
Nor fed on plots of hallowed grasse, to bring
Staines to thy fleece; nor browz'd upon a tree
Sacred to *Pan* or *Pales* Deitie. (ll. 17–22)

The ensuing account of Christ's life is quite unpastoral; but at the end, the Last Judgement is presented in ingenious pastoral guise:

But hoe, I see the Sun ready to set,
Good night to all; for the great night is come;

[24] *Works*, ii. 227.

[25] Fleay took this passage to indicate that Randolph acted as manager's assistant for Prince Charles's Men at Salisbury Court Theatre. See Randolph's *Poems and Amyntas*, ed. J. J. Parry (New Haven, 1917), 363.

[26] ll. 168–70; all refs. to Parry's edn. (see n. 25 above).

Flocks to your folds and shepheards hye you home!
To morrow morning, when we all have slept,
Pan's Cornet's blowne, and the great *Sheepshears* kept. (ll. 90–4)

In William Basse's Eclogues, the poet assumes many personae, but his patrons remain constant: Poemenarcha or the Countess of Pembroke, Sir Richard (later Viscount) Wenman, his wife, and his daughter Penelope. Eclogue I has an inset passage praising the three ladies, and Eclogue III an acrostic on Wenman's name and titles. Eclogue V laments Poemenarcha's departure for Belgium, and the later Eclogue VIII mourns her death as well as Sidney or 'Philisiden's', Wenman's, and Lady Wenman's. The praise of landed patrons often modifies the pastoral in the direction of the country-house poem, especially in Eclogue III.

Simultaneously, the titles of the poems indicate a moral concern: 'Of Gratitude', 'Of Contentment', 'Of Temperance'. There are also intermittent moral observations, among them a curious one, in Eclogue VIII, where sheep are presented as a model of 'Inward agreement': 'And mutuall loue shepheards may learne of sheep'.[27] Basse himself appears most often as Colliden, shepherd-poet and lover. But this persona diffuses the allusive tone even while enforcing it: for Colin has entered pastoral mythology by now, and Basse's concerns absorb the wider strains of art-pastoral. In Eclogue I, Colliden's love of Laurinella finds expression in typical pastoral Petrarchism. In Eclogue VI there is an unusually realistic note in the encounter of Nicco's goat with a wolf, and the ensuing account of shepherds' nostrums and such matters.

But the most notable union of authentic pastoral with extensive allusion is seen in Francis Quarles's *The Shepheards Oracles* (1646). Some earlier accounts give the misleading impression that Quarles's satire is chiefly anti-Puritan. Eclogue for eclogue, there is more satire of Catholicism (Eclogues II, III, IV, IX, with touches elsewhere) than of Puritanism (Eclogues VII, VIII, and XI). In vigour, too, the former can match the Dissenter's anthem in Eclogue XI:

Wee'l exercise within the Groves,
And teach beneath a Tree;
Wee'l make a Pulpit of a Cart,
And, hey! then up goe wee.[28]

[27] Basse, *Poetical Works*, ed. R. W. Bond (London, 1893), 238.
[28] Quarles, *Complete Works*, ed. A. B. Grosart, iii (Edinburgh, 1881), 235. All refs. to this edn. and vol.

In Eclogue VI the somewhat unclear allegory seems to be that Catholic and Dissenter represent equal and opposite aberrations. There is other allusion too, notably in the elegy for Gustavus Adolphus (Eclogue X). In Eclogue VII, the poor shepherd Adelphus appears to be Quarles himself.

The degree to which these themes are pastoralized varies greatly. There is virtually nothing bucolic in Eclogues VIII and IX; Quarles even forgoes the obvious metaphor of shepherd as priest. But in Eclogue I this equation is basic to the poem, pastoral and biblical motifs being closely interwoven (p. 204):

> Did not that Oracle, in times of yore,
> Threaten to send his Foxes from their Holds,
> Into our Vines? and Wolves into our Folds?

In Eclogue VI (p. 218), abuse of the Sabbath follows the common course of rustic pleasures (doubtless coloured by Mantuan II):

> The Musick of the *Oaten Reeds* perswades
> Their hearts to mirth; His wanton *Rams* grow brisk;
> His *Ewes* begin to trip, his *Lambs* to frisk;
> And whilst they sport and dance, the Love-Sick Swains
> Compose Rush-rings and Myrtleberry Chains . . .

For some dozen lines, the allusive purpose is almost lost in a simple (and here unwarranted) sense of pastoral delight. Usually, though, allegory and the pastoral imagination are skilfully combined. This, for instance, is the picture of Gustavus Adolphus's reign in Eclogue X (p. 231):

> neither Wolf, nor Fox
> Disturb the Folds of our encreasing Flocks:
> Our Kids, and sweet-fac'd Lambs can frisk, and feed
> In our fresh Pastures, whilst our Oaten Reed
> Can breath her merry strains, and voice can sing
> Her frolick Past'rals to our Shepheard-King.

The account has a further significance. It suggests Quarles's ideal for his own troubled land. The *Oracles* are said to have been delivered at a feast of Pan in Arcadia; and Arcadian 'love and peace' is desired for 'the disturbed Island of *Britannia*, and grant that each honest Shepheard may again sit under his own Vine and Fig-tree, and feed his own flock, and with love enjoy the fruits of peace, and be more thankfull' (p. 202). These words come from the prefatory epistle, composed after Quarles's death by the co-publisher, John Marriot. Whether retrospectively or not,

Marriot is attributing to the Royalist Quarles a yearning for pastoral peace in troubled times.

Other Royalist poets echo the wish. In Alexander Brome's elegy for Charles I, pastoral anarchy follows the death of 'England's Damon': 'Down scrip and sheep-hook goes, | When foxes shepherds be'.[29] So also George Lauder, lamenting the death of Drummond of Hawthornden, ascribes it to his grief at the Civil War.[30]

Peace could be sought by reviving the pastoral order in poetry. In Lovelace's 'Amarantha. a Pastorall', Alexis and Lucasta withdraw from the turmoil to a pastoral retreat. Carew, writing before the war (*c.*1632), had found such peace actually reigning in England:

> Then let the Germans feare if *Caesar* shall,
> Or the Vnited Princes, rise, and fall,
> But let us that in myrtle bowers sit
> Vnder secure shades, use the benefit
> Of peace and plenty, which the blessed hand
> Of our good King gives this obdurate Land . . .[31]

Carew's context interestingly prefigures Quarles's Eclogue X: he is writing 'In answer of an Elegiacall Letter upon the death of the King of *Sweden* from *Aurelian Townshend*'.

Such conventional pastoral merges into more literal celebrations of country life and the old rural order, of which I shall speak in Chapter 11. The Royalist use of pastoral is nostalgic, idealized, though perhaps set in satiric contrast to present times.

There can be a Puritan nostalgia as well:

> Oh Thou, that dear and happy Isle
> The Garden of the World ere while . . .[32]

But by and large, this pastoral is in a more homely, realistic, 'involved' vein of true rustic concern. There exists from Elizabethan times a collective rural loyalty among country gentlemen, as apparent when they gather in the town as when at home in the country.[33] They display a deep

[29] 'The Pastoral. On the King's Death. Written in 1643', *The Works of the English Poets*, ed. Dr Johnson, with additional lives by A. Chalmers, 21 vols. (London, 1810), vi. 652.

[30] 'Damon: or A Pastoral Elegy'. See Drummond's *Poetical Works . . . with 'A Cypresse Grove'*, ed. L. E. Kastner (Manchester, 1913), i, pp. cix–cx (ll. 35–66).

[31] For title, see text above; ll. 43–8, Carew's *Poems* ed. Rhodes Dunlap (Oxford, 1949; repr. 1970), 75.

[32] Marvell, 'Upon Appleton House', ll. 321–2.

[33] See Michael Walzer, *The Revolution of the Saints* (Cambridge, Mass., 1965), 241–7.

interest in farming and husbandry, a 'new status and businesslike endeavour'[34] in agricultural matters, increased participation as JPs, and generally a pervasive seriousness. This rural ethos is allied to a nascent political opposition as well as to strong Protestantism, culminating from the 1620s in a perceptible 'country' lobby. But the tendency is reflected in pastoral poetry at least a decade earlier.

Wither's Philarete, in *Fair Virtue*, is clearly a country gentleman (the poet) assuming a shepherd's persona:

> though I can well prove my blood to be
> Deriv'd from no ignoble stems to me
>
> . . . .
>
> If any of those virtues yet I have,
> Which honour to my predecessors gave,
> There's all that's left me.[35]

The poet in the framework of William Browne's *Britannia's Pastorals* affords a still clearer image of a conservative countryman, rooted in the soil but taking a critical interest in the court and the nation. The same ethos reigns throughout *The Shepheards Pipe*, of which I shall soon speak, and whose poets all hold strong Protestant views and connections.[36]

The ambivalent possibilities of pastoral diverge in this age to provide contrary mythologies in the great national divide. This may be a unique instance of pastoral that does not merely allegorize but organically incorporates an important social movement. Specific allusion might be absent altogether, and is at best of secondary relevance.

James Turner has given a detailed and persuasive account of the irresponsibility and irrelevance of formal pastoral in the earlier seventeenth century, and the rise of more direct treatments of country life.[37] There is no doubt that the inadequacies of stock pastoral are exposed on a considerable scale. Yet, at this very time, poets of varied politics make original use of pastoral's paradoxical power to reflect the affairs of life.

[34] Ibid. 245. See Appendix E for some account of the matter.

[35] ll. 155–6, 165–7; as in Wither's *Poetry*, selected and ed. F. Sidgwick (1902; repr. New York, 1968), ii.

[36] See Appendix D.

[37] James Turner, *The Politics of Landscape* (Oxford, 1979).

10
Drayton and his Circle: The Earlier Works

1. Idea The Shepheards Garland

THE MOST obvious distinction of Drayton's *Idea The Shepheards Garland* lies in the form. Full-fledged eclogues are rare in the 1590s, eclogue-sequences even more so. Barring Sabie's brief and obscure attempt, Drayton is the only poet of the decade to write a sequence of eclogues, like Spenser's *Calender*, on a consistent pastoral community with well-defined characters.

But though Drayton builds up his pastoral world by Spenser's methods, his purposes seem to be very different. This shows first of all in his allusive or commemorative eclogues. These include the praise of 'Beta' or Elizabeth (Eclogue III), the lament for 'Elphin' or Sidney (Eclogue IV), and the praise of 'Pandora' or the Countess of Pembroke (Eclogue VI). We should also count the praise of 'Idea' or Anne Goodere in Eclogue V. Drayton himself appears through the sequence as 'Rowland'. The *Calender* has quite as much allusion: in fact, the 'Beta' and 'Elphin' eclogues are modelled on Spenser's 'Aprill' and 'November'. What distinguishes Drayton is his treatment of the allusions.

Spenser, as we saw, casts the courtly and ecclesiastical material into a completely pastoral mould. Eliza is markedly a shepherd queen; Dido is the 'shepherds wonted solace' ('November', l. 106). Drayton comes nearest to this in Rowland's elegy for Elphin, sung by Winken. Elphin is presented as a pastoral poet-hero in the manner of Virgil's Daphnis:

> But see where *Elphin* sits in fayre Elizia,
> Feeding his flocke on yonder heavenly playne,
> Come and behold, yon lovely shepheards swayne,
>   piping his fill,
>   on yonder hill,
> Tasting sweete *Nectar*, and *Ambrosia*.[1]

[1] Eclogue IV. 138–43; all refs. to the tercentenary edn. of Drayton's *Works*, ed. J. W. Hebel with Kathleen Tillotson and Bernard H. Newdigate, 5 vols. (Oxford, 1931–41; corrected edn. 1961).

But there is a certain formal elaboration in the praise:

> Immortall mirror of all Poesie:
> the Muses treasure,
> the Graces pleasure,
> Reigning with Angels now in heaven above. (ll. 110–13)

This element is more pronounced in the apparently spontaneous lament with which Winken prefaces Rowland's song:

> Spel-charming Prophet, sooth-divining seer,
> ô heavenly musicke of the highest spheare,
> Sweet sounding trump, soule-ravishing desire,
> Thou stealer of mans heart, inchanter of the eare. (ll. 62–5)

This fulsome panegyric continues through several stanzas. Here Sidney becomes more important than Elphin: his virtues, and the poetry they inspire in Winken, are the very reverse of pastoral.

The two other commemorative pieces mark off the courtly from the pastoral still more clearly. In Eclogue III 'Beta' is placed far *above* the shepherds who adore her, a monarch and a deity:

> *Beta* long may thine Altars smoke, with yeerely sacrifice,
> And long thy sacred Temples may their Saboths solemnize . . . (ll. 115–16)

Even the 'shepheards' and 'Mayds' who worship her are clearly courtiers and court ladies. The setting grows accordingly artificial and half-symbolic:

> Wee'l straw the shore with pearle where *Beta* walks alone,
> And we wil pave her princely Bower with richest Indian stone,
> Perfume the ayre and make it sweete,
> For such a Goddesse it is meete . . . (ll. 103–6)

A stanza on flowers, straight out of Spenser's 'Aprill', seems incongruous in such a context. Perkin and Rowland's closing dialogue still presents Beta as 'The shepheards Goddesse', akin to Virgil's Augustus rather than Spenser's Eliza. We may contrast the easy two-way rapport between Eliza and her 'daintie Damsells': 'Let dame *Eliza* thanke you for her song' ('Aprill', l. 150).

Spenser's rare achievement is to make pastoral convention a genuinely governing and transforming factor in royal panegyric as in other allusions. Royal matters find expression only as they adapt themselves to the pastoral mode. In Drayton's *Garland*, pastoral loses this easy primacy. It must adapt or even deny itself when courtly matters are introduced. The independence of the pastoral world is gone: it is no longer supreme even within the limits of its own convention.

The same is true of the praise of Idea and Pandora. The praise of Idea in Eclogue V is highly sophisticated, almost aureate:

> Oh hie inthronized *Jove*, in thy *Olympicke* raigne,
> Oh battel-waging Marte, oh sage-saw'd *Mercury* . . .
>
> Moyst-humord *Cinthya*, Author of Lunacie,
> Conjoyne helpe to erect our fair *Ideas* trophie. (ll. 71–2, 75–6)

Idea is far removed from Spenser's 'Widdowes daughter of the glenne' ('Aprill', l. 26). Here again, the pastoral in Drayton's last two stanzas appears incongruous. The praise of Pandora in Eclogue VI has only one pastoral reference:

> When hils shall heare no more our shepheards tales,
> Nor ecchoes with our Roundelayes shall ring . . . (ll. 135–6)

Earlier we have a Parnassus-setting with shepherds (ll. 73–4), but this is only a symbol for the Countess's life and spirit. Neither mistress nor patron can be truly pastoralized. The pastoral has definite limits matching those of the shepherd's rank in society. Exceptional virtue or exceptional rank demands that these limits be exceeded.

This also leads to a more important deviation from the spirit of Spenser's *Calender*: the *Garland* is almost fundamentally moral and didactic. This shows first of all in the treatment of Rowland's love. Though Idea is the 'Purest of purest' (Eclogue V. 109), Rowland's love for her is seen by himself and others as sheer folly. This is partly because she will not return his love; it is therefore mere hopeless infatuation.

> She sees not shepheard, no she will not see,
> Her rarest vertues blazond by thy quill . . . (ll. 167–8)

But beyond this, love is presented as fundamentally evil, a moral aberration. For old Winken, in Eclogue II, the lover's hell provides a cautionary tale: 'So may they be which can so lewdly faine' (l. 97). Borrill in Eclogue VII takes up an even more purely moral stand, though there, as I shall later show, the effect is rather different.

Interestingly, in Eclogue II Winken uses lines that echo Spenser's Piers ('October', ll. 91 ff.) to oppose Motto's praise of love:

> Oh divine love, which so aloft canst raise,
> And lift the minde out of this earthly mire . . . (ll. 82–3)

There too, Cuddie had opposed Piers, but by citing the emotional demands of 'Tyranne' love rather than its moral evil. Spenser presents Colin's love as much as an emotional experience as a moral one. Rowland's love in Eclogue I is more clearly conceived as sinful, creating a sense of guilt and repentance:

> Submission makes amends for all my misse,
> Contrition a refined life begins . . . (ll. 49–50)

In fact, this eclogue is not concerned with love but with a general sense of sin and penitence in orthodox religious terms, Pan standing for the Christian God:

> Thus time, beleefe, death, Justice, shall surcease,
> By date, assurance, eternity, and peace. (ll. 71–2)

In Eclogue IX, indeed, Rowland is afflicted solely by the pains of scorned love. Spenser had worked a more subtle Petrarchan balance between the pleasures and pains of love, and its equivalent effects on poetic composition. Drayton does not relate Rowland's poetry to his love. His is a world of more simple values, and, accordingly, of more clear-cut and extended didacticism.

There is other didactic material as well. The *Garland* discusses the conflict and relative value of the gifts of Nature and Fortune. It is introduced in Eclogue V. 11–12, and taken up *in extenso* in the first half of Eclogue VI:

> Vertue and Fortune never could agree . . .
> They fall which trust to fortunes fickle wheele,
> But staied by vertue, men shall never reele. (ll. 31, 35–6)

Several other themes follow from this. In Eclogue VI, Perkin revives the old eclogue-debate on providential justice: 'why should she [Virtue] not be more regarded, | Why should men cherish vice and villanie' (ll. 37–8). Gorbo appears to agree, and this leads on to a more basic matter:

> Where been those Nobles, *Perkin*, where been they?
> Where been those worthies, *Perkin*, which of yore,
> This gentle Ladie did so much adore? (ll. 43–6)

Drayton is invoking an ideal of ancient virtue, lost in the present degenerate age. He echoes Spenser's 'October'; Spenser was echoing Mantuan, and the theme goes back to Theocritus XVI. In Drayton, however, the past is not an abstract concept but a recent and specific ideal. Virtue, otherwise dead, is still alive in Pandora, the Countess of Pembroke. Two poems earlier, Drayton had mourned the death of Sidney. We may already discern the outlines of a moral traditionalism allied to the cult of Sir Philip Sidney. I have noted in Appendix C how this cult was a powerful impulse behind the pastoral of the 1590s. In the lyric poets it remained largely a literary ideal, in a vein of pastoral very different from Sidney's own. In Drayton it becomes a social and moral ideal.

Although the figure of Elphin is imperfectly pastoralized, he is honoured among shepherds and himself becomes the founding shepherd-poet of the tradition: 'Of Pastorall, the lively springing sappe' (Eclogue IV. 60). But this is in a double sense: as actual pastoral poet, and as exemplar of the virtue that Drayton finds imaged in the pastoral ideal. In the other eclogues, this is related to a much broader ideal of traditional virtue.

For this, let us go back to Motto's words in Eclogue V:

> To Fortunes Orphanes Nature hath bequeath'd,
> That mighty Monarchs seldome have possest . . . (ll. 11–12)

'Fortunes Orphanes' are poets of the old school: 'a grayne, | Of the olde stocke of famous poesie' (ll. 3–5). They are not distracted by the search for tawdry wealth and fame,

> the troupes of paynted Imagerie,
> Nor these worlds Idols, our worlds Idiots gazes (ll. 16–17)

but pursue the old ideal of 'honour' and 'True valeur', which 'lodgeth in the lowlest harts' (ll. 21, 28). Traditional poetic values are related to ethical values, and these to the humility and stoic content of pastoral life. Pastoral becomes the truest or purest poetry by its ability to convey this conservative, even nostalgic moral ideal. The 'lowly pastoral' becomes a positive expression of the virtuous will:

> Worlds fawning fraud, nor like deceitfull guiles,
> No, no, my muse, none such shall sojourne here,
>
> Ambitious thoughts to clime nor feares to fall,
> A minde voyde of mistrust, and free from servile thral. (ll. 38–9, 44–5)

This does not preclude shepherd-poets from reaching the loftiest plane of thought, as in Elphin's songs (Eclogue IV. 59–60) or Rowland's own praise of Idea (Eclogue V. 175).

These themes recur even more clearly in Eclogue VIII. In an opening reminiscent of Spenser's 'Maye' (though the context is quite different) Motto describes the strutting 'yonkers' who 'rave it out in rime' while he and Gorbo 'creepe . . . in this lowly vaine' (ll. 1–8). The next stanza clearly alludes to the new poetry of the age:

> Those mirtle Groves decay'd, done growe againe,
> their rootes refresht with *Heliconas* spring,
> Whose pleasant shade invites the homely swayne,
> to sit him downe and heare the Muses sing. (ll. 9–12)

Gorbo's reply is involved, obscure, and in parts illogical. He begins in the typical vein of pastoral humility:

> But this hie object hath abjected me,
> and I must pipe amongst the lowly sorte . . . (ll. 21–2)

But what follows is more complex. After mentioning a number of the ancient worthies whom he is unfit to celebrate, he associates them with the Golden Age. But then, by a *non sequitur*, brave deeds and their fame-crazy chroniclers are condemned as degenerate:

> The Infant age could deftly caroll love,
> till greedy thirst of that ambitious honor,
> Drew Poets pen, from his sweete lasses glove,
> to chaunt of slaughtering broiles & bloody horror. (ll. 65–8)

Innocent love now becomes the prime feature of the Golden Age:

> Then simple love with simple vertue way'd,
> flowers the favours which true fayth revayled,
> Kindnes with kindnes was againe repay'd,
> with sweetest kisses covenants were sealed. (ll. 77–80)

The contrast with Rowland's love is obvious. Explicit condemnation comes from the old shepherds Winken in Eclogue II and Borrill in Eclogue VII, who play precisely the same role as Gorbo in Eclogue VIII.

This also highlights the debates between young and old shepherds. Drayton takes Spenser's sole example in 'Februarie' and extends it into a leading motif. In Eclogue VII, Batte scoffs at Borrill much as Spenser's Cuddie did at Thenot; Motto in Eclogues II and VIII is more reverent towards Winken and Gorbo. But, in all three pieces, an aged shepherd praises the traditional virtues and laments the degeneration of present times. The contrast of young and old lends special point to Drayton's nostalgic ideal. We may also place here the dialogue between two old men, Winken and Gorbo, in Eclogue IV, lamenting the death of Elphin, who represented this ideal. In Eclogue VI, Gorbo again mourns for the dead worthies: it is left to Perkin to tell how virtue survives in the Countess of Pembroke.

Drayton fully accepts the moral primitivism of pastoral. It becomes the vehicle of an ethical, and to some extent historical, ideal. In other words, he gives unusually organic embodiment in pastoral form to the standard tradition of the didactic eclogue. We have seen how important this is in continental theory and practice. We have also seen how common English practice departs radically from this model. But, as in the better-known case of Elizabethan drama, what there is of English theory reflects continental classicism. Puttenham postulates an allusive and a didactic eclogue, but no other. Webbe also says that the eclogue deals with weighty matters, allowing praise without flattery and censure without bitterness. He praises Spenser for following these ends, combing the *Calender* for 'Many good Morrall lessons' not only from the moral eclogues but even from 'Iune', which shows 'the dissolute life of young men, intangled in loue of women'.[2]

Earlier still, E. K. emphasizes Spenser's moral and didactic concerns. In his 'generall argument' to *The Shepheardes Calender*, he divides the eclogues into plaintive, recreative, and moral. But the love-plaints are interpreted in a moralizing spirit, and the 'recreative' eclogues 'conceiue matter of loue, or commendation of special personages'. Ultimately *all* the eclogues are seen to be moral—and, except for 'August', are described in such terms in their separate 'Arguments'.

It is this model of the *Calender*, interpreted in a consistently moral and didactic spirit unlike Spenser's own, that Drayton imitates in the *Garland* and retains in the older and more substantial stratum of the 1606 *Pastorals*. He even repeats this view in the Preface to the Reader appended to the latter in 1619. Commonplace in itself, the Preface is important in determining the light in which Drayton saw his work. Though pastoral uses language 'of the coursest Woofe', says Drayton, 'the most High, and most Noble Matters of the World may bee shaddowed in them'. His own work goes further: '*detracto velamine*, he speakes of most weightie things'. So far, all is clear. But in between comes a most curious overstatement: these 'weightie' themes mean that Drayton 'hath almost nothing Pastorall in his Pastorals, but the name' (*Works*, ii. 517). I can only explain this by the fact that (as we shall see in

[2] *A Discourse of English Poetrie*, Gregory Smith (ed.), *Elizabethan Critical Essays*, i. 262, ll. 29–33, pp. 263–5.

the next section) Drayton was turning by 1619 to a more lyrical, more remote pastoral. By contrast, the earlier eclogues must have appeared all the more didactic, a departure from what in 1619 was seen by him as the true nature of the pastoral.

The signs of these new developments may already be detected in 1593, chiefly in one or two 'inset' lyrics. When Spenser's shepherds sang or told stories, these were substantial pieces taking up the major part of the eclogue. This is often the case in the *Garland* as well, notably in the songs for Beta, Idea, and Pandora. But already in the lament for Elphin, the poem has grown shorter: less than half the total length, and written in a lighter and more varied stanza-form than Winken's apparently spontaneous lament that precedes it. The four songs in Eclogues II and VII are all brief lyrics on love. Within the comprehensive form of the eclogue, Drayton is acknowledging the lyric model that reigns in the pastoral of the age.

He also makes some concession to the dominant spirit of this pastoral. The songs in Eclogue II are arranged to make a moral point, the praise of love succeeded by a frustrated lament. In Eclogue VII, however, Borrill first condemns love in crabbed verse; Batte replies with a much more graceful lyric praising love, and he also has the last word in the final exchange. Interpretations based purely on stylistic features run the risk of subjective judgement, and the simple chance of uneven writing on the poet's part. But here the difference is so marked,[3] and further supported by the verse-forms and order of occurrence, that it does seem that Drayton is inducing a suspension of judgement. Certainly we cannot conclude from this eclogue that love is wholly evil. The witty Batte is clearly the dominant speaker, and makes Borrill appear an inept Polonius rather than a 'wise shepherd' like Winken or Gorbo.

Thus Eclogue VII points the way to a clearly amoral celebration of love, the ballad of Dowsabell in Eclogue VIII. 'In this poem Drayton first discovers his happiest pastoral manner', writes Kathleen Tillotson,[4] and goes on to note its occurrence in the 1606 Daffodil Song and *The Muses Elizium*. I shall attempt to define this manner in a little more detail.

A subsidiary source of pleasure in 'Dowsabell' lies in the story itself: the popular appeal of any tale where a shepherd wins an aristocratic maiden. But beyond this we take delight in the method of narration and the spirit of the love expressed through it. It is a happy, inconsequential

[3] I should point out, however, that R. L. Heffner, jun., considers Batte's song to be 'woodenly constructed': 'Michael Drayton as Pastoral Poet' (D.Phil. Yale, 1953), 54.

[4] Drayton's *Works*, v. 12, col. 1. Cf. Grundy, *The Spenserian Poets*, p. 96.

love, expressed with complete spontaneity on both sides. Dowsabell runs out to the shepherd with whom she has fallen in love; he declares his love for her with easy candour. In fact, this is like love in the Golden Age, as described by Gorbo earlier in Eclogue VIII:

> Kindnes with kindnes was againe repay'd,
> with sweetest kisses covenants were sealed. (ll. 79–80)

There is no impediment laid by shyness, distrust, or social difference: we are in a truly egalitarian world where the shepherd is the unquestioned equal of the knight's daughter. The moral balance of court and country that we find in more self-conscious pastoral is replaced by a total absence of barriers.

Allied to this is the easy idealizing of Dowsabell and her shepherd in looks, accomplishments, and gaiety of spirit. The ease is more remarkable than the idealizing itself: the poem seems to take such perfection for granted. The use of the *Sir Thopas* stanza, with its facile rhymes and loose phrasing ('a mayden fayre and free', 'a frock of frolicke greene'), guided by alliterative whimsy as much as sense, has sometimes been taken to indicate satire or burlesque.[5] To me it seems simply to ensure that there is no sense of strain or over-seriousness. It is all easy, natural, and flawless, a world where happy shepherds love without hindrance, in a state of innocence that scarcely admits the possibility of any obstacles.

This is the spirit that lies at the core of the Elizabethan pastoral lyric. Here, for once, Drayton surrenders to the dominant spirit of contemporary pastoral. Obviously, the *Garland* as a whole has a very different purpose. The shepherds in the lyrics live in a carefree present of innocent hedonism; Drayton's other shepherds look back to the past and moralize upon a complex and even threatening present. They belong to the didactic and allusive pastoral, whereas the lyrics present a different, independent world, a genuinely alternative mode of being. I have earlier tried to show how, despite its allusive elements, *The Shepheardes Calender* rehabilitates this latter vein of pastoral. It appears, then, that *The Shepheards Garland*, for all its imitation of the *Calender*, actually points away from its most notable innovations; while the contemporary lyric, formally so different and even disruptive, preserves its spirit in a notable body of art-pastoral, quite contrary to the general direction of European Renaissance pastoral.

This indicates a feature that we shall find all through Drayton's

[5] See Heffner, pp. 79ff. Tillotson, more cautiously, speaks of a 'burlesque-realistic strain' interacting with other elements: Drayton's *Works*, v. 12, col. 1.

varying, evolving pastoral modes. Commonly taken to embody the quintessence of Elizabethan pastoral, he actually stands contrary to its course at many points. His pastorals follow a unique, deeply personal line of progress. In fact, he uses them to react against the times as represented by other pastoralists including his close associates. As times and fashions change, so does his pastoral, but in this inverse or reactionary manner. His next group of eclogues show a marked advance in the lyrical, undidactic, art-pastoral vein.

2. *Drayton's 1606 Pastorals*, Poly-Olbion

In 1606 Drayton published a radically revised version of *The Shepheards Garland* in his *Poemes Lyrick and pastorall*, adding a new eclogue. These were reprinted in the 1619 *Poems*. According to Heffner, the chief purpose of the revisions (other than stylistic) is 'increased autobiographical and topical allegory' (p. 90). Eclogues I and X (earlier IX) become more specific laments for Drayton's frustrated poetic career. This is echoed in Winken's apostrophe to Rowland in Eclogue VI and the vehement attack on 'Selena' and 'Olcon' in Eclogue VIII. (That on 'Selena', the Countess of Bedford, was removed in 1619; that on 'Olcon', James I, remained.) The lament for Sidney (Eclogue VI, earlier IV) turns into sharp satire of the times. There is also more praise: the eulogy of 'Pandora' is extended to the Goodere sisters (daughters of Drayton's patron Sir Henry Goodere), Elizabeth Beaumont, and an unidentified 'Sylvia' (Eclogue VIII, formerly VI).

It seems necessary to stress some very different innovations in the 1606 *Eglogs*. Eclogue II illustrates them well. In the *Garland*, this poem had pointed to a clear condemnation of love. In 1606 it retains the sense of *memento mori*, though some striking lines are removed. But the two songs are replaced by significantly new ones.

The first of these marks an improvement in quality rather than any change of intention. Instead of a 'crude catalogue'[6] of Idea's moral virtues, there is a memorable cosmic image related to her beauty. The change in the second song goes further. In 1593 we had the simple lament of a scorned shepherd-lover. In 1606 Cupid himself lies wounded by the beloved's scorn of Rowland:

> Vppon a bank with roses set about
> where pretty turtles ioyning bil to bill,

[6] Tillotson's phrase: Drayton's *Works*, v. 184, col. 2.

> and gentle springs steale softly murmuring out
> washing the foote of pleasures sacred hill:
> there little loue sore wounded lyes,
> his bowe and arrowes broken
> bedewd with teares from Venus eyes
> oh greeuous to be spoken.[7]

He proceeds to write his last will and testament.

This is obviously not a simple lament. The conceit of Cupid suggests conscious poetic ingenuity and even delight, exceeding the pain of the ostensible theme. It is almost a wooing-poem, intended to please the mistress and win her over rather than mourn an irrevocable rejection. The 1593 lament had mentioned 'loves Religion' with complete seriousness; now it becomes part of the conceit (sig. D 3^{r-v}):

> His chappell be a mournefull Cypresse shade
> and for a chauntry Philomels sweet lay
> where prayers shall continually be made
> By pilgrim louers passing by that way. (ll. 121–4)

As Tillotson points out, the phrase 'loves Idolatrie' is now omitted.[8] Though the first song uses celestial imagery, even talking of 'The Host of Heavenly Beauties', it avoids anything as direct and extreme as the corresponding assertion in 1593:

> Yea she alone, next that eternall he,
> The expresse Image of eternitie. (ll. 80–1)

Most tellingly, 1606 omits the last four lines of 1593, where Winken categorically dismisses love and Motto agrees. Instead we have the much more qualified warning that 'Beauty and wealth been fraught with hy disdayn' (sig. D 3^{v}, l. 135).

All in all, there is much less moral condemnation of love. It becomes more—though not fully—an attractive, amoral experience. Eclogue IX of 1593 (now Eclogue X) is turned from a love-lament into a complaint against ill-fortune and neglect. The reference to Idea's scorn in Eclogue V. 167ff. in 1593 is now removed. Eclogue VII is a more uncertain case. As we saw above, this was already a less moral poem in

[7] Sig. D 3^{r}, ll. 105–12; as Hebel uses the 1619 edn. as his copy-text, I have quoted the 1606 *Eglogs* from *Poemes Lyrick and pastorall* (London, [1606]): refs. to the signatures of this edn. followed by line-refs. to Hebel.

[8] *Works*, v. 184, col. 2. The phrase occurred in Eclogue II. 69 of 1593.

1593: in fact, it acquires a more moral ending in 1606. Earlier, Batte had boasted

> But I will watch the next time thou doost ward,
> And sing thee such a lay of love as never shepheard heard. (ll. 203–4)

He now admits (sig. F6[v]):

> vppon thy Judgment much I shall rely,
> because *I* finde such Wisdome in thy words . . . (ll. 209–10)

This comes incongruously after 'Away old fool . . .' Perhaps Batte is being ironic; but his new song contains an entirely serious Platonic defence of love, making up in weight what it loses in lyric grace (sig. F6[r]):

> whose hie virtue number teaches
> in which euery thing dooth mooue,
> from the lowest depth that reaches
> to the height of heauen aboue: . . . (ll. 181–4)

This echoes Rowland's first song sung by Winken in the new Eclogue II. The 1606 *Eglogs* present love from two favourable aspects: a simple lyric grace and, at a more complex level, an elevating Platonic force. This is clearest in the three songs set in Eclogue IX, describing the Cotswold pastorals. This poem had no counterpart in 1593.

The first, the Daffodil Song, is at the light, inconsequentially pleasing end of the spectrum. It does not elaborate on the nature of love; this would have been quite inappropriate, as the song relies for its effect on its totally unstudied quality. The naïve pleasure in the confusion between the flower and the maiden named Daffodil indicates a special innocence. Such pastoral is not merely set in a different world; it embodies a different mode of response and communication. Its substance is partly Petrarchan, partly drawn from the celebratory love-eclogue and epithalamium:

> Whose presence as she went along,
> The prety flowers did greet,
> As though their heads they downward bent,
> With homage to her feete.
>
> And all the shepheards that were nie,
> From toppe of euery hill,
> Vnto the vallies lowe did crie,
> There goes sweet *Daffadill*. (sig. G4[v], ll. 121–8)

Objectively considered, this is an elaborate pageant. But the artless lucidity of tone makes it a simple, unplanned, *natural* reaction on the part of both flowers and men. Setting and human life are unselfconsciously blended. The girl Daffodil is made very like the flower to flatter the shepherds' simple delight.

The next song, between Motto and Perkin, turns on more elaborate images and hyperboles. Sylvia endows the flowers with their colours and perfume, and preserves them in eternal spring; the flocks leave their grazing to draw nourishment from her sight, and the streams pause to hear her voice. Such hyperboles preclude the innocent abandon of the Daffodil Song. Instead they suggest a miraculous presence, an extraordinary power emanating from the object of love if not from love itself. This power is closely linked to the pastoral setting, the only proposed and apparently only possible setting for such a presence. Indeed, all three songs in this eclogue have a vivid pastoral setting, unlike the songs in Eclogues II and VII.

In the third song, Rowland invests Idea with a clearly moral innocence. Her dove's collar reads 'Only like me, my mistris hath no gaule' (sig. G5^{v}, l. 188). Idea, like Sylvia in the second song, is the shepherds' queen; like Sylvia, she outshines the sun (also, later, the moon) and prolongs the spring. With this, however, goes a grander vein of conceit where Jove sounds her praises. Finally the two lines of imagery are combined by installing Idea as the 'shepheards starre', 'Aboue where heauens hie glorious are' (sig. G6^{r}, ll. 229–31). Hence this song too reaches the pitch of the praise of Idea in Eclogue II, or Batte's praise of love in Eclogue VII.

In other words, the unhappy or evil aspects of love are reduced in 1606 to treatment in just two songs, by Winken (Eclogue II) and Borrill (Eclogue VII), and even these are balanced by songs in praise of love. The moral concerns of the *Garland* are countered by two new aspects of love, both positive: a spontaneous, amoral joy and a higher idealism. The two veins remain stylistically separate; they merge only in Drayton's last pastorals. But it is important to note their simultaneous presence at this point.

With this goes a changed conception of poetry. In the *Garland* the shepherds were already conscious poets; the nature of their songs changes in 1606. The *Garland* had two debate-eclogues but no light-hearted singing games. The new Eclogue IX fills this gap. The theme of its three songs is happy love; the motive is communal poetic enjoyment of

> The easie turnes and queyntnes of the song,
> And slight occasion whereupon t'was raysed . . . (sig. G4^v, ll. 133–4)

Valuing a song because of its 'slight occasion' is a notable new development. Other small but telling changes suggest a new pastoral aesthetic. In the *Garland* Motto 'Joy'd my lovely feeres, | Chanting sweete straines of heavenly pastorall' (Eclogue II. 3–4). In 1606 the last line becomes 'when to their sports they pleased mee to call' (sig. D1^r: Eclogue II. 4). In Eclogue V of 1593, Motto had asked Rowland to sing

> if the prayse of worthy pastorall,
> May tempt thee now, or moove thee once at all. (ll. 9–10)

In 1606 he hopes that

> the delight of simple pastorall,
> May thee reuiue, whom care seems to apall. (sig. E3^v, ll. 9–10)

In Eclogue VI (Eclogue IV in 1593) there is a new brief image of a happy shepherd world: 'Merry was it when we those toys might tell . . .' (sig. E8^r, l. 42). This happiness is shattered by Elphin's death; but the idea remains, and in the new Eclogue IV (corresponding to the old Eclogue VIII) Motto identifies himself rather more with the 'singing shepherds' of the Renaissance:

> not as twas wont now rurall be our rymes
> Sheapheards of late are waxed wondrous neate.
> though they were richer in the former tymes,
> we be inraged with more kindly heate . . . (sig. D7^r, ll. 5–8)

Also, Gorbo is made Motto's equal in years; in the *Garland* he was an old man who addressed Motto as 'my boy'. This slightly mitigates the didactic tone.

By a parallel process, the rhetoric of the old Eclogue IV is scaled down in the new Eclogue VI, which corresponds to it. Winken's former hyperbolic, non-pastoral lament for Sidney, and Rowland's pastoral but formal elegy, are jointly replaced by a more informal lament in a simpler pastoral vein. Even the hyperboles are relatively artless bucolic ones:

> And for his sake the early wanton lambs,
> That mongst the hillocks wont to skip and play,
> Sadly runne bleating from their carefull dams
> Nor will theire soft lips to the vdders lay. (sigs. E8^v–F1^r, ll. 81–4)

Topical allusions emerge from an uncomplicated pastoral background:

The closing euening ginning to be dark,
When as the small birds sing the Sun to sleepe,
You fould your lambs: or with the early Larke
Vnto the fayre fields driue your harmlesse sheep . . . (sig. F2r, ll. 153–6)

Yet in the last analysis, these innovations fail to fulfil their potential. Far too much remains of the old themes and conventions. There is no total redirection of purpose, only the sporadic appearance of new elements modifying the old ones or lying in uneasy tandem.

Eclogue IX therefore deserves special attention, as it had no counterpart in 1593. We would expect Drayton's new intentions to emerge most clearly in this poem. As we have seen, this proves true of the inset songs. The 'framework', with its account of the Cotswold shearing-feast, is in a different though equally novel vein of specific, localized nostalgia.

Although so highly idealized, the account of the feast has a certain documentary quality. It enumerates the details of a 'folk' festival sentimentally conceived as such. That this self-conscious 'folk' element does not turn oppressive is partly owing to Drayton's lightness of touch: the details are never too esoteric, the relatively unfamiliar ones never crowded too close. The shepherds prove to be the familiar Batte, Gorbo, Motto, and the rest. Their concerns are quite different from the moral ones expressed elsewhere, but their very presence lends a substantiality to the scene, making the shearing-feast part of the wider pastoral life built up through the sequence of eclogues.

At the same time, the nature of the songs, the Daffodil Song in particular, transfers the entire setting to the plane of pure art-pastoral. We no longer risk the embarrassment of being asked to admire simultaneously the 'reality' of the scene and its soothing departure from reality as we know it. Authenticity of detail does not always strengthen the basis of idyllic pastoral. What is welcome as pure imagination becomes unacceptable as the distortion or dressing-up of reality. The strength of Drayton's pastoral imagination and the unfaltering delicacy of his lyric form enable him to avoid this risk: the 'real' details are drawn into a self-contained pastoral world.

In creating this world of singing lover-shepherds, and epitomizing its nature in the songs he puts on their lips, Drayton is obviously adopting the aesthetic of the Elizabethan pastoral lyric, which he had so largely eschewed in 1593. The change seems to have come about in the heyday of such lyrics in the 1590s: the first two songs from Eclogue IX appear in *England's Helicon*, as does 'Upon a Banke . . .' from the new Eclogue II and another idyllic lyric never reprinted, '*Rowlands* Madrigall' (*Helicon*, no. 74). For a rare moment, Drayton is in harmony with the pastoral of the age.

But his new work does not appear in volume form till 1606 and, as I have said, it is ambiguous in tone. Or to put it more correctly, Drayton turns the new lyric impulse to serve his abiding seriousness of purpose. The Cotswold Eclogue (no. IX) is his most sustained piece of art-pastoral among these eclogues. But even here, the moral implications are made plain:

> In cotes such simples simply in request,
> Wherewith proude courts in greatnes scorn to mel
> For country toyes become the cuntry best,
> and please poor shepheards and becom them wel . . . (sig. G2ᵛ, ll. 25–8)

The implicit superiority of this humble life is very clear. It is, of course, considerably clearer from the happy spirit of the eclogue as a whole. The withdrawn, unreflective amorality of this pastoral carries its own moral charge.

As we saw, this is implicit in all Elizabethan pastoral lyrics. In Drayton's more sustained, and sustainedly serious, pastoral, it comes continually to the surface. The Ballad of Dowsabell was related in theme to the preceding account of the Golden Age and present decadence. In *The Shepheards Sirena*, a delicate song bridges two passages of cogitation, satire, and probable allegory. *The Quest of Cynthia* is escape as well as quest: 'Here from the hatefull world wee'll live . . .' (l. 173). *The Muses Elizium* marks the climax of this remarkable duality of moral involvement and imaginative withdrawal, the former leading to the latter. I shall treat these poems in Chapter 20.

In *Poly-Olbion* the paradox achieves its most unusual form. Except for the historical characters on a different plane altogether, the landscape of *Poly-Olbion* is curiously depopulated. A cumulative account like Alice d'Haussy's gives a misleading impression of a plentiful supply of rustics.[9] There are a few very brief allusions to happy rural societies in Somerset, Oxfordshire, and Lincolnshire,[10] and a pastoral vignette of Newmarket Heath (XXI. 35). Skiddaw has its 'poore Shepheards Pipes, and harmlesse Heardsmans tales' (XXX. 226). The account of Lancashire festivities (XXVII. 248ff.) is a little more detailed; but the only scene that stands out from Drayton's surprising neglect of popular

[9] *Poly-Olbion ou l'Angleterre vue par un Élisabéthain* (Paris, 1972), 154ff.

[10] III. 5–10, XV. 214, and XXV. 262 respectively.

customs and festivals is the Cotswold shearing-feast in XIV. 265–78. It is also unusual in being illustrated on a map: nearly all the other figures on the maps stand for personified geographical features, though often depicted as rustics in a very realistic manner.

Here, then, is a carry-over of the new concerns of the 1606 Eclogues into *Poly-Olbion*. But shearing and shearing-supper together get only fourteen lines. Drayton's basic mode in *Poly-Olbion* is not the simple pastoralism that centres on a rustic community, real or imaginary. Instead, he personifies the geographical features, makes myths out of them to interact with his account of human history in an intricate pattern of contrast and connection. A grand and original variant of the pastoral ideal is attributed to the pristine landscape: human life represents a decline.

One curious feature is a landscape with flocks but no herdsmen. In Wales, the Oreades tend the flocks, though '*Cambrian* Shepheards' are briefly mentioned (IX. 71–96). In the forests of Skiddaw, the animals, while not ownerless, look after themselves: 'Which there their owners know, but no man hath to keepe' (XXX. 247). Thus specifically pastoral settings share in the independent life with which all nature is endowed.

As R. F. Hardin has noted,[11] *Poly-Olbion* seems to have been written with a double purpose, historical and geographical. The former demands the celebration of human settlement and progress; the latter finds the spirit of the land to be embodied in nature, with human activity as a degenerate force. The praise of London as a rich port leads directly to censure of the 'idle Gentry' (XVI. 342). The destruction of 'Andreds-weald' is linked not only to the Danish invasion but the ensuing agriculture and industry: this prosperity constitutes an implicit fall (XVIII. 61 ff.). In a superficially anti-pastoral passage, the reduction of Canke Forest to pastureland becomes the shameful adoption of a 'Neatheards life' (XII. 529). But the deeper purpose of such passages is allied to the pastoral, and emerges in lines like these from Song XIX:

> Fooles gaze at painted Courts, to th' countrey let me goe,
> To climbe the easie hill, then walke, the valley lowe;
> No gold-embossed Roofes, to me are like the woods;
> No Bed like to the grasse, nor liquor like the floods:
> A Citie's but a sinke, gay houses gawdy graves,
> The Muses have free leave, to starve or live in caves: . . . (ll. 21–6)

[11] 'The Composition of *Poly-Olbion* and *The Muses Elizium*', *Anglia* 86 (1968), 160–2.

The general intent of *Poly-Olbion* is what we may call trans-pastoral. Orthodox pastoral embodies its nostalgic ideals in the lives of shepherds. Drayton moves back to the landscape itself, mythologized to yield an even grander and more fundamental primitivism. He looks back beyond history to the primeval past when the mountains were young and nature unpeopled.[12] From this vantage-point of elemental wisdom, the mountains and rivers recite the course of human history—sometimes with apparent pride, sometimes with regret and indignation. They know all and see all: human beings play their parts before these recording presences.

The sylvan gods of common pastoral are here most often identified with the features of the landscape. The woods themselves are seen as dryads, rivers as nymphs, mountains as giants. They take their place alongside the classical gods: Diana, Apollo, above all Neptune. But, very significantly, they may also be common rustics. Sometimes we cannot tell: the 'neat *Lancastrian* Nymphes' (XXVII. 21–4) curiously combine the natures of water-deities and country girls. But the River Cunno is unambiguously a 'lustie *Cambrian* Lasse' (IV. 160). Clent is a shepherd (XIV, 'Argument', l. 3), and the islands of Sheppey and Canvey shepherdesses (XVIII. 765 ff., XIX. 12).

This occasional feature of the text becomes a consistent principle behind the maps prefacing each song. As I have said, they depict no rustic scenes worth mentioning except the Cotswold shearing-feast. Briefer pictures sometimes appear: harvesting (Maps 2, 14), picking flowers and weaving chaplets (7, 10), grazing animals (12, 13, 24), hunting (17). Except for one harvest-scene (14) and the hunting-scene, each vignette contains a single figure: is this a representative rustic or the personification of the place itself?

In most cases it is clearly the latter. Many hills and mountains are obviously shepherds (from their crooks), the rest presumably so. There are a few touches of puckish humour: Marcely Hill is tumbling off his perch (7) and Wrekin balances his hat upon his crook (12). Several other features are presented as shepherdesses, generally no doubt becase they are famous for their sheep: Cankwood, Moreland, Romney Marsh, the 'full-flocked *Oulds*' of Leicestershire (XXVI. 38) and the Yorkshire Wold—also others, including Salisbury Plain (12, 12, 18, 26, 28, 3, respectively).

Most interesting are the forests. Some in the earlier maps of Part I are

[12] e.g. in XII. 541, XVI. 86, XVIII. 62, 711, XXII. 47.

obviously dryads, with trees sprouting from their heads; but one or two carry a bow, and are huntresses as well.[13] By far the greatest number are huntresses pure and simple; by the end of Part I, they have lost their classical attire and become becapped figures dressed in more contemporary style.

The maps confirm that the rustic spirit of normal pastoral is here embedded in the landscape and aggrandized as myth. Many of Drayton's settings are explicitly compared to Eden or some classical paradise: the hill and forest of Cowdra, the Vale of Monmouth, the Vale of Evesham, the gardens of Kent, and Gisborough.[14] The last with its eternal summer may stand as typical:

> . . . *Gisboroughs* gay Scite, where Nature seemes so nice,
> As in the same shee makes a second Paradice,
> Whose Soyle imbroydered is, with so rare sundry Flowers,
> Her large Okes so long greene, as Summer there her Bowers,
> Had set up all the yeare, her ayre for health refin'd . . .
>
> (XXVIII. 339–43)

Some of these places are obviously populated, the valleys and gardens in particular. But Drayton makes the paradisal quality adhere to the landscape itself. These passages therefore provide a virtual obverse to the many laments for the destruction of the landscape, usually a forest, which have often been remarked upon.[15] I shall confine myself to two or three instances where the lament is specially combined with satire of the times.

The first is the lament of the dispossessed sylvans of the 'Andredsweald' or Anderida: 'These yron times breed none, that minde posteritie' (XVII. 396). In Part II the theme is taken up still more strongly. In Song XIX Waltham Forest tells Hatfield Forest:

> Gainst Lunatiks, and fooles, what wise folke spend their force;
> For folly headlong falls, when it hath had the course:
> And when God gives men up, to wayes abhor'd and vile,
> Of understanding hee depriveds them quite, the while
> They into errour runne, confounded in their sinne . . . (ll. 51–5)

[13] e.g. New Forest (2), Cardith Forest (5).

[14] V. 221 ff., VII. 205 ff., XIV. 169, XVIII. 671, XXVIII. 339ff. respectively.

[15] e.g. in Heffner, ch. vi; J. A. Berthelot, *Michael Drayton* (New York, 1967), 96ff.; R. F. Hardin, *Michael Drayton and the Passing of Elizabethan England* (Laurence, Kan., 1973), 98.

The destruction of forests becomes, as it were, a prototype of the Fall of Man.

Such long passages of satire make up the bulk of the contemporary references in the poem. By contrast, the landscape with its sylvan population is linked to the Golden Age. As in Drayton's orthodox pastorals, the poem puts forward a traditional, indeed nostalgic ideal.

Two passages are specially interesting. In one the River Grant, 'like a *Satyre*' (XXI. 130) launches a bitter invective against the neglect of poets. This common theme of eclogues is here charged with the full weight of the poem's moral concerns. The Fall of Man is especially related to the neglect of poets:

> That curse the Serpent got in Paradise for hire,
> Descend upon you all, from him your devillish Sire . . . (ll. 161–2)

The other passage is the last invective in the book, summing up Drayton's fury against the 'Bestiall Rout' of 'this last yron Time' (XXX. 6ff.).

In all these instances, Drayton strikes a satiric vein like that of the Spenserian pastoralists associated with him. Song XVII (published in 1612) actually has the image of 'savage swine' (l. 400) used to link *The Shepheards Sirena* with Browne's Eclogue II in *The Shepheards Pipe* (1614).[16]

But in their contexts, these passages take a uniquely Draytonian turn. The last invective, in Song XXX, opens and closes in very different vein: the Muse has traversed

> so sundry soiles,
> Steep Mountains, Forrests rough, deepe Rivers, that thy toyles
> Most sweet refreshings seeme, and still thee comfort sent,
> Against the Bestiall Rout . . .
>
> . . . .
>
> . . . leave this Frie of Hell in their owne filth defilde,
> And seriously pursue the sterne *Westmerian* Wilde . . .
>
> (ll. 3–6, 13–14)

Nature, and the spirit of Albion as enshrined in it, become a refuge from the world. The differences between *Poly-Olbion* and *The Muses Elizium* are too obvious to be detailed; but in its own way, the latter work also preserves these deeper motives of pastoral in a setting from which

[16] See below, beginning of sect. 3.

conventional bucolic elements have all but disappeared. Unlike *Poly-Olbion*, it is clearly within the purview of the pastoral tradition. It concentrates more (though not exclusively) on the imaginative retreat, and its mythology is more nearly classical. Above all, it is a populated landscape—whose life is the very reverse of that in Drayton's own world. In his final volume, Drayton fully vindicates the pastoral impulse by freeing it of threatening contact with actual life in a human community.

Meanwhile, contrary tendencies had begun to appear in other poets, even those closest to Drayton. To these I shall now turn.

3. The Shepheards Pipe *and other poems*

As I have just tried to show, Drayton curiously combines the spirit of satire with the spirit of withdrawal. In his pastoral poetry at least, he is not deeply engaged with the times, even in opposition. Rather, he appears as a neglected outcast ('Malice denyes mee entrance with my sheepe')[17] or else a deliberate opter-out:

> I may not sing of such as fall nor clime,
> nor chaunt of armes, and of heroique deeds . . .[18]

When he praises contemporary poets, it is still as exemplars of obsolete virtue in a withdrawn pastoral retreat:

> And gentle shepheards (as sure som there be)
> That liuing yet his [Sidney's] vertues doe inherit,
> Men from base enuy and detraction free,
> Of vpright harts and of as humble spirit . . .[19]

Instances are Melibeus (Daniel), Alexis (Sir William Alexander), and Rowland himself. The shepherds in Eclogue IX of 1606 may stand for actual people. Idea and Rowland are of course real, as may be the '*Moreland* mayden' named as Sylvia in Eclogue VIII. But it seems impossible and indeed irrelevant to identify the others. They have been organically translated into pastoral terms. In Drayton's pastoral, thought of the times induces a creative escape into a world as different as the imagination can make it.

Barring the odd phrase like 'beastly Clownes',[20] only twice in

[17] 1606 *Eglogs*, sig. C8^v (Eclogue I. 54).
[18] Ibid. sig. E4^r (Eclogue V. 31–2).
[19] Ibid. sig. F1^v (Eclogue VI. 113–16).
[20] Ibid. sig. E8^v (Eclogue VI. 67).

Drayton's pastorals do we find direct attack and close involvement with the times. Eclogue VIII in 1606 has a vehement attack on his former patroness 'Selena' (Lucy, Countess of Bedford) and her protégé 'Cerberon' (variously identified as Daniel, Donne, Jonson, and Florio). This incongruous and uncharacteristic passage was removed in 1619; but Drayton retained the more restrained censure of 'Olcon' (James I) for his neglect of Rowland.

The name 'Olcon' occurs again in the second vituperative passage, in *The Shepheards Sirena*. It is often too hastily assumed that here again 'Olcon' is James. But it seems inconceivable that even the strongest resentment would drive Drayton to describe the monarch and his retinue as

> Rougish Swinheards that repine
> At our Flocks, like beastly Clownes . . . (ll. 356–7)

Besides, this Olcon is obviously a poet, and more involved in literary politics than the poetaster king could well be held to be:

> Angry OLCON sets them on,
> And against us part doth take
> Ever since he was out-gone,
> Offring Rymes with us to make. (ll. 368–71)

Raymond Jenkins's guess of Donne, and Hebel's of Jonson,[21] are more obviously along the right lines, whoever the person may really be.

The cryptic story of the thwarted love of Dorilus and Sirena can scarcely be other than allegorical. Interpretations generally involve political figures, making Dorilus the Fourth Earl of Dorset, self-exiled after a fatal duel,[22] or William Seymour, secretly married to Arabella Stuart.[23] Thinking less of precise identity than imaginative affinity, we may see in Dorilus a clear image of Rowland.[24] The melancholy shepherd, in a winter landscape, who casts aside his bagpipe and laments his unhappy love is as much poet as lover. At the end of the poem, the shepherds clearly stand for poets: experts on the pipe, tabor, and 'gittern', rivals of Olcon's crew in making rhymes. Common sense

[21] R. Jenkins, 'Drayton's Relation to the School of Donne', *PMLA* 38 (1923), 557ff.; J. W. Hebel, 'Drayton's Sirena', *PMLA* 39 (1924), 814ff.

[22] See Tillotson, Drayton's *Works*, v. 208; B. H. Newdigate, *Michael Drayton and His Circle* (corrected edn. Oxford, 1961), 213.

[23] See Heffner, pp. 182ff.

[24] A precise identification was suggested, and later rightly withdrawn, by Hebel; see his 'Drayton's Sirena' (as in n. 21 above) and Drayton's *Works*, v. 208 n. 2.

suggests what a parallel from *The Shepheards Pipe* (quoted below) confirms, that they are the poets of Drayton's circle. But it is significant that they are cast in the typical mould of the lyric shepherd: a happy rout that 'for nought but pleasure cared' (l. 150) though faced with impending attack. This carefree happiness, a staple of the pastoral lyric, was, as we saw, growing increasingly important to Drayton.

The song the shepherds sing conveys the same subtle and delicate spirit. The presence of art-pastoral on this scale distinguishes Drayton's work, even at its most allegorical, from that of his younger associates as collected in *The Shepheards Pipe* (1614), containing seven eclogues by William Browne, two by George Wither, and one each by Christopher Brooke and John Davies of Hereford. Wither's two eclogues were reprinted, with three others, in *The Shepherd's Hunting* (1615).

The contrast between Drayton and the younger poets can be illustrated from a passage by Browne in *The Shepheards Pipe* (used to date *Sirena c.*1614, though the latter was not published till 1627).

> Harm take the swine! What makes he here?
> What luckless planet's frowns
> Have drawn him and his hogs in feere
> To roote our daisied downs?
> Ill mote he thrive! and may his hogs,
> And all that e'er they breed,
> Be ever worried by our dogs
> For so presumptuous deed.[25]

This resembles the attack on Olcon in *Sirena*. But Browne keeps up the invective right through the poem. It is reinforced by realistic, even earthy detail: the 'trimmed ass's' vanity over clothes, his cheating Jockie over the alehouse tally. This is no idyllic, amorous pastoral life rudely disturbed by reality. Browne's shepherds lead a vigorous rustic life, close to the soil; their pastoral virtue is bluff and homely, and exerted in much closer involvement with their objectionable fellow-rustics. They live in the present instead of looking to the past. They are more eager to take issue, to castigate rather than lament.

Hence these eclogues pass easily into satire and controversy. Eclogue I presents 'Roget' (George Wither) complaining against the perverse interpretation of his songs:

[25] Eclogue II. 17–24; all refs. to Browne to G. Goodwin's edn. of the *Poems* (London, 1894). *The Shepheards Pipe* is in vol ii.

no sooner can I play
Any pleasing roundelay,
But some one or other still
'Gins to descant on my quill;
And will say, by this he me
Meaneth in his minstrelsy. (ll. 41–6)

In making this complaint, Roget does in fact abandon his 'notes of jollity' and become the satirist he is charged to be. His next speech paints a strife-torn pastoral world, with even gloomier forebodings of the future:

I fear a time ere long,
Shall not hear a shepherd's song,
Nor a swain shall take in task
Any wrong, nor once unmask
Such as do with vices rife
Soil the shepherd's happy life: . . . (ll. 97–102)

In these poems, unlike Drayton's, pastoral life cannot become an absolute ideal.

There are indeed idyllic interludes in *The Shepheards Pipe*. Eclogue I opens with a pleasing springtime scene:

Hark, on knap of yonder hill
Some sweet shepherd tunes his quill;
And the maidens in a round
Sit to hear him on the ground; (ll. 117–20)

Hoccleve is praised first for his 'moral's excellence' (l. 746), but then in more imaginative terms and finally through sheer fantasy:

Many times he hath been seen
With the fairies on the green,
And to them his pipe did sound,
Whilst they danced in a round. (ll. 753–6)

The idyllic strain is always waiting in the wings, so to speak; but against it we have a disturbed shepherd world very close to the real world and often no more than an allegory for it. The 'Wicked swains that bear me spite' (l. 87), though so consistently pastoralized, obviously stand for Roget's poetic rivals. His complaint against critics, quoted earlier, is even less pastoral in purport.

This makes for a strange and ultimately limiting factor in these eclogues. Their pastoralism is not purely formal or nominal: it relates to an authentic pastoral setting, attractive in literal terms. At the same time, it is a fairly direct metaphor for the real life of the poets. This sets up a conflict between the literal and the symbolic functions of the pastoral. Hoccleve's tales or Wither's satires are not actually pastoral. The poetic conflicts and rivalries, and the motives behind them, are practically the reverse of those associated with imaginary shepherd life. The pastoral cannot, therefore, serve simply as a medium for the poetic ideal as in Drayton's work. It functions as point-by-point metaphor rather than the embodiment of a total world of the imagination. In Eclogue V, Willie (Browne) exhorts Cuttie (Christopher Brooke) to 'for a trumpet change thine oaten-reeds' (l. 48). This is clearly based on Spenser's 'October'; but unlike Spenser's Cuddie, Browne's Cuttie is finally persuaded to try this 'higher' strain at their next holiday.

Yet it is a shepherd's holiday after all. Brooke's eclogue 'To his much loued friend Mr W. Browne' is even more ambivalent. Browne is cast as the wise shepherd, 'a true figure ... | Of Contemplation'. His flights 'farre transcend' the common 'lowly traine' of Pan:

> And to this Mount thou dost translate thine Essence
> Although the plaines containe thy corporal presence,
> Where though poore peoples misery thou shewe
> That vnder griping Lords they vndergoe,
> And what content they (that do lowest lye)
> Receiue from Good-men; that do sit on hye.
> And in each witty Ditty (that surpasses)
> Dost (for thy loue) make strife 'mongst Country lasses.
> Yet in thy humble straine; Fame makes thee rise
> And strikes thy mounting forehead 'gainst the skies . . .[26]

Pastoral is considered here from two aspects: as social and moral commentary, and as idyllic love-lyricism. But Browne's efforts exceed both, though he still remains essentially a shepherd-poet. Epic and pastoral, the shepherd world and the wider one, constitute equal and opposite impulses. Browne attempts to resolve this double allegiance in the comprehensive structure of *Britannia's Pastorals*: in contrast to Drayton, whose increasingly pure pastoral makes him carry the eclogue-form to a climax of lyric refinement.

The most obvious duality, of course, lies in the fact that Willie and Cuttie, though brought to life as shepherd-poets, are also Browne and

[26] *The Shepheards Pipe* (London, 1614), sig. F6^r–v^. These lines are closely based on a passage from Sidney's *Defence of Poetry*, quoted at the start of Ch. 15, sect. 3, below.

Brooke, and intended to be recognized as such. The presence of this *à clé* element in certain eclogues leads us to look for it in the rest. The tale of old Neddy in Browne's Eclogue III seems to be a realistic narrative of the 'suffering shepherd' type. In fact, we have here a *rich* shepherd undone by his servants' knavery. This is not presented as a common social trend; nor is there any psychological interest in Neddy's mental state. This makes one surmise that he stands for a real person, perhaps a superseded courtier or a plagiarized poet. There is no clear sign of allegory; but without postulating allegory, it is difficult to see the point of the exercise.

We may possibly take Neddy as a Wordsworthian suffering rustic, as Grundy (p. 99) does. Similarly we may read Eclogue VI, on Philos's disobedient dog, as a simple piece of rustic fun. But, if so, it embodies a quite incongruous degree of triviality. Besides, the Greek name 'Philos' ('beloved', or sometimes 'lover') marks a contrast to Browne's usual English names. Willie in the other eclogues is Browne; why not here? Again one is led to surmise a hidden allegory of misplaced trust.

The important point is that, though we cannot be sure of the allusion, the integrity of the pastoral has been lost. The detailed evocation of the shepherd's life is self-defeating: we keep looking for a key. Allegory apart, the experience of these shepherds, literally read, is deeply set in external reality. For the poets of *The Shepheards Pipe*, unlike Drayton, to be a shepherd is to belong to the world and have a full share of its evils. As John Davies of Hereford puts it in his contribution to the *Pipe*:

> Swaines are now
> So full of contecke, that they wot ne what
> They would; so, if they could; they all would owe.[27]

This spirit is reflected above all in Wither's pastorals. He has two eclogues in the *Pipe*. They are reprinted, with an important addition to the first and with three new eclogues, in *The Shepherd's Hunting* (1615), which centres upon his imprisonment in the Marshalsea after the issue of *Abuses Stript and Whipt* in 1613. Abuses are what the 'shepherd' hunts. In other words, these eclogues are allegorical through and through.

Of course, particularly in Eclogue V of the *Hunting*, the equation of pastoral and poetry can be more than metaphoric. Pastoral life provides an ideal, aesthetic as well as ethical, for the poet's career. Wither, Browne, William Ferrar ('Alexis'), and their circle actually become 'shepherds' in conduct, mentality, and values:

[27] ll. 214–16; as in Davies's *Works*, ed. A. B. Grosart (London, 1878), ii. (*m*), p. 21.

> Thy flock will help thy charges to defray,
> Thy Muse to pass the long and tedious day:
> Or whilst thou tun'st sweet measures to thy reed,
> Thy sheep, to listen, will more near thee feed;
> The wolves will shun them, birds above thee sing,
> And lambkins dance about thee in a ring.[28]

Here sheepkeeping does not stand for poetry but for Alexis's legal career, distinct from cultivation of 'Thy Muse'. But the two are compounded into a single ideal of peace, content, and poetic delight.

In *The Shepheards Pipe*, the poem ends on this note, departing from the disturbed, down-to-earth spirit of the rest of the volume. In Wither's other eclogue in the *Pipe*, however, Roget[29] laments the state of the times and his own difficulties as a satirist, much as in Browne's Eclogue I. How close satire may come to pastoral appears most clearly in another of Wither's early poems (though published in 1622), *Fair Virtue*. The shepherd Philarete is very much a shepherd, living in Wither's native Hampshire and taking time off from his song to attend to his sheep. He is a lover too, and Wither puts upon his and his singing-boy's lips a number of love-lyrics, one or two of them authentically pastoral. But his mistress, however vividly described, is 'Fair Virtue'. A strong moral note dominates the poem, and is supported towards the end by a great deal of satire of the unvirtuous. Indeed, Philarete has trained a troop of satyrs to dance 'the Whipping of Abuse' (l. 4105). He knows courtly ways (ll. 4387ff.) and is familiar with courtiers (ll. 4561ff.). Yet he remains a shy shepherd boy, wishing to 'Enjoy my music by myself alone' (l. 140), however voluble he may finally prove to his audience of ladies. His basic identity is that of lover, not satirist:

> In homely verse expressed country loves,
> And only told them to the beechy groves . . . (ll. 99–100)

His very satyrs have been trained to 'so rare a gentleness' (l. 4098), and their dance is succeeded by a country banquet to the sound of viols.

At such points, the pastoral becomes more idyllic than in *The Shepheards Pipe*, let alone the *Hunting*. The satiric and realistic pastoral of these poets appears to range outward in a number of directions from

[28] ll. 155–60; all refs. to Wither to F. Sidgwick's edn. of the *Poetry*. *The Shepherd's Hunting* is in vol. i.

[29] The *Pipe* names Wither's persona 'Roget' in this eclogue and 'Thirsis' in the other. The *Hunting* has 'Roget' in both, as in the new eclogues; Wither's *Juvenilia* (1622) and subsequent texts have 'Philarete' in all of them.

the core impulse embodied in the *Pipe*. This looks back at *Fair Virtue* and forward to *The Shepherd's Hunting*, and has points of contact with *Britannia's Pastorals* as well, as we shall see.

In *The Shepherd's Hunting*, pastoral life exists for Wither only as an impossible alternative, for he is in prison.

> Alas, thou art exiled from thy flock,
> And, quite beyond the deserts here confined . . . (Eclogue I. 57–8)

Even his former pastoral pursuits, however, prove to be very unusual, for he had been a hunting shepherd. This is without reference to the usual convention of hunting-eclogues: Roget really is a shepherd, but his chief interest lies in

> hunting foxes, wolves, and beasts of prey
> That spoil our folds, and bear our lambs away. (Eclogue II. 61–2)

This is a curious offshoot of the shepherd's trade, reversing the pastoral spirit. 'The shepherd's hunting' is almost a contradiction in terms. Pastoral is being used as a symbol for the sort of poetry most contrary in spirit: satire. Yet the two were commonly related in the age, owing to the association of *satire* (actually from Latin *satura*, a medley) with *satyr*. Eugene Waith gives a detailed account of the association[30] and the consequent relating of satire to pastoral in English tragicomic drama. Richard Jenkyns demonstrates how, by the same confusion, Horace's prescriptions for satyr-plays were applied to pastoral drama.[31] I may also cite John Weever's *Faunus and Melliflora* (1600), a mythological poem drawing freely on the pastoral convention, especially Sidney's *Arcadia*. But Faunus and Melliflora's child is a satyr: the poem closes with an account of satire, and is followed by translations from Horace, Persius, and Juvenal. We have an analogous association of satire and pastoral in Wither's eclogues.

An interesting precedent in a different way are the four eclogues in Lodge's *A Fig for Momus* (1595). Such poems could only be written in the shadow of traditional pastoral; but, barring a few details in the first, they are what we may call depastoralized eclogues. There are no explicit pastoral elements, but there is extensive use of the structure and themes of the debate or discussion-eclogue. Eclogue I illustrates the opposition of youth and age and passes on to a fable against ambition. Eclogue II

[30] *The Pattern of Tragi-Comedy in Beaumont and Fletcher* (New Haven, 1952; repr. 1969), ch. ii.

[31] *Classical Sources for English Pastoral*, pp. 90ff.

treats of youth and age again, and the frustration of a hermit-turned-courtier. Eclogue III treats of the neglect of poetry;[32] Eclogue IV of action versus contemplation. In other words, Lodge is taking certain satiric and didactic themes commonly treated in pastoral, and developing the satiric vein in isolation from the pastoral, without however cutting off all connection with the eclogue form. Satire is said to realize the highest potential of pastoral: 'More pleasant than the verrelay | The shepheard sings vnto his sheepe'.[33]

So too in Eclogue III of *The Shepherd's Hunting*, Roget exchanges contemplation for action, obscurity for fame:

> And not a beauty on our greens shall play
> That hath not heard of this thy hunting day. (ll. 168–9)

He has become a pastoral hero by abandoning the normal course of pastoral life. He keeps such hounds (actually the titles of his satires) as Envy, Choler, Cruelty, and Avarice, and hunts evil monsters not only through the country but

> Through kitchen, parlour, hall, and chamber too.
> And, as they pass'd the city, and the court,
> My prince look'd out, and deigned to view my sport; . . . (ll. 55–7)

The vivid details do indeed capture the spirit of a real hunt. But even if read literally—which is scarcely possible for more than a few lines—they present an active, violent, disturbed world, the very antithesis of the normal pastoral one:

> Some beasts I found lie dead, some full of wounds,
> Among the willows, scarce with strength to move:
>
> . . . .
>
> Lust had bit some, but I soon passed beside them,
> Their fester'd wounds so stunk, none could abide them.
> Choler hurt divers, but Revenge kill'd more:
> Fear frightened all, behind him and before. (ll. 67–8, 72–5)

Then comes the quieter, deeper malice of the poet's enemies, 'Swoll'n with the deepest rancour of despite' (l. 152).

Simple pastoral content cannot survive in such a milieu. It is replaced by a stoic content that can withstand adversity:

[32] Barnfield's *The Complaint of Poetrie* (1598) also has certain pastoral elements. See his *Works* (ed. Summers), pp. 108–9.

[33] Lodge's *Works*, ed. E. W. Gosse (1883; repr. New York 1963), iii: *A Fig for Momus*, p. 19.

That slender Muse of mine, by which my name,
Though scarce deserved, hath gain'd a little fame,
Hath made me unto such a fortune born,
That all misfortunes I know how to scorn . . .[34]

Though allied to pastoral content, this stoicism arises from adverse conditions very different from idyllic pastoral life. It accompanies a crusading moral concern at the opposite pole from the shepherd's care-free *otium*. Rather, it pertains to another rustic trait, homely and out-spoken honesty. Lodge's Damian had struck the same note: 'For shepheards only sing for sence'.[35]

More generally, rural life as depicted in the *Pipe* and the *Hunting* is allied to a new, realistic, Mantuanesque pastoral that seems to develop in the Jacobean age. Francis Sabie had anticipated the vein in *Pan's Pipe* (1595). His first eclogue is an earthier retelling of Mantuan I: Phillida, made pregnant by Alexis, marries Tyterus to save her honour. In the second, a synod of the gods sits incongruously over a shepherd's-son-turned-apprentice.

The best Jacobean example is Richard Brathwait's *The Shepheards Tales* (1621).[36] Six shepherds relate their loves: all unhappy, involving lust, jealousy, unfaithfulness, and broken promises. These anti-romantic plots are acted out against a background of rural life, which is even aggressively realistic at times. Sapphus and Dymnus have a vulgar squabble over their common love Sylvia. Dorycles' dog breaks wind just as its master is about to propose. Coridon, unlike his Elizabethan namesakes, knows so little of internal joy that he confuses it with 'infernal'.[37] Yet the shepherds have classical names, they worship Pan, they know of '*Siluans, water-nimphs, fairies* and *faunes*' (Part II, Eclogue I, p. 184). There are picturesque glimpses of the countryside and country festivities. These poems cannot really be called anti-pastoral, but they throw the pastoral convention into quizzical and ultimately endearing compound with the realities of life that shepherds share with other men. It is a cruder, more garish version of the scenario of *The Shepheards Pipe*.

[34] Eclogue V. 209–12: cf. Eclogue I. 148ff., Eclogue III. 206–13, 258–88; *Fair Virtue*, ll. 227–8, 4655–60. Cf. also Davies's and Brooke's eclogues in the *Pipe*. See Grundy, p. 171 for Wither's role of 'shepherd Stoic'.

[35] *A Fig for Momus*, Eclogue I: ed. Gosse, iii. 19.

[36] Published in two parts, both 1621: the 1st separately, the 2nd along with *Natures Embassie*. Each part contains three tales, and Part II other poems as well.

[37] See, respectively, Part II, Eclogue II (pp. 191–2); Part I, Eclogue II (p. 26); Part I, Eclogue I (p. 7).

Brathwait seems to have known and admired the poets of the *Pipe*. In *A Strappado for the Devil*, he singles them out for praise amid general censure.[38] His satire, says M. W. Black,[39] was clearly modelled on Wither (although Brathwait later became a Royalist and Wither a Puritan). Perhaps we may postulate a similar influence of Wither and his associates on *The Shepheards Tales*. In any case, their work all belongs to the same vein of pastoral, very different from any of those practised by Drayton.

I do not think it possible to group together all the pastorals of the Spenserian poets. Even Joan Grundy, who does so, distinguishes Drayton's 'magical quality' from Browne and Wither's 'light of common day' (pp. 96, 98). Drayton's pastoral has a consistent seriousness of purpose. But it is basically nostalgic, recreating a morally and, more and more, poetically independent shepherd world. Browne and Wither are much more fundamentally allusive, and always involved with reality in a manner that transcends specific allusions. Their shepherds are enquiring and critical, and shepherd life is not for them an unquestioned ideal. They are exponents of a new vein of pastoral, whereas Drayton is reviving the idyllic pastoral of Elizabeth's last years, given a new seriousness owing to the moral nostalgia with which he imbues it: it is made to embody the vanished ideals he ascribes to that age. His shepherds too can criticize and moralize, but as philosophic old men turning a contemplative eye upon a world that has passed them by. And, increasingly, he conjures up a romantic pastoral world of song, love, and idyllic happiness.

In the seventeenth century, as in the sixteenth, pastoral is too widespread a phenomenon to be gathered under a single head or influence, even where relations exist between the authors. Browne and Wither, though differing among themselves, seem to illustrate one special development of the pastoral, incorporating an active rustic ethos and an engagement with affairs. But alongside them, and once or twice swayed by their concerns, Michael Drayton pursues his deeply original pastoral career.

[38] 'To the Poet-asters of Brittaine', *A Strappado*, ed. J. W. Ebsworth (Boston, Lincs., 1878), 23–4.

[39] M. W. Black, *Richard Brathwait* (Philadelphia, 1928), 65.

11

The Diffusion of Pastoral in the Earlier Seventeenth Century

1. *Lyrics and country poems*

THE WORK of the Spenserians apart, Jacobean and Caroline poetry shows a feebler and less felicitous working of the pastoral tradition. Yet it is a substantial body of work, leading on to other related genres. I shall treat here of poetry composed or published up to the middle of the seventeenth century.

The most apparent vein of pastoral lyric during this period bears a superficial resemblance to the 'classic' Elizabethan style of light innocence and abandon:[1]

> Woods renew
> Hunter's hue,
> Shepherds' grey
> Crowned with bay,
> With his pipe
> Care doth wipe,
> Till he dream
> By the stream.[2]

A closer look, however, reveals important differences. Here is a characteristic instance from Thomas Randolph. Lalage explains to Thirsis why he burns in love for her while she is unaffected:

> Can *Thirsis* in Philosophy
> A Truant bee,
> And not have learn'd the power of the Sun?
> How he to sublunary things,

[1] J. B. Leishman (*The Art of Marvell's Poetry*, ch. iii) argues persuasively for the continuity of pastoral from Elizabethan through Jacobean and Caroline to Restoration times; yet he too grants important differences.

[2] Jasper Fisher, 'Song' from *Fuimus Troes* (1633): see H. J. Massingham (ed.), *A Treasury of Seventeenth-Century English Verse* (London, 1931), 96.

A fervour brings,
Yet in himselfe is subject unto none?[3]

An involved idea shows through the delicate, song-like form and relaxed fancy. Thomas Stanley's nymph admits and even invites her shepherd's love with a flutter of Petrarchan conceits far removed from Drayton's Dowsabell:

> Choose one whose Love may be allur'd
> By thine: who ever knew
> Inveterate Diseases cur'd
> But by receiving new?[4]

These shepherds are always polished and sometimes conceitful, like the aristocratic lovers of courtly 'sonnets'. They may readily be described in the same terms:

> *Chloris*, the gentlest Sheapherdesse,
> That ever Lawnes and Lambes did blesse;
> . . . .
> Her Lips like coral-gates kept in
> The perfume and the pearle within;
> Her eyes a double-flaming torch
> That always shine, and never scorch . . .[5]

Waller and his 'Phyllis' recall their past amours under the thin poetic veil of

> On what shepherds you have smiled,
> Or what nymphs I have beguiled; . . .[6]

Herrick gives the show away in the title of a poem: 'Mrs. *Eliz. Wheeler*, under the name of the lost Shepardesse'.[7]

In other words, the pastoral element is not organic to these lyrics. It only adds spice to set themes and conceits. At most, it provides a dream-setting for an unquestionably sophisticated ideal of free love. Fancy and

[3] 'A Dialogue. Thirsis. Lalage', ll. 7–12: as in Randolph's *Poems & Amyntas*, ed. Parry, p. 134.

[4] 'The Cure', ll. 25–8: as in Stanley's *Poems and Translations*, ed. G. M. Crump (Oxford, 1962), 12.

[5] Richard Lovelace, 'Amyntor's Grove', as in *Poems*, ed. C. H. Wilkinson (Oxford, 1930), 71.

[6] 'To Phyllis', ll. 17–18: as in Waller's *Poems*, ed. G. Thorn Drury (London, [1893]) i. 84.

[7] Herrick's *Poems*, ed. L. C. Martin (Oxford, 1965), 106. All Herrick refs. to this edn.

nostalgia, the insubstantial embodiment of a courtly dream, nullifies the more deeply 'different' and even subversive functions of pastoral.

Such poems blend into the large body of lyrics—as considerable in this as in earlier phases of the Renaissance—which, without any explicit pastoralism, evoke the basic Petrarchan situations of the beloved walking in a setting of nature, or the lover escaping into one. It is significant that some of these should be entitled pastorals: Randolph's 'A Pastorall Ode', with its gloomy hilltop for a lover's suicide-leap,[8] or Carew's 'A Pastorall Dialogue',[9] whose highly polished exchanges scarcely evoke even a ghost of the amoebean eclogue. Most unbucolic of all is Ben Jonson's 'The Musicall Strife; In a Pastorall Dialogue', whose philosophic conceits would have graced any Italian courtly dialogue.

Shee

Come with our Voyces, let us warre,
And challenge all the Spheares,
Till each of us be made a Starre,
And all the world turne Eares.

Hee

At such a Call, what beast or fowle,
Of reason emptie is!
What Tree or stone doth want a soule?
What man but must lose his?[10]

In another 'Pastorall Dialogue' by Carew,[11] a shepherd and 'nymph' merely repeat the loving farewells of two other lovers. Herrick has an amoebean song-contest from which the songs have disappeared, being merely indicated in parentheses.[12] They may have been supplied from other sources during performance, but are clearly not organic to the poem. The form has lost its *raison d'être*; it is only a polished and lacquered skeleton of its original self.

S[TREPHON]. Come my *Daphne*, come away,
We do waste the Crystal day;
'Tis *Strephon* calls.

[8] Parry's edn., p. 137.

[9] Carew's *Poems*, ed. Dunlap, p. 42. All Carew refs. to this edn.

[10] ll. 1–8; as in Jonson's *Poems*, ed. G. B. Johnston (London, 1954; repr. 1975), 122. All refs. to Jonson's poems to this edn.

[11] *Poems*, p. 45.

[12] *Poems*, p. 243: 'A Beucolick, or discourse of Neatherds'.

DA. What would my love?
S. Come follow to the Mirtle grove,
Where *Venus* shall prepare
New chaplets for thy hair.[13]

We are witnessing a disembodiment of the pastoral tradition, its full-bodied shepherd life reduced to disjunct snatches of an elusive and vestigial world. The shepherds are little more than voices. In so far as they come to life at all, they have exchanged the idyllic for the merely libertine. More often, trying to surpass their original Elizabethan selves, they have declined into the utterly unmemorable.

How then, if at all, is the pastoral tradition kept alive in this period? Significantly, a chief means is the allusive or 'allegorical' eclogue, which I have treated separately. For the rest, we may turn first to Scotland, and to William Drummond of Hawthornden in particular. A number of Drummond's 'madrigals' and 'epigrams' are nothing more nor less than *lusus pastorales* in English:

Neare to a Christall Spring,
With Thirst and Heat opprest,
Narcissa faire doth rest,
Trees pleasant Trees which those greene plaines forth bring
Now interlace your trembling Tops aboue
And make a Canopie vnto my Loue . . .[14]

The poems chiefly concern shepherds in the role of lovers: they make vows, appeals, and sacrifices to the gods, fall in love at first sight, exchange wooing-speeches. But there is also an epitaph on a fisherman; another on a sheep-dog, and a poem chiding a dog for barking at the lover; with one or two in a lustier vein of sexuality. Gods and other mythic characters appear—Venus, Priapus, Hylas—and the shepherds all have classical names. Navagero's *lusus* are not more typical of the genre.

Drummond has the occasional longer poem about shepherd-lovers as well: an eclogue of Damon and Moeris, apparently 'art-pastoral'. (Damon, however, was Drummond's pastoral name.)

My flockes sem'd partneres of ther masters voe:
The Bell-bearer the troupes that vsd to lead
His vsuall feading places did forgoe,

[13] Opening of a poem by James Shirley; as in *Poems*, ed. R. L. Armstrong (1941; repr. Folcroft, Pa., 1970), 6. All refs. to this edn.

[14] Drummond's *Works*, ed. Kastner, ii. 154: 'A Louers Prayer', ll. 1–6 (*Madrigals*, no. xiii).

And loathing three-leu'd grasse hold vp his head;
The valkes, the groues which I did hant of yore
My fate and Phillis hardnesse seemd deplore.[15]

This is conventional; but Drummond's genuine absorption in the terms of the convention demands attention at this date. Feebler but equally genuine are Sir Robert Ayton's Italianate pieces.

In England we find such authentic pastoralism in a few of Herrick's poems. Mirtillo apostrophizes Amarillis:

And here the breth of kine
And sheep, grew more sweet, by that breth of Thine.
This flock of wooll, and this rich lock of hair,
This ball of *Cow-slips*, these she gave me here.[16]

But Herrick best illustrates a more important vitalization of the pastoral. Instead of creating a removed world of the imagination, pastoral convention is applied to actual English country life, in the blend of reality and artefact that we find in Drayton's Cotswold pastorals or *The Winter's Tale*:

At Sheering-times, and yearely Wakes,
When *Themilis* his pastime makes,
There thou shalt be; and be the wit,
Nay more, the Feast, and grace of it.
On Holy-dayes, when Virgins meet
To dance the Heyes with nimble feet;
Thou shalt come forth, and then appeare
The *Queen of Roses* for that yeere.[17]

As I remarked in the context of Drayton's Cotswold pastorals, the attempt to authenticate convention may have the opposite effect of stylizing and falsifying reality. Herrick's poetry is secured from such rejection by the adaptation of metre, movement, and diction to the requisite degree of simplicity—by, shall we say, a happy and deliberate trivialization. His verbal structures promise no more than they deliver; and 'pastoral humility' provides a disarming apology for such diminution of scale, which may be called the operative principle of his poetry.

There on a Hillock thou mayst sing
Unto a handsome Shephardling;

[15] Ibid. ii. 258, 'Eclogue' i, ll. 55–60.
[16] 'A Pastorall sung to the King', ll. 13–16, *Poems*, p. 159.
[17] 'To *Phillis* to love, and live with him', ll. 25–32, *Poems*, p. 192.

Or to a Girle (that keeps the Neat)
With breath more sweet then Violet.
There, there, (perhaps) such Lines as These
May take the simple *Villages*.[18]

Elsewhere there is nothing clearly pastoral, only country maidens telling of Philomela, Phillis, and Jupiter's love alongside such typically English rusticities as a game of draw-gloves, or 'That wedding-smock, this Bridal-Cake'.[19] Or else the lyric call to a feast reflects more earthy rustic festivals:

Morris-dancers thou shalt see,
Marian too in Pagentrie:
And a Mimick to devise
Many grinning properties.[20]

We are approaching a distinct vein of rustic poetry, based much more on the actual stuff of country life and festivals. The neglected Patrick Cary imparts a lyric quality to the love of shepherds for Betty and Nell (though he may weave in a reference to 'Pan's chief feast').[21] Something has passed into such poems from the folk-song and folk-lyric that I discussed in Chapter 8; and these in turn draw upon the authentic country songs preserved for us in collections like Thomas Ravenscroft's.

In a slightly different direction, pastoral passes into the country ode, whose sixteenth-century Latin, French, and Italian examples I have noted earlier. Once the Elizabethan achievement is over, English pastoral poetry follows the standard continental course with the same affinities to related genres. As with continental precedent, these odes of rural retirement show less influence of the pastoral than of Horace's Epode II.[22] Instead of the native innocence of the born shepherd or rustic, we have the conscious withdrawal of a sophisticated poet, courtier, and man of the world: 'The first Wish of *Virgil* . . . was to be a good Philosopher; the second, a good Husbandman; and God . . . made him one of the best Philosophers, and best Husbandmen, and to adorn and communicate both those faculties, the best Poet: He made him besides all this a rich man, and a man who desired to be no richer.'[23] By a perhaps deliberate

[18] 'To his Muse', ll. 11–16, *Poems*, pp. 5–6.
[19] 'To the Maids to walke abroad', *Poems*, p. 215.
[20] 'The Wake', ll. 7–10, *Poems*, p. 255.
[21] 'Jack! nay, prithee, come away', in *Trivial Poems, and Triolets* (1651); see G. Saintsbury (ed.), *Minor Poets of the Caroline Period* (Oxford, 1905), ii. 462.
[22] This matter has been definitively treated in M.-S. Røstvig's *The Happy Man*.
[23] Abraham Cowley, 'Of Agriculture', *Several Discourses by Way of Essays*, as in Cowley's *English Writings*, ed. A. R. Waller (Cambridge, 1905–6), ii. 400.

blurring of phraseology, such a character may be nominally presented as a native rustic, as in Cowley's translation from Virgil's *Georgics* (deliberately phrased to echo Horace's 'Beatus ille . . .'):

> Oh happy, (if his Happiness he knows)
> The Country Swain, on whom kind Heav'n bestows
> At home all Riches that wise Nature needs; . . .[24]

But it is a swain who enjoys 'easie plenty', with herds and flocks undoubtedly his own, and supply of game to boot. More often, the professedly sophisticated poet goes to the countryside for solace and refreshment:

> There from the tree
> Wee'l cherries plucke, and pick the strawbery.
> And every day
> Go see the wholesome Country Girles make hay.
> Whose browne hath lovlier grace,
> Than any painted face,
> That I doe know
> *Hide-Parke* can show.[25]

The poet abandons the persona of the fictional shepherd, or adopts it in patently transparent guise as in Katherine Philips's 'A Dialogue betwixt Lucasia and Rosania',[26] or Sir Edward Sherburne's earlier 'A Shepherd Inviting a Nymph to His Cottage',[27] or Cowley's dream gilding his idealized praise of 'pleasant poverty':

> Here a fresh Arbor gives her amorous shade,
> Which *Nature*, the best *Gard'ner* made.
> Here I would set, and sing rude layes,
> Such as the *Nimphs* and *me my selfe* should please.[28]

Actual shepherds appear, if at all, as external details in a landscape, like the lad and nymph with scrip, leather bottle, and 'guardian . . . *Melampo*' in Eldred Revett's 'The Land-schap between two Hills'.[29] I have noted earlier continental examples of this sort; later ones may be

[24] 'A Translation out of *Virgil*', appended to 'Of Agriculture', ibid. 409.
[25] Randolph, 'An Ode to Mr *Anthony Stafford*', ll. 25–32, *Poems*, ed. Parry, p. 129.
[26] Saintsbury, i. 577.
[27] See Chalmers, *The Works of the English Poets* (1810), vi. 630.
[28] *Sylva*, Ode II, *English Writings*, i. 61.
[29] Quoted in Turner, *The Politics of Landscape*, p. 20.

found in the influential work of Casimire Sarbiewski, of which Maren-Sofie Røstvig has given a cogent account.[30]

A happier vein of country idyll appears in Cowley's prose essays: 'Of Solitude', 'Of Agriculture', or 'The Garden', with accompanying poems. The long poem attached to the last is a not unworthy anticipation of Marvell's. There are other garden-poems as well—by James Shirley, for instance[31]—marking one development of the idyllic and solitary vein usually treated in poems of the open countryside. For the countryside too has been bound within the limits of an urbane and contemplative sensibility:

> When Westwell Downs I 'gan to tread,
> Where cleanly winds the green did sweep,
> Methought a landscape there was spread,
> Here a bush and there a sheep: . . .
>
> Here would I sleep or read or pray
> From early morn till flight of day:
> But hark! a sheep-bell calls me up,
> Like Oxford college bells, to sup.[32]

In all probability, such a grazing-ground would be literally enclosed. We may recall the sinister metamorphosis of a pastoral landscape into depopulated enclosure-land as described by Robert Powell: 'nothing remaines but a champant wildernesse for sheepe, with a Cote, a pastorall boy, his dogge, a crooke and a pipe'.[33]

Elsewhere, a country estate, perhaps lightly pastoralized, provides a milieu for sophisticated repose or love. William Herbert, Third Earl of Pembroke, is an early exponent of the vein, though his poems were not published till 1660:

> Fair starry twins, scorn not to shine
> Upon my Lambs, upon my Kine;
> My grass doth grow, my Corn and wheat,
> My fruit, my vines thrive by their heat.[34]

A little later, Waller similarly transforms Penshurst into a half-Petrarchan, half-pastoral setting for his courtship of 'Sacharissa' (Lady

30 Røstvig, i. 75–80, 126–9, and *passim*.
31 'The Garden', *Poems*, p. 16.
32 William Strode, 'On Westwell Downs', Massingham, p. 209.
33 *Depopulation Arraigned* (1636), 55, quoted in Turner p. 163.
34 'A Sonnet', Herbert's *Poems* (London, 1660), 39.

Dorothy Sidney); and elsewhere turns 'The Country' generally into a suitable habitation for Lady Carlisle-as-shepherdess:

> Carlisle! a name which all our woods are taught,
> Loud as his Amaryllis, to resound;
> Carlisle! a name which on the bark is wrought
> Of every tree that's worthy of the wound.[35]

Thomas Stanley's 'Sylvia's Park' (1651) carries the tendency further, to a notable anticipation of 'Upon Appleton House'.[36]

The sensibility expressed fitfully through this threadbare pastoral finds full form in the country-house poem. Such poems are not pastoral; but they most clearly reveal the factors governing the 'new' pastoral of the seventeenth century.

From being a romantic setting, a country estate may deepen into an Ovidian landscape (though perhaps with fairies as well). Here for instance is Hindlip, William Habington's native place:

> A Satyre here and there shall trip,
> In hope to purchase leave to sip
> Sweete nectar from a Fairie's lip.[37]

There is also a paradisal or Golden-Age element:

> From fruitlesse palmes shall honey flow,
> And barren Winter harvest show,
> While lillies in his bosome grow . . .

Both sylvan and paradisal features are more familiar to us from other works, particularly Jonson's prototypal country-house poems, 'To Penshurst' and 'To Sir Robert Wroth':

> Thy Mount, to which the Dryads doe resort,
> Where Pan, and Bacchus their high feasts have made,
> Beneath the broad beech, and the chest-nut shade;[38]

In 'To Sir Robert Wroth', the mythological references are purely formal (ll. 47–52) but the Golden Age is explicitly invoked:

[35] 'The Country to My Lady of Carlisle', *Poems*, ed. Thorn Drury, i. 21.

[36] The resemblance has been noted by Stanley's editor, G. M. Crump (*Poems and Translations*, p. 396). Stanley's poem was adapted from Théophile de Viau's *La Maison de Silvie*.

[37] 'To Castara', *Castara* (1634), Chalmers, vi. 447.

[38] 'To Penshurst', ll. 10–12.

Such, and no other was that age, of old,
Which boasts t'have had the head of gold.
And such since thou canst make thine owne content,
Strive, Wroth, to live long innocent. (ll. 63–6)

'Innocent' underscores the legacy of paradisal motifs that the country-house poem inherits from the pastoral. The contrast with the court provides an obvious corollary:

And, though so neere the citie, and the court,
Art tane with neithers vice, nor sport;[39]

In 'To Penshurst', the court–country contrast is subtler and less absolute. Penshurst is not haughtily palatial; it reflects and interacts with the spirit of the countryside in a happy ideal of rural plenty and harmony, apparently opposed to the court and the class system:

Now, Penshurst, they that will proportion thee
With other edifices, when they see
Those proud, ambitious heaps, and nothing else,
May say, their lords have built, but thy lord dwells. (ll. 99–102)

Yet needless to say—and this is the paradox of the country-house poem—the feudal order is really being idealized, with the court at its apex.[40] When King James visits Penshurst, he seems to enter a genuinely different, non-courtly world; but the reverence rendered him places this society within the accepted hierarchy after all. The rustics happily acquiesce in an order that consigns them to its lower levels and makes their prosperity derive from the master's, while denying their vital contribution to the master's wealth. As Raymond Williams further notes, country life is closely involved even with the new industrial and mercantile order. In Turner's deeper formal analysis, landscape itself becomes the standing symbol of a stratified social order.[41]

Every feature of the country-house poem becomes clearer as we progress from Jonson to Herrick and Carew. Carew's Saxham, seat of Sir John Crofts, is introduced by the evocation of eternal spring.[42] Wrest, seat of the Earls of Kent, is more lushly paradisal still:

[39] ll. 3–4; cf. ll. 67 ff.

[40] Cf. G. R. Hibbard, 'The Country House Poem of the Seventeenth Century', *Journal of the Warburg and Courtauld Institutes*, 19 (1956), 164. Jonson is presenting two versions of feudalism, the older and better being hyperbolically presented as uncourtly. This remains true even if, as Raymond Williams points out (*The Country and the City* (London, 1973), 40), the 'older' was itself of recent origin.

[41] On these points, see Williams, pp. 32, 48–9; Turner, pp. 38 ff.

[42] 'To Saxham', ll. 1 ff., *Poems*, p. 27.

> Here steep'd in balmie dew, the pregnant Earth
> Sends from her teeming wombe a flowrie birth,
> And cherisht with the warme Suns quickning heate,
> Her porous bosome doth rich odours sweate;[43]

But through such exotic, almost erotic description, there runs the theme of innocence and purified impulse:

> No Volatile spirits, nor compounds that are
> Adulterate, but at Natures cheape expence
> With farre more genuine sweetes refresh the sense.
> Such pure and uncompounded beauties, blesse
> This Mansion with an usefull comlinesse . . . (ll. 16–20)

Carew's dominant concerns, however, are social, economic, and basically feudal. The eternal spring of Saxham grows metaphorical: the house protects the poor from 'The cold and frozen ayre'. Again the poet celebrates a feudal harmony sustained by charity and patronage, with the poor as willing or thankful participants. One of Carew's conceits has been foreshadowed by Jonson: the assent of the poor to a happy inequality is imaged in the willingness of birds and beasts to be killed for the lord's table.[44]

The great reconciling virtue is hospitality,[45] which flows freely at Saxham, 'Both from the Master, and the Hinde' (l. 42). Class divisions are contentedly enshrined in the very act of hospitality: at Wrest, the guests are divided according to rank, and only the highest admitted to the lord's table. At Penshurst, host and guest had shared the same meat. More surprisingly, even in the class-conscious Herrick, all Sir Lewis Pemberton's guests find 'equall freedome, equall fare'.[46] This poem is surely the most elaborate exposition ever of the theme of country-house hospitality.

The feudal relationship is clearest in Herrick, because he has the least concept of a total social and natural order. For him, the country is chiefly a venue for the *personal* content and happiness of a prosperous squire or landed gentleman. Herrick's rural odes to his brother Thomas and to Endimion Porter recall the odes of earlier continental Neo-Latinists (though, as Hibbard points out, Thomas was actually a simple farmer

[43] 'To my friend G. N. from *Wrest*', ll. 9–12, *Poems*, p. 86.

[44] Jonson, 'To Penshurst', ll. 29–38; Carew, 'To Saxham', ll. 21–30. Reversed to telling effect in the 'rails' passage in Marvell's 'Upon Appleton House' (ll. 393 ff.).

[45] On this subject see Turner, pp. 142 ff.

[46] 'A Panegerick to Sir *Lewis Pemberton*', l. 60, *Poems*, p. 147.

and not a country gentleman).[47] Thomas's 'Rurall Sanctuary' shall be as '*Elizium* to thy wife and thee' (l. 138); Porter will be regaled by sports and festivals described chiefly as entertainment for the lord. The common rustic unquestioningly assumes a subservient role—with disconcerting directness in 'The Hock-Cart' (*Poems*, p. 102):

> And, you must know, your Lords word's true,
> Feed him ye must, whose food fils you. (ll. 51–2)

In this poem, the lord's hospitality is obviously no more than a once-a-year event. 'The Wassaile' invokes a more generous ideal, but the actual household visited in the poem is sadly lacking in bounty. The hollowness of such rural harmony and prosperity is most openly if unwittingly exposed in Herrick's poems: his characteristic transparency of texture here serves to reveal rather than redeem the truth.

The country-house ethos reverses that of the pastoral in the latter's most distinctive form. The idyllic elements of rural life no longer mark a fundamental otherness from court or city, but only a special modification of the courtly or feudal ideal. It may have a corrective but certainly not a subversive effect. The country becomes a model for traditional 'merry England'—a merciful survival of the 'good old days'—and hence a symbol of the peace held still to envelop the English polity as a whole:[48]

> And if the Fields as thankfull prove
> For benefits receiv'd, as seed,
> They will, to quite so great a love,
> *A Virgill* breed.
>
> A *Tityrus*, that shall not cease
> Th'*Augustus* of our world to praise
> In equall verse, author of peace
> And *Halcyon* dayes.[49]

Or, even more extravagantly, it is not the peace of old England but a new blessing, a change attributed ironically enough to Caroline rule, as in the opening scene of George Daniel's *The Genius of this Great and Glorious Ile* (1637).[50] Such peace would soon be blasted by the Civil War; but

[47] Hibbard, p. 168. The poems are 'A Country life: To his Brother, *M. Tho*: *Herrick*' and 'The Country life, to the honoured *M. End. Porter*' (*Poems*, pp. 34, 229).

[48] On this subject see Turner, ch. iv.

[49] Sir Richard Fanshawe, 'An Ode, upon . . . His Majesties Proclamation in . . . 1630', Helen Gardner (ed.), *The Metaphysical Poets* (rev. edn. Harmondsworth, 1966), 172.

[50] For an account see Turner, pp. 40–1.

even afterwards—as also in, say, *The Compleat Angler*—the country enshrines the *ideal* of the same peace:

> In such a scorching age as this,
> Who would not ever seek a shade,
> Deserve their happiness to miss,
> As having their own peace betray'd.[51]

This uniquely English peace had found comparable expression from mid-Elizabethan times or even earlier. There the poets had chiefly relied on the poetic convention of pastoral, focused upon Eliza the Shepherds' Queen. Now they concentrate on the actual rural order, with subsidiary use of pastoral and allied conventions. The centrality of the pastoral has been lost. It either survives in a shadowy residue of its authentic state, or as one element out of many in a conglomerate rustic or mythic poetry.

We are approaching the totally anthropocentric landscape-poetry of Denham's *Cooper's Hill*. Here a plain where '*Faunus* and *Sylvanus* keep their Courts'[52] sets the scene for a highly moralized account of a deer-hunt, the whole sandwiched between references to St Paul's, Windsor Castle, Chertsey Abbey, Runnymede, the Magna Charta and the pursuit of liberty. The hill, or nature itself, is merely a vantage-point for the contemplation of social and moral matters.

Twenty years before *Cooper's Hill*, the little-known Patrick Hannay had lamented the danger to the same Thames Valley,

> Whereon the silly sheep do fearless feed,
> While on a bank the shepherd tunes his reed.
>
> Next shady groves where *Delia* hunted oft,
> And light-foot *Fairies* tripping still do haunt:
> There mirthful *Muses* raise sweet notes aloft . . .[53]

The sylvans are disturbed, and sometimes driven away, by Pluto's attendants from the smoky gloom of industrial Croydon. This is the lament writ large in Drayton's *Poly-Olbion*. The progress of the new pastoral, and the new veins of country poetry that overshadow it, witness a parallel movement in the evolution of the landscape itself. The golden

[51] Katherine Philips, 'A retir'd Friendship. To Ardelia', ll. 29–32, Saintsbury, i. 524.

[52] Line 235 of the 1668 text. I have used Denham's *Poetical Works* ed. T. H. Banks, jun. (New Haven, 1928). See pp. 78–81 for the 1642 and 1668 versions of this passage, with their varying approaches to sylvan myth.

[53] Song VIII. 13–17, in the 'Songs and Sonnets' appended to Hannay's *Nightingale* vol. (1622): Saintsbury, i. 722.

age of the pastoral convention is over. It is eking out a life by endless compromises with other genres and modes of sensibility.

2. *Pastoral in religious nature-poetry*

A peripheral but noteworthy development needs separate treatment: the incorporation of pastoral into a rich vein of religious nature-poetry. This owes surprisingly little to the standard motifs of Christ or the clergy as shepherds, or of the shepherds of the Nativity. Such elements can be used as necessary; the first, particularly, features in Henry Vaughan's poetry.[54] The Christian soul can itself become a shepherd by allegory, as in George Herbert's 'Christmas':

> My soul's a shepherd too; a flock it feeds
> Of thoughts, and words, and deeds.
> The pasture is thy word: the streams, thy grace
> Enriching all the place.[55]

But such specific images and allusions are anchored in the spiritual content of the shepherd's life:

> Shepherds are honest people; let them sing.[56]

This is Herbert again. To him goes the credit for infusing spiritual meaning into the simple joy of shepherd life as expressed in the Elizabethan lyric. As a further subtlety, in 'Jordan I' he turns this quintessential pastoral simplicity against the sophisticated trappings of the pastoral convention itself:

> Is it no verse, except enchanted groves
> And sudden arbours shadow course-spunne lines? (ll. 6–7)

But we must turn to slightly later poets for the full development of this spiritual vein, the perfection of one of the shepherd's symbolic roles. Sidney Godolphin has an important poem on the subject: it commences with the Nativity shepherds, contrasts them with the Magi, and progresses to general praise of piety, simplicity, and *docta ignorantia*:

[54] e.g. 'Religion', ll. 49–50; 'Mount of Olives I', l. 16; 'And do they so?', l. 40; 'Holy Communion', ll. 51–2; 'The Shepherds', ll. 45–50. All refs. to Vaughan's *Complete Poems*, ed. Alan Rudrum (Harmondsworth, 1976).

[55] ll. 17–20; all Herbert refs. to the *English Poems*, ed. C. A. Patrides (London, 1974).

[56] Herbert, 'Jordan I', l. 11.

Wise men, all ways of knowledge past,
To the shepherds' wonder come at last:[57]

Exactly the same pattern, based again on the Nativity shepherds, is finely developed in Vaughan's 'The Shepherds'. Here too, 'innocence and pleasure' are attendant upon 'holy leisure' (ll. 1–2):

Only content, and love, and humble joys
  Lived there without all noise,
Perhaps some harmless cares for the next day
  Did in their bosoms play,
As where to lead their sheep, what silent nook,
  What springs or shades to look,
But that was all; . . . (ll. 35–41)

This imaginatively independent shepherd life validates the presentation of Christ as 'their souls' great shepherd' (l. 45)—though he soon becomes, rather inconsistently, the Lamb of God as well.

'The Shepherds' is unusual among Vaughan's poems in being openly pastoral. As a rule, his spiritual nature-poetry relies on a complex of other elements. They may be best approached through the roughly contemporary work of Edward Benlowes: *Theophila's Love-Sacrifice* (1652), with its two cantos (XII and XIII) on 'The Sweetness of Retirement' and 'The Pleasure of Retirement'.[58] The Latin argument to 'Sweetness' already presents nature as a temple, in a deistic conceit as daring as any in Vaughan:

Hoc Nemus est Templum, patuli Laquearia Rami;
  Fit sacrae Truncus quisque Columna Domus
Voce Deum celebro; Concordes sponte Choristae,
  Sunt Praecentores, dum modulantur, Aves.[59]

[This forest is the temple, the spreading branches its panelled ceiling. Each trunk makes a pillar of the holy house. I praise God with my voice: the birds, spontaneously harmonious choristers, are my praecentors as they sing.]

The succeeding cantos have much on the peace, innocence, and blessed humility of country life, drawing on classical as well as biblical allusion: 'The Golden Age, like Jordan's stream, does here reflow' (XII. 120, p. 448). The juxtaposition is Benlowes's own, though the line is based on

[57] 'Hymn': 'Lord, when the wise men came from far . . .', Massingham, p. 115.

[58] Consider also the title of Mildmay Fane's vol., *Otia sacra* (1648), for the spiritualization of an essentially pastoral concept.

[59] Saintsbury, i. 445, ll. 11–12, 25–6.

Sarbiewski.[60] This is contrasted with the life of the 'false shepherds' who incite religious wars. Here we have a pastoral metaphor, but used in a context of falsehood and violence, while actual country life provides the spiritual ideal.

In 'The Pleasure of Retirement', this ideal grows explicitly pastoral, even drawing upon the 'shepherd's holiday' of literary convention:

> With harmless shepherds we sometimes do stay,
> Whose plainness does outvie the gay,
> While nibbling ewes do bleat, and frisking lambs do stray.
>
> . . . .
>
> While swains the burth'ning fleeces shear away,
> Oat-pipes to past'ral sonnets play,
> And all the merry hamlet bells chime holy day.
>
> (XIII. 13–15, 22–4, p. 455)

This, however, is part of an account embracing herds of cattle, ripe crops, and full orchards, a real countryside inhabited by 'the mower, who with big-swoln veins, | Wieldeth the crookèd scythe' and 'hinds' that 'do sweat through both their skins, and shopsters scorn' (XIII. 4–5, 42, pp. 455, 456). Vivid, even earthy details blend with insipid idealization and classical allusion, and these with moral and spiritual lessons drawn from nature. Benlowes's native scenery becomes not only akin to but a type of biblical settings (XII. 241–3, p. 451):

> Friend, view that rock, and think from rock's green Wound
> How thirst-expelling streams did bound:
> View streams, and think how Jordan did become dry ground.

The pastoral takes its place within this variety of elements.

In Benlowes's relatively unsubtle work, the components are easily separated; in Vaughan, they need careful unravelling. Some have been thoroughly investigated. There is nothing I can add to Maren-Sofie Røstvig on the influence of Horace's Epode II or of Casimire Sarbiewski's poetry. The importance of biblical landscapes is equally obvious. Most important in this respect is 'Ascension-Day': Bethany blends with Eden, and that with Brecknockshire:

> I smell her [the Magdalene's] spices, and her ointment yields,
> As rich a scent as the now primrosed fields: (ll. 21–2)

[60] See Røstvig, i. 145.

Angels descend to earth and dwell in nature, not only in the days of Genesis ('Religion', 'Corruption') but in Vaughan's own:

> But *rural shades* are the sweet fence
> Of piety and innocence.
> They are the *meek's* calm region, where
> Angels descend, and rule the sphere:[61]

The paradise-theme is by implication everywhere, and made explicit in a large number of poems[62] with associated themes such as prelapsarian innocence:

> Such was the bright world, on the first seventh day,
> Before man brought forth sin, and sin decay;
> When like a virgin clad in *flowers* and *green*
> The pure earth sat, and the fair woods had seen
> No frost, but flourished in that youthful vest,
> With which their great Creator had them dressed:[63]

From the orthodox Christian standpoint, nature fell with man:

> He drew the curse upon the world, and cracked
> The whole frame with his fall.[64]

This was inevitable, as man was central to the natural order; nature was created to serve man:

> For us the windes do blow,
> The earth doth rest, heav'n move, and fountains flow.
> Nothing we see, but means our good . . .[65]

This is from Herbert, and is the usual and expected position in his poems, as in Vaughan's more orthodox ones (like 'Corruption', quoted before n. 64). But in the latter's most distinctive vein, the order is habitually reversed:

> Herbs sleep unto the *east*, and some fowls thence
> Watch the returns of light;
> But hearts are not so kind:[66]

[61] 'Retirement II', ll. 21–4, from *Thalia Rediviva*.
[62] e.g. 'Ascension-Day', ll. 37–48, 'The Palm-Tree', ll. 2–7, 'Retirement II', ll. 27–8.
[63] 'Ascension-Day', ll. 39–44.
[64] 'Corruption', ll. 15–16.
[65] Herbert, 'Man', ll. 25–7.
[66] 'Sure, there's a tie of bodies . . .', ll. 11–13.

The Great Chain of Being is stood on its head. Man has fallen, but nature retains its original purity. Further, man becomes peripheral to nature's scheme, which is complete and self-justified without his presence:

> In what rings,
> And *hymning circulations* the quick world
> Awakes, and sings;[67]

Man may, however, merge with nature, surrender his fallen self to achieve identity with this superior order.

> I would (said I) my God would give
> The staidness of these things to man! for these
> To his divine appointments ever cleave . . .[68]

Nature being so much more powerful a presence here than in conventional pastoral, the relations between man and nature are bound to change. Standard pastoral—especially classical pastoral, but most Renaissance works too—had been firmly focused on man. He was presented in a setting of nature because such an environment revealed his innate tendencies in certain pure and undiluted forms. But the setting never demanded equal attention in descriptive, let alone thematic terms.

In certain poems, most notably *The Shepheardes Calender*, nature had grown into an object of interest in its own right.[69] It now becomes a superior force, a consistent moral presence, the corrective and purifying agent seen in standard pastoral only through its effects on human life. Obviously, what we are witnessing here is not simply a disintegration of the pastoral into other poetic types but the creation of an entirely new poetic mode, to which the pastoral provides one of many subsidiary, contributing elements. Themes and ideals formerly implicit in the pastoral fiction find a new and more direct vehicle in a version of landscape-poetry; elements of actual pastoral convention occur in particularly hidden guise within it.

Vaughan's awareness of pastoral is obvious from his first volume of verse, *Poems with the Tenth Satire of Juvenal Englished* (1646). The 'Song' beginning '*Amyntas* go, thou art undone . . .' is unmemorably conventional, with involved and slightly incoherent conceits. Even in *Thalia Rediviva* (1678), 'Fida Forsaken' unexpectedly proves to be a pastoral poem, on the strength of a reference to 'our true God, *Pan*'. This

[67] 'The Morning-Watch', ll. 9–11.
[68] Vaughan, 'Man', ll. 8–10.
[69] See above, Ch. 7, sects. 4–5.

trivial pastoralism is turned to better use in 'A Rhapsody' in 1646. A pastoral fresco in the Globe Tavern provides a pleasing contrast with the actual town setting:

> Hark! how his rude pipe frets the quiet air,
> Whilst every hill proclaims *Lycoris* fair.
> Rich, happy man! that canst thus watch, and sleep,
> Free from all cares; but thy wench, pipe & sheep. (ll. 21–4)

Meanwhile, a local scenic poem, 'Upon the Priory Grove', blends topographic description with the conventional account of a love-bower, and that with higher themes closely allied to the pastoral. The Priory Grove shadows Elysium, and the poet hopes it will be transplanted there. The theme of innocence is particularly important: even on earth, all foul creatures and powers are absent from the grove (ll. 5–12), and in heaven it will be a setting for 'our first innocence, and love' (l. 34).

These two strains—picture-pastoral, and spiritualization of a rural setting—blend in 'To the River Isca' (*Olor Iscanus*: published 1651 but composed earlier). This begins with a sophisticated, outward-looking poet glorifying his native river, rather as in Ronsard's addresses to the Loire. But his subsequent prayer for the river is in a different vein. The river-bank is first implicitly, then openly Parnassian (ll. 37–42). A little later, it is given paradisal touches, with the expulsion of all evil creatures and forces (ll. 51–68). With all this goes near-explicit pastoralism:

> May thy gentle *swains* (like *flowers*)
> Sweetly spend their *youthful hours*,
> And thy *beauteous nymphs* (like *doves*)
> Be *kind* and *faithful* to their *loves*;
> *Garlands*, and *Songs*, and *Roundelays* . . (ll. 43–7)

Very much the same combination of elements occurs in 'Retirement' and 'The Bee' in *Thalia Rediviva*. One cannot explain the nature-poems in *Silex Scintillans* in such terms; but surely the poems I have just treated point to pastoral as one element in the complex syntheses of *Silex*. Overt pastoralism may be absent as a rule; but it is introduced from biblical sources in 'The Search':

> *Jacob's well*, bequeathed since
> Unto his sons, (where often they
> In those calm, golden evenings lay
> Waterings their flocks, and having spent
> Those white days, drove home to the tent
> Their *well-fleeced* train;) . . . (ll. 22–7)

'Mount of Olives I' makes a 'competitive' contrast between secular shepherd life and religious-pastoral metaphor:

> *Cotswold*, and *Cooper's* both have met
> With learned swains, and echo yet
>   Their pipes, and wit;
> But thou sleep'st in a deep neglect
> Untouched by any; and what need
> The sheep bleat thee a silly lay
>   That heard'st both reed
>   And sheepward play? (ll. 9–16)

The corrupted stream in 'Religion' is metaphorical too, reversing the blessings showered (in literal terms) upon the Usk in 'To the River Isca'. The succeeding pastoralism, equally metaphorical, follows easily:

> Heal then these waters, Lord; or bring thy flock,
> Since these are troubled, to the springing rock . . . (ll. 49–50)

The pastoral convention, in its biblical and secular-philosophic aspects, plays about Vaughan's strikingly new spiritual interpretations of nature. It is the ultimate instance of the far-reaching influence of pastoral.

PART III

The Extension of Pastoral: Narrative, Drama, and Spectacle

12

Pastoral Romance: The Cyclic Structure

SANNAZARO'S *Arcadia* marks the first step in the development from eclogue to pastoral romance. To accomplish this, Sannazaro links the eclogues by *prose*. Scholars generally hold that the eclogues, or some of them, came first. The *prose* were 'written round' them, acquiring more and more importance as Sannazaro developed his plan.

This formal basis in the eclogue means that Sannazaro's narrative never really gets off the ground. The entire romance bears a lyric, static, contemplative character. The early *prose* have little narrative content, and are sometimes outweighed in bulk by the eclogues. When the prose grows more substantial, it is often by repeating the static patterns of the eclogues. The fourth *prosa* consists almost entirely of a 'blason' of the lovely Amaranta, and long accounts of a stag and a beechen cup staked in a singing-match. The fifth *prosa* has a prose rendering of Nemesianus's Eclogue I; the seventh and eighth are largely introspective accounts of Sincero's and Carino's loves, the latter with a long description of fowling. The prose moves slowly, pausing over each detail of the pastoral dreamland.

There is no continuity of action—indeed, action is almost deliberately suppressed. As David Kalstone remarks, *Arcadia* 'moves from one gathering of shepherds to another'.[1] Each illustrates an aspect of the pastoral world, and is then dismissed for the next. The only recurring factor is the figure of Sincero himself, and he is important only in the last part of the story.

None the less, a pattern does emerge from Sincero's career: faintly as yet, obscured by the static pastoralism, but of potential importance in later works. Sincero is a courtier, who has come to Arcadia 'non come rustico pastore ma come coltissimo giovene' [not as a rustic shepherd but as a most cultured youth].[2] He escapes into the pastoral world out of his unhappy, love-afflicted court life, and returns there at the end.

[1] *Sidney's Poetry*, p. 24.

[2] *Arcadia*, ed. Carrara, p. 153; tr. Nash, p. 153.

This foreshadows a pattern towards which many later plays and romances appear to strive. Characters escape from a corrupt or unhappy court into a pastoral or rural refuge. In this regenerative setting, they undergo a change in their nature and relationships; and finally, their problems resolved, they return to a new, revivified, courtly community. Such a structure captures and puts to organic use the basic pastoral contrast of court and country.[3]

This is simply put, but in view of my later accounts of romance and drama, I should like to stress the extreme importance of what we may conveniently call a cyclic pattern of pastoral. Obviously, Sannazaro does not give us anything like a fully developed example. *Arcadia* shows no resolution or revival: Sincero returns to Naples to hear of his beloved's death, casting him out of one affliction into another. Also, he is not really shown to revisit the court. Instead he hears the Neapolitan shepherds sing, reflecting his own grief in the dirge for Meliseus's dead shepherdess. The courtly world is also presented in pastoral terms. Court and country blend into each other instead of being placed in clear contrast.

But it is important that the two worlds, court and country, should exist, and the central character pass from one to the other and back again. *Arcadia* contains in embryo the formal problem facing later writers of pastoral romance and drama. The eclogue is small enough to revolve, if the poet so desires, on a single point of pastoral metaphor. The court can be presented in terms of the country; the king, lover, or heroic poet in terms of the shepherd—even if the former entity so overlaps the latter that the authentic pastoral world is shut out. The drama or romance is too far-flung to sustain such 'allegory'. Here the pastoral cannot function as metaphor—at least, not for any length of time. The shepherd has to be a shepherd, the courtier a courtier. If the author wants to relate the two worlds, he has to do so in terms not of metaphor but of narrative structure, moving his characters from one world to the other or confronting characters from the two. Such a structure can provide an organic use for the contrast of court and country basic to the pastoral mode.

But this potential proves slow of realization: we must wait for English

[3] For a discussion of this structure, see Peter Marinelli, *Pastoral* (The Critical Idiom; London, 1971), ch. iv. See also Mary Lascelles, 'Shakespeare's Pastoral Comedy', in John Garrett (ed.), *More Talking about Shakespeare* (London, 1959), 75–6, 82; Walter R. Davis, *A Map of Arcadia* (New Haven, 1965), 34–8; David Young, *The Heart's Forest: A Study of Shakespeare's Pastoral Plays* (New Haven, 1972), 18–20; Humphrey Tonkin, *Spenser's Courteous Pastoral* (Oxford, 1972), 284ff., 300ff.

romance and drama, at the close of the century, to see it occur on any scale. Italian pastoral drama, as we saw, eschews the 'cycle' and deals with the shepherd world alone. The continental romance resolves Sannazaro's delicate balance of eclogue and narrative in two ways, both inimical to a genuine development of the pastoral. It may concentrate on the narrative, making it more and more elaborate and correspondingly remote from the pastoral, passing into chivalric romance or a simple narrative of Fortune's vicissitudes. Again, it may lay greater, undemanding emphasis on the verse, and finally disintegrate into a miscellany of lyrics. I shall illustrate these tendencies from the Spanish romance *Diana* and Remy Belleau's *La Bergerie*.

Jorge de Montemayor's *Diana* probably appeared in 1559. Alonso Perez and Gaspar Gil Polo produced two continuations, both in 1564. In the work of all three writers, several strands of action are interlaced: we move backward and forward in time, earlier events being recounted in flashback. The obvious (and indeed only) model, barring the ultimate one in the *Odyssey*, is Heliodorus's third-century Greek romance, the *Aethiopica*.[4] In most medieval and Renaissance romances—or Achilles Tatius's *Clitophon and Leucippe*, for that matter—the various plots progress simultaneously and are related, alternately, as they occur.

The influence of Greek romance also makes *Diana* a largely non-pastoral narrative full of sensational action. Most of its characters are aristocrats, and much of the action stands in *contrast* to the pastoral love of Syrenus, Sylvanus, Diana, and Selvagia. Particularly in Gil Polo and Perez, chivalric and exotic adventure becomes a major ingredient, very much as in Heliodorus. In Gil Polo, the history of Marcelius, Alcida, and her family involves voyages and shipwrecks. Perez's two heroes, Delicius and Parthenius, begin their careers at the court of King Rotindas, and proceed on a quest for their parents involving long journeys, supernatural powers (Crimine and other river-nymphs in their underwater chambers), and the giant shepherd Gorphorost, who partakes of Homer and Ovid's Cyclops no less than Theocritus's.

These far-flung adventures are matched by courtly romance and intrigue. The best instances are Montemayor's story of Felix and Felismena (taken from Bandello) and Perez's of Disteus and Dardanea. In fact, many of the 'shepherds' in *Diana* dwell in sizeable towns, lead the lives of prosperous burghers, and conduct amours in appropriate style:

[4] Heliodorus's story of Cnemon is also the source of Gil Polo's plot of Filenus, Felisarda, and Montanus: a fact overlooked in J. M. Kennedy's edn. of Bartholomew Yong's trans. of Montemayor and Gil Polo.

witness the story of Belisa in Montemayor and of Montanus in Gil Polo. There are true shepherds in *Diana*, of course, and occasional touches of nature and rustic life. Montemayor introduces Syrenus in strongly bucolic vein,[5] of which we find later examples in both Montemayor and Gil Polo. A single example must serve:

> they began to walke over a pleasant and flowrie meade, which caused *Diana* to use these words. They are no doubt marvellous and strange things, which the industrie of man hath invented in populous and great cities, but yet those, which nature hath produced in the wide and solitarie fieldes, are more to bee admired . . . There is indeed (said *Marcelius*) in this pleasant solitude great store of content and joy . . .[6]

Now and then we even hear of rural activities. Arsenius courts Belisa 'sometimes in the fielde, as I was going to carrie the Shepherds their dinner; sometimes againe, as I was going to the river to rince my clothes; and sometimes for water to the fountaine' (p. 113, ll. 2–5).

But when all is said and done, these touches do not amount to much in a long romance. Perez, indeed, has more shepherd characters than the others, and more sense of pastoral life. Delicius and Parthenius were left with their foster-parents by shepherds (even as Cariclea was in Heliodorus), and they disguise themselves and dwell among shepherds while wooing Stela and Crimine. The love-lorn Sylvanus, Selvagia, and Cardenia take heed of their cattle (pp. 161, 326)[7]—an attention to duty unknown in Montemayor or Gil Polo. Parisiles discourses of Pan's divinity (p. 248): a notable instance of the 'pastoral religion' otherwise conspicuously absent in *Diana*. There is also the shepherd Partheus, a genial rustic who wears a hyena's skin to guard against thunder, expounds shepherd lore, and celebrates his humble, chaste, and rational love for his shepherdess (pp. 301 ff.). It is at least a feeble reflection of Sannazaro's world. Yet in the total sweep of Perez's amazingly involved narrative, these shepherds get far less attention than the courtly characters with their exotic adventures.

Again, in Perez as in the others, the quality of the shepherds' love does not differ markedly from the courtiers'; and, crucially, it is the courtiers that set the tone. Between *Ameto* and *Arcadia*, courtly love had crossed the social barrier and become the shepherd's birthright. In *Diana*, however, there is a running debate as to whether shepherds can aspire to

[5] See Kennedy's edn., p. 11, ll. 5 ff. All refs. to Montemayor and Gil Polo to this edn.

[6] Kennedy, p. 292, ll. 23–8, 34–5. Cf. p. 108, ll. 3 ff.; p. 228, ll. 13 ff.; p. 315, ll. 2 ff.; p. 323, ll. 14 ff.

[7] All refs. to Perez to Yong's trans. of *Diana* (London, 1598).

'gentle' love. It is generally granted to be possible,[8] but the aristocratic lover provides the yardstick; the shepherd can at most conform.

Class distinctions are vital in *Diana*. At Felicia's court, the aristocratic Felismena, Marcelius, and Alcida are greeted with luxuries; Sylvanus, Syrenus, and Selvagia get cordial but more Spartan treatment.[9] In Perez, Parisiles faces a dilemma when talking to a socially mixed audience: 'To these Shepherdes I could present some things requisite for their poor estate and vocations, and profitable for them and their flocks . . . To you noble personages, I could present (a thinge (perhaps) which would best fit your desires) whereof loue was first engendred, and how he worketh' (p. 199). Later the shepherds inspect a sheep-hook and hear about Pan, while Felix and Felismena enjoy Crimine's tale of love (pp. 247, 251). There is also a discourse on the 'base estates' of shepherds, and how Parthenius and Delicius are discovered to be of high birth and nature (p. 226). It is difficult to see why Gerhardt describes the characters of *Diana* as 'Tous égaux, tous oisifs' [all equal, all at leisure],[10] though she has many worthwhile things to say about the work.

Unlike Sannazaro's *Arcadia*, *Diana* does not provide a genuinely different set of pastoral values and interests. It caters to the established taste for romances of love, war, and adventure, governed by the usual aristocratic code. The pastoral element is neither marginal nor merely novel, but nor is it basic to the work. The controlling values remain courtly. Shepherds are admitted only as long as they behave themselves, and we are gratified that by and large they do so.

The same balance shows in the structure of the work. There is no real 'cyclic' plot in *Diana*, and the pastoral setting has no regenerative power. The shepherds' weeds that some of the courtiers assume, the shepherds' lives that Delicius and Parthenius lead, only serve to create fresh confusion. The pastoral setting in which the shepherds encounter them is simply another stage in their wanderings. The actual agent of fulfilment is the Lady Felicia, as courtly a character as could possibly be, reigning over her retinue of maidens in a sumptuous palace. Even the shepherds must come to her to solve their problems. We have, in fact, almost an anti-pastoral movement from country to court.

Of course, the prose narrative of *Diana* is only half the story. The other half is provided by the poems embodied in it. There is excellent precedent for this. Both *Ameto* and Sannazaro's *Arcadia* alternate prose

[8] See Kennedy, p. 137, ll. 21–37; p. 290, ll. 8–11; p. 294, l. 24, p. 354, ll. 29–35.

[9] See Kennedy, p. 138; p. 363, ll. 22ff., p. 366, ll. 24ff.

[10] Gerhardt, *La Pastorale*, p. 188.

and verse. *Ameto*, of course, is not primarily a pastoral work, and the poems cover a wide range of themes. The most memorable are the hymns to the ladies' patron-goddesses, tracing out the philosophic pattern of the work. Sannazaro has no clear philosophy, and all his poems are truly pastoral; but they too, as I remarked before, tonally dominate the work.

In *Diana*, on the other hand, the prose narrative comes first. The verse is used to develop the poetic or emotional potential of particular situations within the narrative. True, the action is often held up while its implications are tangentially explored in verse: as far as narrative stylization is concerned, we have not quite stepped out of Sannazaro's world.

But unlike the poems in *Arcadia*, those in *Diana* are only occasionally pastoral. Of the 154 poems in Montemayor, Perez, and Gil Polo, only 22 contain a substantial pastoral element. For the rest, there may be an occasional line on nature or the shepherd's life, or the mention of a 'shepherd' or 'shepherdess' without any other pastoral touch whatsoever. The greater number are purely non-bucolic, belonging to the general tradition of 'sonnets' on love (sometimes true sonnets) with full measure of courtly sophistication. There is nothing to distinguish the shepherds' songs from the courtiers'.

Further, a very large number of poems have no real links with the narrative. These detachable, non-pastoral lyrics recall the miscellaneous 'idylls' that I discussed in Chapter 5. Like them, the poems in *Diana*, bucolic in source but often not in content, contribute to the diffuse borderland of the pastoral: the casual, nominal pastoralism conveyed by the odd 'shepherd' in a context that has nothing of a setting of nature, a radical simplicity of emotion, or even the conventional trappings of pastoral life.

This can be illustrated from *England's Helicon*, which has twenty-four poems from Yong's *Diana*, plus one translated out of Montemayor by Sidney. Only seven belong to the group I have categorized as truly pastoral.[11] A number have no bucolic touch whatsoever. It must have been the counsel of despair to give them headings describing their pastoral narrative contexts.

Because the poems can be readily detached and perhaps anthologized, they also lead to neglect of the romance structure. Pastoral romance is forgotten for pastoral poetry, and pastoral poetry is forgotten for more diverse lyric models. This process is classically exemplified in Remy

[11] *Helicon*, nos. 48, 49, 60, 67, 98, 105, 109.

Belleau's *La Bergerie* (Book I first published 1565; revised and published with Book II in 1572). It was known to associates of Sidney like Daniel Rogers and Abraham Fraunce[12] and, we may assume, to Sidney himself.

Belleau's setting is a château: very recognizably Joinville, the seat of the House of Guise, where Belleau was tutor to the Duke's nephew. The presiding noblewoman is obviously Antoinette de Bourbon, Duchess of Guise. Her attendant 'shepherdesses' are her retinue of young women, and the 'shepherds' are court gallants.

The furthest the poet ventures is to the gardens and woods behind the castle and a little village below it, inhabited by tradesmen and artisans rather than shepherds. A beechen cup and a shepherd's stick are described in eclogue-like detail, but only as wares in a shop. Finally, the poet comes to the Marne and sees a troop of nymphs. Here, very briefly, we have the authentic note of nature-myth, if not of strict pastoral.[13] A nymph's song evokes a series of reminiscences from nature unique in the work:

> j'ay ouy le tin-tin des Cigalles au mois le plus chaut de l'été, j'ay ouy doucement glisser la rosee sur les herbes emperlees de son degout, . . . j'ay ouy couché dessus un ruisselet tapissé de verdure & calfeutré de mousse le murmure d'une eau roulante à petis flots au travers de petites pierrettes & de gravois menu . . .[14]
>
> [I have heard the chirping of grasshoppers in the hottest month of summer, I have heard the dew slide sweetly over the grass beaded with its drops . . . I have heard, lying above a rivulet covered with greenery and clumps of moss, the murmur of a stream flowing in little waves over little stones and fine gravel]

But the songs have nothing pastoral, and the episode is a small fraction of the whole.

There is really no story in *La Bergerie*. The poet simply wanders through the setting described above, meets a number of people (almost all courtiers), and hears, reads, and composes an altogether improbable number of poems, overwhelmingly courtly in spirit. A few make a formal parade of 'suffering' and 'admiring' shepherds who lament the wars of religion, celebrate the Treaty of Cateau-Cambrésis, and eulogize the

[12] For Rogers, see J. A. Van Dorsten, *Poets, Patrons and Professors* (Leiden, 1962), 29; for Fraunce, *The Arcadian Rhetorike*, ed. Ethel Seaton (Oxford, 1950), p. xxxii.

[13] I cannot agree with Gerhardt (pp. 242–4) that Belleau tempers the literary quality of his inspiration with substantial observation of nature, and even attempts to renew the French eclogue by this means.

[14] *La Bergerie* (1565 text), ed. D. Delacourcelle (Geneva, 1954), 128. All refs. for the 1565 version of Part I of *La Bergerie* ('Premier journée') to this text.

House of Guise.[15] 'L'Esté' and 'Description des vendanges' contain vivid country descriptions (Delacourcelle, pp. 42, 58). Finally we have one notable piece of pastoral, a love-song imploring Pan's aid: 'si pastoralle, si passionnee, & faitte si à propos' [so pastoral, so impassioned, and so appropriate]: p. 91. The 'bergeres' react by bursting into laughter! Apparently this is the correct and appreciative response. Rustic plainness is merely comic in that milieu, and 'si à propos' means simply that the piece conforms to 'pastoral decorum'.

By and large, these shepherdesses form their tastes on very different fare: eulogy of the military expedition of François, Duke of Guise (Delacourcelle, pp. 37 ff.); epitaphs on the first two Dukes (pp. 45, 46); an epithalamium for the Duke of Lorraine (p. 63); and a genethliacon and two court masques on the birth of the Duke's son (pp. 101 ff.)—the last of these written by Ronsard. These are supported by a battery of love-lyrics, courtly in spirit if not in specific allusion.

In 1572 some attempt is made to increase the pastoral content of Part I. The 'Chant pastoral', 'L'Esté', and 'Description des vendanges' are expanded with some truly bucolic material, and there is a new delicate nature-lyric, 'Avril'.[16] But the shepherds in 'L'Esté' include Bellot, Tenot, and Perrot: Du Bellay, Baïf, and Ronsard. Bellin (Belleau himself) and Toinet (Baïf) are interlocutors in an eclogue that replaces Ronsard's royal masque (Marty-Laveaux, i. 293 ff.). In fact, these poems are allegories of the relations between contemporary poets. As commonly with the pastoral of the Pléiade, Belleau's gaze is turned to external matters.

In any case, the new pastoralism in Part I is more than offset by the contents of Part II. Here we have one poem, 'L'Hyver', of markedly rustic witch-lore (ii. 80–5). A mysterious fisherman offers some authentic piscatory material (ii. 52–72), and the 'Eclogue, sur la guarison d'amour' is properly bucolic (ii. 43); but Ianot, Thenot, Bellin, and Perrot occur more than once among the characters. Finally, an elegy for Du Bellay is strongly pastoral, full of echoes of Moschus's Lament for Bion (ii. 133 ff.).

Against this, there are eminently courtly epicedia and epithalamia. But what really stifles the pastoral is the sheer weight of miscellaneous

[15] See Delacourcelle, p. 29; the extension of this poem in 1572 (Belleau's *Œuvres poetiques*, ed. C. Marty-Laveaux (Paris, 1878; repr. 1965), i. 187–8); Delacourcelle, pp. 43 ff. The first two items are taken from Belleau's *Chant pastoral de la paix* (1559).

[16] Marty-Laveaux (ed.), *Œuvres poetiques*, i. 201 ff. All refs. to this edn. for the 1572 revision of Book I and the text of Book II.

poetry: a plethora of short pieces (fifty in a series at one point) matched by a number of long ones, culminating in an interminable 'David and Bersabee'. By the end, the prose connections have lost all importance, disappearing altogether for a long stretch (ii. 112–26) and again well before the end.

Belleau, it seems, has chosen a pastoral setting because he feels he need not take it seriously. It is the undemanding wrapping for a very mixed parcel of poems. A number are borrowed from other authors or reprinted from Belleau's own earlier works. The narrative connecting them dwindles and withers away. The pastoral romance has subsided into the lyric substratum that always threatened to engulf it.

In Sidney we see a new attempt, on an unprecedented scale, at building up a valid pastoral structure. But basically, he retains the courtly bearings of his predecessors in the romance. Thus Sidney's pastoralism is a curiously blended affair, with remarkable innovations and yet sterile and self-destructive elements as well. The same paradoxical combination appears later in d'Urfé's *L'Astrée*; and it may be better, if somewhat unchronological, to look at this and other continental works before moving on to the English pastoral romance.

13
Cervantes

1. Galatea

CERVANTES'S first published work, in 1585, was the first part of the unfinished pastoral romance *Galatea*. He kept promising a sequel almost to the day of his death. His failure to produce it is sometimes taken to imply an innate distaste for the artificial pastoral genre. Yet *Galatea* is a classic example of its kind, and the tensions that it conceals may be deeper and more organic than sheer antipathy.

In *Galatea*, a number of intrigue-plots and romantic adventures are grouped around the central love-story of Galatea, Elicio, and his humbler fellow-suitor Erastro. In some respects, the work leaves an impression of static, Sannazaresque idyllic life. This is no doubt partly the impact of any pastoral work on the modern reader; and due also to the fact that the story is unfinished, so that interest in the plot is necessarily low. But partly too it is owing to the leisured pace and relaxed form. There are no fewer than seventy-eight poems[1] of varying length. There are also a fair number of set speeches, plus debates and discussions on love. *Otium*, and a refined poetic mood, are essential postulates of the work.

But these are belied by the content of much of the narrative, the actual structure of events. Strangely for a pastoral romance, *Galatea* opens with violent death: Lisandro kills his enemy Carino, who had plotted against the life of Lisandro's beloved Leonida. (Lisandro later tells Elicio the whole sordid intrigue.)[2] Scarcely is this episode over when we embark upon the tale of misunderstanding, spite, and conspiracy that keeps Teolinda separated from her lover Artidoro.

Story succeeds story, all in analogous veins: love, adventure, and chivalry prove disturbingly akin to violence, intrigue, and hate. And shepherds are as prone to these evils as courtiers or gentlemen. The idyllic

[1] Three of these are by Francisco de Figueroa: see William Byron, *Cervantes. A Biography* (London, 1979), 262.

[2] i. 21 ff. All refs. by book and (where appropriate) page no. to *Galatea* as tr. by H. Oelsner and A. B. Welford in *The Complete Works* of Cervantes in English trans. (gen. ed. J. Fitzmaurice Kelly), ii (Glasgow, 1903).

marriage of Daranio and Silveria (and there too we have a rejected lover)[3] serves to counterpoint a very different quality in pastoral life and love generally. When the narrative breaks off at the end of Book VI, Elicio is about to make a last peaceful bid for Galatea's hand, failing which he has already planned intimidation and open violence with the aid of his entire community.

It will be seen that Cervantes's shepherds are distinctly martial in training and temperament. They are, of course, skilled and sophisticated in love and love-poetry as well. Indeed, their relation to the 'higher' orders is somewhat ambiguous. Sometimes we find the expected distinction. Florisa invites Teolinda and Leonarda, both shepherdesses, to her house, but apologizes for not entertaining the high-born Grisaldo and Rosaura in befitting manner (iv. 149). Elsewhere, though, the dividing line is blurred. Although Lisandro is of noble birth and Leonida a shepherdess, they seem to be on equal footing, and their fathers were the two governors of the region (i. 21–2). Teolinda too declares she is not of low stock, though her parents are labourers and she has herself herded sheep (i. 33). The shepherds' courtly excellences are sometimes granted only as cause of wonder: an eclogue by Orampo, Marsilio, *et alii* seems, even to shepherds like Damon and Thyrsis, to be 'of more than shepherd wit' (iii. 134). Thyrsis himself, and Lenio, amaze Darinto by their wit—until Elicio explains that they have long been at court (iv. 181). Here we have a notably ambiguous interaction of court and country.

Similarly ambiguous, and inconclusive, is Darinto's debate with Elicio on shepherd life. Darinto, a courtier, praises and envies the shepherds, and it is left to Elicio to object that their life has 'as many slippery places and toils' as the courtier's (iv. 157–8).

There are simpler court–country oppositions, as when we discover that Lauso, singing in praise of country life, is the familiar figure of the disillusioned courtier and warrior (iv. 158). Rural life may be spiritually superior by its very humility, or it may pose a grander challenge to the 'higher' orders. Both positions, of course, are standard and recognized in pastoral. The latter obviously carries potential for more complex treatment, a realization of the higher possibilities of idealized shepherd life. In Cervantes's work, this is partly brought out by the ideal embodied in Galatea herself: though she was brought up in 'pastoral and rustic exercises', noblewomen thought themselves lucky to 'approach her in discretion as in beauty' (i. 10). Perhaps more memorably, we have the

[3] ii. 92ff.; iii. 109ff.

dignified conduct and varied wisdom of the learned shepherds Damon and Thyrsis (and to a lesser extent Elicio himself). Even in appearance, the pair are 'so well dressed, though in shepherd's garb, that in their carriage and appearance they seemed more like brave courtiers than mountain herdsmen' (ii. 60).

All in all, there is the unmistakable sense of a special grace and dignity in shepherd life. The natural setting is appropriately 'golden', sometimes paradisal: 'Here in every season of the year is seen the smiling spring in company with fair Venus, her garments girded up and full of love . . . if in any part of the earth the Elysian fields have a place, it is without doubt here' (vi. 242). This is the crowning perception of a substantial pastoral life, fleshed out with vivid and convincing touches of herdsmanship, idyllic practices, and 'pastoral religion'. The obsequies for the famous shepherd Meliso in Book VI might be straight out of Sannazaro.

Yet it is during these obsequies that Calliope appears through storm and fire and sings her 'Canto' on the great poets of Spain (vi. 251 ff.). The priest Telesio follows this with a discourse on the same subject (vi. 288–9). Such open allusions are rare. But Cervantes himself tells us in the Prologue that 'many of the disguised shepherds . . . were shepherds only in dress' (p. 6). The Meliso whose death is lamented is commonly taken as the historian Diego Hurtado de Mendoza. Other shepherds have been identified with contemporary poets, from a manuscript list found in the Spanish National Library,[4] and still longer lists have been compiled from other sources, with Cervantes as Elicio.[5] Galatea herself is often taken to be Donna Catalina de Palacios, Cervantes's wife-to-be.

The impact of such 'allusive art-pastoral' is less disorienting than the tonal adaptation of pastoral life that I noted earlier. For it should be obvious by now that, in structure, range of material, and general spirit, *Galatea* is more allied to Montemayor than to Sannazaro, and indeed marks an interesting fusion of the two models, which may be said to mark the opposite boundaries of pastoral romance.

The variety of subplots in *Galatea* resembles that in *Diana*; but whereas in Montemayor and his followers, the action frequently ranged outward from the pastoral and left shepherd life far behind, *Galatea* is so constructed that the various strands of action lead up to the pastoral

[4] See Byron, p. 164.

[5] e.g. Fitzmaurice Kelly, Introduction to *Galatea* (cit. n. 2), p. xxxii. For a general identification of features of Cervantes's shepherds with traits and personalities of the age, see G. Shagg, 'A Matter of Masks: *La Galatea*', in D. M. Atkinson and A. H. Clarke (eds.), *Hispanic Studies in Honour of Joseph Manson* (Oxford, 1972), 255–67.

setting. This gives the work a strong central pastoral interest, but at the same time modifies the nature of that interest. We can hardly speculate on the possible course of an unfinished story: no doubt it would have incorporated the 'cyclic' structure in some form. But it could scarcely have been a very simple form, for the quality of shepherd life has been too greatly modified for that.

As I indicated above, Cervantes's shepherds have much that is special to them; but even more that they hold in common with the rest of humanity. They apparently live in a conventional idyllic milieu; but except in the most superficial aspects of behaviour, they seldom behave as we might expect. Their vision and experience have been widened, but accordingly urbanized and, one may say, contaminated. This seems to be the case here to a greater degree than in Montemayor; and, much more than in Montemayor, the shepherds have marked personalities beneath stereotyped patterns of speech and demeanour. Their actions and relations introduce new values, new individual responses to a mixed body of experience, which cannot be captured in a plot-summary or in a selected reading of idyllic passages—nor indeed in the surface register of standard pastoral rhetoric, which Cervantes retains.

'Broken pastoral rules litter the pages', says William Byron of *Galatea*.[6] Its pervasive pastoralism conceals a more radical threat to its own existence than the mixed texture of *Diana*. The pastoral elements are not simply diluted or overshadowed; they are developed along lines that subtly deflect their original thrust. But as long as they survive, and apparently flourish, their inevitable concomitants in terms of form, matter, and rhetoric cannot but impede the free growth of these new concerns, for which pastoral is scarcely the most appropriate medium.

Hence, perhaps, the unfinished state of the work, and maybe the way pastoral is introduced in Cervantes's later work and masterpiece. His reservations about the mode are stated directly in 'The Dogs' Colloquy' in the *Exemplary Novels* (published 1613):

> I took to considering that it could not be true that I had heard say of the life of shepherds, at least of those of whom the mistress of my master[7] used to read in certain books ... [Actual shepherds] sang ... with harsh voices which, whether alone or joined with others, appeared not to sing, but to shriek or grunt. The most of the day they used to spend in getting rid of fleas or patching

[6] Byron, p. 275.

[7] i.e. the dog's first master, a butcher. He is now kept by shepherds and is describing their ways.

their foot-gear . . . From this I came to comprehend, what I think everybody must believe, that all those books are dreams well written to amuse the idle, and not truth at all, for, had they been so, there would have been some trace among my shepherds of that most happy life . . .[8]

Yet on the whole, pastoral romances (including *Galatea* itself) get a kinder reprieve during the book-burning in *Don Quixote* than almost any other class of literature; declaredly because they work less mischief but also, it is plain, because of Cervantes's greater awareness of their purely literary value. The unreality of pastoral is balanced against its aesthetic reality, its currency as a meaningful dream. The specifically pastoral episodes in *Don Quixote* focus and make explicit the tensions between city and country, ideal and rural, fine-spun and demotic values, that pervade the work and take on subtle, mutually modifying relations going far beyond mere burlesque.

2. Don Quixote *as pastoral*

Don Quixote (Part I, 1605; Part II, 1615) contains a number of pastoral and quasi-pastoral interludes. If we view the whole work as mirroring the structure of the chivalric romance, these may be held to correspond to similar interludes in such romances. But, after all, *Don Quixote* is not a chivalric romance *simpliciter*: however complex in its implications, it is essentially a burlesque of the form. The pastoral interludes in such narrative are explicitly satirized more than once (I. iii. 11, pp. 185–6; I. iv. 23, p. 421).[9] But similar interludes in *Don Quixote* are too varied and complex to be dismissed by the same censure. If the premisses of chivalric narrative are designedly inverted, the pastoral element must obviously serve a different function in the whole, and acquire a different significance in absolute terms.

Given the nature of the work, it may for once be fitting to begin with the extended implications of pastoral and work inward to its formal manifestations. *Don Quixote* is a heaven-sent illustration of pastoral in Empson's sense of a balance or contrast of value-systems. Quixote's career provides a deflating parallel to that of aristocrat knights of romance; and this in turn finds an unheroic counterpart in Sancho's

[8] As tr. by N. Maccoll in Cervantes's English *Works* (cit. n. 2), viii (Glasgow, 1902), 163–4.

[9] All refs. by part, book (in Part I), and chapter, with page no. where appropriate, to *Don Quixote* in Ozell's revision of Peter Motteux's trans. ed. H. G. Doyle (New York, 1950). The names of the characters have been given in the forms found in this edn.

jaunts and jollities. The Don's chivalric ideal is opposed to homely rustic reality; at the same time, his ideal is itself an unheroic reality, a comic but authentic *reductio* of the values of 'straight' chivalric fiction.

Quixote makes himself ludicrous by over-acceptance of the chivalric myth, by his attempt to make its symbolizing, epitomizing premisses acquire literal validity in an uncongenial world. He exposes its basic weakness by his mindless re-enactment of the pattern; at the same time, his artless commitment suggests the improbable virtues upheld by its ethos, seen in purer and more telling form than in the actual aristocracy that spawned the myth.

Such idealistic constructs are measured against a demotic, basically rustic reality. This earthy rusticity provides the quasi-pastoral bedrock of judgement in *Don Quixote*. In contrast to pastoralism proper, it does not modify experience by imagination. Such reworking of reality is chiefly reserved for the other side of the contrast, the world of chivalric romance. The most striking 'pastoral' element in the work is reductive, not creative; its viewpoint is that of 'The Dogs' Colloquy'.

However admissible in theory, it is startling in practice to find rusticity highlighted on this scale in terms of its very mundaneness and unheroic quality. Quixote is a gentleman-turned-knight; Sancho a rustic and (by the evidence of at least one passage, in I. iii. 6, p. 130) a shepherd. But for all the drubbings and humiliation heaped on him, for all his own gullibility and dogged hope of attaining a governorship, he provides a constant corrective to his master by his active good sense (most clearly seen during his mock-governorship), his telling candour, and the imbibed wisdom of his proverb-ridden moral observations, which Quixote finds an irksome contrast to his own rhetoric.

Sancho is the 'shepherd' of the narrative, not only literally but in his Empsonian function. He brings a chastening and stabilizing reality to Quixote's imaginative excesses—a function linked to his inferior social station. This fundamental balance or opposition between knight and peasant, mock-chivalric and quasi-pastoral, bourgeois and rustic, is reflected in the structure of several episodes. Quixote's imagined armies reduce themselves to flocks of sheep (I. iii. 4). The aristocratic 'New Arcadians' who 'take their diversion' in shepherd guise, cordially entertain Quixote and Sancho; the actual drovers going past the company trample them down (II. 58).

Quixote draws these harsh realities within his romantic fiction by viewing them as products of enchantment. The greatest instance of this fancied transmogrification is the reduction of Dulcinea del Toboso to one of an uncouth trio of country hussies (II. 10, pp. 504ff.). This conspiracy of the enchanters is of course a reinstatement of Dulcinea in her true rank: she is none other than Aldonza Lorenzo, who cards flax and threshes corn in Quixote's own parish. She reappears to Quixote in her 'enchanted' rustic guise during his curious visionary trip into the Cave of Montesinos, and her companion borrows four reals from him there (II. 23, pp. 595–7). The postulation of 'enchantment' enables Quixote to recognize Dulcinea's rustic identity even while he rejects it, to accommodate disconcerting realities within a satisfying fiction—but it is not a pastoral fiction. Rather, it explicitly rejects the elements of rustic life that provide the starting-point for pastoral; and rustic life accordingly discredits Quixote's stand by glaring contrast. Even within the Don's own visionary fancies, Dulcinea shifts and blends identities, displaying her rustic face as the inevitable choric accompaniment of her role as romantic heroine.

For as Quixote himself knows, poetic mistresses with pastoral names are largely fictitious:

> Dost thou think . . . that the *Amaryllis's*, the *Phyllis's*, the *Sylvia's*, the *Diana's*, the *Galatea's*, the *Alida's*, and the like . . . were Creatures of Flesh and Blood, and Mistresses to those that did and do celebrate 'em? No, no, never think it; for I dare assure thee, the greatest Part of 'em were nothing but the meer Imaginations of the Poets . . . (I. iii. 11, p. 194).[10]

It is ironic that this insight should come from the unquestioning conniver in all possible chivalric fictions; but it recognizes an important truth, that conventional pastoral is a fiction—and though commonly opposite, sometimes allied to chivalric romance. Early in the work, in the book-burning episode, Quixote's niece fears lest her uncle should land in this opposite delusion (I. i. 6, p. 36).

Her fears come true towards the end of his career, when, his chivalric dream thwarted and effectually shattered, he seeks a new outlet for his romanticism. His projected Arcadia is already touched by the ironic incursions of life in La Mancha: 'We grant all this, said the Curate, but we who can't pretend to such Perfections, must make it our Business to find out some Shepherdesses of a lower Form, that will be good-natur'd, and meet a Man half-way upon Occasion' (II. 73, p. 928). Sancho fears for his daughter's chastity among shepherds who are 'more Knaves than Fools' (II. 67, p. 896).

[10] Cervantes makes the same point in his own narrator's role, I. iii. 13, p. 209.

But Quixote's naïve pastoralism breeds aspiration in other breasts too. The Bachelor Carrasco speculates: 'as every Body knows, I am a most celebrated Poet, and I'll write Pastoral in abundance. Sometimes too I may raise my Strain, as Occasion offers, to divert us as we range the Groves and Plains' (II. 73, pp. 927–8). If the pastoral dream is threatened by rustic reality, the reality itself is tinged by a sneaking weakness for the dream. Yet obviously, these tendencies are at odds with the main current of that reality, and the Bachelor Carrasco, once unhorsed by Quixote (II. 14) before he unhorses the latter at a second encounter, is a half-pedantic, half-romantic aspirant with an embryonic Quixote in his make-up.

Rustic reality is contrasted with the alternative romanticism of the pastoral, as much as with the chivalric. It is this contrast that I have emphasized so far. But the design is made complex by an idealization and literary redaction of this genuine rusticity as well. Nabokov (and he alone) recognizes the importance of this function by listing 'The Arcadian (or Pastoral) theme' as one of the ten chief structural devices of *Don Quixote*, however Nabokov may dislike its presence: 'The chivalry theme and the Arcadian theme often mingle in Don Quixote's mind'[11]—and, we may add, in Cervantes's own.

The crasser romanticism that provides the main target of satire carries its redeeming features, particularly apparent in Part II: a curious cogitative dignity in Quixote, pungent good sense in Sancho, a mellower and more sympathetic humanity beneath the slapstick violence and grotesquerie. Their impact is anticipated in certain episodes commencing early in Part I, poised between the earthily rustic and the conventionally pastoral, presenting suggestive possibilities of being that modify genuine rusticity, drawing it towards the sophisticated and the abstractly universal.

The first such sequence opens with the encounter of Quixote and Sancho with the goatherds (I. ii. 3). Here, if anywhere in the work, we find authentic yet credible use of the pastoral convention. Quixote's long speech on the Golden Age (pp. 63–4) demands separate discussion: however opposite in tone to the goatherds' discourse, its premisses clearly apply to the latter's lives. And the goatherds merely provide the setting for the story of Chrysostome who dies for love of Marcella (I. ii. 4–6). Marcella and her suitors are not true rustics. She is a gentlewoman who assumes shepherd guise in quest of freedom—only to find her lovers

[11] Vladimir Nabokov, *Lectures on Don Quixote*, ed. F. Bowers (London, 1983), 30, 43.

following her there in the same disguise. They re-create the hyperbolic world of affected passion so congenial to pastoral, which she had ironically hoped to escape by resort to that very mode. Her dream of freedom lapses into the enactment of a literary artifice and conventional rigidity of conduct.

So far, the paradoxes range within the expected, as indeed does the basic situation of aristocratic lovers in pastoral guise, with real shepherds in the background. There is a partial parallel in *Don Quixote* itself in the linked stories of Cardenio and Dorothea (I. iii. 9–10, iv. 1–9), with their separate retreats to a Petrarchan 'lover's exile' in the mountains of Sierra Morena. Dorothea has gone there in country habit after serving some time as a shepherd (I. iv. 1, p. 234); Cardenio, in the more extreme guise of a half-barbarous 'hermit of love'. But their exiles lead to meeting and union with their loves: the cyclic pattern of pastoral is clearly marked.

In the Marcella story, there is no union. What resoundingly breaks the mould, turning a lachrymose Petrarchan pastoral into a daring critique of basic mores,[12] is Marcella's sudden appearance and impassioned self-defence:

> I was born free, and that I might continue so, I retir'd to these solitary Hills and Plains, where Trees are my Companions, and clear Fountains my Looking-glasses. With the Trees and with the Waters I communicate my Thoughts, and my Beauty. I am a distant Flame, and a Sword far off: Those whom I have attracted with my Sight, I have undeceiv'd with my Words . . . (I. ii. 6, pp. 85–6).

Marcella had set out as a kind of female equivalent of Guarini's unwilling lover Silvio. But, unlike Silvio, she does not subside into happy matrimony. Cervantes leaves his tale open-ended: Marcella withdraws after her speech to an agitated but fulfilling solitude.

There is promise of similar development in the tale of Eugenio the goatherd (I. iv. 24): after Leandra is seduced and subsequently sent to a nunnery, her lovers Eugenio, Anselmo, and many others, men of 'good Family' and 'considerable Estate' (p. 426), turn herdsmen and set up what is expressly declared to be another Arcadia (p. 429). But instead of taking a chastening turn towards realism, Eugenio's Arcadia remains almost a satirically exaggerated version of the Petrarchan frustrated lovers' retreat:

> there is no part of it in which is not to be heard the Name of *Leandra*. This Man curses and calls her Wanton and Lascivious, another calls her Light and Fickle;

[12] Poggioli (*The Oaten Flute*, p. 173) sees it as a seminal instance of a new development, the 'pastoral of the self'.

one acquits and forgives her, another arraigns and condemns her; one celebrates her Beauty, another rails at her ill Qualities; in short, all blame, but all adore her (p. 429).

We do not learn what finally happens to these Arcadians. Within the story, Eugenio is brought to life by fighting with Quixote at table and, immediately after, the latter attacks a ritual procession praying for rain (I. iv. 25). The story returns to its accustomed continuum, the shepherd-lovers having provided a piquant contrast. They can now rest forgotten in their unreal isolation.

In Part II, chapter 58, we find another aristocrats' retreat, the 'New Arcadia' set up by people of quality only to 'take their Diversion' (p. 833). This is little more than a picnic, with camping and bird-watching and the reciting of eclogues out of Garcilaso and Camoens. It is professedly temporary, 'to pass the Time agreeably, and for a while banish Melancholy from this Place' (p. 834).

Even Quixote makes no mention of the Golden Age in such company; and after his shattering encounter with the drovers, he beats a retreat without bidding the Arcadians farewell.

Passing over the nominally pastoral episode of Basil the 'amorous shepherd' (II. 19)—not substantially unlike any novella where a lover defeats his rival by a trick—we come to the last and most significant pastoral motif, Quixote's design for his own Arcadia. I have granted the ironic and unreal implications of his dream; but we must view these in tandem with the driving impulse behind this and his earlier chivalric ideal.

The best way is provided by a much earlier passage: his discourse on the Golden Age while supping with the goatherds in I. ii. 3 (pp. 63–4). Quixote is inspired to hold forth on the subject by the sight of the goatherds, and his discourse, heavily reliant on Virgil IV and Ovid, is unmitigatedly pastoral: 'Then was the Time when innocent beautiful young Shepherdesses went tripping o'er the Hills and Vales: Their lovely Hair sometimes plaited, sometimes loose and flowing, clad in no other Vestment but what was necessary to cover decently what Modesty would always have conceal'd' (p. 64). It was the passing of the Golden Age that brought evil into the world, and the need of knights-errant to fight such evil. Knighthood, then, relates to an inferior state of mankind; but it was instituted to redeem that state and indeed to restore the Golden Age, as Quixote implies here and declares explicitly in a later passage: 'Know, *Sancho*, cry'd he, I was born in this Iron Age, to restore the Age of Gold, or the Golden Age, as some chuse to call it' (I. iii. 6, p. 129). This motive underlies all the follies and mishaps of his career. It is this which, mediated through the increasing good sense and penetration in his own sayings and Sancho's, lends him greater dignity in Part II, matched by the jesting yet preponderantly humane tolerance of his aristocratic interlocutors, especially the Duke and Duchess who shelter him. The same attitude is discernible in the New Arcadians; in Basil the amorous shepherd and his rival Camacho; and in Don Diego, the virtuous and contented country squire (II. 16–18). These quasi-pastoral episodes are individually minor and perhaps inconclusive; collectively they suggest, not perhaps a new order—the controlling, continuing reality will not let us conceive of this—but the possibility of more understanding between man and man.

What qualifies Quixote for his improved stature is precisely what has made him a universal laughing-stock: his role as literary lion, hero of *Don Quixote*, Part I, to which open reference is made continually. His gull's role-playing has been vindicated as aesthetic artefact, lampoon turned celebration. The failure of his knight-errantry now appears not untenably, at times, as more than the defeat of an insane fantasy: it is the failure of an inadequate and unreal myth to express an ill-defined but subtle ethos, moving and estimable in our half-obscured glimpses of it.[13]

It is in this context that Quixote's exchange of the chivalric myth for the pastoral takes on its full significance: it hints at an equally unreal, but alternative and perhaps superior myth. However Quixote may relate the two (and he seems to view the pastoral merely as an interlude, in Part II, chapter 67, p. 894), the narrative line proceeds from one to the other; and the new folly gains forceful validity, at least in the last reckoning, when the Bachelor, Curate, and Barber uphold it in a charitable effort at revitalizing the dying Quixote:

> The Batchelor beg'd him to pluck up a good Heart, and rise, that they might begin their Pastoral Life, telling him, that he had already writ an Eclogue to that Purpose, not inferior to those of *Sanazaro*, and that he had bought with his own Money, of a Shepherd of *Quintanar* two tearing Dogs to watch their Flock, the one call'd *Barcino*, and the other *Butron*; (II. 74, pp. 929–30)

[13] Cf. Turgenev, *Hamlet and Don Quixote*, tr. R. Nichols (London, 1930; repr. Folcroft Press, 1972), 13: 'It matters little that Don Quixote has drawn [his] ideal from the fantastic medley of chivalric romance—nay, it is even by reason of this very fact that the burlesque side of him exists—for he has known how to disengage the pure ideal from all alloy and to conserve it in utter integrity.'

The change in Quixote is noteworthy too: 'all the Use I shall make of these Follies at present, is to heighten my Repentance; and though they have hitherto prov'd prejudicial, yet by the Assistance of Heaven, they may turn to my Advantage at my Death' (II. 74, p. 931). From the martial to the pastoral, and thence to the transcendent and spiritual: this is a well-established cycle, and *Don Quixote* may be seen, unexpectedly, to conform to it. The martial spirit is, of course, presented with fundamental irony, but not simply through satiric and reductive techniques: rather by comparison with other value-systems and categories of experience that can, in one sense or another, be called pastoral. It may not be too fanciful to draw a comparison with that very different work, *The Faerie Queene*, where also the narrative of chivalric adventure appears to be controlled by values basically allied to the pastoral. The 'placing', or even the open rejection, of explicit pastoral interludes does not impair the spirit underlying them.

14
D'Urfé's *L'Astrée*

I SHALL make no attempt at an exhaustive survey of continental pastoral in the late Renaissance, particularly the Italianate elements taken up and transformed in France. Hence I shall say nothing of, for example, the pastoral drama of Alexandre Hardy. But we must take a look at the high point of this development: Honoré d'Urfé's *L'Astrée*, published in five books between 1607 and 1628. (Book V was written after d'Urfé's death, on the basis of his notes and instructions, by his secretary Balthazar Baro. Book IV, published posthumously, may also owe something to Baro.)

L'Astrée had only a late and marginal effect on English pastoral within our period (on some Caroline drama, for instance, where it combines with the influence of plays like Racan's *Bergeries* or Mairet's *Sylvie* and *Silvanire*). Basically, *L'Astrée* points the contrast between English and continental pastoral. For the latter it acquires almost a quintessential importance. It sums up a course of development, not merely aesthetic but clearly ethical, that begins with Boccaccio and runs through Sannazaro and Montemayor. The changes along the way indicate the inherent nature of such pastoral—distant, factitious, often alien to modern taste, but curiously vital and compelling in its own inbred terms.

Though the extent of allusion in *L'Astrée* has been disputed, it cannot but be considerable.[1] D'Urfé deliberately mystifies the reader in a non-committal Preface to Book I 'a la Bergere Astrée'. But against this we can place the clear avowal to Etienne Pasquier: 'Ceste bergère que je vous envoye n'est véritablement que l'histoire de ma jeunesse'[2] [this shepherdess that I send you is indeed nothing but the story of my youth].

[1] See the considered and balanced views of O.-C. Reure, *La Vie et les œuvres de Honoré d'Urfé* (Paris, 1910), 100ff., and Maxime Gaume, *Les Inspirations et les sources de l'œuvre d'Honoré d'Urfé* (Saint-Etienne, 1977), 163–75.

[2] As quoted in Reure, p. 102. Cf. d'Urfé's reported remark to Olivier Patru that *L'Astrée* contained 'tant de secrets d'une si haute importance' [so many secrets of such great importance] as could not be divulged to a youth of 19: see Louis Mercier's Preface to *L'Astrée*, ed. H. Vaganay (Lyons, 1925–8), i, p. xix.

Pasquier's reply is even more revealing: 'Vous estant proposé de célébrer sous noms couvers plusieurs seigneurs, dames et familles de vostre païs de Forest'[3] [You have proposed to celebrate, under concealed names, many lords, ladies and families in your native land of Forez].

D'Urfé's young associate and admirer Olivier Patru compiled a detailed guide to the personal and political allegory of the work. Few scholars have accepted all of Patru's identifications; he himself begins by saying: 'Toutes les histoires de l'Astrée ont un fondement véritable; mais l'auteur les a toutes romancées, si je puis user de ce mot'[4] [all the stories in *L'Astrée* have a true basis; but the author has fictionalized them all, if I may use the word]. Precise allegory is less important than the undeniable, sustained incorporation of d'Urfé's emotional biography. His love of and eventual marriage with his erstwhile sister-in-law Diane de Chateaumorand is not so much allegorized as infused into Celadon's love of Astrée and Silvandre's for Diane. *L'Astrée* shows the expansion in a free imaginative medium of an ethos, a way of life, a distinctive sensibility shadowed in d'Urfé's life and milieu. Authenticity at this fundamental level vitalizes what would otherwise have been a tortuously artificial work.

Mutatis mutandis, this is also true of the setting of d'Urfé's native Forez. Much has been said of the 'realism' thus introduced by d'Urfé into the pastoral.[5] Still more questionably, d'Urfé has also been credited with historical realism by virtue of his fifth-century setting.[6] In fact, d'Urfé never lets actuality impede his pastoral fancy. The locale of the romance may correspond to d'Urfé's own, but what matters is its distancing or transformation at the behest of a perfected imaginative vision—the degree of departure rather than the degree of adherence. The setting becomes the vehicle for a psychological state: 'la passion que tu [the River Lignon] a veue commencer, augmenter, et parvenir à la perfection le long de ton agreable rivage'[7] [the passion that you have seen commence, increase, and attain to perfection along your pleasant bank]. Finally, personal experience of both nature and love pass into a higher if more tenuous reality of aesthetic experience; and this, we feel, reacts in turn upon the actual milieu of the author and his age. There is much

[3] Quoted in Reure, p. 103.
[4] See *L'Astrée*, ed. Vaganay, v. 545.
[5] See e.g. Reure, p. 225; Gaume, pp. 176–204.
[6] See Reure, p. 234, and Henri Bochet, *L'Astrée. Ses origines, son importance dans la formation de la littérature classique* (repr. Geneva, 1967), 122.
[7] 'L'Autheur a la riviere de Lignon', Preface to Book III of *L'Astrée*: ed. Vaganay, iii. 6.

contemporary evidence that *L'Astrée* was read as a textbook of refined manners and had concrete influence as such. D'Urfé's translator John Davies cites Richelieu's opinion 'That he was not to be admitted into the Academy of *Wit*, who had not been before well read in ASTREA'.[8] Roland Desmarets writes to his brother Jean about d'Urfé:

> Je voudrais que notre jeunesse, et surtout notre jeunesse noble, ne quittât jamais son livre, pour y apprendre l'élégance et l'urbanité des mœurs.[9]
>
> [I could wish that our youth, and above all our noble youth, might never relinquish his book, so that they might learn here elegance and urbanity of manners.]

Even in Germany, forty-eight aristocrats set up an 'Académie des parfaits amants' and named themselves after d'Urfé's characters, though none had the temerity to call himself Celadon.[10]

Reure recounts in detail the vogue of *L'Astrée*, though this was inevitably followed by a reaction.[11] D'Urfé was evidently borne out in his assumption that his romance would provide a school for manners and ethics.[12] An unsuspected relevance and authenticity proves to infuse this hyper-refined work.

Accordingly, d'Urfé's shepherds are aristocrats. Their ancestors, descended from noble and martial stock, had sworn to 'flie for euer from all sort of ambition, for that it alone was cause of so much paynes, and to liue, they and theirs, vnder the peaceable habite of shepheards'.[13] This is a collective re-enactment of the classic case of the courtier-turned-shepherd (or hermit). It is repeated by the individual who reverts to court life and chivalry but withdraws again, as Celadon's father Alcippe had done: 'let thy launce be turned into a sheephook, thy sword into a culter, to open the earth, and not the bellies of men; there shalt thou finde that repose, which for so many yeeres thou couldst neuer haue elsewhere' (Pyper, p. 48). Damon, sheltered by a hermit, exemplifies the same tendency on a more limited scale (Davis, ii/1. 126).

[8] *Astrea. A Romance . . . translated by a Person of Quality* (Preface 'To the Reader' signed J[ohn] D[avies]: London, 1657), Preface: i. sig. A2v.

[9] Reure's French trans. of the Latin original: Reure, p. 304.

[10] Ibid. 210.

[11] Ibid. 302ff.

[12] Preface to *L'Astrée*, Book II. 'L'Autheur au Berger Celadon': Vaganay, ii. 3–5. Cf. Baro's 'Epistre' ('A la bergere Astrée'), v. 4.

[13] *The History of Astrea: The First Part, in Twelue Bookes: Newly Translated out of French . . . Printed by N. Okes for Iohn Pyper* (London, 1620), 35. Refs. for Part I of *L'Astrée* to this text, as 'Pyper'. Books XI and XII are separately paginated; this sequence indicated as 'Pyper, ii'. Refs. for the later parts of *L'Astrée* to John Davies's translation (see n. 8 above), as 'Davies'. There are two sequences of pagination in vol. ii, cited as ii/1 and ii/2.

In other words, Celadon, Astrée, and their forebears choose pastoral life much as courtiers and urbanites (like d'Urfé and his audience) choose the pastoral fiction. In a very different manner, we might say of *L'Astrée* what I shall later say of *As You Like It*: that it incorporates within its fiction the motives that normally operate behind a work of pastoral.[14] But whereas Shakespeare uses such insight to question and reassess the mode, d'Urfé simply consolidates its urbane functions. His version of pastoral allows him most direct access to what his audience demands of the mode.

The shepherds of the Lignon are simultaneously rustics and aristocrats, they can eat their cake and have it too. The distinctive virtues of pastoral life are indeed brought out at many points, and contrasted with court life. We have at least one debate, between Florice and Circéne, on the competing merits of the two lives (Davies, ii/2. 90–1). More commonly, the superiority of rustic life is simply accepted: 'And to tell you truly [says Hylas], I have tasted of all waters, and tried all kinds of lives; but I find none comparable to the sweet lives of Shepherds in this countrey' (Davies, iii. 65). On the other hand, Celadon humbly pleads his shepherd stock to Adamas as a reason for renouncing the company of court ladies (Pyper, p. 338). In a few episodes and 'histories', we may even get a genuine sense of idealized rustic life with its occupations, practices, and ceremonies. This is seen in the account of the early love of Celadon and Astrée (Pyper, pp. 98ff.) and more vividly in the history of Diane's parents, Celion and Bellinde (Pyper, pp. 346ff.). The 'finding of the Mistletoe' (Davies, ii/2. 8) shows brief but effective use of imaginary folk-convention. The nature-setting is specifically lauded by Leonide to Paris (Davies, i. 320). Celadon's hermitage (Pyper, ii. 60ff.) is described in vividly sylvan detail, as in more stylized vein is the Temple of Astraea (Davies, ii/1. 81ff.).

There is much fanciful mythic belief and ritual, centred upon the worship of Tautates as well as lesser deities; but all this is rather too abstract and philosophized to constitute authentic 'pastoral religion'. A 'Temple of Love' is entirely secular and courtly in purport. However, it leads to another temple, that of Astraea; and only here, with its rustic-clad goddess merged with the shepherdess Astrée, is a pastoral element introduced—and that at a new sophisticated level of theme and narrative.

Indeed, more often than not, the shepherds act like courtiers and

[14] See below, Ch. 18, sect. 2.

aristocrats, and many episodes point explicit parallels. This is scarcely surprising, as the two groups are of the same stock—unlike all other shepherds, as we are often reminded. When Leonide chides Princess Galathée for loving Celadon, she replies: 'these shepheards are as good as Druides or Knights, & their Nobility is as great as others, being all descended from the antiquity of the same stocke' (Pyper, p. 26). Celadon had left off his shepherd's guise while travelling in Italy, because there 'none but vile persons and Peasants do live in the Country' (Davies, i. 364); and Dorinde is ashamed of her pastoral dress, demeaning everywhere except in Forez (Davies, iii. 64). There is special grace and accomplishment in a shepherd like Silvandre, a veteran in war and a scholar of the 'Phocencian and Massellian Universities' (Davies, i. 200). But the shepherds at large share something of the same nature: 'for though their garments be course, and their conversation smell a little of the village, yet they are more discreet, and more civil, then any I ever conversed withall' (Davies, iii. 65). Celadon's boldness was 'alwayes greater then fitted the name of a shepheard' (Pyper, p. 30); and the shepherds generally show 'courages much above their quality' (Davies, iii. 212) when they respond to Silvandre's call to arms in Amasis's defence. Taumantes, a rich shepherd's son, is brought up like an aristocrat's heir, as indeed in this society he is (Davies, ii/2. 191). Shepherds even share in courtiers' woes: 'as Lakes though lesse then the Sea, have their stormes and tempests; so it is with us, we also have our misfortunes and miseries' (Davies, ii/1. 23–4; cf. Pyper, pp. 235, 342–3).

Thus, at a blow, d'Urfé annuls the opposition of court and country: or, to put it more fairly, provides an unusually direct correlative for the underlying courtly motives actually found in so much pastoral: 'If it be a shame, said *Alcippe*, to be a shepheard, we must be such no more: if it be no shame, the reproach cannot be hurtfull' (Pyper, p. 41). A highly evolved system of conduct and society finds its best matrix in rural or pastoral life. D'Urfé addresses 'la Bergere Astrée' at the opening of his work:

tu n'es pas, ny celles aussi qui te suivent, de ces bergeres necessiteuses, . . . mais que vous n'avez toutes pris cette condition, que pour vivre plus doucement en sans contrainte.[15]

[Neither you, nor those that follow you, are shepherdesses from necessity . . . but you have taken up that state only to live more pleasantly and without constraint.]

[15] Ed. Vaganay, i. 7.

The pastoral ethos no longer offers something autonomous and exclusive, even potentially subversive; it is a purer and more confident assertion of the courtly ethos. D'Urfé creates the strongest possible identification between shepherd and reader, the fictional world and the recipient milieu. Values and concepts can be transferred intact from one to the other: these shepherds think and feel unashamedly in accordance with certain trends in French upper-class culture. 'Pour le lecteur du XVIIe siècle,' writes Jacques Ehrmann, 'le monde pastoral est un prolongement idéal du monde chevaleresque-aristocratique'[16] [for the seventeenth-century reader, the pastoral world was an idealized extension of the chivalric-aristocratic world]. The country becomes the final resting-place of a courtly, or trans-courtly, sensibility.

What are the concepts and values fostered by such a sensibility? We have already seen their beginnings in Italian drama and Spanish romance. The chief characteristic is a preoccupation with love in a pseudo-Petrarchan excess of adoration and sentimentalism, with a complex code of behaviour and a pronounced vein of comment, analysis, and introspection: 'the artificiall practices of Louers and Shepheards giue no place to others' (Pyper, p. 343). The sugary intricacies of love are brought out in amazing length and detail. At one level, this is embodied in improbably complicated intrigue that also serves an exemplary purpose. The various 'histories' illustrate the diverse veins of love.

At another level, a complex and hyper-refined code of love is unfolded through endless meditation and soliloquy, long set-speeches of sentimental oratory, and an unmatched series of love-letters constituting a virtual *ars dictaminis* for lovers. (Astrée and Celadon leave letters for each other in the hollow of a tree—with paper and inkhorn for convenience of reply!) Disputes, exchanges, and recondite discourses on love are indulged in by shepherds even more than by aristocrats; and as in all such romances, characters consistently burst into song, witty, conceitful, and urbane—and, perhaps uniquely even for such a work, devoid of all pastoral content whatsoever.

All these are external expressions of the patterned sentimentalism that operates through the characters' entire conduct and psychology. Celadon and Astrée's love makes sense only in terms of exaggerated fidelity to an impersonal and abstract code: indeed, their woes start from his taking too literally her command never to enter her sight again. His

[16] J. Ehrmann, *Un paradis désespéré. L'Amour et l'illusion dans l'Astrée* (New Haven and Paris, 1963), 18. Cf. Bochet, p. 106.

subsequent attempt at suicide, his life as love's eremite, his erection of a temple to Astrée–Astraea are an obvious pastoral parallel to the obsessive love and loyalty which knights and courtier-lovers (like those in L'Astrée itself) express through the trials and vicissitudes of their chivalric careers.

Celadon proceeds to disguise himself as Alexis, daughter of the Druid Adamas, and dwell among women including Astrée herself. From this point, if not earlier, d'Urfé's fine-spun Platonism[17] is consistently tinged with a prurient awareness of sexual presences, far removed from the frank sexuality of simpler pastoral. Celadon–Alexis's physical proximity to Astrée feeds their erotic relationship under cover of his disguise and her ignorance. Still more telling, because more concentrated in effect, is the earlier episode where Celadon disguises himself as a woman to watch the naked Astrée in a ceremonial enactment of the Judgement of Paris. Here lurks the 'serpent in the sheepfold' spotted by Gérard Genette in a notable essay on *L'Astrée*:

> Il y a donc dans *l'Astrée* une contradiction très sensible entre un idéal spirituel cent fois proclamé qui vise à la sublimation totale de l'instinct amoureux, et une conduite réelle . . . qui semble traiter cet idéal . . . comme un instrument non de perfection spirituelle, mais de raffinement érotique.[18]

> [There is, therefore, in *L'Astrée* a patent contradiction between a spiritual ideal, proclaimed a hundred times, which aims at total sublimation of the erotic impulse, and an actual conduct . . . which seems to regard that ideal . . . as an instrument not of spiritual perfection but of erotic refinement.]

D'Urfé never explores this oblique eroticism or its implications for the nature of the relationship he depicts. On the contrary, it is blended unquestioningly with the postulates of mock-Platonic *fin amour*. The almost obsessive psychological exploration proves to be shallow and limited. The self-analysis reduces itself to self-dramatization and role-playing, a working-out of set models of conduct and sensibility: 'Here thou hast a jealous and distrustfull ASTREA; a despairing, yet faithfull CELADON; a fickle and unconstant HYLAS; and such intricate scenes of *Courtship*, *Love*, *Jealousie*, and the other *passions*, as cannot but raise in thee a consideration of humane Affairs, sutable to the severall emergencies'.[19]

I remarked that the characters in Cervantes's *Galatea* have begun to

[17] For the nature and extent of this Platonism, see Bochet, pp. 60ff.; Gérard Genette, 'Le Serpent dans la bergerie', prefatory to *L'Astrée. Textes choisis* (Paris, 1964), 12ff.

[18] Genette, p. 19.

[19] John Davies's preface 'To the Reader', Davies, i. sig. A2^{v}.

develop personalities, work individual variations upon set patterns of behaviour. In one respect, the characters in *L'Astrée* are more vivid still: the voluminous narrative follows each turn of their behaviour.[20] Yet the moment we put the book down, they recede into a faceless uniformity: they have been fashioned to illustrate a contrived ethos above and beyond them. Even eccentrics like the cynical shepherd Hylas are part of the pattern. Myriam Jehenson talks of d'Urfé's practice of 'distancing the reader from involvement with the characters and of making him concentrate on the formal procedures used rather than on the significance of the characters or the events'.[21]

D'Urfé very obviously wrote his romance to embody an abstract system of traits, codes, and values, rather than the full imaginative experience of the pastoral convention. This is where he departs decisively from his Italian and Spanish predecessors, though they may have tended in that direction at times. And because of this changed purpose, he can (as I observed earlier) embody his conceptions in his fiction with unusual directness. I have noted the specifically pastoral content of *L'Astrée*; but it affords no sustained sense of shepherd life or a setting of nature. Characters ingrow or interact, unmindful of their pastoral life and surroundings or else treating them in a purely factual spirit. Their medium of existence is verbal, not environmental. D'Urfé's shepherd, writes Ehrmann, 'mène sa *quête* dans l'univers des mots'[22] [conducts his quest in the universe of words].

Yet such detailed expatiation of conduct and character calls for a story of appropriate length and intricacy. Like *Diana* or Sidney's *New Arcadia*, *L'Astrée* has a bewilderingly involved network of subplots consisting chiefly of courtly intrigue (political as well as amatory) and chivalric or martial adventure. There are numerous 'histories' told in flashback, in instalments, interlaced with each other as well as with the narrative present. But so intricate are the connections that they create no sense of courtly or chivalric affairs *leading into* the pastoral or culminating in it. Indeed, the opposite is often the case. The 'present' narrative focuses more and more on political and military affairs centred upon the court of the ruling 'Nymph' Amasis, culminating in full-scale war with

[20] Gerhardt notes this feature: within the framework of Arcadian pastoral, 'il [d'Urfé] se charge de les rendre aussi vraisemblables, aussi proches de la réalité générale et contemporaine que possible' [he undertakes to make them as lifelike, as close to universal and contemporary reality as possible]: *La Pastorale*, p. 262.

[21] M. Y. Jehenson, *The Golden World of the Pastoral. A Comparative Study of Sidney's New Arcadia and d'Urfé's L'Astrée* (Ravenna, n.d.), 143–4. Cf. p. 150.

[22] Ehrmann, p. 19.

the rebel Polemas in Books IV and V. The outstanding precedent, of course, is the siege of Amphialus in the *New Arcadia*.[23]

The shepherds come to the aid of Amasis and Adamas against Polemas. The pastors themselves change the pastoral ethos, as well as the pastoral location, to suit the new direction of the narrative: 'so strange a Metamorphosis, which in a moment turned a company of Shepherds into a company of Souldiers' (Davies, iii. 212).

The love of Celadon–Alexis and Astrée is interlaced with the martial action; but its static self-absorption has made it a subsidiary motif by this time. A more compelling logic of dynamic narrative has taken over, as in the *New Arcadia* or earlier in a piecemeal manner in *Diana*.

This new action is non-pastoral not only in content but, more important, in its formal postulates. It rests upon the normal assumptions of time, causality, and external realities, in place of the arrested intricacies of erotic self-contemplation. Needless to say, we are still plunged in romantic fictions, passing in Baro's Book V into a pronounced vein of magic and sensationalism. *Diana* yields a similar compound at times; but in this as all else, the fancy in *L'Astrée* is more extreme, more uncompromising in its aesthetic. The pastoral elements take their place in a narrative of very different intent, and the pastoral note at the end is merely a formal admission of origin: 'we see that the God of love is no lesse pleased to have his power admired in the homely Cottages of our Shepherds, as well as in great Palaces: Nay, to break the force of an inchantment hee casts his eye only upon them, as taking most delight in their innocency' (Davies, iii. 458).

L'Astrée provides the tide-mark of continental pastoral of the late Renaissance: its luxuriant introverted sentimentalism, the unhurried, almost static unfolding of its design, its fanciful adaptations and embellishments of human conduct, but, underneath, a thin residual assertion of naïve human impulse such as more demanding realities cannot allow. *L'Astrée* exposes and magnifies the basic courtly impulse of such pastoral, accommodating a varied courtliness of allusion and inviting self-destruction through direct civilities and complexities. Its ethos appears self-sustaining but is wholly reliant on an ethos in the external world.

This gives d'Urfé's highly wrought, tenuous artefact a unique validity; but in the process, the self-contradictory, self-defeating propensities of such pastoral myth stand revealed.

[23] See Ch. 15 below. Sidney's *Arcadia* was tr. into French by Jean Baudoin and G. Chappuis in 1624, and by 'un Gentil-homme François' and Geneviève Chappelain in 1625.

15
Sidney's *Arcadia*

1. *The structure of the two* Arcadias

SIDNEY'S *Arcadia*, particularly the *Old Arcadia* which he first composed for his sister *c.*1577–81, seems at first sight to come very close to the 'cyclic' pattern I defined in the last chapter. The pastoral setting provides a refuge from the court: 'But the peace wherein they [the shepherds] did so notably flourish, and especially the sweet enjoying of their peace to so pleasant uses, drew divers strangers, as well of great as of mean houses, especially such whom inward melancholies made weary of the world's eyes'.[1] This is best seen in Basilius's retreat from court to country on hearing the ominous oracle: 'being so cruelly menaced by fortune, he would draw himself out of her way by this loneliness, which he thought was the surest mean to avoid her blows' (Robertson, p. 6, ll. 23–5). In the *Old Arcadia*, a number of courtly characters arrive by different means at a pastoral retreat. The setting of nature, and the freedom from normal courtly restraints, seem to inspire a special predilection to love. The course of their amours involves disguises, misunderstandings, multiple loves, and apparent death. In the end, the complications are resolved, the lovers are united, and Basilius returns to his kingdom with morale restored.

But this is obviously a misleading account, for pastoral plays little part, regenerative or otherwise, in the *Arcadia*. The principal lovers are not shepherds; we hear little of the pastoral setting, and that little is not closely related to the action. It is almost as though Sidney 'depastoralizes' the love-plot and plays down the setting to prevent any pattern of genuine pastoral regeneration. To an extent, the 'Eclogues' balance and rectify the non-pastoral spirit of the 'Books'. But the two are so obviously placed in alternation and contrast that it seems advisable to consider them separately. I shall discuss the 'Eclogues' in the next section, completing the perspective.

[1] *The Countess of Pembroke's Arcadia (The Old Arcadia)*, ed. Jean Robertson (Oxford, 1973), 56, ll. 18–27. All refs. to the *Old Arcadia* to this text.

In the main narrative, all the serious characters are courtiers. Among them, Musidorus alone assumes pastoral disguise, and that in an act of conscious stooping and self-denial: 'he clothed himself in a shepherd's weed, that under the baseness of that form he might at least have free access to feed his eyes' (Robertson, p. 105, ll. 33–5). Basilius abandons his responsibilities but retains his feudal station, attended and entertained by his chosen shepherds. Pamela and Philoclea do not enter joyfully into pastoral life, but rather chafe at the inversion of social order and the indignity of being ruled by their inferiors: 'She answered him [Dametas the comic shepherd] he should be obeyed, since such was the fortune of her and her sister' (Robertson, p. 33, ll. 33–4).

In Sannazaro, the courtier Sincero had to take the shepherd world very much on the latter's terms. Even in Montemayor, the shepherds provide one important strand in the plot. But the only shepherds in Sidney's narrative (as opposed to the Eclogues) are the degenerate trio of Dametas, Miso, and Mopsa. The model for Dametas is surely Montemayor's Delius, Diana's coarse and jealous husband, though Sidney transfers the trait of jealousy to Dametas's wife Miso. More generally, Sidney's treatment of shepherds in a courtly tale seems closer to another, neglected precedent. Many critics have noted Sidney's debt to *Amadis de Gaule*; but very little attention has been paid to the long pastoral episode in Book IX, where Prince Florisel de Niquée assumes a shepherd's garb to woo the supposed shepherdess Silvie, actually of noble birth.[2] His rival is the shepherd Darinel—at first an honourable and dignified figure, but soon reduced to a foolish yokel, a constant comic foil to Florisel. He receives blows which Florisel avenges, runs away from dangers that Florisel fights. His very love is mean and timid. When six knights carry off Silvie and another damsel, Darinel hides in a bush,[3] just as Dametas does to escape from a bear. Again, Darinel's absurd love for Silvie (an aristocrat in shepherd's weeds) is paralleled, with the sexes reversed, in Mopsa's love of Musidorus. These resemblances need not necessarily indicate direct influence; but they do suggest an affinity in mode and basic assumptions.

Sidneys' dismissive view of the lower orders also shows in his account of the rebellion in Book II. In the *New Arcadia* (Sidney's unfinished

[2] It is mentioned, along with other borrowings from *Amadis*, in *The Countess of Pembroke's Arcadia (The New Arcadia)*, ed. Victor Skretkowicz (Oxford, 1987), pp. xix–xx; also in J. J. O'Connor, *Amadis de Gaule and Its Influence on Elizabethan Literature* (New Brunswick, 1970), 188, 190, 192, 263, and Robertson, p. xxi.

[3] See *Le Neufiesme Liure d'Amadis de Gaule* (Paris, 1553), fo. 59r.

expansion and recasting of the work) this is embellished with new touches of grotesque humour, such as an artist with his hands cut off. Nor is it offset by the new episode of the Helots' revolt. The Helots are a separate people or nation, conquered by the Lacedaemonians. Sidney obviously distinguishes between such subjugation of one nation by another and the God-given order of the estates within a single nation or society.

In the *Arcadia*, the only values that matter are the courtier's. There is nothing of Empson's 'double attitude . . . of the complex man to the simple one ("I am in one way better, in another not so good")'.[4] The nominally pastoral setting merely ensures that the courtiers are released from their normal restraints. They can express their love in untrammelled, romantically exciting ways: the princes' disguise, Basilius's relinquishing of dignity, Gynecia's explicit declarations of love. The same open amorousness is seen in the shepherds of Italian drama; but nothing in the *Arcadia* suggests that the courtiers' love is shaped by the quality of shepherd life. Rather, shepherd-lovers like Lalus and Kala illustrate a very different and modest love.

Nor does the pastoral setting serve any inspiring or regenerative function. As critics have pointed out,[5] it motivates the courtiers only to intrigue, confusion, degradation, and neglect of duty. There are remarkably few references to the surroundings of nature, and even these seem to show deliberate irony. Two idyllic *loci amoeni* are rudely disturbed by violence and danger: a lion and a bear, and later the rebellious Phagonians.[6] Elsewhere the nature-settings relate to particularly disastrous points of the love-plot. In Book II 'a number of trees so thickly placed together' (Robertson, p. 92, l. 30) is the scene of an awkward meeting between Gynecia and 'Cleophila'. A little wood with its altar to the sylvan gods is a witness to Philoclea's agitated sense of her 'fall' (Robertson, p. 110, l. 14). Similarly, for 'Cleophila', the objects of nature become a Petrarchan mirror of the lover's torment (Robertson, p. 118, ll. 31–2):

> Since stream, air, sand, mine eyes and ears conspire:
> What hope to quench where each thing blows the fire?

[4] William Empson, *Some Versions of Pastoral* (1935; repr. Harmondsworth, 1966), 19.

[5] e.g. A. C. Hamilton, *Sir Philip Sidney* (Cambridge, 1977), 46–7.

[6] See Robertson, p. 46, ll. 2ff., p. 124, ll. 22ff. The point has been made by Franco Marenco, *Arcadia puritana* (Bari, 1968), 200ff.; J. A. Galm, *Sidney's Arcadian Poems* (Salzburg, 1973), 174–5.

Book III opens 'among the sweet flowers . . . under the pleasant shade of a broad-leaved sycamore' (Robertson, p. 168, ll. 11–12), where Pyrocles had first told Musidorus of his love. (The irony in that first conversation has been pointed out by critics.)[7] This time they talk mainly of unhappy love and their impending parting. A later 'touch of nature' is more ironic still. Pyrocles visits the cave round which he will weave his plot, leading to the half-comic, half-sordid bed-trick, Basilius's apparent death, and Pyrocles' own downfall. This ominous trip is reported by Sidney as 'early visit[ing] the morning's beauty in those pleasant deserts' (Robertson, p. 215, ll. 14–15).

Finally we have the 'fair thick wood' where Pamela and Musidorus rest on their flight and sing love-songs—and where, after that, Musidorus plans to rape Pamela, and is prevented only by 'a dozen clownish villains' who take them captive (Robertson, p. 197, l. 29–p. 202, l. 16). This scene raises another important point. Musidorus and Pamela plan to *escape* from Arcadia. Far from being the ideal cradle of their loves, it is a scene of shame, confusion, and restraint from which they want to flee: 'one of the greatest matters had won her to this was the strange humours she saw her father lately fallen into, and unreasonable restraint of her liberty . . . added to the hate of that manner of life' (Robertson, p. 172, ll. 28–31).

In the *Old Arcadia* Pyrocles does not plan to elope, but he does so in the 1593 revision of the bedchamber scene (Robertson, p. 236, ll. 28 ff.).[8] That nobody succeeds in fleeing, that the final reconciliation takes place within the geographical confines of Arcadia, is the result of a series of narrative turns that have nothing to do with the pastoral setting.

None the less, the *Old Arcadia* shows a nominal presence of the 'cyclic' structure in its full sweep. The characters have emphatically moved away from the court, even if with little sense of moving into the country, and still less of the beneficial effects of such a withdrawal. The *New Arcadia*, on the contrary, is guided by a different plan dominated by heroic and courtly elements.

First of all, the early career of the princes is greatly developed, in a gigantic retrospective sequence in five instalments in the middle of Book

[7] See Kalstone, *Sidney's Poetry*, 51; R. A. Lanham, *The Old Arcadia* (New Haven, 1965; with Davis's *A Map of Arcadia*), 247–8.

[8] The 1593 revisions are now generally credited to Sidney's own pen, or at least to his express design. See W. A. Ringler, jun. (ed.), Sidney's *Poems* (Oxford, 1962), 377–8; W. L. Godshalk, 'Sidney's Revision of the *Arcadia*, Books III–V', *PQ* 43 (1964), 183; P. Lindenbaum, 'Sidney's *Arcadia*: The Endings of the Three Versions', *HLQ* 34 (1971), 205–18; Robertson, pp. lxi–lxii.

II. The first large instalment (chs. 6–10, as divided in the 1590 edition) is recounted by Musidorus to Pamela, the second (chs. 18–24) by Pyrocles to Philoclea. Philoclea, Pamela, and Basilius fill in the background story of Erona, Antiphilus, and Plangus, with the Battle of the Six Princes (chs. 13, 15, 29). Between the accounts, there are chapters where the main story makes progress.

The narrative moves back and forth as it did in Heliodorus or Montemayor.[9] This completely breaks up the outline of the main pastoral narrative, such as it was in the *Old Arcadia*. There we left the heroic world behind and entered the rustic, once and for all; in the *New*, our interest continually returns to the heroic. This provides the staple interest of the crucial Book II, where the loves of the princes and princesses develop and mature. In fact, the princesses may be said to fall in love with the heroes progressively as they learn of their feats: 'Therefore, dear Pyrocles (for what can mine ears be so sweetly fed with, as to hear you of you?) be liberal unto me of those things which have made you indeed precious to the world'.[10] This implies a new relation between love and heroic action. In the *Old Arcadia*, love is largely opposed to chivalry. In the *New*, however, we (like the princesses) are continually kept in mind of the princes' heroic nature, even when we see them disguised and in love. In Book III they actually fight for their loves. This provides a contrast between their noble affections and the ignoble, enfeebling passion of Basilius and Gynecia. In the *Old Arcadia*, the young and old lovers had struck much the same vein of misguided courtship.

There is a deal of other heroic action, both past and present, in the *New Arcadia*. The Helots' rebellion, the early history of Argalus and Parthenia, and that of Amphialus and Helen, are recounted before the main plot has got underway. With Phalantus and Artesia, martial action is actually brought within the confines of Basilius's pastoral retreat. This ludicrous incursion foreshadows the tragic blow to pastoral peace delivered by Amphialus in Book III.

In the *Old Arcadia*, 'Cleophila' had been a simple anagram of the beloved's name. In the *New*, the princes' assumed names—Palladius, Daiphantus and Zelmane—argue loyalty to the memories of a heroic life.

[9] See S. L. Wolff, *The Greek Romances in Elizabethan Prose Fiction* (New York, 1912), 352–3; also V. Skretkowicz, 'Sidney and Amyot', *RES* NS 37 (1976), 170–4. Wolff's claim for a 'Heliodorian frame' in the *Old Arcadia* seems untenable.

[10] Skretkowicz's edn., p. 233, ll. 35–8. All refs. to the *New Arcadia* to this edn.; see n. 2 above for details.

Again, the whole spectrum of 'heroic' subplots is brought together in Phalantus's tournament, in the pictures of the defeated beauties: Andromana, Artaxia, Erona, Helen, Parthenia, Zelmane, even Baccha and Leucippe. The pastoral is no more than a strand in this vast web of chivalric action.

The 'flashback' almost complete, the rest of Book II is taken up with an expanded account of the revolt in Arcadia. What we have of Book III is concerned solely with the capture of the princesses and the Amphialian war. Part of it is moral and philosophic discussion; part action in high martial vein. There is nothing even remotely pastoral—except the false invitation to pastoral games with which the princesses are lured away!

The pastoral sequence provides the vantage-point from which the author tells his story, looking before and after. But it is in no sense a culmination, not even a carefully demarcated area of experience; merely one episode out of many. This suggests the structure of another kind of romance.

In Canto XI of *Orlando Furioso*, Angelica stays for a while in rustic dress in a herdsman's humble cottage, nursing the wounded Medor back to health. She thus becomes a model of the princess disguised as a shepherdess, her high-born beauty exceeding anything the truly rustic maiden has to offer:

> Non le può tor però tanto umil gonna,
> che bella non rassembri e nobil donna.
>
> Taccia chi loda Fillide, o Neera,
> o Amarilli, o Galatea fugace;
> che d'esse alcuna sí bella non era,
> Titiro e Melibeo, con vostra pace.

[Even so humble attire, however, could not disguise her natural beauty and nobility. You who praise Phyllis, Neiera, Amaryllis, or elusive Galatea, be silent! For beauty none of them can touch Angelica—saving your presence, Tityrus, and yours, Meliboeus.][11]

Nor is she attracted by any lofty pastoral ideal. She simply falls in love with Medor, making the most of the convenient idyllic setting. The actual rustics remain very much in the background, ministering to the courtiers' needs. The herdsman's wife stands sponsor to Angelica when she marries Medor.

[11] Canto XI, stanzas 11–12; as in the edn. by L. Caretti (Turin, 1966). Trans. as by Guido Waldman (Oxford, 1974).

It is a brief episode, occupying only some fifteen stanzas out of the enormous poem. But later Orlando comes to the spot, and the sight of the lovers' names carved on the trees is what actually sends him mad. In Canto XXIII, stanzas 100–1, Ariosto describes the setting with just the sort of irony we find later in Sidney:

> Giunse ad un rivo che parea cristallo,
> ne le cui sponde un bel pratel fioria
>
> . . . . . .
>
> Quivi egli entrò per riposarvi in mezzo;
> e v'ebbe travaglioso albergo e crudo,
> e piú che dir si possa empio soggiorno,
> quell' infelice e sfortunato giorno.

[He came to a stream which looked like crystal; a pleasant meadow bloomed on its banks . . . Here he stopped, then, to rest—but his welcome proved to be harsh and painful, indeed quite unspeakably cruel, on this unhappy, ill-starred day.]

I am not arguing that Sidney used Ariosto as a conscious model, though we must admit the possibility. In terms of bulk, the pastoral sojourn is considerably more important even in the *New Arcadia*. But I do claim an aesthetic kinship between the two works. They make the same assumptions about the functions of pastoral in a heroic romance: to provide an occasion for royal disguise, a striking—perhaps ironic—contrast of mood and setting, a useful instrument for introducing a love-plot, but scarcely a competing scale of values or an equivalent source of interest.

Tasso too has a pastoral episode in *Jerusalem Delivered*, Book VII. Erminia, escaping from Poliferno while she is seeking Tancred in Clorinda's armour, is sheltered by a family of shepherds. There is much more genuine pastoralism in Tasso. The shepherds' life presents a superior alternative to the court and battlefield. The elder shepherd, in fact, has deliberately withdrawn from the court: 'la nostra povertà' is

> Altrui vile e negletta, a mi sì cara
> che non bramo tesor né regal verga,
> né cura o voglia ambiziosa o avara
> mai nel tranquillo del mio petto alberga.
> Spongo la sete mia ne l'acqua chiara,
> che non tem' io che di venen s'asperga,
> a questa greggia e l'orticel dispensa
> cibi non compri a la mia parca mensa.

[O poverty! chief of the heav'nly brood,
Dearer to me than wealth or kingly crown,
No wish for honour, thirst of other's good,
Can move my heart, contented with mine own:
We quench our thirst with water of this flood,
Nor fear we poison should therein be thrown;
These little flocks of sheep and tender goats
Give milk for food, and wool to make us coats.][12]

The very accentuation of the pastoral ideal makes Tasso's pastoralism less like Sidney's.[13] Rather, Tasso provides a model for Book VI of *The Faerie Queene*. Also, Tasso's pastoral is more removed from the rest of the action than Ariosto's was, just as Erminia is less central to *Jerusalem* than Angelica and Orlando were to Ariosto's poem.

More important in Sidney's context is *Amadis de Gaule*, Book IX.[14] The young Florisel hears of Silvie's beauty, disguises himself as a shepherd and serves her for three years. Then—largely because of Silvie's own desire to seek Anastarax, whom she loves, neglecting Florisel—they set out, attended by Darinel, on a series of non-pastoral chivalric adventures. Presently they are separated. Silvie attains to the hand of Anastarax, while Florisel pursues his famous career.

The differences from Sidney's plot are obvious. Most notably, Sidney's princes reach Arcadia after many adventures, just as they undertake others later. Florisel, on the contrary, is dubbed knight after leaving the herdsman's life. But, because the *New Arcadia* begins with the princes' entry into Arcadia, the impact of the narrative comes to resemble that of *Amadis* IX: a pastoral prelude to a long and involved sequence of chivalric deeds.

I do not wish to press the parallel too far. I repeat that I am not proposing structural models for the *New Arcadia* in Ariosto or *Amadis*. I am merely suggesting that here rather than in Sannazaro or Montemayor are the formal affinities of Sidney's romance.

The *New Arcadia* marks the final stage in the self-defeating expansion of the pastoral romance. The pastoral is enriched by bringing in an array

[12] Canto VII, stanza 10; as in Tasso's *Poesie*, ed. F. Flora (Naples, n.d.). Edward Fairfax's trans. as ed. R. Weiss (London, 1962).

[13] On some further implications of Tasso's passage see Ettin, *Literature and the Pastoral*, pp. 111–12. Cf. also Poggioli, *The Oaten Flute*, pp. 10–12.

[14] I may point out another minor resemblance here. The portraits of vanquished beauties in Phalantus and Artesia's train may well have been suggested by the row of similar portraits that line the path to the throne in the castle of the 'Mirror of Love'; see *Amadis*, Book IX (1553), fos. 32^r, 36^v–37^r (ch. xii).

of impressive themes; but these are developed so as to destroy or at least severely restrict the original spirit of the mode. In the process, we obtain a complex narrative of weighty thematic concerns, perhaps of greater value and potential than the pastoral romance itself. But the more successfully it realizes these other concerns, the less can it claim to be a work of the pastoral imagination.

2. *The poems in the* Arcadia

The *Old Arcadia* contains seventy-seven poems by Ringler's count, though one or two, like the versified oracle, scarcely deserve the name. Only twenty-seven are from the 'Eclogues'; the other fifty occur in the main narrative. The *New Arcadia* being so different as well as incomplete, comparison is difficult; for what it is worth, the 1590 narrative has twenty-five poems, with a blank space for another one, replacing an extent of the *Old Arcadia* that had twenty-one. The 1593 version fills the blank, but leaves out one of the 1590 poems. The unique Cambridge manuscript of the *New Arcadia* has twenty-six poems or blank spaces for poems, following the 1590 pattern. Among the additions are such peripheral pieces as the epitaph of Argalus and Parthenia and the single comic hexameter of Dametas' *impresa*. Also, as the *New* text is much longer than the *Old*, the poems make up a smaller proportion of the whole.

In general effect, even the *Old Arcadia* is much less verse-studded than Montemayor's *Diana*. Moreover, whereas the poems in *Diana* are often very long, those in the *Old Arcadia* narrative are generally quite short.[15] The *New Arcadia* is less particular in this respect,[16] but the expanded prose narrative absorbs the new long pieces to a considerable extent. Also, the poems are better placed.[17] The account of the rebellion is no longer delayed by the songs exchanged between 'Dorus' and Philisides. Nor do we have to read through songs that merely flash through somebody's mind at a critical moment: 'do not think, fair ladies, his thoughts had such leisure as to run over so long a ditty; the only general fancy of it

[15] Barring a 146-line poem (*OA* 62) praising Philoclea's beauty (originally that of Philisides' mistress) and Agelastus's 39-line lament for Basilius (*OA* 70), the longest piece has 22 ll., and most are sonnets or shorter still. (Poems numbered as in Ringler's edn. of Sidney's *Poems*.)

[16] It introduces into the narrative, in this order, *OA* 30 (180 ll, omitting the *OA* framework), *OA* 8 (48 ll.), *OA* 74 (86 ll.), *OA* 73 (186 ll.), and (in 1590 only) *OA* 75 (142 ll.). See Skretkowicz, pp. 199, 212, 311, 346, 446.

[17] Cf. Galm, p. 18.

came into his mind' (Robertson, p. 242, ll. 30–2). This is said of a 146-line poem recounted as Pyrocles climbs into Philoclea's bed—the one long poem embedded in the *Old Arcadia*. In the *New* it is transferred to a leisurely bathing scene. Other long poems are read in books (*OA* 8, 30), sent in letters (*OA* 74), or sung as prearranged serenades (*OA* 73).[18] Even the shorter poems, in both the *Old* and the *New Arcadia*, are often premeditated rather than extempore.

Unlike *Diana*, the *Arcadia* narrative has few detachable, independent lyrics. Almost invariably the poems bear marks of their contexts. All this, together with the smaller proportion of verse to prose generally, gives the *Arcadia* a very different texture from *Diana*. The narrative is punctuated by verse, but there is little sense of lyric verse being part of the basic medium. Characters do not burst into poetry as a habitual means of communication or even self-expression. Songs occur as songs, to heighten or comment upon certain moments and situations, or simply lend relief and fill a pause in the action.

Sidney thus frees his prose from the impediment of constant lyric elaboration. This makes it a more efficient medium not only for story-telling but for analysis of character and motive. The narrative that seems impossibly slow to today's novel-reader marks, in terms of Renaissance pastoral romance, not only a new briskness of pace but more fundamentally, a new recognition of the autonomy of the action.

At the same time, the groups of 'Eclogues' preserve the lyrical element that readers would have expected of a pastoral romance. Sidney separates the lyric and narrative impulses that had been impeding each other in earlier pastoral romance, and allows both free play within their respective spheres. This separation opens up exciting formal possibilities for the pastoral. The prose and verse, narrative and lyric, can conform readily to an opposition of action and contemplation, action and art, *negotium* and *otium*, court and country. Critics like Kalstone, Marenco, and Galm interpret the Eclogues in just this way.[19] Unfortunately, it seems an over-simple view.

There is no doubt that the Eclogues set out to present the traditional image of literary shepherds. We are duly told that they are not hirelings but owners of their flocks, and also informed of 'the peace wherein they did so notably flourish, and especially the sweet enjoying of their peace to so pleasant uses' (Robertson, p. 56, l. 19–20).

[18] See, respectively, Skretkowicz, pp. 212, 199, 311, 346.
[19] Kalstone, p. 60; Marenco, pp. 152–4; Galm, p. 10.

The happy pastoral community abides. In fact, in the Third and Fourth Eclogues, it is sharply marked off from the courtly interlopers. Book III contains the unhappy love-tangles of the princes; the Third Eclogues present the happy love and marriage of Lalus and Kala. Similarly Book IV describes the confusion among the courtiers after Basilius's apparent death; whereas in the following eclogues, 'The shepherds, finding no place for them in these garboils, to which their quiet hearts (whose highest ambition was in keeping themselves up in goodness) had at all no aptness, retired themselves from among the clamorous multitude' (Robertson, p. 327, ll. 2–5).

Thus the Eclogues seem to perform the classic function of pastoral by providing a purer, fuller expression of the confused elements of our normal experience. In Walter Davis's words, they 'relate this particular action of two Greek princes to the timeless themes of man's life on earth'.[20] From one point of view, this is correct; but it implies that the Eclogues provide the controlling values and perspective of the work. A detailed analysis leads to a very different conclusion. Such an analysis can only be made with respect to the *Old Arcadia*, as the order of the poems in the *New Arcadia* is uncertain, and differs in the 1590 and 1593 versions. (However, I have argued elsewhere for partial authorial sanction for the 1590 order.)[21]

The First and Second Eclogues are royal entertainments. They present the shepherds' traditional art and pastimes within a quasi-feudal structure. The pastimes are enhanced by 'divers strangers, as well of great as of mean houses' (Robertson, p. 56, ll. 20–1). Early on, in the second poem of the First Eclogues, the 'higher' love of Philisides is placed alongside the pastoral courtship of Lalus and Kala.[22] The pastoral details of the shepherds' love are turned to metaphor by Philisides (Robertson, p. 62, ll. 20–2):

> Despair my field; the flowers spirit's wars;
> My day new cares; my gins my daily sight,
> In which do light small birds of thoughts o'erthrown.

In later poems, by 'Dorus' and other courtiers like Philisides, Strephon, and Klaius, there is more of actual landscape, but pictured in Petrarchan

[20] *A Map of Arcadia*, p. 113.

[21] See my 'The Eclogues in Sidney's *New Arcadia*', *RES* NS 35 (1984), 185–202.

[22] The contrast has been noted, though in somewhat different terms, by Kalstone, p. 64; Neil L. Rudenstine, *Sidney's Poetic Development* (Cambridge, Mass., 1967), 84; Galm, pp. 48–52.

fashion as the lover's retreat rather than the shepherd's habitual milieu.[23] From another angle, the country provides a contrast to the court: 'Here no treason is hid, veiled in innocence' (Robertson, p. 166, l. 25). Finally, country life holds an elevated philosophic attraction, again a matter that would hardly have struck Lalus and his mates (Robertson, p. 166, ll. 15–17):

> Contemplation here holdeth his only seat,
> Bounded with no limits, borne with a wing of hope,
> Climbs even unto the stars; nature is under it.

In fact, the poems are ranged in a sort of hierarchy. The shepherd-singers occupy the homeliest level. Above them come Strephon, Klaius, and Philisides. The first two are 'gentlemen', and Philisides seems to be one as well: 'of such patronage as neither left me so great that I was a mark for envy nor so base that I was subject to contempt' (Robertson, p. 334, ll. 14–16). They bridge the gap between the rustics and the princely characters. Like the princes, they can handle intricate verse-forms, quantitative metre, and courtly sentiments. Of course it is in the songs of Dorus and Cleophila that these features find full expression. But in all these sophisticated lyrics, the pastoral concerns are the merest offshoot of the Petrarchan content. One poem briefly, and another extensively, refers to a nature-setting.[24] Only one has an intermittent pastoral content: 'Lady, reserved by the heav'ns . . .' (*OA* 13).

In bulk, these poems of 'courtly' orientation balance or even exceed those sung by the true shepherds. In terms of impact, they are still more important. They are placed to attract maximum attention, at the beginning and end of each group. They are sung by the heroes and by Philisides, the author's own persona. They reflect the courtly interests of the main narrative and the poems embedded in it.

Above all, in the *Old Arcadia*, the courtly narrative continues through the Eclogues as well. Through substantial prose interludes, we are told of Erona and Plangus, and the early history of the princes. Even more important, the princes' present loves are advanced through the Eclogues; their songs form part of their courtship and love-entanglements. 'Dorus' picks up a lute from the blushing Pamela's feet 'with a dismayed grace, all his blood stirred betwixt fear and desire' (Robertson, p. 79, ll. 18–19).

[23] Briefly in Philisides' 'Fair rocks, goodly rivers, sweet woods . . .' (*OA* 31), *in extenso* in Dorus's 'O sweet woods . . .' (*OA* 34) and Strephon and Klaius's sestina 'Ye goatherd gods . . .' (*OA* 71).

[24] 'Fair rocks, goodly rivers . . .' (*OA* 31) and 'O sweet woods . . .' (*OA* 34).

'Cleophila' sings to Philoclea but impresses all three of her lovers (Robertson, p. 82, ll. 15–17). Histor's narration of the princes' exploits helps the progress of their loves. Pamela asks for the story: 'And when she had asked thus much, having had nothing but vehement desire to her counsel, her sweet body did even tremble for fear lest she had done amiss. But glad was her shepherd, not to have his doings spoken of, but because any question of him proceeded out of that mouth' (Robertson, p. 152, ll. 28–33).

Thus the first two groups of 'Eclogues' do not really provide a pastoral world to counter the courtly nature of the 'Books' or 'Acts'. The pastoralism is more marked than in the 'Acts'; but ultimately the sequences come to bear upon the princely characters. Few poems convey any sense of a pastoral or even natural setting. One or two others are clearly linked to the plot, though they contain nothing pastoral. The rest, including all the quantitative poems, are completely detachable as well as non-pastoral.

In other words, as in so many earlier pastoral romances, the range of poems passes beyond the truly bucolic into a wide range of miscellaneous verse, especially love-lyrics. Ringler extols the Arcadian Eclogues as 'a more extensive and varied pastoral work than Spenser's' (p. xxxviii). It is difficult to agree if we take the term 'pastoral' at all strictly.

With the Third and Fourth Eclogues the case is somewhat different. To begin with, the princes do not participate in them. The highest-ranking characters are Philisides, Strephon, and Klaius. Secondly, the shepherds are not performing before a royal audience but singing to please or console themselves. Thirdly, the contrast with the court is much more clearly drawn.

Even so, there is very little of the truly pastoral. In the Third Eclogues, Dicus's epithalamium 'Let mother earth . . .' (*OA* 63) has only ten properly pastoral lines out of ninety-nine.[25] In Nico's tale of his neighbour (*OA* 64), a courtly 'shepherd', favoured by the prince, cuckolds a simple yokel. This is really anti-pastoral, more like the bourgeois *fabliau*. Philisides' fable of man (*OA* 66) has a detachable bucolic framework but is intrinsically non-pastoral. Geron and Histor's debate on women (*OA* 67) treats the theme of many Renaissance eclogues, but is not itself pastoral.

The Fourth Eclogues fall into two clear sections. Of the four love-poems, I have already mentioned 'Ye goatherd gods . . .' (*OA* 71), with its Petrarchan, non-pastoral nature-setting. The other three (*OA* 72, 73,

[25] See Robertson, p. 245, l. 29; p. 246, ll. 23–4; p. 246, l. 32–p. 247, l. 5.

74) are complex and extremely sophisticated love-poems, as far removed from a shepherd's cares as may be. Of the two poems on Basilius's death, the latter ('Farewell O sun . . .', *OA* 76) is also non-pastoral. Alone in strong contrast stands the markedly pastoral 'Since that to death is gone the shepherd high' (*OA* 75), which follows the movement of Moschus's Lament for Bion as mediated by the eleventh eclogue in Sannazaro's *Arcadia*.[26]

Only one properly pastoral poem among the eleven, then, with a few intermittent or superficial touches in three others. It is not a great tally. Nor is it supplemented much by the prose framework of the Eclogues, or their general location in the work.

The Third Eclogues open with a substantial prose account of Lalus's wooing of Kala:

> Thus the first strawberries he could find were ever in a clean washed dish sent to Kala. Thus posies of the spring flowers were wrapped up in a little green silk and dedicated to Kala's breasts . . . As for her father's sheep, he had no less care of them than his own . . . But if he spied Kala favoured any one of the flock more than his fellows, then that was cherished . . . (Robertson, p. 244, ll. 6–9, 20–1, 22–4)

The community supports this picture of the happy couple: 'there needed no inviting of the neighbours in that valley; for so well was Lalus beloved that they were all ready to do him credit. Neither yet came they like harpies to devour him, but one brought a fat pig, the other a tender kid, a third a great goose' (Robertson, p. 245, ll. 1–5). It is too single-noted, almost contrived in its happy idyllic tone. Sidney may have recalled the elegant *naïveté* of *Daphnis and Chloe* as he wrote this passage; but even that romance introduced checks and complications along its length. In any case, Sidney's general tone is markedly more serious and balanced than in *Daphnis*. By contrast, the encapsulated sweetness of this two-page account, its prettiness and diminution of scale, suggest a less than total commitment to the potential of the pastoral setting. It is presented externally, as a useful counter to the life of the courtiers and the 'fiery agonies' of their love. It is unsubtly idealized, while at the same time its limitations are made clear: 'But among the shepherds was all honest liberty; no fear of dangerous telltales . . . but one questioning with another of the manuring his ground, and governing his flock. The highest point they reached to was to talk of the holiness of marriage' (Robertson,

[26] See Ringler, p. 419.

p. 245, ll. 22–6). Instead of reflecting a wide range of experience, pastoral life becomes a temporary respite from it: deliberately simple, almost unreal. As an object of independent interest, it would cloy after a couple of pages. It is acceptable only as setting off the courtier's life that is the author's central concern.

Similarly, in the Fourth Eclogues, the shepherds are the 'suffering commons' of the political eclogue, standing to their king as their sheep stand to them. Sheep and shepherd, the literal and the metaphoric, merge in Geron's lament: 'Alas, poor sheep . . . You are now not only to fear home wolves but alien lions; now, I say, now that Basilius, our right Basilius is deceased. Alas, sweet pastures, shall soldiers that know not how to use you possess you? Shall they that cannot speak Arcadian language be lords over your shepherds?' (Robertson, p. 327, ll. 15, 19–23). The shepherds' lives have no meaning except in relation to the court. The latter is the basic reality, the shepherds' laments only a reflection. Further, as Basilius is not really dead, we may even find a retrospective irony in the shepherds' innocent grief.

The *Old Arcadia* is not a story about shepherds. It is a story about princes who find themselves among shepherds—or, to be more accurate, who find themselves away from the court. Shepherds there are indeed, but Sidney confines them to the interludes. This indicates their irrelevance, not only in terms of direct involvement with the plot, but in providing a milieu that influences the main characters. In the earlier books, we may at least feel that the nature-setting somehow affects the quality of the princes' love. The action in Books IV and V would not have varied in any essential way if there had not been a field, tree, or shepherd within a hundred miles. (The one possible exception is the grim case of Musidorus's plan to seduce Pamela, and even this occurs away from the central Arcadian setting.) At the climax of the story, the action affects the shepherds, but is not affected by them in the slightest.

3. *Pastoral themes and concerns in the* Arcadia

Sidney's views on the function of the pastoral are most clearly expressed in *A Defence of Poetry*:

> Is the poor pipe disdained, which sometime out of Meliboeus' mouth can show the misery of people under hard lords or ravening soldiers, and again, by Tityrus, what blessedness is derived to them that lie lowest from the goodness of them that sit highest; sometimes, under the pretty tales of wolves and sheep, can

include the whole considerations of wrong-doing and patience; sometimes show that contentions for trifles can get but a trifling victory . . .[27]

Sidney justifies the pastoral entirely in terms of moral and allegorical purpose—which, as we have seen, is the general approach of practically every theorist of the age.

In his account of the Arcadian Eclogues, Sidney is less insistent on their serious inner purpose. This appears only as one of many motives: 'sometimes they would contend for a prize of well singing, sometimes lament the unhappy pursuit of their affections, sometimes, again, under hidden forms utter such matters as otherwise were not fit for their delivery' (Robertson, p. 56, ll. 6–9). Kalander's account in the *New Arcadia* (Skretkowicz, p. 24) does not differ substantially from this. Sidney's Eclogues show a great variety of subject; but the *Arcadia* as a whole, particularly the *New Arcadia*, obviously adopts the more serious aims stated in the *Defence*. These, we should note, are based almost entirely on the eclogue, particularly Virgil's Eclogues as interpreted in the Renaissance. Romance and drama are not mentioned.

Not that allusion and 'inner purpose' are absent in pastoral romance and drama, especially the former. I have indicated how even Sannazaro's *Arcadia* has a certain amount of it, and both Bartholomew Yong and Thomas Wilson speak of courtly allusions in *Diana*.[28] Moreover, *Diana* contains several discussions and debates, particularly on the nature of love and its relation to noble birth.[29] But all this is subsidiary to the romantic and narrative impulse, and there is little or no discussion of other themes, political, moral, or philosophical.

Sidney fills his romance with a far greater body of intellectual concerns, allied to those of the humanist eclogue and humanist theories of pastoral. Yet these are incorporated into the courtly, but lighter and essentially pleasure-oriented form of the pastoral romance. The *Arcadia*, especially the *New Arcadia*, is important for bringing together these two lines of development.

By being writ large, the courtly and intellectual concerns of the eclogue are clearly seen to be inimical to the true pastoral vein.[30] This latter, in so

[27] Sidney's *Miscellaneous Prose*, ed. Katherine Duncan-Jones and Jan Van Dorsten (Oxford, 1973), 94, l. 35–p. 95, l. 6.

[28] Yong, ed. Kennedy, p. 5, l. 31–p. 6, l. 1; Wilson, in introducing his trans. of *Diana*, Book I (BL MS Addl. 18638), as ed. H. Thomas (New York, 1921), 10.

[29] T. P. Harrison relates these to the 'Italian courtly symposium': see 'A Source of Sidney's *Arcadia*', *Studies in English* (Univ. of Texas), 5 (1926), 55.

[30] Without specific ref. to the eclogue, this is roughly Peter Lindenbaum's thesis in

far as it survives, is relegated to the Eclogues. Nor can a long narrative sustain the allegoric or metaphoric use of the pastoral. This can only occur in a passing comment (like Musidorus's on 'shepherds of men': Skretkowicz, p. 24, ll. 7–8) or limited passages of concentrated rhetoric—either verse ('Since that to death is gone the shepherd high') or highly wrought prose related to the verse, like Geron's lament in the Fourth Eclogues (Robertson, p. 327). For the rest, the concerns of the 'allegorical' eclogue must be treated openly in courtly, heroic terms.

It is important to realize this continuous influence of the humanist eclogue on what is purportedly a pastoral romance: an influence seen primarily not in Sidney's Eclogues but in the thematically dense narrative. It is a difficult influence to trace, as it concerns the non-pastoral themes of the humanist and courtly eclogue, largely divorced from their pastoral setting. How can we trace them back to the eclogue rather than to any other source? Despite an obvious uncertainty, I think we can make out a plausible case.

Some episodes in the *Arcadia* clearly read as modified eclogues (sometimes partly or wholly in prose) embedded in the text. The best example is the singing-match of Dorus and Philisides in the *Old Arcadia*, interrupted by the rebels' attack (Robertson, pp. 124–5). This is a piece of extraneous pastoralism that markedly disturbs the flow of the narrative. Sidney has briefly abandoned one formal model, the romance, for another, the amoebean eclogue.

Later on we have a similar 'set piece' in the imaginary wooing of Dametas and Charita in Musidorus's concocted tale to Miso (Robertson, pp. 190–1). Equally if less obviously based on the eclogue is an exchange between Musidorus and Pyrocles, a sort of competition in the quality of their loves, embodied in two antithetical songs (Robertson, pp. 170–1).

There are, of course, no hidden political or philosophic themes in any of these sequences. But the last one in particular leads on to clear theoretical discussions, often on subjects commonly treated in the Renaissance eclogue. One such topic was the morality of love. Pyrocles and Musidorus have a long debate on the subject after the former divulges his love of Philoclea, ending in a piece of stichomythia reminiscent of the amoebean eclogue:

> 'Alas! Let your own brain disenchant you', said Musidorus.
> 'My heart is too far possessed', said Pyrocles.

Changing Landscapes. Anti-Pastoral Sentiment in the English Renaissance (Athens, Ga., 1986), chs. ii and iii.

'But the head gives you direction.'
'And the heart gives me life', answered Pyrocles.
(Robertson, p. 23, ll. 25–8)

Immediately before this, they had discussed their varying attitudes to the pastoral setting; before that, the respective merits of action and withdrawal. Here are three important debates within the first twenty pages of the *Old Arcadia*, all retained in the *New*. In fact, there are even earlier ones. The theme of 'action versus withdrawal' is inaugurated in Philanax's debate with Basilius, and accompanied by a discussion on fate and providence (Robertson, pp. 6–9).

This last theme is taken up by Pyrocles and Musidorus in Book V (Robertson, pp. 370ff.). The imprisoned princes debate the power of providence as shepherds had done in so many eclogues.[31] From there they move on to discuss the possibility of life after death. Earlier, in Book IV, Philoclea and Pyrocles had conducted a long debate on the morality of suicide (Robertson, pp. 294ff.).

The *New Arcadia* abandons one or two of these debates: for instance, Philanax's argument with Basilius is presented in a letter. On the other hand, a number of important new debates are introduced—above all, that between Pamela and Cecropia in Book III on hedonism and morality, atheism and faith (Skretkowicz, pp. 356ff.), on a par with the princes' prison discourses. I may add here the different but equally serious vein of judicial or forensic rhetoric in the trial scene of the *Old Arcadia*.

In these last, it would be absurd to claim any influence of the amoebean debates of the moral eclogue. We have passed by slow stages from obvious or highly probable eclogue-models to the equally obvious absence of such models. We have seen the incidence of many themes current in the didactic eclogue: the morality of love, love versus chastity, the beauty of nature, action versus *otium*, fate and providence. These themes have been absorbed, apparently without trace, in a still wider set of concerns. We come back to the externally oriented, centrifugal nature of Sidney's pastoral.

But it is still pastoral, by Sidney's own criteria. Let us go back to the account of pastoral poetry in the *Defence*. Every theme that Sidney lists there is important in the *New Arcadia*: good and bad government, 'wrong-doing and patience', trifling contentions and trifling victories for 'this world's dunghill'. There is a very telling passage in the *Old Arcadia*.

[31] See p. 47 above.

Gynecia, her daughters, and the princes have gone to the shepherd's meet. Basilius, left behind, 'had a sufficient eclogue in his own head betwixt honour, with the long experience he had had of the world, on the one side, and this new assault of Cleophila's beauty on the other side' (Robertson, p. 45, ll. 8–11). Here is the clearest possible testimony that Sidney considered 'eclogue' to be a loose synonym for 'debate' or even more generally 'moral conflict'.

I described in Chapter 3, section 3, how in the humanist eclogue, shepherds' dialogues and song-contests are turned to the purpose of debate or argument. Courtly English eclogues in manuscript often show the same feature.[32] The most notable is perhaps Fairfax's 'Hermes and Lycaon'. But examples occur at dates closer to Sidney's, like the eclogue by Gorges printed in *A Poetical Rhapsody* (no. 10) where a shepherd declares his exalted love for 'Daphnee' against a goatherd's remonstrance: love-confession turns to a debate between humble and ambitious pastors. Another eclogue in the *Rhapsody* (no. 11) is a debate 'Concerning Olde Age' between two aged shepherds.

More generally, English practice at this time shows a tendency to confine the term 'eclogue' to dialogues, or at least matched, answering verses, between shepherds. Greene's *Menaphon* and Lodge's *Rosalynde* use the word exclusively in titles to such poems. (Curiously, it never occurs among the titles in *England's Helicon*.) *Menaphon*, indeed, has another occurrence close to Sidney's: the love-lorn Menaphon spends 'whole Eclogues in anguish'.[33]

Such practice is confirmed by critical theory, which commonly identified the eclogue with dialogue. There was indeed an equally common practice, derived from Probus[34] and repeated in every textbook, dividing bucolic poetry into dialogue, poet's monologue, and a mixture of the two. But dialogue was more commonly stressed, perhaps owing to such models as Petrarch and Mantuan. Cooper's *Thesaurus* defines 'Ecloga', after 'electio' [selection, choice] and 'explanatio' [explanation], as 'sermocinatio seu colloquium' [dialogue or conversation].[35] So also Ramus explains '*ἐκλογή*, electio, separatio, explanatio: hic autem collocutio est'[36] [Eclogue: selection, extract, explanation; here, however, a dialogue]. Such ideas are reflected in Webbe's 'Dialogues or speeches

[32] See above, Ch. 7, sect. 3, and Ch. 9 *passim*.

[33] *Menaphon*, ed. G. B. Harrison (with Lodge's *A Margarite of America* (Oxford, 1927), 74.

[34] See Thilo (ed.), Servius, III. ii. 329. 10–14.

[35] T. Cooper, *Thesaurus linguae Romanae et Britannicae* (London, 1565), sig. 2R4^r^.

[36] Ramus's edn. of Virgil's Eclogues (1582), p. 29.

framed or supposed betweene Sheepeheardes, Neteheardes, Goteheardes',[37] and Puttenham's 'base and humble stile by maner of Dialogue'.[38] Puttenham indeed goes on to speak of 'priuate and familiar talke', but it is a short step from the concept of dialogue to that of debate.[39] Probus's equivocal use of 'disputo' could have helped to bridge the gap.[40] Hessus, in the Argument to his Latin translation of Theocritus, had said of Idyll I: 'introducitur cum Thyrside colloquens . . . caprarius' [A goatherd is brought in talking to Thyrsis]. Andreas Divus, otherwise cribbing from Hessus, changes 'colloquens' [talking] to 'disputan[s]' [disputing].[41]

The 'eclogue' in Basilius's head carries another set of implications. It is not an abstract argument so much as an emotional conflict, embodied in personality and the action of the story. Nor is it peculiar to Basilius. The princes' abstract discussion of the same issue, love versus honour, is rooted in their own situation. Gynecia suffers a similar opposition between her marital faith and her illicit passion, as does Pamela between her love and her royal dignity and Philoclea between her love and her virgin modesty. The *New Arcadia* adds another character to the list: Amphialus, involved in the most complex conflict of all.

These conflicts are not confined to particular speeches or episodes but embodied in the basic action of the romance. Sidney's moral debates are primarily exemplified, only incidentally discussed or theorized over. 'In all these creatures of his making,' writes Fulke Greville, 'his intent, and scope was, to turn the barren Philosophy precepts into pregnant Images of life.'[42] The action involving them is long, romantic, courtly. It has little that is even remotely pastoral, little apparently eclogue-like. Yet an improbable influence from the didactic debate-eclogue seems to have passed into the plot-structure of the *Arcadia*.

It is perhaps better to call it an association or overtone rather than an influence: we can hardly say that the action is dictated by any such model. But I think we can claim that the treatment of the action is affected by a quibbling extension of pastoral terms and themes. Back-

[37] *A Discourse of English Poetrie*, Gregory Smith (ed.), *Elizabethan Critical Essays*, i. 262, ll. 16–18. [38] *The Arte of English Poesie*, Gregory Smith, ii. 27, ll. 16–17.

[39] For the course of such a progress in the Middle Ages, see J. H. Hanford, 'Classical Eclogue and Medieval Debate', *Romanic Review*, 2 (1911), 16–31, 129–43.

[40] 'Opportunum fuit ergo ei, qui pastores inferebat, ea lingua disputasse.' [It was therefore befitting for him [Theocritus], who brought in shepherds, to *disputare* [examine, discuss, dispute] in that language [Doric]]: Thilo, III. ii. 327. 2–3.

[41] *Theocriti . . . Eidyllia trigintasex*, tr. Eobanus Hessus, sig. A7^r; *Theocriti . . . Idyllia trigintasex*, tr. Andreas Divus (Basle, 1554), 10.

[42] *The Life of . . . Sir Philip Sidney*, ed. N. Smith (Oxford, 1907), 15.

ground association with the didactic eclogue serves to point and perfect the themes inherent in the conflicts of the narrative. It lends weight to the intellectual content of the action, and crystallizes it from time to time in actual debates or dialogues.

The *Arcadia* thus acquires the full range of intellectual concerns to be found in the Renaissance eclogue—a range it could never have acquired from the obvious model of the pastoral romance. And, curiously enough, it is through this fusion of concerns that ultimately, in the *New Arcadia*, Sidney revalidates the pastoral at a somewhat rarefied level. It acquires no absolute validity; it provides a remarkable new element in the courtly ideal, but indicates at the same time why a pastoral vehicle remained essential to Sidney's purpose. Two suggestive pages by Mark Rose[43] are about all that has been said about the subject. Here is a field waiting to be explored.

Between the *Old* and the *New Arcadia*, the status of the shepherd is considerably revalued. In the *Old*, the shepherds had merely played a part—the most unexpected and hence noteworthy part—in the general achievement of the Arcadians: 'Even the muses . . . bestow[ed] their perfections so largely there that the very shepherds themselves had their fancies opened to so high conceits' (Robertson, p. 4, ll. 14–17). The *New Arcadia* repeats this (Skretkowicz, p. 16, ll. 13–18); but in a new passage soon after, Kalander declares that the shepherds are specially favoured by the Muses: 'no sort of people so excellent in that kind as the pastors, for their living standing but upon the looking to their beasts, they have ease, the nurse of poetry' (Skretkowicz, p. 24, ll. 24–6). Most excellent among them are Strephon and Claius,[44] who now become shepherds (in the *Old Arcadia* they had been gentlemen): 'having neglected their wealth in respect of their knowledge, they have not so much impaired the meaner as they bettered the better' (Skretkowicz, p. 24, ll. 12–14). Urania too had earlier been 'thought a shepherd's daughter, but indeed of far greater birth' (Robertson, p. 328, l. 7). Now she becomes a shepherdess, but apparently stands for a transcendent, Platonic spiritual force.[45] The *New Arcadia* opens with the love-lament of Strephon and Claius: the shepherd's new dignity is affirmed right at the outset. They describe their lofty passion in consistently pastoral terms:

> her eyelids are more pleasant to behold than two white kids climbing up a fair tree and browsing on his tenderest branches, and . . . her breath is more sweet

[43] *Heroic Love: Studies in Sidney and Spenser* (Cambridge, Mass., 1968), 42–3.

[44] Generally so spelt in the *New Arcadia*.

[45] See Katherine Duncan-Jones, 'Sidney's Urania', *RES* NS 171 (1966), 123–32.

than a gentle south-west wind which comes creeping over flowery fields and shadowed waters in the extreme heat of summer . . . [but not] to be matched with the flock of unspeakable virtues laid up delightfully in that best-builded fold (Skretkowicz, p. 5, ll. 3–14).

Such 'virtues' in shepherds were unthinkable in the *Old Arcadia*.

Even in the *New*, the pastoral setting and characters are never Platonized again. The lovers soon follow Urania out of Arcadia. But in less mystic spirit, a new dignity is given to the shepherd. Sometimes this can be equivocal, as where (in both versions) the disguised prince 'Dorus' is taken as an embodiment of pastoral virtue: 'he hath manifested: that this estate is not always to be rejected, since under that veil there may be hidden things to be esteemed' (Robertson, p. 106, ll. 1–3). There is at least an association through paradox, the recognition of pastoral graces as an embellishment of Musidorus's royal nature: 'Tell me, sweet Philoclea, did you ever see such a shepherd? Tell me, did you ever hear of such a prince?' (Skretkowicz, p. 155, ll. 1–3; cf. p. 151, ll. 19–35).

An episode in the Artesia–Phalantus story takes us much further. The shepherd girl Urania's portrait is carried among the defeated royal beauties. This time we have a genuine tension of royal and pastoral: 'with all that poverty, beauty played the prince, and commanded as many hearts as the greatest queen there did' (Skretkowicz, p. 97, ll. 29–31). Moreover, Lalus the shepherd boy appears to defend the portrait. He is not permitted to fight, but he presents a new image of valiant grace: '(doing all things with so pretty grace that it seemed ignorance could not make him do amiss, because he had a heart to do well), . . . coming with a look full of amiable fierceness (as in whom choler could not take away the sweetness)' (Skretkowicz, p. 99, ll. 22–6).

By this time, we may feel that Sidney has in mind a distinctive ideal of 'pastoral' excellence. This incorporates a grace and prowess worthy of the court, but in a special setting of simplicity and native innocence, perhaps rising (as with Strephon and Claius) to a height of philosophic perception. It is not a genuinely pastoral ideal but the perfection of a courtly one. The pastoral contributes that touch of perfection, a pristine or unspoilt version of the standard courtly virtue.

In fact, like the political eclogue-writers, Sidney falls prey to the divisions of the pastoral metaphor. His narrative preserves the social hierarchy, treating kings as kings and shepherds as shepherds. Basilius's pastoral retreat thus indicates disorder and neglect of duty, the confusion implied by Greville's phrase 'a Princely Shepherd, or Shepherdish

King'.[46] Marenco shows how Sidney rejects the king-shepherd metaphor with its implicit equation of the active and contemplative lives.[47] But the very fact that the kingdom in question is Arcadia gives the whole setting a symbolic quality, invests the king with the shepherd's aura. It modifies the royal ideal by pastoral values, playing as a disembodied force around events and characters.

The *Arcadia* proves to contain several distinct veins of courtly and humanist concerns, all of which could lead to pastoral or something like it. These disparate concerns are embodied in the form of a romance. That romance was revised piecemeal at several points before being drastically expanded and rewritten. To complete the confusion, the revision is incomplete.

Small wonder that our gaze, like Sidney's own, moves from one concern and one level of response to another. Small wonder too that our attempts to treat the *Arcadia* as pastoral must be intermittent and even inconsistent. The work approximates to the pastoral from several angles, none of them affording much scope for genuine development of the mode. We are soon lost in a maze of non-pastoral and anti-pastoral concerns.

Sidney gives the pastoral a great new charge of themes and subjects, while the pastoral vehicle does not develop in proportion. We lose the delicate balance between pastoral life and other modes of experience implicitly playing about it. A whole new world is opened up before us; but in the process, the primacy of the pastoral is lost.

[46] Greville's *Life*, p. 12. Cf. Toliver's memorable remark: 'Thus as we are shown knighthood as shepherds practice it and eclogues as knights sing them, it is clear that each is and will remain basically foreign to the other' (*Pastoral Forms and Attitudes*, p. 52).

[47] *Arcadia puritana*, pp. 41–2.

16
Other English Romance

In this chapter and the next I shall define a vitally important development of the pastoral: the spiritually active pastoral setting of English romance and drama. This is obviously different from the spiritual themes of the allegorical eclogue, as well as from pathetic fallacy and the 'landscape of the mind'. It differs from the mere sense of pastoral life as conducive either to the formal moral virtues—labour, honesty, humility, content—or to idyllic hedonism. Instead, it views the pastoral setting as directly nurturing spiritual states in man through a special power or function.

The closest major continental analogue is in Sannazaro's *Arcadia*; but there the setting is much more a simple reflection of human states of mind. It does not exude an independent power that can create or change mental states or affect human actions.

1. *The progress of the pastoral romance*

The new spiritual landscape arises out of what I have defined as the 'cyclic' structure, from court to country and back again. In the most embryonic instances we have a mere pastoral sojourn of no special significance, set in a course of adventures. Barnabe Riche's Don Simonides rescues the shepherd Titerus from Venus's prison and attends his pastoral wedding; but he is unaffected by the experience, and 'the next daie beyng wearie of the Desert, curteously tooke his leaue of Titerus'.[1] Lodge's *Forbonius and Prisceria* (1584) appears to be more 'cyclic' in its movement: a frustrated love affair achieves success after the heroine is removed to the country, the hero following in shepherd's guise. But the country setting serves no organic function: it merely provides a change of scene and a pleasant detachable poem about two shepherd-lovers, Corulus and Corinna.

[1] Barnabe Riche, *The Straunge and Wonderfull Aduentures of Don Simonides* (London, 1581), sig. P2^r.

Elsewhere, however, the setting assumes a special significance, at first by contrast with the outer world, then by assuming a special power that *affects* the surrounding action. The arbitrary linear sequence of romantic action thus comes to be unified round a pastoral centre, earlier events leading up to it and later ones deriving from it.

There is some approach to this in the story of Argentile and Curan in William Warner's *Albion's England* (1586).[2] The dispossessed Princess Argentile and her lover Prince Curan woo and marry after severally fleeing the court and turning shepherds. Here the pastoral retreat is organic to the plot, though there is little sense of a special reconciling influence. What is remarkable, however, is that there should be any pastoral at all. As Ward noted long ago, Warner's story is a version of the Havelok legend.[3] But the pastoral sojourn is Warner's own invention. It is very significant that he should have chosen this as an appropriate setting for the resolution of the love-plot.

Sometimes the setting is truly invested with spiritual meaning, as in Brian Melbancke's *Philotimus* (1583). After many wasted years, Philotimus comes to a *locus amoenus* where dwells the old shepherd Laurus. He tells Philotimus of his own wasted youth and eventual rest: 'The fragrant fieldes, the rurall lawnes, where Zephyrus inspires the fruitful earth, and doeth attire eache bushe with budde and bloomie braunch, where the purple Columbine, and the oriente cowsloppe, the daffadillie and the pretie lillie, the dazie and the violet, do may in aray, shalbe my pallace and my paradise.'[4] Though eccentrically constructed, this vivid sentence stands out from Melbancke's customary euphuism. Philotimus himself chooses a more active course under a virtuous prince; but rustic life remains a valid, indeed transcendent ideal, significantly placed near the end of the narrative.

There is also a striking sequence near the end of William Warner's *Syrinx* (1584). Dircilla, cast on an island, is at first shocked by its savage inhabitants; but gradually she perceives their grace and beauty. The men are 'nimble lads', 'right *fauni* or *satyrs*', the women like nymphs, and all of 'harmless manners and dispositions': 'amongst woods, casting themselves into a ring, they danced their roundelays; or

[2] *Albions England* (London, 1586), 83–7; IV. XX.

[3] A. W. Ward, *History of English Dramatic Literature* (rev. edn., London, 1899), iii. 55. For many analogous versions of the story, see W. W. Skeat (ed.), *Havelok* (EETS ES 4; 1868), pp. ivff. Skeat says (p. xviii) that Warner adopted the version in Caxton's *Chronicles*.

[4] Brian Melbancke, *Philotimus* (London, 1583), sig. 2F 1^{r-v}.

gathering sweet gays, they decked themselves with flowers; or that they couched their white sides on the soft herbs'.[5] This picture of 'soft primitivism' obviously owes much to the shepherds and sylvan gods of pastoral tradition. The island itself is a 'second *Elysium*', enjoying eternal spring. Dircilla takes 'the liberty of these woods as a supersidias against the world' (p. 182). The savages worship her as a god, and she teaches them to combine the benefits of civilization with their primitive virtue and innocence.

This very notable episode looks back to Montaigne's 'Des cannibales' (published 1580) and forward to the enlightened sylvans of *The Faerie Queene*. Though not strictly pastoral, it is in a closely analogous vein, and has been surprisingly overlooked so far: Greg (p. 147) dismisses *Syrinx* as unworthy of notice. Yet some uncertainty remains. The setting is still tentative and half-incidental, not allowed to dominate the work, performing its regenerative function almost in spite of itself. The breakthrough does not come till later in the decade.

It is very likely that Lodge wrote *Rosalynde* in 1587, though the work was not published till 1590.[6] By then, Greene had brought out *Pandosto* (1588) and *Menaphon* (1589). There are also briefer pastoral sequences in Greene's *Ciceronis Amor* (1589) and *Francesco's Fortunes* (1590) and Lodge's *Euphues' Shadow* (1592).

Early scholars traced this crop of romances to the manuscript circulation of Sidney's *Arcadia*. Certainly it is difficult to account otherwise for certain features of *Menaphon* at least.[7] Another influence increasingly appreciated is Angel Day's version of Longus's Greek pastoral romance, *Daphnis and Chloe* (1587).[8] This would give a pastoral bent to Greene's earlier fondness for Heliodorian romance, and probably affect his friend Lodge as well. I may add another possible factor here. Bartholomew Yong's translation of Montemayor's *Diana*, though not published till 1598, appears to have been finished by 1582, when Yong was at the Middle Temple.[9] Lodge might still have been at Lincoln's Inn, or in touch

[5] William Warner, *Syrinx or a Sevenfold History*, ed. W. A. Bacon (Evanston, Ill., 1950), 185.

[6] See Paula Burnett (ed.), *Rosalynde* (B.Litt. Oxford, 1972), pp. xxxiiff., cxcix–ccv, adopting the suggestion of E. A. Tenney, *Thomas Lodge* (Ithaca, 1935), 96–8.

[7] See Robertson (ed.), *Old Arcadia*, p. xxxviii.

[8] See S. L. Wolff, *The Greek Romances in Elizabethan Prose Fiction*, pp. 375, 432ff. for Greene; Burnett, pp. lxvi–lxvii, for Lodge.

[9] Kennedy (ed., Yong's trans. of *Diana*, pp. xxxixff.) suggests the influence of Montemayor on Lodge's *Rosalynde*. She also says (p. xxxi) that the trans. was 'finished in May 1583'. But Yong plainly writes in 1598 'it hath lyen by me finished *Horaces* ten and sixe yeeres more' (p. 5).

with Inns-of-Court circles at any rate. Melbancke was at Gray's Inn. Warner probably never attended an Inn, but moved in legal circles as an Attorney of Common Pleas.[10]

Yet another possible factor has also escaped notice. Though not published till 1590, Sidney's *Arcadia* was entered in the Stationer's Register on 23 August 1588. It seems more than likely that this spurred Greene and his publishers to anticipate the market. No SR entry survives for *Pandosto*. It has been identified with 'A booke intitled the complaint of tyme', entered on 1 July 1588 to Thomas Orwin (who merely printed *Pandosto* for Thomas Cadman).[11] Even if one accepts this doubtful identification, Greene and his publishers may easily have heard in advance of the registration of the *Arcadia*. A well-known letter from Fulke Greville to Walsingham indicates that the matter was being talked of as early as November 1586.[12] It is even possible that Day, himself a publisher, translated *Daphnis and Chloe* in 1587 in anticipation of the same event. Greene's efforts followed, using Day's own work as a model. Greene also seems to have revised *Rosalynde*.[13] I may add the conjecture that Lodge was persuaded to publish his romance after the actual appearance of the *Arcadia* in 1590. A copy of the latter survives marked 'May. 29. 1590'.[14] *Rosalynde* was entered on 6 October 1590. With the pastoral romance, as with the lyric, the publication of Sidney's *Arcadia* may have been a crucial impetus to growth.

In Greene, Longus is subsidiary to Heliodorus. *Pandosto*, the source of *The Winter's Tale*, lacks the latter's 'cyclic' coherence because the two main stories are kept quite separate.[15] Shakespeare lets Hermione live: her union with Leontes crowns Florizel's with Perdita, and the whole action works towards the same happy ending. The pastoral scene sets the upward movement in operation. In *Pandosto*, Bellaria dies after her trial. The pastoral belongs to a fresh sequence of events, creating new complications instead of resolving the old.

Moreover, the value of the pastoral life is asserted only in a partial and equivocal manner. Dorastus wonders that 'so courtly behaviour could be found in so simple a cottage', and agonizes over marrying a

[10] See *Syrinx*, ed. Bacon, p. xxxiii.

[11] See A. F. Allison, *Robert Greene . . .: A Bibliographical Catalogue of the Early Editions* (Folkestone, 1975), 53.

[12] See Ringler (ed.), Sidney's *Poems*, p. 530.

[13] See Burnett, pp. clx–cxcviii, confirming the earlier work of H. C. Hart (*NQ* Mar.–June 1906) and Alice Walker (*RES* 9–10 (1933–4); *MLQ* 22 (1927)).

[14] Now Huntington Lib. 69441; see Ringler, p. 532.

[15] David Young, however, takes the opposite view in *The Heart's Forest*, p. 116.

shepherdess.[16] Fawnia has an even deeper struggle, between her accustomed humility and her innate royal pride: 'thy shepherds hooke sheweth thy poore state, thy proud desires an aspiring mind' (Bullough, p. 180). She commends the shepherd's state to Dorastus in a memorable speech (pp. 181–2), and later, in Pandosto's clutches, she longs for pastoral peace and quiet (p. 194). But her 'desires reach as high as Princes' (p. 185): 'Fawnia poore soule was no less joyful, that being a shepheard, fortune had favoured her so, as to reward her with the love of a Prince, hoping in time to be advaunced from the daughter of a poore farmer to be the wife of a riche King' (p. 186). This is a less than total vindication of the pastoral from the heroine. Fawnia feels unmixed pleasure in assuming royal status, and the reader presumably rests in simple satisfaction that the lost princess should regain her birthright.

In *Menaphon*, the courtly and the shepherdly are even more clearly demarcated. Structurally, indeed, *Menaphon* assumes for the first time the primacy of pastoral. Instead of the arbitrary, infinitely extensible action of Heliodorian romance, it concentrates on a single setting, and that a pastoral one. Other settings and events take on meaning in relation to this, leading up to or out of it. Pastoral becomes the organizing principle of the work.

There is also much on the values and attractions of shepherd life, beginning with Menaphon's opening meditation on how he 'by being a shepheard find[s] that which Kings want in their royalties'.[17] Princess Sephestia, disguised as Samela, gradually comes to prize the pastoral life: 'finding such content in the cotage, began to despise the honors of the Court' (p. 45). Such is her 'content in *Arcadie*' that she refuses to leave the country as her son Pleusidippus wants (pp. 64–5).

Yet he does want to leave, at the end of a childhood when his lordly nature found vent in bullying the shepherd boys. Much more clearly than in *Pandosto*, royal nature breaks through shepherd guise. This is reinforced by the education he receives at the court of King Agenor, where his kidnappers take him. He returns to Arcadia as a prince in conscious shepherd's guise, carries off Samela like a knight and mocks the pursuing shepherds: 'Are sheepe transformed into men . . . ?' (p. 95). The shepherds are led by Melicertus, who also is a disguised courtier and,

[16] Geoffrey Bullough (ed.), *Narrative and Dramatic Sources of Shakespeare*, viii (London, 1975), 178. All refs. to *Pandosto* to this text.

[17] *Menaphon*, ed. G. B. Harrison (with Lodge's *A Margarite of America*), p. 25. All refs. to *Menaphon* to this edn.

in fact, Pleusidippus's father Maxim[i]us. In the denouement, the operative values are courtly rather than pastoral.

Samela prizes the content of Arcadia, but she is both amused and repelled when Menaphon woos her (pp. 40, 43, 44). She admits the love of Melicertus because of his innate nobility: 'his browes containe the characters of nobilitie, and his lookes in shepheards weeds are Lordlie, his voyce pleasing, his wit full of gentrie: weigh all these equallie, and consider *Samela* is it not thy *Maximus*?' (pp. 56–7). It is Maxim[i]us indeed. As in Greene's probable model, Warner's story of Argentile and Curan,[18] the pastoral sojourn simply brings together two parted courtier-lovers. The shepherds set out by speaking as fine euphuisms as the courtiers; but they descend to a rustic crudity treated with condescension if not contempt.

Though the pastoral world is central to *Menaphon*, we feel it is not fully vindicated. All through the story, courtly values provide a parallel, unassimilated movement. The pieces are all there, but have not quite fallen into place. They are assembled, and the joints smoothed over, in Lodge's *Rosalynde*. This is the more remarkable in that *Rosalynde* was probably composed before Greene's two romances.

Rosalynde reduces the 'pastoral cycle' to its quintessence, without any Heliodorian additions. A number of courtly characters, dissatisfied with or driven out from a corrupt court, gather in a half-pastoral, half-sylvan setting where their problems are solved with mysterious ease. Even the final battle is transacted with the same smoothness. There had been a deal of fighting all through Lodge's source, *The Tale of Gamelyn*.

Rosalynde has been criticized for this lack of action; but Lodge puts it to good use, eschewing external events to concentrate on settings, relationships, and states of mind. The pastoral milieu is as idyllic as the world of the Elizabethan pastoral lyric. Most of the lyrics, of course, are later in date: in fact, *Rosalynde* provides some of the earliest memorable specimens. The prose context bears out their spirit. There is much about pastoral content: 'Envie stirres not us, wee covet not to climbe, our desires mount not above our degrees, nor our thoughts above our fortunes. Care cannot harbour in our cottages, nor doo our homely couches know broken slumbers'.[19] This is accompanied by an endemic state of love. As Montanus informs 'Ganimede' soon after, shepherd life combines opportunity with loyalty, the chief requisites to love (p. 189).

[18] On this point see J. Q. Adams, 'Greene's "Menaphon" and "The Thracian Wonder"', *MP* 3 (1905–6), 317–18; Wolff, p. 442. Cf. Chambers, *Elizabethan Stage*, iv. 49.

[19] Bullough, ii (1958), 189. All refs. to *Rosalynde* to this text.

Or, as 'Aliena' tells Saladyne: 'we heere love one, and live to that one so long as life can maintain love, using few ceremonies because we know fewe subtilties, and little eloquence for that wee lightly accompt of flatterie: only faith and troth, thats shepheards wooing' (p. 234). Such innocent love is inseparable from the simple morality of shepherd life; but it also removes the inhibitions of more mundane codes. Social distinctions disappear, mistress and servant freely exchanging places: 'I will buy thy farme and thy flockes, & thou shalt still (under me) be overseer of them both: onely for pleasuresake I and my Page wil serve you, lead the flocks to the field, and folde them: thus will I live quiet, unknowen, and contented' (p. 189). 'Lodge is unique in that he elevates his major rustic characters to the same level as his noble characters.'[20] Sexual stereotypes are annulled as well, and women court as freely as men. 'Aliena' virtually declares her love to Saladyne at first meeting (p. 223). Rosalynde, of course, can freely court and bait Rosader in her disguise.

This brings us to a matter more important than the idyllic setting: the unusual response of the characters. I may usefully cite W. R. Davis here: in *Rosalynde*, he says, 'a conscious pose may be a way of being "natural" . . . [E]ach character enters Arden under a conscious mask, finds his true self and thus achieves meaningful discipline. Each of them therefore finds his proper nature by acting it out dramatically.'[21] The disguise adds a new dimension to pastoral as release. It permits the characters, Rosalynde above all, a degree of heightened yet unselfconscious sensation and frank utterance. In earlier romances, pastoral disguise was usually a surrender to circumstance. Characterization was rudimentary, and we accepted it all as a romantic action operating at some remove from ourselves. In *Rosalynde*, the characters are unusually immediate, individual personalities. Their disguises lead to active role-playing, a conscious participation in the pastoral ethos after a discriminating assessment of it.

The pastoral conventions cannot seem too naïvely accepted when a disguised princess invokes pastoral simplicity in love to coax a declaration from an aristocratic lover: 'But sir our countrey amours are not like your courtly fancies, nor is our wooing like your suing' (p. 234). The rapport between shepherd and flock becomes the more acceptable by

[20] Burnett, p. xcii. Cf. W. R. Davis, *Idea and Act in Elizabethan Fiction* (Princeton, 1969), 84–5.

[21] W. R. Davis, 'Masking in Arden: The Histrionics of Lodge's *Rosalynde*' *SEL* 5 (1965), 157, 163. Cf. the briefer account in Davis's *Idea and Act*, pp. 81, 83ff.

being part of the true-to-life chaffing of one girl by another: 'I . . . am glad *Rosader* is yours: for now I hope your thoughts will be at quiet; your eye that ever looked at Love, will nowe lende a glaunce on your Lambes: and then they will prove more buxsome and you more blythe, for the eyes of the Master feedes the Cattle' (p. 215).

Rosalynde recognizes the pastoral ideal as an ideal: not an absolute external state but an assumption or convention, an attractive way of adapting to the circumstances of the shepherd's life, using it to serve her more sophisticated needs. She, and in large measure Alinda, thus enter into their roles with creative zest, turning the assumptions of pastoral life and disguise to the purpose of imaginative fulfilment, release of personality, and, through this, success in love.

It is customary to contrast Lodge's 'consistent, moralistic and mannered treatment'[22] of pastoral with Shakespeare's discriminating use of the story in *As You Like It*. It seems to me, however, that Lodge himself is reordering and revaluing the mode. He recognizes the idealizing nature of the convention, letting his unusually vivid characters (especially the heroines) accept it as such and humanize it in their conduct. The narrative thus acquires an immediacy, even at times a tonic irony, all too rare in pastoral romance. At the same time, pastoralism becomes unassailable by its acceptance as a convention of conduct, a state of mind: it will be real as long as it is felt to be real by the characters.

Shakespeare's accredited achievement in *As You Like It* thus appears to have been partly anticipated by Lodge. This may help us the better to assess Shakespeare's real genius. I shall turn very soon to *The Faerie Queene* and the drama, for that is where further development lies. Pastoral romances after *Rosalynde* are largely unmemorable, their thematic potential unrealized.

Two partial exceptions are the pastoral interludes in Greene's *Ciceronis Amor* or *Tullies Loue* (1589) and Lodge's *Euphues' Shadow* (1592). In Greene's romance, the idiot Vatinius or Fabius is transformed by the 'diuine influence'[23] of the sleeping Terentia in a *locus amoenus*. The story comes from *Decameron*, v. i, and reflects Boccaccio's own *Ameto*. But Greene extends Boccaccio's setting into a pastoral 'vale of Loue' with a background story of Coridon and Phillis (pp. 177–84).[24]

[22] Young, p. 39.

[23] Greene's *Life and Complete Works*, ed. A. B. Grosart (London, 1881–3), vii. 207. The episode occurs on pp. 184–9.

[24] Phillis is rich and Coridon is poor: names, setting, and situation are all very similar to those in certain of Breton's lyrics, like 'Fair in a morne . . .' or 'On a hill there grows a

In *Euphues' Shadow*, the heroes Philamis and Philamour feel the pastoral scene to be a peaceful, resuscitating influence: 'Ah place of content, the very Court of my Paradise'.[25] Philamis dwells there as a hermit. There too, he forgives Philamour for having once attempted to kill him, and they return reconciled to the city. In the background is a shepherds' holiday, and the wise shepherd Celio who cites Tasso and Ariosto.

We need not linger over the Host's pastoral tale in Part II of *Greenes Neuer Too Late* or *Francescos Fortunes* (1590). The shepherdess Mirimida dismisses all her suitors, holding 'that there was no Goddesse to *Diana*, no life to libertie, nor no loue to chastitie'.[26] Nothing is made of the idea: Greene's sole motive is to tell a story.

Later romances can be dealt with as briefly. They repeat the two unpromising patterns we saw in continental romance. Sometimes they decline into a mere rag-bag of lyrics linked by a thin narrative. We can see this happening through John Dickenson's *Arisbas* (1594) to his *The Shepheardes Complaint* (1596). Elsewhere, chivalric and courtly interests take over from the pastoral. Francis Sabie's two-part verse-tale, *The Fisher-mans Tale* and *Flora's Fortune* (both 1595), retells *Pandosto* with chivalric additions. By beginning *in medias res*, the pastoral episode comes close to the beginning and is soon forgotten. William Basse's *Three Pastoral Elegies* (1602) tell a connected story of the courtier Anander's frustrated love for the court lady Muridella. The chief shepherd character, Anetor, is merely a confidant. There is nothing in these works to distract us from more important developments elsewhere.

Something, however, needs to be said of a much later work, *The Countesse of Montgomeries Urania* (1621). Its very title evokes the *Arcadia*, no doubt specially because its authoress, Lady Mary Wroth, is 'Neece to the euer famous, and renowned S^r^. Phillips Sidney knight'.[27] *Urania* is not really a pastoral romance, though Urania, a royal waif, first appears as a shepherdess. We see her commiserating with a motherless lamb (p. 16). But within twenty-three pages, she has left on a voyage with Parselius, Prince of Morea, and there follows a bewildering farrago

flower'. The account of their wooing (pp. 183–4) is reminiscent of 'In the merry month of May'. It seems possible that Greene knew Breton's work in manuscript. The poems in BL MS Addl. 34064 appear to have been composed in the mid- and late 1580s: see Black, *Studies in . . . Manuscript Poetic Miscellanies*, i. 269.

[25] Lodge's *Works*, ed. Gosse, ii. 78.

[26] Greene's *Life and Complete Works*, ed. Grosart, viii. 220.

[27] Title-page of the 1st (1621) edn. All refs. to this text.

of adventures, scores of subplots crowding upon each other. The effect is particularly daunting because few episodes are expanded in terms of character, description, or moral observation: the excitement of events seems the chief end, and the more dizzying complications the better.

As may be expected, a few of the episodes and subplots are pastoral—sometimes only nominally so, like the story of Liana (pp. 204ff.). Elsewhere the pastoral setting is properly defined, but the interest is solely in the plot: such is the tale of 'Cross-eyed Cupid'[28] centring round the shepherdesses Celina, Derina, and Lemnia, with Leurenius the Venetian prince (pp. 541 ff.).

In most other cases, however, the pastoral setting is seen as specially significant. The shepherds usually prove to be princes or aristocrats. Exceptions are the young shepherd who enjoys yet laughs at love and at his social betters (pp. 482ff.), and the people in the tale of Allarina (pp. 181 ff.). These are all shepherds, though there is 'difference, and distinction made of their degrees' (p. 184). Lady Mary draws upon both the amorous and the love-free serene aspect of pastoral life, apparently as alternating fictions with no great sense of the power of either theme. After being crossed in love, Allarina vows herself to Diana and liberty (p. 187); but in a later episode (pp. 408ff.), her wedding is celebrated with pastoral pomp, her lover having returned to her.

Where aristocrats retreat to pastoral life, they are obviously more conscious of its implications. Sometimes these are purely negative. Lady Pastora retreats to a rather melancholy island rock to cure her passion for a married man (pp. 355ff.). Sirelius draws his friend Procatus to shepherd life with him, to feed his own love-melancholy (pp. 438ff.). Elsewhere, more fruitfully, the beloved herself dwells in the country, and the withdrawal is in quest of love. Such is the case of the happy 'Forester', actually a courtier in charge of the King's forest lodge, who dwells with his companions in a 'delightfull kind of wildnesse' (p. 297). Such too is Leonius, Prince of Naples, who falls in love with Veralinda, chief shepherdess of a pastoral company, and disguises himself as the nymph Leonia to be near her (pp. 362ff.).

Unsurprisingly, Veralinda proves to be the Princess of Frigia. Even in pastoral life, these noble shepherds scarcely declass themselves. The King's Forester lives in an elaborate lodge; his servants merely imitate the true fellowship of Sherwood or Arden, 'shewing fellowshippe in their

[28] The phrase is Hallett Smith's: *Elizabethan Poetry*, p. 17. Smith is not, of course, talking of the *Urania* in particular.

apparell, but obedience in their fashions' (p. 298). Lady Pastora keeps a herd of goats 'for her pleasure, or rather to passe her time withall' (p. 357). It is a refreshing change to find Procatus complain 'I am tired with rurall mirth, and passionate ditties, I had rather heare a horse neigh, then all the Sheephardesses in this Island sing' (p. 440).

But this is not a meaningful divagation, merely one episodic possibility out of many. We cannot be sure whether these pastoral passages, a mere fraction of the romance, are viewed as serving even a collective narrative function, let alone a meaningful role in the design, if there be a design. While owning allegiance to Sidney's *Arcadia*, *Urania* imitates the eclecticism of, say, the *Amadis* romances, in its use of pastoral interludes. Clearly, Lady Mary has lost whatever sense her uncle affords of a pastoral presence underlying his own courtly romance.

2. The Faerie Queene

The Faerie Queene has an important pastoral interlude in Book VI; but there is much else in the work for students of the pastoral. Settings of nature and rural life occur at many decisive points of the action, with varying degrees of allegoric or symbolic meaning. By a curiously self-deprecatory touch, Spenser declares, almost at the end of his poem as it stands,

> And, were it not ill fitting for this file,
> To sing of hilles and woods, mongst warres and Knights,
> I would abate the sternenesse of my stile,
> Mongst these sterne stounds to mingle soft delights; (VII. vi. 37. 1–4)

Yet he does proceed to tell the tale in question, of Arlo Hill; and indeed *The Faerie Queene* abounds in elements that we may at least call quasi-pastoral, investing with special significance a setting of nature or a life lived in nature, as either enlightening contrast to the main action or else its symbolic concentration. Spenser's concept of chastity, worked out through romantic adventure, has for one of its chief referents the Diana-like sylvan figure of the uncompromisingly chaste Belphoebe. (Diana herself appears in a wood in III. vi. 16ff.). A minor but crucial point of bearing is provided by the country maiden whom alone, of all women, the Squire of Dames found truly chaste (III. vii. 59). Similarly, a defining point of the courtly ideal is the disillusionment (however conventional) of the courtier-turned-hermit who shelters Calepine and Serena (VI. v.

34ff.), or even of the shepherd Meliboe in the Pastorella episode (VI. ix. 24–5).

Less obviously, but much more fundamentally, the whole course of action is picked out by recurrent similes from pastoral life.[29]

> As gentle Shepheard in sweete euen-tide,
> When ruddy *Phoebus* gins to welke in west,
> High on an hill, his flocke to vewen wide,
> Markes which do byte their hasty supper best; (I. i. 23. 1–4)

The romantic landscape also bears the implicit presence of shepherds and other rustics, an untold continuum of humble existence behind the main action:

> The fearefull Shepheard often there aghast
> Vnder them neuer sat, ne wont there sound
> His mery oaten pipe, but shund th'vnlucky ground. (I. ii. 28. 7–9)

Right through *The Faerie Queene*, we sense the operation of this spirit alongside the romantic and epical. As I noted in Chapter 9, readers commonly detect a fundamentally pastoral element in Spenser's sensibility, suffusing and modifying all his subject-matter. It is as though he must validate his chivalric theme by corroborative parallels with a humbler but more stable order, which is also the indispensable food for his own imagination. In the Prologue to Book I, while casting aside his pastoral 'maske', he declares *The Faerie Queene* to be a 'far vnfitter taske' for one used to 'Oaten reeds' (Prol. 1); and the latter seems to remain for him a more significant as well as more congenial strain.

Sometimes a rural sojourn serves simply as an interlude in a courtly tale, a temporary retreat for the unhappy, like Arthur's squire spurned by Belphoebe. But his forest home conveys the very spirit of this sentimental episode:

> a gloomy glade,
> Where hardly eye mote see bright heauens face,
> For mossy trees, which couered all with shade
> And sad melancholy: there he his cabin made. (IV. vii. 38. 6–9)

In the tale of Tristram, hiding in the woods from his vindictive usurping uncle, there is a subtler mingling of courtly and pastoral veins. Calidore gauges correctly that Tristram is of 'Heroicke sead'. Even in his

[29] See e.g. *FQ* I. ii. 16, 28, I. vi. 10, I. viii. 11. II. viii. 40, II. ix. 14, IV. iv. 18, 35, VI. viii. 12, VII. vi. 28. All refs. to Smith and Selincourt's 1-vol. edn.

exile, he has 'trayned bene with many noble feres | In gentle thewes, and such like seemely leres' (VI. ii. 31. 4–5), and we first see him punishing a discourteous knight. In his forester's dress, he reminds Calidore of a disguised god of pastoral myth, like Apollo on 'woodie *Cynthus*' (VI. ii. 25. 5). We may remind ourselves that the Red Cross Knight too was brought up as a ploughman until his higher nature asserted itself (I. x. 66).

The early life of Sir Satyrane shows a more organic infusion of the courtly in the primitive—one may say the genesis of the courtly in the primitive nature of man. Satyrane is a satyr's son by a human mother, 'nourseld vp in life and manners wilde' yet renowned through Faerie for his 'famous worth' (I. vi. 23. 8–9, 29. 9). His early savage training seems directly to foster his chivalric career, and after each adventure he returns as though for sustenance to his 'natiue woods . . . | To see his sire and ofspring auncient' (I. vi. 30. 3–4). Here he finds Una holding the satyrs in thrall by her beauty and virginity. Spenser depicts her influence over the whole range of mythic sylvans, embellished with touches of clear pastoralism:

> about her dauncing round,
> Shouting, and singing all a shepheards ryme,
> And with greene braunches strowing all the ground . . . (I. vi. 13. 6–8)

Their idolatry, not only of Una but of her ass, is of course misguided, but indicates a fundamental rightness of nature. There is also the 'saluage man' who aids Calepine and Serena against Turpin in VI. iv. 2ff. He had never known virtue or compassion, nor learnt the use of arms; but being born of unspecified noble blood (VI. v. 1–2), he comes instinctively to the aid of virtue in distress.

There is a complex nature-and-nurture puzzle here. In each of these examples, Spenser is using quasi-pastoral or mythic primitivism for unexpected confirmation of the elements of 'vertuous and gentle discipline', his theme as declared in his letter to Ralegh. There is a more questionable primitivism as well. At an easy, indeed pleasurable, level we have Hellenore's band of satyrs with their shepherd-like ways:

> The iolly *Satyres* full of fresh delight,
> Came dauncing forth, and with them nimbly led
> Faire *Hellenore*, with girlonds al bespred,
> Whom their May-lady they had newly made: (III. x. 44. 3–6)

They have much in common with Una's satyrs, though their very different queen encourages their primitive impulses in the opposite direction. Beyond this, however, we find downright violent evil in the wild man who carries Amoret away (IV. vii. 5 ff.) and the cannibals who capture Serena (VI. viii. 35 ff.).

These rural and sylvan interludes lay open deep sources of psychic energy, whether for good or evil: pristine impulses which the chivalric action reflects in modified, moderated forms. In the nature-episodes, we glimpse a deeper and more enduring existence than the romantic staple of Spenser's narrative.[30] The main action draws its strength and supplies its defects from the hidden reserves of nature, rural life, and contemplative withdrawal—which open up from time to time into a vision of total nature against which to view the romantic narrative, *sub specie aeternitatis*.

We pass by easy gradation from heightened half-allegorized nature-settings to the descriptive and narrative mythopoeia of the marriage of the Thames and the Medway (IV. xi. 8 ff.) or the legend of Arlo Hill (VII. vi. 36 ff.): Ovidian interludes expressive of the vital presences operating in 'inanimate' nature. These in turn lead on to fully symbolic and allegoric landscapes: Spenser's profoundest embodiments of the primary forces of created nature, cosmic energies mystically guiding the ethical postulates of the chivalric action. Such are the Garden of Adonis (III. vi), the island with Venus's temple (IV. x), the pageant of the seasons and months in the Mutabilitie Cantos (VII. vii). The meretricious artifice of Phaedra's island or the Bower of Bliss can be destroyed by moral or even physical strength; but the truly paradisal, philosophic landscapes are inviolate. They constitute the 'allegorical cores'[31] of certain books of the poem: conceptual centres for the linear romantic narrative, points of rest which the diffuse and changing forces of action are striving to reach.

This function is clearest in the formal, indeed emphatic use of pastoral in the 'core' landscape of the last complete book of *The Faerie Queene*. The Pastorella episode obviously belongs to the romances of royal foundling and disguised courtier. Various elements have been traced to *Daphnis and Chloe*, 'Argentile and Curan', *Pandosto*, and *Amadis*, IX.[32] None of these models (except *Pandosto* in a notable speech by Fawnia)[33]

[30] See Kathleen Williams, *Spenser's Faerie Queene: The World of Glass* (Berkeley, 1966; repr. 1973), 265–6, as well as Donald Cheyney, *Spenser's Image of Nature. Wild Man and Shepherd in 'The Faerie Queene'* (New Haven, 1966), *passim*.

[31] The expression is C. S. Lewis's: *The Allegory of Love* (Oxford, 1936; repr. 1958), 334.

[32] For the last of these, see J. J. O'Connor, *Amadis de Gaule and ... Elizabethan Literature*, pp. 167–8. The other suggestions are widely current.

[33] See p. 308 above.

treats at length, as Spenser does, of the peace and moral virtue of the shepherd's life. For this, he draws upon the Erminia episode in *Jerusalem Delivered* (the direct source of the old shepherd Meliboe's speech on the subject); on such material in *Menaphon*; and more generally on the humble content of moralizing shepherds all through the eclogue tradition, including Spenser's own shepherds in the *Calender* and *Colin Clout*.

The theme of virtuous content is not in itself particularly notable; more so is its juxtaposition with a festive happiness. When Calidore first sees the shepherds, their conventional singing in the shade is presented as their primary activity:

> shepheards singing to their flockes, that fed,
> Layes of sweet loue and youthes delightfull heat . . . (VI. ix. 4. 3–4)

This impression is heightened by the appearance of Pastorella. She must be a familiar sight to the shepherds; yet they fête her continuously with wonder and excitement (VI. ix. 8). It is like a permanent May Game with Pastorella as Queen. Later, the shepherds' joyful pastimes are again presented as their primary concern:

> One day when as the shepheard swaynes together
> Were met, to make their sports and merrie glee,
> As they are wont in faire sunshynie weather,
> The whiles their flockes in shadowes shrouded bee,
> They fell to daunce: (VI. ix. 41. 1–5)

This 'merrie glee' and Meliboe's graver content combine to provide a comprehensive depiction of the pastoral world. The 'cyclic' plot, with pastoral as the source of regeneration, was well advanced by 1596; Spenser gives an unusually clear account of what this regenerative power consists in. The pastoral scene is made 'special' in nature, not merely in function.

Yet there is a basic problem to solve. The Pastorella story affords a perfect romantic 'cycle'. But it is set within a larger framework of chivalric narrative—where, moreover, the chivalric action carries the strongest moral implications. Calidore's pastoral sojourn stalls his quest: the setting proves akin to Armida's bower as well as Erminia's retreat. Can this pastoral be called regenerative at all?

Interpretations of Calidore's truancy usually ring the changes on Greg's simple account: the pastoral is 'not allowed to afford more than a temporary solace to the knight; . . . [he] is driven once again to resume his arduous quest' (Greg, p. 101). A more sophisticated version proposes that the 'solace' and the 'quest' represent competing value-systems, reconciled only in the pervasive cosmic symbol of the Dance of the Graces.[34]

I shall presently come to the Dance. As for the normal pastoral milieu, it appears to me that the conflict between chivalric duty and pastoral repose is that between the actual and an ideal order. The superiority of the pastoral life is strongly asserted:

> For who had tasted once (as oft did he)
> The happy peace, which there doth ouerflow,
> And prou'd the perfect pleasures, which doe grow
> Amongst poore hyndes, in hils, in woods, in dales,
> Would neuer more delight in painted show
> Of such false blisse . . . (VI. x. 3. 3–8)

It is undutiful for Calidore to follow this life, simply because he must restore order in an inferior, fallen world. The innocent retreat becomes a place of distraction and temptation not by its own shortcomings but those of the outer world.[35]

Ultimately, of course, the pastoral world is destroyed. As Tonkin puts it: 'Spenser gives the lie to the pastoral world in the final cruel and unforgettable emblem of the cowardly Coridon driving his sheep out into the desolated countryside where the shepherds once dwelt' (p. 292). To me it seems rather that this pushes the idyllic pastoral world further back in time, further into the realms of the ideal. The mean figure of Coridon in a desolate landscape emblems the degenerate reality of country life in a fallen world haunted by the Blatant Beast. It does not destroy the pastoral ideal; it makes it more clearly an ideal, a state of mind or of a society governed by content and charity, not simply the physical condition of life where men tend sheep. We are again faced with the 'inner', ideal nature of Elizabethan pastoral at its highest, imposing complex values upon a life (the shepherd's) with the symbolic potential to absorb them.

The simplest level at which the ideal operates is the conventionally moral: Meliboe's life. As in the *Calender*, this is used to provide

[34] See Tonkin, *Spenser's Courteous Pastoral*, pp. 122–3.

[35] Cf. Toliver, *Pastoral Forms and Attitudes*, p. 15: 'A poet who would remain true both to his idyllic vision and to the normative world of social strife and moral conflict may endorse feudal society as the best conceivable social arrangement, but he casts a longing eye on the simple life of Arcadia and the higher paradise that Arcadia at times seems to foreshadow.'

perspective to the higher reaches of the ideal, in terms of love and poetry. The richest gifts of the pastoral world—and here we may agree with Tonkin (p. 292)—are provided by Pastorella and the Dance of the Graces.

Pastorella, like Shakespeare's Perdita, presents an obvious paradox: the shepherdess of royal or noble birth. She intensifies and perfects within herself the spirit of the pastoral world; at the same time, she stands outside that world, not only by birth but by an innate superiority of nature. In lesser romances and dramas, there would have been no ambiguity, as they maintain a clear hierarchy of classes: Pastorella's own birth mirrors the feudal class-structure as embodied in romance convention. At another level, however, her perfections are symbolic of a deeper and more general state of being fostered by the pastoral milieu, and partaking almost of a mystic quality. The shepherds know nothing of the Blatant Beast (VI. ix. 6). Theirs is an unfallen world, and dwelling among them in love with Pastorella, Calidore seems to be rendered immaculate, free from sin, brought by Pastorella's love to a state of grace:

> Thus *Calidore* continu'd there long time,
> To winne the loue of the faire *Pastorell*;
> Which hauing got, he vsed without crime
> Or blamefull blot, but menaged so well,
> That he of all the rest, which there did dwell,
> Was fauoured, and to her grace commended. (VI. ix. 46. 1–6)

The word 'grace' recurs constantly in this canto. It is also significant that Calidore is the only one of Spenser's hero-knights who does not need the assistance of Prince Arthur, commonly taken to symbolize the power of grace.[36] The pastoral sojourn and love of Pastorella may be taken to provide a substitute.

Pastorella must prove an aristocrat so that she may be effectively united with the knight Calidore; but her distinctive, almost supra-natural virtue emanates essentially from the pastoral scene. It is this virtue that justifies and validates her noble birth. As in Spenser's allusive pastorals, the pastoral qualities are organic; the courtly affinities are secondary in conception, though central to this particular fiction.

The full force of the supernatural power inherent in the pastoral setting appears, of course, in the Dance of the Graces. I shall make no attempt to elucidate the symbolic and mystic significance of the scene. I have nothing to add to the full account by Tonkin, who gathers together the

[36] See P. C. Bayley, 'Order, Grace and Courtesy in Spenser's World', in J. Lawlor (ed.), *Patterns of Love and Courtesy* (London, 1966), 196ff.

researches of earlier commentators. I shall only consider the consequences for the form of Spenser's work, and for the history of the pastoral, of this heightened scene of Platonic Christian mysticism.

The first point to note, of course, is its very presence: the most remarkable piece of philosophic symbolism of any work I have considered, perhaps of any pastoral work ever composed. The conceptual implications of pastoral could scarcely be carried further. The second important point is that this symbolic scene is located on Mount Acidale, a special 'inner circle' of the pastoral world, where wild beasts and 'ruder clowne' (VI. X. 7. 4) may not tread. This again emphasizes the depth to which Spenser explores his setting, and the way he isolates its philosophic implications.

These implications are brought out through the symbolic complexity of the scene. Some elements are common to the mythic settings of classical pastoral, like the nymphs sitting by the stream (along with the more English fairies: VI. X. 7. 6). But the setting as a whole is obviously a close evocation of the earthly paradise. Venus's damsels (with Venus herself in the background) and the Graces provide a thematic context very different from that of common mythological pastoral.

Another relevant point is the presence of Venus. Acidale is her playground, where she sports with the Graces (VI. X. 9).[37] Considering the symbolism of the Dance, this is no doubt Venus Urania or Coelestis; but, as Tonkin says (p. 218), Venus Vulgaris or Pandemos as well, for erotic love itself is here made perfect and 'innocent' as traditionally in the pastoral. The undefiled stream (VI. X. 7) may be a symbol of this. The figure round whom the Graces, 'Handmaides of *Venus*', dance embodies

> Diuine resemblaunce, beauty soueraine rare,
> Firme Chastity, that spight ne blemish dare; (VI. X. 27. 4–5)

The central theme of Books III and IV is symbolically recapitulated here.

But this maiden is Colin Clout's beloved, 'certes but a countrey lasse' (VI. X. 25. 8). This is where Spenser's pastoral reaches its point of apotheosis. Pastorella, the royal shepherdess, is superseded by a genuine country maiden. At the highest point of his philosophic design, Spenser abandons all extraneous elements and relies upon the unquestionably pastoral.

The other important point is that she is *Colin Clout's* beloved:

[37] On this matter see James Nohrnberg, *The Analogy of The Faerie Queene* (Princeton, 1976), 510–11, 514–15.

> He pypt apace, whilest they him daunst about.
> Pype iolly shepheard, pype thou now apace
> Vnto thy loue, that made thee low to lout . . . (VI. x. 16. 5–7)

In the *Calender*, Spenser blended the pastoral setting with Parnassus ('Iune', ll. 25–9):

> frendly Faeries, met with many Graces,
> And lightfote Nymphes can chace the lingring night,
> With Heydeguyes, and trimly trodden traces,
> Whilst systers nyne, which dwell on *Parnasse* hight,
> Doe make them musick, for their more delight . . .

(Cf. 'Iune', ll. 57–64.) The process reaches its climax here in *The Faerie Queene*. The shepherd-poet's piping controls the entire dance, just as the pastoral maiden stands at its centre. There are two related matters here: the participation of the artist in the order of nature (or even the union of the artistic and natural orders) and the celebration of pastoral as the highest form of art, that which allies itself most deeply to the natural order. Colin, the figure of the poet—further, of the pastoral poet—is the only person who can observe this vision of harmony and even direct it with his pipe. When it disappears, he breaks his instrument in the shepherd's conventional gesture of frustration. It commonly notes frustration in love; here, the passing of the vision of cosmic love and harmony. In Calidore's response, the common idyllic inversion of the social order also finds its acutest expression: the knight asks forgiveness of the shepherd for shattering his vision.

One last and most important point remains to be made. I drew attention earlier to the presence of the pastoral 'cyclic' structure within Spenser's linear romance plot. But the Acidale episode lies beyond all plots and time-sequences, an inviolable world. Eternal spring reigns there. Supernatural figures tread a circular dance (compared to Ariadne's unchanging starry crown) and flee human approach. This removed world has a kind of penumbral influence on the common pastoral setting surrounding it, but it is essentially incompatible with normal life. The gracing spirit that, in conventional pastoral, shows normal experience in a new light is here isolated and presented in its pure state with the most nearly approximate symbols. This remains even when the orthodox bucolic world has been shattered by marauders from without. The pastoral imagination has received its ultimate, unshakable vindication.

3. Britannia's Pastorals

Britannia's Pastorals is generally viewed as an imitation of *The Faerie Queene* in full pastoral dress. Like his master, Browne left his poem incomplete. Book I appeared in 1613. It was reprinted, and Book II appended to it, in 1616. The incomplete Book III remained in manuscript.

Britannia's Pastorals is not a collection of eclogues but a full-scale romance, with a bewildering tangle of plots. Shepherds predominate, especially near the outset, but are by no means the only characters. Browne's debt to Spenser is easy to discern all through the far-flung and complex narrative, set against a background of nature and myth. Specific major borrowings from Spenser have been listed by F. W. Moorman, Herbert Cory, and Joan Grundy.[38]

All this, however, must not obscure the great difference between the two works even in structure, let alone tone and import. Ironically, the difference arises from the desire to imitate Spenser: to put *The Faerie Queene* into pastoral dress is to change its orientation. Not only must the martial and chivalric elements be removed; the treatment of the pastoral itself changes profoundly.

In section 2, I described the pastoral, quasi-pastoral, and primitivist elements in *The Faerie Queene*. They make up a heterogeneous group of settings, motifs, and episodes. But, except perhaps for the mythological tales, they all have one point in common. Spenser is in every case departing from his normal chivalric narrative for a special purpose: either a significant contrast, or a summing-up in concentrated symbolic form. At their most operative, such passages provide centres around which the linear chivalric narrative arranges itself.

Obviously, these episodes can serve important functions precisely because they are *not* the common element of the narrative. Their very occurrence serves as a signpost: they indicate a heightened level of significance, even a special controlling power. In the last Book, they reach their climax in an openly pastoral sequence, one of the highest points ever reached in philosophic pastoral.

By making pastoral the basic medium of his narrative, Browne largely forgoes its more particular role in pointing special significations. The

[38] F. W. Moorman, *William Browne. His Britannia's Pastorals* (Strasbourg, 1897), 19–38; H. E. Cory, 'Browne's *Britannia's Pastorals* and Spenser's *Faerie Queene*', *University of California Chronicle*, 13 (1911), 189–200; Grundy, *The Spenserian Poets*, pp. 146–7.

pastoral world now takes on the uncertain, transient, often threatened and violent quality of general romance narrative. While Doridon woos Marina like a typical shepherd-lover, a lustful 'cruel swain' attacks them, leaves him bleeding, and carries her away to a boat.[39] After riding out a fearsome storm, she is abandoned on the island of Mona and imprisoned in Famine's den (II. i. 46ff.). Fida, sheltering in an arbour with her pet hind, is attacked by Riot and the hind killed (I. iv. 39ff.).[40] Remond and Doridon find its bloody traces, fear for Fida's safety, and set out on her quest. They come upon a shepherd weeping over a wounded tree (perhaps his beloved metamorphosed?) and threatened by a wild man (II. ii. 581ff.).

Particularly significant is the ending to the story of Philocel and Caelia, with the lovers wishing to die for each other (II. v. 651ff.). Grundy cites many analogues;[41] but in those, the lovers are vindicated where they were condemned—which, except in *Jerusalem Delivered* and *Menaphon*, is a pastoral scene. Only Browne leads us out of the pastoral to seek resolution elsewhere. The lovers *are* condemned and thrown off a cliff. Luckily, Thetis rescues them below, just as soon after she rescues Marina from the Cave of Famine. Browne's pastoral world cannot solve its own problems, let alone those of the outer world.

Given Browne's ambitious plan, his concept of the pastoral convention is unambitious and largely derivative. The pronouncedly pastoral elements in his work fall into two classes. One is the Italianate, derived from Sannazaro and Italian pastoral drama. About this I have nothing to add to Grundy's study.[42] The other strain comes from the idyllic shepherd life of the Elizabethan pastoral lyric. This appears at its

[39] *Britannia's Pastorals*, I. ii. 405–648. All refs. to Goodwin's edn. of Browne's *Poems*, by book, song, and line no. I have used this edn., with numbered lines and the text of Book III, for convenience of reference, despite its shortcomings. The most obvious of these is the fact that Goodwin was unaware of the existence of two separate edns. of Book I, from 1613 and 1616. (See G. Tillotson, 'Towards a Text of Browne's Britannia's Pastorals', *The Library*, 4th ser. 11 (1931), 193–202, incorporating the original findings of E. M. Cox and Hugh Candy. See also the more detailed account in Tillotson's B.Litt. thesis 'William Browne of Tavistock: His Life and Pastorals' (Oxford, 1930). Goodwin's text follows 1616. I have compared all my citations from Book I with the 1613 text and noted the few variants that occur in the quoted passages.

[40] Although Fida is specifically said to remain silent during this attack (I. iv. 117–18), the shepherds' festivities are broken just at this point by a distressed maiden's screams. This may simply be Browne's carelessness, but it creates the impression of other dangers in this ominous wood that we know nothing of. (For the disturbed festival, see the end of I. iii: 1613 edn., p. 62. Goodwin omits this passage, apparently through inadvertence.)

[41] Joan Grundy, 'William Browne and the Italian Pastoral', *RES* NS 4 (1953), 313.

[42] Ibid., *passim*.

gayest in Doridon's wooing of Marina at first sight (I. ii. 489ff.), but also in the wooing-song of Remond and Fida (I. iii. 241–82), Aletheia's meeting with Riot-transformed-to-Amintas (I. v. 863ff.), and above all in the festivals and singing-contests.

But Browne's shepherds and shepherdesses are curiously passive. They seldom do anything to influence their states, except offering themselves for martyrdom like Philocel and Caelia. It may be a telling sign that Browne abandons the Remond–Doridon plot after bringing a huntress and a wild man on the scene. Some action seems imperative after this, and action would have sorted very ill with the general bent of the work. As a rule, Browne's shepherds are merely acted upon: if lucky, by benevolent forces like Thetis or the spring-god who rescues Marina, but quite as often by evil ones like the 'cruel swain', Riot or Limos.

This is an inevitable result of the attempt to pastoralize the entire romance structure. Browne introduces in full strength the hostile forces which, in the standard romance plot, oppose the central characters. At the same time, he dispenses with the martial chivalry which defeats these forces in the standard romance. Instead, his central 'good' characters are peaceful shepherds. Yet he eschews the 'cyclic' structure which had allowed the pastoral world to control the real or external one. His idealization of shepherd life does not go beyond the standard praise of humble content. When this is placed next to the more powerful and active agents that he introduces, it is bound to appear as a subsidiary, 'suffering' element.

As in Sidney's *Arcadia*, so here in a different way, the pastoral is destroyed by its very expansion. It collapses under the alien burden it must carry. These extraneous elements fall into two classes: one taking us back to old didactic functions of the pastoral, the other introducing completely new concerns. We must obviously consider both for a full understanding of the *Pastorals*. It is simpler to commence with the first.

A good part of this consists of moralizing and satire. The speeches of the characters, especially in Book I, are full of moral tags and *sententiae*. These can extend to full-scale discourses, sometimes on accustomed themes of the didactic eclogue. Remond satirizes women (I. i. 569ff.), and Doridon warns Marina against an ill-matched marriage, leading to a debate on the advisability of love (I. ii. 521ff.). Remond comforts the mysterious weeping shepherd with a long moral speech, including a quite irrelevant censure of avarice (II. ii. 687ff.). In the manuscript Book III,

'Celadyne'[43] rails against 'vain dreams' (III. i. 159ff.), and the unnamed mournful swain laments the injustice of the world (III. i. 580ff.).

All these may be explained in terms of didactic theories of pastoral, with the moralizing 'wise shepherd' or the lamenting lover-swain dwindling (as so often) into a mere mouthpiece for ideas. Even this link with pastoral disappears in the song of the well-god and river-nymph on the life of man (I. ii. 185ff.), or the direct allegory of Browne's most substantial moral sequence, Aletheia's wanderings and Riot's repentance, as well as in the less prominent figure of Athliot (wretchedness) in II. v. Aletheia's encounter with a miller, a tailor, and a weaver (I. iv. 515ff.) introduces a satiric realism not impossibly distant from the pastoral; but the general bent of the allegory has nothing pastoral about it.

In other moral and satiric digressions, the poet himself speaks. Some of these indeed use the ideal shepherd's life as a 'positive' contrast to the corrupt times.[44] A vehement passage of satire and lament for the times makes him determine again to sing one day of his native country, of

> the crystal wells,
> The fertile meadows and their pleasing smells,
> The woods delightful and the scatter'd groves,
> Where many nymphs walk with their chaster loves . . . (II. iv. 21–4)

Most notable is the passage in II. iii. 217ff. explicitly equating the Golden Age with shepherd life. This is one of the few instances where the satire, though extensive, is matched in length by the praise of pastoral innocence and description of nature. More usually we would have only a brief reference to this after a long diatribe on the world's evils:

> And free there's none from all this worldly strife,
> Except the shepherd's heaven-bless'd happy life. (II. i. 883–4)

This couplet concludes one of Browne's most wide-ranging passages of satire:

> The devilish politician all convinces,
> In murd'ring statesmen and in pois'ning princes;
> The prelate in pluralities asleep,
> Whilst that the wolf lies preying on his sheep . . . (II. i. 867–70)

(We may note in passing the purely local and incidental use of the pastoral metaphor.) Elsewhere, Browne satirizes the 'British swains' who

[43] So spelt here, though 'Celandine' in Book I.
[44] e.g. I. iii. 295ff., II. iv. 326ff.

barter their wool for such 'base trumperies' as 'pois'nous weeds, roots, gums and seeds unknown' (II. iv. 939ff.). Browne may almost be said to embed in the *Pastorals* a number of detachable satires. He recognizes this more than once, coming back with a start from 'satyr's vein' to shepherd's.[45] He also vows to follow *Britannia's Pastorals* with 'rough hewn satires' (II. i. 1043), or calls on other poets to write such works (II. i. 1028).

Even in the *Pastorals*, much of the satire bears no reference to pastoral matters. In II. iv. 51ff., the contrast is with the old Devonshire heroes. Book III has a fantasy of 'ballad-makers, rhymers, drinkers' inhabiting the Den of Oblivion (III. i. 311ff.), followed by Gulliverian satire of the Fairy court. In the last, the witty fancy of Mercutio's Queen Mab speech or Drayton's *Nymphidia* is adapted to the purpose of topical court satire.[46] The Den of Oblivion satirizes contemporary poets. Politics and poetry, indeed, are Browne's two major fields of satire and allusion.

The first important piece of political satire is Aletheia's account of the 'valley of grieving wights' (I. iv. 679ff.). Ralegh and Essex sit lamenting their estrangement from Elizabeth; an unidentified 'shepherdess'[47] makes up the trio. In the centre of the valley sits 'Idya', England herself, singing a dirge for Henry, Prince of Wales.

There is nothing pastoral about the dirge. It is a revised version of one already published by Browne in 1613.[48] But the scene as a whole, though based on the larger allegorical models of *The Faerie Queene*, has as much pastoral and mythological admixture as many allegorical eclogues. The later political passages, however, are purely non-bucolic digressions introduced by the poet, generally speaking in his own person. In the Aletheia story itself, a eulogy of Elizabeth changes imperceptibly from Aletheia's utterance to the poet's own:

> Ye suckling babes, for ever bless that name
> Releas'd your burning in your mothers' flame!
> Thrice-blessed maiden, by whose hand was given
> Free liberty to taste the food of Heaven. (I. v. 383–6)

[45] e.g. II. i. 885, II. iv. 961 (where the speaker is a shepherd in the story, not the poet).

[46] See Joan Mary Ozark, 'Faery Court Poetry of the Early Seventeenth Century' (D.Phil. Princeton, 1973), ch. i.

[47] David Norbrook suggests she may be Arabella Stuart; see his 'Panegyric of the Monarch and Its Social Context under Elizabeth I and James I' (D.Phil. Oxford, 1978), 268.

[48] With another elegy by Christopher Brooke, as *Two Elegies, Consecrated to the Never-dying Memorie of . . . Henry Prince of Wales* (London, 1613).

As customarily in Browne and the other Spenserians, Elizabeth's reign is being opposed to James's—here in the language of militant Protestantism and anti-Spanish politics.[49] The marauding heroes of such politics are praised again and again: in the Valley of Grief, and at II. iii. 609, II. iv. 211, and III. i. 879. This pastoral poem includes some fairly plain warmongering.

Browne's shepherd-poets are also formed in the light of contemporary allusion, and formed ambivalently, as in *The Shepheards Pipe*. On the one hand, we have a community of singing shepherds entertaining Thetis. On the other hand, this community is explicitly identified with Browne's own. The account opens with a list of continental poets, both classical and Renaissance (II. i. 932ff.), as a frame of reference for the 'English shepherds' that follow. The first poet to sing is Colin Clout. His panegyric is followed by an enigmatic passage on how Avarice thwarted the erection of a memorial to Spenser, concluding in a satiric attack on that vice, 'That gulf-devouring offspring of a devil' (II. i. 1032). This may be an untraced allusion or a general reference to Spenser's detractors.[50] In either case, it brings us back from the idyllic world of the poet-shepherd to the real world of envy, death, and calumny. The 'swain of name | Less than of worth' (II. ii. 72) also lacks his deserts. Astrophel, 'Th'admired mirror, glory of our Isle' (II. ii. 249), has fallen prey to death. The poets after him—Chapman, Drayton, Jonson, Daniel, Brooke, Davies, Wither—are highly praised, but at the end comes a significant malediction:

> Then base contempt (unworthy our report)
> Fly from the Muses and their fair resort,
> And exercise thy spleen on men like thee. (II. ii. 329–31)

Again we are brought back from the happy shepherds singing for Thetis to the real world of Browne and his fellow-poets. As in *The Shepheards Pipe*, they form an authentic, contemporary community, facing opposition and neglect and involving themselves in the problems of the times.

This is best seen from Browne's own presence in his work. He occurs in a number of personae, most if not all of them noted by Grundy (pp. 75–

[49] On this subject see Joshua McClennen, 'William Browne as a Satirist', *Papers of the Michigan Academy*, 33 (1949), 358; Joan O. Holmer, 'Internal Evidence for Dating William Browne's *Britannia's Pastorals* Book III', *Papers of the Bibliographical Society of America*, 70 (1976), 347–64; David Norbrook, *Poetry and Politics in the English Renaissance*, pp. 207–9.

[50] It may be a hit at Robert Cecil. See Norbrook, *Poetry and Politics*, p. 199, though Norbrook makes no mention of this passage.

6). An interesting though subsidiary one is the sad lover in the Den of Oblivion in Book III. Though I have not seen it suggested, this appears to be the unnamed shepherd who falls in love with Marina in I. i. (The other character in Book III, 'Celadyne', is clearly Celandine from I. i.) Yet he also seems an *alter ego* of the poet. Ramsham Wood is close to Tavistock.[51] We are also told that the swain knew Celadyne 'On Isis' banks, | And melancholy Cherwell' (III. i. 698–9).[52] This gratuitous reference suggests an unsuspected personal allegory in the narrative itself.

We can scarcely read the allusion back into I. i, unless it is of impenetrable coterie interest. But how far can we carry it in Book III either? The swain is grieving for a scorned love in Devon; earlier in the same song, Browne says *in propria persona* that he is mourning a dead love in France (III. i. 107–34). There is also the mystery of the 'Willy' whose verses on the dead Alexis are carved on a rock in Anglesey (II. i. 238–318). This is Browne mourning the death of William Ferrar, of course. But within the narrative, can we identify this 'Willy' with the one who dwells by the Tavy and sings the Tale of Walla? The problem does not seem to bother Browne: he sets up both figures as necessary to project his own identity. In III. ii. 105 he brings in 'a shepherd that was born by-west' who also seems to be himself.

Browne writes more or less 'autobiographically' in the digressions, and at the same time injects just as much autobiography as he chooses into characters who undergo emotions and experiences akin to his own. He is both controller and participant. He sees himself in terms of a transforming pastoral fiction, but also stands outside it and, in fact, guides the course of that fiction by the wider experience reflected in the digressions.

Hence he can speak in the same line of 'I' and 'Willy' as two separate persons (II. iii. 1285; cf. III. i. 973–84). The details of Willy's life correspond to Browne's (see II. iii. 748 ff.). But Willy is the idealized shepherd-poet of a distanced, mythologized, pastoral world, wooed by the nymphs of the Tavy and singing of Walla's metamorphosis. Browne in his own person expresses the same local patriotism with immediate involvement and at times a certain stridency:

[51] III. i. 281: see John Shelly's note in W. C. Hazlitt's edn. of Browne's *Works* (London, 1868), ii. 374.

[52] According to Wood (*Athenae Oxonienses*, ed. P. Bliss (London, 1815), ii. 364–6), Browne was at Oxford shortly after James's accession and again in 1624 as tutor to Robert Dormer.

And, Tavy, in my rhymes
Challenge a due; let it thy glory be,
That famous Drake and I were born by thee! (III. i. 1000–2)

Here Browne speaks like the morally engaged shepherd-poet of Wither's work. Like him, Browne says,

No thirst of glory tempts me: for my strains
Befit poor shepherds on the lowly plains;
The hope of riches cannot draw from me
One line that tends to servile flattery . . . (II. iv. 147–50)

His retirement involves a critical rejection of the community, the stance of satirist-shepherd. The pastoral ideal has grown active and even belligerent.

'Willy' and the narrator 'I' project the two extremes of Browne's poetic sensibility. His total concept of the pastoral, and of *Britannia's Pastorals*, emerges from a combination of the two: a static, remote existence passing into myth, and an involvement with the fluid, disturbed reality of contemporary life. The varying but ubiquitous presence of the poet's personality underpins the whole, provides the axis on which the poem turns.

In the last analysis, the poet's various roles prove to be allied. Even where Browne speaks *in propria persona*, he presents himself as a shepherd, and his song as a tale told to other shepherds in a vividly realized rustic setting.

But, shepherds, I have wrong'd you; 'tis now late,
For see our maid stands hollowing on yond gate. (II. ii. 849–50)

He feeds his flock at the 'cistern' (I. v. 909), extricates his lambs from the bushes (II. i. 1047), and hurries home to supper in the evening (II. ii. 849).[53] Structurally, the closest parallel is with Wither's *Fair Virtue*. There too, an intermittent pastoral framework encloses matter of a simultaneously moral and romantic nature, however different in actual content. Philarete too breaks off his tale to attend to his sheep, or go home in the evening.[54] Again, *Fair Virtue* has many embedded poems, many moral digressions, and at least one long simile (of a man picking flowers, ll. 3847ff.) very reminiscent of Browne's. The Hampshire scene

[53] See also I. i. 1ff., II. iii. 1285ff., II. iv. 47, 133ff., III. i. 975ff. For II. i. 1047, cf. Drayton, *The Shepheards Garland*, Eclogue IV. 154–5. See also the end of *Britannia's Pastorals*, I. iii (1613 edn., p. 62).

[54] See ll. 691–7, 2253ff., 3309ff., 4111ff. (as in Wither's *Poetry*, ed. Sidgwick).

of the opening is depicted with much the same combination of local detail and mythological veneer as Browne's Devonshire.

Grundy (p. 62) thinks that Browne, when writing Book I of the *Pastorals*, 'did not yet know either Wither or his poetry'. It is of course possible that the reference to the *Pastorals* in *Fair Virtue* (l. 1936) is a later insertion to support the (true or feigned) early date of the latter poem. But in the absence of evidence to the contrary, it seems best to take this mention at face value, and assume that Browne and Wither did know each other *c.*1612. In that case, we may suppose that the two young poets wrote their respective works in response to a common formal ideal, even a mutually discussed programme of song, romance, and moral matter in a pastoral framework. The results, of course, are very different. Wither's pastoral framework, in *Fair Virtue* at least, inclines more towards the idyllic, while the subject of Philarete's song is more directly allegorical than the *Pastorals*. (We must remember, though, that the Aletheia story takes up a large proportion of Book I.) Browne's pastoral framework is much closer to the world of *The Shepheards Pipe*, a community of working rustics idealized slightly or not at all.

In these passages, we have a version of pastoral no less notable than that in Marina's loves or the song-festival for Thetis. 'In *Britannia's Pastorals*,' writes Grundy, 'mixed up with all the unreal shepherds and their adventures, is a rendering of rural life that is astonishing in its realism and its particularity' (p. 150). Browne introduces himself (as distinct from 'Willy') into Thetis's festival too, as the friend of Brooke, Davies, and Wither (II. ii. 303 ff.). This allusive and mythic context seems one exalted extreme of a friendship that is essentially part of the easy rural life of the 'framework': 'For yonder's Roget [i.e. Wither] coming o'er the stile' (II. iii. 1286).

Because of its versatility, this concept of 'the poet as shepherd' acquires an unusual importance in relating the disparate parts of the poem. It promises a clue to some broader principle of unity. Judged in terms of earlier pastoral, Browne's poem is a confusing mixture. An excessively literal-minded poet seems to be attempting a pastoral romance by inserting passages of pastoral into expanses of romance. Moreover, with his satire and moral allegory, he seems to take us back to the didactic and allegorical pastoral, based upon the humanist eclogue, that we found to influence Sidney's *Arcadia*. These didactic and allusive passages are mostly digressions from the narrative. It is as though, in the same literal-minded way, he thinks he can create 'allegorical' pastoral by varying the pastoral passages with direct allusion, moralizing, and satire.

Some of this criticism must be granted in absolute terms. Browne's warmest admirer cannot praise his formal control. Unlike *The Faerie Queene*, with its strong conceptual framework, *Britannia's Pastorals* adopts and abandons themes in a local and temporary fashion. Yet, the last paragraph suggested a grossly distorted and unfair view of Browne's work, owing to the inadequacy of the terms of reference.

In fact, the poem seems to be governed by a new set of concerns, basically incompatible with conventional pastoral and the romance form. These new concerns disturb without adequately reordering the elements of convention. None the less, we can make sense of the *Pastorals* only in their terms.

As the first of these new formal principles, we may select the peculiarly proleptic quality of *Britannia's Pastorals*. It moves simultaneously in two time-worlds, roughly coinciding with the narrative and the digressions, but actually balanced and adjusted much more subtly against each other. It is hard to determine when the action takes place. At several points, shepherd life is explicitly compared to the Golden Age; but the action is often as explicitly associated with the fallen world, sometimes directly with the course of history, as in the pictures in the Cave of Famine (II. i. 671 ff.). The mythic element also indicates a distant age; yet the poets Thetis meets are Browne and his contemporaries, and Idya sits grieving for Prince Henry near Ralegh and Essex.

Ultimately, there seem to be at least three time-planes in the *Pastorals*: the unquestionable present, where Browne lives and writes; the distanced pastoral and mythical world that he writes about; and the even more remote mythic past of certain inset tales told in the past tense: the rise of the two rivers in I. ii. 649 ff., the metamorphosis of Walla (II. iii. 763 ff.), the story of Pan's tree (II. iv. 405 ff.). But the three worlds fuse, merge, and overlap, take on new relations, alter relative distances, as though seen through a continually refocused set of lenses. An element allotted to one plane suddenly moves to another or curiously straddles the two.

As we saw, Browne's poetic personae provide one important proleptic instrument, alternating between the half-mythic Willy and the contemporary shepherd-narrator. Even more important is that celebrated feature of the *Pastorals*, the digressive 'epic similes'.

While a few similes are explanatory or illustrative in nature, most of them operate on a much more immediate, realistic plane than the narrative they purport to illumine. Browne is elucidating the world of romance by reference to one more familiar to him and to ourselves.

Further, the similes are sometimes so long, and so tenuously connected with their subject, that they acquire an independent importance.

A few similes have a realistic or satiric content. Most of them, however, describe country life, often in close and vivid detail, always with an immediacy of apprehension. Some of them extend over an entire landscape, like the memorable one of a 'landskip'-painting itself (I. ii. 819ff.).[55] Others include the cycle of the seasons in I. iv. 775, the storms and floods in I. v. 307, the spring scenery of II. v. 433, and the autumnal of II. iv. 481 (though in the last two cases, the main point of the simile lies elsewhere).

More often, though, Browne presents smaller, sharply realized scenes. Two features may strike us here. The first is the way Browne endows creatures of nature with individual lives and personalities: fledgling wrens learning to fly (I. iv. 13), a squirrel fleeing from a pack of boys (I. v. 697) or sparrows from a brood of eaglets (II. iv. 59), a martin building her nest (II. v. 1), a chorus of singing birds with subtly distinguished motives:

> Here have I heard a sweet bird never lin
> To chide the river for his clam'rous din;
> There seem'd another in his song to tell,
> That what the fair stream did he liked well;
> And going further heard another too,
> All varying still in what the others do; (II. iii. 713–18)

Even trees and stones are credited with action and volition: rocks that 'Grumbling . . . fall o'er each other's back' (I. v. 317), 'new-cloth'd trees' that 'stand wistly list'ning' to bird-song (II. v. 434–5; cf. I. iv. 776), 'A widow vine stand in a naked field' (II. v. 320), and 'the plough'd-lands lab'ring with a crop of corn' (I. iv. 310). These self-contained nature-scenes have little human participation. The creatures of nature play leading roles instead. But, unlike in *Poly-Olbion*, there is very little use of mythopoeia, whether standard legend or the author's nonce-creations. In I. v. 32, the swan sings as he dies in legendary manner; a hundred lines later, a real dying swan on the Tamar performs no such feat. Instead of weaving extraneous stories around the creatures of nature, Browne credits them with more literal motives and actions.

Images of rustic human life are still more numerous, and coincide at times with the nature-descriptions. It is hard to tell whether certain hunting-scenes focus upon the hunter or his prey.[56] In the fruit-picking

[55] There may be elements of conventional pastoral *within* these realistic images: see I. ii. 825, II. iii. 160.

[56] e.g. I. ii. 639, I. v. 697.

scene (II. iv. 133ff.), the woodland setting and description of fruits engage us as much as the human participants. Setting and figures merge in the pictures of village children at play:

> As children on a play-day leave the schools,
> And gladly run unto the swimming pools;
> Or in the thickets, all with nettles stung,
> Rush to despoil some sweet thrush of her young;
> Or with their hats (for fish) lade in a brook . . .[57]

Other images focus entirely on humans, generally workmen: miller (II. i. 418, II. ii. 164), irrigator (II. ii. 171, II. v. 77), forester (III. ii. 273), or 'merry milkmaid' (II. v. 265). Particularly memorable are the smiths of I. v. 501ff., the sawyers of III. i. 915ff., or the ballad-mongers at a fair:

> (with as harsh a noise
> As ever cart-wheel made) squeaks the sad choice
> Of Tom the Miller with a golden thumb,
> Who, cross'd in love, ran mad and deaf and dumb . . . (II. i. 389–92)

There are festive images too: a rustic wedding (I. ii. 671), a wrestling-match (I. v. 33), and a May Game with the Lady of the May presenting gifts (II. iv. 269). Such descriptions merge with the idyllic scenes in the main narrative: the May Games during which Caelia elopes with Philocel (II. v. 131ff.), the shepherds' meets in I. iii and II. ii:

> Some from the company removed are
> To meditate the songs they meant to play,
> Or make a new round for next holiday.
> Some tales of love their love-sick fellows told:
> Others were seeking stakes to pitch their fold.
> This, all alone was mending of his pipe:
> That, for his lass sought fruits most sweet, most ripe. (II. ii. 26–32)

This passes well into the realm of convention. The following lines are directly influenced by Sidney's description of Arcadia.[58] But the immediately preceding passage combines striking natural detail—'The milk-white gossamers not upwards snow'd' (II. ii. 3)—with the vivid impression of a village at dawn.

These images and descriptions lead on in turn to the rustic framework of the shepherd-narrator's world. In the same way, the similes drawn

[57] I. v. 63ff.; cf. I. v. 3ff., 697ff., II. iv. 481ff.

[58] As first noted by D. L. Richardson in *Literary Leaves* (London, 1840), ii. 181.

from nature connect with similar descriptions set in the narrative. The birds who sing and flutter their way through the similes are close kin to the robin and oyster-catcher that feed Marina in her prison. And there are a memorable set of birds in I. iii. 197–202:

> The mounting lark (day's herald) got on wing,
> Bidding each bird choose out his bough and sing.
> The lofty treble sung the little wren;
> Robin the mean, that best of all loves men;
> The nightingale the tenor, and the thrush
> The counter-tenor sweetly in a bush.

A cliff near the Cave of Famine is pictured with nesting seafowl (II. i. 619ff.). These are vivid, multi-noted rustic scenes, particularly four memorable pictures of early dawn, morning, evening, and night.[59] The well-god's curse in I. i. 718ff., when he fears his stream has been polluted, weaves in properly pastoral matters with the description of the stream.

More important, the god's subsequent love-song carries a reference to the Tavy, locating the stream in Browne's home territory and suggesting that it may be based on an actual stream he knew. There are many explicit accounts of Devon scenes: Inescombe (II. iii. 1103ff.), local rivers (II. v. 273ff.), above all, a spirited description of the Tavy (I. ii. 715ff.). The narrative is clearly set in the West Country. As Browne says at the outset, his Muse will 'homely pipen of her native home' (I. i. 14).[60]

This prompts an interesting question. The *Pastorals* have other, equally vivid descriptions: the cave where Marina's lover mourns (I. i. 445ff.), the 'Scornful Hill' (I. iii. 89ff), the seacoast in II. i. 619ff., the gloomy valley where the bereaved Pan retires (II. iv. 689ff.), the creek from where Philocel and Caelia elope (II. v. 153ff.). Are these too based on actual scenes known to Browne? The possibility is increased by the fact that an analogous description can be confidently identified. In I. ii. 649ff., the two varying rivers running from the same source are surely the Tamar and the Torridge.[61]

[59] See II. ii. 1ff., I. iv. 483ff., I. v. 413ff., and II. iv. 575ff. respectively.

[60] The 1613 text reads 'onely' instead of 'homely' (p. 2).

[61] Mr C. E. Hicks, Hon. Sec. of the Devonshire Assoc., has confirmed this identification in a letter. See R. Polwhele, *History of Devonshire* (Exeter, 1797), i. 30; J. L. W. Page, *The Rivers of Devon* (London, 1893), 272–3. Polwhele quotes a set of verses first printed 'Ex Dono Amici' in T. Risdon's *Chorographical Description . . . of Devon*, giving a mythic picture of the rivers analogous to Browne's. Risdon was Browne's contemporary; one wonders whether Browne could have been the 'amicus'. Page also describes a similar legend.

The matter is of more than pedantic local-naturalist's interest. It shows how Browne bases his romantic narrative upon the authentic image of his native countryside. This may even be the case where the landscape aspires to symbol or moral allegory. It is worth noting that Mrs Bray cites the allegorical setting of the 'Valley of Grief' as a 'scene in our neighbourhood'.[62] Moorman considers that the abbey from which Aletheia is shut out resembles Tavistock Abbey.[63] Doridon talks of 'the griping carl | That spoils our plains in digging them for marl' (II. ii. 444). According to Goodwin, this was a common Devonshire pursuit, and Doridon's 'our' would seem to make him a native of that county.[64]

Local topography apart, romantic or allegoric scenes often seem to draw out Browne's basic awareness of real nature and rustic life. He describes the grove through which the river-nymph conducts Marina as an earthly paradise, 'With sweeter scents than in Arabia found'—but compares this to the smell

> Within a field which long unploughed lies,
> Somewhat before the setting of the sun; (I. ii. 334–5)

The description of bird-song in I. iii. 197ff. is combined with the reflection

> Had Nature unto man such simpl'ess given,
> He would, like birds, be far more near to heaven. (I. iii. 219–20)

In such passages, Browne discovers paradise in nature as he knows it. He can also discover the fallen world in rustic life. The hunting-images reflect the disturbed, threatened universe of the romantic narrative. Some of the best accounts of village life occur in Aletheia's allegorical story, so that its moral action seems to crystallize the actual quality of village life as Browne knew it.

In every way, the passages on nature and rustic life prove more basic and substantial than those of conventional pastoralism. The former seems the point of entry into Browne's poetic world, the latter a secondary growth. In the latter he is conventional, borrowing his mode, setting, and even specific episodes from earlier poets, while missing the significance they draw from them. In the former he uncovers a new source of poetry in the vivid, personally experienced reality of country life.

[62] A. E. Bray, *The Borders of the Tamar and the Tavy* (New edn. London, 1879), ii. 204.
[63] Moorman, p. 44.
[64] Goodwin, ii. 333, quoting Shelly's note in Hazlitt's edn.

Behind the romance and allegory of Browne's narrative, there is a new poetic world struggling to break out. It does not achieve integrated form, but appears through a fragmented series of digressions, images, and (at their most organic) descriptions of settings for the action. This is because Browne cannot break loose from formal pastoral. Among the genres and conventions open to him, it is the only one that, however superficially and misleadingly, approaches his interest in nature and rustic life. He is led to adopt it, though it is basically incompatible with his deeper interests. The integrity of the mode suffers as a result.

Browne may be said to mark the first step in the decline of the pastoral into a vaguer and less demanding convention where a 'real', recognizable countryside, often the poet's native district, is presented with classical names and other conventional trappings. I have noted signs of the process in shorter Jacobean and Caroline poems. At its best, this vein constitutes little more than a pleasant periphrasis; at its worst, an objectionable gilding of the harsh realities of country life. This is the vein practised by Pope and condemned by Crabbe.

Dr Johnson could not admit an independent world of the pastoral imagination: 'We knew that they never drove a field, and that they had no flocks to batten; and though it be allowed that the representation may be allegorical, the true meaning is so uncertain and remote that it is never sought because it cannot be known when it is found.'[65] He praises *Windsor Forest* primarily as a descriptive poem, derived from Denham's *Cooper's Hill* and (perhaps justly, in this case) finds the mythological admixture to be the parts that 'deserve least praise'.[66] He also praises Gay's *The Shepherd's Week* for its 'just representations of rural manners and occupations'.[67] Wordsworth cites this praise with approval,[68] and Hazlitt finds *The Compleat Angler* the finest work of English pastoralism.[69] It is not surprising that Hazlitt should also praise Browne for his 'natural tenderness and sweetness', his 'Poetical beauties . . . scattered, not sparingly, over the green lap of nature': the hunted squirrel, the flowers, the description of the night.[70] Keats, it has been shown, was

[65] 'Life of Milton', *Lives of the English Poets*, ed. G. Birkbeck Hill (1905; repr. Hildesheim, 1968), i. 164.

[66] 'Life of Pope', ibid. iii. 225.

[67] 'Life of Gay', ibid. ii. 269.

[68] 'Essay, Supplementary to the Preface', in Wordsworth's *Prose Works*, ed. W. J. B. Owen and J. W. Smyser (Oxford, 1974), iii. 72, ll. 390–6.

[69] Hazlitt, *Complete Works*, ed. P. P. Howe (London, 1930), iv. 56, v. 98.

[70] Ibid. vi. 311, 315 (*Lectures on the . . . Age of Elizabeth*).

strongly affected by Browne,[71] and Coleridge thought it worth his while to claim a tenuous kinship.[72]

For all their differences over the treatment of nature, Augustan and Romantic agree in the primacy of the real landscape in pastoral. In this they differ from the Elizabethan. Browne stands at the parting of the ways. His work provides a fascinating mixture of elements illustrating the transition from the old pastoral to the new.

[71] See Joan Grundy, 'Keats and William Browne', *RES* NS 6 (1955), 44–52.

[72] See Coleridge's *Notebooks*, ed. K. Coburn, iii (London, 1973), item 3652, text and notes.

17

Pageants and Entertainments

IN THIS chapter, I shall give an account of the peculiarly simplified and extravagant pastoral of court entertainments and pageantry. I shall use the term 'pageantry' to cover a wide range of spectacles, progresses, and festivities. A proper classification lies beyond my scope, though I shall of course make basic distinctions of form, occasion, and convention.

My approach may smack of the obsolete. Modern scholarship has penetrated the façade of court spectacle to study the political ideals and purposes behind it and in it. I may seem to turn the clock back in my concern with spectacle and courtly play. I shall indeed pay appropriate heed to the themes underlying such displays; but an exclusive concern with these serious purposes can be as distorting as a romantic obsession with spectacle. We may consider the explicit themes or symbolic content to the neglect of deeper formal assumptions and their implied ethos. Formally, court pageants were extravagant, simplistic, and unreal. Their endemic presence in Renaissance court life is itself an important pointer to the spirit of contemporary statecraft, as important as their more direct political ends.

Again, the recurrent use of pastoral motifs in court pageantry marks an obvious reversal of the basic assumptions of the pastoral mode. Yet the fact that reversal is possible on such a scale may indicate the instability of those assumptions, the fragile sophistication of the mode itself.

In the whole range of Renaissance pageantry, the most extensive and integral use of pastoral seems to occur in the country progresses of Queen Elizabeth. On the one hand, they mark a withdrawal from court to country, the basic movement of all pastoral. On the other, they carry the court into the country, the actual tendency of much pastoral. The tension between the two can be genuinely resolved by what Jean Wilson calls a 'mutual validation of experience':[1] values inherent in the country itself are perfected and articulated by the coming of the Queen. Court and

[1] *Entertainments for Elizabeth I*, ed. Jean Wilson (Woodbridge, 1980), 47. See also E. C. Wilson, *England's Eliza*, pp. 154–6; Cooper, *Pastoral*, pp. 200ff.

country seem able to fortify each other, producing a joint affirmation instead of the usual ambiguity.

The best-known Elizabethan pastoral pageant is Sidney's *The Lady of May*. It is also the earliest notable one on record, though not necessarily the first to be composed.[2] Shorn of the non-pastoral satire of the pedant Bombus, and the touch of folk-custom in the election of the Lady of May, the piece resolves itself into a love-contest and singing-match on the classic model of the eclogue: Therion and Espilus vie for the hand of the Lady of May. The fact that the suitors are a shepherd and a forester lends the contest a debate-like structure and a thematic interest. Both occupations are germane to pastoral; but the contrast permits Sidney to cast a critical glance at the actual shepherd's life. Here is pastoral convention appearing—if untenably in the last analysis—to view itself in a flexible and humorous light. This creates a sense of genial realism, of actual rusticity in considered and dignified submission to the Queen, rather than an artificial world inhabited by creatures of compliment.

When all is said and done, the specifically pastoral content of *The Lady of May* is limited. This is even truer of an undatable entertainment in the 'Ditchley Manuscript'[3] where a knight 'clowneshly Clad' leads a troop of 'Shepardes, and heardmen' to the Accession Day Tilts. The knight, like the hermit who introduces him, is a disillusioned courtier, withdrawn to pastoral peace. The herdsmen clamour to join in the jousting. The monarch's (and courtier's) country retreat, the intimate presence of rustics, and the simultaneous martial display could hardly be more closely related. Later, in another entry in the manuscript, we have a shepherd who invites the gathered 'soldiors' to his humble fare (fo. 11^{r-v}).

The most fully pastoral of all Elizabethan progress-entertainments are those staged at Bisham and Sudeley in 1592. The sheepkeeping activities of the Cotswolds here provide occasion to ring every possible change on pastoral themes. The Bisham entertainment is the more mythic and romantic: a Wild Man speaks of Pan and Sylvanus; Pan himself then appears, courting two shepherdesses. At Sudeley too there is a show of Apollo and Daphne; but the tenor of the spectacle is more humble and factual. Idealization takes the customary form of extolling the shepherd's

[2] It has, however, been taken as such by e.g. Ringler (ed.), Sidney's *Poems*, p. 361; R. Kimbrough and P. Murphy, 'The Helmingham Hall Manuscript of Sidney's *The Lady of May*', *Renaissance Drama*, NS 1 (1968), 104.

[3] BL MS Addl. 41499A fos. 2^rff. (transcript in MS Addl. 41499B). The piece in question is *not* the 'Ditchley Entertainment' of 1592 from the same MS.

peace and content: 'The country healthy and harmeles; a fresh aier, where there are no dampes, and where a black sheepe is a perilous beast; no monsters; we carry our harts at our tongues ends, being as far from dissembling as our sheepe from fiercenesse'.[4] The High Constable of Cotswold himself unbends so far as to dress like a sheep and bleat a eulogy in 'the Rammish tongue'. The Queen is invited to participate in the shepherds' games and choose their festive King and Queen; she is also presented with 'Shepheards weeds', no doubt in cloth very different from russet and kersey.

These are fully pastoral outcrops of a larger body of royal progresses and entertainments at least semi-pastoral in nature. At Elvetham in 1591, musicians 'in auncient countrey attire' sing a song of Coridon and Phyllida.[5] At West Horsley in 1559 there had been a masque of country maids, with two 'grasyers or gentillmen of the cuntrye',[6] and at the Shrovetide revels of 1559–60 a masque of 'clowns', hinds, and shepherds.[7] At Harefield in 1602 we find a dialogue between a bailiff and a dairy-maid,[8] and Chambers alludes to another between a gardener and a mole-catcher.[9] In 1600 the Countess of Pembroke composed an eclogue, 'Astraea', on hearing of the Queen's intended visit to Wilton.[10] It has nothing pastoral beyond the speakers' names, Thenot and Piers: all the more significant that she should use the pastoral form at all. The Queen's country progresses seem to have been freely interpretable as a pastoral withdrawal.

Thus Elizabeth infused serious image-building and public relations into the simple May Games of her father Henry VIII. Henry was particularly fond of appearing as Robin Hood, perhaps with a train of 'outlaws'; or else as some other 'foster', or a green-clad champion of May. He is said to have first met Anne Boleyn in shepherd's costume at a feast arranged by Cardinal Wolsey.[11] In 1515 Henry and his brother-in-law Charles Brandon entertained their wives and retinue in a 'forest'.[12] In 1515, too, a group of revellers invited the royal couple to a Maying banquet in the woods outside Greenwich.[13]

[4] John Nichols, *The Progresses and Public Processions of Queen Elizabeth* (London, 1823), iii. 136.

[5] Ibid. iii. 116.

[6] E. K. Chambers, *The Elizabethan Stage* (Oxford, 1923), i. 157.

[7] Ibid. i. 157–8.

[8] Nichols, iii. 586 ff.

[9] Chambers, i. 124.

[10] See Nichols, iii. 529. Printed in *A Poetical Rhapsody* (1602), no. 4.

[11] Greg, *Pastoral*, p. 370.

[12] See Marie Axton, 'The Tudor Mask and Elizabethan Court Drama', in M. Axton and R. Williams (eds.), *English Drama, Forms and Development: Essays in Honour of Muriel Clara Bradbrook* (Cambridge, 1977), 28.

[13] See Sydney Anglo, *Spectacle, Pageantry, and Early Tudor Policy* (Oxford, 1969), 119.

Of course, nature and pastoral life enter into continental pageantry as well. The Valois court held lavish festivities at Fontainebleau, Bayonne, and other such royal 'country houses', and the entertainments there often made use of explicit pastoralism. In the Emperor Charles V's welcome to Fontainebleau at Christmas 1539, the winter landscape suddenly came alive with sylvan gods who performed a 'danse rustique'.[14] At Bayonne in 1565, when Catherine de' Medici met her daughter Elizabeth of Spain, she arranged a banquet on an island where they were greeted and served by shepherds and shepherdesses.[15] At a dinner at Binche in 1549, the gods of field, garden, and woods served three successive courses.[16]

But such celebrations differ in quality from Elizabeth's progresses. The French shepherds and sylvans lack personality. They are partly footmen or waiters, partly ornaments, partly symbols of rural wealth and a contented peasantry. These motives cannot be discounted in Elizabeth's progresses; but there the Queen meets the rustics on their own territory in every sense. She enhances and perfects the real England instead of imposing a courtly artefact.

The best precedent is the King's visit to Sherwood Forest, as enacted in Henry VIII's revels or in Chettle and Mundy's play *The Death of Robert Earl of Huntingdon* (Act I). There is also a literary tradition of a 'shepherd's holiday' celebrating the Queen, as in Spenser's 'Aprill'. The most elaborate instance is the 'Shepherds' Holiday' inserted in Angel Day's translation of *Daphnis and Chloe*, which seems to pastoralize an actual Accession Day celebration.[17] The Sudeley entertainment also incorporates such a 'holiday'.

The characters in these feasts and pageants may represent courtiers, but the rustic mask and setting are complete. They are denizens of the woods and lanes where they appear, throwing open their lives, their communities, even their problems and eccentricities, in welcome to the Queen. She is engaged, with apparent spontaneity, to solve the marital dilemma of Sidney's Lady of May, or choose the shepherds' King and Queen at Sudeley. At Elvetham in 1591, she is herself greeted as the May Queen. The rout that follows the 'clownesh' knight in the Ditchley Manuscript approaches her with more ardour than deference. There is assumed to be a special rapport or ease of access between the commons and their ruler.

[14] See Jean Jacquot (ed.), *Les Fêtes de la Renaissance* (Paris, 1956–75), ii. 436.

[15] See F. Yates, *The Valois Tapestries* (2nd edn. London, 1975), 56–8.

[16] See Jacquot, ii. 317.

[17] See Cooper, pp. 201 and 233 n. 18.

We find the same spirit in some entertainments of James's reign as well: for instance, Thomas Campion's welcome to Queen Anne at Caversham House in April 1613.[18] At a more popular level, there is Greg's instance of the 'pleasant pastorall' with which the villagers of Bishops Cannings, Wiltshire, entertained the Queen the same year (Greg, pp. 379–80). As late as 1636, Charles I and Henrietta Maria were greeted in even more demotic fashion at Richmond (Greg, p. 385).

The rustic spirit being allowed its free dignity, pastoral life can be extolled openly, if equivocally in the context. Dorcas the shepherd and Rixus the forester speak in much the same vein in *The Lady of May*: 'where it is lawful for a man to be good if he list, and hath no outward cause to withdraw him from it; where the eye may be busied in considering the works of nature, and the heart quietly rejoiced in the honest using them'.[19] The court is unfavourably contrasted with the country in the play of Diana in the Kenilworth Revels.[20] The Ditchley rustics claim to be as good as knights and gentlemen, and the Ditchley Manuscript contains another, fragmentary praise of country life,[21] presumably from a speech at a country progress. At Cowdray in 1591, an Angler and a Netter were to repeat the same themes, with much satire of the court.[22]

The dissatisfied courtier in rural retirement appears over and over in the pageants and progresses. There is at least one poem from Henry VIII's court where a forester spurned by Beauty turns into a beadsman—and a forester, in the courtly games of the time, suggested the King.[23] There is a knight dressed as a recluse in the 1511 Westminster joust of 'Les quater Chivalers de la forrest salvigne'.[24] Frances Yates shows how Sir Henry Lee ('Loricus'), being the Queen's Ranger of Woodstock, could mingle the personae of knight, rustic, and hermit: the first at Woodstock in 1575, the last at Ditchley in 1592.[25] The Ditchley Manuscript has a number of other hermits and disillusioned knights, and Peter Beal has

[18] Campion, *Works*, ed. W. R. Davis (New York, 1967), p. 238.

[19] Sidney, *Miscellaneous Prose*, ed. Duncan-Jones and Van Dorsten, p. 28, ll. 12–15.

[20] Nichols, i. 504.

[21] Fo. 8^{r}: the first part of the discourse is missing.

[22] See Nichols, iii. 94–5.

[23] See Axton, pp. 28, 39–40; J. E. Stevens, *Music and Poetry in the Early Tudor Court*, pp. 408–9.

[24] See F. H. Cripps-Day, *The History of the Tournament in England and in France* (London, 1918), 118.

[25] Hemetes the hermit in the Woodstock Entertainment had also once been a knight. See Frances Yates, 'Elizabethan Chivalry: The Romance of the Accession-Day Tilts', *Astraea* (1975; repr. Harmondsworth 1977), 88–111; also J. W. Cunliffe, 'The Queenes Majesties Entertainment at Woodstocke', *PMLA* 26 (1911), 92–141.

discovered an important knight-turned-hermit in the Ottley Manuscript.[26] In *The Lady of May*, Sidney makes Dorcas speak of disillusioned men who 'of young courtiers . . . grew old shepherds'.[27]

Yet basically, of course, the pageants retain, and even exaggerate, the trappings of court life. The courtly concerns are translated into a rustic context, but without for a moment threatening their centrality. The literal pastoralism of the entertainments merges imperceptibly into the ruler-shepherd metaphor. The Queen herself becomes the greatest shepherdess: her presence turns country life into the Golden Age.[28] This metaphoric or symbolic pastoralism is central to many non-progress entertainments, most notably Peele's *Descensus Astraeae* (1589). But it forms part of the implicit context of the progress entertainments as well.

Hence the fine fusion of court and country slides imperceptibly into the unequal compound of common courtly pastoral. The royal milieu simply adopts a piquant, playful disguise for its essential courtliness. This appears most tellingly in outdoor 'banquets' or light repasts where the garden setting encourages such flights of fancy. Basilius's banqueting-house in Sidney's *Arcadia*, with its 'excellent waterwork', rainbow fountain, and mechanical birds, had analogues in many large Renaissance gardens.[29] Special ones would be built for festivals. As early as 1515, one of Henry VIII's May Day banquets was held in a special arbour made of boughs, surrounded by more artificial bowers with singing birds.[30] At the Bayonne festivities of 1565, 'shepherds' served the royal guests in an octagonal semi-alfresco banquet-house with tables set among the trees.[31] At Woodstock in 1575, a banquet-house doubles as the hermit Hemetes' 'poor home'.[32] It was built round an oak whose branches were bent down to form a roof, walled with lattice-work covered with flowers and ivy, and furnished with a half-moon-shaped table 'couered with green turues'.

Such rustic intrusions are reassuringly self-defeating. Still more telling is the common practice, in court entertainments, of introducing shepherds or other rustics as background, choric figures, or simply as interludes in a programme of different bent. All over Europe, musicians attending upon court entertainments frequently dress in shepherd's garb,

[26] Peter Beal, 'Poems by Sir Philip Sidney', *The Library*, 5th ser. 33 (1978), 288.
[27] *Miscellaneous Prose*, p. 28, l. 26.
[28] See Jean Wilson, p. 23.
[29] *New Arcadia*, ed. Skretkowicz, p. 86, ll. 10–18, and note on p. 524.
[30] See Anglo, p. 119.
[31] See Yates, *Valois Tapestries*, pp. 56–8.
[32] Cunliffe, pp. 99–100.

whatever the nature of the entertainment. When Mary, Louis XII's queen, entered Paris in 1513, she was greeted with a garden-pageant representing 'le vergier de france' [the orchard of France], with the King, Queen, and other figures, and 'plusieurs bergiers et bergieres lesquelz chantoient melodieusement' [many shepherds and shepherdesses who sang melodiously].[33] At the Shrovetide celebrations at the English court in 1559–60, a shepherd as minstrel accompanied eight 'clowns' and eight 'hinds'.[34] Such choric shepherds commonly appear in the *intermezzi* of Italian court drama: as in a comedy played for Prince Philip at Milan in 1549, another at the wedding of Duke Cosimo I of Florence in 1539, and yet another for Virginia de' Medici's wedding to Cesare d'Este at Florence in 1586.[35] The first two also have *intermezzi* of sylvan gods—as at Bayonne in 1565, or the wedding of the Duke of Joyeuse in 1581.[36]

Both in *intermezzi* and in other contexts, the morris dance or moresco features prominently. As Welsford noted long ago,[37] this was equally popular with courtiers and rustics, and thus a staple of courtly pastoralism. At Lucrezia Borgia's marriage with Alfonso of Ferrara, there were several morescos: by horned satyrs, by shepherds, and by 'peasants performing the whole round of their agricultural labour'.[38] In 1531 we hear of a 'morisque de Satyres' at Paris.[39] In 1542, Giulio Romano designed an elaborate moresco for a carnival at Mantua, with eight shepherds led by Pan.[40] Once again, English royal progresses adapted the courtly entertainment to a more popular context. At Kenilworth, Pan's special gift to Her Majesty consists of 'His mery morrys-dauns, with theyr pype and taber'.[41] Chambers (i. 124) cites several morris dances in Elizabeth's progresses, and notes how such dances pass into formal pastoral.

But the most paradoxical, indeed perverse, use of pastoral occurs in martial contexts—though the martial element too is largely decorative, turned into the opposite of itself. Shepherd and soldier can merge because both roles have ceased to matter, become passing affectations of the courtier. We may recall that, of the quaintly accoutred knights in

[33] See R. Withington, *English Pageantry* (London, 1918), i. 172.

[34] See Chambers, i. 157–8.

[35] See respectively: Jacquot, vol. ii. 443; A. C. Minor and B. Mitchell (eds.), *A Renaissance Entertainment* (Columbia, Miss., 1968), 245–6; Roy Strong, *Splendour at Court* (London, 1973), 186.

[36] See, respectively, Yates, *Valois Tapestries*, p. 58; Yates, 'The Joyeuse Magnificences', *Astraea*, p. 171.

[37] Enid Welsford, *The Court Masque* (Cambridge, 1927), 25.

[38] Ibid. 89.

[39] Jacquot, ii. 437.

[40] See A. d'Ancona, *Origini del teatro italiano* (rev. edn. Turin, 1891), ii. 438–9.

[41] Nichols, i. 470.

Sidney's *Arcadia*, two come in shepherds' guise. Philisides in Book II of the *New Arcadia* (Skretkowicz, p. 255) has been identified with Sidney himself as he appeared at the Accession Day Tilts in 1581.[42] There is also the 'Knight of the Sheep' (who might have proved to be Philisides) accompanying the 'forsaken knight' (Musidorus) in the war against Amphialus (Skretkowicz, pp. 411–12). Moreover, we have a poet-knight dressed as a Wild Man (Skretkowicz, p. 256).

There is no direct report of Sidney's own garb at the Accession Day Tilts; but recent evidence makes it clear that he must have appeared as a shepherd-knight at one tournament and possibly two.[43] Such pastoral masquerade was well established, not only in courtly exercises but in actual warfare. In a battle at St.-Omer in 1487, a group of Flemish knights came dressed as shepherds.[44] Among tournaments, the most celebrated is the 'Pas d'Armes de la Bergère' organized by King René of Anjou at Tarascon in 1449.[45] There are many later instances. A Monsieur Florengis jousted as a shepherd at the Field of Cloth of Gold.[46] The Wild Man disguise also occurs several times, as does the analogous Green Knight.[47] Moving from tournament to masque and festival, the Binche entertainment of 1549 incorporated not only wild men but also four knights 'alla pastorale'.[48] Close to Sidney's own day we find the knight 'clowneshly Clad' of the Ditchley Manuscript.

Such costumes illustrate the decorative vein of court pastoral. Philisides' attendants in the *New Arcadia* are 'apparelled like shepherds (for the fashion, though rich in stuff)' (Skretkowicz, p. 255, ll. 7–8). So, too, in the 'Pas d'Armes de la Bergère, the 'shepherds' and 'shepherdess' had been costumed in fur and gold embroidery, silver crook, and ostrich feathers.[49] A hundred years later in Binche, the knights 'alla pastorale' are dressed in 'brocato d'oro' [gold brocade].[50] In the 1511 Westminster masque of the 'Chivalers de la forrest salvigne', the Wild Men are 'covered with grene Silke flosshed', and the trees made of silk, satin, and damask, even silver and gold.[51] Henry VIII's Robin Hood costume is

[42] But see Skretkowicz (ed.), *New Arcadia*, p. xv, for objections to this view.

[43] See Beal, pp. 287–8; also D. Coulman, 'Spotted to be known', *Journal of the Warburg and Courtauld Institutes*, 20 (1957), 179–80.

[44] See Cooper, p. 68.

[45] See G.-A. Crapelet (ed.), *Le Pas d'armes de la bergère* (2nd edn. Paris, 1835).

[46] J. H. Hanford and S. Watson, 'Personal Allegory in the Arcadia', *MP* 32 (1934), 7.

[47] See Nichols, ii. 322–4; R. Coltman Clephan, *The Tournament, Its Periods and Phases* (London, 1919), 75; Withington, i. 75–6; Yates, 'Elizabethan Chivalry', *Astraea*, p. 91; Yates, *Valois Tapestries*, p. 59; Jacquot, ii. 338.

[48] Jacquot, ii. 340.

[49] Crapelet, p. 41.

[50] Jacquot, ii. 340.

[51] See Welsford, p. 123; Anglo, p. 111.

made of green velvet and gold.[52] Serlio describes an Urbino pastoral where the shepherds were similarly dressed. Even the rustic backcloth for a 'satyric' play, says Serlio, should be made of costly stuffs:

Et queste cose quanto saranno di maggior spesa: tanto piu lodeuoli saranno, perche (nel uero) son proprie di generosi, magnanimi, & ricchi Signori, nemici della brutta Auaritia.[53]

[And the more costly these things are, the more praiseworthy they will be, because in truth they befit generous, great-hearted, and wealthy lords, enemies of ugly avarice.]

Much later, d'Urfé describes the pastoral plays he has seen, where

s'ils leur donnent une houlette en la main, elle est peinte et dorée, leurs juppes sont de taffetas, leur pannetiere bien troussée, et quelquefois faite de toile d'or ou d'argent.[54]

[if they [the dramatists] give them a sheep-hook to hold, it is painted and gilt, their smocks are of taffeta, their pouch neatly tucked, and sometimes made of cloth of gold or of silver.]

Shepherd life can embellish the hyper-courtly masque and tournament only because it has ceased to count as a living entity. It can therefore be used as a decoration, a tame paradox, contributing a pleasing *frisson* of the contrary and the ingenious. It would be preposterous to reduce Sidney's *Arcadia* to these terms; equally, it would be wrong to deny the presence of such an element in the work. At one level, the pastoral is laid under contribution to create an exotic, poetically removed, highly wrought romantic atmosphere that lies like a lacquer over the surface of the work.

But elsewhere, in dramatic spectacle as well as narrative, pastoral can be oriented to the world of courtly romance in a totally different way, by separating and reorganizing the components. Instead of mingling or coalescing, they can take on new relations of contrast or meaningful interaction. In particular, they can incorporate the two worlds in new and exciting versions of the 'cyclic' structure. Let us turn from the ephemeral fictions of court entertainment to the deeper concerns of pastoral drama.

[52] See Axton, p. 28.

[53] Serlio, *Libro . . . d'architettura* (1560), Book II, fo. 27^r.

[54] 'L'Autheur a la Bergere Astrée', *L'Astrée*, ed. Vaganay, i. 7–8.

18
English Pastoral Drama

1. *Elizabethan drama*

IN HIS account of English Renaissance pastoral drama, Greg concentrated on strictly Italianate works, compressing the rest into a final half-chapter with two pages on Shakespeare. The reverse procedure might yield a truer account of things; for English pastoral drama, unlike the Italian, was not established early on as a consciously defined tradition. Rather, it may be seen as an inevitable but, in the initial stages, almost incidental development, proceeding through a relatively small and disparate number of examples from several lines of growth originating in other rustic, romantic, and mythological drama. Such multiple origin accounts for the many unusual features of these pastoral plays, giving them their peculiar strength and making Shakespeare's achievement possible. The Italian element is subsidiary, derivative, and relatively unexciting, except where woven in with the other strands in the design.

We may not be entirely convinced by Richard Cody's attempt (in *The Landscape of the Mind*) to extend the Neoplatonism infusing Italian pastoral drama to Shakespeare's early comedies. In *The Two Gentlemen of Verona*, a potentially pastoral episode of a more obvious sort—Valentine's sojourn among the outlaws—is dismissed in less than a page; and the elements Cody emphasizes in *A Midsummer Night's Dream* are not those that lead on to the clear pastoralism of *As You Like It*.

Formally, no doubt, the Italian element is one of the earliest to appear, in the court plays of Lyly and Peele. (Even earlier, in 1573, Italian players had presented pastoral drama at the English court.)[1] Violet Jeffery provides what is still the best (if somewhat over-stretched) account of Lyly's borrowing from Italian pastoral plays;[2] this consists chiefly in mythology and the love-theme rather than strictly pastoral elements, and

[1] They 'ffollowed the progresse and made pastyme fyrst at Wynsor and afterwardes at Reading' (*Revels Accounts*, ed. A. Feuillerat (Louvain, 1908), 225).

[2] Violet M. Jeffery, *John Lyly and the Italian Renaissance* (Paris, 1928), ch. v.

still less an ideal of pastoral life.[3] In *Gallathea* (*c.*1585), Tyterus and Melibeus are both shepherds, and their daughters are disguised as such to escape the clutches of a monster. In *Love's Metamorphosis* (*c.*1588–90), described as a pastoral on the 1601 title-page, the chief male characters are foresters. But all this hardly matters. *The Woman in the Moon* (*c.*1590–5) has a little more pastoral detail, but even here the Arcadian shepherds are scarcely shepherds to any purpose.

The pastoral elements are clearer and more promising in Peele's *The Araygnement of Paris*,[4] though it is probably earlier than Lyly's plays (*c.*1581–4; printed 1584). We cannot forget that Paris is a shepherd on Ida: though in fact (the prototype of this figure in English drama) a prince disguised as such to woo a nymph. The situation is half-romance and half-*pastourelle* (for Paris deserts Oenone). In either case, we have a contrast of court and country—another central pastoral situation in embryo. Still more interestingly, a similar contrast, almost along class lines, appears between the Olympians and the rural gods: Pallas, Juno, and Venus visit Pan and the sylvans like royalty on a country progress.[5] The humans seem to provide a mere underplot to the real action among the gods. This too foreshadows the later use of pastoral subplot in a tragic or courtly action.

There are many descriptions of nature, though they tend to pass into the mythological.[6] There is at least one notable passage (ll. 935–43) on a shepherd's humble content. Above all, there is a substantial shepherd community, particularly the love-lorn Colin who dies of a broken heart. This is clearly an extension of *The Shepheardes Calender* along the lines of Italianate sentiment. In a word, Peele is taking his pastoralism seriously, inaugurating certain functions of pastoral in drama that will become operative principles in later works.

The seed sown by Lyly and Peele burgeons in the anonymous *The Maid's Metamorphosis* (1599–1600?; printed in 1600). Eurymine, supposedly low-born, is condemned to death for attracting the love of Prince Ascanio. Spared by the assassins, she becomes a shepherdess beloved by both Apollo and the shepherds. She makes Apollo reluctantly

[3] This was pointed out long ago by Homer Smith: 'Pastoral Influence in the English Drama', *PMLA* 12 (1897), 377.

[4] It also seems to have been so in Peele's lost *The Hunting of Cupid*, judging by the surviving fragments. See *Malone Society Collections*, Parts 4 and 5 (Oxford, 1911), 309–12, and *England's Helicon*, no. 18.

[5] *The Araygnement of Paris*, ll. 181 ff., as ed. R. M. Benbow in Peele's *Dramatic Works* (New Haven, 1970; vol. iii of Peele's *Life and Works*, ed. C. T. Prouty).

[6] ll. 78–9, 253–77, 320ff.

turn her into a man, but finally change her back again so that she can marry Ascanio. She proves to be the daughter of the hermit Aramanthus, who is a deposed prince.

Here the mythological element is matched by the purely pastoral. A full-fledged 'cyclic' plot revolves round the pastoral sojourn, with every possible conventional complication. Other conventions are introduced locally: a debate between a shepherd and a forester; another between a shepherd's boy, a forester's boy, and a court page. The courtship of Silvio and Gemulo, as described by their servants, is typically bucolic:

> FRISCO. Faith and I am foundered with a flinging too and fro, with Ches-nuts, Hazel-nuts, Bullaze, and wildings, for presents from my maister to the faire shepherdesse.
>
> MOPSO. And I am tierd like a Calfe, with carrying a Kidde euery weeke to the Cottage of my maisters sweete Lambkin.[7]

The three elements interacting from the earliest days of Renaissance Italian pastoral are juxtaposed here as well: the pastoral, the courtly, and the mythological. The pastoral element cannot stand by itself, but it holds its own with the others at last.

With minor variations of emphasis, the same may be said of *The Thracian Wonder*, published in 1661 but plausibly attributed to the Renaissance.[8] It is closely based on Greene's *Menaphon*, with extensive pastoral scenes and even a new pastoral subplot of Palemon and Serena. But country scenes are interspersed with those of court and battle, and the ending is purely martial. The pastoral setting, though still central to the plot, is blurred by the intervention of other elements.

Although there is yet no full and secure reliance on the pastoral, it has by now become a primary source of dramatic inspiration. Its extent can be gauged from lost pastoral titles like *Phyllida and Corin*, *Clorys and Orgasto* (Ergasto?), Chettle and Haughton's *The Arcadian Virgin*, and Chapman's 'pastrall tragedie'.[9] The titles suggest a basis in Italianate 'Arcadian' convention. 'A pastorell or historie of A Greeke maide' may indicate an admixture of Heliodoran romance.[10]

[7] III. ii. 52–6, as in Lyly's *Complete Works*, ed. R. W. Bond (Oxford, 1902; repr. 1973), iii. 368.

[8] Estimates of the date range from *c.*1600 (Chambers, *Elizabethan Stage*, iv. 49) to after 1611 (C. Crupi in *Archiv für . . . Neueren Sprachen und Literaturen* (1971) 341–7). The ascription to Webster on the title-page is not taken seriously.

[9] See G. M. Sibley, *The Lost Plays and Masques 1500–1642* (Ithaca, 1933), 122, 28, 9, and 118 respectively. For the sources of information, see *Revels Account* for 1584 (ed. Feuillerat, p. 365); Henslowe's *Diary* for 1599, ed. R. A. Foakes and R. T. Rickert (Cambridge, 1961), 16, 128, 122 respectively.

[10] See Sibley, pp. 67–8; Revels Accounts for 1578–9 (ed. Feuillerat, p. 286).

But as I said before, it is the interaction of other conventions, often not primarily pastoral, that gives English pastoral drama its peculiar strength and makes Shakespeare's achievement possible. There is, for instance, a pattern of romantic action involving withdrawal into a natural or desert setting, perhaps in disguise. This could be an easy development from any love-plot involving elopement, a scorned lover's retreat, a threatened maiden's escape, or a simple romantic quest or journey. In *Sir Clyomon and Sir Clamydes* (perhaps by Thomas Preston: composed between 1570 and 1583) the Princess Neronis, disguised as a youth, serves the coarse comic shepherd Corin.[11] This is an explicitly pastoral instance of a basic situation which could appear in a number of versions, most notably in a forest setting. Clifford Leech[12] compares Neronis's state to that of the spurned Queen Dorothea in *James IV* (*c.*1590), though the latter's forest sojourn is restricted to a single scene where the assassin Jaques attacks her.

Common Conditions (hitherto overlooked by historians of pastoral drama) affords a clearer example, though it is considerably earlier (SR entry, 26 July 1576). The exiled Prince Sedmond, his sister Clarisia, and the Vice, Common Conditions, reach a *locus amoenus* where they are attacked by tinkers, and brother and sister separated. Later, in a forest, Clarisia is united with her lover Lamphedon, while Sedmond meets Sabia, who loves him in vain.

Pace David Young,[13] we may also place here, rather than among properly pastoral plays, the somewhat later, extraordinarily popular *Mucedorus* (*c.*1590?; seventeen editions between 1598 and 1668). The princely hero turns shepherd, but only as an unlikely means of courting Princess Amadine at the court of Aragon. Later he dons hermit's garb, but again only in order to elope. Captured by the wild man Bremo, they endure an unwilling captivity in the forest, though their love is strengthened during it. This is the closest we come to a 'pastoral sojourn'. There is absolutely nothing of shepherd life or the values appropriate to it.

But already in *The Rare Triumphs of Love and Fortune* (1583?), the forest retreat has assumed an operative role. True, the hermit Bomelio professes to find his retreat a place of woe; he is, moreover, an evil

[11] *Clyomon and Clamydes*, 1599 Quarto (Malone Soc. Repr.; Oxford, 1913), sig. F1^{r}ff. Conjectural dates for this and all other plays as in A. Harbage, *Annals of English Drama*, rev. S. Schoenbaum (London, 1964).

[12] In the New Arden edn. of *The Two Gentlemen of Verona* (London, 1969), p. xli.

[13] *The Heart's Forest*, pp. 24–6.

magician. All the same, his cave becomes a gathering-point for the characters and a centre of regeneration, though the inept dramatist requires no fewer than three *dei ex machina*. We may also place here the later, and far superior, *The Old Wives' Tale* (*c.*1590–5) by George Peele. In Peele's central action, the evil abode of the magician Sacrapant is set in the heart of a normal and even attractive rural scene, with convincing rustic figures and a chorus of harvesters. The framing narrative is quasi-pastoral as well: three court pages are entertained by Clunch the Smith, who 'leades a life as merrie as a King with Madge his wife'.[14]

Here too comes *A Knack to Know an Honest Man* (1594), again overlooked by scholars. The play of courtly romance and intrigue opens with a dialogue of shepherds, suddenly interrupted by the courtier Lelio's duel with Sempronio. The pastoral world is clearly contrasted with the violence of the court. We also have a hermit, Phillip, who rescues, heals, and converts Sempronio.

During the same years,[15] Shakespeare ascribes complex functions to the forest in *The Two Gentlemen of Verona*, where Valentine resorts with the outlaws. It is a variation upon the Petrarchan lover's retreat (see v. iv. 1 ff.), but more importantly a place of resolution, a setting explicitly placed against the court. The characters gather there in situations—and consequent frames of mind—not possible at court, thereby allowing a resolution of the tangled plot. The last scene admittedly has an air of haste. The epidemic forgiveness seems as much due to the dramatist's urge to wind up as to the spiritual influence of the forest scene. All the more notable that Shakespeare should have chosen this as the best setting for swiftly resolving a complex situation.

The possibilities of such a setting are more fully realized in Beaumont and Fletcher's *Philaster* (*c.*1609), written many pastoral plays after *The Two Gentlemen*. We must avoid an over-simple analysis of *Philaster*. The events in the forest do, after all, continue the distrustful misunderstandings of the earlier action, negating the quest for peace and solitude which brings Philaster, Arathusa, and 'Bellario' to the forest. But this very climax of the confusion is also, we may feel, a symbolic turning-point. 'In the same forest where all seems confused, the feet of the plot somehow find a way, and bring everything to a happy ending.'[16] It is also

[14] *The Old Wives Tale*, ll. 69–70: as ed. F. S. Hook in Peele's *Dramatic Works* (*Life and Works*, iii).

[15] *The Two Gentlemen* is commonly dated 1594, though Clifford Leech (New Arden edn., p. xxxv) suggests 1592–3.

[16] John Danby, *Poets on Fortune's Hill* (London, 1952), 177.

significant that the dramatists bring in an honest rustic, whose chivalrous intervention in Arathusa's defence is the means of keeping the bloodshed within the limits of comedy. Some three decades later, the same combination of confusion and resolution is conveyed in Richard Brome's *The Love-Sick Court*, in the abortive duel in the North Vale of Tempe and the appearance of protective rustics.[17]

The close alliance of forest and pastoral in English drama, the ease with which the former could suggest the latter's functions and thus pass into it, should now be clear. The forest is equally important in another line of development leading up to Shakespeare's mature pastoral: the Robin Hood plays. An outlaw in *The Two Gentlemen* swears 'By the bare scalp of Robin Hood's fat friar' (IV. i. 36), and the whole idea of a band of outlaws obviously smacks of the Robin Hood legend. The Duke Senior in *As You Like It* is explicitly compared to Robin Hood.[18] The *Tale of Gamelyn*, the source of *Rosalynde* and thus of *As You Like It*, is well known for its relation to the Robin Hood legend.[19]

The Robin Hood plays go back to formal extensions of folk-drama like the manuscript 'Robin Hood and the Knight'[20] and the two plays printed by William Copland as 'the play of Robyn Hoode'.[21] They provide a dramatic parallel to the popular ballads and songs that exercise such a decisive influence on the English pastoral lyric. Explicit connection with the pastoral is indicated by the SR entry on 14 May 1594 for the lost 'pastorall plesant commedie of Robin Hood and Little John'.[22] The appellation suggests a formal, full-scale comedy, unlike the earlier popular pieces; and we may deduce the same for William Haughton's 'Robin Hood's Pen'orths', also lost, written for the Admiral's Men.[23]

The important point, though, is not the pastoralization of the Robin Hood story, but the legacy of the Robin Hood plays to other pastoral drama: a homely outdoor atmosphere, a spirit of release—above all, a

[17] Greg's account of the play (*Pastoral*, p. 408) is somewhat misleading: the characters do not seek a cure for love among country folk. The 'cyclic' nature of the plot is much vaguer than Greg's description suggests.

[18] I. i. 116. All refs. to the New Arden edn. by Agnes Latham (London, 1975). The phrase 'greenwood tree' also suggests outlawry and the tales of Robin Hood.

[19] See L. A. Hibbard, *Mediaeval Romance in England* (1924; repr. New York, 1960), 158–61.

[20] See J. M. Manly, *Specimens of the Pre-Shakespearean Drama* (1897; repr. New York, 1967), i. 279. The title, of course, is modern.

[21] As part of *A mery geste of Robyn Hoode and of hys lyfe*. See W. W. Greg, *A Bibliography of the English Printed Drama to the Restoration* (London, 1939), i. 108–9.

[22] See Greg, *Bibliography*, ii. 966.

[23] Sibley, p. 136. (Henslowe's Diary, fo. 70^v, 71^r, ed. Foakes and Rickert, p. 138.)

strong and unusually antinomian contrast of corrupt court and virtuous country. Most significant are Mundy and Chettle's twin plays, *The Downfall* and *The Death of Robert Earl of Huntingdon* (both 1598). These explicitly reject the usual jests for more serious themes.[24] Significantly, they follow the minority tradition (traced back to Grafton)[25] of making Robin Hood a nobleman. This makes his career a special version of the 'court to country' plot. Robin's ordered egalitarian brotherhood contrasts with the vicious disordered court. Marian's vow of chastity may be a purely fortuitous parallel to the theme of purity in pastoral, but A. H. Thorndike is surely right in finding a theme of forgiveness running through the play.[26]

Court evil finally invades the forest. Robin is poisoned in Act I of *The Death*, and the succeeding acts unfold a courtly tragedy. The 'cycle' is a tragic one; but at least the two worlds are clearly juxtaposed, the nature-retreat acquiring a moral significance:

> For what in wealth we want, we haue in flowers,
> And what wee loose in halles, we finde in bowers. (ll. 1380–1)

And at the beginning of *The Death* there is a moment's harmony when King Richard visits Sherwood and feasts with Robin.

These two plays, we are told, were written at the royal instance,[27] but they are allied to a vein of popular drama (linked in turn to the balladic tradition)[28] where an honest rustic gains court favour: *George-a-Greene* (between 1587 and 1593: ascribed to Robert Greene), where Robin Hood makes an appearance, or *Edward IV* (between 1592 and 1599), featuring the Tanner of Tamworth. There are similar plays where a country maiden matches her noble sister in love. We may readily guess the stories of lost plays like *Jack and Jill*, *Joan as Good as My Lady*, and *The Blacksmith's Daughter*,[29] though perhaps the heroine of the last work proved to be a noblewoman, as in *Fair Em the Miller's Daughter*.

This romantic variant passes into clear and significant pastoral in Greene's *Friar Bacon and Friar Bungay* (*c*.1589–92). Margaret of

[24] See *The Downfall* (Malone Soc. Repr., ed. J. C. Meagher; Oxford, 1965 for 1964), ll. 2208–33. All refs. to this edn.

[25] See R. H. Hilton, 'The Origins of Robin Hood', *Past and Present*, 14 (1958), 31.

[26] A. H. Thorndike, 'The Relation of "As You Like It" to Robin Hood Plays', *JEGP* 4 (1901), 62.

[27] See *The Downfall*, ll. 2215 ff.

[28] Of the plays mentioned in this paragraph, the following share their material with ballads: *George-a-Greene*, *Edward IV* (with the Tanner of Tamworth), *Joan as Good as My Lady*.

[29] See respectively Sibley, pp. 81 (Revels Account, 1567–8), 84 (Henslowe's Diary, 1598–9), 16 (mentioned in Gosson's *School of Abuse*, 1597).

Fressingfield is a real country maiden, not a royal foundling. Yet the King and court concur heartily to her marrying Lacy, Earl of Lincoln, and even to combining the wedding with the Prince's own.

This egalitarianism is more than outweighed by other factors. The Prince himself clearly may not marry Margaret. Court and country provide parallel but distinct worlds, related only by coexistence within the polity. The country is attractive, but the court is essentially superior. It needs no regeneration from the country: the Prince's retreat to Fressingfield is an act of truancy. Contact with Margaret does indeed strengthen him in his future role as king, adding her happy rusticity to his awareness of state and society. But he does not, and cannot, take back to court Margaret or what she stands for.

In other words, the Margaret story provides a kind of underplot to the courtly action, affecting our assessment of the latter without controlling its course. The pastoral or rustic subplot probably originated as a kind of chorus, from the use of shepherds, rustics, and sylvan gods in the interludes in court plays and masques.[30] This could easily be expanded into a subplot, at its simplest one of unambitious comedy: clownish actors in *John a Kent and John a Cumber* (*c*.1587–90), the wise men of Gotham in *A Knack to Know a Knave* (1592). But in *A Midsummer Night's Dream*, the same subplot of rustic actors is organically linked to the rest of the play by the Titania–Bottom plot, and performs very complex functions indeed. In Lyly's *Midas* (1589–90), IV. ii, shepherds provide a scene of choric comment on the action. Much later, the woodmen in Philaster, IV. ii, and still later the rustics in Brome's *The Love-Sick Court*, IV. ii and V. iv, serve a similar function. And *Fair Em the Miller's Daughter* (*c*.1589–91) provides us, however ineptly, with a double action very like that of *Friar Bacon and Friar Bungay*.

The use of pastoral and rustic subplots may remind us of Empson's characterization of all Elizabethan subplots as 'pastoral' by his own broad definition.[31] In fact, he discusses *Friar Bacon* at some length, but only to compare the Margaret and Friar Bacon subplots, and that chiefly as concerns ironic parallels. Even so, the 'dramatic ambiguity' of such double irony produces 'a complexity of sympathy'. It 'can give the individual a rich satisfaction at one time, and therefore different satisfactions at different times from different "points of view" . . . And yet, since the separation of ambiguity . . . is never complete, at each level you

[30] See Greg, *Pastoral*, p. 409.
[31] *Some Versions of Pastoral*, ch. ii.

would feel that there were others that made the play "solid"'.[32] We may not follow Empson in his over-catholic concept of the pastoral; but his remarks certainly apply to the truly pastoral subplot. Through a subtle play of parallel and contrast, it can provide an enriching commentary on the main courtly action.

Thus there seem to be two major functions of pastoral in the cyclic plots that bring courtly characters into a setting of nature and rustic life. First, as we have repeatedly seen, such plots contrast corrupt court with regenerative country over the entire time-sequence of the action. Secondly, within the pastoral section, they can compare and contrast the visitors and the native rustics, court and country values, evaluating each against the other. The first function, however important, is relatively simple, tending to idealize the country. The second is potentially very subtle and ambiguous. It may present the country in a more equivocal light, and conclude—if it reaches a conclusion at all—with a fine adjustment of court and country values. This will specially be the case where, as generally in romantic comedy, the country characters only provide a subplot to the main courtly action. The narrative interest in the courtly characters can interact with the central presence of the pastoral setting in very complex ways. We have seen the interesting possibilities of such patterns in Lodge's *Rosalynde*.

What makes Shakespeare's pastoral remarkable is that he simultaneously sets at work all the possibilities I have outlined in the last paragraph. He does not move away from the central pastoral tradition, as has sometimes been suggested. Rather, he adopts it as his chief concern, probes and exploits it with a thoroughness never employed before, except perhaps in Book VI of *The Faerie Queene*. Finally, both Shakespeare and Spenser arrive, on the further side of conventional pastoral, at a new philosophic sense of harmony and simplicity that is expressed in a few outstanding pastoral works.

2. *Shakespeare*

It hardly needs saying that an adequate treatment of Shakespeare's pastoral is impossible within the compass of such a book as this. There are also innumerable studies on the subject. I have therefore confined myself to remarks at what may be called a secondary or even tertiary stratum of analysis, on themes and viewpoints of directly pastoral bearing beneath the surface play of plot and character.

[32] Empson, *Some Versions of Pastoral*, pp. 58–9.

The first Shakespearean play important for our purposes is *A Midsummer Night's Dream*. I have already drawn attention to the rustic subplot of the play. In fact, two of the three main groups of characters may be called 'pastoral' in Empson's sense: the fairies and the 'mechanicals'. The multiple implications of pastoral plots are thus, as it were, split between two levels. At first sight, this seems conveniently to separate the contrasting functions of poetic idealization and tonic realism. In fact, both strands are equivocal. Bottom and his crew offer some positive values, and the fairy world very many negative ones. But a basic distinction of tone and orientation obviously remains, making for a two-pronged, mutually poised commentary on the central 'courtly' action.

The rustics play more roles than they are aware of. They amuse us with their folly; but they convey an instinctual viability, a homely worth suggested rather than exemplified by their speech and action, buckram for the fragile fancies of love and fairyland:

> For never anything can be amiss
> When simpleness and duty tender it.[33]

This is the very substance of pastoral ethics. But the reassuring substantiality becomes a threat, further entangling and endangering the romantic fancies, when Titania falls in love with Bottom; and their union appears as an ironic commentary on the third group, the human lovers.

Yet it may be a strengthening irony, allied to the confusion that purifies the humans' love and prepares the way to their final happy union. Elements from the subplot are being used to probe and question the romantic and courtly action, leading to a deeper though perhaps equivocal understanding.

Equivocal too is the embryonic 'cyclic' plot.[34] Unhappy lovers escape from Athens into a wood which forms the chief setting of the play. Here, love-tangles are sorted out under openly supernatural influence, and they return to happy marriage at court. In the process, the woodland setting and fairy spells may be thought to have touched their petty and jealous loves with a delicacy and a remoter charm.

What complicates this apparently neat pattern is that the wood is presented simultaneously as a place of disorder.[35] Its presiding spirits are

[33] v. i. 82–3; all refs. to the New Arden edn. by Harold F. Brooks (London, 1979).

[34] Noted by David Young, *Something of Great Constancy: The Art of 'A Midsummer Night's Dream'* (New Haven, 1966), 87, 90.

[35] This double function is best noted by C. E. Ramsey, 'A Midsummer Night's Dream', in M. Seidel and E. Mendelson (eds.), *Homer to Brecht: The European Epic and Dramatic Traditions* (New Haven, 1977), 224–8.

Oberon and Titania, whose wrangles have disturbed the seasonal cycle itself, and Puck, best pleased by 'things . . . | That befall prepost'rously' (III. ii. 120–1). Magic is employed through spite and error in the service of disorder. The night becomes a time of fear and confusion when evil spirits roam (III. ii. 381–7). Titania's elves charm away snakes and hedgehogs to create a bower of innocence for their Queen—only to have it invaded by the inner evil of irrational love.

Behind all this we glimpse a more stable rhythm of nature and human life. It is ultimately a benevolent scheme. Oberon and Titania are finally reconciled, and their dance signifies a restoration of order (IV. i. 84), which is then conveyed to the human couples in the final scene. Beyond this we have the higher spirituality of the 'imperial votress' (II. i. 163). At an earthier level, there is the solid reality of rustic life as apparent in the homely activities of Puck (II. i. 34–7). The imagery gives astonishingly vivid glimpses of daylight nature.[36] This is a world of Maying-rites and happy pastoral love where Oberon disguises himself as Corin to woo Phillida (II. i. 66–8).

But we view all this intermittently though the magic glass of the fairy scenes. Even at the end, we may suspect the fragility of any order, cosmic or human, that relies upon the humour of these alien spirits.[37] Shakespeare undermines the power and stability of the pastoral setting itself, even as he exploits the disturbing possibilities of the 'pastoral subplot' in the fairies and rustics. We seem to have moved far from an idealized, spiritual world. Yet this undermining of standard pastoral idealization is the first step towards a new, deeper concept of pastoral life that finally vindicates the idyllic setting of *The Winter's Tale*.

As You Like It marks the next, much greater step in this direction. Shakespeare turns at last to formal pastoral, if only to disturb and rework its premisses. The implications of Empson's 'pastoral' subplot are fully realized in *As You Like It*. Here, says Harold Jenkins, 'the art of comic juxtaposition is at its subtlest'.[38] Courtly, pastoral, and realistic elements mingle in complete topsy-turvydom. Two pairs of courtier-lovers are balanced by a pair of egregiously Petrarchan shepherd-lovers and another of earthy burlesque clown-lovers. The ironic parallels are more

[36] e.g. I. i. 183–5, II. i. 249–52, III. ii. 20–3, IV. i. 52–3.

[37] Cf. R. F. Miller, '*A Midsummer Night's Dream*: The Fairies, Bottom, and the Mystery of Things', *Shakespeare Quarterly*, 26 (1975), 255. Obviously, this is directly contrary to Thomas MacFarland's reading of the *Dream* as Shakespeare's happiest play, and 'very possibly the happiest work of literature ever conceived' (*Shakespeare's Pastoral Comedy* (Chapel Hill, 1972), 78).

[38] Harold Jenkins, 'As You Like It', *Shakespeare Survey*, 8 (1955), 43.

pronounced than ever. Orlando's verses are no better than Phebe's, and his courtship can be made to appear as earthy as Touchstone's by an easy parody:

> If a hart do lack a hind,
> Let him seek out Rosalind. (III. ii. 99–100)

It is Orlando the courtier, not Silvius the shepherd, who is charged with talking in blank verse (IV. i. 29). Again, Touchstone patronizes Corin, Audrey, or William, just as Jaques patronizes Touchstone. This is obviously a very special version of the egalitarianism of much idyllic pastoral. There, it was a premiss of firm if naïve validity; here it leads to a deeper questioning of all premisses and distinctions, a genuine confusion of values.

Jacques further holds that the Duke Senior is a usurper in the forest no less than his brother at court (II. i. 27–8). Even the deer, the 'native burghers' of the forest, show the worst traits of civic life: 'Sweep on you fat and greasy citizens . . .' (II. i. 55). Orlando, new-come from the court, breaks in rudely with drawn sword upon an eminently civilized gathering of seasoned forest-dwellers: yet even the latter are courtiers after all.

All this results in a complete blurring of lines. We cannot arrive at any assessment of attitudes and life-styles, court and country, satiric and romantic pastoral. This is where the ambiguities of the pastoral subplot (and *As You Like It* has more than one subplot) have led us. As I have said before, the 'cyclic' plot at its simplest implies a fairly direct idealization of the country and of shepherd life. This may be said to be the root impulse behind *all* pastoral literature. Here, however, a special development of the cyclic plot, bringing court and country into a deep and complex confrontation, has led to a new, ambiguous, self-exploratory pastoral[39] that seeks a new basis for its undoubtedly valid premisses because it can no longer naïvely accept the old basis: 'in respect of itself, it is a good life; but in respect that it is a shepherd's life, it is naught' (III. ii. 13–15).

We can scarcely rest in such a sardonic balance of negatives. Touchstone himself is not doing so in this speech. He is deliberately playing the courtier foxing the peasant actually no inferior to himself. The joke is really against courtiers, and Touchstone knows it: 'to be bawd to a

[39] On this point cf. Lerner, *The Uses of Nostalgia*, pp. 21–7, and Ettin, *Literature and the Pastoral*, ch. v generally, though Lerner's and Ettin's specific analyses of *As You Like It* scarcely overlap with mine.

bell-wether, and to betray a she-lamb of a twelvemonth to a crooked-pated old cuckoldly ram, out of all reasonable match' (III. ii. 78–81). This is a fantastic charge against the shepherd, but embodies a perfectly valid one against the courtier.

The mere fact that the resolution takes place in Arden, and obviously could only take place there, implies a bias towards the country setting. Yet this is no idyllic paradisal world. As critics commonly point out, winter winds blow in Arden, and nature is unquestionably red in tooth and claw. The new-comers' opening dialogue with Corin could scarcely have come out of *England's Helicon*:

CORIN. Who calls?
TOUCHSTONE. Your betters sir.
CORIN. Else are they very wretched. (II. iv. 64–6)

In a doubtless deliberate reversal of a cherished pastoral assumption, Corin is a hireling shepherd, not an owner-grazier; and his wisdom is inherently pessimistic: 'I know the more one sickens the worse at ease he is; and that he that wants money, means, and content is without three good friends; that the property of rain is to wet and fire to burn' (III. ii. 23–6). But this is the basis for not only reluctant content but an assertion of genuine country values: 'Those that are good manners at the court are as ridiculous in the country as the behaviour of the country is most mockable at the court' (III. ii. 44–7). Here is the positive side of Touchstone's neither/nor opposition of court and country. And Corin's side of it is as positive as anything in the play: 'Sir, I am a true labourer: I earn that I eat, get that I wear; owe no man hate, envy no man's happiness; glad of other men's good, content with my harm; and the greatest of my pride is to see my ewes graze and my lambs suck' (III. ii. 71–5). These are the standard moral values of pastoral life: it may be Tasso's old shepherd or Spenser's Meliboe speaking. Yet it is based on a rejection of the standard idyllic setting. Corin's world is, to a unique extent, a place of adversity.

The exiled courtiers draw their happiness from the same source as Corin:

Seeking the food he eats,
And pleas'd with what he gets . . . (II. v. 37–8)

The Duke's philosophy is declaredly based on adversity; and Amiens echoes his words:

> Happy is your Grace,
> That can translate the stubbornness of fortune
> Into so quiet and so sweet a style. (II. i. 18–20)

The centre of the pastoral state has passed within the mind.

So had it done in Sannazaro, or more briefly and unsubtly in certain Elizabethan lyrics; but there it had imposed a uniform state of mind. In *As You Like It*, as in *The Shepheardes Calender*, the nature-setting produces a whole range of possible reactions. This is not what is usually meant by Renaissance pastoral providing a 'landscape of the mind'. Rather, the landscape is emphatically *not* a reflection of the mind: the mind reacts to the landscape out of its own resources, producing a state of mind very different from what the landscape, directly interpreted, would induce.

Rosalind's conduct in Arden is the most striking instance of this independent development of mental resources usually linked with a nurturing pastoral milieu. The escape from court, and the assumption of disguise, allow Rosalind to give full flow to the penetrating simplicity of utterance which has always formed part of her nature, but which she can truly exercise only when free of all duties and pressures of identity.[40]

The fact that she is specifically in shepherd's (or rather forester's) disguise goes for nothing—in contrast to Lodge's Rosalynde, who often reminded Rosader of it. Lodge's heroine was immersed in the situation, balancing with excited delight her feminine, courtly nature against her male, rustic role. Shakespeare's Rosalind uses both as stepping-stones to express a much more comprehensive personality.

This free expression of her spirit comes to follow the lines traced more lightly by the conventional shepherds of *England's Helicon*. She, a woman, courts a man. She addresses the noble Orlando and the rustic Silvius with the same frankness. But, in *As You Like It*, these qualities are not inherent in the pastoral milieu; they are special to Rosalind herself. Her humorous romanticism is alien to both Phebe and Audrey. She expresses the frank confidence of courtly sophistication as well as a firm faith in her love, secure of surviving the mockery. The country mistress feels the duty of priggishness: 'I am not a slut, though I thank the gods I am foul.' (III. iii. 33–4). Yet Princess Rosalind *in propria persona* could scarcely have wooed and wed Orlando with such easy initiative: 'Come, woo me, woo me; for now I am in a holiday humour and like enough to

[40] See D. J. Palmer, '"As You Like It" and the Idea of Play', *Critical Quarterly*, 13 (1971), 242; David Young, *The Heart's Forest*, p. 57.

consent' (IV. i. 65–6). She can also express, and expel, the doubts that would have remained unaired in an orthodox courtship: 'No, no, Orlando, men are April when they woo, December when they wed. Maids are May when they are maids, but the sky changes when they are wives' (IV. i. 138–41).

Disguised in Arden, Rosalind passes beyond the necessarily restricted values of both court and country. Commentators talk of the 'spirit of Arden'. But although the forest is presented as a perceptible entity, almost a personification, it does not impose a set pattern of conduct but rather allows a secure liberty: 'Are not these woods | More free from peril than the envious court?' (II. i. 3–4); '. . . there's no clock in the forest' (III. ii. 295–6); '. . . let the forest judge' (III. ii. 119–20). The forest is gloriously unexacting, non-committal. It does not impose a pattern of events but simply, in Helen Gardner's useful phrases, 'a space in which to work things out', a 'comic space of encounters where time seems to stand still'.[41]

It is very important that there is 'no clock in the forest'. Even Touchstone's observations on his 'dial' indicate a sameness, an absence of urgency or of a meaningful sequence of events in time: 'And so from hour to hour, we ripe, and ripe . . .' (II. vii. 26). Thus the sense of *otium* is restored to the operative centre of a time-bound cyclic scheme of recovery and regeneration. The extreme importance of internal, subjective time in this play has often been pointed out.[42] As John Shaw has noted, the forest is also free of the vagaries of Fortune: that is reserved for the court, while 'the magical forest shields the contented, worthy followers of Nature',[43] and fosters virtuous relations worked out by their own inner rhythm and causality.

The paucity of action which Shakespeare inherits from Lodge (and considerably enhances, leaving out a robber-episode and a final battle) is a positive advantage here. It frees the characters from all pressures of circumstance and habitual identity, all motives dictated by external factors, so that, as Helen Gardner puts it (p. 27), 'each man finds himself and his true way'. With Oliver and Duke Frederick, this may even be a goodness unsuspected in their earlier selves: ''Twas I: but 'tis not I . . .'

[41] Helen Gardner, 'As You Like It', *More Talking about Shakespeare* (cit. Ch. 12 n. 3), pp. 22, 23.

[42] See e.g. Rawdon Wilson, 'The Way to Arden: Attitudes towards Time in *As You Like It*', *Shakespeare Quarterly*, 26 (1975), 16–24; Paul Turner, *Shakespeare and the Nature of Time* (Oxford, 1971), 29–31.

[43] John Shaw, 'Fortune and Nature in *As You Like It*', *Shakespeare Quarterly*, 6 (1955), 48.

(IV. iii. 135). In the last analysis, there *is* something benevolent—indeed providential—about the setting of the play; but this benevolence operates through inner development and states of mind rather than the physical details of the pastoral scene. Shakespeare rejects the surface minutiae of the pastoral convention in order to intensify its basic functions.

This is the full measure of Shakespeare's achievement in *As You Like It*: he has expressed *within* the terms of a pastoral work the mental processes commonly operating *behind* it. In the pastoral convention generally, the courtier creates a dream of life in nature to embody a security he cannot find at court. The harshness of the peasant's life is adapted (by himself or others) into a philosophy of reconcilement and a view of nature benevolent enough to accommodate it. In other words, the landscape and rural life are reshaped and idealized into a suitable symbolic artefact for reflecting certain states of mind, certain values held precious. Shakespeare goes behind the works and actually presents the artefact in the process of creation. He does not afford a finished pastoral landscape, but nature and rustic life much more as they are. (The fantastic touches—palms beside oaks, lions in Arden, and so on—are entirely superficial.) His characters weave their ideals and states of mind around this landscape, turning it into pastoral, as it were, by the force of their minds and personalities, directly presenting the impulses which must elsewhere be deduced from the completed work of art.

That is why a play as realistic, as remote from philosophic symbolism, as *As You Like It* is so important to an understanding of the philosophy of pastoral. There is no actual magic in Arden, but the resolution is so inexplicable in terms of the 'working-day world' that Rosalind can fitly present it to her companions as magic. That is the only possible external explanation of a mystery whose key she actually holds in her hand.

As the process of regenerative pastoral comes to be explored, it cannot but demand more heightened correlatives. Such exploration is bound to grow more explicitly philosophic, even symbolic. It will use new elements from mythology and give new meaning to old ones like the Golden Age and the earthly paradise. This is seen most clearly in *The Faerie Queene*, Book VI; but Shakespeare follows the same path. The line runs directly from *As You Like It* to *The Winter's Tale*.

The story of *The Winter's Tale*, as I said in the context of *Pandosto*, was not originally a 'pastoral cycle'. The split in the middle is avoided by Shakespeare partly by keeping Hermione alive and making her restoration the climax of the entire plot. But it is also transcended in good measure by thematic and symbolic links binding the action together.

Looking back upon the play from the final scene, we clearly see the power of romantic providence guiding the action. The speech of Time suggests this half-way through.

The very title *The Winter's Tale* evokes a seasonal motif, suggesting that the entire cycle of events is somehow parallel to the cycle of nature. The early court scenes occur in winter, the pastoral scene in summer. The older and younger generations are identified with winter and spring respectively: in Perdita's flower-speech, but also more broadly over the entire action.[44]

There is no strong network of seasonal and nature-images running through the play as we might have expected. Spurgeon failed to find any such, and relied chiefly on 'the most imaginative similes' for her sense of 'the likeness between human and natural processes and characteristics'.[45] All the same, Wilson Knight gathers an important crop of nature-images from the first three acts, including significant images of diseased or repellant nature—but all placed within 'creation's firmamental and earthly steadfastness'.[46] Act IV then provides a free and joyful celebration of this creative force, centred on the flower-speech and the art-and-nature debate.

The two halves of the play thus complement each other within a single movement, and the pastoral Act IV symbolically opens the upward turn of the action. The new complications of the plot (Polixenes' wrath, the elopement of Florizel and Perdita) are dwarfed by the relief of the passage from court to country, winter to summer, tragic jealousy to happy love; also by the strong sense of nature's bounty and fruitfulness. Even in the plot, Shakespeare replaces Dorastus's uncertain voyage with Camillo's counsel to Florizel to sail to Sicily. A happy ending seems in sight.

Wolfgang Clemen points out another interesting feature of the imagery of Act IV, in contrast to the earlier acts. Whereas the earlier imagery was a functional 'expression for thought and passion', Act IV brings in images for their own sake, 'often . . . [so] that the effect and the impression of [a] passage seems to lie solely in the imagery'.[47] In other words, the images are being used to create an independent concept of nature over and above the implications of the strict narrative.

[44] On the seasons-motif, see W. O. Scott, 'Seasons and Flowers in *The Winter's Tale*', *Shakespeare Quarterly*, 14 (1963), 411–17; E. Schanzer, 'The Structural Pattern of "The Winter's Tale"', *REL* 5 (1964), 72–82.

[45] Caroline Spurgeon, *Shakespeare's Imagery* (Cambridge, 1935; repr. 1971), 306.

[46] G. Wilson Knight, *The Crown of Life* (1947; repr. London, 1982), 89.

[47] Wolfgang Clemen, *The Development of Shakespeare's Imagery* (2nd edn. London, 1977), 196.

Though Paulina talks earlier of 'good goddess Nature' (II. iii. 103),[48] this mythic figure is absent from the pastoral scene. Though it contains some of Shakespeare's best descriptions of flowers, scenes, and seasons, it presents 'great creating nature' as an abstract or transcendent force, almost a philosophic entity. The pastoral setting becomes the symbol of this force—and, more particularly, of its promise of benevolent fulfilment.

This sense of nature as a marked, positive force—indeed a controlling one—is a major point of difference from *As You Like It*. With it goes another, the alliance between nature and man. In *As You Like It* the forest setting was physically a source of adversity. There were suggestions of a seasonal cycle, but the action followed the rhythm of human relations. Pastoralism in a narrow sense—the keeping of sheep, life in a rustic community—was a minor factor.

In *The Winter's Tale*, on the other hand, the shepherds' lives are ordered by a largely benevolent nature. Their lives can thus be pastoral in a much more obvious way. We see them on holiday, but they clearly keep sheep and form a viable rustic community, reliant on the fostering power of nature.

Shakespeare's treatment of nature in *The Winter's Tale* is simultaneously direct, literal—as an actual beneficent life-force—and symbolic, as the correlative of an idealized pattern of human life. In the latter function, it corresponds to the traditional pastoral landscape. But because it has the former function too, it gives the landscape and pastoral life a unique philosophic charge, invests it with meanings that conventional pastoral knows nothing of.

Perdita herself is emphatically presented as the child of nature, the subject of this controlling force. She is dressed as Flora; she distributes flowers appropriate (as far as possible) to the various seasons, linked to the stages of a man's life. As Wilson Knight points out (p. 106), the Proserpina allusion highlights the seasonal theme, making the flower-description more than the incidental topos of the standard eclogue. Various references link Perdita to all times of the year: April, January, Whitsuntide,[49] as well as June, when presumably the shearing-supper would be held.[50] In the argument with Polixenes, she takes the side of nature.

[48] All refs. to the New Arden edn. by J. H. P. Pafford (London, 1963; repr. 1968).

[49] IV. iv. 3, 111, and 134 respectively.

[50] Tusser includes sheep-shearing in 'Junes Husbandrie': see *Five Hundred Points of Good Husbandry*, ed. Geoffrey Grigson (Oxford, 1984), 110. See also Appendix B, n. 17.

As with Spenser's Pastorella, Perdita's royal origin presents a problem: a superiority of spirit inseparable from her lowly pastoral milieu yet contrary to its premisses. Perdita's superiority, however, expresses itself in spontaneous identification with nature. The force of nature controls the entire action, though it appears with special clarity in the pastoral scene. This is reflected in Perdita, a product of the highest generative discrimination of that force.

The aristocratic foundling intensifies and perfects within herself the spirit of pastoral life. At the same time, pastoral life provides—and it alone could provide—a fostering medium for Perdita's spirit. She provides the pastoral setting with the human qualities with which it can interact to their mutual perfection. Significantly, her latent royalty of spirit reveals itself in defending the shepherd's state:

> I was not much afeard; for once or twice
> I was about to speak, and tell him plainly,
> The self-same sun that shines upon his court
> Hides not his visage from our cottage, but
> Looks on alike. (IV. iv. 443–7)

It is a spirit that can accommodate itself to any human state.

Though the pastoral in *The Winter's Tale* is dominated by the presence of nature, it also implies strong spiritual qualities in man. This is suggested early in the play in Polixenes' celebrated speech on his and Leontes' boyhood, 'as twinn'd lambs that did frisk i' th' sun':

> What we chang'd
> Was innocence for innocence; we knew not
> The doctrine of ill-doing, nor dream'd
> That any did. Had we pursu'd that life,
> And our weak spirits ne'er been higher rear'd
> With stronger blood, we should have answer'd heaven
> Boldly 'not guilty', the imposition clear'd
> Hereditary ours. (I. ii. 67–75)

The state of innocence is expressed in pastoral terms. The pastoral of Act IV, functioning in the plot as a restoration of life, indicates a new birth of innocence as well. The pastoral setting takes on a paradisal significance.

This is nowhere overtly stressed, and there are apparent arguments against it. Because of the seasonal imagery, the pastoral operates undeniably in time. (There was said to be eternal spring in paradise.) Perdita even evokes Fortune at one point (IV. iv. 51). But the various seasons are conjured within a single scene, and largely through the single figure of Perdita.

> the year growing ancient,
> Not yet on summer's death nor on the birth
> Of trembling winter . . . (IV. iv. 79–81)

The controlling force of nature behind the *entire* action emerges in this scene with unusual vividness. The scene thus takes on a symbolic function at a level higher than the rest of the action. The force of nature appears perfect and inviolate, beyond the local turns and changes of the plot.[51] Spenser actually places an inviolable symbolic centre, Mount Acidale, in the middle of his orthodox time-bound pastoral landscape. Shakespeare has none such, but he invests the setting with a similar sense of unchanging spiritual power.

It is in this spiritual dimension to the pastoral that *The Winter's Tale* marks an advance over *Cymbeline*, where the same pattern appears in a more rudimentary way. Already in *Cymbeline* we have two princes brought up in a natural retreat. Their sister, in male disguise, finds shelter there from an unfriendly court, apparently dies, and is 'brought to life' again in a burial-and-rebirth sequence charged with vegetation imagery. Finally, the princes return to court in a triumphant assertion of their martial spirit. Unlike Perdita, they had found their life in nature cramping and uncongenial, and there was no explicit sense of the power of nature.

The Tempest comes after *The Winter's Tale* and goes beyond it. The themes that Shakespeare had hitherto barely contained within natural and pastoral settings here find expression in the openly supernatural: or, to be more accurate, in 'natural magic', the literal assumption of the latent power of nature suggested philosophically in the *Tale*. *The Tempest* is too far removed from conventional pastoral to be treated here; but it develops the same pattern, and is treated by David Young, in *The Heart's Forest*, as a pastoral play.

The presence of Shakespeare's work alters the entire perspective of English Renaissance drama. The more conventional Italianate plays appearing alongside them become part of a larger conception of the pastoral. Standard pastoral mythopoeia is seen as an adjunct to Shakespeare's philosophic patterns, the usual love-tangles as a more commonplace exploitation of the potential realized in *As You Like It*.

[51] See Young, *The Heart's Forest*, pp. 136–7.

And, Shakespeare apart, the various lines of rustic drama provide a much more broad-based body of work, with many alternative traditions to the Italianate one.

3. *Jacobean and Caroline drama*

Elizabeth's reign had seen very little drama that was formally pastoral; there is a great deal under her successors. Much of it is of indifferent quality: the orthodox pastoral proves less stimulating than its combinations and transformations in the earlier reign. The Italian element is much more pronounced, though an Englishness of tone appears in Randolph's *Amyntas*, and of setting as well in Jonson's *The Sad Shepherd*. This later body of drama is also more courtly in spirit. Virtually all the plays were acted before the King, and many were composed for that purpose.

It is often hard to draw the line between pastoral drama and pastoral masque. Daniel's *The Queen's Arcadia* was composed as a court entertainment, as the title indicates;[52] and the love-tangles of the plot are schematized to suit the quasi-allegoric theme. Yet this very theme requires the creation of an autonomous, romantic pastoral world.

This Arcadia, with its sentimental shepherd-lovers and nymphs, recalls Italian drama, *Aminta* in particular: Carinus saves Cloris from a satyr, Palaemon the frustrated lover goes to throw himself from a rock.[53] Yet it is an English Arcadia, land of the rustic who

> Knowes but to keepe his sheepe, and set his fold,
> Pipe on an Oaten Reede some Rundelayes,
> And daunce a Morrice on the holy dayes.[54]

This world is invaded by a band of city-bred rogues. Their anti-pastoral evil can take on a highly contemporary guise, as in the dialogue in III. i between Alcon the quacksalver and Lincus the pettifogger. Alcon has even introduced tobacco into Arcadia! There is also Pistophoenax, a religious agitator. Such explicit social satire is rare in pastoral plays.

[52] The title refers primarily to the Queen of Arcadia in the play; but there is surely a simultaneous reference to James's Queen, before whom it was acted in 1605.

[53] Greg, *Pastoral*, pp. 253–5, and Violet M. Jeffery, 'Italian and English Pastoral Drama of the Renaissance, III: Sources of Daniel's "Queen's Arcadia" and Randolph's "Amyntas"', *MLR* 19 (1924), 436–40, also note parallels from *Il pastor fido* and *Il pentimento amoroso*.

[54] II. ii: 650–2; all refs. for *The Queen's Arcadia* and *Hymen's Triumph* to Daniel's *Complete Works in Verse and Prose*, ed. A. B. Grosart (London, 1885), iii.

The court–country contrast is made pointedly ethical, and at the same time topical, not by allegorizing pastoral metaphor but by incorporating such issues into a pastoral fantasy. Hence, in a deeper sense too, this Arcadia is England, with new fangled threats to its happy insularity: 'shut vp here | Within these Rockes, these vn-frequented Clifts' (v. iii: 2202–3). That the threats should be defeated is an article of the romanticized patriotism of this entertainment for the Queen.

In other words, the topical satire paradoxically demands the contrasted setting of a removed world of the imagination, a survival of the Golden Age (l. 1031), 'An euerlasting holy day of rest, | Whiles others worke' (III. i: 1035–6). It may seem to us, however, that this Arcadia is threatened not by the presence of the actual, but by its simplistic and trivialized presence. The countering pastoral ideal seems too lightly won. It was left to Drayton much later, in his opposition of Elizium and Felicia, to intensify this conflict effectively.

In Daniel's other pastoral play, *Hymen's Triumph* (acted in 1614 as a royal entertainment at the marriage of the Earl of Roxburgh), the pastoral setting is largely ignored. Daniel borrows from Italianate drama its complicated tangle of love-intrigue, with a wider romantic perspective in Silvia's encounter with pirates. But the specifically pastoral touches are few and largely formal. There are one or two vividly realized instances of the Petrarchan lover's nature-retreat (ll. 1346ff., 1421ff.) and at least one eulogy of an Arcadian Golden Age—now, alas, threatened by avarice (ll. 507ff.). We touch lightly here upon the satiric concerns of *The Queen's Arcadia*. These are also implicit in a marked opposition of shepherds and foresters, whereby the former become (for the latter at least) a suspect upper class, 'vnsinowed amorous heardsmen' (l. 478): a curious indictment of pastoral Petrarchism within a work composed in that very spirit.

But all this does not add up to very much. Action, intrigue, and disguise overshadow all concern with setting and spirit. The locale is formally pastoral, it seems, only to introduce a nondescript romantic remoteness and a free play of narrative fancy. It is worth noting that the songs between the acts have no pastoral matter, nor the naïve delight that the Elizabethan lyric had taught us to admit as pastoral in spirit. Instead, they savour of the lightweight but finished urbanity of the Jacobean pastoral lyric. This indeed is generally true of the songs in these later pastoral plays—in contrast to, say, the Elizabethan romance, where the songs had played a leading part in setting the pastoral tone.

Greg is right in holding *Hymen's Triumph* to be a better play than *The Queen's Arcadia*; but its specific contribution to pastoralism is small.

This places it curiously at variance with the play to which Daniel's Italianate pastorals may seem most closely allied: Fletcher's *The Faithful Shepherdess*,[55] unsuccessfully produced at Blackfriars *c.*1608 and then with applause at Somerset House on Twelfth Night 1633. In this play, Italianate refinement reaches its height in English drama. But it is best defined by beginning with the non-Italianate features. Critics have noted some important parallels with Shakespeare, especially the supernaturalism and 'wood of errors' plot of *A Midsummer Night's Dream*.[56] What seems to have passed without note is the parallel with *As You Like It* in the patterned disposition of the plot, several pairs of lovers graded according to their concepts and ethics of love. This is not a a superficial structural point, for the use of such conceptual distinctions as a formal principle exceeds anything in Italian pastoral drama. The nearest precedent is in *Il pastor fido*; but there we have contrasts of character rather than pronounced ethical stands. Greg rightly holds (pp. 269–70) that Fletcher's characters are not formal allegoric figures; but there is much ethical type-casting. Only Amarillis shows an authentic complexity of character.

The ethical frame of reference is related to Fletcher's concern with chastity. The power of chastity magically controls Clorin's already magical nostrums; further, it is the dominant component in the religion of Pan, though not (as many readers have noted)[57] in Pan's own practice. It enters as a force into the very setting, the 'holy wood' and 'vertuous Well' that 'coole looser flames'.[58] The distinction between chaste love and varieties of lust or passion is the running theme of the play: chastity is important as an abstract concern distinct from its embodiment in

[55] In *Hymen's Triumph*, Daniel may have been consciously influenced by Beaumont and Fletcher's tragicomic models: *The Faithful Shepherdess*, with its important prefatory remarks on the subject, had appeared some four years previously. Daniel's heroine Silvia tells the tale of Isulia, a thinly veiled version of her own story, in response to a plea for a tale neither merry nor too sad, 'But mixed, like the tragicke Comedies' (l. 1469).

[56] L. B. Wallis, *Fletcher, Beaumont and Company* (Morningside Heights, 1947), 187; Lerner, *The Uses of Nostalgia*, pp. 88, 90; Lee Bliss, 'Defending Fletcher's Shepherds', *SEL* 23 (1983), 298; and in greatest detail, D. M. McKeithan, *The Debt to Shakespeare in the Beaumont-and-Fletcher Plays* (1938; repr. New York, 1970), 86–100.

[57] e.g., Clifford Leech, *The John Fletcher Plays* (London, 1962), 43; Lerner, p. 91.

[58] See I. ii. 100–19. All refs. to *The Dramatic Works in the Beaumont and Fletcher Canon*, gen. ed. F. Bowers. *The Faithful Shepherdess*, ed. Cyrus Hoy, is in vol. iii (Cambridge, 1976).

particular characters.[59] It expands near the end into a wider moral and ethical ideal: Clorin exhorts the priest of Pan to

teach them how to cleare
The tedeous way they passe through, from suspect:
Keepe them from wrong in others, or neglect
Of duety in them selves; correct the bloud,
With thrifty bitts and laboure . . . (v. v. 169–73)

These ideas are echoed in the priest's reply and the final Hymn to Pan (v. v. 194ff.). Chastity becomes a formal symbol of the purifying of experience that constitutes a basic function of pastoral. Concern for chastity guides the total life of this shepherd community, entails a select, ordered, almost rigid response to the endlessly sensuous substance of its way of life. Italian pastoral drama at its best evinces a subtlety and refinement of perception, a play of philosophic forces and concepts around a delicately complex set of love-relations; seldom, to my knowledge, is there such clear and crucial reliance on a well-defined moral issue. *Il pastor fido*—at least as interpreted by Guarini in his apologetics—provides a partial exception.[60] But, broadly speaking, Fletcher's practice can be seen as a characteristically English modification—perhaps an unsubtilizing—of Italianate pastoral.[61]

Viewed in a truer perspective, however, this moral element in turn is shaped and transformed by an Italianate spirit. In the cross-play of love-tangles, poetic justice, and supernatural interventions, chastity itself becomes an aesthetic rather than a moral principle, a criterion for the sympathetic selection and romantic reward of chosen characters as in any comedy. Such naïvely romanticized morality simply withdraws us into a Never Never Land, embodying the reductive tendency in the pastoral simplification of experience. Our engagement with moral and philosophic issues, as with rustic life, is subsumed by an opposite-tending, fantasized counterpart of itself.[62] Finally, we are led furtively

[59] Bliss (pp. 298ff.) gives a clear account of the structural contrast of these versions of chastity, love, and lust, showing how Fletcher exchanges Guarini's concern with fate and romantic providence for a more 'humanist orientation'. Bliss rather overlooks the supra-human, abstract power of certain moral values in this play.

[60] See Toliver, *Pastoral Forms and Attitudes*, pp. 29–30.

[61] It is seen as such by Violet M. Jeffery, 'Italian Influence in Fletcher's "Faithful Shepherdess"', *MLR* 21 (1926), 150–1.

[62] Danby (pp. 42–4), and more forcefully Lerner (pp. 88–91), would see the opposition in unhappier terms of contradiction and inconsistency. It seems to me that, in his precarious and fragile way, Fletcher succeeds in synthesizing the opposites, as—no doubt frivolously—they often are synthesized in pastoral. Cf. also the more sympathetic account of the duality in Bliss, pp. 300–1.

back to a sanctified and holy sensuousness. The *locus amoenus* to which the light-of-love Cloe tempts Thenot (I. iii. 26 ff.) is not so different from the general setting of the play: and this is the keynote for the poise between spiritual and aesthetic, or even sensual, all through.[63] Clorin and Thenot invoke a hard primitivism even in this setting; but the governing force in each case is love, and Clorin's chastity is scarcely separate in appeal from her beauty, whether to Thenot, Alexis, or the satyr.

The supernatural and divine elements must also be viewed in this light. The chastity of the play has nothing Christian about it, barring a single reference to Heaven's blessings (V. V. 192). That Pan should be its improbable patron indicates the rootlessness of Fletcher's pleasing myth. The pattern of reforms and rescues worked by Clorin's herbs and the satyr's errands takes on the fluidity and ephemerality of the amoral tangles of *A Midsummer Night's Dream*. 'Truth . . . | . . . I charme thee from this place' (III. i. 27–8) says the Sullen Shepherd as he transforms Amarillis into Amoret's shape.

The moral purpose declaredly guiding the play becomes in effect a vehicle of free fancy, the instrument of a pleasurable poetic justice. The unusually virtuous satyr[64] makes an attractive attendant figure, but robs the play of the moral depth and contrast that a supernaturally evil creature would have supplied. Such vicious characters as exist—the Sullen Shepherd, Cloe to an extent, Alexis and Amarillis but slightly—are fitted into a balanced and symmetrical plot, their every move countered immediately by often supernatural forces. From the outset, their lusts and conspiracies are bounded by a reassuring frame of romantic excitement.

Yet, as Greg noted long ago,[65] nothing is actually worked out in the course of the plot. The Sullen Shepherd is banished at the end, but otherwise the characters remain exactly where they began. The impulse to effective action has disappeared. The unvirtuous characters want active satisfaction for their lust, but otherwise the lovers (and Clorin the bereaved lover) seek their end in the perfection of a mood, a state of suspension, like the lovers on Keats's urn. Longings, deprivations, even promised requital or satisfaction remain innocent by remaining unfulfilled. Hence too we sense a wistfulness, as of creatures clinging to their set veins of love in a world that offers no value or support outside

[63] Cf. the general remarks on the pastoral interaction of sensuality and innocence in Ettin, pp. 150–1; and Lerner's discussion of Italian drama from this angle (pp. 83–7).

[64] Though not without precedent in Italian drama: see Jeffery, *MLR* 21 (1926), 148–9.

[65] Greg, *Pastoral*, pp. 268–9. Wallis disagrees (p. 188), but not very convincingly.

the formal chastity vowed to Pan. This static, stylized, unrealized emotion is quintessentially the product of art. Here drama deliberately forgoes its mobility and complexity (despite the intricate symmetry of the plot) for the unchallenging stasis of the masque or a kind of long dramatized lyric. Swinburne aptly describes the work as 'a lyric poem in semi-dramatic shape'.[66]

The Faithful Shepherdess marks the final point of development of one line of pastoral drama. What in Daniel was a vein of courtly compliment deepening into entertaining dramatized narrative, is intensified by Fletcher into an independent, self-contained world of art. This is perhaps the ultimate end of the pastoral imagination; and when as fully realized as in *The Faithful Shepherdess*, we see clearly how it requires a form inimical to the truly dramatic. At the same time, it is too utterly devoid of the popular or native elements demanded of pastoral drama by contemporary audiences. Though in some ways the purest product of dramatic pastoral in England, Fletcher's play marks a closed road ahead.

The road actually taken appears after a gap of some two decades, bridged only by one or two minor works. James Shirley's first play, *Love Tricks: or the School of Compliment* (February 1625), has a pastoral sequence. A number of characters enter the shepherd world—sometimes in uncalled-for sex-disguise—as a respite from frustrated love or escape from an unwanted match. But this is done casually, mechanically, out of a kind of inertia of narrative tradition: it is a set recourse for the lovesick. Equally routine are the brief depictions of pastoral peace and innocence (IV. ii, pp. 64–6),[67] shepherds' interest in matters of love (IV. ii, p. 66), magic remedies (IV. ii, p. 69; V. i, pp. 77–8), and 'pastoral religion' and the Feast of Pan (V. iii, pp. 91–2). Towards the end, a number of characters are simply called to the country by a shepherd (V. ii, p. 86) without forewarning or dramatic preparation. The reconciling 'pastoral cycle' has been reduced to a stereotype.

The play is not without points of interest, like the unexpected ironic counterpoint provided by the comic servant Gorgon masquerading as a shepherdess. But all in all, it constitutes a tired, conventional use of pastoral—the more tellingly so in being a young dramatist's first work.

Thomas Goffe's *The Careles Shepherdess* (*c*.1625–9; printed 1656)

[66] A. C. Swinburne, 'Beaumont and Fletcher', *Studies in Prose and Poetry* (London, 1894), 77. Cf. Orie Latham Hatcher, *John Fletcher: A Study in Dramatic Method* (Chicago, 1905), 30–1, and Freda L. Townsend, 'Ben Jonson's "Censure" of Rutter's *Shepheards Holy-Day*', *MP* 44 (1946), 241–2.

[67] All refs. to Shirley's *Dramatic Works*, ed. A. Dyce (London, 1833), i.

has a few striking passages exemplifying the theme of pastoral purity and innocence. The hero Philaretus (who is not a shepherd) says of Arismena (who is):

> Can she be base, whom Nature
> Hath grac'd with all perfections of the first
> Creation? I tell you Sir, were all
> As she, *Pandora* should receive her ills
> Into her Box again, and man as at
> The first, should be exempted from a fear
> Of death.[68]

But the difference of origin between hero and heroine provides nothing more than a petulant exchange between their parents. Indeed, the dramatist seems scarcely aware of the implications of any of his themes. We are presented with a love-tangle of indifferent interest and many loose ends. The only sustained motif at all akin to pastoral is the conflict between humans and satyrs, and even the latter include humans so disguised. The songs are chiefly refined lyrics of no bucolic content; only one[69] shows a simple gaiety reminiscent of Elizabethan pastoral lyrics, and this, tellingly, is sung by the servant Graculus.

In the early 1630s we again find a considerable body of formal pastoral drama. Among them is a notable attempt to blend Italianate pastoral with standard English comedy in Thomas Randolph's *Amyntas; or The Impossible Dowry* (acted *c.*1633–4 before the King and Queen at Whitehall).[70] I have little to add to Greg's perceptive account of this fusion of traditions (Greg, pp. 283, 286–90). Specific parallels with Italian drama have been pointed out by V. M. Jeffery.[71] Greg has drawn special attention to the humour and burlesque that enleavens the romantic tone, injecting unusual realism and good sense into the closed world of pastoral Petrarchism. The reluctant, self-deprecating love of the aging Thestylis balances the stock amours of Laurinda and Amaryllis, Damon, Alexis, and Amyntas; yet Thestylis is sensitive and sympathetic to the young lovers, Amaryllis in particular. Laurinda herself shows a witty, Rosalind-like irony in discussing her love; and there is something genially comic in the clash between the impulses of friendship and rivalry in her two lovers, Damon and Alexis.

[68] All refs. to *The Careles Shepherdess. A Tragi-Comedy . . . Written by T. G. Mr. of Arts* (London, 1656). This passage is from I. iii, p. 16.

[69] p. 44. There is some pastoral admixture in Sylvia's song, p. 23.

[70] I have used Randolph's *Poems and Amyntas*, ed. J. J. Parry.

[71] 'Sources of Daniel's "Queen's Arcadia" and Randolph's "Amyntas"', pp. 442–4.

The characters of the underplot acquire unusual importance, particularly in the way they set the comic and ironic tone of the play through extensive appearances at the outset. Mopsus's love, and Iocastus's follies as a parallel to Amyntas' own madness, serve the typical parodic function of the subplot in English Renaissance drama. Above all, the fake orchard-robbing 'fairies' led by the mischievous page Dorylas debunk the supernaturalism of the main plot through bold counterpoint. By these sharp contrasts and variety of tones, the formal structure of Italian pastoral drama is modified to suit the multi-noted English comedy. We are scarcely surprised to be regaled, at the end of this Sicilian play, with a morris dance featuring Maid Marian and the Clown.

However, this is the only clear note of English rustic life in the play. Conventional references to shepherd life are also surprisingly few. This points to a self-defeating quality in Randolph's attempt at anglicizing Italianate pastoral. He thereby robs the play of the unified atmosphere, stylized setting, and patterned, aesthetically oriented way of life that, however prone to artificiality or trivialization, was the vital principle of such pastoral. In other words, we are deprived of the actual pastoralism: what remains is the external framework of intrigue, adventure, and supernatural wonders that such pastoral had adopted—in potential self-destruction—to lend it dramatic body for the stage. The pastoral setting threatens to become a mere formal convenience to permit a greater than usual intervention of the sentimental, exotic, or supernatural.

The Faithful Shepherdess had preserved a quintessential pastoralism at a certain cost to its nature as drama. *Amyntas* affirms the dramatic potential of pastoral—but in the process depletes its pastoral content and spirit. The process is repeated in most contemporary plays without Randolph's quickening wit and realism. We obtain more and less attractive versions of Italianate romance, action, and intrigue, commonly outshining pastoral setting and atmosphere. There is a plethora of oracles, turning the reader's mind to suspense and puzzle-solving rather than to setting and situation. Pastoral drama is being assimilated more and more closely to general comedy. Its pastoral content becomes 'given', axiomatic, unserious—a process already noted in Shirley's *Love Tricks*.

This atrophy of the pastoral is apparent in John Tatham's *Love Crowns the End*, acted in 1632 by the schoolchildren of Bingham, Nottinghamshire, and printed in *The Fancies Theater* (1640). It is an almost cryptically compressed version of the standard pastoral love-plot of 'cross-eyed Cupid'. There are good and bad shepherds, pursued and pursuant nymphs; a 'lustful shepherd' who disguises himself as a satyr; a 'Lovers Valley'; and a hermitage where the wise shepherdess Claudia cures a remarkable number of characters deranged by love. We can discern a faintly sketched 'cyclic' movement from court to country and back again, as well as a certain amount of pastoral detail and the familiar spirit of idealized shepherd life. The notional influence of *The Faithful Shepherdess* is particularly obvious. But it is all hurried, uninspired, hustled together, a sequence of scenes that do no more than recall for readers the jaded possibilities of the pastoral romance plot.

Even this vestigial pastoralism is missing from *Love in It's Extasie*, ascribed to William Peaps, printed in 1649 but 'written long since'. Described on the title-page as 'A kind of Royall Pastorall', its royal and noble characters make their way variously to the woods in shepherd's guise. But, barring two or three perfunctory expressions of pastoral content, there is absolutely no reference to the setting or to shepherd life. One must search hard even to find the word 'shepherd'. To such sketchy and mechanical rituals has the 'cyclic' plot of pastoral been reduced.

One play which does remain vividly pastoral, despite a fair share of oracles, adventures, and intrigue, is Joseph Rutter's *The Shepherds' Holiday* (printed 1635). Inferior to Randolph's *Amyntas* in literary merit, it shows a more pleasing and genuine interest in the pastoral. This is partly due to a clear-cut two-tier plot: at one level, genuine shepherd-lovers such as Nerina, Hylas, and Daphnis; at another, a supposed princess disguised as a shepherdess and a shepherd who proves to be a prince. The authentic shepherds can thus keep clear of intrigue and oracles, while the 'royal' characters are intimately linked to the pastoral setting. This means, however, that the autonomy of the shepherd world is lost. In *The Faithful Shepherdess*, or even *Amyntas*, all the characters were shepherds or rustics.

Rutter creates a sustained presence of nature, shepherd life, sylvan myth, and 'pastoral religion'. He even shows some awareness of the common thematic or philosophic implications of a pastoral setting. Near the outset, he presents a suitably moralized version of the libertine 'Golden Age' familiar from Tasso's chorus: it now marks the triumph of monogamous true love:

> Pure, uncompounded love—that could despise
> The whole world's riches for a mistress' eyes.[72]

[72] Refs. to Dodsley's *A Select Collection of Old English Plays*, 4th edn. by W. Carew Hazlitt (London, 1875), xii. This quotation is from I. iv, p. 378.

Ironically, this is spoken by Mirtillus the would-be libertine. But the sense of liberty merges quite seriously with the theme of innocence and chaste love that runs through the play, even to the point of affectation. In the Prologue, the author proclaims his own Muse to be 'virgin' and 'innocent', while the Epilogue to the King and Queen fears lest these patrons of 'chaste innocuous sports' should have been offended even by such blameless fare.

Rutter also touches on the theme of noble birth versus noble conduct. Sylvia sees true nobility to reside in the latter, the gift of Nature even if Fortune does not concur (pp. 416–17). When first she saw Thyrsis, she observed in him 'such civility and friendship, | As one would little look for of a shepherd' (III. i, p. 397). But Thyrsis is really a prince, embodying the common ambiguity of all such royal shepherd-figures. *The Shepherds' Holiday* touches, fleetingly but tellingly, on all the basic themes of pastoral romance and drama; and supports this with a conventional but genuine delight in idealized shepherd life.

This can also be said of Abraham Cowley's youthful work, *Love's Riddle* (composed 1634–5). The plot is a text-book illustration of the 'cross-eyed Cupid' situation, brought about by the heroine Callidora's male disguise and resolved by her casting it off. There is an almost laboured pairing-off of four pairs of lovers, falling (as in Rutter's play) into two groups. The larger consists of noble characters, wittingly or unwittingly transformed into shepherds; and their fortunes involve lost children, piracies, and seductions—a wide sweep of romantic action. The genuine rustics are again reduced to subplot status.

The thematic possibilities of such parallel and contrast, whether between individual couples or classes, are brought out to some extent. Court and country values can be critically contrasted, as where the merry shepherd-clown Alupis fears 'some ragges of the Court fashions | Visibly creeping now into the woods' (Act II, p. 87; cf. pp. 72 ff., 98 ff.).[73] Yet he satirizes shepherd life and loves as well, and rejects marriage even as he joins in the final merrymaking. Callidora's equivocal response to pastoral life is more deeply ambiguous. She prizes pastoral peace and content, in terms suggesting a 'pastoral purification' of other modes of experience: the shepherd sits upon

> His rurall throne, arm'd with his crooke, his scepter,
> A flowry garland is his country crowne;
>
> . . . .

[73] All refs. to Cowley's *English Works*, ed. A. R. Waller, ii.

> Thus in an humble statelinesse and majestie
> He turns his pipe, the woods best melody,
> And is at once, what many Monarches are not,
> Both King and Poet.

But Callidora is really of noble birth, like her lover Philistus; and thoughts of him arouse her to a higher love and aristocratic values; then

> The woods seeme base, and all their harmlesse pleasures
> The daughters of necessity, not vertue. (Act II, p. 89)

Philistus too regrets the appearance of 'Court, and Citie follies' (Act V, p. 135) in shepherds—who are not really such. Bellula, the nobleman's daughter brought up among shepherds, is praised by Florellus as being too beautiful for a shepherdess (Act III, p. 101). Yet she only wishes to marry 'some plaine vertuous shepheard', and Florellus wishes to be one for her sake.

Every now and then, the play evokes tensions and ambiguities of response, touching upon the deeper concerns of pastoral. Yet these seem half-unwitting, engendered by the terms of the standard pastoral paradigm. We cannot credit the young author with any searching critique of the mode, merely a competent exercise in a pleasing convention.

William Montague's *The Shepheard's Paradise* is neither pleasing nor competent. It was acted in 1632–3, with Henrietta Maria in the heroine's role. It is a tedious work in unreadably turgid prose, which makes the plot more incomprehensible than ever. But the controlling concept demands attention as a very inept but very clear expression of certain deeper themes of pastoral.

Montague's lovers congregate in an intensified pastoral setting, the Shepherd's Paradise. This is 'a heavenly Institution that extends it selfe to all strangers, whose births are such, as may be worthy fortunes prosecution, and the distresse seeme so desperate as it may bring honor to the remedy' (Act I, p. 15).[74] First and foremost, then, this paradise is exclusively for aristocrats. Secondly, it is for those crossed in love; questions of love—of a sentimentally Platonic bent—are debated before a Queen elected each May Day, chiefly on the basis of her beauty. We are reminded partly of the medieval courts of love, partly of the more varied courtiership of the Renaissance; partly too of religious orders with their

[74] All refs. to *The Shepheard's Paradise. A Comedy* (London, 1659).

set rituals and observances, which have curious parallels in the practices of this community.

It is significant that Montague gives his setting a pastoral cast, though its inhabitants would clearly not recognize a sheep if they saw one. The play is totally devoid of rustic characters and details of shepherd life. But the subtler thematic concomitants of the 'cyclic' pastoral plot are, as it were, distilled into an insubstantial, delicately abstract fantasy. It indicates a perceptive reading of the tradition, though it is Montague's failure that the imaginative escape should be so remote and unviable, a pedantic Platonist's parody of *As You Like It*.

Royalty and noblemen gather in disguise in the Shepherd's Paradise. They hold all possessions in common, and have endless leisure to discourse of the philosophically pure and innocent love we have learnt to associate with pastoral. Belleza the heroine (actually the Princess Saphira) addresses the trees in the copse called 'Love's Cabinet' as emblems of this purified eroticism: 'your so pure innocence as ill can ne're come so neere, as to be withstood. For in your veine runneth water instead of blood' (Act V, p. 134). There are many wearisome debates on the nature of love. Not surprisingly, these languid votaries of love learn, as Belleza puts it, to measure time 'with your soul, not your sense' (Act II, p. 40), just as the radiant lovers of *As You Like It* had done.

It is a far cry from *The Shepheards Paradise* to *The Sad Shepherd*, though Jonson's unfinished play is probably later only by a year or two. Here at last is an original attempt at true pastoral in dramatic form. The Italianate element has been sharply reduced. Indeed, it inheres in the single figure of Aeglamour, the sad shepherd himself, with his Petrarchan melancholy for a supposedly dead mistress. Perhaps we should add Amie's lovesickness, though this is treated with a robust dose of *double entendre*. In other words, stock pastoral love and sentiment are reduced—as in *As You Like It* in a different way—to one among many elements, no longer the dramatic continuum. The Prologue decries the fashion for banishing mirth from pastoral, and argues

> whence can sport in kind arise,
> But from the Rurall Routs and Families?
> Safe on this ground then, wee not feare to day,
> To tempt your laughter by our rustick *Play*.[75]

[75] ll. 35–8; all refs. to Jonson's *Works*, ed. C. H. Herford and P. and E. Simpson, vol. vii (Oxford, 1941; repr. 1970).

Clearly, Jonson intends to modify Italianate traditions. He will weave the wool of 'meere [i.e. pure] *English* Flocks', 'it being a Fleece, | To match, or those of *Sicily*, or *Greece*' (ll. 9–14). To what extent does this constitute a new vein of pastoral, as opposed to a mere transfer of locale?

The picture of shepherd life is full of conventional details. The shepherds are masters of their flocks, not hirelings (II. v. 15), and Alken is the 'wise shepherd' of convention. At the same time, he is cast in a typically English mould, like Spenser or Drayton's shepherds. At least one detail, the prize for the earliest-born lamb, is directly out of Drayton (Eclogue IX of 1606). Others are poeticized versions of actual folk-customs, reminiscent of Spenser's 'Maye' eclogue:

> to awake
> The nimble Horne-pipe, and the Timburine,
> And mixe our Songs, and Dances in the Wood,
> And each of us cut downe a Triumph-bough? (I. iv. 13–16)

But reversing Spenser's sympathies, Jonson makes this the prelude to bitter satire of the Puritans who would ban such gaiety. One is reminded of the anti-Puritan strain in Drayton's pastorals, as more pronouncedly in the *Annalia Dubrensia* (1636), a collection of poems relating to the Cotswold Games revived by Captain Robert Dover around 1604.[76] Jonson castigates the Puritans not only as killjoys but as hypocrites and exploiters of society:

> Would they, wise *Clarion*, were not hurried more
> With Covetise and Rage, when to their store
> They adde the poore mans Eaneling, and dare sell
> Both Fleece, and Carkasse, not gi'ing him the Fell. (I. iv. 22–5)

We return fleetingly to the world of Barclay's Eclogues, or even the Wakefield Second Shepherds' Play. Jonson is taking pains, almost gratuitously, to link his pastoral to contemporary reality—especially no doubt to the Puritan opposition to the theatre, which lends an unexpected touch of allegory to the fable.

This realistic note is linked to the English orientation of the pastoral. The specifically English touches in Jonson's shepherd life are reinforced by non-pastoral legend and folk practices. First among these, of course, is the Robin Hood story, featured in the very subtitle, 'A Tale of Robin-

[76] See T. P. Harrison, 'Jonson's *Sad Shepherd* and Spenser', *MLN* 58 (1948), 260. Harrison cites Greg's edn. of *The Sad Shepherd* in vol. xi of Bang's *Materialien zur Kunde des älteren Englischen Dramas* (Louvain, 1905). See also Greg, *Pastoral*, p. 408.

Hood'. The recurrent connection between Robin Hood and the pastoral here achieves its most integrated form. Robin appears as the friend and protector of shepherds. His feast is virtually a shearing-supper:

> My friends and neighbours, to the Jolly Bower
> Of *Robin-hood*, and to the greene-wood Walkes:
> Now that the shearing of your sheepe is done,
> And the Wash'd Flocks are lighted of their wooll . . . (I. iv. 3–6)

Robin's huntsmen are courteous to the wise shepherd Alken. George-a-Greene, another rural hero (and leading figure in an Elizabethan play) provides a subsidiary motif. The pastoral ideal is reinforced by rustic myths and values of stronger native currency.

Yet these latter can end up by submerging the pastoral. *The Sad Shepherd* does not quite escape the danger. The foresters' life, of course, is conventionally if paradoxically allied to the shepherd's, and Jonson blends the two with particular skill. But the play's structure is radically changed by the presence of a third strand, the magical. Magic and witchcraft have links with pastoral, though it would be misguided to cite the Pharmaceutria eclogues here. More pertinent is the supernatural element in pastoral and quasi-pastoral plays: *A Midsummer Night's Dream*, *The Tempest*, *The Faithful Shepherdess*—even Rosalind's profession of magical arts in *As You Like It*. But in all these, the supernatural is of a romantic or numinous cast, and contributes directly to the pastoral ambience. In *The Sad Shepherd* the witchcraft is mundane, a comic machiavellism opposed to the values of the main plot. No doubt it was put in Jonson's mind by his own antimasques, as in the *Masque of Queens*. As the source of the play's most obvious action, it could have dissipated our interest in the pastoral and ideal dimension, reducing the play to a comedy of intrigue bordering on magical farce.

That this does not happen is due to the skill with which Jonson develops the magical in *organic* opposition to the pastoral: the former is made to define the latter's values, a disorder opposing the latter's happy order. We may indeed relate the subplot of Maudlin and her children to the designedly low or uncouth vein of pastoral which we have met before from time to time—sometimes with a reductive ethnicity, sometimes with purely comic purpose. In dramatic function, Maudlin and her children are akin to Shakespeare's Audrey and William; but they partake also of the comic wrangling shepherds in Theocritus IV and V and Virgil III, or the lover of Nencia di Barberino. Lorel is a swineherd, on the lowest rung of the herdsmen's hierarchy. His wooing directly echoes that of Theocritus's Polyphemus, though (as with Polyphemus) it can take on an unironical colouring of pastoral happiness:

An hundred Udders for the payle I have,
That gi' mee Milke and Curds, that make mee Cheese

. . . .

Twa trilland brookes, each (from his spring) doth meet,
And make a river, to refresh my feet:
In which, each morning ere the Sun doth rise,
I look my selfe, and cleare my pleasant eyes,
Before I pipe; (II. ii. 15–16, 28–32)

There is a subtle ambiguity of tone here. Broader ambiguity appears in the satire of rustic life vented by Maudlin-as-Marian:

beare the Venison hence. It is too good
For these course rustick mouthes that cannot open,
Or spend a thanke for't. A starv'd Muttons carkasse
Would better fit their palates. (I. vii. 5–8)

This hostile but not invalid view supplements the idyllic one, setting the latter in perspective. Here too, Jonson is carrying on the techniques of *As You Like It*.

This is apparent yet again, and most tellingly, in his plotting of the shepherd and forester characters of the main action, the lovers in particular. More pronouncedly than in *As You Like It*, it is the foresters who most advance the pastoral ideal. The love of Robin and Marian is a happy and ideal relationship, a symbol of order:

CLA[RION]. Hee, and his *Marian*, are the Summe and Talke
Of all, that breath here in the Greene-wood Walke.
MEL[LIFLEUR]. Or *Be'voir* Vale.
LIO[NEL]. The Turtles of the Wood.
CLA[RION]. The billing Paire.
ALK[EN]. And so are understood
For simple loves, and sampled lives beside. (I. v. 106–10)

Opposed to this is the disorderly passion of Aeglamour the shepherd for his lost Earine. Its destructive power is conveyed through a recurrent spring-motif. The play opens with Aeglamour's praise of Earine (from Greek *earinos*, spring): 'The world may find the Spring by following her' (I. i. 3). She is the source of nature's vitality, and perhaps of paradisal virtue and innocence as well, for there was eternal spring in Eden. Earine's death thus becomes the death of spring: 'A Spring, now she is dead: of what, of thornes?' (I. v. 33). The common pathetic fallacy of pastoral epicedia is heightened to suggest the decay of nature:

> Did not the whole Earth sicken, when she died?
>
> . . . .
>
> And all the Flowers, and Sweets in *Natures* lap,
> Leap'd out, and made their solemne Conjuration,
> To last, but while shee liv'd: Doe not I know,
> How the Vale wither'd the same Day? (I. v. 37, 49–52)

Aeglamour himself threatens to 'Quite alter the complexion of the Spring' (I. v. 12) by bringing on magical extremes of heat and cold to avenge himself for his grief. Earlier, too, he had threatened the shepherd world with such vindictive destruction (I. iii. 52–77).

By contrast, the pastoral sports convey 'all the profer'd solace of the Spring' (I. v. 32). In the previous scene, the pastoral ideal embodied in the sports and threatened by the Puritans is more radically identified with the Golden Age:

> a happy age, when on the Plaines,
> The Wood-men met the Damsells, and the Swaines
> The Neat'ards, Plow-men, and the Pipers loud . . . (I. iv. 42–4)

Even if the shepherds compromised their lasses,

> all these deeds were seene without offence,
> Or the least hazard o' their innocence. (I. iv. 53–4)

Tasso's Golden Age chorus has been completely naturalized. Within the framework of the play, however, this happy ordered universe is disturbed by Aeglamour's love. His destructive sentimentalism is set against Robin and Marian's ordered and idyllic love, and both against Amie's naïve and untutored longing.

But clearly, Aeglamour's passion is not intrinsically destructive; it is made so only by Earine's supposed death. Between the lines of Aeglamour's deranged speeches, Jonson is putting forward a valid ideal of pastoral love, along more Petrarchan and indeed more conceptualized lines than that of Robin himself. Once again we are reminded of *As You Like It*, in the way pairs of lovers are set off against each other to indicate levels and versions of love.

Anne Barton has recently drawn attention[77] to the way such a structure is anticipated in other comedies of Jonson's old age, *The New*

[77] Anne Barton, *Ben Jonson, Dramatist* (Cambridge, 1984), 271 ff.

Inn in particular. In *The New Inn* and *A Tale of a Tub*, Jonson may be observed to approach the condition of pastoral in a number of interesting ways—a palpable Elizabethan nostalgia being not the least important—even while formally keeping well clear of the pastoral convention.

It must be remembered that the settings of these plays—Barnet and Finsbury Hundred respectively—were at that time far outside London, and Jonson turns to them as a conscious change from city life. As Barton says of *The New Inn*: 'Like Arden, Illyria or the wood near Athens, this [Barnet] is a place to which people journey, most of them, by implication, from the city, and in which they can be transformed. The inn provides a heightened and extraordinary environment where characters discover . . . who they really are' (p. 259).

The cyclic pattern is obvious. But unlike in Arden, or the wood near Athens, the setting is not the agent of transformation. The high spirits of Lady Frampul and her crew, or of Goodstock the host for that matter, are imported from the realms of the aristocracy; and Prudence the maid, to whom the same manner seems inborn, is first appointed the sovereign of the sports and then truly translated to that level by marriage with Lord Latimer, as many high-souled shepherd maids had been earlier. The disputations on love also recall the aristocratic Platonized contentions in pastoral romance from *Diana* onwards, and indeed the erotic-philosophic element in Renaissance pastoral generally. It is as though Jonson were out to create a tantalizing parallel to pastoral narrative structures, that never quite meets the terms of the convention.

A Tale of a Tub is a more complex case. Jonson's Prologue would be equally applicable to a true pastoral:

old Records,
Of antick Proverbs, drawne from *Whitson-Lord's*,
And their Authorities, at *Wakes* and *Ales*,
With countrey precedents, and old Wives Tales;
Wee bring you now, to shew what different things
The *Cotts* of *Clownes*, are from the *Courts* of *Kings*.[78]

The characters range from Squire and Justice to a range of rustics that anticipates Hardy. There is no shepherd among them. The humbler characters interact with the higher in intricate patterns of contrast, irony, and mutual reinforcement. The parallel with the rustics in *A Midsummer Night's Dream* is pronounced in the final masque but perceptible all through.

[78] ll. 7–12; as in vol. iii (Oxford, 1927; repr. 1954) of Jonson's *Works* (edn. cit. n. 75).

Beneath their folly and *naïveté*, Turfe the constable, his neighbours and servants display an appealing innocence and communal solidarity, suffused with nostalgic remoteness in contrast to even the modest sophistication of Squire Tub and Justice Preamble. And it is the humble orders that finally win, when Awdrey Turfe marries neither judge nor squire but Lady Tub's man Pol Marten. It is a classic instance of Empson's pastoral puzzle of 'better and not so good'.

The Sad Shepherd marks the explicitly pastoral, explicitly nostalgic climax of an increasing withdrawal and idyllic rusticity in Jonson's Caroline plays. In this he matches Spenser and Shakespeare: pastoral answers to a special and organic growth of their sensibilities at their ripest and most comprehensive, the pursuit of a simplicity that lies on the further side of experience.

19
More Court Spectacles and the Masque

I HAVE excluded from the last chapter some slight compositions that afford little more than a pleasant glow of stylized pastoralism: sketches or dramatic entertainments rather than fully fledged plays. The nature of such pieces may be seen from the fictional instance of 'Gripus and Hegio', 'A *Pastorall* Acted by the Lady Iulias Servants, for the entertainment of Flaminius' in Robert Baron's romance, *ἐροτοπαίγνιον or The Cyprian Academy* (printed 1647). It contains a rudimentary plot of shepherdly love-tangles. Venus and Cupid appear at the outset and Ceres and Hymen at the close, with a chorus of fairies and much stock detail of setting and diction. (There are echoes not only of Sidney's *Arcadia* but of Milton's 'Nativity Ode'!)

'Gripus and Hegio' is more substantial in plot but not very different in spirit from William Denny's *The Shepherd's Holiday* (1651?).[1] Here the chief action, if such it may be called, is a debate on marriage versus virginity, with associated songs, games, and rites, such as take place every year on the Ide (*sic*) of May. The 'Genius . . . unto these plains' appears as a palmer and then a young shepherd: we may be reminded of the Attendant Spirit in Milton's masque of Comus. A chorus of sylvans appear, and finally the nymph Pega, both virgin and wife, binds the shepherds in an appropriate blessing of married chastity and innocence.

There is some praise of pastoral content, still more of 'Our chaste-hatch'd love . . . warm'd by pure desire' (p. 73). The latter theme is expanded, almost to fantastical lengths, in a 'key or clavis to this Pastoral or Eclogue' (dedicatory letter, p. 62). Theme and spirit far exceed the action in importance: undemanding intellectual elaborations upon a static, conventional scene.

Denny aptly says of this piece that it 'might heretofore have passed as a masque had it not been for vizards' (p. 62). It continues the line descending from Sidney's *The Lady of May* through Heywood's

[1] The date of the dedicatory letter in the MS. The piece was printed in the *Inedited Poetical Miscellanies* (1870); all refs. to this edn.

Amphrisa the forsaken Shepheardesse.[2] *Amphrisa* in turn has links with Daniel's *The Queen's Arcadia*: masque and entertainment shade imperceptibly into drama proper. In Heywood's piece, pastoral love has an unhappy outcome; but Amphrisa, forsaken by Panasius, forgets her grief as her companions crown her with willow, and joins them in a song praising the shepherd's life as commanded by the gracious Queen of Arcadia, who comes visiting among them.

We are not certain of the date and occasion when *Amphrisa* was performed; but its spirit is that of an Elizabethan royal progress, whether or not it formed part of one. There is the same ease of relationship with the monarch, the same coexistence of royal virtue and happy rusticity presented as the implicit state of England. At the same time, there is more sugary Petrarchism than in *The Lady of May*—as later there will be still more in Denny's play. We find change even in continuity.

Elsewhere pastoral values may be clearly rejected. In *Deorum iudicium*, another of Heywood's *Pleasant Dialogues and Dramma's*, the goddesses are 'fairer much' than shepherdesses (l. 4897), and Venus promises Paris 'No Shepherdesse or rustick Damsell' but a 'Grecian Queen' (ll. 5093–5). In *Iupiter and Ganimede* Ganymede yearns for his flock and rustic life, while Jove tempts him to a higher order of existence:

> No more of cheese and milke from henceforth thinke,
> Ambrosia thou shalt eat, and Nectar drinke . . . (ll. 3604–5)

Pastoral has subsided to a marginal embellishment in a mythic, quasi-Ovidian setting (as also when Mercury appears as a shepherd in *Iupiter and Io*). Heywood has moved, albeit in a restrained manner, into the world of ornate myth that serves as the common setting of the Jacobean masque.

The masque proper is distinguished from the foregoing works by the explicit, overriding purpose of courtly compliment. The entertainments described above reflect the courtly taste and ethic in their somewhat feeble and fine-spun grace; the ones I shall now cite adapt and distort legend and literary convention into an ostentatious, designedly simplistic exercise in the self-gratification of the ruling class. They open up a highly stylized landscape eked out with much artifice; an abundance of mythology in both action and allusion; studiedly simple symbols of great

[2] I have used Heywood's *Pleasant Dialogues and Dramma's*, vol. iii of Bang's *Materialien* (1903; repr. Vaduz, 1963), for this and later pieces cited from the vol. There is a single sequence of line-nos. running through all the pieces in this edn.

potential complexity; and a cast of gods and refined rustics mouthing polished blank verse or sophisticated lyrics.

This may seem to afford fair territory for a pronounced vein of mythic pastoral. Yet, as Greg noted long ago (*Pastoral* p. 378), pastoral is surprisingly rare in the masque. We may at once dismiss some false or unpromising trails. The Jacobean entertainment entitled *A Pastorall Sonnet. Containing a Parliament of the Gods* concerns the dispute between Mars and Vulcan, and has nothing pastoral except an unimportant 'jury' of twelve shepherds.[3] In Beaumont's *Masque of the Inner Temple and Gray's Inn*, a band of comic rustics, ranging from 'A Country Clown, or Shepherd' to a 'She-Baboon' and a 'She-Fool', provide the second antimasque.[4] The Haberdashers' pageant at the Lord Mayor's inauguration in 1620 had a shepherd and sheep alongside carders, spinners, knitters, and other participants in the wool trade.[5] In the Drapers' Pageant composed by Heywood for the Lord Mayor's Pageant of 1638, there was a shepherd's speech and, in the printed copy, much factual account of sheepkeeping and the wool trade, out of deference to the draper-mayor (Greg, p. 385).

All this is unpromisingly literal. The only notable instance of a pastoral masque is Jonson's *Pans Anniversarie or The Shepherds Holy-Day*. Pan is James I; the masque was doubtless composed for his birthday. The shepherds' songs and dances are unusually elaborate, as may be expected, and set off by an antimasque of Boetians who seem to represent the city as opposed to the country, as well as the bourgeoisie in contrast to the aristocrats. We hear of the 'harmonie' and 'innocence' of Arcadia (ll. 162, 164),[6] rising to the standard philosophic quibble on the name of Pan:

> PAN is our All, by him we breath, wee live,
> Wee move, we are; (ll. 191–2)

All through, the metre demands that the last word of the subtitle should be pronounced 'holy day'. At another level, there is much literal detail of shepherd life, including the longest flower-catalogue I have come across (ll. 12–45). At two levels, then, the thematic and the descriptive, authentic pastoral lends body to the allegory. The prayers and vows cannot always be decoded point for point:

[3] See John Nichols, *The Progresses, Processions, and Magnificent Festivities, of King James the First* (London, 1828), iii. 162ff.

[4] See *A Book of Masques in Honour of Allardyce Nicoll* (Cambridge, 1967), 138.

[5] Nichols, *Progresses of James*, iv. 623–4.

[6] All refs. for Jonson's Masques to vol. vii of his *Works*, ed. Herford and the Simpsons.

So may our Ewes receive the mounting Rammes,
And wee bring thee the earliest of our Lambes:
So may the first of all our fells be thine,
And both the beestning of our Goates, and Kine . . . (ll. 260–3)

Although the age produced no other memorable pastoral masque, quasi-pastoral settings and myths are endemic. In Chapter 17 I described the realistically pastoral or rustic end of the spectrum. Here I shall trace the more exotic and mythic strand. I shall not attempt even a partial listing of innumerable continental models. Two notable instances are the wood-gods who burst upon the winter landscape at Fontainebleau in 1539, and Pan and his crew falling prey to Circe in the 1581 Joyeuse wedding revels.[7]

Turning to England, the 1575 Kenilworth revels provide a good starting-point. A whole gallery of gods assemble here, from Pan and Sylvanus to Neptune, Mars, and Phoebus. There is also a Savage Man's speech and a play of Diana and her nymphs.[8] Nymphs and fairies appear more than once on the Queen's Suffolk and Norfolk progress of 1578.[9] At Elvetham in 1591, water-gods and forest-gods hold battle; and the Graces and the Hours sing Thomas Watson's song, turning the estate into a paradise peopled by sylvans:

Now th'Ayre is sweeter then sweet Balme,
And Satires daunce about the Palme,
Now earth with verdure newly dight,
Giues perfect signes of her delight.[10]

Pan, Sylvanus, and a wild man, Ceres and her nymphs, Apollo and Daphne, appear alongside human rustics in the Bisham and Sudeley entertainments of 1592.[11] At Harefield Place in 1602, a troop of satyrs complain against the nymphs in a speech adapted from the Italian of Giraldi Cinthio.[12]

Such entertainments continued in the next reign, though they were overshadowed by the (largely non-pastoral) masque. Jonson wrote an entertainment for Queen Anne and Prince Henry at Althorp in 1603. The

[7] See, respectively, Jacquot (ed.), *Les Fêtes de la Renaissance*, ii. 436, and Strong, *Splendour at Court*, p. 161.

[8] Nichols, *Progresses of Elizabeth*, i. 432ff.

[9] Ibid. ii. 199, 211.

[10] Quoted from *England's Helicon*, ed. Rollins, no. 26, p. 46, ll. 2–5.

[11] Nichols, *Progresses of Elizabeth*, iii. 131ff.

[12] See V. M. Jeffery, 'Italian and English Pastoral Drama of the Renaissance', *MLR* 19 (1924), 56–62.

park setting becomes a mythological landscape with satyrs as well as Queen Mab and her fairies: precisely the compound of Jonson's future *Masque of Oberon* or Campion's masque for Lord Hayes's wedding. In an entertainment for the King and Queen at Highgate the next year, Jonson introduced a broad vein of humour in Pan alongside a more delicate classical fancy in Aurora, Flora, and Zephyrus, while Mercury drew out the Arcadian, paradisal implications of the scene: 'This place . . . is the *Arcadian* hill CYLLENE, . . . Where, now, behold my mother MAIA, sitting in the pride of her plentie, gladding the aire with her breath, and cheering the spring with her smiles. At her feet, the blushing AVRORA, . . . accompanied with that gentle winde, FAVONIVS' (ll. 60–71).

As may be expected from their themes, masque settings commonly acquire clear, even explicit, Elysian or paradisal overtones. In Jonson's *Masque of Beauty* there is a grove with musicians representing 'the *Shades* of the olde *Poets*', a 'new *Elysium*' restoring the 'spirits of the antique *Greekes*' (ll. 245–6, 137–8, respectively). In *The Golden Age Restored*, old poets sit in 'Elysian bowres' (l. 127). *The Fortunate Isles*, celebrating Prince Charles's betrothal to Henrietta Maria, is chiefly marine, but the isle of Macaria (France) that joins itself to Britannia is a veritable paradise. In Campion's masque for Lord Hayes's wedding, Flora's bower lies beyond the reach of seasonal change and mortality. In William Browne's Inner Temple Masque, Circe's island takes on an Elysian character. In Aurelian Townshend's *Tempe Restored*, the Vale of Tempe itself becomes subject to Circe and is finally restored to the Muses.

City entertainments had their paradises too. In James's London progress on 15 March 1604, Sylvanus invited the King into the Garden of the Muses.[13] In Middleton's Easter pageant for 1621 Flora, elected queen of the seasons, presides over a springtime scene as 'Vertues true Paradise',[14] while Dekker in *London's Tempe*, written for the Mayor 'Camp-belle's' inauguration in 1629, puns on the latter's name to present a 'field of happiness' enjoying eternal spring.

Eternal spring reigns in the court masque as well. It provides an excellent conceit for winter entertainments like Jonson's *The Vision of Delight* (Christmas 1617) or the anonymous *Masque of Flowers* (Twelfth Night 1614), *Masque of the Twelve Months*, and *Masque of the Four Seasons*.

[13] Nichols, *Progresses of James*, i. 361–4.

[14] Thomas Middleton, *Honourable Entertainments*, ed. R. C. Bald (Malone Soc. Repr., Oxford, 1953), 96.

In some of these examples, Paradise mingles with Parnassus. The Garden of the Muses that James entered in Cheapside foreshadowed many others in his halls. I have already noted the ancient poets in Jonson's *Masque of Beauty* and *The Golden Age Restored*. Macaria in *The Fortunate Isles* has not only poets but Apollo himself, and

> Here all the day, they feast, they sport, and spring;
> Now dance the *Graces* Hay, now *Venus* Ring . . . (ll. 515–16)

Jonson's *Chloridia* (1631) has Poetry, History, Architecture, and Sculpture in a Parnassian spring-setting, while Townshend's Tempe is 'the happie retreat of the Muses and their followers'.[15]

Even commoner is a Golden Age of justice, virtue, and innocence—a concept readily turned to court-compliment. *The Golden Age Restored* declares its theme in the title. Let me quote instead from *Pans Anniversarie*:

> And come you prime Arcadians forth
> . . . .
> Commending so to all posteritie
> Your innocence from that faire Fount of light,
> As still you sit without the injurie
> Of any rudenesse, Folly can, or spight; (ll. 159, 163–6)

Here is a clear declaration of the 'innocence' or purity of pastoral experience.

Particularly important and recurrent is the theme of chaste love, invaluable for wedding-masques and compliments to the female aristocracy. I shall confine myself to instances with 'Elysian' settings. Jonson's *Masque of Beauty* and *The Golden Age Restored* treat clearly of the subject. Campion's masque for Lord Hayes's wedding includes a hymn to Cynthia, goddess of 'single chastitie'. There is a debate on marriage versus virginity, as later in Denny's *The Shepherds' Holiday*.

The clearest treatment of chastity occurs in Robert White's *Cupid's Banishment*, presented before the Queen in 1617. Hiller gives an informative account of the work,[16] with its banishment of Cupid, its surprising toleration of Bacchus and his crew (as in Drayton's Nymphal III in *The Muses Elizium*), above all the chaste wedding of the King and Queen of the masque, for 'theire revells did wholly tend to chastity,

[15] Aurelian Townshend, *Poems and Masks*, ed. E. K. Chambers (Oxford, 1912), 97.

[16] Geoffrey G. Hiller, 'Drayton's *Muses Elizium*: A New Way over Parnassus', *RES* NS 21 (1971), 1 ff.

beeing a sporte the Goddesse and hir Nymphs did use in bowers and retir'd places without any prejudice to virginity or scandall to any entire vow'.[17]

Most of these masques are only tangentially related to the pastoral convention; but they make explicit—almost to the point of overkill—some of its underlying themes. By their emphatic celebration of court life, they totally forfeit the imaginative integrity of pastoral; yet their setting and ambience are akin to that of the pastoral drama of the age, or its Italian antecedents. These are chiefly art-pastoral, apparently at the farthest remove from allegory or even allusion. But the contemporary courtier-spirit has coloured their content: that may be the reason for the enervation of the pastoral imagination they display.

[17] Nichols, *Progresses of King James*, iii. 291.

PART IV

Last Fruits: Three Versions of Pastoral

20

Drayton's Late Pastorals

WHILE treating of Drayton's earlier pastorals, I remarked that they express two distinct veins: a simple lyric delight and a higher idealism, increasingly merged in his later work. *The Shepheards Sirena*, *The Quest of Cynthia*, and *The Muses Elizium* are pastorals—the first most clearly so—but placed at the furthest border of the genre. Specifically bucolic elements maintain a slender, almost dispensable presence in a more complex setting. Uniquely for lyric, ballad, or eclogue, they re-create the most ambitious themes of pastoral romance and drama.

In the *Battaile of Agincourt* volume of 1627, *The Quest of Cynthia* precedes *The Shepheards Sirena*; but the latter is the simpler piece and seems to have been composed earlier, at least in part. The poem falls into three sections: the lament of the lovesick Dorilus; his merry friends' song praising his beloved Sirena; and their call to help protect their flocks from 'Rougish Swinheards'. In Chapter 10, section 3, I discussed the first and last parts to show how, even there, the tone modulates respectively to the romantic sentiment and carefree joy of standard Elizabethan art-pastoral. The two veins are finely merged in the intermediate song in Sirena's praise, said to be composed earlier than the enclosing framework.[1]

The praise of Sirena is like a heightened, lapidary version of the Daffodil Song of 1606:

> And every little Grasse
> broad it selfe spreadeth,
> Proud that this bonny Lasse
> upon it treadeth:
> Nor flower is so sweete
> in this large Cincture
> But it upon her feete
> leaveth some Tincture.[2]

[1] See Kathleen Tillotson in Drayton's *Works*, ed. Hebel *et al*., v. 206–8.

[2] ll. 237–44; all refs. as before to the tercentenary edn., ed. J. W. Hebel *et al*. The poems treated in this chapter are in vol. iii.

The phrasing is a little more full, a little more stylized; but a limpid ease and joy lightens even such artificial touches as gravel turning to pearls and fishes leaping onto land to swallow Sirena's bait. Her presence calms raging tempests, and the Muses weave an 'Anadem' to crown her.

The world of the singers is homely and recognizable, if inevitably stylized; but their more delicate spirit transcends this milieu to suggest a paradise of the lyric imagination. This setting is fully realized in *The Quest of Cynthia*.

The Quest has no clear touch of pastoral, except that 'the Shepheards on the Downes' are among those whom the poet taught to sing of Cynthia. In contrast to the allegoric obliquities of *Sirena*, we have here the poet-lover's direct quest for his beloved. Her very name suggests chastity, perhaps touched by the Platonic concerns of Drayton's own *Endimion and Phebe*. Her trail is truly a miraculous heightening of Daffodil's: she makes lilies white, turns hemlock plants to roses, lines a black stream with seed-pearl, and gives it the power to restore maidenheads. The pastoral quest for innocence or purity of impulse is given an almost mythic validation:

> here our sports shall be:
> Such as the golden world first sawe,
> Most innocent and free. (ll. 182–4)

This is opposed to the 'hatefull world'

> Where onely villany is wit,
> And Divels onely thrive. (ll. 179–80)

Interestingly, however, the details of Cynthia's paradise are simple, natural and rustic, with only a passing mention of fairies (l. 219). *The Muses Elizium* has a more complex, more artificial setting; but its substance is already present in this 1627 piece.

Drayton's Elysium is clearly modelled on the traditional earthly paradise. 'The Description of Elizium' opens with the words 'A Paradice on earth'. Drayton is indeed inconsistent on one crucial point: the 'Description' talks of eternal spring, while the Nymphals allude to seasonal change. For the rest, the abundance of flowers and fruits, with streams for them to grow by, a chorus of bird-song, and 'sweets' emanating from the barks of trees and the earth itself, are all typical features of the earthly paradise.[3]

[3] See A. Bartlett Giamatti, *The Earthly Paradise and the Renaissance Epic* (Princeton, 1966), *passim*. There is a useful summary of the standard features of such paradises on p. 52: 'birds, flowers, springs, Zephyr, perfume, eternal springtime, grass, shade, trees'.

Other conventional settings, however, may be seen to mingle with this basic one. Very different in purport from Eden and Paradise, yet interacting with them at every point, is a tradition of secular Gardens of Love. Giamatti traces it back to the classical epithalamium (the *locus classicus* being in Claudian),[4] and forward through the Garden of Mirth in the *Roman de la Rose*[5] to the enchanted 'false paradises' of Renaissance epic, like Spenser's Bower of Bliss. Drayton would have known the pseudo-Chaucerian *Romaunt of the Rose* if none other of the earlier sources. In *The Quest of Cynthia*, he presents a virtuous equivalent to such enchanted bowers. So too in Elysium—obviously a 'true' paradise—'continuall Youth' flourishes, and ('Description', ll. 105–8):

> happy soules, (their blessed bowers,
> Free from the rude resort
> Of beastly people) spend the houres,
> In harmelesse mirth and sport . . .

The wooing in Nymphal II, the intensity of the nymphs' virginal friendships, their mirth in the swains' company in Nymphal VI, and the 'higher' festivities of Nymphal III—all this presents Elysium as a purified Garden of Mirth.

Again, this Elysium is reached by 'a new way over Parnassus', as the subtitle tells us. We need look no further than Plato's *Ion* for the source: 'like Bacchic maidens who draw milk and honey from the rivers when they are under the influence of Dionysus but not when they are in their right mind . . . the lyric poet[s] . . . bring songs from honeyed fountains, culling them out of the gardens and dells of the Muses'.[6] In Nymphal III, 'Apollo's draught' comes from the Helicon. Elysium is the 'Poets Paradice', with Apollo and the 'thrice three Virgins'. The poem describes a festival of the Muses. Nymphal X spells out the way to Parnassus, over 'the craggy by-clift Hill'. The remote and elevated situation, ringed by mountains, is also characteristic of earthly paradises.[7]

Paradise and Parnassus: these points of reference crystallize the latent symbolism of conventional pastoral. Several other lines of development also converge upon the Nymphals. Italianate pastoral is one, though we must gauge it in general terms rather than specific borrowings, often

[4] See ibid. 50ff.

[5] ll. 631ff., 1323ff., as numbered in E. Langlois's edn. I have used R. Sutherland's parallel-text edn. of the English *Romaunt* and the French *Roman* (Oxford, 1967; repr. 1968).

[6] *Ion*, 534; B. Jowett's trans., as in the *Dialogues* (New York, 1937), i. 289.

[7] See Giamatti, pp. 53–4.

postulating English intermediaries. There is specific borrowing in Nymphal VII. Venus and Cupid's disguised infiltration of the nymphs takes us back to Cupid's similar trick in Lyly's *Gallathea*, whose Italian precedents have been cited by Violet Jeffery.[8] *Gallathea*, III. iv. 74–6, is also the most probable source for Cupid's punishment—bow broken, arrows seized, wings clipped—though Drayton's lines verbally echo *The Tempest*, IV. i. 99–101. Tillotson suggests that Codrus's ferrying of Venus and Cupid may derive from Lyly's *Sapho and Phao*, though here the ultimate source is classical, in Aelian.[9] It has not been pointed out that a detail from Lyly's play, Phao's disconcerting reference to Venus, Mars, and Vulcan, has been borrowed in Lelipa's story.[10]

More generally, Italian influence is suggested by the stylized, heightened nature-setting, the pronouncedly idealized 'nymphs', the easy mingling of gods and mortals. The chaste company of nymphs recalls Diana's followers in the Italian plays. In Nymphal I. 103, Dorida talks of 'our chaste *Diana*'. In Nymphal VII, the nymphs actually go hunting—though line 29, comparing the disguised Cupid to one of Diana's votaries, need not imply that they are accompanying Diana. This mixture of myth and pastoral goes back, as we saw, to Boccaccio's *Ameto* and *Il ninfale fiesolano*, and it is more than likely that Drayton derives the word 'Nimphall' from that source. (It does not occur in the *OED* in this sense outside Drayton.)

But Diana's followers in Italian pastoral oscillate between fierce virginity and an equally fierce amorousness. Drayton's nymphs see love and chastity as elements in a very different compound that I shall presently define. Again, though men and gods freely intermingle, there is a curious lack of sylvan gods to bridge the gap between human and celestial. We are told in Nymphal X. 51 that sylvans never set foot in Elysium: the satyr lived with 'wild *Silvanus* and his woody crue' (Nymphal X. 57) in the forests of Felicia. This illustrates a new purpose in Drayton. His gods—Apollo and the Muses, Venus and Cupid—stand for important themes and forces, mythology being used as symbol. He does not feel the need to eke this out with the full trappings of the mythic pastoral landscape. Pan himself is not mentioned, except incidentally in Nymphal V. 81: *Elizium* operates on a higher plane, raising traditional

[8] In *John Lyly*, pp. 80–1. See *Gallathea*, II. ii, III. iv, as in Lyly's *Works*, ed. Bond.

[9] Tillotson, Drayton's *Works*, v. 222.

[10] *Sapho and Phao*, I. i. 66 (ed. Bond). This would seem to be a point in favour of Lyly as a precedent, rather than 'Eurymachus fancie' in Greene's *Francescos Fortunes*, as suggested by Hardin in *Michael Drayton and the Passing of Elizabethan England*, p. 130.

themes to a new level of symbolic concentration. Italianate elements play no more than a contributory part in the process.

A more important element, fitting into Drayton's own pastoral progress, is the English pastoral lyric. The themes I traced in those poems in Chapter 8 come back, strengthened and often transformed, in the *Elizium*.

The commonest theme of the Elizabethan pastoral lyric is love, sometimes credited with an almost prelapsarian innocence. We observed this in *The Quest of Cynthia*. In *Elizium*, the 'purification' is apparent from the very 'Description of Elizium'. The proud flowers vie in beauty and pelt each other with perfumes. Martial and amorous pride are both reduced to a fanciful contest among flowers, as later in Marvell's 'Upon Appleton House'.[11] The 'proud and wanton' brooks meander in 'Gambols and lascivious Gyres' (compare the brooks in Milton's Paradise),[12] and the sun comes to 'coole his glowing face' in them ('Description', ll. 53–68).

Yet sun, flowers, and streams *are* all proud, and the streams in particular suggest a lively sexuality: a nice tension repeated in the human loves of the Nymphals. The Elysian nymphs get married; they pay their vows to 'the bright Queene of love' (Nymphal I. 7); they admit suitors, and even multiple suitors, with a sense of teasing power, as in Nymphal II:

> And if e'r I be in love,
> With one of you I feare twill prove,
> But with which I cannot tell,
> So my gallant Youths farewell. (ll. 355–8)

They joke about their power to dissemble (Nymphal I. 145 ff.). When their tongues are loosened by Apollo's draught in Nymphal III, they can be openly sexual:

> The Robin and the Wren,
> Every Cocke with his Hen,
> Why should not we and men,
> Doe as they doe. (ll. 189–92)

Yet they also banish Venus and Cupid from their soil in Nymphal VII. However, this is done not with a rigorous show of chastity but an easy, almost playful mastery over the situation that suggests a happier spirit of

[11] Discussed in Ch. 22.
[12] See below, Ch. 21, sect. 4.

love. Venus and Cupid, on their part, show a curious innocence, almost a hangdog vulnerability. Cupid's threatened punishment, commonly a revenge taken by victims of love (as in the *locus classicus*, Ausonius's *Amor cruciatus*), belongs also to the iconography of chastity.

But chastity can imply not total virginity but a chastened and purified love, and that at two levels, human as well as divine.[13] Cupid himself may break his weapons in despair at the sight of chaste love, as in the betrothal masque in *The Tempest*, closely echoed in Drayton's lines:

> Her waspish-headed son has broke his arrows,
> Swears he will shoot no more, but play with sparrows,
> And be a boy right out.[14]

Drayton can use complex symbols with disarming lightness of touch. The associations of the 'chastised Cupid' answer to Drayton's theme of chaste love, love that is not love.

The anti-erotic Nymphal VII thus proves to be perfectly compatible with the treatment of love and woman's beauty elsewhere in *Elizium*.[15] This is already clear in Nymphal I. As Buxton points out, Drayton reverses the purpose of the song-contest so that Rodope and Dorida are vying in compliment, each trying to *give* the other victory.[16] This at once creates a sense of innocence and amity. Similarly, Nymphal V draws on the common encounter of youth and age in pastoral (seen in Drayton's own earlier eclogues). But here, the aged hermit and the young nymphs are in perfect concord: they greet him with respect, and he responds with high compliments.

Apart from the benign reworking of convention, these instances also point to the way experience is wrought into poetry in *Elizium*. The exchange of praise in Nymphal I is a modified *blason*, with a latent eroticism becoming faintly explicit at a few points. But the nymphs' charms are presented chiefly in an aesthetic light, as the substance of poetic conceits. The true competition seems to be neither in beauty nor in friendship but in poetic fancy, the turning of ingenious compliments. The same may be said of the contest between Mertilla and Cloris in Nymphal IV in 'wishes of each others good' (another competitive amoebean eclogue turned to altruistic friendship). Again, in Nymphal II, Lalus and

[13] See Edgar Wind, *Pagan Mysteries in the Renaissance* (rev. edn. Harmondsworth, 1967), 146 ff.; Erwin Panofsky, *Studies in Iconography* (1939; repr. New York, 1962), 95–128. Also consider Spenser's conception of chastity in *The Faerie Queene*, Books III–IV.

[14] IV. i. 99–101; as in the New Arden edn. by Frank Kermode (corr. edn. London, 1961; repr. 1970).

[15] Cf. Hiller, 'Drayton's *Muses Elizium*', pp. 7 ff.

[16] John Buxton, *A Tradition of Poetry* (London, 1967), 67–8.

Cleon woo Lirope with gifts. This, of course, harks back to classical pastoral. But the descriptions of the gifts come in carefully balanced pairs, each pair followed by Lirope's witty rejection. This creates the impression of a patterned contest in wit and repartee. Within it, Lalus and Cleon woo Lirope less with the value of the gifts than with the attractive vignettes they weave round them.

In Nymphal VI the forester, fisherman, and shepherd extol their lives in terms of beauty and pleasure. They have no arguments, only extended descriptions. There is practically no moralizing. Appropriately, the purpose of the contest is to win the favour of a troop of nymphs, who crown them with flowers. The nymphs and their companions respond to experience on the basis of its aesthetic potential. In fact, they reorder experience so as to bring out this potential, live their whole lives on that plane.

Elysium thus becomes 'the Poets Paradice' in a deeper sense. Nearly every Nymphal incorporates some sort of poetic 'set piece': descriptions, songs, song-contests, accounts of artefacts, at the very least a piece of rounded narrative like that of Codrus or the nymphs in Nymphal VII. I have earlier noted the importance of these 'set pieces' in *The Shepheardes Calender*.[17] Drayton's nymphs, apparently so different from Spenser's shepherds, share with them this faculty of shaping experience into art. The paradisal setting provides an external symbol for this aesthetic order, but—by a refinement of pastoral we have met before—it is essentially a faculty of the mind, the way in which the inhabitants of paradise describe and respond to experience.

Art and nature are subtly mingled to indicate this aesthetic ordering of life. In Nymphal II, as Heffner has noted, Lalus stands more for nature and Cleon for art.[18] But the contrast is largely lost in a common sense of artifice in the gifts and other objects they describe: flowers fashioned into garments, reeds into a boat, jewels shaped like objects of nature. In Nymphal V, Claia's and Lelipa's lists of flowers convey a happy sense of nature's abundance, but are ordered in terms of the garland and chaplet they are weaving. Notable in a different way is the exchange of wishes between Mertilla and Cloris in Nymphal IV. In their imagination, they both endow nature with artificial, lapidary embellishments. Elsewhere the landscape is literally endowed with such features, turning it into a poetic artefact.

[17] See above, the first part of Ch. 7, sect. 3.

[18] Heffner, *Drayton as Pastoral Poet*, p. 243.

Appropriately enough, the greatest amount of lapidary detail is lavished on Nymphal IX, 'Upon *Apollo* and his prayse'. Here Drayton practically abandons the landscape for the Temple of Apollo. The first hymn draws its matter from myths; the second is a catalogue of the gems with which Apollo's shrine is built. We learn that Elysium abounds in such precious stones (Nymphal IX. 89–92, 165–8). These were a standard feature of the earthly paradise: their absence in the 'Description of Elysium' is made good here, in the temple of the presiding deity.

Yet this artifice, apparently contrary to the spirit of pastoral, serves to concentrate in symbolic form the basic postulates of the pastoral convention. The idealizing and distancing quality of pastoral had always served to highlight the recasting of experience in art. *The Muses Elizium* simply makes this function more prominent.

At the same time, it retains the basic commitment to simplicity and an innocent hedonism. Tillotson has drawn vital attention to the element of play in the *Elizium*,[19] the delight conveyed through the sheer lyric simplicity of the form. Drayton uses octosyllables much more than decasyllables; also a balladic stanza (though rhyming in the first and third lines) generally accompanied by feminine rhymes in the second and fourth lines. All this creates the sense of an unforced, slightly fanciful, and even exuberant lyric flow, and the resultant bouyancy is conveyed to the setting and the happy ordering of life in Elysium. Potentially disruptive experience, be it the 'monstrousness' of Felician women or censure of the nymphs themselves (as in Nymphal I. 137–56 or Nymphal III. 299–354) is turned into the stuff of art.

It is therefore entirely appropriate that the other Nymphal on the cult of Apollo should celebrate the independent imagination in the most direct way. The rhyming bouts in Nymphal III seem to derive from the burlesque amoebean eclogue. They have been treated as *exempla* for serious theories of poetry.[20] It seems better to take them at face value, as examples of total poetic abandon, freeing the lyric impulse that elsewhere plays more cautiously upon normal subject-matter. Freed from all restraints of theme and actual reference, it now finds expression in exaggerated and even grotesque whimsy, an inconsequential exercise in abstract poetic energy. These deliberately absurd pieces can therefore inaugurate a Bacchic celebration of Apollo, culminating in a solemn hymn to the Muses. Again we see the seriousness behind Drayton's artefact of the unserious.

[19] Drayton's *Works*, v. 219.

[20] See Heffner, pp. 246ff.; Berthelot, *Michael Drayton*, pp. 66–7.

His basic seriousness emerges most clearly from the contrast between Elysium and Felicia. It is commonly recognized that Felicia is the actual England of the time, and 'Elizium' (doubtless with a pun on 'Eliza') the vanished Elizabethan ideal. The satire itself is not specially original; Cloris's dispraise of Felician women in Nymphal IV, the common pastoral allegorizing of moral matters in Nymphal X. In the latter the satyr strayed from Felicia describes how

> With wild *Silvanus* and his woody crue,
> In Forrests I, at liberty and free,
> Liv'd in such pleasure as the world ne'r knew . . .
>
> . . . .
>
> Till this last age, those beastly men forth brought,
> That all those great and goodly Woods destroy'd (ll. 57–9, 62–3)

In this Nymphal, Drayton repeats the common equation of *satyr* and *satire* (ll. 33–5).

What is remarkable is the opposite element in the balance, the ideal opposed to this satire. Instead of the homely honesty of Mantuanesque shepherd life, it is the Elysian ideal of total withdrawal into a poetic universe. The satyr himself is not a ranting cynic, nor the lascivious evil-doer of Italian drama, nor Fletcher's elfin agent of Pan. Instead he is a broken creature—'Sadly he sits, as he were sick or lame'—who desires nothing but a peaceful refuge. He may or may not be a persona of the aged Drayton,[21] but he obviously stands for Drayton's ideal of total withdrawal into a removed world of aesthetic fulfilment.

The withdrawal is as important as the fulfilment, and a full account of the poem must take note of it. As William Oram says, Drayton's career resembles the better-known cases of Spenser, Shakespeare, and Jonson.[22] All these poets turn significantly to pastoral, conventionally the exercise of a young poet, at the end of a long career. We have seen how Spenser and Shakespeare expand the convention into a versatile symbolic medium; it becomes more than ever a measure of reality. By contrast, Drayton's work indicates an *escape* into art, reducing rather than comprehending life, stepping back from a total confrontation.

It is over eighty years since Greg wrote 'with all its exquisite justness, as of ivory carved and tinted by the hand of a master and encrusted with the sparkle of a thousand gems, the *Muses' Elizium* remains a toy' (p. 109). Later readings have modified this view, and I myself have read

[21] As suggested by Hiller, p. 13.
[22] W. A. Oram, '*The Muses Elizium*: A Late Golden World', *SP* 75 (1978), 12.

the work in the light of its many deep concerns. But Drayton's heightened pastoral setting reorders experience so radically, and at the same time so selectively, as to lose all commitment to life as it is. The criticism-by-contrast reduces itself to total condemnation and escape: 'Elizium appears merely lovely or precious; its radical exclusions make it representative of a state of mind unable to deal with what it excludes—to risk its pleasing dreams in the context of normal existence'.[23] Drayton's achievement is to escape into more than the trivial, to express through the escape a deeply felt moral condition and a profound commitment to art.

Scholars have suggested the indebtedness of *The Muses Elizium* to the Jacobean masque.[24] The Elysian, Parnassian, and Golden-Age associations of the masque, its frequent treatment of chaste love and virtue, will have emerged from my account in Chapter 19. The themes could be transplanted into actual rustic settings. It seems eminently possible that *Elizium* was written as an outdoor courtly entertainment. Tillotson and Newdigate suggest that Elysium might be Knole Park, the seat of Drayton's last patron Edward Sackville, Fourth Earl of Dorset.[25] Hiller (pp. 4–6) repeats the idea. Mary Ozark doubts the dramatic purpose, but suggests that Nymphal VIII celebrates an actual wedding, perhaps that of Anne Clifford, widow of the Third Earl, to Philip Herbert, Fourth Earl of Pembroke.[26] (There is some trouble in making the dates fit, however.)

It is not impossible that Elysium stands for Knole or at least absorbs features of the landscape there. One or two points are suggestive, like the preservation of the woods around Knole amidst general deforestation,[27] and the possibility that 'Th'Arch Flamyne of Elizium' (Nymphal VIII. 174) is the Archbishop of Canterbury.[28] But Drayton does not force the association upon us: indeed, he does everything to discourage it, presenting Elysium as a remote realm of the imagination. In other words, he takes the most pronouncedly courtly tradition of poetry and spectacle in the age and turns it to a purpose as different as could be: withdrawal, imaginative isolation, and (in the satire of Felicia) total condemnation of the court culture of his day.

Drayton's use of masque material has been noted before, but not this

[23] Oram, pp. 21–2.
[24] See Tillotson, Drayton's *Works*, v. 219; Hiller, pp. 1 ff.
[25] Tillotson, Drayton's *Works*, v. 220; Newdigate, *Drayton and His Circle*, p. 214.
[26] J. M. Ozark, *Faery Court Poetry*, pp. 331 ff.
[27] Hiller, p. 5.
[28] See Tillotson, Drayton's *Works*, v. 223.

reversal of its intentions. He is isolating masque themes and symbols from their local and ephemeral contexts, restoring their imaginative integrity through an emphatic rejection of court and contemporary life.

Viewed in this light, Drayton's poets' paradise ceases to appear as a merely restrictive escape into art. Rather, it enriches and renders permanent a still more restricted and transient vein. Drayton is preserving the pastoral imagination from Felician venality, though he can only preserve it in a remote world of artefact. To the very end of his career, his pastoral follows a course of its own.

21
Milton

THERE is a fair sprinkling of pastoral and semi-pastoral elements in Milton's work—almost as much as in Spenser. But in Spenser, the pastoral (despite its equivocal treatment in *The Faerie Queene*, Book VI) appears basic to the poet's sensibility. In Milton—even in 'Comus' or 'Lycidas'—it is tangential to his central concerns. A continuous though low-key critique of pastoral runs through the corpus of Milton's poetry. Yet his guarded and critical acceptance implies acute understanding of the nature of pastoral, and creates some very original versions of the mode.

1. *Some early poems*

The lightest and simplest vein may be introduced through its least consequential expression, the Fifth Latin Elegy 'In adventum veris' [On the Coming of Spring]. As part of the poetic furniture of spring, we have a shepherd watching the dawn from a rock (ll. 41–2)[1] and another piping while Phyllis sings (ll. 113–14). There is extended reference to Pan, Sylvanus, satyrs, and dryads (ll. 119ff.), with a concluding evocation of the Golden Age.

We can match this from innumerable continental Neo-Latin elegies, odes, and lyrics. The Phillis of 'L'Allegro'—and Corydon, Thyrsis, and Thestylis too—obviously serves a different function. Pastoral is not central to 'L'Allegro'; but it plays an organic role in a markedly original poetic structure, unlike the conventional design of the Fifth Latin Elegy.

Early in 'L'Allegro', Milton introduces motifs involving spring, outdoor settings, and sylvan myth, as in the second 'sager' version of the birth of Euphrosyne (ll. 17–24). There follows the staider but equally animated figure of 'The mountain nymph, sweet Liberty' (l. 36). Gradually—reversing the usual progress of, say, a spring ode—the

[1] All refs. to Milton's *Poems*, ed. John Carey and Alastair Fowler (London, 1968), including trans. from the Latin.

mythic setting passes into idealized nature-description and thence into a realistic account of the English countryside. The shepherd 'tell[ing] his tale' (counting his sheep), the whistling ploughman, the singing milkmaid, the 'nibbling flocks', are all conventional details, but of a kind that confirm actuality. Milton is turning his poem inward from mythic and allegorical evocations of nature to the Cheerful Man's joyous engagement with the real countryside, involving no more than a light stylization.

But he reaches out again to a removed and literary plane when recognizably English rustics appear as Corydon and Thyrsis, Phillis and Thestylis. By implication, their life is assimilated to the idyllic design of classical pastoral; and under the cachet of this analogy, the succeeding account of rural English sports and pleasures becomes a version of the all-time ideal of pastoral harmony.[2] The Cheerful Man had first looked outward at the external world of nature; now he turns the elements of this world into the stuff of poetic tradition as answering to his own sensibility.

Later in the poem, even city sights appear as the products of rural poetic inspiration:

> Such sights as youthful poets dream
> On summer eves by haunted stream. (ll. 129–30)

And Shakespeare himself 'warble[s] his native wood-notes wild'. The Cheerful Man's sensibility grows in range, extending to courtly, chivalric, and urban pursuits; but these acquire rural affinities within his mind. This primacy of nature and the rural life marks the imaginative constitution of the Cheerful Man, and guides the limited but organic use of formal pastoral in the poem.[3]

'Il Penseroso', on the contrary, has nothing pastoral or even clearly akin to it. The Pensive Man's pleasures touch at many points upon outdoor and rural settings; but these are depopulated, withdrawn retreats, rejecting the common course of nature and rural life instead of

[2] Cf. David Daiches, 'Some Aspects of Milton's Pastoral Imagery', *More Literary Essays* (Edinburgh, 1968), 109: 'The cottage between the two oak trees is a highly stylised image of rustic content, stylised to a point where it in fact transcends local landscape and becomes an embodiment of a universal concept of peaceful rusticity.'

[3] Rosemond Tuve (*Images and Themes in Five Poems by Milton* (Cambridge, Mass., 1957), 21) admits the pastoral bent of the images and descriptions in 'L'Allegro', and the fundamentally different orientation of 'Il Penseroso'. M.-S. Røstvig (*The Happy Man*, i. 101–2) interestingly shows how Milton's picture of the Cheerful Man is allied to 'A Shepheard' in Wye Saltonstall's *Picturae loquentes* (1631).

assimilating it as in 'L'Allegro'. The woods may inspire his 'strange mysterious dream'; but that very dream leads him beyond embodied nature. The hermit-figure at the end shows features of the 'wise shepherd':

> Where I may sit and rightly spell
> Of every star that heaven doth shew,
> And every herb that sips the dew; (ll. 170–2)

But once again, his 'prophetic strain' seems to transcend star and herb for a more abstract, mystical plane of experience.

This transcendence indicates a more complex and highly evolved state of mind than in 'L'Allegro'.[4] It is significant that Milton reduces his range of nature-references as he scales the higher reaches of his sensibility.[5] Nature is reduced from a poetic end to a poetic means; and conventional pastoral (or anything like it) occurs only in the earlier and simpler phases of the first stage. It is already 'placed' within a wider frame of sensibility.

2. *The masques*

It is interesting that in his final speech in *Arcades*, the Genius of the Wood should pass from 'L'Allegro' parallels (ll. 45–60) to 'Il Penseroso' parallels (ll. 61–73), confirming that these two poems present a single evolving design. In *Arcades* itself, the speech clearly presents a conceptual progress organic to the work at large and its use of pastoral in particular.

Arcades opens like a typical courtly pastoral masque. The shepherds are members of the Egerton family, and their 'bright honour sparkle[s] through [their] eyes' (l. 27). But the courtly mock-rustic is transformed into a bolder vein of spiritual pastoral, an intenser compliment to Alice, Dowager Countess of Derby.

We have advanced here from the Nativity Ode, where pastoral seems conceived as essentially pagan. There, the shepherds' 'silly thoughts' correspond to the pagan phase of history, as do the sylvan gods expelled at Christ's advent (ll. 181–8). True, Christ himself is 'mighty Pan' (l. 89); but this seems an 'accommodational' device, a means of conveying

[4] The case for this has perhaps been most persuasively argued by Don Cameron Allen, *The Harmonious Vision: Studies in Milton's Poetry* (Baltimore, 1954), ch. i.

[5] Rosenmeyer (*The Green Cabinet*, p. 228) thinks, however, that 'Milton links the pastoral tradition with melancholy rather than mirth'.

Christ's divinity to the untutored shepherds.[6] Essentially, the new Christian disposition has no bearing on the pastoral, except that the shepherds doubtless continue to be shepherds.[7]

In *Arcades*, however, we find a truly post-redemptive pastoral. The vein is introduced through indirect allusion, almost subconscious association. The shepherds approaching the Countess suggest the shepherds of the Nativity, seeing the angels ('What sudden blaze of majesty') or even approaching the manger ('Here our solemn search hath end'). At this stage, to be sure, they are pagan in outlook, guessing the Countess to be Latona or Cybele. But they have in fact encountered a higher divinity, and recognize it in the final song. The nymphs and shepherds are specifically summoned from Arcadia to England to serve a greater deity:[8]

> Though Syrinx your Pan's mistress were,
> Yet Syrinx well might wait on her. (ll. 106–7)

The refrain in lines 94–5 (repeated in lines 108–9) is also ambiguous:

> Such a rural queen
> All Arcadia hath not seen.

This may mean that she is the highest in Arcadia, or that she exceeds the highest there. In either case, we have a new pastoral adapting and elevating the pagan convention while reversing its intent.

The deification of the Countess may seem disconcerting, but it is more than idolatrous compliment. It reflects the impersonal spiritual concerns present in the Genius's speech and thus woven deeply into the substance

[6] This has been suggested by Kathleen M. Swaim, '"Mighty Pan": Tradition and an Image', *SP* 68 (1971), 491. Swaim explores the range of philosophic, mystic, and Christian interpretations of Pan. See also J. B. Broadbent, 'The Nativity Ode', in Frank Kermode (ed.), *The Living Milton* (London, 1960; repr. 1967), 25. One should, of course, note that these 'higher' associations of Pan seem to be operating in the reference to 'Universal Pan' in *Paradise Lost*, IV. 266—a passage which explicitly dismisses other classical myths and mythic settings as inferior to Paradise.

[7] Organically Christian interpretations of the pastoral in the 'Ode' have, of course, been attempted, as by Poggioli (*The Oaten Flute*, pp. 124–34). At another level the entire 'Ode' may be read as a 'Golden Age Eclogue' in the manner of Virgil IV: Patrick Cullen makes out a detailed case in 'Imitation and Metamorphosis: The Golden-Age Eclogue in Spenser, Milton and Marvell', *PMLA* 84 (1969), 1559–70. But this convention is only obliquely related to pastoral proper.

[8] On the Englishness of this revivified pastoral, see Brooks and Hardy, cited in the *Variorum Commentary* on Milton's Poems, ii/2 (Cambridge, 1972), 525. On the higher spiritual and philosophic implications of 'a new poetic voice, the special Puritan voice of regenerate eloquence', see S. D. Blau in ibid. 529.

of Milton's pastoral. Milton is not simply using pastoral for allegoric purpose, whether courtly-allusive or spiritual. For this, needless to say, there is precedent without number. More interestingly, Milton grants the primacy of art-pastoral in classical examples, but proposes a new Christian pastoral of serious bent, a practical, 'committed' vehicle of Christian—specifically, Puritan—ethics and poetics. This involves a revision of the very modal basis of pastoral, not merely its application in allusive manner to different or contrary-spirited material.

The process appears most clearly and completely in 'Lycidas', where the thrust of the pastoral is ethical and practical. But it may be discerned in the spiritually oriented pastoral conceit of *Arcades*[9] and the direct, extended treatment of the substance of that conceit in *A Masque presented at Ludlow Castle* (Comus). All these works belong to a well-defined tradition of 'Protestant pastorale', which I have traced briefly in Appendix E.

The pastoral concerns of *A Masque* are those of *Arcades* writ large.[10] Again we have an underlying courtly allegory, the actors being members of the Egerton family. The action is set in the Earl of Bridgewater's estate. The Attendant Spirit assumes the shape of the Earl's shepherd Thyrsis, who in turn stands for Henry Lawes, music teacher to the Earl's children. Near the end, the 'rural sports' at Ludlow evoke in literal terms the milieu of the country-house poem, but also suggest allegorically the more sophisticated pastoral entertainment of the masque itself. The country dancers—stylized shepherds—also evoke the country-house set-up in the heightened terms of pageant and spectacle.

These are obvious links between *A Masque* and the general run of pastoral masque and pageant. What is remarkable is that they should appear so marginal to the work. Other concerns prevail, leading us towards a new concept of the pastoral.[11]

Rather confusingly, pastoral is used to treat both the parties in the action. Comus appears as a shepherd just like the Attendant Spirit. The Lady associates pastoral revelry with 'riot, and ill-managed merriment':

[9] Obviously, this view is totally opposed to that of A. S. P. Woodhouse, who sees *Arcades* as 'the most purely aesthetic of all Milton's great poems' (ibid. 524).

[10] For the (moderate) formal debt of *A Masque* to pastoral dramatists like Tasso, Guarini, and Fletcher, see J. B. Leishman, *Milton's Minor Poems* (London, 1969), 199–209. Leishman's angles of interest seldom if ever coincide with mine.

[11] Milton's innovative treatment of the courtly masque has been considered from a different angle by John Creaser, '"The Present Aid of this Occasion": The Setting of *Comus*', in D. Lindley (ed.), *The Court Masque* (Manchester, 1984), 111–34.

> the loose unlettered hinds,
> When for their teeming flocks, and granges full,
> In wanton dance they praise the bounteous Pan,
> And thank the gods amiss. (ll. 173–6)

Unlike in the Nativity Ode, Pan here is emphatically pagan, like the later 'Pan, or Sylvan' (l. 267)—lustful creatures cohabiting with goddesses. Earlier (ll. 118–20), fairies and elves, as well as nymphs, had been associated with Comus's night-flying rout.

But the nature-setting at this point differs markedly from that in other passages of pastoral and quasi-pastoral (for example, ll. 290–2, 336–47, 496–8). Significantly, the shepherd folds his sheep (l. 93) as Comus and his crew appear. In the Attendant Spirit's speech to the brothers (ll. 530ff.), Comus's revelry is seen as alien to the pastoral landscape and rhythm of life. In spite of Comus's pastoral guise or the degenerate rusticity he represents, he is opposed to the dominant vein of pastoral in the poem.

> Was this the cottage, and the safe abode
> Thou told'st me of? What grim aspects are these,
> These ugly-headed monsters? (ll. 692–4)

Indeed, Comus's claims to pastoral identity may seem to rest on an ironical reference to his 'herd' of monsters:

> I shall ere long
> Be well stocked with as fair a herd as grazed
> About my mother Circe. (ll. 151–3)

Hence 'the blind mazes of this tangled wood' (l. 180) come to be set against 'the kind hospitable woods' (l. 186). Comus's rout, needless to say, brings out the former aspect (ll. 115 ff., 519ff.). Gradually, the wood becomes an evil setting contrasted with the pastoral and rural milieu:

> might we but hear
> The folded flocks penned in their wattled cotes,
> Or sound of pastoral reed with oaten stops
>
> . . . .
>
> 'Twould be some solace yet some little cheering
> In this close dungeon of innumerous boughs. (ll. 342–4, 347–8)

The influence of Fletcher's *The Faithful Shepherdess* is obvious; behind it we may glimpse the wood of confusion in *A Midsummer Night's Dream*, or even Spenser's allegorical Wood of Error. The pagan pastoral and sylvan gods dwell in these woods; but genuine shepherd life affords a godlier vein of pastoral.

A second, even clearer opposition lies between two versions of primitivism outlined in Comus's temptation-speech:

> Wherefore did Nature pour her bounties forth,
> With such a full and unwithdrawing hand,
> Covering the earth with odours, fruits, and flocks,
> Thronging the seas with spawn innumerable,
> But all to please, and sate the curious taste? (ll. 709–13)

and

> if all the world
> Should in a pet of temperance feed on pulse,
> Drink the clear stream, and nothing wear but frieze . . . (ll. 719–21)

Soft and hard primitivism are dramatically contrasted, the former of course being Comus's ideal. Indeed, the hedonistic bent of Comus's entire speech, with its spirit of *carpe diem*, recalls the lusher pagan vein of pastoral primitivism as realized in, say, Italian drama or romance. Against this we find an ascetic primitivism characteristic of Milton's new godly pastoral. Once more Milton presents a hierarchy within pastoral, superior Christian above inadmissible pagan, recasting and reconceiving the terms of the convention.

However, as befitting the formally profane context of a masque, this higher pastoral is not presented in doctrinal terms. Instead, Milton intensively associates the pastoral with concord and harmony, rising to a celestial and mystical plane. It also extends to personal allegory, for Thyrsis represents the musician Lawes, as the latter's prefatory letter to the Viscount Brackley states. By assuming his shape, the Attendant Spirit becomes a pastoral embodiment of music, order, and harmony.

Early on, the Spirit virtually describes the real Thyrsis as a second Orpheus

> Who with his soft pipe, and smooth-dittied song,
> Well knows to still the wild winds when they roar,
> And hush the waving woods . . . (ll. 86–8)

(Compare this with ll. 493–5.) Later on, Thyrsis's songs are said to inspire 'even to ecstasy' (l. 624). This is the harmony destroyed by Comus's 'barbarous dissonance' (l. 549).

To the singer-shepherd is assimilated a second persona, the 'wise shepherd' skilled in tales and curious lore: 'soothest' Meliboeus[12] (l. 822) or, more youthfully, the shepherd lad who gave Thyrsis the harmony (ll. 618ff.). But the chief context is musical, with philosophic and mystic overtones.[13] Through a different course of development, Milton comes to conceive of the singing or piping shepherd much as Spenser had in *The Faerie Queene*, Book VI. But Colin Clout had himself entered—indeed, directed—the highest mystic vision, moving away from the mundane pastoral setting to do so. Thyrsis (or the Attendant Spirit in his guise) appears confined to the stock pastoral routine:

> This evening late by then the chewing flocks
> Had ta'en their supper on the savoury herb
> Of knot-grass dew-besprent, and were in fold,
> I sat me down to watch upon a bank
> With ivy canopied, and interwove
> With flaunting honeysuckle, and began
> Wrapt in a pleasing fit of melancholy
> To meditate my rural minstrelsy . . . (ll. 539–46)

To realize its full extent, the theme of harmony has to embrace much more than the figure of Thyrsis; yet it always retains pastoral or quasi-pastoral implications. Quite early on, the Lady's song to Echo pictures the nymph in a lush, Ovidian, romantic landscape, from which she may ascend to the skies to 'give resounding grace to all heaven's harmonies' (l. 242). But by 'warbled song', such harmony can be evoked on earth in the figure of Sabrina, dweller in a similar landscape and herself the heroine of an Ovidian transformation. She is also a specifically pastoral goddess:[14]

> the shepherds at their festivals
> Carol her goodness loud in rustic lays,
> And throw sweet garland wreaths into her stream . . . (ll. 847–9)

Above all, quasi-pastoral elements appear in the earthly paradise as described by the Attendant Spirit after casting aside his garb of Thyrsis. We may indeed call this supra-pastoral, to which the formal pastoral

[12] Probably Spenser: see J. F. Bense in *Neophilologus*, 1 (1916), 62–4 (cited by Carey and Fowler, p. 218), and Tuve, p. 122.

[13] On the use and implications of music in *A Masque*, see David Norbrook, *Poetry and Politics*, pp. 259ff.; but Norbrook is not interested in the pastoral associations of the music. See also Ellen Harris, *Handel and the Pastoral Tradition* (Oxford, 1980), 118–22.

[14] On the wider pastoral affinities of the Sabrina figure (ex Spenser, Fletcher, and William Browne) see Tuve, pp. 122–3.

expression of virtue and harmony had tended at the mundane level. As in the songs to Echo and Sabrina, Christian moral concepts are here woven into a tissue of classical allusion and nature-myth.

Milton's great achievement in *A Masque* is to translate an Ovidian setting into Christian moral terms by presenting the moral forces as mythic realities. The landscape is vitalized by these forces; classical elements are functionally subsidiary no matter how pervasive. Yet the latter lend depth and colour to the scene, turning abstract homiletic concepts into living powers in a romantically charged setting of nature.[15]

Compared to Spenser, indeed, Milton forgoes a range of formal intricacies, the symbolic and iconic content of 'pagan mysteries': Colin Clout in concert with Venus and the Graces. But Milton's more selective mythography, closely focused on a specific moral end, affords the same easy commerce of contraries from homely rusticity to celestial virtue.

> Or if Virtue feeble were,
> Heaven itself would stoop to her. (ll. 1021–2)

Pastoral is used organically in *A Masque*: it is the vital agent in the fusion of moral doctrine with a pageant entertainment in a memorable setting of nature. Christian pastoral has gracefully come of age.

3. *'Lycidas'*

At first reading, 'Lycidas' may embarrass a historian of the pastoral convention. For a poem of its eminence, it seems to offer no new version of pastoral, conforming instead to the standard allegorical or allusive eclogue. Like most such poems, it is only intermittently pastoral. Further, there seems to be the usual fluctuation between various levels of pastoral metaphor: the shepherd is now poet, now priest, and now (it seems) simply a shepherd, though the poem clearly operates within a non-pastoral sphere of experience.

It is worth spelling this out at the start, if only to drive home again the unpropitious nature of the allusive mode adopted by Milton, the incongruities merged in his fine formal synthesis. For a special synthesis there does appear to be. This comes out clearly through contrast with a later poem which ostensibly shares many of its concerns: the Latin 'Epitaphium Damonis' on the death of Charles Diodati.[16] It is as though

[15] For a somewhat different, more pagan-oriented interpretation of Milton's syncretism, see Lerner, *The Uses of Nostalgia*, pp. 165–9, 177–80.

[16] The distinction between the two poems has been brought out by A. S. P. Woodhouse,

when writing in the common language of Renaissance humanism, Milton can forgo the special bias of his English pastoral. In particular, his Puritan concerns would have been inappropriate.

Needless to say, the 'Epitaphium Damonis' is not art-pastoral. It is a pronounced case of allegorical pastoral, not only in referring to actual persons, but as bringing out the scholarly and poetic overtones of the 'shepherd's trade'. The implicit contradictions in such allegory appear here as elsewhere: sometimes conscious paradox ('Dicite Sicelicum Thamesina per oppida carmen' [Now sing your Sicilian air through Thames-side towns]: l. 3), sometimes latent confusion as in the Tuscan city, 'Thusca urbs' (l. 13) which is later treated *in extenso* in pastoral terms. But city and country are explicitly opposed as well, and in the same context: it is in this *urbs* that Milton–Thyrsis was away when Damon died, and Milton blames himself for the desertion:

> Ecquid erat tanti Romam vidisse sepultam?
> Quamvis illa foret, qualem dum viseret olim,
> Tityrus ipse suas et oves et rura reliquit; (ll. 115–17)

[Was it so very important for me to see buried Rome? Would it have been, even if the city had looked as it once did when Tityrus himself left his flocks and fields to see it?]

The shepherd's trade is described in detail in lines 37ff.:

> Frigoribus duris, et per loca foeta pruinis,
> Aut rapido sub sole, siti morientibus herbis?
> Sive opus in magnos fuit eminus ire leones
> Aut avidos terrere lupos praesepibus altis . . . (ll. 39–42)

[through the hard winter weather, in fields stiff with frost, or under the fierce sun when plants were dying of thirst, whether our job was to stalk the fully grown lions, or to scare the hungry wolves away from our high sheepfolds?]

Barring a single counterpointing detail of a snoring farmhand (l. 54), the passage progresses steadily from realistic to idyllic, or (one may say) from native to classical. The succeeding picture of mourning nature and neglected farmstead is also drawn from classical epicedia, as is the contrasted setting of happy pastoral life (echoing Virgil X. 42ff.):

'Milton's Pastoral Monodies' (*Studies in Honour of Gilbert Norwood* (1952), 261–78, cited in *Variorum Commentary*, i (Cambridge, 1970), 293, ii/2. 593–5). On the underlying Virgilian affinities of the 'Epitaphium', see Daiches, pp. 101–2, and Louis Martz, 'The Rising Poet, 1645', in J. H. Summers (ed.), *The Lyric and Dramatic Milton* (New York, 1965), 9–12. Martz refers to McKellar's annotations in his edn. of Milton's Latin poems (1930).

Tityrus ad corylos vocat, Alphesiboeus ad ornos,
Ad salices Aegon, ad flumina pulcher Amyntas,
Hic gelidi fontes, hic illita gramina musco,
Hic Zephyri, hic placidas interstrepit arbutus undas; (ll. 69–72)

[Tityrus is calling me to the hazels, Alphesiboeus to the ash-trees, Aegon to the willows, lovely Amyntas to the streams: 'Here are cool fountains! Here is turf covered with moss! Here are soft breezes! Here the wild strawberry tree mingles its murmurs with the mild streams.']

Tityrus and the rest may be members of Milton and Diodati's circle, and their happy repose represent the pleasures of poetry and scholarship. But in terms of poetic validity, allusion is submerged here in an independent creation of the pastoral imagination. Though not art-pastoral, such poetry accepts the validity, even the primacy, of art-pastoral and allows the aesthetic bent of the latter to shape its own allusive concerns. This also applies to the account of the earlier activities of Damon and Thyrsis in lines 140–52, and *a fortiori* to the account of Milton's Tuscan experiences, where an entire ethos of letters and scholarship seems to evolve out of a more fundamental pattern of pastoral life:

Quamquam etiam vestri nunquam meminisse pigebit
Pastores Thusci, musis operata iuventus,
Hic charis, atque lepos; et Thuscus tu quoque Damon.

. . . .

O ego quantus eram, gelidi cum stratus ad Arni
Murmura, populeumque nemus, qua mollior herba,
Carpere nunc violas, nunc summas carpere myrtos,
Et potui Lycidae certantem audire Menalcas. (ll. 125–7, 129–32)

[And yet I shall never be regretful when I remember you, shepherds of Tuscany, young men formed by the muses: grace and charm dwell with you. You too, Damon, were a Tuscan . . . O how grand I felt, lying by the cool, murmuring Arno, in the shade of a poplar grove, on the soft turf, where I was able to pluck violets and myrtle-tips, and listen to Menalcas and Lycidas having a singing-match.]

Late Florentine humanism is justified by being shown to match the rhythms of shepherd life, the purity of its apprehensions and responses, its inviolate absorption in its own essential pursuits. And its orientation is literary, imaginative, and liberal, rather than ethical and ecclesiastic as in 'Lycidas'.

This freely humane orientation appears even in the implicitly Christian sequences. The two 'cups' given to Thyrsis by Manso (ll. 181 ff.) are not only books but, it seems, books of specifically spiritual bent.[17] But the description is its own justification, the cups engage our attention as simple shepherds' trophies. Much more significantly, the resurrectional movement in lines 198 ff. is treated in pagan vein—towards the end, almost sacrilegiously so for an account of the Christian heaven:

> Cantus ubi, choreisque furit lyra mista beatis,
> Festa Sionaeo bacchantur et orgia thyrso. (ll. 218–19)

[where singing is heard and the lyre rages in the midst of the ecstatic dances, and where the festal orgies rave in Bacchic frenzy under the thyrsus of Zion]

Needless to say, Milton is here moving beyond pastoralism; but ever since Virgil V, this has been a permissible development from the pastoral and compatible with it:

> Diodotus, quo te divino nomine cuncti
> Coelicolae norint, sylvisque vocabere Damon. (ll. 210–11)

[Diodati, the divine name by which all the hosts of heaven will know you, though the woods still call you Damon.]

Ultimately the pastoral is set in the total context of Milton's poetic projects: 'Ipse ego Dardanias Rutupina per aequora puppes | Dicam' [I shall tell of Trojan keels ploughing the sea off the Kentish coast]: ll. 162–3. He has sounded these epic notes on pastoral pipes, albeit 'novis . . . cicutis' [a new set of pipes], l. 157; but the fastening broke and the pipes fell apart, so that 'nec ultra | Ferre graves potuere sonos' [they could bear the grave notes no longer]: l. 159. Indeed, he dreams of clearly rejecting the pastoral:[18]

> O mihi tum si vita supersit,
> Tu procul annosa pendebis fistula pinu
> Multum oblita mihi, aut patriis mutata camoenis
> Brittonicum strides . . . (ll. 168–71)

[17] They are taken to be 'two of Manso's books, the *Erocallia* (twelve Platonic dialogues about love and beauty), and the *Poesie Nomiche*, which include an Italian translation of Claudian's *Phoenix*': John Carey's note (Milton's *Poems*, p. 277), citing M. De Filippis's article in *PMLA* 51 (1936), 745–56.

[18] This has been noted by Ettin, *Literature and the Pastoral*, p. 123, and earlier by R. W. Condee, 'The Structure of Milton's "Epitaphium Damonis"', *SP* 62 (1965), 577–94. Condee reads the poem as moving away from shared patterns of pastoral experience to a private, profounder relationship between Milton and Diodati and the symbol of Amor (interpreted as Heavenly Love) in the two cups. I cannot agree that this movement is incompatible with the patterns of pastoral experience.

[O, if I have any time left to live, you, my pastoral pipe, will hang far away on the branch of some old pine-tree, utterly forgotten by me, or else, transformed by my native muses, you will whistle a British tune.]

Pastoral against epic, classical against British: this dual change of intent is reflected in the very different pastoralism of 'Lycidas'.[19] Here Milton shows himself to be unusually aware of the varying, even conflicting scope of various orders of pastoral, and controls them within a sustained design rather than an arbitrary shift from tone to tone. This critical awareness of the full pastoral spectrum, the judicious use of each element in the service of a larger unity, releases a new poetic energy in 'Lycidas', makes it profoundly original while at the same time profoundly conventional.

This dual response appears subtly in the opening lines. The premature culling of the laurel, myrtle, and ivy (especially if, as Warton suggested, they stand not for threnodic poetry but for all poetry) symbolizes King's untimely death; but further, the early, almost precocious nature of the poem itself—a pastoral, as customarily in early work. The 'harsh and crude' exercise reflects the crudeness demanded of pastoral by decorum, and also the crudity associated with a young poet's earliest efforts. Pastoral thus becomes, almost by definition, an imperfect genre, threatening as much as inaugurating the graceful evolution of a pöetic career, as the seasonal rhythm is 'shattered' by King's untimely death. King, by contrast, could 'build the lofty rhyme'—in superior genres or kinds, needless to say. The status of pastoral is questioned at the outset of this pastoral poem. How can it accommodate the greater concerns of 'loftier' poetry—King's concerns, and therefore Milton's in this poem?

To answer this question, we must specify the various modes or levels of poetic utterance in 'Lycidas', pastoral and non-pastoral. The first and most obvious is the literal treatment of the sea and shipwreck:

> He must not float upon his watery bier
> Unwept, and welter to the parching wind . . . (ll. 12–13)

and again more elaborately near the close:

[19] In a different way, of course, change of intent from the norms of pastoral convention appears also in *Arcades* and *A Masque*; but 'Lycidas' is different again. See C. F. Stone III, 'Milton's Self-Concerns and Manuscript Revisions in *Lycidas*', *MLN* 83 (1968), 869–70, for a valuable interpretation of the relations between the poems, though I cannot agree when he goes on to speak of a 'loss of the pastoral' in 'Lycidas' and a disruption of its pastoral entity by higher concerns.

> Ay me! Whilst thee the shores, and sounding seas
> Wash far away, where'er thy bones are hurled . . . (ll. 154–5)

It is mingled with pastoral, somewhat awkwardly, in lines 182–5: the shepherds can rejoice because Lycidas, 'genius of the shore', will protect all who 'wander in that perilous flood'. It is also incongruous that the 'pilot of the Galilean lake' should speak in expressive pastoral metaphor. We may invoke the model of the piscatory eclogue; Sannazaro I has been cited as a specific antecedent. Basically, though, the 'perilous flood' seems to indicate a destructive element, a substratum of uncontrolled reality: it is the poet's purpose to control and overcome it by his pastoral art.[20]

Pastoral first occurs clearly in the account of King and Milton's life at Cambridge:

> For we were nursed upon the self-same hill,
> Fed the same flock; by fountain, shade, and rill. (ll. 23–4)

This is allegorical or 'applied' pastoral of the most obvious sort; but idyllic, uncomplicated, Theocritean in tone. It embodies, if not a direct response to nature, a fresh glimpse of the stylized landscape of pastoral poetry:

> Together both, ere the high lawns appeared
> Under the opening eye-lids of the morn,
> We drove a-field, and both together heard
> What time the grey-fly winds her sultry horn . . . (ll. 25–8)

The 'rough satyrs' and 'rural ditties' also suggest a simple, conventional level of pastoral. The contrasted passage on nature's lament (ll. 39–49) does not, for all the vividness of its pathetic fallacy, make any extraordinary demand of the convention. Indeed, it closely follows the 'Lament for Bion'. An assessment of this conventional vein occurs by implication in lines 50–63:

> What could the muse herself that Orpheus bore,
> The muse herself for her enchanting son . . . (ll. 58–9)

[20] Cf. Isabel MacCaffrey, 'Lycidas: The Poet in a Landscape', *The Lyric and Dramatic Milton*, p. 73: the ocean is 'a feature of the literal level; it is also connected, of course, with Milton's feelings about the uncontrollable events of human life', contrasted with 'the fountains, dews and friendly rivers that mourn for Lycidas in the unsullied pastoral world' (p. 79). Brooks and Hardy had also viewed the ocean as 'unfriendly and alien': surely the impression is not overcome by Woodhouse and Bush's literal-minded objection that the sea was singularly calm when King was shipwrecked (see *Variorum Commentary*, ii/2. 591).

Though not explicitly pastoral, this passage sounds a number of associations: the marine or piscatory eclogue, topographical myth, the figure of Orpheus so often conceived (though not here) as a shepherd. We feel the ineffectuality of the mythologized poetic world of which standard pastoral forms a part.

Although allusive, such pastoral is thematically undemanding in any deeper sense. It does not incorporate what, for Milton, are the deepest concerns of King's and his own life. But the mention of Orpheus raises this world to a more elevated station. A new worth and seriousness now appear in the concept of poetry as pastoral:

> Alas! What boots it with uncessant care
> To tend the homely slighted shepherd's trade,
> And strictly meditate the thankless muse,
> Were it not better done as others use,
> To sport with Amaryllis in the shade,
> Or with the tangles of Neaera's hair? (ll. 64–9)

As in Comus's temptation-speech, two aspects of conventional pastoral are being placed in opposition: its pristine *otium*, even libertinism, as developed in the Arcadian strain distilled from classical pastoral, and the actual labours of the herdsman, exemplifying a higher virtue. The 'shepherd's trade' fleetingly suggests the proletarian pastoral of Barclay and Plowman literature. Of course, these suggestions are not developed, for the shepherd's trade is here patently allegorical for the poet's; but it is significant that the 'homely' and earthy implications of shepherd life constitute the strain associated with the 'clear spirit' and the higher thematic reaches of pastoral.[21]

Here, then, we reach a new level of pastoral allegory—more purely allegorical, more restricted in its aesthetic and descriptive scope, but carrying a deeper thematic charge, an allegory of ethos and not merely an allegory of fact. The more conventional pastoral of the 'Epitaphium Damonis' had served a similar function; but now we have a rarer if more rigid ethos and a divergent vein of pastoral to match it. Lycidas's 'lofty rhyme' is linked to the pastoral after all. Indeed, Phoebus's speech (Apollo has significantly replaced Pan's rout of 'rough satyrs' and old Damaetas) presents the poet's career as a hubristic, tragic progress, and

[21] Poggioli (p. 89) would hold that this strain is actually unpastoral. The earlier chapters of my book should disprove this notion, though we may agree with Poggioli that in ll. 67–9 Milton is dismissing the 'pastoral of love'.

its frustration as a kind of nemesis. That is why Milton makes a Fury, not a Fate, wield 'th'abhorred shears'.

Though Phoebus's speech is introduced by an intensified metaphor of the poet as shepherd, the speech itself is not pastoral. We are, as it were, being led beyond the pastoral at this point, though we shall return to it at a still higher stage of the argument, in St Peter's speech and the description of heaven. This appears to be Milton's customary mode of progression in 'Lycidas'. He introduces a 'lofty' concern, apparently beyond the reach of pastoral, but finally incorporated within the mode. Thus, stage by stage, he builds up an intricate structure of various versions of pastoral reflecting increasingly serious and complex themes.[22]

Milton recognizes the 'higher note' in Phoebus's speech, in contrast to Sicilian and Roman pastoral, Arethusa and the Mincio. There can be no easy return to this simple strain: his 'oat proceeds', faces the question of why Lycidas died, by reverting to the literal 'marine' strain that, I suggested earlier, represents the intractable reality challenging the poet's art. Here Milton uses a standard premiss going back to Virgil IV. In the Golden Age, man had not acquired the art of navigation, so that 'that fatal and perfidious bark | Built in the eclipse, and rigged with curses dark' (ll. 100–1) shadows the fallen state of man.

From this point, Milton gradually readopts the pastoral again. The satyr-ridden Arcady of Cambridge life is replaced by the figure of 'Camus, reverend sire'. Such nature-myth is allied to pastoral, though still in an aquatic context. We may be specially reminded of Giles Fletcher's Father Cam.[23]

We remain on the water with the 'pilot of the Galilean lake'; but his speech introduces the most intense and serious use of pastoral in the poem. In content, of course, it is the usual Church-pastoral metaphor. Its importance lies in its function in Milton's total scheme. Another level of pastoral is opened up: a religious and moral concern, expressed through indignation at the corruption of the clergy. The 'lean and flashy songs' may still allude to poetry, though more probably to sermons or religious

[22] A. S. P. Woodhouse finds the first two of the three movements in 'Lycidas' to 'shatter the pastoral tone' (*Variorum Commentary*, ii/2. 594). Similarly, J. S. Lawry, '"Eager Thought": Dialectic in *Lycidas*', PMLA 77 (1962), 27–32, also holds that, through most of the poem, pastoral proves unequal to the 'thrust of reality'; but through the priest-shepherd and paradisal motifs, it is incorporated in the final synthesis. Cf. also MacCaffrey, pp. 65–92, that many readers feel that in 'Lycidas', the pastoral is 'repeatedly left behind as new ranges of awareness open' (p. 71) but that ultimately the poem 'can be read as a reassessment of the pastoral mode itself' (p. 78).

[23] Description quoted in Ch. 6, sect. 1.

works and doctrines generally. In any case, the songs are being dismissed in religious and ethical terms rather than literary ones. The dominant metaphor is that of shepherd as cleric, not shepherd as poet.

Already in Phoebus's speech, the hero-poet's aspiration had been seen, ultimately, in moral and religious terms; it 'lives and spreads aloft by those pure eyes, | And perfect witness of all-judging Jove' (ll. 81–2). In St Peter's speech, the concept is given pastoral guise. The progress from non-pastoral to pastoral is also a progress from pagan to Christian, Phoebus to St Peter. For Milton, the higher thematic reaches of the pastoral appear to be distinctively Christian. We shall see this more strikingly later on.

St Peter's speech is followed by the flower-passage with its delicate but restricted lyricism. The Arcadian strain is consciously reinvoked: 'Return, Alpheus . . .'. This part of the poem conceals a paradox. Despite the lyric energy and profusion of detail, it actually describes a desecration of nature, flowers plucked or shed for Lycidas's hearse, giving up their beauty in self-destructive homage:

> Bid amaranthus all his beauty shed,
> And daffadillies fill their cups with tears . . . (ll. 149–50)

This indicates the futility of a return to Arcadianism so late in the poem.

> For so to interpose a little ease,
> Let our frail thoughts dally with false surmise. (ll. 152–3)

Is this again an allusive reference to poetry, the elegies and tributes to King's memory? If so, it constitutes a dismissive comment on the entire *Justa Edouardo King naufrago*, a self-deprecatory parallel to the 'Orpheus' passage. It is followed by the harrowing account of King's drifting corpse, overwhelming the lyric fiction of an Arcadian funeral.

This destructive reality is finally overcome in a vision of heaven:

> Where other groves, and other streams along,
> With nectar pure his oozy locks he laves,
> And hears the unexpressive nuptial song,
> In the blest kingdoms meek of joy and love. (ll. 174–7)

This is not pastoral, but a paradisal topos that touches one end of the pastoral spectrum, like the Elysium at the end of *Comus*. It is further anchored to pastoral by the formal correspondence in superiority of the 'solemn troops' of saints to the earlier rout of fauns and satyrs. We may even see a transformation of pastoral humility in the 'blest kingdoms meek of joy and love'. One strand of Phoebus's non-pastoral speech had progressed to St Peter's pastoral metaphor. Another strand—'Fame is no plant that grows on mortal soil'—culminates in the paradisal image of this sequence.[24]

By this transformation into paradisal terms, the pastoral is vindicated at the end. And, we may note, it is no longer an allusive mode: the terms of the convention have been literally realized in the description of heaven.

I may recapitulate the levels of pastoral in the poem. There are four at least: a simple Arcadianism, aesthetic and mythic in conception though already allusive in function; a sterner, more demanding assessment of the 'homely slighted shepherd's trade', artistic discipline deepening into moral; the fervid religious and ecclesiastical concerns of St Peter's pastoral metaphor of the sheepfold; and above these, the trans-pastoral, paradisal setting of the descripton of heaven. These are placed in a climactic series, mediated through non-pastoral passages like Phoebus's speech, and counterpointed by that image of destruction, the sea. Milton shows a master's control of the various possibilities of pastoral in a structure that will best answer his general concerns as a poet. As Rajan says of Milton generally, it is his 'habit to strain at the form, to oblige it to surpass its own dimensions; yet the impression given is not of violation but of a highly individual fulfilment, of something latent being raised into imaginative actuality'.[25]

But we may view the same structure in a very different light. Rajan himself notes in 'Lycidas' 'the angry challenge of the poem to the tradition which it inherits'.[26] What in 'Lycidas' becomes an ascending or progressive design is, in terms of pastoral generally, a restrictive or retrogressive one. Growing more and more allusive and externally oriented, it marks a decline of the special quality of the pastoral imagination as I have defined it throughout this book. The basic pastoral fiction is for Milton an inadequate and undemanding Arcadianism. Grappling with deeper concerns, he turns to specific, increasingly rigid and reductive *applications* of a fertile and suggestive mode. One may almost say that Milton achieves success by narrowing and diverting the possibilities of pastoral, exploiting certain specific potentials while

[24] We may even see Heaven in *Paradise Lost* as the ultimate supra-pastoral perfection of the earthly paradise, supra-pastoral in itself. See, in this connection, John R. Knott, jun., *Milton's Pastoral Vision* (Chicago, 1971), 53–5, and ch. iii *passim*. Knott mentions many other instances of pastoral and quasi-pastoral heavens (pp. 78–82).

[25] B. Rajan, *The Lofty Rhyme* (London, 1970), 26.

[26] Ibid. 46.

professing minimal adherence to its basic assumptions. 'Lycidas' becomes an unlikely instance of a 'self-consuming artefact'. It operates on the periphery of the genre to which it lays such resounding claim by its perfection of form.

The animating principle of the poem lies elsewhere. The opposition of classic Arcadianism and 'higher' moral and religious allegory reflects a contrast between the easy exercise of poetic fancy and the pervasive intellectual and moral rigour that Milton prescribes for the true poet:

> whatsoever in religion is holy and sublime, in vertu amiable, or grave, whatsoever hath passion or admiration . . . all these things with a solid and treatable smoothnesse to paint out and describe . . . And what a benefit this would be to our youth and gentry, may be soon guest by what we know of the corruption and bane which they suck in dayly from the writings and interludes of libidinous and ignorant Poetasters . . .[27]

Further, such an opposition foreshadows Milton's habitual 'competitive' method as later applied to epic in *Paradise Lost*, Book IX:

> The skill of artifice or office mean,
> Not that which justly gives heroic name
> To person or to poem. Me of these
> Not skilled nor studious, higher argument
> Remains . . . (ll. 39–43)

So also in 'Lycidas', pastoral is carefully adapted to Milton's own greater poetic programme. This makes it entirely appropriate that the poet should occur as a character and indeed the principal speaker of the elegy. Since Tillyard, readings of 'Lycidas' have brought out the operation of Milton's private ambitions and fears. These are reinforced by more general fears for the state of the clergy. 'Lycidas', says Michael Lloyd, deals chiefly 'with the salvation of the shepherd rather than the sheep'.[28]

The shepherd-speaker of 'Lycidas' is brought into unusually close affinity with Lycidas himself:

> So may some gentle muse
> With lucky words favour my destined urn,
> And as he passes turn,
> And bid fair peace be to my sable shroud.

[27] *The Reason of Church Government*, Preface to Book II, as ed. H. M. Ayres in Milton's *Works* (Columbia edn., ed. F. A. Patterson *et al.*), iii/1 (New York, 1931), 238–9.

[28] 'The Two Worlds of *Lycidas*', *Essays in Criticism*, 11 (1961), 390.

For we were nursed upon the self-same hill,
Fed the same flock; by fountain, shade, and rill. (ll. 19–24)

References to this 'I' recur at every stage of the poem. He is participant (ll. 3, 56, 88) as well as listener or observer (ll. 77, 87, 154), a steady monitoring presence and yet himself one of the poem's direct concerns. Indeed, the enclosing framework of the poem reflects Milton's concern with his own poetic career. The opening 'Yet once more' draws us back to his earlier elegies and early poetry generally. At the close, 'fresh woods, and pastures new' points forward to his future work—perhaps specifically to a new, fortified religious poetry of which the later portion of 'Lycidas' marks the inception. (To what extent does this line echo the 'other groves, and other streams' where Lycidas now walks?) The poem is thus presented as an episode in the 'true poem' of Milton's life,[29] the overriding term of reference in relation to which all the other themes are viewed.

Thus 'Lycidas' illustrates not simply a personal allegory in pastoral terms, but the adaptation of the convention to a new personalized mode of apprehension. The poet's personality is, as it were, outgrowing the confines of a pastoral persona, the designedly oblique or objectified presentation of the self which earlier poets including Spenser had sought in pastoral. The fact that the speaker in 'Lycidas' has no name is significant: he is not sufficiently realized as a distinct character or persona, but is much more closely identifiable with the poet.[30]

Dr Johnson grasped the wrong end of the stick. If 'passion runs not after remote allusions and obscure opinions',[31] 'Lycidas' may be said to succeed by an unusually direct expression of personality, passion, and ambition breaking through the set forms. John Crowe Ransom made the point in a celebrated if controversial essay.[32]

The wrought classical grace of Milton's poem conceals fertile dissensions and contradictions. Milton brings us into a new poetic realm of more direct personal concern and direct grappling with serious themes. Here pastoral, with its graceful indirections and speculative play of

[29] '. . . he who would not be frustrate of his hope to write well hereafter in laudable things, ought him selfe to bee a true Poem' (*Apology for Smectymnuus*, ed. H. M. Ayres, Columbia edn., iii/1. 303).

[30] But contrast M. H. Abrams's view: 'Milton is at considerable pains to identify [the 'uncouth swain'] as someone other than himself': 'Five Types of *Lycidas*', as cited in the *Variorum Commentary*, ii/2. 610.

[31] 'Life of Milton', *Lives of the Poets*, ed. Birkbeck Hill, i. 163.

[32] 'Lycidas: A Poem Nearly Anonymous'; see *Variorum Commentary*, ii/2. 573–4.

symbols, is no more than a strategy of expression, however consummate in form. Milton provides an interesting parallel with Marvell, his co-pastoralist and political associate. Marvell deliberately, and flamboyantly, breaks the conventional forms of pastoral, weaves new concerns and energies into components levered from their standard settings by his poetic play. Milton, on the other hand, brings conventional devices and ingredients to their last refinement but places them in new combinations, dictated by new poetic habits and purposes.

The formal pastoral of the Restoration and eighteenth century appears to be in the same classic strain as 'Lycidas'; but there is between the two all that marks the original, creative working-out—even working-through—of a convention from the mechanical manipulation of its elements in set depersonalized patterns.

4. Paradise Lost *and* Paradise Regained

Paradise Lost contains little or nothing truly pastoral; but the account of Paradise shows subterraneous use of pastoral details and assumptions. Explicit references to pastoral or sylvan myth can be dismissive, in Milton's habitual contrast with Christian (here paradisal) myth. Adam and Eve's bower is superior to the 'feigned' ones of Pan or Silvanus, nymph or Faunus (IV. 705–8), and Eve's beauty exceeds that of the wood-nymphs, or the goddesses on Mount Ida (V. 379–83). On the other hand, we have 'Universal Pan' leading the Graces and the Hours in dance (IV. 266–8). This emblems the use of pastoral elements in the accounts of Paradise.

The landscape of Paradise can be utterly Theocritean:

> Another side, umbrageous grots and caves
> Of cool recess, o'er which the mantling vine
> Lays forth her purple grape, and gently creeps
> Luxuriant; mean while murmuring waters fall
> Down the slope hills . . . (IV. 257–61)

Immediately before this comes the modified pastoral of the country-house poem: 'A happy rural seat of various view', with 'lawns, or level downs, and flocks | Grazing the tender herb' (IV. 247, 252–3). Here we approach the private impulse behind Milton's pastoral, nurtured upon his own rural observation as directly presented in 'L'Allegro' and worked into the spirit of Paradise as observed by Satan in Book IX:

As one who long in populous city pent,
Where houses thick and sewers annoy the air,
Forth issuing on a summer's morn to breathe
Among the pleasant villages and farms
Adjoined, from each thing met conceives delight,
The smell of grain, or tedded grass, or kine,
Or dairy, each rural sight, each rural sound;
If chance with nymph-like step fair virgin pass,
What pleasing seemed, for her now pleases more . . . (ll. 445–53)

This passage, more clearly than any other, places Paradise in line with Milton's earliest and simplest versions of pastoral. Penetrating the suspect zone of classical pastoral, Milton reinstates the basic pastoral impulse as unfallen and paradisal. Significantly, in Book XI, the vision of strife in lines 638 ff. is largely presented as the destruction of a pastoral landscape.

One way a band select from forage drives
A herd of beeves, fair oxen and fair kine
From a fat meadow ground; or fleecy flock,
Ewes and their bleating lambs over the plain,
Their booty; scarce with life the shepherds fly . . . (XI. 646–50)

It is also significant that Satan should often be alluded to in images of pastoral destruction (III. 434–5, IV. 403–4, and the wolf-image in IV. 183–7).

The distinctive nature of paradisal innocence must be made clear. It incorporates a sensuality or even libertinism within its pristine 'Simplicity and spotless innocence'. The very vines in Paradise are 'luxuriant' (IV. 260), while the brooks run in 'mazy error' (IV. 239):

A wilderness of sweets; for nature here
Wantoned as in her prime, and played at will
Her virgin fancies, pouring forth more sweet,
Wild above rule or art; enormous bliss.[33]

In this setting, Eve wears her hair 'in wanton ringlets . . . | As the vine curls her tendrils' (IV. 306–7); and her bearing, while quintessentially innocent, seems to prolepsize the dalliance of the conventional shepherdess: 'sweet reluctant amorous delay'.[34] Indeed, Eden affords the

[33] V. 294–7; cf. IV. 629–31, V. 212–15.

[34] Giamatti (*The Earthly Paradise*, pp. 302 ff.) sees this as an anticipation of the Fall, the presence of ensnaring and corrupting elements in Paradise itself. But this is a proleptic view: before the Fall, these possibilities are contained within a purifying and transforming innocence.

ultimate prototype of the primary impulses enshrined in pastoral, reduced to their greatest clarity, simplicity, and innocence by use of the most compelling of allied Christian myths:[35]

> O innocence
> Deserving Paradise! If ever, then,
> Then had the sons of God excuse to have been
> Enamoured at that sight; but in those hearts
> Love unlibidinous reigned, nor jealousy
> Was understood, the injured lover's hell. (v. 445–50)

A similar, typically pastoral paradox inheres in the joyful and unexacting labours of Adam and Eve in the garden, an activity twin to *otium*.[36] At certain points, we see them virtually as rustic labourers:[37]

> Adam, in what bower or shade
> Thou find'st him from the heat of noon retired,
> To respite his day-labour with repast . . . (v. 230–32)

Eve preparing dinner reminds us of Thestylis in 'L'Allegro' (see v. 303–7); and their hospitality to Raphael in Book V recalls (or should we say foreshadows?) that of innumerable shepherds of pastoral convention. The fare formalizes rude pastoral plenty in mythic terms: 'where store, | All seasons, ripe for use hangs on the stalk' (v. 322–3). Even the animals playing around Adam and Eve as they eat indicate a transmogrified pastoral:

> others on the grass
> Couched, and now filled with pasture gazing sat,
> Or bedward ruminating: for the sun
> Declined was hasting now with prone career . . . (iv. 350–3)

Such details show the clear infusion of pastoral convention into what may otherwise be regarded simply as a parallel exercise in soft primitivism. A full analysis of the paradisal landscape is beyond the scope

[35] Cf. Knott, p. 22: 'Every action of Adam's—eating, labouring, even lovemaking—is an implicit affirmation of his love for God and dependence upon him.' Cf. also pp. 111–14, where Knott compares Eve to Pastorella and Perdita in terms of 'an instinctive sympathy with nature that seems both the proof and the source of innocence' (p. 112).

[36] I cannot agree with Knott (pp. 11, 48) that Adam's state differs from *otium* because of his awareness of, and obedience to, God.

[37] Knott points out (pp. 92–3) how Adam and Eve's labours follow the conventional pattern of the 'pastoral day', and how Milton departs from standard accounts of Paradise by introducing a hot noon. Cf. the labourers in 'L'Allegro', ll. 82–8, and the sleeping farmhand in the 'Epitaphium Damonis', l. 54.

of my study. (It has already been attempted with fair success by John Knott in *Milton's Pastoral Art*.) I have only to note the presence of pastoral elements and analogies. Here in his *magnum opus*, Milton has interwoven the pastoral with his dominant myths, fables, and conventions.

Pastoral in *Paradise Regained* is much more in line with that in *Arcades* or *A Masque*. Classical pastoral, and allied topoi chiefly drawn from later romances, are clearly linked to Satan and his temptations. Like Comus to the Lady, Satan first appears to Christ in shepherd's weeds (I. 314ff.). 'Pan, | Satyr, or Faun, or Sylvan' (like other classical gods) provide disguises for Belial during his escapades

> In wood or grove by mossy fountain-side,
> In valley or green meadow to waylay
> Some beauty rare . . . (II. 184–6)

Indeed, 'sylvan pipe or song' are early associated with hypocrisy, the mere profession of virtue, in contrast to the hard ways of truth (I. 478–80); and to add further irony, the contrast is drawn by Satan himself.

When Christ awakes from sleep in Book II, he finds himself in a pleasing rural setting and searches for 'cottage, herd or sheep-cote' (II. 288). He comes upon a 'pleasant grove', a *locus amoenus*, a setting for sylvan myth: 'to a superstitious eye the haunt | Of wood-gods and wood-nymphs' (II. 296–7). This is the scene laid by Satan to tempt Christ with 'A table richly spread'. Satan now appears 'Not rustic as before, but seemlier clad, | As one in city, or court, or palace bred' (II. 299–300). The scene is evocative of a courtlier pastoralism, the alfresco banquet of Renaissance potentates:

> And at a stately sideboard by the wine
> That fragrant smell diffused, in order stood
> Tall stripling youths rich-clad, of fairer hue
> Than Ganymede or Hylas, distant more
> Under the trees now tripped, now solemn stood
> Nymphs of Diana's train, and Naiades
> With fruits and flowers from Amalthea's horn . . . (II. 350–6)

Yet at the end of his trials, Christ is truly refreshed in a *locus amoenus* to which he is borne by angels, a Godly bower conjured up in exact parallel to the satanic one:[38]

[38] Knott (p. 23) also compares this meal with that offered to Raphael by Adam and Eve in *Paradise Lost*, Book V.

> Then in a flowery valley set him down
> On a green bank, and set before him spread
> A table of celestial food, divine . . . (IV. 586–8)

Much earlier, and still more tellingly, Christ's disciples are depicted as 'plain fishermen' in a piscatory–pastoral analogy to Satan's shepherd guise. A single line (II. 26) conjures up an idyllic landscape, set however in a context of appropriately 'hard' primitivism:

> Then on the bank of Jordan, by a creek:
> Where winds with reeds, and osiers whisp'ring play
> Plain fishermen, no greater men them call,
> Close in a cottage low together got
> Their unexpected loss and plaints outbreathed. (II. 25–9)

The implications are not developed, and the apostles-to-be disappear from the poem; but once again, Milton's central concern in *Paradise Regained*—the spiritual struggle born of primary humane impulse at the basic level of existence—is fleetingly allowed to validate and redeem the pastoral convention.

22
Andrew Marvell

MARVELL is the only Metaphysical poet to use pastoral on a large scale. Although his poems predate much of Milton's work, I am treating him after the latter as he provides a fitter conclusion to my survey. Pastoral is far more central to Marvell's poetry: Laurence Lerner calls him the most pastoral of seventeenth-century poets.[1] Coming at the end of the Renaissance, he provides a comment on all that has gone before, as well as an intensely individual exploration of new directions. This often takes him beyond the confines of formal pastoral; and departing from my usual practice, I must follow him there to gauge his total response to the mode.

The orthodox potential of the convention exhausted, it provides matter for Marvell's Metaphysical wit. He vitalizes pastoral by the only means remaining to him: working against its grain, exploiting its tensions and paradoxes, replacing its simple finished forms by probing, teasing, open-ended explorations. Even a light piece like 'Ametas and Thestylis making Hay-Ropes', formally reminiscent of Elizabethan pastoral lyrics, uses a substantial metaphor to explore the nature of love ('Love binds Love as Hay binds Hay')[2] instead of simply accepting it with joyful abandon.[3] Marvell is working an alert variation upon the light, sophisticated lyric usual in Jacobean and Caroline pastoral poetry.

In more complex poems, Marvell re-examines conventional pastoral by presenting a truer confrontation of man and nature. If they finally harmonize, it is along radically new lines.

First of all, Marvell lays far greater stress on the natural setting, sometimes conceiving it as an entirely separate entity. It can conflict or contrast with man, as in the Mower poems or 'The Garden'. I have noted in Chapter 11, section 2, how Metaphysical poets, particularly Vaughan, reverse the relation between man and nature found in orthodox pastoral. In a less openly Christian or religious form, we find the same relation in Marvell. Most simply put, nature exemplifies a moral force or order

[1] Lerner, *The Uses of Nostalgia*, p. 17.
[2] All refs. to Marvell's *Poems*, ed. Hugh Macdonald (The Muses' Lib.).
[3] Cf. Leishman, *The Art of Marvell's Poetry*, p. 119.

while human impulse displays what we may call a pristine impurity, an unregulated, subversive state allied to original sin.

These opposite forces are then brought into contact, sometimes in an archetypal conflict between nature and man: a paradoxical pastoral of disharmony and alienation. Marvell challenges the basic assumptions of pastoral beneath an audacious play with its surface conventions. Man's resort to nature might not re-create Paradise but re-enact the Fall. Hence the chief figure of man in contact with nature is no longer the shepherd but the mower, destroyer not feeder, although in a curious state of empathy with nature. Where a shepherdess appears, like Juliana in 'Damon the Mower', she too has a destructive effect on nature:

> Not *July* causeth these Extremes,
> But *Juliana's* scorching beams. (ll. 23–4)

Occasionally nature itself is sullied, fallen—as in the same poem:

> Only the Snake, that kept within,
> Now glitters in its second skin. (ll. 15–16)

This counters in advance the defanged, harmless snake that makes an orthodox pastoral gift in lines 35–6.[4] The 'heat' of Damon's unrequited love has scorched the natural world as well. In 'The Mower against Gardens', the ordering of nature by 'luxurious [lustful] Man' perverts life and fertility, leaving nature sterile beneath a debased luxuriance: witness the 'dead and standing pool of Air', the eunuchs in the 'green *Seraglio*', the sexless cherry. But the '*Fauns* and *Faryes*'—potentially sinister creatures in that age—are miraculously unspoilt by contrast, exuding 'A wild and fragrant Innocence' (l. 34).

Usually, nature is not corrupted but simply suppressed or destroyed. It suffers at the hand of man: the Mower in 'Upon Appleton House', 'carving' the rail with his scythe (ll. 393–400), brings death into paradise and fears his own death in consequence. The same pattern is magnified in 'The Mower's Song', where the Mower destroys nature and is destroyed by the same violence, now operating ironically through his own love:

> For *Juliana* comes, and She
> What I do to the Grass, does to my Thoughts and Me. (ll. 23–4)

[4] Patrick Cullen discounts such symbolism, along with virtually all other philosophic or other serious concerns in the Mower poems (*Spenser, Marvell, and Renaissance Pastoral*, p. 192). I find it impossible to share his view.

The Fall appears in Marvell in many guises, and man's desecration of nature is one of them. The death of the rail parallels that of the fawn in 'The Nymph Complaining'. In 'Upon Appleton House' England itself is an Eden destroyed by the Civil War, its violence displacing the 'sweet *Militia*' of flowers.

But paradisal nature survives outside the range of human influence. Man might even undo the effects of the Fall by union with this pristine nature—as in at least one poem, 'The Garden'.

However, 'The Garden' also illustrates how unfallen nature does not embody any autonomous ideal but a purer version of *human* traits and experiences.

> No white nor red was ever seen
> So am'rous as this lovely green. (ll. 17–18)

We have here the paradox of eminently human attributes which can, however, be embodied in nature only by excluding man from the scene.[5] Humanity achieves perfection by surrendering its proper medium, human life.

Hence Marvell's descriptive mode is peculiarly anthropocentric: nature's values are adapted from man's. She can display not only human warmth but lushness and even eroticism: 'Insnar'd with Flow'rs, I fall on Grass' ('The Garden', l. 40) The green of the garden is more amorous than any human mistress. The very fawn in 'The Nymph Complaining' has a markedly erotic tinge to its innocent affection. At Appleton, the River Denton embraces the meadows in 'wanton harmless folds'. This latency of the unspiritual affords scope for witty play; at a deeper level, it reflects a subtle engagement between innocence and experience, action and contemplation.

Nature and man love and hate each other in Marvell. Their spirits come together, move apart, enter into union and into conflict, alternately subjugate each other. Sometimes this results in a plausible imitation of conventional pastoral forms; sometimes the elements are rent apart so as to spite convention or question the very basis of pastoral.

Nature seems to devise her paradisal delights only to offer them to man. In 'Upon Appleton House' the poet walks through the woods as the lord of nature:

[5] Contrast the simple purification of human impulse in, say, Mildmay Fane. See Røstvig, *The Happy Man*, i. 133ff.

Then, languishing with ease, I toss
On Pallets swoln of Velvet Moss;
While the Wind, cooling through the Boughs,
Flatters with Air my panting Brows. (ll. 593–6)

The fruits in 'The Garden' offer themselves seductively to the poet; and 'Damon the Mower' sees all nature as ministering to him alone:

On me the Morn her dew distills
Before her darling Daffadils.
And, if at Noon my toil me heat,
The Sun himself licks off my Sweat.
While, going home, the Ev'ning sweet
In cowslip-water bathes my feet. (ll. 43–8)

This passes into a darker alliance where nature corrupts herself in ready sympathy with Damon's love:

This heat the Sun could never raise,
Nor Dog-star so inflame's the dayes

Not *July* causeth these Extremes,
But *Juliana's* scorching beams. (ll. 17–18, 23–4)

Needless to say, it is in the Fairfax poems that human influence upon nature is most apparent. Bilborough Hill presents an archetype of the world, and a 'securer Glory' invests its slopes than those of proud, upstart heights.[6] But this reflects the spirit of its master Fairfax. Humanity works even more decisively on the landscape in 'Upon Appleton House'. The chaos of greater nature contrasts with the purged and ordered microcosm of the estate:

'Tis not, what once it was, the *World*:
But a rude heap together hurl'd;

Your lesser *World* contains the same.
But in more decent Order tame; (ll. 761–2, 765–6)

Appleton and Bilborough matter to the poet because they embody the genius of the Fairfaxes better than any building can:

Him *Bishops-Hill*, or *Denton* may,
Or *Bilbrough*, better hold then they:
But Nature here hath been so free
As if she said leave this to me. (ll. 73–6)

[6] 'Upon the Hill and Grove at Bill-Borow', ll. 1–16.

The landscape must enter into relation with man, acquire significance or indeed its very being from this source alone. In 'Upon Appleton House', Marvell abjures the basic premiss of the country-house poem, the social structure binding together man and the countryside. Fairfax's genius works directly upon the land, not as mediated through the life of a rustic community. Instead we have a larger theatre of nature shaped to express an exceptional humanity. Indeed, as is seen in 'Bill-borow', man is capable of greater glories than nature can accommodate:

> For all the *Civick Garlands* due
> To him our Branches are but few.
> Nor are our Trunks enow to bear
> The *Trophees* of one fertile Year. (ll. 69–72)

Maria Fairfax also embodies a perfection which is inadequately mirrored in the woods in 'Upon Appleton House':

> *She* streightness on the Woods bestows;
> To *Her* the Meadow sweetness owes;
> Nothing could make the River be
> So Chrystal-pure but only *She*:
> *She* yet more Pure, Sweet, Streight, and Fair,
> Then Gardens, Woods, Meads, Rivers are. (ll. 691–6)

She enforces what we can only call a moral discipline over nature:

> See how loose Nature, in respect
> To her, it self doth recollect;
> And every thing so whisht and fine,
> Starts forth with to its *Bonne Mine*.
> The *Sun* himself, of *Her* aware,
> Seems to descend with greater Care . . . (ll. 657–62)

Theophila Cornewall, we may recall, is to 'Reform the errours of the Spring' ('The Picture of little T. C. in a Prospect of Flowers', l. 27). In all these instances, nature is shaped and governed by the human spirit: a paradise originating in man and partially communicating itself to nature. Man may have corrupted nature by his fall; but he redeems it again by his own transforming virtue. Maria's virtue is not merely dominant but seminal and original, its unmoved perfection activating the world around her. Indeed, she 'vitrifies' nature, as the purifying Last Fire will do.[7]

Marvell's most substantial nature-poem being cast as a compliment to

[7] See Thomas Browne, *Religio Medici*, i. 50.

an aristocrat and military hero, there cannot but be a realignment of the active and contemplative ideals. Standard pastoral had been wedded to the latter. The supremacy of the active life was perversely upheld in much allusive pastoral, but only by undermining and impoverishing the mode. Marvell, on the contrary, achieves a true balance of opposites.

The 'Battle of Flowers' in 'Upon Appleton House' (stanzas 37–46) affords an obvious illustration. The innocent militarism of the flowers suggests a virtue of which nature is the fit resort and embodiment. It can, however, be exceeded by human virtue as embodied in Fairfax. This is partly a matter of moral discipline, an enhanced spiritual application of the gardener's own art:

> For he did, with his utmost Skill,
> *Ambition* weed, but *Conscience* till.
> *Conscience*, that Heaven-nursed Plant,
> Which most our Earthly Gardens want. (ll. 353–6)

Here again is an 'inner Paradise'. But already in the preceding stanza, Marvell has advanced a superior active ideal, cultivating the 'Gardens' of England through warfare and government. He regrets that Fairfax 'preferr'd to the *Cinque Ports* | These five imaginary Forts' (ll. 349–50). Contemplative discipline should be a preparation for the exercise of active, even military energy.[8] Man exceeds nature, perfects the latter's vein of innocence and pure virtue, restores the Golden Age—and this through engagement with the world in place of retreat to a symbolic flower-garden.

The 'paradise within' is no longer projected on to nature but embodied in human action, among 'Groves of Pikes' and mountains of corpses for which Bilborough Hill is a humble substitute. Even in a landscape-poem, Marvell has moved a long way towards 'An Horatian Ode upon Cromwell's Return from Ireland', with its celebration of martial activity and rejection of the rural retreat:

> Much to the Man is due.
> Who, from his private Gardens, where
> He liv'd reserved and austere,

[8] It seems inescapable that the active virtues are indeed held superior, though the contrary has sometimes been suggested: e.g. M. C. Bradbrook and M. G. Lloyd Thomas, *Andrew Marvell* (Cambridge, 1961), 36, 'the General's highest glory is that he gave up his command'. See also John M. Wallace, *Destiny His Choice: The Loyalism of Andrew Marvell* (Cambridge, 1968), 242–8. Cf. n. 9 below.

As if his highest plot
To plant the Bergamot,
Could by industrious Valour climbe
To ruine the great Work of Time . . . (ll. 28–34)

Yet, as Friedman points out,[9] there is a sense of fitness, indeed of fulfilment of one virtue by another, in that Fairfax should abandon the battlefield for Bilborough:

But Peace (if you his favour prize)
That Courage its own Praises flies.
Therefore to your obscurer Seats
From his own Brightness he retreats:
Nor he the Hills without the Groves,
Nor Height but with Retirement loves. (ll. 75–80)

Bilborough outshines the 'Mountains more unjust' by the same modesty born of perfection. It is the perfect symbol of Fairfax's ethical state; or, more accurately, an extension or enshrinement of that state in nature. Worldly and unworldly, human and 'natural' preoccupations, war and peace, engagement and withdrawal—these opposites are reconciled, or at any rate associated, by placing a martial and aristocratic culture in a rural setting.

The fusion occurs most subtly in the passage in 'Upon Appleton House' on the surrounding woods. It is a 'Sanctuary', a 'Temple green', and an 'Ark'—that is, an equivalent of the Church, as 'Natures mystick Book' is of the revealed scriptures (stanza 73). But the wood is also an epitome of the natural or material world:

where all Creatures might have shares;
Although in Armies, not in Paires. (ll. 487–8)

It is a 'yet green, yet growing Ark': sanctity is combined with, indeed expressed through, physical vitality. There is even a sardonic ring to this benediction, a whimsical insistence upon unheroic physical detail.

The Oak-Leaves me embroyder all,
Between which Caterpillars crawl:
And Ivy, with familiar trails,
Me licks, and clasps, and curles, and hales. (ll. 587–90)

[9] Donald M. Friedman, *Marvell's Pastoral Art* (London, 1970), 201–2, 208–9. For other admissions of the equivocal nature of Marvell's judgement, see e.g. Ruth Wallerstein, *Studies in Seventeenth-Century Poetic* (Madison, 1950; repr. 1961), 286–7; John Dixon Hunt, *Andrew Marvell* (London, 1978), 188–9; Annabel M. Patterson, *Marvell and the Civic Crown* (Princeton, 1978), 95–110.

These are the vestures of the 'great *Prelate of the Grove*'. Later we have clear sexual or erotic overtones:

> Bind me ye *Woodbines* in your 'twines,
> Curle me about ye gadding *Vines* . . . (ll. 609–10)

Is this a negation of the paradisal purity of the woods, or a confirmation of its purifying power over the baser emotions? Earlier, the woodpecker's foraging had re-enacted the Fall:

> Who could have thought the *tallest Oak*
> Should fall by such a *feeble Strok*'!
>
> Nor would it, had the Tree not fed
> A *Traitor-worm*, within it bred.
> (As first our *Flesh* corrupt within
> Tempts impotent and bashful *Sin* . . .) (ll. 551–6)

But this parallel is part of the poet's 'easie Philosophie'—the gift of *otium*, relaxed meditation born of an 'unfallen' peace of mind. The Fall itself is rendered innocent in the woods: the tone of the comparison negates the premisses, drawing the poet into the happy rhythm of life among 'lower' nature.[10]

The pervasive sense of peace and withdrawal evokes echoes of 'The Garden':

> How safe, methinks, and strong, behind
> These Trees have I incamp'd my Mind;
> Where Beauty, aiming at the Heart,
> Bends in some Tree its useless Dart . . . (ll. 601–4)

This may intensify to an ecstatic pain, like a felicitous Passion:

> Do you, O *Brambles*, chain me too,
> And courteous *Briars* nail me through. (ll. 615–16)

Generally, however, the poet enjoys a serene expansion of being. He surrenders human articulation for spontaneous communion with the creatures:

> Already I begin to call
> In their most learned Original:
> And where I Language want, my Signs
> The Bird upon the Bough divines . . . (ll. 569–72)

[10] Cf. John Dixon Hunt, pp. 111–12.

This is the return to 'Natures Cradle', a kind of paradisal womb-state, prefigured in the Ark-image. In a different way, Marvell is re-enacting a fundamental premiss of Vaughan's poetry: a creative retrogression along the scale of being to its vital source, as fostered by communion with the lower orders of life:

> Give me but Wings as they, and I
> Streight floting on the Air shall fly:
> Or turn me but, and you shall see
> I was but an inverted Tree. (ll. 565–8)

Is this a conceitful parallel or true nature-mysticism? The very trees lose their individual forms—'It seems indeed as *Wood* not *Trees*'—asserting instead a primordial state of vegetable being. We are being led towards the primal apprehension of 'a green Thought in a green Shade'.

Yet even as the poet loses his human identity, he enjoys the privileges of a master of the woods, served by the powers of nature.[11] The mossy banks yield him rest while the wind cools his brow and creepers embrace him. He is both the chained slave of nature and its 'Lord' before whom the trees divide (l. 620). This happy equipoise makes the setting explicitly paradisal, a restored Eden:

> No *Serpent* new nor *Crocodile*
> Remains behind our little *Nile*;
> Unless it self you will mistake,
> Among these Meads the only Snake. (ll. 629–32)

It exceeds heaven itself, so that the sun pines for its reflection in the stream (ll. 639–40).

The compelling force behind this paradise becomes apparent only in the next sequence, when '*young Maria* walks to night'. Her innocence, unlike the lamenting nymph's, is not the absence of experience but the triumphant perfection of experience.

> *She* that already is the *Law*
> Of all her *Sex*, her *Ages Aw*. (ll. 655–6)

Such virtue will find its culmination in a future union of great houses. Her virgin life in the woods marks a mere interim:

> Mean time ye Fields, Springs, Bushes, Flow'rs,
> Where yet She leads her studious Hours,

[11] Cf. Kitty Scoular, *Natural Magic* (Oxford, 1965), 170, 185.

(Till Fate her worthily translates,
And find a *Fairfax* for our *Thwaites*) . . . (ll. 745–8)

The landscape does not act upon or interact with man: it reflects his (or her) superior being. Humanity also provides the final cause for such a landscape: it permits man to realize or recover his higher nature.

From the poet's point of view, it affords an endless fund of symbols for the operation of the human spirit. Beyond the influence of a Maria or a Fairfax, the poet asserts his own imaginative dominance over nature. The landscape is shaken, dissolved, and realigned:

No Scene that turns with Engines strange
Does oftner then these Meadows change. (ll. 385–6)

The shifts of size and perspective, and apparently of matter itself, provide some of the best-known passages of the poem: giant grasshoppers and puny men, cows likened to constellations and then to fleas, 'unfathomable Grass' that turns into a sea, and the actual transformation of the meadow during a flood—much as Appleton House grows spherical when Fairfax appears. Marvell frees his subject from the laws of space, time, matter, and causality. This endlessly pliable material can supply fanciful compliments to the Fairfaxes; or it can become the medium of a greater intellectual release. To a lesser extent, this release is seen in 'The Garden' and the Mower poems.

Beyond all specific concern with man and nature, the creation of this intellectual dreamland is a major purpose in Marvell. Its freedom is a holiday freedom: it argues an intellectual irresponsibility, a disinclination for single-minded commitment to a theme or approach. Marvell's poetic forms are not final and absolute. They are in a teasing state of flux: a series of images, approaches, glimpses from various perspectives in various lights, hinting at possible truths concealed in a moment's illusion. Marvell's unfailing lightness of tone, the quizzical exaggeration of his poetic conceits, his very preference for octosyllabics over the pentameter, are means of absolving himself from full commitment to his own speculations. Instead he indulges himself in the tangential pursuit of whims and conjectures: an endless withdrawal from, as well as endless engagement with, the possibilities of experience.[12]

This avoidance of certitudes recalls the imaginative release of orthodox pastoral. There the 'holiday' is often total: a deceleration of

[12] Cf. Friedman, p. 32: Marvell's 'genius was stirred more immediately by complex choices than by the passion of certainty'. Cf. also the interpretation of the Mower poems in Barbara Everett, 'Marvell's "The Mower's Song"', *Critical Quarterly* 4 (1962), 219–24.

mental activity, a fastidious seeking after ease, not the demanding creation of a poetic world so much as an escape from the intellectually taxing world of reality. Human experience is selected and simplified: hence the lucidly representative or symbolic function that pastoral often assumes. But even as it reveals the design, it softens and modifies the contours, invites easy acquiescence in what becomes thereby a spurious simplicity.

In place of these easy certainties, Marvell introduces new, disconcerting elements into his poetic universe. This stimulating disorder provokes fresh questions, introduces new viewpoints and perhaps new facts, embarks on an uncommitted exploration of possibilities and alternatives. He turns to nature as the setting most conducive to such liberty, unattainable in the set patterns of social intercourse. The freedom with which he treats nature is a reflection of the freedom which he finds in nature.

In the standard country poem or rural idyll, country life had provided rest and relief from complex activity: at most, it fostered a meditative stasis born of *otium*. To Marvell, on the contrary, the relief provided by nature consists in its unique stimulation of mental activity. He may talk of *otium*, but his 'easie' philosophy is subtle and complex, an indefinitely extensible course of speculation. His pastoral is an open-ended process, the continual provocation of new and challenging patterns of experience through which man realizes the power and extent of his faculties. Here resides the true humanity of 'Upon Appleton House': not Fairfax's valour or Maria's saintly virtue, but a more general fulfilment of man's powers through interaction with nature.

'The Garden' marks the furthest point in Marvell's cultivation of humanity in nature. This is all the more remarkable as the poem opens with a simple contrast between man and nature. Human endeavour is partial, crowned with a 'single Herb or Tree'; the Garden provides 'all Flow'rs and all Trees'. These, moreover, weave 'Garlands of repose'. The contemplative ideal does not merely surpass but subsumes or incorporates the active. Civilization is 'all but rude', compared with the solitude of nature: a paradox heightened in the Latin 'Hortus', where the city becomes the haunt of bestial herds: 'Me . . . | Non Armenta juvant hominum, *Circique* boatus, | Mugitusve Fori' [the herds of men give me no pleasure, nor the bellowings of the circus nor the mooings of the market-place]: ll. 16–18. As in the Appleton woods, the poet deliberately reverses the scale of being. Vegetable life is superior to the human: spiritual fulfilment is achieved by a progression *down* the scale.

Hence the garden restores our imperfect human impulses to a purer and more perfect state:

> When we have run our Passions heat,
> Love hither makes his best retreat.
> The *Gods*, that mortal Beauty chase,
> Still in a Tree did end their race. (ll. 25–8)

The tree, then, offers a more than mortal consummation, a metamorphosis of fulfilment rather than frustration. This might almost be the deliberate purpose of the chase:

> *Apollo* hunted *Daphne* so,
> Only that She might Laurel grow. (ll. 29–30)

The love-pursuit becomes a philosophic progress, as more generally in the pattern of the entire poem.

Yet, by Marvell's accustomed paradox, nature is not autonomous: her virtues and those of man realize themselves through each other. Man can commit his being to nature and enter the world of harmony and innocence:

> Fair Quiet, have I found thee here,
> And Innocence thy Sister dear! (ll. 9–10)

In this recreated Eden, the poet recovers the pleasures of his own earlier life, purified and perfected. Erotic and epicurean elements mingle in the delights nature holds out to him:

> The Luscious Clusters of the Vine
> Upon my Mouth do crush their Wine:
> The Nectaren, and curious Peach,
> Into my hands themselves do reach;
> Stumbling on Melons, as I pass,
> Insnar'd with Flow'rs, I fall on Grass. (ll. 35–40)

Despite the tonic sensuality which I noted earlier, this is an innocent recreation of the Fall, as in the 'woods' passage in 'Upon Appleton House'. Here too the poet is the lord of nature, and she his handmaid and paramour. Nature grows anthropocentric again. The setting is, after all, a garden, not the wilds.[13] Even more clearly than at Appleton, we are imbibing not the spirit of free nature but the spirit of man as sublimated

[13] And, as Pierre Legouis points out, the fruits mentioned grow in England only with careful art (*Andrew Marvell: Poet, Puritan, Patriot*, (Oxford, 1965), 45).

in nature. The garden is another version of Marvell's philosophic dreamland, the symbol of an essentially mental configuration of experience.

Nature serves as setting for a philosophic ascent of the human mind; and still more notably, that setting itself passes from the material to the immaterial. I have earlier pointed out how, in the Appleton woods, nature is reduced to formless, quintessential matter, the paradox of the abstractly sensory. A similar, totally conceptualized yet totally sensory apprehension reduces the Garden to the celebrated 'green Thought in a green Shade'. 'Annihilation' becomes a creative process, a release of the shaping energies of nature in a newer, fuller dimension: 'Far other Worlds, and other Seas'.[14]

The process occurs chiefly within the human mind, 'that Ocean where each kind | Does streight its own resemblance find'. The mind becomes a womb of creation—going beyond the primal crucible of the Appleton woods to a totally internal world.[15] Earlier, human impulses and perceptions had been translated to the purer plane of nature; we now have the opposite, countering process—the recovery, amounting to a re-creation, of the natural world on the superior plane of the mind. Although the forms of nature retain the essence of their physical entities, they represent a totally spiritual, disembodied level of experience, leading to the Platonic ecstasy of stanza 7. Stanza 8 proposes a higher, totally asexual existence, beyond even the purified eroticism of the garden:

> Two Paradises 'twere in one
> To live in Paradise alone. (ll. 63–4)

We cannot tell how much genuine loss or wistfulness lies behind the rather forced jest. The last stanza returns to a more modest hortulianism; but the zodiac-image recalls the higher sally from which we have just returned.

Thus by a new and original path,[16] Marvell provides a Platonic pastoral unlike that of Italian poetry and drama. Marvell's Platonism draws him away from the formal refinements of conventional pastoral;

[14] Røstvig (i. 167) cites the Hermetic concept of the *benedicta viriditas*, the creative spirit as descended into the vegetable world in the form of greenness. This is one of the more plausible points of Røstvig's Hermetic interpretation of the poem.

[15] Cf. the notable Cartesian account of this internalization in Daniel Stempel, '*The Garden*: Marvell's Cartesian Ecstasy', *JHI* 28 (1967), 99–114.

[16] Perhaps not entirely original. Røstvig (i. 129 ff.) notes Marvell's predecessors in this respect, particularly Henry More.

but his more general settings and flexible lyric forms allow readier play of the free intellect.

Such free flight is circumscribed, but therefore stabilized, in some of his Christian pastorals and paradise-poems.[17] 'Bermudas' extends and modifies the stock paradise myth in topical terms. The New World is an unspoilt Eden as well as the new Promised Land: it combines pristine abundance with the bounty of ultimate grace. 'The Garden' clearly evoked the first paradise of Adam and Eve. 'Bermudas' as clearly presents a postlapsarian one, the gift of redemption. It is reached over the sea: navigation was unknown in the original Golden Age. But it affords safety from the 'Prelat's Rage': the Fall lamented is specifically doctrinal and ecclesiastical. The Bermudas become the seat of the Church Triumphant.

This highly evolved state of spiritual fulfilment is presented in terms of pristine nature. In this lies the complexity of the poem. Redemption is made real in deeply sensory terms: the rocky coast is itself a temple, built by God himself. 'Natures mystick Book' is integrated with revelation more intimately than in 'Upon Appleton House' or 'The Garden'. More teasingly still, the landscape veers between symbolic stylization and the true if unfamiliar features of an exotic land. Paradoxically, the unfamiliarity makes Marvell's theme more vivid and immediate, because it allows direct description in place of conscious symbolism as in Vaughan or Benlowes:

> Friend, view that rock, and think from rock's green Wound
> How thirst-expelling streams did bound:
> View streams, and think how Jordan did become dry ground.[18]

In Marvell, we do not have to read lessons or mnemonics into nature; her actualities function simultaneously as metaphoric counters, and blend with the world of pure metaphor. 'The Gospels Pearl' is poetically akin to the real 'Ambergris on shoar', and both these with the pomegranates, transformed to 'Jewels more rich than *Ormus* show's'. We move between various levels of image and sensory detail: nature's verities are vehicles of divine grace.

For what distinguishes this landscape, at points so reminiscent of 'The Garden', is a different play of forces. Nature and man do not simply interact; they both serve the designs of God, one as instrument and the other as recipient:

[17] I cannot agree with those who find a marked Christian vein in 'The Garden': e.g. Cullen, pp. 153–63.

[18] Benlowes, *Theophila's Love-Sacrifice*, Canto XII, ll. 241–3, as in Saintsbury (ed.), *Minor Poets of the Caroline Period*, i.

He lands us on a grassy Stage;
Safe from the Storms, and Prelat's rage.
He gave us this eternal Spring,
Which here enamells every thing;
And sends the Fowl's to us in care,
On daily Visits through the Air. (ll. 11–16)

Despite the excitement of the metaphor in 'Bermudas', it is no different in function from the orthodox Christian pastoral of 'A Dialogue between Thyrsis and Dorinda' or the other dialogue of 'Clorinda and Damon'. The former, indeed, is not without subtlety in the way it plays off heavenly against earthly pastoral. Celestial pastoral makes good the imperfections of the earthly:

Oh, ther's, neither hope nor fear
Ther's no Wolf, no Fox, nor Bear.
No need of Dog to fetch our stray,
Out Lightfoot we may give away;
No Oat-pipe's needfull, there thine Ears
May feast with Musick of the Spheres. (ll. 21–6)

Yet both poems present no more than rectified versions of the common pastoral experience. As Cullen says of 'Clorinda and Damon', 'Ultimately, Damon's argument directs itself not to a repudiation but to an assimilation of the pagan garden of natural delights with the Christian garden of the spirit' (p. 166).

Even in their rustic ignorance, Thyrsis and Dorinda possess, as it were, a native virtue that makes them naturally receptive to the heavenly state. Their heaven can thus mark a symbolic heightening of their actual shepherd lives,[19] once again a landscape of the mind: 'Heaven's the Centre of the Soul.' But again Marvell modifies the impact of the idea, this time by an over-sweetness of tone. The somewhat precious spirituality of the central metaphor is rounded off with a quasi-romantic death-wish.[20]

'Clorinda and Damon' is early work. The ambiguity here is scarcely more significant than the common mixture of metaphoric planes in allegorical pastoral.[21] From these seeds in convention—we may even say

[19] Much the same point is made by Lerner, *The Uses of Nostalgia*, p. 183.

[20] This can have disconcerting implications if read in a more serious light: see Legouis, pp. 41–2.

[21] I cannot follow Cullen (pp. 165–7) in his discovery of doctrinal intricacies in the poem.

the abuse or decline of convention—Marvell builds up his subtle and complex assessment of man in nature.

With Marvell our study can fittingly end. As I observed earlier, he illustrates not the central line of Renaissance pastoral but a late and largely eccentric reworking. In previous chapters, I noted the mergers, compromises, and simple dilution whereby formal pastoral survived in and after the mid-seventeenth century. Marvell's mixed and 'impure' pastoral may appear as another instance of this trend. But he preserves the central concerns of pastoral to a remarkable degree; and this creative engagement with the mode marks him off from most of his contemporaries. Although he found his way into 'The Golden Treasury', it is significant that the nineteenth century did not respond to him as it did, for instance, to William Browne. Despite his innovations, Marvell's pastoral relates to the earlier exercise of the pastoral convention. The vein he works is emphatically Renaissance, and some of its treasures have never been so cunningly retrieved as by this last prospector in the field.

APPENDIX A

Allusions in Neo-Latin Art-Pastorals

This appendix lists the allusions I have found in Neo-Latin eclogues classified by Grant as art-pastorals. It will be seen that Grant himself often recognizes the allusions. Even this list does not indicate the full extent to which we must qualify our view of Neo-Latin art-pastoral: see my remarks in Chapter 3, section 1. Also, while a number of eclogues contain no specific allusions, they have such a strong realistic and/or moral note that they scarcely qualify as art-pastoral. Several pieces by Mantuan and Camerarius fall into this category.

I have included dedicatory openings to real people only where they are very long (see Mario, Sainte-Marthe, below). References are to Oporinus, *Bucolicorum autores XXXVIII*; *Carmina illustrium poetarum italorum*; Carrara, *La poesia pastorale*; and Grant, *Neo-Latin Literature and the Pastoral*.

AMALTEO, GIAMBATTISTA. Eclogue I: Complimentary opening to Cosimo de' Medici. 'Lycidas' leaving his country for Spain is surely a figure of the poet himself, though the journey remains untraced. (See Carrara, p. 403; Grant, p. 155.)

ANISIO, GIANO. Eclogues V and VI: Both contain veiled figures from Anisio's Neapolitan circle and his times. (See Grant, pp. 137–8.)

ARCUCCI, GIAMBATTISTA. Eclogue III: Complimentary, allusive opening; praise of a playwright 'Amyntas' who seems to be a real person. (See Grant, pp. 153–4.)

—— Eclogue IV: Complimentary, allusive opening; Grant (p. 154) sees allusion to a specific love affair or official matter.

BOIARDO, MATTEO MARIA. Eclogue II: Laments a bereavement suffered by Tito Vespasiano Strozzi. (See Ch. 4 n. 37.)

—— Eclogue III: Includes compliments to Ercole d'Este before whom the song-contest is held. (See Grant, p. 120.)

—— Eclogue V: References to Strozzi (Tityrus), Boiardo (Bargus), Ercole d'Este. (See Ch. 4 n. 36 and Grant, p. 122.)

—— Eclogue VII: Contains compliment to Ercole. According to Grant (pp. 121–2) 'several quite pointed allusions to living persons' were omitted in revision.

CAMERARIUS, JOACHIM. Eclogue IV: In the second part of the poem, a shepherd laments his brother's death. Allusion indicated by Camerarius's remark in his note on the poem: 'De huius autem scribendae occasione nihil nunc est dicendum' [but nothing should be said now of the occasion for writing this]. (*Libellus continens eclogae* (1568), p. 128.)

CORDUS, EURICIUS. Eclogue III: References to Cordus, Hessus, and their circle. (See Grant, p. 170.)

—— Eclogue IV: References to Gosius Horlus, said (Oporinus, p. 366) 'Primus . . . Hessa nouem duxisse per arua sorores' [to have first led the Nine Sisters through the fields of Hesse] and to his pupil. The song of praise is composed by 'Simithusius Aegon'—Cordus, from Simsthausen in Hesse.

DE SLUPERE, JAKOB. Eclogues I–V: Many if not all the shepherds seem to be members of the poet's circle. (See Ch. 3, sect. 4.)

FIERA, BATTISTA. Eclogue I (Oporinus, pp. 333ff.): Alcippus laments his mother Meliboea's death. May safely be assumed to be autobiographical, or at least to refer to a real death.

FORCADEL, ESTIENNE. 'Amyntas': Letter from 'Amyntas' (the poet) to 'Corydon' (his patron, Charles, Cardinal of Lorraine). (See Grant, p. 196.)

GUARINO, GIOVAN BATTISTA. Eclogue I: 'Pan' is Borso d'Este, and 'Tyrus' the poet protected by Pan because of his father, the scholar Guarino da Verona. (See Carrara, p. 245.)

—— Eclogue II: Laments the death of 'Leontes' or Leonello d'Este; compliments 'Borsius' or Borso d'Este. (See Carrara, p. 245).

HESSUS, EOBANUS. Eclogue II: 'Eobanus' (so named) repeats the song of 'Philetas' (the poet's friend Burkhard Spalatin). (See Grant, p. 166.)

—— Eclogue III: Philaegon, just back from Fulda, and Cygnus, who sings 'carmina . . . Romula Teutonicas . . . per oras' [Roman songs on Teutonic shores], are surely real poets.

MARIO, ANTONIO. 'Thyrsis': Long dedicatory opening to the Governor of Verona, with details of the poet's life. (See Ch. 3 no. 9 and Grant, p. 124.)

SAINTE-MARTHE, SCÉVOLE DE. 'Damoetas': 29-line complimentary opening. (See Ch. 3 n. 9.)

STROZZI, TITO VESPASIANO. Eclogues I, II, III. 'Chronidon' is Guarino da Verona. (See Grant, p. 119.)

SUSANNEAU, HUBERT. 'Sylvius': According to Grant (p. 193), might refer to a real though unidentified physician from Picardy.

URCEO, ANTONIO. 'ecloga unica' (Oporinus, pp. 47ff.): Grant (p. 125) finds autobiographical reference.

VINTA, FRANCESCO. 'Amyntas' (*Carmina illustrium poetarum italorum*, xi. 249ff.): Laments the death of 'Amyntas', whom both Carrara (p. 396) and Grant (p. 152) consider to be a real though unidentified person.

APPENDIX B

Months and Seasons in *The Shepheardes Calender*

The 'seasonal' framework of *The Shepheardes Calender* does not affect my reading of the poem. I have therefore ignored it in my chapter on the *Calender*. But the matter looms so large in recent criticism that I feel bound to pay some heed to it.

'The year with its cycle of seasons determines the form of the poem', says A. C. Hamilton.[1] Most recent critics have agreed with his view, often in more elaborate and questionable form. There is a strong temptation to deduce the theme and structure of the *Calender* from the title rather than the text, to credit Spenser with a very simple scheme of human life harmonized with and controlled by nature.

There were many poetic, artistic, and philosophic traditions concerning the cycle of the year. We may agree with Rosemond Tuve[2] that ultimately they all assume the same basic premisses, the same 'world-picture'. A comprehensive view appears in the common iconographical motif of an allegorical figure of the year ('Annus'). He holds the sun and the moon, and is surrounded by the signs of the zodiac and the four seasons or twelve months; sometimes also the four elements, four humours, four quarters of the day, or the stages of a man's life. Tuve gives many examples from tapestries and other textiles, manuscript illustrations, and mosaics. Byrhtferth's eleventh-century manual provides an important English instance.[3]

One hesitates to draw upon such examples, centuries older than the period of this study. But this cosmic, synoptic view survived to Spenser's day in a humble but exceedingly common application. In the popular calendars and almanacs, the accounts of the months and the movement of the heavenly bodies would be accompanied by woodcuts of the labours of the months. Such labours are consistently associated with the

[1] 'The Argument of . . . the *Calender*' (*ELH* 23), p. 174.

[2] *Seasons and Months. Studies in a Tradition of Middle English Poetry* (Paris, 1933), 136ff. For another account, concentrating on literary sources, see Nils Erik Enkvist, *The Seasons of the Year. Chapters on a Motif from Beowulf to the Shepherd's Calendar* (Helsinki, 1957).

[3] See S. J. Crawford's edn. (EETS os 177; Oxford, 1929), diagram opposite p. 86.

zodiac in painting, sculpture, and tapestry as well. Human activities are obviously being placed under heavenly influence, but the degree of association varies a great deal. We find now a cosmic application of the 'seasons' theme, now a more local attention to its reflection in created nature or the life of man. In calendars and books of hours the zodiac sign may be relegated to an obscure corner or placed *below* the labour for the month.[4] We may even find a single sign for two months.[5] Clearly, the associations were growing lax.

It is difficult to assign precise divisions to a subtly graded range of applications. But we may distinguish some important stages and emphases, and consider *The Shepheardes Calender* in relation to each.

At its most philosophic, the seasons-motif may illustrate a divine or cosmic scheme. Boethius's address to God provides the *locus classicus*: 'Tua vis varium temperat annum'[6] [Your power rules the changing year]. Medieval encyclopaedists expand upon the theme. Byrhtferth's design, mentioned above, is shared by Bartholomeus Anglicanus and Vincent of Beauvais.[7] In the Renaissance, the rediscovery of Lucretius would reinforce the notion:

> At vigiles mundi magnum versatile templum
> sol et luna suo lustrantes lumine circum
> perdocuere homines annorum tempora verti
> et certa ratione geri rem atque ordine certo.

[But those watchful sentinels sun and moon, travelling with their light around the great revolving region of heaven, taught men well that the seasons of the year come round, and that all is done on a fixed plan and in fixed order.][8]

Virgil, Horace, and Ovid could all yield lines in support.[9] Spenser himself was to give the idea its classic English expression in the Mutabilitie Cantos; but how far does it appear in *The Shepheardes Calender*?

It scarcely seems an exaggeration to say that it appears chiefly in the signs of the zodiac in the woodcuts. The poetry itself seldom admits such a philosophic scheme. Old Thenot in 'Februarie' does recognize it:

[4] e.g. in the Peterborough Psalter and the Duc de Berry's *Belles Heures*.

[5] e.g. in a printed book of hours published by Simon Vostre of Paris in 1501.

[6] *De consolatione philosophiae*, i. 5. 18; my trans.

[7] *De proprietatibus rerum*, IX. v–xx; *Speculum maius*, xv. lxiv–lxviii.

[8] *De rerum natura*, v. 1436–9; text and translation as in the Loeb edn. by M. F. Smith (rev. edn. Cambridge, Mass., 1975). Cf. i. 174ff., v. 737–50.

[9] Virgil, *Georgics*, i. 257–8; Horace, *Odes*, IV. vii. 9–12; Ovid, *Metamorphoses*, i. 116–20, xv. 199ff.

> Must not the world wend in his commun course
> From good to badd, and from badde to worse,
> From worse vnto that is worst of all,
> And then returne to his former fall?
> Who will not suffer the stormy time,
> Where will he liue tyll the lusty prime? (ll. 11–16)

But Thenot's emphasis is on homely morality. The philosophic contemplation of change and order does not interest him. In 'November', the yearly renewal of spring is contrasted with man's mortality; but this is no more than a borrowing from the 'Lament for Bion'. Embarrassingly for the 'seasonal' exegetists, the opening lines of 'November' name the wrong sign for the month. The concept of a cosmic cycle may deeply underlie the form of *The Shepheardes Calender*; but it is not the evident thematic link binding the work together.

Of course, the great body of the 'seasons and months' tradition is concerned not with cosmic change but with the human 'labours of the months'. I shall not attempt even a brief history of the artistic tradition.[10] For Spenser, the two most likely sources would be tapestries and calendars. The seasons or months provide an ideal theme for a series of tapestries hung along a wall or gallery. Tapestries had notoriously short lives; the earliest relevant survivals of English manufacture are the 'Four Seasons' from Hatfield House, made around 1611, but undoubtedly reflecting a set theme, and based on engravings by Maerten de Vos.[11] Records go back to 1620 for the occurrence of the same theme in the famous Mortlake tapestries.[12] There are many extant examples from the continent.[13]

The most important calendars, artistically speaking, were those prefixed to psalters and books of hours. Rosemond Tuve has shown that such works, with other illuminated manuscripts, belonged to several great Elizabethan families with which Spenser was associated.[14] The

[10] For a convenient account, see R. van Marle, *Iconographie de l'art profane au Moyen-Age et à la Renaissance* (1931; repr. New York, 1971), i, ch. viii.

[11] See J. Humphreys, *Elizabethan Sheldon Tapestries* (Oxford, 1929), 14ff.

[12] See H. C. Marillier, *English Tapestries of the Eighteenth Century* (London, 1930), 61–3.

[13] e.g. the 'Trivulzio tapestries' designed by Bramantino (Trivulzio Family Palace, Milan); a suite by Il Bachiacca (Egyptian Museum, Florence); the 'Lucas months', once attributed to Lucas van Leyden and often copied by the Gobelins in the 17th cent.; the 'Grotesque months' designed by Giulio Romano (National Garde Meuble, Paris); a suite in the Metropolitan Museum of Art, New York (see at n. 21 below). Information from E. Müntz, *A Short History of Tapestry* (London, 1885).

[14] 'Spenser and Some Pictorial Conventions', *Essays by Rosemond Tuve: Spenser, Herbert, Milton* (Princeton, 1970).

common calendars and almanacs, of course, were works of household reference.

The shepherd participated in the labours of the months. June was commonly devoted to sheep-shearing. Some early medieval calendars[15] present the care of sheep, though not their shearing, in May. In the Duc de Berry's *Très riches heures*, sheep and cattle are driven to the pasture in March (they had been prominently confined to their fold in February). This may be connected to the sign of Aries (which rules from mid-March to mid-April): in Queen Mary's Psalter we have a pastoral scene to indicate the constellation.

More important is the pervasively pastoral context of the medieval handbook, *Le Bon Berger*,[16] where the whole year is described in terms of the shepherd's duties, month by month, though the illustrations are conventional. (May, not June, is shearing-time.) I have also described, in Chapter 3, section 3, a number of continental eclogues which describe rural activities season by season; their closest classical model, Calpurnius V, is concerned entirely with sheepkeeping. For Spenser, the most familiar account of this nature must have been the homely English one in Thomas Tusser's *A hundreth* (later *Fiue hundreth*) *good pointes of Husbandry*. Here the shearing-month is again June, no doubt in consideration of the English climate, but the precepts for May contain instructions for the care of sheep and cattle.[17]

It is remarkable that all this finds little or no reflection in Spenser's *Calender*. The woodcuts, indeed, are obviously within the 'labours' convention. In most of them, the unknown artist has finely merged the subject of the eclogue with the labour for the month: wood-cutting in February, haymaking in June, reaping in July, threshing in August. There is a courtly pageant in April and a maying procession in May. (These two months often portrayed courtly and festive themes.) Other woodcuts depict seasonal scenery if not activity, as in January and December. But the shepherd's activities are totally omitted from this scheme. Of course, sheep and shepherds appear in every picture; but the shepherds are absorbed in talk or contemplation, often in pointed contrast to the 'labours' in the background.

The poems themselves ignore the 'labours'. Eight eclogues allude to the month or season, but not in connection with work. (The exceptions

[15] e.g. BL MS Cott. Tiberius B. v, Cott. Julius A. vi.

[16] See p. 42 above.

[17] See Tusser, ed. Grigson, pp. 104, 109. Later, June is the shearing-month in Drayton's *Eglogues* (1606), IX. 1, and Jonson's *The Sad Shepherd*, I. iv. 1–17.

are 'Iulye', 'August', 'September', and 'October'. There is no explicit reference in 'Aprill' or 'Iune', but surely one assumes a springtime, the other a summer setting.) In the 'labours' convention, the shepherd resumes his activities in March. In Spenser, Willy and Thomalin talk of love, and Thomalin recounts his experience on a holiday. The roundelay in 'August' also begins (ll. 53–4):

> PERIGOT. It fell vpon a holly eue,
> WILLYE. hey ho hollidaye . . .

The woodcut for 'March' shows no sheep at all, and that for August only the 'spotted Lambe' staked in the singing-match. May, like April, was traditionally devoted to courtly pleasures—hunting, hawking, wooing, or walking with ladies in a garden. In May, says Bartholomeus Anglicanus, 'wel nyȝe alle þingis þat beþ alyue beþ imeued to ioye & to loue'.[18] But Spenser departs violently from this pattern. His May eclogue is the most solemnly didactic of the twelve. He is obviously working his own vein, leaving the 'cycle of labours' aside. In fact, given the nature of his pastoral, he could hardly do otherwise. His pastoral demands just that *otium* that the 'labours' deny to man. The shepherds must have leisure for contemplation, poetry, and love.

A more metaphorical use of the seasonal cycle is suggested by Spenser's title. It involves a viewpoint expressed in the old *Kalender of Shepardes*: 'the age of a man is .lxxii yere, and that we lyken but to one hole yere, for euer more we take .vi. yeare for euery moneth . . . so doth a man channge hym selfe twelue tymes in hys lyfe, by twelue ages, & euery age lasteth .vi. yeare'.[19] Other calendars and books of hours often carried verses to this effect.[20] There is also an interesting set of Brussels tapestries, *c*.1520, now in the Metropolitan Museum of Art, New York.[21] Here the four seasons, twelve months, signs of the zodiac, and labours of the months are linked to the 'twelve ages of man' by Latin mottoes and illustrative historical scenes. The theme seems to have been common in Brussels tapestries: two months from another suite are in the Musée des Arts Décoratifs in Paris.

[18] *De proprietatibus rerum*, tr. John Trevisa, ed. M. C. Seymour *et al*. (Oxford, 1975), i. 531.

[19] *The Kalender of Shepardes*, printed by Thomas Este for John Wally (London, 1570?), sig. A7r.

[20] The very same set of verses occurs in the Hours printed in Paris by Simon Vostre in 1508 and Gillet Hardouyn in 1510. See also the 1545 Hours printed in Paris by Kerver, described by Standen (see n. 21 below).

[21] See E. Standen, 'The Twelve Ages of Man', *Bulletin of the Metropolitan Museum of Art*, 12 (1954), 241–8.

A less elaborate division based on the four seasons is more common. We find it in Byrhtferth and in Vincent of Beauvais.[22] More pertinently, it occurs along with the twelvefold division in the *Kalender of Shepardes*,[23] and also in Tusser's *Good pointes of Husbandry*.[24] Among poetic sources, a passage from Horace, no doubt familiar in the original, was also available in translation in Tottel's Miscellany.[25] There is a longer passage in Ovid's *Metamorphoses*, though this reverses the direction of the metaphor, describing the seasonal cycle as 'aetatis peragentem imitamina nostrae' [in imitation of our own lifetime].[26] These are the most likely sources for the early Elizabethan examples that I described in Chapter 6, section 3. Marot may also have had them in mind when writing his 'Eglogue au Roy', Spenser's immediate source for 'December':

> So now my yeare drawes to his latter terme,
> My spring is spent, my sommer burnt vp quite:
> My harueste hasts to stirre vp winter sterne,
> And bids him clayme with rigorous rage hys right. (ll. 127–30)

There is a sore temptation to read this image into the whole *Calender* and elaborate it into a twelvefold division by month. The most notable attempts have been made by Mary Parmenter and Helena Shire.[27] Their efforts may convince us that, illuminating though such comparisons may be at points, the *Calender* cannot really be interpreted in such terms. Both Parmenter and Shire have constantly to shift their premisses—now relying literally on the nature of the month or season, now on a metaphorical meaning, now on an incidental remark in the *Kalender of Shepardes*, now on the zodiacal sign for the month, now on a mere reference to Church or folk festivals. No work could be knit together by such ropes of sand. Patrick Cullen's attempt is more cautious but basically similar. He widely varies the degree of metaphor from one point of his reading to another, leading sometimes to over-interpretation or even interpretation by contraries. June marks the sun's ascent but Colin's descent; September is the month of harvest, but Diggon has 'wrecked his harvest'.[28]

[22] Byrhtferth, EETS, p. 11; *Speculum maius*, xv. lxiv–lxviii.

[23] As in n. 19 above.

[24] Tusser, ed. Grigson, p. 59.

[25] Horace, Odes, IV. vii. 9–12; Tottel, ed. Rollins, no. 197.

[26] *Metamorphoses*, xv. 200: text and tr. as in the Loeb Classics edn., ed. F. J. Miller (Cambridge, Mass., 1916; repr. 1976).

[27] Parmenter, 'Spenser's *Twelve Aeglogves Proportionable to the Twelve Monethes*', *ELH* 3 (1936), 190–217; Shire, *A Preface to Spenser* (London, 1978), 102–3.

[28] See Cullen, *Spenser, Marvell, and Renaissance Pastoral*, pp. 134, 141.

I may also point out that the eclogues bear no relation to the age of the participants, such as the 'twelve ages' conceit would demand. How does the youthful love of 'August' (whether happy or sad) relate to man's life from forty-three to forty-eight? Is Diggon Davie's state in 'September' that of man at his 'most ioyfull and couragious estate'?[29]

One last line of approach remains. In certain late medieval artistocratic books of hours, notably those made for the Duc de Berry, the nature-settings are pictured in splendid detail, genuine landscapes whose spirit dominates the human action. Even the small miniatures of the *Belles heures* impart depth and character to the landscape. In the *Grandes heures*, human figures disappear from all but one month, so that the artist can concentrate fully on the natural scene. This interest in the exact material appearances of nature has been traced back to Italian scientific and medical works.[30] It has also been related to 'scientific' discourses like that in the late classical *Secreta secretorum*.[31]

In the other direction, it has been traced forward to the rise of landscape painting in Holland and Flanders, and the application of Italian artistic theory to such paintings to create a feeling for landscape and an established artistic genre of such works.[32] Still more relevantly, a variety of Middle English and Scottish works show an interest in landscapes and seasons, either for their own sake or as a controlling power behind human life. Gavin Douglas's Prologues to books of the *Aeneid* are the most memorable products of a considerable body of poetry that has been explored by authors such as Tuve, or Pearsall and Salter.[33]

My account in Chapter 7, section 5, attempts to demonstrate that Spenser shows little of this direct apprehension of nature (barring a few remarkable touches). His landscape shades off into the idealized, mythic, and symbolic. This has been described in some detail in Chapter 7.

[29] *Kalender of Shepardes* (edn. cit. n. 19), sig. A7v.

[30] See Otto Pächt, 'Early Italian Nature Studies and the Early Calendar Landscape', *Journal of the Warburg and Courtauld Institutes*, 13 (1950), 13–47.

[31] See Tuve, *Seasons and Months*, ch. ii.

[32] See E. H. Gombrich, 'Renaissance Artistic Theory and the Development of Landscape Painting', *Gazette des beaux arts*, 6th ser. 41 (1953), 335–60.

[33] Tuve, *Seasons and Months*; Derek Pearsall and Elizabeth Salter, *Landscapes and Seasons of the Medieval World* (London, 1973).

APPENDIX C

Sidney and the Elizabethan Pastoral Lyric

The dates of certain commemorative pieces in Sidney's honour point to the importance of the first publication of his works, between 1590 and 1593. Sidney died in 1586. Spenser's *Astrophel* and the poems accompanying it appeared along with *Colin Clouts Come Home Againe*—and this, curiously, is dated 1591 in the Dedication, though apparently not published till 1595. In 1593 came *The Phoenix Nest*, another volume commemorating Sidney and duplicating some of the poems in *Astrophel*. Thomas Watson mourns Astrophel alongside Meliboeus in his elegy on the latter[1] as well as in certain of the *Italian Madrigalls Englished*,[2] both published in 1590. Sidney's own pieces are set to music more often than those of any other poet;[3] Campion, Weelkes, and John Dowland even write music for imitations of poems from the *Arcadia*.[4]

This reflects a greater Sidney cult in the mainstream of English pastoral. As late as in *A Poetical Rhapsody*, we find two new pastorals by Sidney and one by his sister, three poems continuing the story of Strephon, Claius, and Urania in the *New Arcadia*, and a lament for a 'Willy' who may well be Sidney. (The later editions actually read 'Sidney'.)[5]

Astrophil and Stella is nearly as important as the *Arcadia*, though only one poem in *Astrophil* (Song IX) is properly pastoral. Even in shepherd's guise, Sidney is commonly called 'Astrophel' rather than 'Philisides'. The two roles are combined to yield the classic figure of a shepherd-lover. In Barnes's Sonnet 95 he is 'Th'Arcadian Shepherd Astrophel' guided by Venus; in Canzon 2, Astrophel's birthday is added to the shepherd's

[1] Watson's *Poems*, ed. Arber, pp. 154–5.

[2] Nos. 23–4, 27 (Fellowes, *English Madrigal Verse*, pp. 277–8). Song I is also about Astrophel and Stella (Fellowes, p. 272).

[3] Fellowes, pp. 764–5, lists 17 pieces from 14 song-books between 1588 and 1624.

[4] Campion, 'What faire pompe have I spide' (*Works*, ed. W. R. Davis (New York, 1967), 7); Weelkes, 'I love, and have my love regarded' (Fellowes, p. 289); Dowland, 'O sweet woodes . . .' (Fellowes, p. 470).

[5] See, respectively, *A Poetical Rhapsody*, ed. Rollins, nos. 1 and 2; 4; 5, 6, and 7; 9.

calendar.[6] Barnfield in 'The Shepherd's Content' laments Astrophel's unhappy love as well as his death.[7] Later Wither talks of Stella's poet-lover alongside Spenser, Drayton, and Browne, all described as pastoral poets.[8]

Barnfield surprisingly describes Astrophel as having 'sung the louely Layes | Of simple Shepheards in their Countrey-Farmes'.[9] This indicates the unexpected nature of Sidney's influence, encouraging art-pastoral rather than the courtly and intellectual concerns of the *Arcadia* itself. As we have seen, the pastoral of the 1590s was chiefly occupied with very different themes, closer to those of *The Shepheardes Calender*: love, poetry, an independent pastoral world.

There is another important factor to consider. Apart from Francis Sabie, about whom virtually nothing is known, nearly all the poets on the preceding list are associated, directly or at one remove, with Sidney's sister Mary, Countess of Pembroke. The exceptions are Watson, Barnfield, and Lodge. But the last two were Drayton's friends,[10] and Sidney's father-in-law Walsingham was Watson's patron. We may dismiss Harry Morris's weak attempt to relate Watson and Barnfield to the Wilton circle.[11] But Marlowe dedicates *Amintae gaudia* to Mary because 'moribundus pater, illius tutelam humillime tibi legauerat'[12] [its dying father most humbly bequeathed its guardianship to you].

Fraunce's position in the Wilton circle is well known. He goes so far as to incorporate the Countess in his pastoral world, weaving 'pleasant Yuychurches park' and 'fayre Pembrokiana' into the setting of *Amyntas*.[13] The same 'Matchles lady regent'[14] presides over the shepherds' tales in *Aminta's Dale*: are the shepherds, then, part of her circle?

Breton dedicated three books to the Countess between 1592 and 1601. The pirated *Bowre* and *Arbor* are not among them, but their composition may have been inspired by Mary or her brother in Breton's courtly days. Manuscript poems by Breton occur significantly often

[6] *Parthenophil*, ed. Doyno, pp. 54, 94.

[7] Barnfield's *Poems*, ed. Summers, pp. 29, 32.

[8] *Fair Virtue*, ll. 1933–8, in Wither's *Poetry*, ed. Sidgwick, ii. 76.

[9] Barnfield, *Poems*, p. 28.

[10] See Newdigate, *Michael Drayton and His Circle*, pp. 88–9.

[11] 'Richard Barnfield, "Amyntas" and the Sidney Circle', *PMLA* 74 (1959), 318–24. See also the ensuing correspondence between Morris and W. F. Staton, jun., in *PMLA* 76 (1961), 150–3.

[12] *Amintae gaudia* (London, 1592), sig. A 2^{r-v}.

[13] *The Countesse of Pembrokes Yuychurch* (London, 1591), sig. L 1^{v}.

[14] *The Third part of . . . Yuychurch Entituled, Amintas Dale* (London, 1592), fo. 1^{r}.

alongside pieces by Sidney and Dyer.[15] William Smith seems to have enjoyed or at least solicited Mary's patronage: some time before 1600 he sent her a *New Years Gift* of manuscript poems.[16] Barnes makes her one of the eight recipients of dedicatory sonnets in *Parthenophil and Parthenophe*. While scarcely proof of exclusive allegiance, this again shows patronage or hope of such. Morley dedicates to Mary his first book of madrigals. I may also point out that either Mundy ('Sheepheard Tonie')[17] or the editor or publisher of *England's Helicon* entitles a poem (no. 127) 'The Countes of Pembrookes Pastorall'.

Drayton had access to the Sidneys through the Gooderes and the Haringtons, and later to the Herberts through the Astons. Lady Mary is praised as 'Pandora' in *The Shepheards Garland* and *Ideas Mirrour*, and as 'Meridianis' ('Mari Sidnei') in the latter work.[18] Spenser had dedicated his *Calender* to Sidney. In the prefatory material to *The Faerie Queene* and *The Ruines of Time*, he honours Mary specifically in the light of her brother's memory. But he mentions her own 'manie singular fauours and great graces' to him,[19] and the appearance of 'The Doleful Lay of Clorinda' in the *Astrophel* volume also argues a direct relationship.

While these poets stood in different relations to the Countess—perhaps with nothing more than a hope of patronage—they could all aim to please her by writing in the vein with which her brother was best associated.

> the *Arcadian* Swaines with rytes adore
> *Pandoras* poesy, and her living fame.[20]

Does this imply the actual cultivation of pastoral poetry inspired by Sidney, to please the Countess? Or it is merely Drayton's pastoral allegory (occurring, however, in a non-pastoral work) for the Countess's general patronage? If the former, does it imply active encouragement on her part? It seems likely that the poets acted on their own initiative. After all, at least one important poet in Mary's retinue, Samuel Daniel, wrote

[15] L. G. Black, *Studies in . . . Poetic Miscellanies*, i. 256.

[16] See Smith's *Poems*, ed. Sasek, pp. 29–31, 91–6.

[17] For the latest confirmation of Mundy's authorship of the 'Sheepheard Tonie' poems, see R. Hosley, 'The Authorship of *Fidele and Fortunio*', *HLQ* 30 (1967), 315–30.

[18] For 'Pandora' see *The Shepheards Garland*, Eclogue VI, and *Ideas Mirrour*, opening sonnet ('Ankor tryumph . . .': Drayton's *Works*, ed. Hebel *et al.*, i. 97); for 'Meridianis', *Ideas Mirrour*, Sonnet 51 (*Works* i, 124), and Jean Robertson, 'Drayton and the Countess of Pembroke', *RES* NS 16 (1965), 45.

[19] Dedication to *The Ruines of Time*.

[20] *Ideas Mirrour*, opening sonnet, ll. 3–4.

no pastorals during this period, barring a short translation from Tasso's *Aminta*.[21] Nor does the Sidney cult necessarily produce pastoral poetry. *The Phoenix Nest* has very little pastoral. Seven of its poems recur in *England's Helicon*, one or two with pastoral touches added, the rest relying on a Petrarchan nature-setting.

[21] 'A Pastorall' in the *Delia* vol., 1592: see *Works*, ed. A. B. Grosart (London, 1885), i. 260.

APPENDIX D

Protestantism in the Spenserian Poets

The poets of *The Shepheards Pipe* were members of the Inns of Court (except John Davies of Hereford, whose occupation of writing-master brought him in contact with the others).[1] At this time, a considerable part of the population of the Inns of Court consisted of the sons of landed gentry,[2] like our poets. There also appears to have been a substantial Puritan presence at the Inns, though it was, in W. R. Prest's words, chiefly 'conservative, erastian and moderate (differing little from the typical cast of thought among the country gentry, with whom the lawyers predominantly identified themselves)'.[3]

By the reign of Elizabeth, there seems to be an appreciable sense of a collective rural loyalty among country gentlemen, as apparent when they gather in the town as when at home in the country. Michael Walzer describes their presence in the Inns of Court, their informal county-based meetings and dicussions of affairs when they came to London. But the growing ethos binding them together was a new, independent rural spirit: a deep interest in farming and husbandry, a 'new status and businesslike endeavour' in agricultural matters, an increase in the number of JPs, more generally 'a pervasive seriousness'.[4] In an anonymous 1579 dialogue *Of Cyuile and Uncyuile Life*, a country gentleman says: 'You know the vse and auncient custome of this Realme of England was, that Noble men and Gentlemen, (not called to attendance in our

[1] Browne entered the Inner Temple in 1611 after an unspecified time at Clifford's Inn. Wither was in London, probably at a minor Inn, from *c.*1606 (see his *Poetry*, ed. Sidgwick, i. p. xxii), though he entered Lincoln's Inn only in 1615. Brooke was at Lincoln's Inn by 1609, and remained as a Bencher after 1614. Richard Brathwait, incidentally, was at Gray's Inn from 1609 for an indeterminate time.

[2] See K. Charlton, 'Liberal Education and the Inns of Court in the Sixteenth Century', *British Journal of Educational Studies*, 9 (1960), 26, 38; P. J. Finkelpearl, *John Marston of the Middle Temple* (Cambridge, Mass., 1969), 6. W. R. Prest, though more cautious, provides material to support this view: see his *The Inns of Court under Elizabeth I and the Early Stuarts* (London, 1972), 27–32.

[3] Prest, p. 214. See his chs. ix–x. Cf. Michael Walzer, *The Revolution of the Saints* (Cambridge, Mass., 1965), ch. vii, and Finkelpearl, pp. 64–5.

[4] Walzer, p. 245.

Princes seruice) did continually inhabite the countryes, continuing there, from age to age, and from Auncester, to auncester, a continuall house, and hospitallitie' (sig. B 2ᵛ). In the ensuing dialogue, the countryman is defeated at every point. In Breton's similar dialogue of 1618, *The Court and Country*, he wins all the way: 'I thinke we haue more ancient and true Gentlemen that hold the plough in the field then you haue in great places that waite with a trencher at a Table'.[5] Wither's Philarete in *Fair Virtue* is clearly a country gentleman—the poet himself—assuming a shepherd's persona:

> though I can well prove my blood to be
> Deriv'd from no ignoble stems to me
>
> . . . . . .
>
> If any of those virtues yet I have,
> Which honour to my predecessors gave,
> There's all that's left me. (ll. 155–6, 165–7)

Our poets also had specific associations with political figures and trends. John Selden, prominent lawyer-politician and frequent opponent of the Crown, seems to have been Browne's close friend, from the extent of his prefatory contributions to *Britannia's Pastorals*. Much later, in 1640, Browne wrote a letter of congratulation to another outspoken parliamentarian, Sir Benjamin Rudyard.[6] John Hoskins, leader of the Parliamentary opposition in the earlier part of James's reign, was Christopher Brooke's friend, and Davies wrote an epigram to him. (Brooke himself sat in six parliaments from 1604.) William Ferrar, the Spenserians' 'Alexis', was an adherent of Sir Edwyn Sandys, another Parliamentary leader and royal opponent. The names of Brooke and Ferrar appear in the records of the Virginia Company alongside those of Hoskins and Sandys, as well as Henry Goodere, son-in-law of Drayton's patron, and William Herbert, Third Earl of Pembroke. The anti-Spanish bent of this group reinforced their commercial interests in New World expeditions, and the Virginia Company in particular was 'a focus for opposition to the court'[7] and of political Puritanism.[8]

The Earl of Pembroke has a special position and importance. Browne dedicated Book II of *Britannia's Pastorals* to him in 1616, was later tutor

[5] Breton's *Works*, ed. Grosart, ii. (*u*), p. 6, col. 1.

[6] See Browne's *Poems*, ed. Goodwin, i. p. xxv.

[7] Norbrook, *Panegyric of the Monarch*, p. 249. In *Poetry and Politics*, pp. 211–12. Norbrook also notes the close relations between various Spenserians and the members of the Merchant Adventurers' Company, including Sandys.

[8] See S. L. Adams, 'The Protestant Cause' (D.Phil. Oxford, 1972), 180–2.

at Oxford to his brother's ward and subsequently in residence at Wilton. In the 1640 letter to Rudyard, Browne prays for 'my honoured lord the Lord Chamberlain', that is, Philip Herbert, Fourth Earl of Pembroke and William's brother. And, of course, Browne is the probable author of the famous epitaph on 'Sidney's sister, Pembroke's mother'.[9] Wither dedicated *Abuses Stript and Whipt* to William Herbert, who secured his release from the subsequent imprisonment.[10] Davies was one of the Herberts' adherents, dedicating many volumes to William, his mother, and other members of the family.

Although one of the most powerful peers of his day, made Privy Councillor in 1611 and Lord Chamberlain in 1615, Pembroke was already a prominent opponent of many royal policies: anti-Spanish, anti-Catholic, anti-Somerset, with strong Protestant and Parliamentary sympathies. On 20 May 1613, the Viscount Fenton writes that Pembroke and Southampton 'haue vith them sume of the moste discontented of the nobillmen of the younger sort and all the Parlement mutineers'.[11]

In 1613 and 1616, Browne published vehement attacks on the Spanish in *Britannia's Pastorals*, and commented on English politics in line with this.[12] Wither's political commitment, even at this stage, does not need to be proved in detail, and Brooke was himself a parliamentarian. Norbrook points out how the Spenserian poets were adherents of Prince Henry, in whom the Protestant 'opposition' found a champion; and in particular, how the poets played a part in a more general reaction against the court in 1613–14.[13]

Here then are two lines of contact verging upon Browne, Wither, and their circle: a social and moral ideal centred on country life and loyalties, and elements of a nascent political opposition connected with strong Protestantism. I do not wish to argue for a general affinity between these two sets of phenomena at this date, or enter into the historians' debate on 'Court' and 'Country'. But as far as Browne and Wither are concerned,

[9] See Browne's *Poems*, ed. Goodwin, ii. 350, for a summary of the evidence for Browne's authorship. Grundy (*Spenserian Poets*, pp. 6–7, 144) accepts it unquestioningly. See also Allan Holaday, 'William Browne's Epitaph on the Countess of Pembroke', *PQ* 28 (1949), 495–7.

[10] See J. M. French, 'Wither in Prison', *PMLA* 45 (1930), 960.

[11] Historical Manuscripts Commission, Supplementary Report (1930), on the collection of the Earl of Mar and Kellie, p. 51.

[12] See above, Ch. 16, sect. 3.

[13] Norbrook, *Poetry and Politics*, pp. 203ff., 207ff. See his chs. viii and ix for an informative account of the anti-court, anti-Spanish, and 'Puritan' tendencies of the Spenserians, especially as expressed in pastoral.

both lines of association exist and appear to be reflected in their pastoral poetry. In both *The Shepheards Pipe* and *Britannia's Pastorals*, Browne affords a clear image of a conservative rural poet, physically and ideologically rooted in the country, but applying the resultant values and preoccupations to a critical interest in the court and the nation. The two lines of influence that I am arguing for become entirely explicit there. Wither's eclogues show this quality still more clearly. Unlike Browne, his loyalties are not exclusively or even primarily rural; when he writes pastoral, it therefore becomes all the more imbued with the paradox of the 'hunting shepherd'.

Barring a few passages noted in Chapter 10, section 3, Drayton's pastoral is very different in nature. He was indeed associated with the *Shepheards Pipe* poets. They addressed poems to one another, wrote prefatory verses for one another's books, and expressed mutual admiration elsewhere.[14] Drayton too had relations with, and support for, the political 'opposition'. Prince Henry was his patron and Selden his friend. Hardin and Norbrook give detailed accounts of this, basing themselves, as might be expected, on the satires and occasional poems, and *Poly-Olbion* to some extent.[15] Hardin suggests further that Drayton's dissatisfaction with the court made him long for a pastoral retreat. He even identifies Drayton with a special brand of 'country patriotism' shared with Browne and Wither.[16]

At this point, I feel we can no longer follow Hardin. At the very least, we should refrain from associating Drayton too closely with Browne and Wither's treatment of pastoral and country life, or the censure of court and politics expressed through that medium.

Drayton did not himself belong to the Inns of Court, and was a generation older than Browne and Wither (though not Brooke and Davies). Among his patrons, the Sackvilles were Royalists, though Sir Edward had his differences with James.[17] The Astons became Catholics some time after Drayton's death. Drayton's friends were drawn from all camps, and his biographer Newdigate finds it 'difficult to attach him to any one of the creeds or sects into which England had become divided' (p. 215). In some manuscript lines to a friend—surely a place for sincerity—he sees Catholic and Puritan as equal threats:

[14] See Newdigate, *Drayton and His Circle*, pp. 194–6, for a full account.

[15] Hardin, *Drayton and ... Elizabethan England, passim*; Norbrook, *Poetry and Politics*, ch. viii.

[16] Hardin, pp. 27–8.

[17] To which Hardin draws attention (p. 90).

When Brownistes banisht be,
Sectes and disloyalty,
Scizme and popery,
Then shall we flourish . . .[18]

He does not take sides, but deplores all faction and disturbance. Contemplation of the times leads him, in his pastorals, towards withdrawal and nostalgia. Though Drayton kept up links with the Pembroke circle, and had access to William Herbert through the latter's friend Aston, his contact with the family goes back a generation to the Countess Mary. His younger contemporaries write a new, 'committed' pastoral with enquiring, critical shepherds symbolic of a new awareness in the 'countryman'. Its practitioners look to the Earl of Pembroke. Drayton looks back instead to a Golden Age associated with 'Elphin', the reign of Elizabeth, and its last great survivor in the Countess of Pembroke.

Nostalgia for Elizabeth's reign was not uniformly escapist.[19] It could be made the weapon for pragmatic anti-James politics, as in Greville's Life of Sidney, where Sidney's political position is identified, with unhistorical irony, as the Queen's own. I might mention here a curious satiric pastoral added to *Albion's England* by William Warner in 1606. A shepherd falls asleep and sees a crowd of evil Popish fairies. They deplore English Protestantism, but (rather perversely for such creatures of evil) also condemn the rampant social abuses. It is implied that Elizabeth's reign was free of such evils, although (by another inconsistency) she is emphatically a Protestant queen. Protestant loyalty, satire, and Elizabethan nostalgia form a compound in a pastoral framework.[20]

Satire and nostalgia enter here and there in *The Muses Elizium*; but the tone, as I have tried to demonstrate, is world-weary, meditative, disengaged. Drayton is not committed to the new cause in the manner of his younger contemporaries.

[18] Lines added in MS at the end of 'The Ballad of Agincourt' in a copy of *Poems* (1619), presented by him to the antiquary Richard Butcher. See Drayton's *Works*, ed. Hebel *et al.*, v. 291.

[19] On its extent and implications, especially among the Spenserians, see Norbrook, *Poetry and Politics*, pp. 199, 207.

[20] *A Continuance of Albions England* (London, 1606), xiv. 91.

APPENDIX E

'Protestant *Pastorale*'

Michael Walzer points out the interesting phenomenon of a 'Protestant *pastorale*' from Du Bartas and Buchanan to Milton's *Masque* of Comus, reflecting an early and deep undercurrent in the Protestant ethos.[1] For Protestants in Catholic countries and Puritans in England, the country came to represent an alternative moral and political ideal, as well as a physical refuge from court corruption and hostility. Theodore Beza presents Abraham as living the morally ideal shepherd's life, in a Christian parallel to Horace's *Beatus ille*:

O l'homme heureux au monde
Qui dessus Dieu se fonde,
Et en fait son rampart:
Laissant tous ces hautains,
Et tant sages mondains
S'esgarer à l'escart.

[O happy is the wight
That grounds him selfe aright
On God, and maketh him his shield:
And lets the worldly wize,
Which looke aboue the skies,
Goe wander where they list in field.][2]

There is little or no explicit pastoralism in *Abraham sacrifiant*. What such *pastorale* borrows from the tradition are the underlying values of simplicity, purity, faith, and content. Roger Howell's interpretation of the 'shepherd knight' of Protestant chivalry can extend to all Protestant shepherd-figures:

It had religious overtones with its echoes of the Good Shepherd. He was gentle, he was beneficent, and he tended faithfully to his master's business, preserving

[1] Walzer, *The Revolution of the Saints*, pp. 241 ff.

[2] *Abraham sacrifiant*, ll. 289–94. Quoted from *A Tragedie of Abrahams Sacrifice* (Arthur Golding's trans. with Beza's text), ed. M. W. Wallace (Toronto, 1906).

his charges against any dangerous and popish wolf, risking his life for any helpless ones who strayed. And, too, he represented the potential purity of the country against the possible corruption of the court.[3]

So too in Buchanan's *Baptistes*:

> Non Sceptra spectat, non parentum stemmata,
> Decusve formae, aut regias opes DEUS,
> Polluta nullo corda sed contagio
> Crudelitatis, fraudis & libidinis:
> Hoc ille templo SPIRITUS capitur SACER.[4]

[God does not regard either sceptre, lineage, beauty of form, or regal wealth, but a heart unpolluted by any touch of cruelty, fraud, or lust; the Holy Ghost is attracted by such a temple.]

We may compare the Protestant Golden Age of Spenser's 'Maye', ll. 103–16. Du Bartas (whose first *Semaine*, from which the next two quotations are taken, was translated by Sidney) elaborates on the common pastoral motif of

> Great Kings, and Consuls, who have oft, for blades
> And glist'ring Scepters, handled hookes and spades.[5]

The courtly ideal is perfected in the country. So too, one may add, is the economic. Du Bartas rejects 'Miser's Idols, golden Ingots ram'd' (l. 1136) but makes it clear that

> heere I sing the happie Rusticks weale,
> Whose handsome house seemes as a Common-weale:
> And not the needie, hard-racke-rented Hinde,
> Or Copie-holder, whom hard Lords doo grinde . . . (ll. 1141–4)

The second line may apply to Sidney's Kalander.

Walzer suggests in a brief sentence (p. 241) that Protestant courtiers like Duplessis-Mornay and Sidney felt the frustrations of court life in an ideological, not merely personal sense and featured something of the same spirit of Protestant *pastorale*. The kingdom of Arcadia seems to embody a similar ideal. Already in the *Old Arcadia*, the Arcadians

[3] Roger Howell, *Sir Philip Sidney. The Shepherd Knight* (London, 1968), 10–11.

[4] ll. 105–9: as in Francis Peck, *New Memoirs of the Life and Poetical Works of Mr. John Milton* (London, 1740), 312.

[5] Third day of the first week: quoted from Sylvester's translation of *The Divine Weeks and Works*, ed. S. Snyder (Oxford, 1979), ll. 1043–4. These lines are represented in Du Bartas's original.

(finding how true a contentation is gotten by following the course of nature, and how the shining title of glory, so much affected by other nations, doth indeed help little to the happiness of life) were the only people which, as by their justice and providence gave neither cause nor hope to their neighbours to annoy them, so were they not stirred with false praise to trouble others' quiet . . . (Robertson, p. 4, ll. 6–12)

Here again we have a quasi-pastoral ideal of peace, content and humility. We may recall the praise of country life in *The Lady of May*: 'O sweet contentation, to see the long life of the hurtless trees; to see how in straight growing up, though never so high, they hinder not their fellows; they only enviously trouble, which are crookedly bent'.[6]

The *New Arcadia* extends this view of the Arcadian polity, and makes it more exclusively Arcadian and pastoral. The description of Arcadia at the opening is rhetorically strained and factitious; but it symbolizes a social and ethical order in which, in McCoy's words, 'the material, social, and aesthetic realms harmoniously combine'.[7] Some of Claius's remarks to Musidorus in the *New Arcadia* are significant too. The Arcadians are 'a happy people, wanting little because they desire not much'. Though shepherds, they are not quite shepherds, but men 'that live upon the commodity of their sheep, and therefore in the division of the Arcadian estate are termed shepherds' (Skretkowicz, p. 11, ll. 31–3). After all, a nation must embrace more than the shepherd's estate. Yet the whole is kept close to the pastoral station and mode of life, and enjoys its blessings: 'peace and, the child of peace, good husbandry'.

Idealized shepherd life is a happy leaven to the social and political design of the *New Arcadia*. It is not a dominant or persistent element, nor does it alter the basically courtly nature of the work. Basilius's abdication of his duties is clearly condemned; and Euarchus, the princes, and even Helen of Corinth pursue programmes of war and foreign relations reflecting a different Protestant militancy. Thus Euarchus 'begat of a just war, the best child—peace' (*New Arcadia*: Skretkowicz, p. 162, l. 30).

We may even conjecture—though this can be no more than conjecture—that the Arcadian state in the *New Arcadia* embodies Sidney's ultimate concept of the ideally ordered state in a world of peace. We can certainly hold that he is incorporating some of his most cherished political principles in the picture of an enlarged and modified pastoral

[6] Sidney, *Miscellaneous Prose*, p. 29, ll. 18–21.

[7] Richard C. McCoy, *Rebellion in Arcadia* (New Brunswick, 1979), 201.

community. It is wrong of Basilius to withdraw to the shepherd world, but something of the pastoral ideal is to be incorporated in the kingdom as a whole. Kalander's remark on Basilius in the *New Arcadia* thus acquires a deeper truth: 'there is no cause to blame the prince for sometimes hearing them [the shepherds]. The blameworthiness is that to hear them he rather goes to solitariness than makes them come to company' (Skretkowicz, p. 25, ll. 8–10).

Later we see how the Spenserian poets express their critical and dissenting politics through versions of pastoral. The shepherd is poet and philosopher but also critic and satirist and, above all, the country gentleman who regards himself, not undeservedly, as the nation's strength and arbiter. A moral ideal clearly underlies the socio-political.

It was Milton's achievement to extract this ideal, simply and purely expressed in Beza and Buchanan's biblical plays, and give it new expression in mythic and classical terms. This is the process I have tried to highlight in my section on *A Masque* in Chapter 21 above.

Index